Microsoft® Excel Data Analysis and Business Modeling

Wayne L.
Winston

PUBLISHED BY
Microsoft Press
A Division of Microsoft Corporation
One Microsoft Way
Redmond, Washington 98052-6399

Library of Congress Cataloging-in-Publication Data
Winston, Wayne L.
    Microsoft Excel Data Analysis and Business Modeling/ Wayne Winston.
       p. cm.
    Includes index.
    ISBN 0-7356-1901-8
    1. Industrial management--Statistical methods--Computer programs. 2. Decision making--Computer programs. 3. Microsoft Excel (Computer file) I. Title.

    HD30.215.W56 2004
    005.54--dc22   2003064860

Printed and bound in the United States of America.

1 2 3 4 5 6 7 8 9   QWT   8 7 6 5 4

Distributed in Canada by H.B. Fenn and Company Ltd.

A CIP catalogue record for this book is available from the British Library.

Microsoft Press books are available through booksellers and distributors worldwide. For further information about international editions, contact your local Microsoft Corporation office or contact Microsoft Press International directly at fax (425) 936-7329. Visit our Web site at www.microsoft.com/mspress. Send comments to *mspinput@microsoft.com*.

Acquisitions Editor: Alex Blanton
Project Editors: Jean Trenary and Kristine Haugseth
Technical Editor: John Pierce
Indexer: Liz Cunningham

Body Part No. X10-21791

Table of Contents

Introduction

Whether you work for a Fortune 500 corporation, a small company, a government agency, or a not-for-profit organization, if you're reading this introduction, the chances are that you use Microsoft Excel in your daily work. Your job probably involves summarizing, reporting, and analyzing data, and it might also involve building analytical models to help your employer increase profits, reduce costs, or just manage operations more efficiently.

Over the past decade, I've taught thousands of analysts at organizations such as Bristol-Myers Squibb Company; Cisco Systems, Inc.; Eli Lilly and Company; Ford Motor Company; General Motors Corporation; Intel Corporation; Microsoft Corporation; NCR Corporation; Owens Corning; Pfizer, Inc.; Proctor & Gamble; the U.S. Army; and the U.S. Department of Defense how to use Excel more efficiently and productively in their jobs. At each of these organizations, my classes have received uniformly positive evaluations. Students have often told me that using the tools and methods I teach in my classes has saved them hours of time each week and has provided them with new and improved approaches for analyzing important business problems.

I've used the techniques described in this book in my own consulting practice to solve many business problems. We even use Excel to help the Dallas Mavericks basketball team and its owner Mark Cuban evaluate NBA referees, players, and lineups! I have also taught an Excel business modeling and data analysis course to MBA students for many years at the Indiana University Kelley School of Business. (As proof of my teaching excellence, I have received an MBA teaching award for 18 consecutive years.)

The book you have in your hands is an attempt to try and make these successful classes available to everyone. Here is why I think this book will help you learn how to get more from Excel:

- The materials have been tested and used successfully in the classes I've taught for the U.S. Army and a number of Fortune 500 companies.

- I've written the book as though I'm talking to the reader. This approach hopefully transfers the spirit of a successful classroom environment to the written page.

- I teach by example, which makes concepts easier to master. These examples are constructed to have a "real-world" feel. Many of the examples are based on questions sent to me by former students working at Fortune 500 corporations.

■ For the most part, I lead you through the approaches I take to set up and answer a wide range of data analysis and business questions in Excel. You can follow along with my explanations by referring to the sample worksheets that accompany each example. However, I've also included template files for the examples presented in this book on the book's companion CD. If you want, these templates enable you to work directly with Excel and complete each example on your own.

■ For the most part, the chapters are short and organized around a single concept. You should be able to master the content of most chapters with at most two hours of study. By looking at the questions that begin each chapter, you'll gain an idea about the types of problems you'll be able to solve after mastering a chapter's topics.

■ You won't just learn about Excel formulas in this book. You will learn some important math in a fairly painless fashion. For example, you'll learn something about statistics, forecasting, optimization models, Monte Carlo simulation, inventory modeling, and the mathematics of waiting in line. You will also learn about some new developments in business thinking (real options, computing customer value, mathematical pricing models, and so on).

■ At the end of each chapter, I've provided a group of problems (a total of nearly 400 in all) that you can work through on your own. These problems will help you determine whether you've mastered the concepts in each chapter. Answers to all the problems are included on the CD that accompanies this book.

■ Most of all, learning should be fun. If you read this book, you will learn how to predict U.S. presidential elections, how to set football point spreads, how to determine the probability of winning at craps, and how to determine the probability of each team winning the NBA finals. These examples are interesting and fun, and they also teach you a lot of useful things about Excel.

You can follow almost all of the examples in this book whether you are working with Microsoft Office Excel 2003 (the newest version of Excel), Microsoft Excel 2002 or Microsoft Excel 2000.

What You Should Know Before Reading This Book

To follow the examples in this book, you don't need to be an expert in Excel. Basically, the two key actions you should know how to perform are the following:

- **How to enter a formula**   You should know that formulas must begin with an equal sign (=). You should also know the basic mathematical operators. For example, you should know that an asterisk (*) is used for multiplication and a forward slash (/) is used for division.

- **How to work with cell references**   You should know that when you copy a formula that contains a cell reference such as $A$4 (an absolute cell reference, which is created by the dollar signs), the formula will still refer to cell $A$4 in the cells you copy it to. When you copy a formula that contains a cell reference such as $A4 (a mixed cell address), the column (A) will remain fixed, but the row number (4) will change. When you copy a formula that contains a cell reference such as A$4 (a mixed cell address), the row will remain fixed, but the column will change. Finally, when you copy a formula that contains a cell reference such as A4 (a relative cell reference), both the row and the column of the cells referenced in the formula will change.

Essentially, that's all you need to know about Excel to read and benefit from this book. Starting from this narrow base of knowledge, I'll show you the amazing things you can do with Excel.

How to Use This Book

As you read along with the examples in this book, you can take one of two approaches. You can open the template that corresponds to the example you are studying and complete each step of the example as you read the book. You will be surprised how easy this process is and how much you'll learn and retain. You can also follow my explanations as you look at the final version of each sample file instead of filling in the template.

Using the Companion CD

The CD-ROM that accompanies this book contains the sample files you use in the book's examples (both the final Excel workbooks and the template files you can work with on your own). The workbooks and templates are organized in folders that are named for each chapter. The answers to all chapter-ending problems in the book are also included on the book's CD. Each answer file is named so that you can identify it easily. For example, the answer to problem 2 in Chapter 10 is in the file named S10_2.xls.

To use the CD, insert it into your CD-ROM drive. If AutoRun is not enabled on your computer, double-click the file StartCD.exe in the root folder of the CD. (You'll be presented with a licensing agreement that you need to accept before you can install the files that come on the CD.) The sample files will be copied to the folder C:\Microsoft Press\Excel Data Analysis by default.

The CD also contains a version of *Microsoft Excel Data Analysis and Business Modeling* in PDF format. Adobe Reader is required to view the PDF version of the book. The CD includes a link to Adobe's Web site, where you can download a copy of Adobe Reader if you don't already have a copy installed on your computer. (You can download Adobe Reader free of charge.)

System Requirements

To work with this book's sample files, your computer must meet the following minimum system requirements:

- A minimum of 40 MB of available hard disk space is required to install the sample files.

- A copy of Microsoft Excel 2000, Microsoft Excel 2002, or Microsoft Office Excel 2003 needs to be installed.

Support Information

Every effort has been made to ensure the accuracy of this book and the contents of the companion CD. To provide feedback on the book's content or the companion CD, you can send e-mail to *mspinput@microsoft.com*, or write to us at the following address:

Microsoft Excel Data Analysis and Business Modeling Editor
Microsoft Press/Microsoft Learning
One Microsoft Way
Redmond, WA 98052

Microsoft Press provides corrections for books through the World Wide Web at *http://www.microsoft.com/learning/support/*. To connect directly to the Microsoft Press Knowledge Base and enter a query regarding a question or issue that you might have, go to *http://www.microsoft.com/learning/support/search.asp*. For support information regarding Microsoft Excel, you can connect to Microsoft Technical Support on the Web at *http://support.microsoft.com/*.

Acknowledgments

I'm eternally grateful to Jennifer Skoog and Norm Tonina, who had faith in me and first hired me to teach Excel classes for Microsoft finance. Jennifer in particular was instrumental in helping me design the content and style of the classes on which this book is based. Keith Lange of Eli Lilly and Company, Pat Keating and Doug Hoppe of Cisco Systems, Inc., and Dennis Fuller of the U.S. Army also helped me refine my thoughts on teaching data analysis and modeling with Excel.

I am grateful to my many students at the organizations where I've taught and at the Kelley School of Business. Many of them have taught me things I did not know about Excel.

Alex Blanton of Microsoft Press championed the project and shared my vision of developing a user-friendly text designed for use by working business analysts. An author could not ask for a better editor than John Pierce. He unfailingly corrected my grammatical shortcomings and did not hesitate to make necessary changes. Microsoft Press did a great job with the production process and made writing a book as painless as possible.

Finally, my wonderful family put up with my long absences during the year in which the book was written. My lovely and talented wife, Vivian, is always patient and inspiring. My daughter, Jennifer, and son, Gregory, inspired many of the book's examples. Even our dog, Honey, helped by barking less when she saw I was working!

1

Range Names

- I want to add up sales in Arizona, California, Montana, New York, and New Jersey. Can I use a formula to compute total sales in a form such as *AZ+CA+MT+NY+NJ* instead of *SUM(A21:A25)* and still get the right answer?

- To compute total sales for a year, I often average the 12 monthly sales below the current cell. Can I name my formula *annualaverage* so that when I enter *annualaverage* in a cell the appropriate average is computed?

- How can I easily select a cell range?

- How can I paste a list of all range names (and the cells they represent) into my spreadsheet?

You have probably received spreadsheets that use formulas such as *SUM(A5000:A5049)*. Then you have to struggle to understand what's contained in cells A5000:A5049. If cells A5000:A5049 contain sales in each U.S. state, wouldn't the spreadsheet be easier to understand if the formula was *SUM(USSales)*? In this chapter, I'll teach you how to name individual cells, ranges of cells, constants, and formulas. I'll also show you how to use range names in formulas.

How Can I Create Range Names?

There are three ways to create range names:

- Entering a range name in the Name box

- Choosing the Name, Create command from the Insert menu

- Choosing the Name, Define command from the Insert menu

Using the Name Box to Create a Range Name

The Name box is located directly above the label for column A, as you can see in Figure 1-1. (To see the Name box, you need to display the Formula bar.) To create a range name using the Name box, simply select with the mouse the cell or range of cells that you want to name, click in the Name box, and then type the range name you want to use. Press Enter, and you've created the range name. Clicking on the drop-down arrow for the Name box displays the range names defined in the current workbook. You can also display all the range names in a workbook by pressing the F3 button, which displays the Paste Name dialog box. When you select a range name from the Name box, Excel selects the cells corresponding to that range name. This enables you to check that you've chosen the cell or range that you intended to.

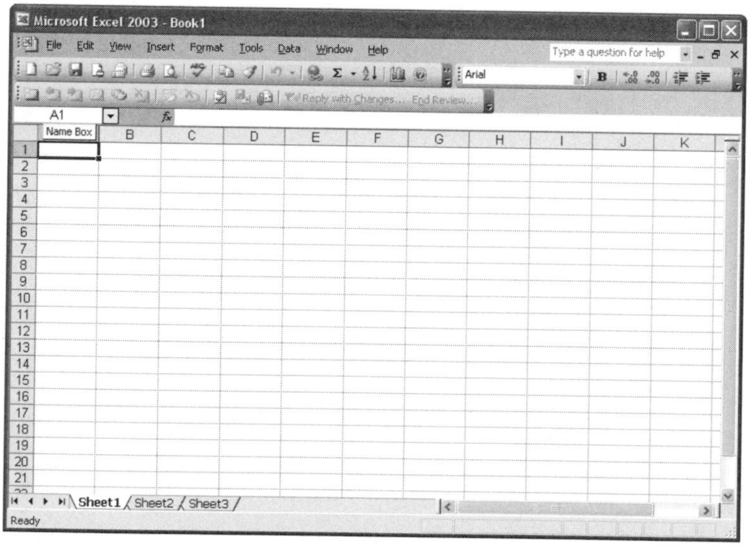

Figure 1-1   You can create a range name by selecting the cell range you want to name and then typing the range name in the Name box.

Creating Range Names by Using the Name Create Command

The spreadsheet States.xls contains sales during March for each of the 50 U.S. states. Figure 1-2 shows a subset of this data. We would like to name each cell in the range B6:B55 with the correct state abbreviation. To do this, select the range A6:B55, choose Insert, Name Create, and then choose the Create Names In Left Column option, as indicated in Figure 1-3.

	A	B
1		
2		
3		
4		
5	State	March Sales
6	AL	$ 915.00
7	AK ·	$ 741.00
8	AZ	$ 566.00
9	AR	$ 754.00
10	CA	$ 687.00
11	CO	$ 757.00
12	CT	$ 786.00
13	DE	$ 795.00
14	FL	$ 944.00
15	GA	$ 624.00
16	HI	$ 663.00
17	ID	$ 895.00
18	IL	$ 963.00
19	IN	$ 854.00

Figure 1-2   By naming the cells that contain state sales with state abbreviations, you can use the abbreviation when you refer to the cell rather than the cell's column and row number.

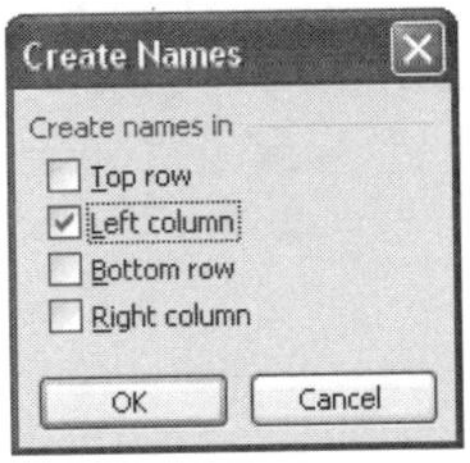

Figure 1-3   Use the Name, Create command on the Insert menu to name cell ranges. The Create Names dialog box provides options for naming cell ranges.

Excel now knows to associate the names in the left column of the selected range with the cells in the second column of the selected range. Thus B6 is assigned the range name *AL*, B7 is named *AK*, and so on. Note that creating these range names in the Name box would have been incredibly tedious! Click on the drop-down arrow in the Name box if you don't believe that these range names have been created.

Creating Range Names by Using the Name Define Command

If you choose the Insert, Name Define command, the dialog box shown in Figure 1-4 comes up.

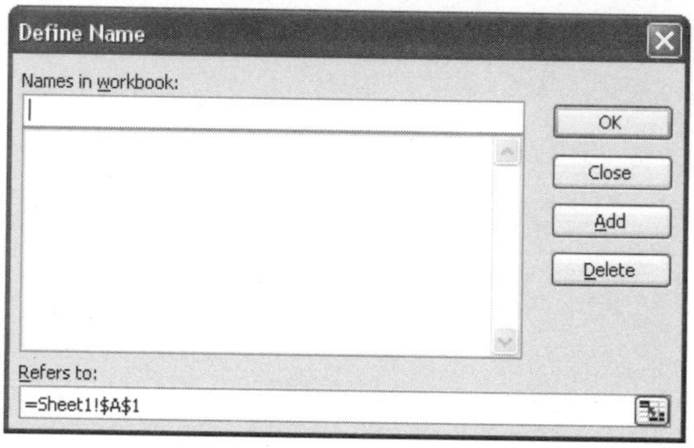

Figure 1-4   The Define Name dialog box before creating any range names.

Suppose you want to assign the name *range1* (range names are not case sensitive) to the cell range A2:B7. Simply type *range1* in the Names In Workbook box and then go down to the Refers To area and point to the range or type in *=A2:B7*. Click Add, and you're done. The Define Name dialog box will now look like Figure 1-5.

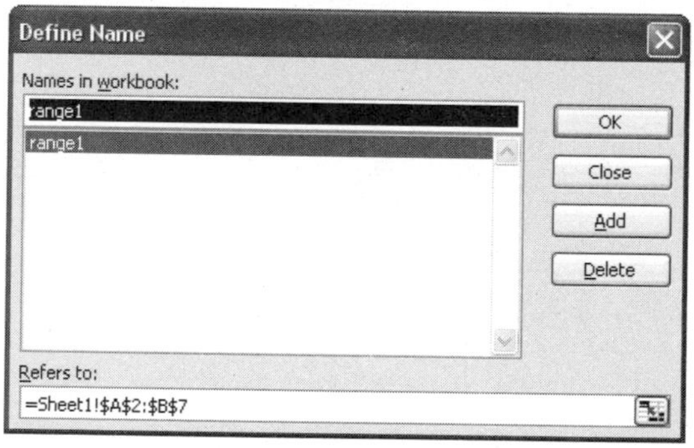

Figure 1-5   Define Name dialog box after creating a range name.

Of course, if you now click in the Name box, the name *range1* will appear. Now let's look at some specific examples of how to use range names.

I want to add up sales in Arizona, California, Montana, New York, and New Jersey. Can I use a formula to compute total sales in a form such as *AZ+CA+MT+NY+NJ* instead of *SUM(A21:A25)* and still get the right answer?

Let's return to the file States.xls in which we assigned each state's abbreviation as the range name for the state's sales. If we want to compute total sales in Alabama, Alaska, Arizona, and Arkansas, we could clearly use the formula *SUM(B6:B9)*. We could also point to cells B6, B7, B8, and B9, and the formula would be entered as *=AL+AK+AZ+AR*. The latter formula is, of course, much easier to understand.

As another illustration of how to use range names, look at the file HistoricalInvest.xls, shown in Figure 1-6, which contains annual percentage returns on stocks, T-Bills, and bonds. (The rows for years 1935–1996 are hidden.)

	A	B	C	D
4				
5				
6		Annual Returns on Investments in		
7	Year	Stocks	T.Bills	T.Bonds
8	1928	43.81%	3.08%	0.84%
9	1929	-8.30%	3.16%	4.20%
10	1930	25.12%	4.55%	4.54%
11	1931	-43.04%	2.31%	-2.56%
12	1932	-8.64%	1.07%	8.79%
13	1933	49.98%	0.96%	1.86%
14	1934	-1.19%	0.30%	7.96%
77	1997	31.86%	4.91%	9.94%
78	1998	28.34%	5.16%	14.92%
79	1999	20.89%	4.39%	-8.25%
80	2000	-9.03%	5.37%	16.66%
81	2001	-11.85%	5.73%	5.57%
82				
83		stocks	tbills	bonds
84	averages	12.05%	3.96%	5.21%

Figure 1-6   Historical investment data.

After selecting the cell range B7:D81 and choosing Insert, Name Create, we choose to create names in the top row of the range. The range B8:B81 is named *Stocks*, the range C8:C81 *T.Bills*, and the range D8:D81 *T.Bonds*. Now we no longer need to remember where our data is. For example, in cell B84, after typing *=AVERAGE(*, we can press F3 and the Paste Name dialog box appears, as shown in Figure 1-7.

Figure 1-7   You can add a range name to a formula by using the Paste Name dialog box.

Then we can select Stocks in the Paste Name list and click OK. After entering the closing parentheses, our formula, *=AVERAGE(Stocks)*, computes the average return on stocks (12.05 percent). The beauty of this approach is that even if we don't remember where the data is, we can work with the stock return data anywhere in the workbook!

If we use a column name (in the form A:A, C:C, and so on) in a formula, Excel treats an entire column as a range name. For example, entering the formula *=AVERAGE(A:A)* will average all numbers in column A. Using a range name for an entire column is very helpful if you frequently enter new data into a column. For example, if column A contains monthly sales of a product, as new sales data is entered each month, our formula always computes an up-to-date monthly sales average. I caution you, however, that if you enter the formula *=AVERAGE(A:A)* in column A, you will get a circular reference message because the value of the cell containing the average formula depends on the cell containing the average. You will learn how to resolve circular references later in the book, in Chapter 11.

How Do I Delete a Range Name?

To delete a range name, simply choose Insert, Name Define to bring up the Define Name dialog box. (See Figure 1-5.) Select the range name you want to delete, and then click Delete. Unfortunately, Excel lets you delete only one range name at a time.

How Do I Change a Range Name?

To change a range name, select Insert, Name Define to bring up the Define Name dialog box. (See Figure 1-5.) Select the range whose name you want to change, and then enter a new name or the cell range to which the range name refers. You can change the range by typing in the new range or by selecting the new range in the worksheet. Click OK, and the range is changed.

How Do I Name a Constant?

In many spreadsheets a value occurs so often that you might want to name it to use it as a constant. For example, suppose sales during the current year are $10 million and sales are growing 10 percent a year. (See the file Growth.xls.) We can name the annual growth rate *Growth* by choosing Insert, Name Define, filling in the Names In Workbook box and the Refers To area as shown in Figure 1-8, and then clicking OK.

Figure 1-8   You can name a value that occurs frequently in a workbook and use it as a constant.

Now everywhere in your spreadsheet, *Growth* will be interpreted as 1.1.

If you haven't already, open the file Growth.xls. Copying from F11 to G11:H11 the formula *E11*Growth* generates the sales for years 1–6 that grow at 10 percent a year, as you can see in Figure 1-9.

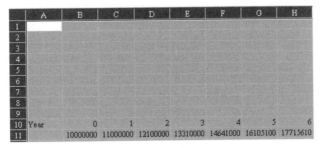

	A	B	C	D	E	F	G	H
1								
2								
3								
4								
5								
6								
7								
8								
9								
10	Year	0	1	2	3	4	5	6
11		10000000	11000000	12100000	13310000	14641000	16105100	17715610

Figure 1-9   Sales growth was calculated using a named constant.

To compute total sales for a year, I often average the 12 monthly sales below the current cell. Can I name my formula *annualaverage* so that when I enter *annualaverage* in a cell the appropriate average is computed?

Often you perform the same type of operation over and over. Wouldn't it be nice if you could name the formula that performs the operation? Then, whenever you needed to use the formula, you could call up the formula from the Paste Name dialog box. Here's an example.

Suppose that we repeatedly average 12 cells below the current cell to compute average monthly sales for several products during a calendar year. (See the file Sales.xls and Figure 1-10.) We would like to start 2 rows below the current cell and average 12 cells to get an average of monthly sales. To name this operation, we begin by going to any cell. I used cell B2 in this example. Choose Insert, Name Define to bring up the Define Name dialog box. Select the name *annualaverage,* and then look at the Refers To area, as indicated in Figure 1-11.

	A	B	C	D	E
1					
2	average		261.75	254.3333	256.3333	218.1667
3	Month	Product 1	Product 2	Product 3	Product 4
4	Jan	171	231	281	257
5	Feb	292	226	303	223
6	Mar	285	393	175	196
7	Apr	100	260	370	153
8	May	358	238	317	105
9	Jun	253	205	242	180
10	Jul	317	301	398	312
11	Aug	397	385	296	269
12	Sep	393	163	350	259
13	Oct	155	387	113	132
14	Nov	169	150	131	321
15	Dec	251	113	100	211

Figure 1-10 Data for naming a formula to average 12 months of sales.

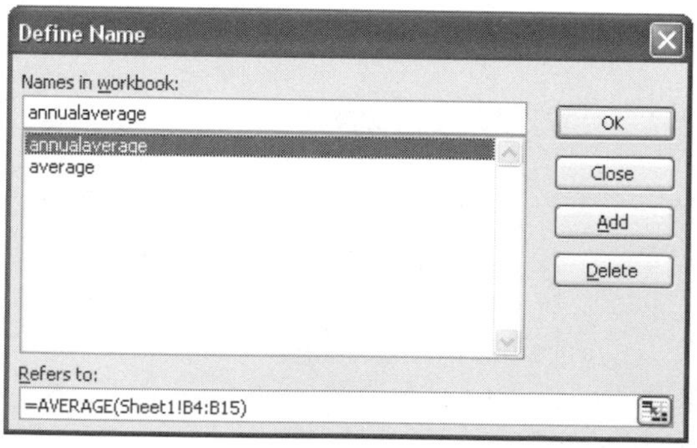

Figure 1-11 Naming a formula to average 12 months of sales.

You enter the formula that performs the operation given the current cell location. Because we are in cell B2, we want to average cells B4:B15, so we enter the formula *=AVERAGE(B4:B15)*. You must type in the formula you want rather than enter the formula by pointing. Now, if we enter the name *annualaverage* in any cell, the formula will drop down 2 cells and average the next 12 cells below the current cell. To illustrate how this named formula works, I've entered the formula *=annual average* in cells C2:E2. You now obtain the annual average of sales for products 2–4. Note that if you are in cell E2 and you select Insert, Name Define, the Refers To area indicates that the range *annualaverage* refers to the formula *=Average(E4:E15)*, which is the correct formula!

How can I easily select a cell range?

If you have selected a cell within a cell range, press Ctrl+Shift+* to select the entire range.

How can I paste a list of all range names (and the cells they represent) into my spreadsheet?

Press F3 to display the Paste Name box, and then click the Paste List button. A list of range names and the cells each corresponds to will be pasted into your spreadsheet, beginning at the current cell location.

Remarks

- Excel does not allow you to use the letters r and c as range names. Instead it will create a range name r_ or c_.

- If you use Insert, Name Create to create a range name and your name contains spaces, Excel inserts an underscore (_) to fill in the spaces. For example, the name Product 1 is created as Product_1.

- Range names cannot begin with numbers or look like a cell reference. For example, 3Q or A4 are not allowed as range names.

- The only symbols allowed in range names are periods (.) and underscores (_).

Problems

1. The file Stock.xls contains monthly stock returns for General Motors and Microsoft. Name the ranges containing the monthly returns for each stock and compute the average monthly return on each stock.

2. Create a formula to add up the six numbers below a given cell.

3. Suppose you want to name the range containing the cells A1:B3 and A6:B8. You can select multiple ranges in Excel by holding down the Ctrl key between the selection of different ranges. Use this technique to give the cell range consisting of A1:B3 and A6:B8 the name *Red*.

2

Natural Language Range Names

- How do I create a name for a range of cells based on a spreadsheet label and use that name in formulas?

- How do I use natural language range names to incorporate a relationship such as *Month(t) Ending Inventory = Month(t) Beginning Inventory + Month(t) Production –Month(t) Demand* in a spreadsheet formula?

Microsoft Excel 2002 and Microsoft Office Excel 2003 give you the ability to create "natural language" range names based on labels already present in your spreadsheet. I'll illustrate the use of natural language range names with two examples.

> **Note** This feature is available only in Excel 2002 and Excel 2003.

How do I create a name for a range of cells based on a spreadsheet label and use that name in formulas?

In the file NaturalRange.xls, shipments from three plants to four cities are listed. We want to find the total amount shipped from each plant and the total shipped into each city. Figure 2-1 shows the information in NaturalRange.xls.

	A	B	C	D	E	F
1						
2						
3						
4		City 1	City 2	City 3	City 4	
5	Plant 1	174	102	197	100	573
6	Plant 2	162	197	103	159	621
7	Plant 3	189	185	163	175	712
8		525	484	463	434	
9						
10	Plant 1 City 1	174				

Figure 2-1   Shipments from plants to cities.

To use the natural language range feature, choose Tools, Options. On the Calculation tab, select the Accept Labels In Formulas option. Clearing this option makes the natural language range names invalid.

Next we enter in cell F5 the formula *SUM(Plant 1)*. Note that the total shipments from Plant 1 (573 units) have been tabulated. Excel sensed from the Plant 1 label in row 5 that you wanted to name the range B5:E5 *Plant 1*. This is amazing, but there's more! Copy the formula in F5 to the range F6:F7. In F6 you will see the formula *SUM(Plant 2)*, and in F7 you will see *SUM(Plant 3)*. You can see that Excel is smart enough to determine the "natural" way to copy the formula in F5, and it adjusted the range names used in F6 and F7 accordingly. In a similar fashion, copying the formula *SUM(City 1)* from B8 to C8:E8 computes the total shipments into each of the four cities. This use of natural range names makes the logic of the spreadsheet much easier to understand.

Finally, suppose we want to enter the amount shipped from Plant 1 to City 1 into a cell. We could just use the formula *=B5*. Alternatively, we could use the formula *=Plant 1 City 1*. Excel now looks for the cell at the *intersection* of the natural language names defined by Plant 1 and City 1. Of course, this is the spreadsheet entry in cell B5.

How do I use natural language range names to incorporate a relationship such as *Month(t) Ending Inventory = Month(t) Beginning Inventory + Month(t) Production –Month(t) Demand* in a spreadsheet formula?

Often, spreadsheets contain modeling relationships that relate quantities at different points in time. For example, if we are trying to update our ending inventory each month, an appropriate formula is:

```
Month(t)Ending Inventory = Month(t)Beginning Inventory + Month(t)Production -
Month(t)Demand
```

If we are updating a toy store's cash on hand at the end of every month, an appropriate formula is:

```
Month(t)Ending Cash = Month(t)Beginning Cash + Month(t)Cash Inflow -Month(t)Cash
Outflow
```

Natural language range names make it easy for a person viewing a spreadsheet to see how this logic was included in the spreadsheet. The file NatRangeII.xls (see Figure 2-2) shows how to model the computation of monthly inventory levels with natural language range names. We begin month 1 with 100 units in inventory and produce 150 units each month. Monthly demands are given in column D of the spreadsheet.

	A	B	C	D	E
1					
2					
3					
4	Month	Beg Inv	Prod	Demand	End Inv
5	1	100	150	149	101
6	2	101	150	172	79
7	3	79	150	175	54
8	4	54	150	146	58
9	5	58	150	136	72
10	6	72	150	126	96

Figure 2-2   Computing inventory with natural language range names.

In cell B6 we set month 2 beginning inventory equal to month 1 ending inventory by entering the formula =E5. Copying this formula to the range B7:B10 computes beginning inventory for months 3–6. We use natural language range names to compute ending inventory by copying from E5 to E6:E10 the following formula:

```
=Beg Inv ı Prod   Demand
```

To see what this formula does, focus on any of rows 5–10. For example, to evaluate the formula in cell E5, Excel finds the number in row 5 from the column headed Beg Inv, adds this number to the number in row 5 from the Prod column, and then subtracts the number in row 5 from the Demand column. Copying this formula down to rows 6 through 10 now computes the correct ending inventory level for each month. Note that if we had copied =B5+C5-D5 down to E6:E10, few people would have understood the logic of our computations. The formula =Beg Inv+ Prod - Demand makes our logic more apparent.

Problems

1. A small candy store has $6,000 in cash on hand on January 1. Cash inflows and outflows for the months January–June are shown in the following table. Use natural language range names to compute each month's ending cash position.

Month	Inflow	Outflow
January	$5,000	$4,500
February	$6,000	$5,000
March	$5,200	$6,500
April	$7,200	$7,000
May	$8,000	$8,000
June	$9,000	$7,500

2. The following table gives the dollar sales of three products in four regions of the country: East, Midwest, South, and North. Use natural language range names to compute total sales of each product and the total dollar volume of sales in each region.

	East	Midwest	South	North
Product 1	$500	$600	$700	$650
Product 2	$600	$536	$665	$888
Product 3	$999	$834	$432	$326

3

Lookup Functions

- How do I write a formula to compute tax rates based on income?

- Given a product ID, how can I look up the product's price?

- Suppose that a product's price changes over time. I know the date the product was sold. How can I write a formula to compute the product's price?

Syntax of the LOOKUP Functions

Lookup functions enable you to "look up" values from worksheet ranges. Excel allows you to perform both vertical lookups (using VLOOKUP functions) and horizontal lookups (using HLOOKUP functions). In a vertical lookup, the lookup operation starts in the first column of a worksheet range. In a horizontal lookup, the operation starts in the first row of a worksheet range. Because the great majority of formulas using lookup functions involve vertical lookups, we'll concentrate on VLOOKUP functions.

VLOOKUP Syntax

The syntax of the VLOOKUP function is as follows. The brackets ([ ]) indicate optional arguments.

```
VLOOKUP(lookup value, table range, column index,[range lookup])
```

- *Lookup value* is the value that we want to look up in the first column of the table range.

■   *Table range* is the range that contains the entire lookup table. The table range includes the first column, in which we try and match the lookup value, and any other columns in which we will look up formula results.

■   *Column index* is the column number in the table range from which the value of the lookup function is obtained.

■   *Range lookup* is an optional argument. If *range lookup* is True or is omitted, the first column of the table range must be in ascending numerical order. If *range lookup* is True or omitted and an exact match to the lookup value is found in the first column of the table range, Excel keys the lookup off the row of the table in which the exact match is found. If *range lookup* is True or omitted and an exact match does not exist, Excel keys the lookup off the largest value in the first column that is less than the lookup value. If *range lookup* is False and an exact match to the lookup value is found in the first column of the table range, Excel keys the lookup off the row of the table in which the exact match is found. If no exact match is obtained, Excel returns an #N/A response (Not Available).

HLOOKUP Syntax

For an HLOOKUP function, simply change "column" to "row." Thus, in an HLOOKUP function, Excel tries to locate the lookup value in the first row (not the first column) of the table range.

Let's explore some interesting examples of lookup functions.

How do I write a formula to compute tax rates based on income?

The following example shows how a VLOOKUP function works when the first column of the table range consists of numbers in ascending order. Suppose that the tax rate depends on income as follows:

Income Level	Tax Rate
$0-$9,999	15 percent
$10,000-$29,999	30 percent
$30,000-$99,999	34 percent
$100,000 and over	40 percent

To see how to write a formula that computes the tax rate for any income level, open the file Lookup.xls, shown in Figure 3-1.

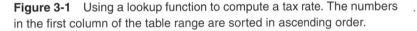

Figure 3-1   Using a lookup function to compute a tax rate. The numbers
in the first column of the table range are sorted in ascending order.

I began by entering the relevant information (tax rates and break points) in
cell range D6:E9. I named the table range D6:E9 *lookup*. I recommend that you
always name the cells you're using as the table range. Then you need not remember the exact location of the table range, and when you copy any formula involving
a lookup function, the lookup range will always be correct. To illustrate how the
lookup function works, I entered some incomes in the range D13:D17. By copying
from E13:E17 the formula *VLOOKUP(D13,Lookup,2,True)*, we compute the tax
rate for the income levels listed in D13:D17. Let's examine how the lookup function worked in cells E13:E17. Note that because the column index in the formula
is 2, the answer always comes from the second column of the table range.

■   In D13, the income of -$1,000 yields #N/A because -$1,000 is less than
    the lowest income level in the first column of the table range.

■   In D14, the income of $30,000 exactly matches a value in the first col-
    umn of the table range, so the function returns a tax rate of 34 percent.

■   In D15, the income level of $29,000 does not exactly match a value
    in the first column of the table range, which means the lookup func-
    tion stops at the largest number less than $29,000 in the first column
    of the range; $10,000 in this case. This function returns the tax rate in
    column 2 of the table range opposite $10,000, or 30 percent.

■   In D16, the income level of $98,000 does not yield an exact match in
    the first column of the table range. The lookup function stops at the
    largest number less than $98,000 in the first column of the table
    range. This returns the tax rate in column 2 of the table range oppo-
    site $30,000, 34 percent.

- In D17, the income level of $104,000 does not yield an exact match in the first column of the table range. The lookup function stops at the largest number less than $104,000 in the first column of the table range, which returns the tax rate in column 2 of the table range opposite $100,000, 40 percent.

- In F13:F17, we changed the value of the *range lookup* argument from True to False and copied from F13 to F14:F17 the formula *VLOOKUP(D13,Lookup,2,False)*. Cell F14 still yields a 34 percent tax rate because the first column of the table range contains an exact match to $30,000. The other entries in F13:F17 all display #N/A because none of the other incomes in D13:D17 have an exact match in the first column of the table range.

Given a product ID, how can I look up the product's price?

Often the first column of a table range does not consist of numbers in ascending order. For example, the first column of the table range might list product ID codes or employee names. In my experience teaching thousands of financial analysts, I've found that many people don't know how to deal with lookup functions when the first column of the table range does not consist of numbers in ascending order. In these situations, you need to remember only one simple rule: use False as the value of the *range lookup* argument.

Here's an example. In the file Lookup.xls (see Figure 3-2), you can see the prices for 5 products, listed by their ID code. How do you write a formula that will take a product ID code and return the product price?

	H	I	J	K	L	M	N	O	P
5									
6									
7									
8									
9			Lookup2=H11:I15						
10	Product ID	Price							
11	A134	$ 3.50							
12	B242	$ 4.20							
13	X212	$ 4.80							
14	C413	$ 5.00							
15	B2211	$ 5.20							
16									
17	ID	Price							
18	B2211	3.5							
19	B2211	5.2							
20									
21									

Figure 3-2 Looking up prices from product ID codes. In cases like these, when the table range isn't sorted in ascending order, enter False as the last argument in the lookup function formula.

Chapter 3 Lookup Functions

Many people would enter the formula as I have in cell I18, *VLOOKUP(H18,Lookup2,2)*. However, note that when you omit the fourth argument (the *range lookup* argument), the value is assumed to be True. Because the product IDs in the table range *Lookup2* (H11:I15) are not listed in alphabetical order, an incorrect price ($3.50) is returned. If we enter in cell I18 the formula *VLOOKUP(H18,Lookup2,2, False),* the correct price ($5.20) is returned.

You would also use False in a formula designed to look up an employee's salary using the employee's last name or ID number.

Suppose that a product's price changes over time. I know the date the product was sold. How can I write a formula to compute the product's price?

Suppose the price of a product depends on the date the product was sold. How can you use a lookup function in a formula that will pick up the correct product price? More specifically, suppose the price of a product is as follows.

Date Sold	Price
January-April 2005	$98
May-August 2005	$105
September-December 2005	$112

We'll write a formula that will determine the correct product price for any date on which the product is sold in the year 2005. For variety, we'll use an *HLOOKUP* function. I've placed the dates when the price changes in the first row of the table range. See the file DateLookup.xls, shown in Figure 3-3.

	A	B	C	D	E	F
1						
2	Date	1/1/2005	5/1/2005	8/1/2005		
3	Price	98	105	112		
4						
5			Lookup:B2:D3			
6						
7		Date	Price			
8		1/4/2005	98			
9		5/10/2005	105			
10		9/12/2005	112			
11		5/1/2005	105			
12						

Figure 3-3 Using an HLOOKUP function to determine a price that changes depending on the date it's sold.

I copied from C8 to C9:C11 the formula *HLOOKUP(B8,lookup,2,TRUE)*. This formula tries to match the dates in column B with the first row of the range

B2:D3. At any date between 1/1/05 and 4/30/05, the lookup function will stop at 1/1/05 and return the price in B3; for any date between 5/01/05 and 7/31/05, the lookup stops at 5/1/05 and returns the price in C3; and for any date later than 8/01/05, the lookup stops at 8/01/05 and returns the price in D3.

Problems

1. The file Hr.xls gives employee ID codes, salaries, and years of experience. Write a formula that takes a given ID code and yields the employee's salary. Write another formula that takes a given ID code and yields the employee's years of experience.

2. The file Assign.xls gives the assignment of workers to four groups. The suitability of each worker for each group (on a 0-10 scale) is also given. Write a formula that gives the suitability of each worker for the group to which the worker is assigned.

3. You are thinking of advertising Microsoft products on a sports telecast. As you buy more ads, the price of each ad drops as described in the following table.

Number of Ads	Price Per Ad
1-5	$12,000
6-10	$11,000
11-20	$10,000
More than 20	$9,000

For example, if you buy 8 ads, you pay $11,000 per ad, but if you buy 14 ads, you pay $10,000 per ad. Write a formula that yields the total cost of purchasing any number of ads.

4. You are thinking of advertising Microsoft products on a popular TV music program. You pay one price for the first group of ads, but as you buy more ads, the price per ad drops as described in the following table:

Number of Ads	Price Per Ad
1-5	$12,000
6-10	$11,000
11-20	$10,000
More than 20	$9,000

For example, if you buy 8 ads, you pay $12,000 per ad for the first 5 ads and $11,000 for each of the next 3 ads. If you buy 14 ads, you pay $12,000 for each of the first 5 ads, $11,000 for each of the next 5 ads, and $10,000 for each of the last 4 ads. Write a formula that yields the total cost of purchasing any number of ads. Hint: You will probably need at least three columns in your table range and your formula might involve two lookup functions.

5.   The annual rate your bank charges you to borrow money for 1, 5, 10, or 30 years is given in the following table.

Duration of Loan (Years)	Annual Loan Rate (Percent)
1	6
5	7
10	9
30	10

If you borrow money from the bank for any duration between 1 and 30 years that's not listed in the table, your rate is found by interpolating between the rates given in the table. For example, let's say you borrow money for 15 years. Because 15 years is one quarter of the way between 10 years and 30 years, the annual loan rate would be calculated as follows:

$$\frac{3}{4}(9) + \frac{1}{4}(10) = 9.25\%$$

Write a formula that will return the annual interest rate on a loan for any period between 1 and 30 years.

6.   The distance between any two U.S. cities (excluding cities in Alaska and Hawaii) can be approximated by the formula

$$69* \sqrt{(\textit{difference in latitudes})^2 + (\textit{difference in longitudes})^2}$$

The file CityData.xls contains the latitude and longitude of selected U.S. cities. Create a table that gives the distance between any two of the listed cities.

4

The INDEX Function

- I have a list of distances between U.S. cities. How do I write a function that returns the distance between, say, Seattle and Miami?

- Is there any way I can write a formula that references the entire column containing the distances of each city to Seattle?

Syntax of the INDEX Function

The INDEX function allows you to return the entry in any row and column within a rectangular array of numbers. The most commonly used syntax for the INDEX function is:

```
INDEX(Array, Row Number, Column Number)
```

To illustrate, the formula *INDEX(A1:D12,2,3)* would return the entry in the second row and third column of the array A1:D12. This entry is the one in cell C2.

I have a list of distances between U.S. cities. How do I write a function that returns the distance between, say, Seattle and Miami?

The file Index.xls (see Figure 4-1) contains the distances between eight U.S. cities. The range C10:J17, which contains the distances, is named Distances.

	A	B	C	D	E	F	G	H	I	J
1										
2										
3										
4		Boston-Denve	1991			T Dist to Seattle	15221			
5		Seattle-Miami	3389			T Dist to Seattle	15221			
6										
7										
8										
9			Boston	Chicago	Dallas	Denver	LA	Miami	Phoenix	Seattle
10	1	Boston	0	983	1815	1991	3036	1539	2664	2612
11	2	Chicago	983	0	1205	1050	2112	1390	1729	2052
12	3	Dallas	1815	1205	0	801	1425	1332	1027	2404
13	4	Denver	1991	1050	801	0	1174	2100	836	1373
14	5	LA	3036	2112	1425	1174	0	2757	398	1909
15	6	Miami	1539	1390	1332	2100	2757	0	2359	3389
16	7	Phoenix	2664	1729	1027	836	398	2359	0	1482
17	8	Seattle	2612	2052	2404	1373	1909	3389	1482	0

Figure 4-1 You can use the INDEX function to calculate the distance between U.S. cities.

Suppose that you want to enter the distance between Boston and Denver in a cell. Because distances from Boston are listed in the first row of the array named Distances, and distances to Denver are listed in the fourth column of the array, the appropriate formula is *INDEX(distances,1,4)*. We find that Boston and Denver are 1991 miles apart. Similarly, to find the (huge) distance between Seattle and Miami, you would use the formula *INDEX(distances,6,8)*. Seattle and Miami are 3389 miles apart.

Imagine that the Seattle Sonics basketball team is embarking on a road trip in which they play games in Phoenix, Los Angeles, Denver, Dallas, and Chicago. At the conclusion of the road trip, the Sonics return to Seattle. Can we easily compute how many miles they travel on the trip? As you can see in Figure 4-2, we simply list in order the cities the Sonics visit (8-7-5-4-3-2-8), starting and ending in Seattle, and copy from D21 to D26 the formula *INDEX(distances,C21,C22)*. The formula in D21 computes the distance between Seattle and Phoenix (city number 7), the formula in D22 computes the distance between Phoenix and Los Angeles, and so on. The Sonics will travel a total of 7112 miles on their road trip. By the way, I used the INDEX function to show that the Miami Heat log more miles during the NBA season than any other team.

	A	B	C	D
18				
19			**Road Trip!!**	
20			City	Distance
21			8	1482
22			7	398
23			5	1174
24			4	801
25			3	1205
26			2	2052
27			8	
28			Total	7112

Figure 4-2 Distances for a Seattle Sonics road trip.

Is there any way I can write a formula that references the entire column containing the distances of each city to Seattle?

The INDEX function makes it easy to reference an entire row or column of an array. If we set the row number to 0, the INDEX function references the listed column. If we set the column number to 0, the INDEX function references the listed row. To illustrate, suppose we want to total the distances from each listed city to Seattle. We could enter either of the following formulas:

```
SUM(INDEX(distances,8,0))
SUM(INDEX(distances, 0,8))
```

The first formula adds up the numbers in the eighth row (row 17) of the Distances array; the second formula adds up the numbers in the eighth column (Column J) of the Distances array. In either case we find the total distance from Seattle to the other cities is 15,221 miles, as you can see in Figure 4-3.

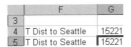

	F	G
3		
4	T Dist to Seattle	15221
5	T Dist to Seattle	15221

Figure 4-3   Total distances of cities to Seattle.

Problems

1. Use the INDEX function to compute the distance between LA and Phoenix and between Denver and Miami.

2. Use the INDEX function to compute the total distance from Dallas to all cities.

3. Mark Cuban and the Dallas Mavericks are embarking on a road trip that takes them to Chicago, Denver, Los Angeles, Phoenix, and Seattle. How many miles will they travel on this road trip?

4. The file Product.xls contains monthly sales for six products. Use the INDEX function to compute the sales of product 2 in March. Use the INDEX function in a formula that computes total sales during April.

5

The MATCH Function

■ Given monthly sales for several products, how do I write a formula that will calculate the sales of a product during a given month? For example, how much of product 2 did I sell during June?

■ Given a list of baseball player salaries, how do I write a formula that yields the player with the highest salary? How about the player with the fifth highest salary?

■ Given the annual cash flows from an investment project, how do I write a formula that returns the number of years required to pay back the project's initial investment cost?

Suppose you have a spreadsheet with 5000 rows containing 5000 names. You need to find the name John Doe, which you know appears somewhere (and only once) in the list. Wouldn't you like to know a formula that would return the row number at which John Doe is located? The Excel MATCH function enables you to find within a given array the first occurrence of a "match" to a given text string or number. You should use the MATCH function instead of a LOOKUP function in situations in which you want the position of a number in a range rather than the value in a particular cell. The syntax of the match function is:

```
Match(lookup value, lookup range, match type)
```

In the explanation that follows, we'll assume that all cells in the lookup range are located in the same column. In this syntax,

■ *Lookup value* is the value you're trying to match in the lookup range.

■ *Lookup range* is the range you're examining for a "match" to the lookup value.

■ *Match type =1* requires your lookup range to consist of numbers listed in ascending order. The MATCH function then returns the row location in the lookup range (relative to the top of the lookup range) that contains the largest value in the range that is less than or equal to the lookup value. *Match type = -1* requires the lookup range to consist of numbers listed in descending order. The MATCH function returns the row location in the lookup range (relative to the top of the lookup range) that contains the last value in the range that is greater than or equal to the lookup value. No matter in what order the values or text in the lookup range are listed (ascending, descending, or no order), *match type = 0* returns the row location in the lookup range that contains the first exact match to the lookup value. When no exact match exists and *match type = 0*, Excel returns #N/A. The great majority of MATCH function applications use *match type = 0*, but if *match type* is not included, *match type = 1* is assumed.

The file MatchEx.xls, shown in Figure 5-1, contains three examples of the MATCH function's syntax.

	A	B	C	D	E	F	G
1							
2							
3							
4		Boston			-5		6
5		Chicago			-4		5
6		Dallas			-3		4
7		Denver			-1		3
8		LA			3		-1
9		Miami			4		-3
10		Phoenix			5		-4
11		Seattle			6		-5
12				last number<=0	4	last number>=-4	7
13	Boston	1					
14	Phoenix	7					
15	Pho*	7					

Figure 5-1 Examples of using the MATCH function to locate the position of a value in a range.

In cell B13, the formula *MATCH("Boston",B4:B11,0)* returns 1 because the first row in the range B4:B11 contains the value *Boston*. Notice that text values must be enclosed in quotation marks (""). In cell B14, the formula *MATCH("Phoenix",B4:B11,0)* returns 7 because cell B10 (the seventh cell in B4:B11) is the first cell in the range that matches *"Phoenix"*. In cell E12, the formula *MATCH(0,E4:E11,1)* returns 4 because the last number that is less than or equal to 0 in the range E4:E11 is in cell E7 (the fourth cell in the lookup range). In cell G12, the formula *MATCH(-4,G4:G11,-1)* returns 7 because the last number that is greater than or equal to -4 in the range G4:G11 is contained in cell G10 (the seventh cell in the lookup range).

Unlike LOOKUP functions, the MATCH function can work with an inexact match. For example, the formula *MATCH("Pho*",B4:B11,0)* returns 7. The asterisk is treated as a wildcard, which means that Excel searches for the first text string in the range B4:B11 that begins with *Pho*.

If the lookup range is contained in a single row, Excel returns the relative position of the first match in the lookup range, moving left to right. As shown in the following examples, the MATCH function is often very useful when it is combined with other Excel functions, such as VLOOKUP, INDEX, or MAX.

Given monthly sales for several products, how do I write a formula that will calculate the sales of a product during a given month? For example, how much of product 2 did I sell during June?

The file ProductLookup.xls (shown in Figure 5-2) lists sales of four NBA bobble-head dolls for January through June. How can we write a formula that computes the sales of a given product during a given month? The trick is to use one MATCH function to find the row in which the given product is located and another MATCH function to find the column in which the given month is located. We can then use the INDEX function to return the product sales.

	A	B	C	D	E	F	G
1							
2							
3		January	February	March	April	May	June
4	Shaq	831	685	550	965	842	804
5	Kobe	719	504	965	816	639	814
6	MJ	916	906	851	912	964	710
7	T-Mac	844	509	991	851	742	817
8							
9	Product	Month	Row # of product	Column # of month	Product Sales		
10	Kobe	June	2	6	814		
11							

Figure 5-2   The MATCH function can be used in combination with functions such as INDEX and VLOOKUP.

We have named the range B4:G7, which contains sales data for the dolls, as *Sales*. We enter the product we want to know about in cell A10 and the month we're examining in cell B10. In C10, we use the formula *MATCH(A10,A4:A7,0)* to determine which row number in the range Sales contains sales figures for the Kobe doll. Then, in cell D10, we use the formula *MATCH(B10,B3:G3,0)* to determine which column number in the range Sales contains June sales. Now that we have the row and column numbers that contain the sales figures we want, we can use the formula *(INDEX(Sales,C10,D10))* in cell E10 to yield the piece of sales data we want. For more information on the INDEX function, see Chapter 4.

Given a list of baseball player salaries, how do I write a formula that yields the player with the highest salary? How about the player with the fifth highest salary?

The file Baseball.xls (see Figure 5-3) lists the salaries paid to 401 major league baseball players during the 2001 season. The data is not sorted in order of salary, and we want to write a formula that returns the name of the player with the highest salary as well as the name of the player with the fifth highest salary. To find the name of the player with the highest salary we proceed as follows:

■ Use the MAX function to determine the value of the highest salary.

■ Use the MATCH function to determine the row that contains the player with the highest salary.

■ Use a VLOOKUP function (keying off the data row containing the player's salary) to look up the player's name.

We have named the range C12:C412, which includes the players' salaries, as *Salaries*. We've named the range used in our LOOKUP function (range A12:C412) as *Lookup*.

	A	B	C	D
3				
4				
5				
6		name	Alex Rodriguez	dl-Derek Jeter
7			highest	5th highest
8		player position	345	232
9		amount	22000000	12600000
10				
11		name	salary	
12	1	dl-Mo Vaughn	13166667	
13	2	Tim Salmon	5683013	
14	3	Garret Anderson	4500000	
15	4	Darin Erstad	3450000	
16	5	Troy Percival	3400000	
17	6	Ismael Valdes	2500000	
18	7	Pat Rapp	2000000	
19	8	Glenallen Hill	1500000	

Figure 5-3 This example uses the MAX, MATCH, and VLOOKUP functions to find and display the highest value in a list.

In cell C9, we begin by finding the highest player salary ($22 million) with the formula *MAX(Salaries)*. Next, in cell C8, we use the formula *MATCH(C9,Salaries,0)* to determine the "player number" of the player with the highest salary. We use *match type = 0* because the salaries are not listed in ascending or descending order. We find that player number 345 on the list has the highest salary. Finally, in cell C6, we use the function *VLOOKUP(C8,Lookup,2)* to look up the player's name in the second column of the lookup range. Not surprisingly, we find that Alex Rodriguez was the highest paid player in 2001.

To find the name of the fifth highest player, we need a function that yields the fifth largest number in an array. The LARGE function does that job. The syntax of the large function is *LARGE(cell range, k)*. When the LARGE function is entered in this fashion, it returns the kth largest number in a cell range. Thus, the formula *LARGE(salaries,5)* in cell D9 yields the fifth largest salary ($12.6 million). Proceeding as before, we find that Derek Jeter is the player with the fifth highest salary. (The *dl* indicates that at the beginning of the season, Jeter was on the disabled list.)

Given the annual cash flows from an investment project, how do I write a formula that returns the number of years required to pay back the project's initial investment cost?

The file Payback.xls, shown in Figure 5-4, shows the cash flows for an investment project over the next 15 years. We assume that at time 0, the project required a cash outflow of $100 million. During year 1, the project generated a cash inflow of $14 million. We expect cash flows to grow at 10 percent per year. How many years will pass before the project pays back its investment?

The number of years required for a project to payback an investment is called the *payback period*. In high-tech industries, payback period is often used to rank investments. (You'll learn in Chapter 8, however, that payback is flawed as a measure of investment quality because payback ignores the value of money over time.) For now, let's just concentrate on how to determine the payback period for our simple investment model.

	A	B	C	D	E
1	Year 1 cf	14			Payback Period
2	Growth	0.1			6
3	Initial investment	100			
4	Year	Cash flow	Cum cash flow		
5	0	-100	-100		
6	1	14	-86		
7	2	15.4	-70.6		
8	3	16.94	-53.66		
9	4	18.634	-35.026		
10	5	20.4974	-14.5286		
11	6	22.54714	8.01854		
12	7	24.80185	32.820394		
13	8	27.28204	60.1024334		
14	9	30.01024	90.11267674		
15	10	33.01127	123.1239444		
16	11	36.31239	159.4363389		
17	12	39.94363	199.3799727		
18	13	43.938	243.31797		
19	14	48.3318	291.649767		
20	15	53.16498	344.8147437		

Figure 5-4 In this example, we'll use the MATCH function to calculate an investment's payback period.

To determine the payback period for the project, we proceed as follows:

- In column B we compute the cash flows for each year.

- In column C we compute the cumulative cash flows (total to date) for each year.

- We use the MATCH function (with *match type =1*) to determine the row number of the first year in which cumulative cash flow is positive. This calculation gives us the payback period.

We gave the cells in B1:B3 the range names listed in A1:A3. Our year 0 cash flow (-Initial_investment) is entered in cell B5. Our year 1 cash flow (Year_1_cf) is entered in cell B6. Copying from B7 to B8:B20 the formula *B6*(1+Growth)* computes the cash flow for years 2-15.

To compute the year 0 cumulative cash flow, we enter the formula *B5* in cell C5. For later years we calculate cumulative cash flow by using a formula such as *Year t cumulative cash flow = Year t – 1 cumulative cash flow + Year t cash flow.* To implement this relationship, simply copy from C6 to C7:C20 the formula *=C5+B6.*

To compute the payback period, we use the MATCH function (with *match type = 1*) to compute the last row of the range C5:C20 containing a value less than 0. This calculation will always give us the payback period. For example, if the last row in C5:C20 that contains a value less than 0 is the sixth row in the range, that means the seventh value marks the cumulative cash flow for the first year the project is paid back. Because our first year is year 0, the payback occurs during year 6. Therefore, the formula in cell E2, *MATCH(0,C5:C20,1)* yields the payback period (6 years). If any cash flows after year 0 were negative, this method would fail because our range of cumulative cash flows would not be listed in ascending order.

Problems

1. Using the distances between U.S. cities given in Chapter 4, write a formula with the MATCH function to determine (based on the names of the cities) the distance between any two of the given cities.

2. The file MatchType1.xls lists in chronological order the dollar amount of 30 transactions. Write a formula that yields the first transaction for which total volume to date exceeds $10,000.

3. The file MatchTheMax.xls gives the product ID code and unit sales for 265 different products. Use the MATCH function in a formula that yields the product ID of the product with the largest unit sales.

6

Text Functions

- I have a spreadsheet in which each cell contains a product description, a product ID, and a product price. How can I put all the product descriptions in column A, all the product IDs in column B, and all the prices in column C?

- Every day I receive data about total U.S. sales, which is computed in a cell as the sum of East, North, and South region sales. How can I extract East, North, and South sales to separate cells?

- I download quarterly gross national product (GNP) data from the Web. The cell containing first quarter data for 1980 contains the entry 1980.1 5028.8. How can I place the date and GNP value in different cells?

- In the spreadsheet I use for a mailing list, column A contains people's names, column B contains their street address, and column C contains their city and zip code. How can I create each person's full address in column E?

When someone sends you data or you download data from the Web, often the data isn't formatted the way you want. For example, when downloading sales data, dates and sales amounts might be in the same cell but you need them to be in separate cells. How can you manipulate data so that it has the format you need? The answer is to become good at using Excel's set of text functions. In this chapter, I'll show you how to use the following

Excel text functions to magically manipulate your data until it looks the way you want:

- LEFT
- RIGHT
- MID
- TRIM
- LEN
- FIND
- SEARCH
- CONCATENATE
- REPLACE
- VALUE

Text Function Syntax

The file Reggie.xls, shown in Figure 6-1, includes examples of text functions. You'll see how to apply these functions to a specific problem later in the chapter, but let's begin by describing what each of the text functions do. Then we'll combine these functions to perform some fairly complex manipulations of data.

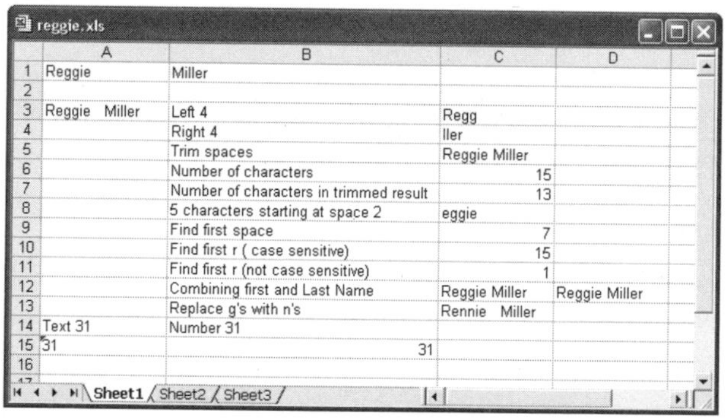

reggie.xls

	A	B	C	D
1	Reggie	Miller		
2				
3	Reggie Miller	Left 4	Regg	
4		Right 4	ller	
5		Trim spaces	Reggie Miller	
6		Number of characters	15	
7		Number of characters in trimmed result	13	
8		5 characters starting at space 2	eggie	
9		Find first space	7	
10		Find first r (case sensitive)	15	
11		Find first r (not case sensitive)	1	
12		Combining first and Last Name	Reggie Miller	Reggie Miller
13		Replace g's with n's	Rennie Miller	
14	Text 31	Number 31		
15	31	31		
16				

Sheet1 / Sheet2 / Sheet3

Figure 6-1 Examples of text functions.

The LEFT Function

The function *LEFT(text,k)* returns the first *k* characters in a text string. For example, cell C3 contains the formula *LEFT(A3,4)*. Excel returns *Regg*.

The RIGHT Function

The function *RIGHT(text,k)* returns the last *k* characters in a text string. For example, in cell C4, the formula *RIGHT(A3,4)* returns *ller*.

The MID Function

The function *MID(text, k, m)* begins at character *k* of a text string and returns the next *m* characters. For example, the formula *MID(A3,2,5)* in cell C8 returns characters 2-6 from cell A3, the result being *eggie*.

The TRIM Function

The function *TRIM(text)* removes all spaces from a text string except for single spaces between words. For example, in cell C5 the formula *TRIM(A3)* eliminates two of the three spaces between Reggie and Miller and yields *Reggie Miller*.

The LEN Function

The function *LEN(text)* returns the number of characters in a text string (spaces are included). For example, in cell C6 the formula *LEN(A3)* returns 15 because cell A3 contains 15 characters. In cell C7, the formula *LEN(C5)* returns 13. Because the trimmed result in cell C5 has two spaces removed, cell C5 contains two less characters than the original text in A3.

The FIND and SEARCH Functions

The function *FIND(text to find, actual text, k)* returns the location at or after character *k* of the first character of *text to find* in *actual text*. FIND is case sensitive. SEARCH has the same syntax as *FIND*, but it is not case sensitive. For example, if we enter *FIND ("r",A3,1)* in cell C10, Excel returns 15, the location of the first lowercase *r* in the text string *Reggie   Miller*. (The uppercase *R* is ignored because *FIND* is case sensitive.) Entering *SEARCH("r",A3,1)* in cell C11 returns 1 because *SEARCH* matches *r* to either a lowercase or an uppercase character. Entering *FIND(" ",A3,1)* in cell C9 returns 7 because the first space in the string *Reggie   Miller* is the seventh character.

CONCATENATE and & Functions

The function *CONCATENATE(text1, text2, . . ., text30)* can be used to join up to 30 text strings into a single string. The & operator can be used instead of *CONCATENATE*. For example, entering in cell C12 the formula *A1&" "&B1* returns *Reggie Miller*. Entering in cell D12 the formula *CONCATENATE(A1," ",B1)* yields the same result.

REPLACE Function

The function *REPLACE(oldtext, k,m, newtext)* begins at character *k* of *oldtext* and replaces the next *m* characters with *newtext*. For example, in cell C13 the formula *REPLACE(A3,3,2,"nn")* replaces the third and fourth characters (*gg*) in cell A3 with *nn*. This formula yields *Rennie Miller*.

VALUE Function

The function *VALUE(text)* converts a text string that represents a number to a number. For example, entering in cell B15 the formula *VALUE(A15)* converts the text string *31* in cell A15 to the numerical value 31. You can tell that the value 31 in cell A15 is text because it is left-justified. Similarly, you can tell that the value 31 in cell B15 is a number because it is right-justified.

Text Functions in Action

You can see the power of text functions by using them to solve some actual problems that were sent to me by former students working in Fortune 500 corporations. The key to solving each problem is to combine multiple text functions in a single formula.

I have a spreadsheet in which each cell contains a product description, a product ID, and a product price. How can I put all the product descriptions in column A, all the product IDs in column B, and all the prices in column C?

In this example, the product ID is always defined by the first 12 characters and the price is always indicated in the last 8 characters (with two spaces following the end of each price). Our solution, contained in the file Lenora.xls and shown in Figure 6-2, uses the LEFT, RIGHT, MID, VALUE, TRIM, and LEN functions.

It's always a good idea to begin by trimming excess spaces, which we do by copying from B4 to B5:B12 the formula *TRIM(A4)*. The only excess spaces in column A turn out to be the two spaces inserted after each price. The results of using the TRIM function are shown in Figure 6-2.

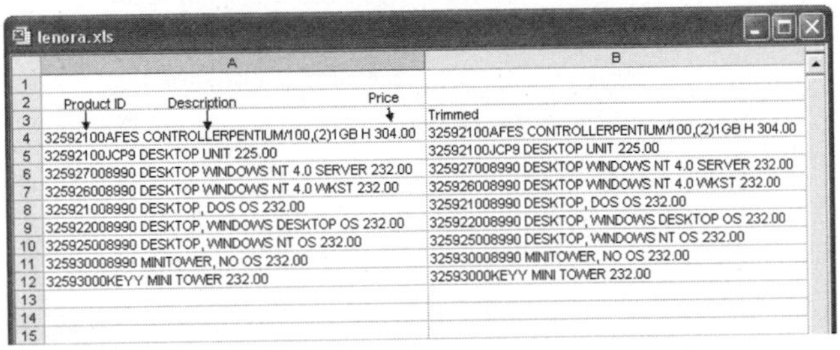

Figure 6-2   Use the TRIM function to trim away excess spaces.

To capture the product ID, we need to extract the 12 leftmost characters from column B. We copy from C4 to C5:C13 the formula *LEFT(B4,12)*. This formula extracts the 12 leftmost characters from the text in cell B4 and the following cells, yielding the product ID, as you can see Figure 6-3.

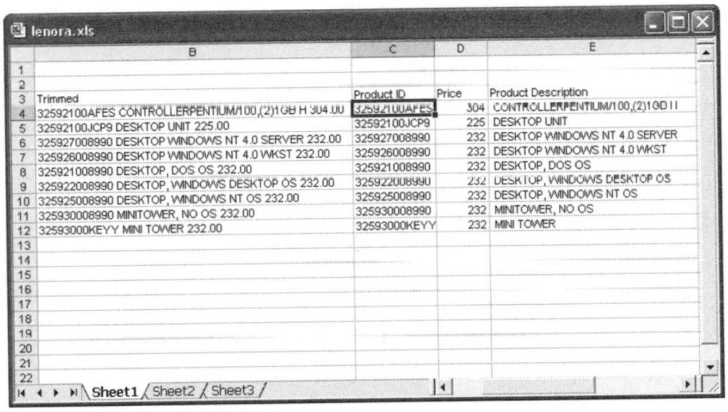

Figure 6-3   Text functions extract the product ID, price, and product description from a single text string.

To extract the product price, we first note that the price occupies the last 6 digits of each cell, so we need to extract the rightmost 6 characters in each cell. I copy from cell D4 to D5:D12 the formula *VALUE(RIGHT(B4,6)*. I use the *Value* function to turn the extracted text into a numerical value. Without converting the text to a numerical value, you couldn't perform mathematical operations on the prices.

Extracting the product description is much trickier. By examining the data, we can see that if we begin our extraction with the 13th character and continue until we are 6 characters from the end of the cell, we will have the data we want. Copying the following formula from E4 to E5:E12 does the job: *MID(B4,13,LEN(B4)-6-12)*. *Len(B4)* returns the total number of characters in the trimmed text. This formula (*MID* for Middle) begins with the 13th character and then extracts the number of characters equal to the total number less the 12 characters at the beginning (the product ID) and the 6 characters at the end (price). This subtraction simply leaves the product description!

Now suppose we are given the data with product ID in column C, the price in column D, and the product description in column E. Can we put these values together to recover our original text?

Text can easily be combined by using the CONCATENATE formula. Copying from F4 to F5:F12 the formula *CONCATENATE(C4," ",E4," ",D4)* recovers our original (trimmed) text, which you can see in Figure 6-4.

	C	D	E	F
1				
2				
3	Product ID	Price	Product Description	Concatenation
4	32592100AFES	304	CONTROLLERPENTIUM/100,(2)1GB H	32592100AFES CONTROLLERPENTIUM/100,(2)1GB H 304
5	32592100JCP9	225	DESKTOP UNIT	32592100JCP9 DESKTOP UNIT 225
6	325927008990	232	DESKTOP WINDOWS NT 4.0 SERVER	325927008990 DESKTOP WINDOWS NT 4.0 SERVER 232
7	325926008990	232	DESKTOP WINDOWS NT 4.0 WKST	325926008990 DESKTOP WINDOWS NT 4.0 WKST 232
8	325921008990	232	DESKTOP, DOS OS	325921008990 DESKTOP, DOS OS 232
9	325922008990	232	DESKTOP, WINDOWS DESKTOP OS	325922008990 DESKTOP, WINDOWS DESKTOP OS 232
10	325925008990	232	DESKTOP, WINDOWS NT OS	325925008990 DESKTOP, WINDOWS NT OS 232
11	325930008990	232	MINITOWER, NO OS	325930008990 MINITOWER, NO OS 232
12	32593000KEYY	232	MINI TOWER	32593000KEYY MINI TOWER 232

Figure 6-4 Using concatenation to recombine product ID, product description, and price.

The concatenation formula starts with the product ID in cell C4. The empty quotation marks (" ") insert a space. Next we add the product description from cell E4 and another space. Finally, we add the price from cell D4. We have now recovered the entire text describing each computer! Concatenation can also be performed by using the & sign. We could also recover the original product ID, product description, and price in a single cell with the formula *C4&" "&E4&" "&D4*.

If the product IDs did not always contain 12 characters, this method of extracting the information would fail. We could, however, extract the product IDs by using the FIND function to discover the location of the first space. Then we could obtain the product ID by using the LEFT function to extract all characters to the left of the first space. The example in the next section will show how this approach works.

If the price did not always contain precisely six characters, extracting the price would be a little tricky. You would need to use the OFFSET function, which you will learn about in Chapter 21.

Every day I receive data about total U.S. sales, which is computed in a cell as the sum of East, North, and South region sales. How can I extract East, North, and South sales to separate cells?

This problem was sent to me by an employee in Microsoft's finance department. She received a spreadsheet each day containing formulas such as =50+200+400, =5+124+1025, and so on. She needed to extract each number into a cell in its own column. For example, she wanted to extract the first number (East sales) in each cell to column C, the second number (North sales) to column D, and the third number (South sales) to column E. What makes this problem challenging is that we don't know the exact location of the character at which the second and third numbers start in each cell. In the first cell in our example, the second number begins with the fourth character. In the second cell, the second number begins with the third character. The data we're using in this example is in the file SalesStripping.xls, shown in Figure 6-5. By combining the FIND, LEFT, LEN, and MID functions, we can easily solve this problem as follows:

- Use the Edit, Replace command to replace each equal sign with a space. This converts each formula into text.

- Use the FIND function to locate the two plus (+) signs in each cell.

- East sales are represented by every character to the left of the first plus sign.

- North sales are represented by every character between the first and second plus sign.

- South sales are represented by every character to right of the second plus sign.

	A	B	C	D	E	F	G	H	I
1	Extracting Sales in Three Regions								
2	East+North+South	First +	Second +	East	North	Total Length	South		
3	10+300+400	3	7	10	300	10	400		
4	4+36.2+800	2	7	4	36.2	10	800		
5	3+23+4005	2	5	3	23	9	4005		
6	18+1+57.31	3	5	18	1	10	57.31		
7									
8									
9									

Figure 6-5   Extracting East, North, and South sales with a combination of the FIND, LEFT, LEN, and MID functions.

We begin by finding the location of the first plus sign for each piece of data. By copying from B3 to B4:B6 the formula FIND("+",A3,1), we can locate the first plus sign for each data point. To find the second plus sign, we begin *one character* after the first plus sign, copying from C3 to C4:C6 the formula *FIND("+",A3,B3+1)*.

To find East sales, we use the LEFT function to extract all the characters to the left of the first plus sign, copying from D3 to D4:D6 the formula *LEFT(A3,B3-1)*. To extract the North sales, we use the MID function to extract all the characters between the two plus signs. We begin one character after the first plus sign and extract the number of characters equal to *(Position of 2nd plus sign)-(Position of 1st plus sign) – 1*. If you leave out the –1, you'll get the second + sign. (Go ahead and check this.) So, to get the North sales, we copy from E3 to E4:E6 the formula *MID(A3,B3+1,C3-B3-1)*.

To extract South sales, we use the RIGHT function to extract all the characters to the right of the second plus sign. South sales will have the number of characters equal to *(Total characters in cell) – (Position of 2nd plus sign)*. We compute the total number of characters in each cell by copying from F3 to F4:F6 the formula *LEN(A3)*. Finally, we obtain South sales by copying from G3 to G4:G6 the formula *RIGHT(A3,F3-C3)*.

Using the Text To Columns Command to Extract Data

There is an easy way to extract East, North, and South sales (and data similar to this example) without using text functions. Simply select cells A3:A6, and then choose Text To Columns on the Data menu. Select Delimited, click Next, and then fill in the dialog box shown here:

Entering the plus sign in the Delimiters area directs Excel to separate each cell into columns, breaking at each occurrence of the plus sign. The result is shown here.

	A	B	C	D	E
	salesstripping.xls				
1	Extracting Sales in Three Regions				
2	Data Text to Columns Results				
3	10	300	400		
4	4	36.2	800		
5	3	23	4005		
6	18	1	57.31		
7					

Problems

1. Cells B2:B5 of the workbook Showbiz.xls contain the fictitious addresses of some of our favorite people, as shown here. Use text functions to extract each person's name to a single column and each person's street address to a single column.

	A	B
1		
2		Ally McBeal 1200 Lawyer Drive
3		Drew Carey 1000 Hollywood Lane
4		Britney Spears 300 Singer Road
5		Peyton Manning 500 QB Street

2. The workbook IDPrice.xls contains the product ID and prices for various products. Use text functions to put the product IDs and prices in separate columns. Use the Text To Columns command on the Data menu to accomplish the same goal.

	A	B
1		
2		ID and Price
3		xa1 304
4		za23 23
5		xa13 4123
6		zzx 12
7		a12q 374

3. The workbook QuarterlyGnpData.xls contains quarterly GNP data for the United States (in billions of 1996 dollars) in the format shown here. Extract this data to three separate columns, where the first column contains the year, the second column contains the quarter number, and the third column contains the GNP value.

	A	B	C	D	E
1	http://forecasts.org/data/index.htm				
2					
3	Real Gross National Product				
4					
5	Billions of Chained 1996 Dollars, Seasonally Adjusted Annual Rate				
6	Source: U.S. Department of Commerce, Bureau of Economic Analysis				
7					
8	DATE GNPC96				
9					
10	1950.1 1618.4				
11	1950.2 1667.2				
12	1950.3 1733.1				
13	1950.4 1763.9				
14	1951.1 1782.9				
15	1951.2 1814.9				
16	1951.3 1851.6				

4. The file TextStylesData.xls contains information about the size, color, and style for a variety of shirts. For example, the first shirt is style 100 (indicated by digits between the colon and the hyphen). Its color is 65, and its size is L. Use text functions to extract the style, color, and size of each shirt.

	A
1	**Item**
2	100's:100-65L
3	100's:100-65XL
4	100's:100-65XXL
5	100's:100-06M
6	100's:100-06L
7	100's:100-06XL
8	100's:100-06XXL
9	100's:100-05M
10	100's:100-05L
11	100's:100-05XL
12	100's:100-05XXL

7

Dates and Date Functions

■ When I enter dates into Excel, I often see a number such as 37625 rather than a date such as 1/4/2003. What does this number mean, and how do I change 37625 to a normal date?

■ Can I enter a formula that automatically displays today's date?

■ How do I determine a date that is 50 workdays after another date? What if I want to exclude holidays?

■ How do I determine the number of workdays between two dates?

■ I have 500 different dates entered in Excel. What formulas can I use to extract the month, year, day of the month, and day of the week from each date?

To illustrate the most commonly used month-day-year formats in Excel, suppose today is January 4, 2004. We could enter this date as any of the following:

■ 1/4/2004

■ 4-Jan-2004

■ January 4, 2004

■ 1/4/04

> **Note**   If you enter a year with only two digits, for years entered as 30 or higher, Excel assumes the digits represent years in the twentieth century. For example, 1/1/29 is treated as January 1, 2029, but 1/1/30 is treated as January 1, 1930. Each year, the year treated as dates in the twentieth century increases by one.

If you want to walk through the explanations for the problems in this chapter in Excel, open the file Date.xls. (Be sure you open the correct file. There is a similarly named file named Dates.xls, which is used in the next section.)

When I enter dates into Excel, I often see a number such as 37625 rather than a date such as 1/4/2003. What does this number mean, and how do I change 37625 to a normal date?

The way Excel treats calendar dates is sometimes confusing to the novice. The key is understanding that Excel can display a date in a variety of month-day-year formats, or it can display a date in *serial format*. A date in serial format, such as 37625, is simply a positive integer that represents the number of days between the given date and January 1, 1900. Both the current date and January 1, 1900, are included in the count. For example, Excel displays January 3, 1900, in serial format as the number 3, which means there are three days between January 1, 1900, and January 3, 1900 (including both days).

> **Note**   Excel assumes that 1900 was a leap year containing 366 days. In reality, 1900 contained only 365 days.

Figure 7-1 shows the worksheet named Serial Format in the file Dates.xls. Suppose you are given the dates shown in cells D5:D14 in serial format. For example, the value 37622 in cell D5 indicates a date that is 37,622 days after January 1, 1900 (including both January 1, 1900, and the current day). To display these dates in month-day-year format, copy them to E5:E14. Select the cell range E5:E14, choose Format Cells, and then select the date format you want from the list shown in Figure 7-2. The dates in E5:E14 will now be displayed in date format, as you can see in Figure 7-1. If you want to format dates in the serial number format, select E5:E14 and then choose Format Cells General.

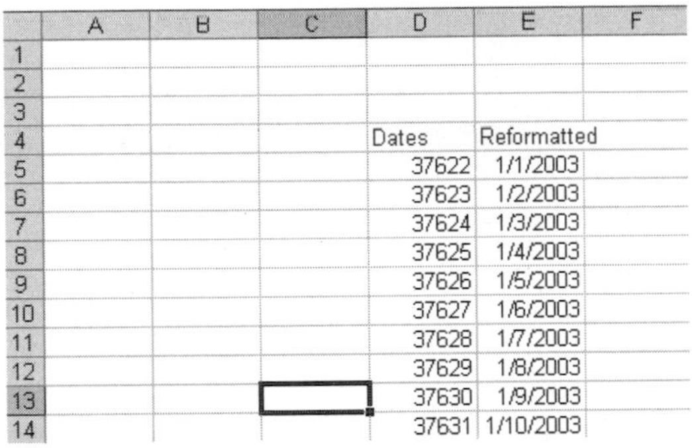

	A	B	C	D	E	F
1						
2						
3						
4				Dates	Reformatted	
5				37622	1/1/2003	
6				37623	1/2/2003	
7				37624	1/3/2003	
8				37625	1/4/2003	
9				37626	1/5/2003	
10				37627	1/6/2003	
11				37628	1/7/2003	
12				37629	1/8/2003	
13				37630	1/9/2003	
14				37631	1/10/2003	

Figure 7-1   Use the Format Cells command to change dates from serial number format to month-day-year format.

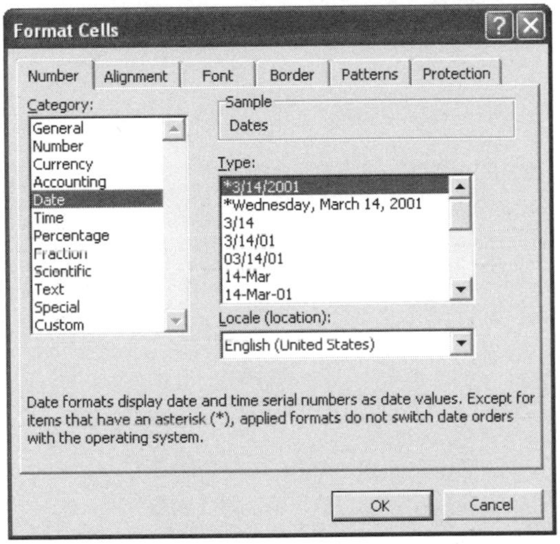

Figure 7-2   Reformatting a serial number to month-day-year format.

As I mentioned previously, simply changing the format of a cell in a date format to General will yield the date in serial format. Another way to obtain the date in serial format is to use the DATEVALUE function. Enclose any date in quotation marks, and this function will return the date's serial number. For example, cell I5 in the worksheet named Date Format contains the formula *DATEVALUE("1/4/2003")*. Excel yields 37625, which is the serial format for January 4, 2003.

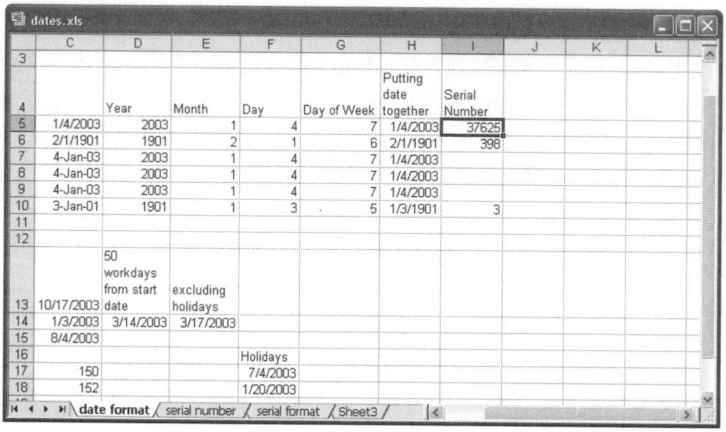

Figure 7-3 You can use the DATEVALUE function to format a date in serial format.

Can I enter a formula that automatically displays today's date?

Displaying today's date with a formula is easy, as you can see by looking at the worksheet Date Format, shown in Figure 7-4. Entering the *TODAY()* function in a cell will display today's date. Of course, whenever you open the workbook, the cell displays the current date. If you update a worksheet every day and want the current date to be displayed, use *TODAY()*.

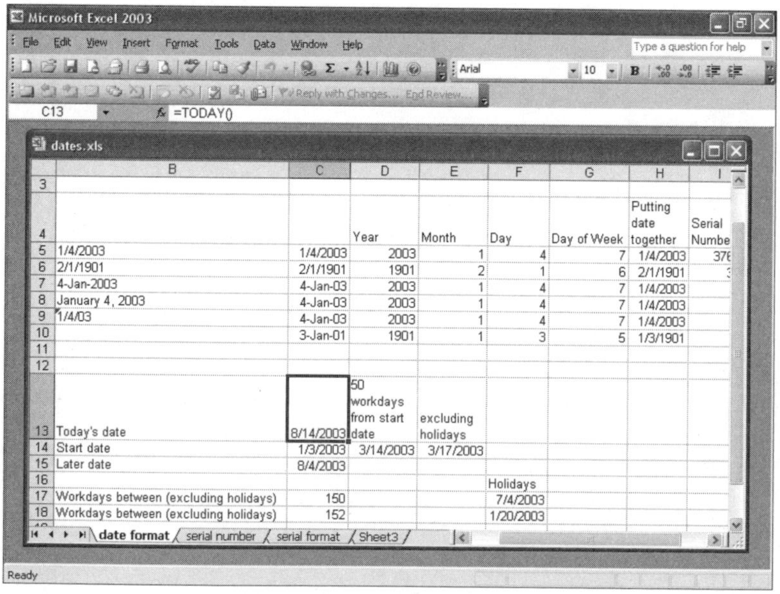

Figure 7-4 Use the TODAY function to display today's date. Use the WORKDAY and NETWORKDAYS functions to calculate dates a certain number of days from today.

How do I determine a date that is 50 workdays after another date? What if I want to exclude holidays?

The function *WORKDAY(start_date, #days, [holidays])* displays the date that is the number of workdays indicated in *#days* (a workday is a nonweekend day) after a given start date. *Holidays* is an optional argument for the function that allows you to exclude from the calculation any dates that are listed in a cell range. Thus, entering the formula *WORKDAY(C14,50)* in cell D14 of the Date Format worksheet tells us that 3/14/2003 is 50 workdays (Monday–Friday dates) after 01/03/2003. If we believe that the only two holidays that matter are Martin Luther King Day and the 4th of July, we can change the formula to *WORK-DAY(C14,50,F17:F18)*. With this addition, Excel does not count 01/20/2003 in its calculations, making 03/17/2003 the 50th workday after 01/03/2003.

> **Important**   To use the WORKDAY function, you must have the Analysis Toolpak installed. To install the toolpak, run Tools Add-Ins and select Analysis ToolPak and Analysis ToolPak VBA.

How do I determine the number of workdays between two dates?

The key to solving this problem is to use the NETWORKDAYS function. The syntax for this function is *NETWORKDAYS(start_date, end_date, [holidays])*, where *holidays* is an optional argument identifying a cell range that lists the dates you want to count as holidays. The NETWORKDAYS function returns the number of working days between *start_date* and *end_date* excluding weekends and any listed holidays. As an illustration of the NETWORKDAYS function, look at cell C18 in the Date Format worksheet, which contains the formula *NETWORKDAYS(C14,C15)*. This formula yields the number of working days between 1/3/2003 and 8/4/2003, which turns out to be 152. The formula *NETWORKDAYS(C14,C15,F17:F18)*, which is entered in cell C17 of the worksheet Date Format, yields the number of workdays between 1/3/2003 and 8/4/2003 excluding Martin Luther King Day and the 4th of July. The answer is 152 -2 = 150. The NETWORKDAYS function also requires installation of the Analysis Toolpak.

I have 500 different dates entered in an Excel worksheet. How do I write formulas that will extract from each date the month, year, day of the month, and day of the week?

The worksheet Date Format (see Figure 7-4) lists several dates in the cell range C5:C10. In C5 and C7:C9, I've used four different formats to display January 4, 2003. In columns D:G, I've extracted the year, month, day of the month, and day of the week for each date. By copying from D5 to D6:D9 the formula *YEAR(C5)*, we extract the year for each date. By copying from E5 to E6:E9 the formula *MONTH(C5)*, we extract the month (1 = January, 2 = February, and so on) part of each date. By copying from F5 to F6:F9 the formula *DAY(C5)*, we extract the day of the month for each date. Finally, by copying from G5 to G6:G9 the formula *WEEKDAY(C5,1)*, we extract the day of the week for each date.

> **Note**   When the last argument of the Weekday function is 1, 1 = Sunday, 2 = Monday, and so on. When the last argument is 2, 1 = Monday, 2 = Tuesday, and so on. When the last argument is 3, 0 = Monday, 1 = Tuesday, and so on.

Suppose you are given the year, month, and day of the month for a date. Is there an easy way to recover the actual date? The DATE function, whose arguments are *DATE(year,month,day)*, will return the date with the given year, month, and day of the month. In the worksheet Date Format, copying from cell H5 to cells H6:H9 the formula *DATE(D5,E5,F5)* recovers the dates we started with.

Problems

1. What is the serial format for January 25, 2006?

2. What is the serial format for February 14, 1950?

3. To what actual date does a serial format of 4526 correspond?

4. To what actual date does a serial format of 45000 correspond?

5. Determine the day that occurs 74 workdays after today's date (including holidays).

6. Answer question 5 but exclude the current year's Christmas, New Year's Day, and the 4th of July.

7. How many workdays (including holidays) are there between July 10, 2005, and August 15, 2006?

8. Answer question 7 but exclude Christmas, New Year's Day, and the 4th of July.

    File DateP.xls contains several hundred dates. Use this file for the next set of problems.

1. Determine the month, year, day of the month, and day of the week for each date.

2. Express each date in serial format.

3. A project will begin on December 4, 2005. The project consists of three activities: Activities 1, 2, and 3. Activity 2 can start the day after Activity 1 finishes. Activity 3 can start the day after Activity 2 finishes. Set up a spreadsheet that will accept as inputs the duration (in days) of the three activities and output both the month and year during which each activity is completed.

Evaluating Investments with Net Present Value Criteria

■ What is net present value (NPV)?

■ How do I use NPV to compare the merits of investments for which cash flows are received at several points in time?

■ How do I use the Excel NPV function?

■ How can I compute NPV when cash flows are received at the beginning of a year or in the middle of the year?

■ How can I compute NPV when cash flows are received at irregular intervals?

Consider the following two investments, whose cash flows are listed in the file NPVExample.xls and shown in Figure 8-1.

■ Investment 1 requires a cash outflow of $10,000 today and a cash outflow of $14,000 two years from now. One year from now, investment 1 yields $24,000.

■ Investment 2 requires a cash outflow of $6,000 today and a cash outflow of $1,000 two years from now. One year from now, investment 2 yields $8,000.

Which is the better investment? Investment 1 yields total cash inflow of $0, while investment 2 yields a total cash flow of $1,000. At first glance, investment 2 appears to be better. But wait a minute. Most of the cash outflow for investment 1 occurs two years from now, while most of the cash outflow for investment 2 occurs today. Spending $1.00 two years from now doesn't seem as costly as spending $1.00 today, so maybe investment 1 is better than it first appears. To determine which investment is better, we need to compare the values of cash flows received at different points in time. That's where the concept of net present value proves useful.

	A	B	C	D	E	F
1						
2						
3		r	0.2			
4	NPV	Time	0	1	2	Total cf
5	277.7778	Inv 1 CF	-10000	24000	-14000	0
6	-27.7778	Inv 2 CF	-6000	8000	-1000	1000
7		PV Inv 1	-10000	20000	-9722.22	
8		PV Inv 2	-6000	6666.667	-694.444	
9						
10		PV beginning of Year				
11		Inv 1	$277.78	$277.78		
12		Inv 2	($27.78)	($27.78)		
13		PV End of Year				
14		Inv 1	$231.48			
15		Inv 2	($23.15)			
16		PV Middle of year				
17		Inv 1	$253.58			
18		Inv 2	($25.36)			

Figure 8-1 To determine which investment is better, we need to calculate net present value.

What is net present value?

The net present value (NPV) of a stream of cash flows received at different points in time is simply the value *measured in today's dollars* of the stream of cash flows. Suppose we have $1.00 today and we invest this dollar at an annual interest rate of r percent. This dollar will grow to $1 + r$ dollars in the first year, $(1+r)^2$ in two years, and so on. We can say in some sense that $1 now equals $(1+r)$ a year from now and $(1+r)^2$ two years from now. In general, we can say that $1 now is equal to $(1+r)^n$ n years from now. As an equation, we can express this calculation as follows:

\$1now = \$(1+r)^n received n years from now

If we divide both sides of this equation by $(1+r)^n$, we get the following important result:

$$\frac{\$1}{(1+r)^n} \, Now = \$1 \; received \; n \; years \; from \, now$$

This result tells us how to compute (in today's dollars) the NPV of any sequence of cash flows. You can convert any cash flow to today's dollars by multiplying the cash flow received n years from now (n can be a fraction) by

$$\frac{1}{(1+r)^n}$$

You then add up the value of the cash flows (in today's dollars) to find the investment's NPV. Let's assume r is equal to 0.2. We could calculate the NPV for the two investments we're considering as follows:

$$Investment\,1\,NPV = -10,000 + \frac{24,000}{(1+0.20)} + \frac{-14,000}{(1+0.2)^2} = \$277.78$$

$$Investment\,2\,NPV = -6,000 + \frac{8000}{(1+0.2)} + \frac{-1000}{(1+0.2)^2} = \$-27.78$$

On the basis of NPV, investment 1 is superior to investment 2. Although total cash flow for investment 2 exceeds total cash flow for investment 1, investment 1 has a better NPV because a greater proportion of investment 1's negative cash flow comes later and the NPV criterion gives less weight to cash flows that come later. If we use a value of .02 for r, investment 2 has a larger NPV because when r is very small, later cash flows are not discounted as much and NPV returns results similar to those derived by ranking investments according to total cash flow.

Note   I made up the interest rate $r = 0.2$, skirting the issue of how to determine an appropriate value of r. You would need to study finance for at least a year to understand the issues involved in determining an appropriate value for r. The appropriate value of r used to compute NPV is often called the company's *cost of capital*. Suffice it to say that most U.S. companies use an annual cost of capital between 0.1 (10 percent) and 0.2 (20 percent). If the annual interest rate is chosen according to accepted finance practices, projects with NPV>0 increase the value of a firm, projects with NPV<0 decrease the value of a firm, and projects with NPV=0 keep the value of a firm unchanged. A firm should (if it had unlimited investment capital) invest in every available investment having positive NPV.

To determine the NPV of investment 1 in Excel, I first assigned the range name r_ to the interest rate (located in cell C3). I then copied the Time 0 cash flow from C5 to C7. I determined the NPV for investment 1's year 1 and year 2 cash flow by copying from D7 to E7 the formula *D5/(1+r_)^D$4*. (The symbol ^, located over the number 6 on the keyboard, raises a number to a power.) In cell A5, I computed the NPV of investment 1 by adding the NPV of each year's cash flow with the formula *SUM(C7:E7)*. To determine the NPV for investment 2, I copied the formulas from C7:E7 to C8:E8 and copied the formula from A5 to A6.

How do I use the Excel NPV function?

The Excel *NPV* function uses the syntax *NPV(rate, range of cells)*. Given a rate, the function determines the NPV for the given rate of the cash flows in the range of cells. The function's calculation assumes that the first cash flow is one period from now. In other words, entering the formula *NPV(r_,C5:E5)* will not determine the NPV for investment 1. Instead, this formula (entered in cell C14) computes the NPV of the following sequence of cash flows: -$10,000 a year from now, $24,000 two years from now, and -$14,000 three years from now. Let's call this investment 3. The NPV of investment 3 is $231.48. To compute the actual cash NPV of investment 1, I entered in cell C11 the formula *C7+NPV(r_,D5:E5)*. This formula does not discount the Time 0 cash flow at all (which is correct because Time 0 cash flow is already in today's dollars), multiplies the cash flow in D5 by

$$\frac{1}{1.2}$$

and then multiplies the cash flow in E5 by

$$\frac{1}{1.2^2}$$

The formula in cell C11 yields the correct NPV of investment 1, $277.78.

How can I compute NPV when cash flows are received at the beginning of a year or in the middle of the year?

To use the NPV function to compute the net present value of a project whose cash flows always occur at the beginning of a year, you can use the approach we followed to determine the NPV of investment 1: separate out the year 1 cash flow and apply the NPV function to the remaining cash flows. Alternatively, observe that for any year n, $1 received at the beginning of year n is equivalent to $(1+r)$ received at the end of year n. Remember that in one year, a dollar will grow by a factor $(1+r)$. Thus, if we multiply the result obtained with the NPV function by $(1+r)$, we can convert the NPV of a sequence of end-of-year cash flows to the NPV of a sequence of cash flows received at the beginning of the year. We can also compute the NPV of investment 1 in cell D11 with the formula *(1+r_)*C14*. Of course, we again obtain an NPV of $277.78.

Now suppose the cash flows for an investment occur in the middle of each year. For an organization such as MSN, which receives monthly subscription revenue, we can approximate the 12 monthly revenues received during a given year as a lump sum received in the middle of the year. How can we use the NPV function to determine the NPV of a sequence of mid-year cash flows? For any year *n*,

$$\$\sqrt{1+r}$$

received at the end of year *n* is equivalent to $1 received at the middle of year *n* because in half a year $1 will grow by a factor of

$$\sqrt{1+r}$$

If we assume the cash flows for investment 1 occur mid year, we can compute the NPV of the mid-year version of investment 1 in cell C17 with the formula *SQRT(1+r_)*C14*. We obtain a value of $253.58.

How can I compute NPV when cash flows are received at irregular intervals?

Cash flows often occur at irregular intervals, which makes computing the NPV or internal rate of return (IRR) of these cash flows more difficult. Fortunately, the Excel XNPV function makes computing the NPV of irregularly timed cash flows a snap.

> **Note**   To use the XNPV function, you need to first install the Analysis Toolpak. To install the Analysis Toolpak, select Tools, Add-Ins and then check the options for the Analysis Toolpak and Analysis Toolpak VBA.

The XNPV function uses the syntax *XNPV(rate,values,dates)*. The first date listed must be the earliest. Other dates need not be listed in chronological order. The XNPV function computes the NPV of the given cash flows assuming the current date is the first date in the sequence. For example, if the first listed date is 2/15/03, the NPV is computed in February 15, 2003, dollars.

To illustrate the use of the XNPV function, look at the example on Sheet 1 in the file XNPV.xls, which is shown in Figure 8-2. Suppose that on 4/08/01 we paid out $900. Later we receive the following amounts:

- $300 on 8/15/01
- $400 on 1/15/02

- $200 on 6/25/02

- $100 on 7/03/03

If the annual interest rate is 10 percent, what is the NPV of these cash flows? We enter the dates (in Excel date format) in D3:D7 and the cash flows in E3:E7. Entering the formula *XNPV(A9,E3:E7,D3:D7)* in cell D11 computes the project's NPV in 4/08/01 dollars because 4/08/01 is the first date listed. This project would have an NPV, in 4/8/2001 dollars, of $20.63.

	A	B	C	D	E	F	G
1							
2	XNPV Function		Code	Date	Cash Flow	Time	df
3			36989.00	4/8/2001	-900		1
4			37118.00	8/15/2001	300	0.353425	0.966876
5			37271.00	1/15/2002	400	0.772603	0.929009
6			37432.00	6/25/2002	200	1.213699	0.890762
7			37805.00	7/3/2003	100	2.235616	0.808094
8	Rate						
9		0.1					
10				XNPV	Direct		
11				20.62822	20.628217		

Figure 8-2 XNPV function example.

The computations performed by the XNPV function are as follows:

1. Compute the number of years after April 8, 2001, that each date occurred. (We did this in column F.) For example, 8/15/01 is .3534 years after 04/08/01.

2. Discount cash flows at the rate

$$\left(\frac{1}{1+rate}\right)^{years\,after}$$

For example, the 8/15/2001 cash flow is discounted by

$$\left(\frac{1}{1+.1}\right)^{.3534} = .967$$

3. Sum up in cell E11 overall cash flows, *(cash flow value)*(discount factor)*.

Suppose that today's date is actually 2/14/01. How would you compute the NPV of an investment in today's dollars? Simply add a row with today's date and 0 cash flow and include this row in the range for the XNPV function. (See Figure 8-3 and the worksheet Today.) The NPV of the project in today's dollars is $20.34.

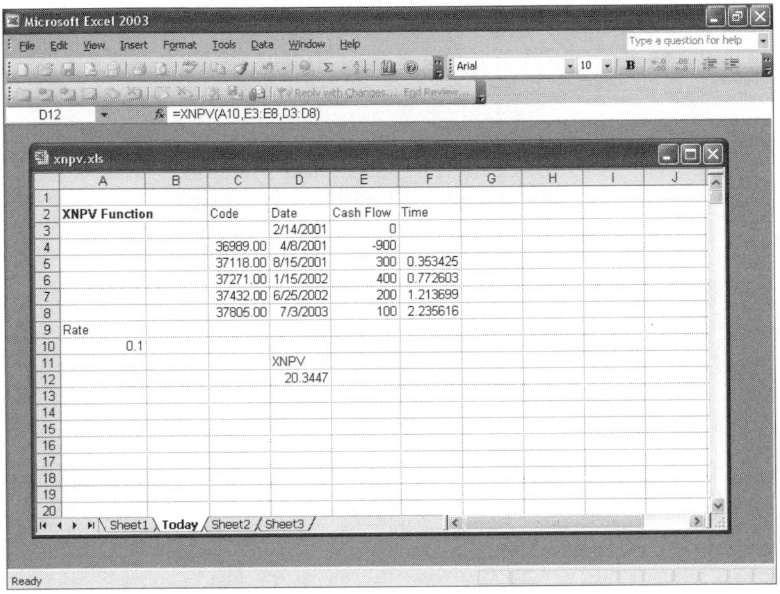

Figure 8-3   NPV converted to today's dollars.

Problems

1. An NBA player is to receive a $1,000,000 signing bonus today and $2,000,000 one year, two years, and three years from now. Assuming r = .10 and ignoring tax considerations, would he be better off receiving $6,000,000 today?

2. A project has the following cash flows:

Now	1 Year From Now	2 Years From Now	3 Years From Now
-$4 million	$4 million	$4 million	-$3 million

   If the company's cost of capital is 15 percent, should they do the project?

3. Beginning one month from now, an MSN customer pays $25 per month in revenues to MSN for the next five years. Assuming all revenue for a year is received at the middle of a year, estimate the NPV of these revenues. Use r = .15.

4.   Use the XNPV function to obtain an exact answer to problem 3.

5.   Consider the following set of cash flows over a four-year period:

Year	1	2	3	4
	($600.00)	$550.00	($680.00)	$1,000.00

Determine the NPV of these cash flows if r = .15 and cash flows occur at the end of the year.

6.   Solve problem 5 assuming cash flows occur at the beginning of each year.

7.   Consider the following cash flows:

Date	Cash Flow
12/15/01	($1,000.00)
1/11/02	$300.00
4/07/03	$600.00
7/15/04	$925.00

If today is November 1, 2001, and r = .15, what is the NPV of these cash flows?

8.   After earning an MBA, a student will begin working at an $80,000-a-year job on September 1, 2005. She expects to receive a 5 percent raise each year until she retires on September 1, 2035. If the cost of capital is 8 percent a year, determine the total present value of her before tax earnings.

Internal Rate of Return

- What is internal rate of return (IRR)?

- How can I find the IRR of cash flows?

- Does a project always have a unique IRR?

- Are there conditions that guarantee a project will have a unique IRR?

- If two projects both have a single IRR, how do I use the projects' IRRs?

- How can I find the IRR of irregularly spaced cash flows?

The net present value (NPV) of a sequence of cash flows depends on the interest rate (r) used. For example, if we consider cashflows for projects 1 and 2 (see the worksheet IRR in the file IRR.xls, shown in Figure 9-1), we find that for r = 0.2, project 2 has a larger NPV, and for r = 0.01, project 1 has a larger NPV. When we use NPV to rank investments, the ranking of investments can depend on the interest rate. It is the nature of human beings to want to boil everything in life down to a single number. The *internal rate of return* (IRR for short) of a project is simply the interest rate that makes the NPV of the project equal to 0. If a project has a unique IRR, the IRR has a nice interpretation. For example, if a project has an IRR of 15 percent, we receive an annual rate of return of 15 percent on the cash flow we have invested. In this chapter's examples, we'll find that project 1 has an IRR of 47.5 percent, which means that the $400 we have invested at *time 1* is yielding an annual rate of return of 47.5 percent. Sometimes, however, a project might have more than one IRR or even no IRR. In these cases, speaking about the project's IRR is useless.

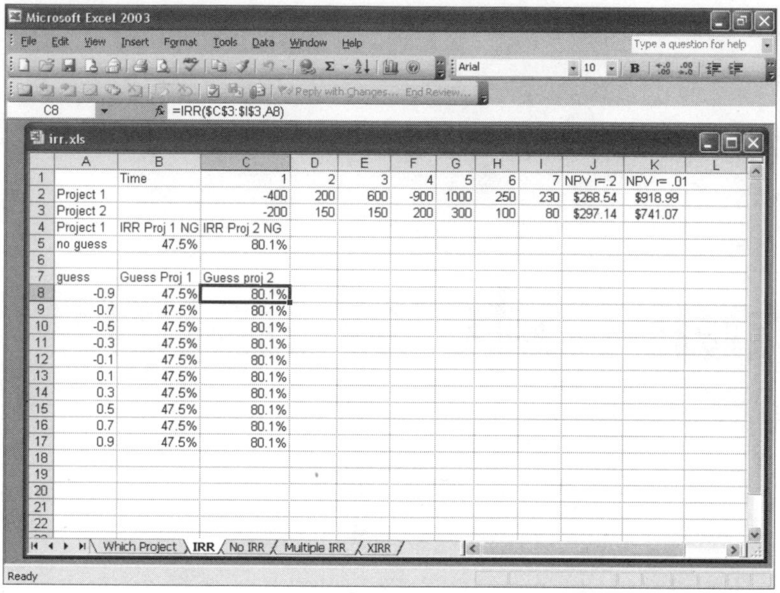

	A	B	C	D	E	F	G	H	I	J	K
1		Time	1	2	3	4	5	6	7	NPV r=.2	NPV r= .01
2	Project 1		-400	200	600	-900	1000	250	230	$268.54	$918.99
3	Project 2		-200	150	150	200	300	100	80	$297.14	$741.07
4	Project 1	IRR Proj 1 NG	IRR Proj 2 NG								
5	no guess	47.5%	80.1%								
6											
7	guess	Guess Proj 1	Guess proj 2								
8	-0.9	47.5%	80.1%								
9	-0.7	47.5%	80.1%								
10	-0.5	47.5%	80.1%								
11	-0.3	47.5%	80.1%								
12	-0.1	47.5%	80.1%								
13	0.1	47.5%	80.1%								
14	0.3	47.5%	80.1%								
15	0.5	47.5%	80.1%								
16	0.7	47.5%	80.1%								
17	0.9	47.5%	80.1%								

Figure 9-1 Example of the IRR function.

How can I find the IRR of cash flows?

The Excel IRR function calculates internal rate of return. The function has the syntax *IRR (range of cash flows, [guess])*, where *guess* is an optional argument. If you do not enter a guess for a project's IRR, Excel begins its calculations with a guess that the project's IRR is 10 percent and then varies the estimate of the IRR until it finds an interest rate that makes the project's NPV equal 0 (the project's IRR). If Excel can't find an interest rate that makes the project's NPV equal 0, Excel returns #NUM. In cell B5, I've entered the formula *IRR(C2:I2)* to compute project 1's IRR. Excel returns 47.5 percent. Thus, if we use an annual interest rate of 47.5 percent, project 1 will have an NPV of 0. Similarly, we find that project 2 has an IRR of 80.1 percent.

Even if the IRR function finds an IRR, a project might have more than one IRR. To check whether a project has more than one IRR, you can vary the initial guess of the project's IRR (say from -90 percent to 90 percent). I varied the guess for project 1's IRR by copying from B8 to B9:B17 the formula *IRR($C$2:$I$2,A8)*. Because all the guesses for project 1's IRR yield 47.5 percent, we're fairly confident that project 1 has a *unique* IRR of 47.5 percent. Similarly, we can be fairly confident that project 2 has a unique IRR of 80.1 percent.

Does a project always have a unique IRR?

In the worksheet Multiple IRR in the file IRR.xls (see Figure 9-2), you can see that project 3 (cash flows of -20, 82, -60, 2) has two IRRs. I varied the guess about project 3's IRR from -90 percent to 90 percent by copying from C8 to C9:C17 the formula *IRR($B$4:$E$4,B8)*.

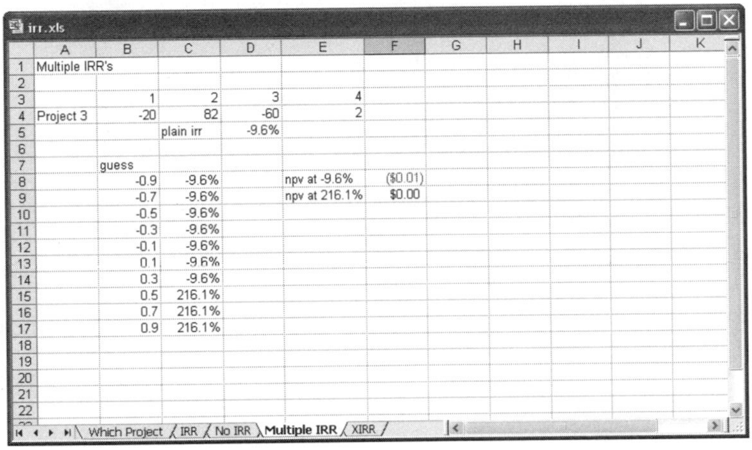

	A	B	C	D	E	F
1	Multiple IRR's					
2						
3		1	2	3	4	
4	Project 3	-20	82	-60	2	
5			plain irr	-9.6%		
6						
7		guess				
8		-0.9	-9.6%		npv at -9.6%	($0.01)
9		-0.7	-9.6%		npv at 216.1%	$0.00
10		-0.5	-9.6%			
11		-0.3	-9.6%			
12		-0.1	-9.6%			
13		0.1	-9.6%			
14		0.3	-9.6%			
15		0.5	216.1%			
16		0.7	216.1%			
17		0.9	216.1%			

Figure 9-2 Project with more than one IRR.

Note that for a guess of 30 percent or less, the IRR is -9.6 percent. For other guesses, we find an IRR of 216.1 percent. For both these interest rates, project 3 has an NPV of 0.

In the worksheet No IRR in the file IRR.xls (shown in Figure 9-3), you can see that no matter what guess we use for project 4's IRR, we receive the #NUM message. This message indicates that project 4 has no IRR.

When a project has multiple IRRs or no IRR, the concept of IRR loses virtually all meaning. Despite this problem, however, many companies still use IRR as their major tool for ranking investments.

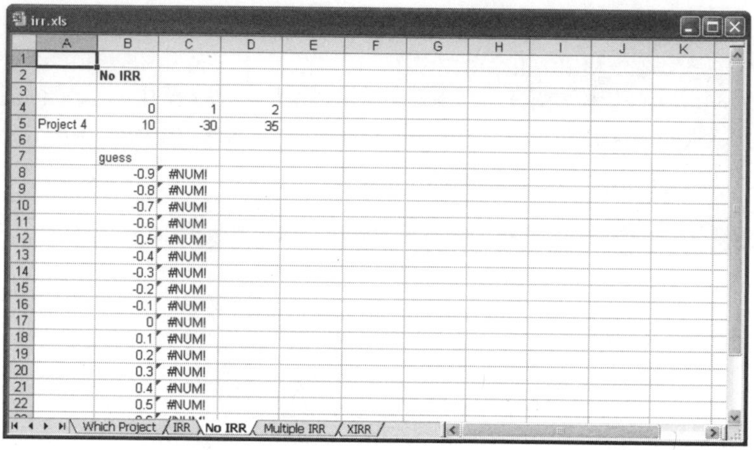

Figure 9-3   Project with no IRR.

Are there conditions that guarantee a project will have a unique IRR?

If a project's sequence of cash flows contains exactly one change in sign, the project is guaranteed to have a unique IRR. For example, in projects 1 and 2, the sign of the cash flow sequence is - + + + + +. There is only one change in sign (between Time 1 and Time 2), so both projects have a unique IRR. For project 3, the signs of the cash flows are - + - +. Because the sign of the cash flows changes three times, a unique IRR is not guaranteed. For project 4, the signs of the cash flows are + - +. Because the signs of the cash flows change twice, a unique IRR is not guaranteed in this case either. Most capital investment projects (such as building a plant) begin with a negative cash flow followed by a sequence of positive cash flows. Therefore, most capital investment projects will have a unique IRR.

If two projects both have a single IRR, how do I use the projects' IRRs?

If a project has a unique IRR, we can state that the project increases the value of the company *if and only if* the project's IRR exceeds the annual cost of capital. For example, if the cost of capital for a company is 15 percent, both projects 1 and 2 would increase the value of the company.

Suppose two projects are under consideration (both having unique IRRs), but we can undertake at most one project. It's tempting to believe that we should choose the project with the larger IRR. To see that this belief can lead to incorrect decisions, look at Figure 9-4 and the worksheet named Which Project in IRR.xls. Project 5 has an IRR of 40 percent, and project 6 has an IRR of 50 percent. If we rank projects based on IRR and can choose only one project, we would choose project 6. Remember, however, that a project's NPV measures the amount of value the project adds to the company. Clearly, project 5 will (for virtually any cost of capital) have a larger NPV than project 6. Therefore, if only a single project can be chosen, project 5 is it. IRR is problematic because it ignores the scale of the project. While project 6 is better than project 5 on a per-dollar-invested basis, the larger scale of project 5 makes it more valuable to the company than project 6. IRR does not reflect the scale of a project, while NPV does.

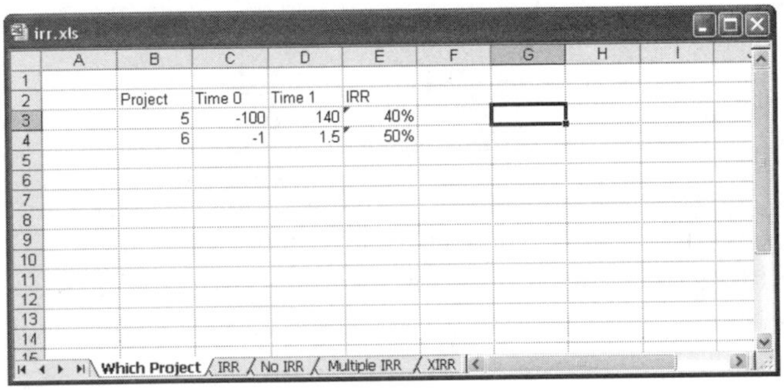

Project	Time 0	Time 1	IRR
5	-100	140	40%
6	-1	1.5	50%

Figure 9-4 IRR can lead to an incorrect choice of which project to pursue.

How can I find the IRR of irregularly spaced cash flows?

Cash flows occur on actual dates, not just at the start or end of the year. The XIRR function has the syntax

```
XIRR(cash flow, dates, [guess])
```

The XIRR function determines the IRR of a sequence of cash flows that occur on any set of irregularly spaced dates. As with the IRR function, *guess* is an optional argument. As with the XNPV function, the XIRR function cannot be used unless you have installed the Analysis Toolpak. For an example of how to use the XIRR function, look at Figure 9-5 and sheet XIRR of the file IRR.xls.

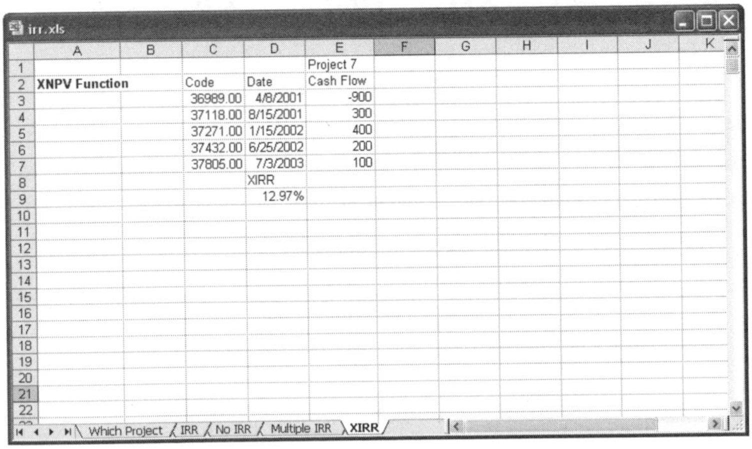

XNPV Function	Code	Date	Project 7 Cash Flow
	36989.00	4/8/2001	-900
	37118.00	8/15/2001	300
	37271.00	1/15/2002	400
	37432.00	6/25/2002	200
	37805.00	7/3/2003	100
		XIRR	
		12.97%	

Figure 9-5 Example of the XIRR function.

The formula *XIRR(E3:E7, D3:D7)* in cell D8 shows that the IRR of project 7 is 12.97 percent.

Problems

1. Compute all IRRs for the following sequence of cash flows:

Year 1	Year 2	Year 3	Year 4	Year 5	Year 6	Year 7
-$10,000	$8,000	$1,500	$1,500	$1,500	$1,500	-$1,500

2. Consider a project with the following cash flows. Determine the project's IRR. If the annual cost of capital is 20 percent would you undertake this project?

Year 1	Year 2	Year 3
-$4,000	$2,000	$4,000

3. Find all IRRs for the following project:

Year 1	Year 2	Year 3
$100	-$300	$250

4. Find all IRRs for a project having the given cash flows on the listed dates.

1/10/ 2003	7/10/ 2003	5/25/ 2004	7/18/ 2004	3/20/ 2005	4/1/ 2005	1/10/ 2006
-$1,000	$900	$800	$700	$500	$500	$350

5. Consider the following two projects. Assume a company's cost of capital is 15 percent. Find the IRR and NPV of each project. Which projects add value to the company? If the company can choose only a single project, which project should it choose?

	Year 1	Year 2	Year 3	Year 4
Project 1	-$40	$130	$19	$26
Project 2	-$80	$36	$36	$36

6. 25-year-old Meg Prior is going to invest $10,000 in her retirement fund at the beginning of each of the next 40 years. Assume that during each of the next 30 years Meg will earn 15 percent on her investments and during the last 10 years before she retires, her investments will earn 5 percent. Determine the IRR associated with her investments and her final retirement position. How do you know there will be a unique IRR? How would you interpret the unique IRR?

7. Give an intuitive explanation of why project 6 (on the worksheet Which Project in the file IRR.xls) has an IRR of 50 percent.

8. Consider a project having the following cash flows.

Year 1	Year 2	Year 3
-$70,000	$12,000	$15,000

Try to find the IRR of this project without using a guess. What problem arises? What is the IRR of this project? Does the project have a unique IRR?

10

Functions for Personal Financial Decisions: The PV, FV, PMT, PPMT, and IPMT Functions

- Should I pay $11,000 today for a copier or $3,000 a year for 5 years?

- If I invest $2,000 a year for 40 years toward my retirement and earn 8 percent a year on my investments, how much will I have when I retire?

- I am borrowing $10,000 on a 10-month loan with an annual interest rate of 8 percent. What will my monthly payments be? How much principal and interest am I paying each month?

When we borrow money to buy a car or a house, we always wonder whether we're getting a good deal. When we save for retirement, we're curious how large a nest egg we'll have when we retire. In our daily work and personal life, financial questions similar to these questions often arise. Knowing how to use the PV, FV, PMT, PPMT, and IPMT functions in Excel makes answering these types of questions easy.

Should I pay $11,000 today for a copier or $3,000 a year for 5 years?

The key to answering this question is attributing a value to the annual payments of $3,000 per year. Let's assume the cost of capital is 12 percent per year. We could use the NPV function to answer this question, but the PV function provides a much quicker means to solve this problem. (For more information about the NPV function, see Chapter 8.)

The PV function returns the value in today's dollars of a series of future payments, assuming periodic, constant payments and a constant interest rate. A stream of cash flows that includes the same amount of cash outflow (or inflow) each period is called an *annuity*, and assuming that each period's interest rate is the same, an annuity can be valued using the PV function. Here's the syntax for the PV function:

```
PV(rate,#per,[pmt],[fv],[type])
```

- *Rate* is the interest rate per period. If you borrow money at 6 percent per year and the period is a year, *rate* equals 0.06. If the period is a month, *rate* equals 0.06/12, or 0.005.

- *#per* is the number of periods in the annuity. In our copier example, *#per* equals 5. If payments for the copier are made each month for 5 years, *#per* equals 60. Your rate must be consistent with *#per*, of course. In other words, if *#per* implies that a period is a month, you need to use a monthly interest rate. If *#per* implies that a period is a year, use an annual interest rate.

- *Pmt* is the payment made each period. In our example, *pmt* is $5,000. A payment is a positive number, while money received is a negative number.

- *Fv* is the cash balance (or future value) that you want to have after the last payment is made. In our copier example, *fv* equals 0. (If we want a $5,000 cash balance after the last payment, *fv* would equal $5,000.) If *fv* is omitted, it's assumed to equal 0.

- *Type* is either 0 or 1. *Type* indicates when payments are made. If *type* is omitted or equal to 0, payments are made at the end of each period. When *type* equals 1, payments are made at the beginning of each period.

The solution to the question about the best way to pay for the copier is included in the file PV.xls, shown in Figure 10-1.

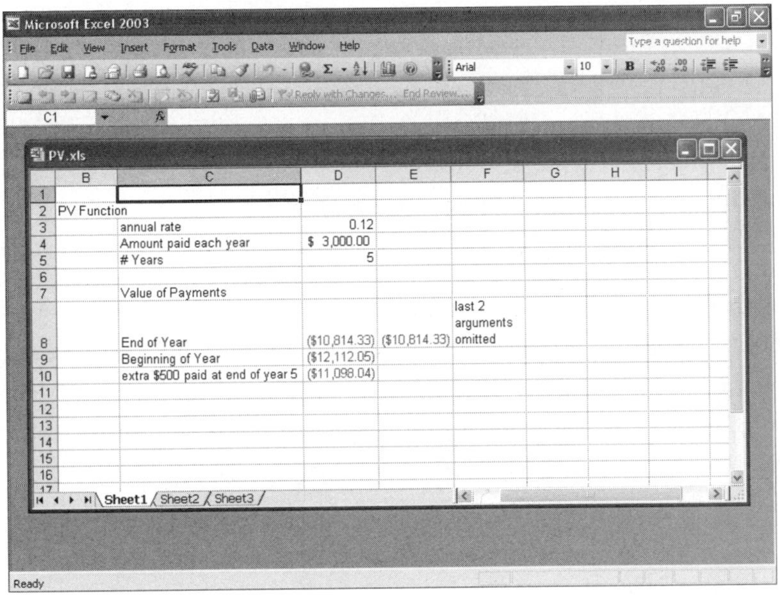

Figure 10-1   The PV function calculates the present value of payments.

In cell D8, I computed the present value of paying $3,000 per year for 5 years (at the end of each year) with a 12 percent cost of capital. Here's the formula I used:

```
PV(annual_rate,Years,Amount_paid_each_year,0,0)
```

I named the cells D3:D5 with the labels in C3:C5 by using the Insert, Name Create command. (See Chapter 1 for information about creating range names.) Excel returns a net present value of -$10,814.33. (The negative sign means we are paying money out.) By omitting the last two arguments, I obtain the same answer in cell E8 with the formula

```
PV(annual_rate,Years,Amount_paid_each_year)
```

Making payments at the end of the year is a better deal than paying out $11,000 today.

To calculate the net present value of the payments if we make payments of $3,000 on the copier for 5 years at the beginning of each year, I used the formula in cell D9:

```
PV(annual_rate,Years,Amount_paid_each_year,0,1)
```

Changing the last argument from a 0 to a 1 changes the calculation, which is now based on payments at the beginning of the year rather than payments at the end of the year. With this change, the present value of the payments is

$12,112.05, so it's better to pay $11,000 today than to make payments at the beginning of the year.

Suppose we pay $3,000 at the end of each year and we have to include an extra $500 payment at the end of year 5. We can find the present value of all our payments by including a future value of $500, using the following formula:

```
PV(annual_rate,Years,Amount_paid_each_year,500,0).
```

In this calculation, the present value of the payments equals $11,098.04.

If I invest $2,000 a year for 40 years toward my retirement and earn 8 percent a year on my investments, how much will I have when I retire?

In this situation, we want to know the value of an annuity in future dollars (40 years from now) and not in today's dollars. This is a job for the FV or *future value* function. The future value function calculates the future value of an investment assuming periodic, constant payments with a constant interest rate. The syntax of the FV function is as follows:

```
FV(rate,#per,[pmt],[pv],[type])
```

- *Rate* is the interest rate per period. In our example, *rate* is 0.08

- *#per* is the number of periods in the future at which you want to compute the future value. *#per* is also the number of periods during which the annuity payment is received. In our case, *#per* equals 40.

- *Pmt* is the payment made each period. In this example, *pmt* is -$2,000. The negative sign indicates we are receiving money.

- *Pv* is the amount of money (in today's dollars) owed right now. In our case, *pv* equals $0. If we owed someone $10,000 today, *pv* would equal $10,000. If we had $10,000 in the bank today, *pv* would equal -$10,000. If *pv* is omitted, it's assumed to equal zero.

- *Type* is 0 or 1, and it indicates when payments are due or money is deposited. If *type* equals 0 or is omitted, money is deposited at the end of a period. In our example, *type* is 0 or omitted. If *type* equals 1, payments are made or money is deposited at the beginning of a period.

The file FV.xls, shown in Figure 10-2, contains the resolution to this question. In cell B7, I've entered the formula *FV(Rate,Years,-Annual_deposit,0,0)* to find that in 40 years our nest egg will be worth $518,113.04. Notice that I entered a negative value for our annual payment because a deposit can be viewed as a negative payment. In cell C7, I obtained the same answer by omitting the last two (unnecessary) arguments. The formula entered in C7 is

FV(Rate,Years,-Annual_deposit). If deposits are made at the beginning of each year for 40 years, the formula entered in cell B8, which is *FV(Rate,Years,-Annual_deposit,0,1)*, yields the value of our nest egg in 40 years, $559,562.08.

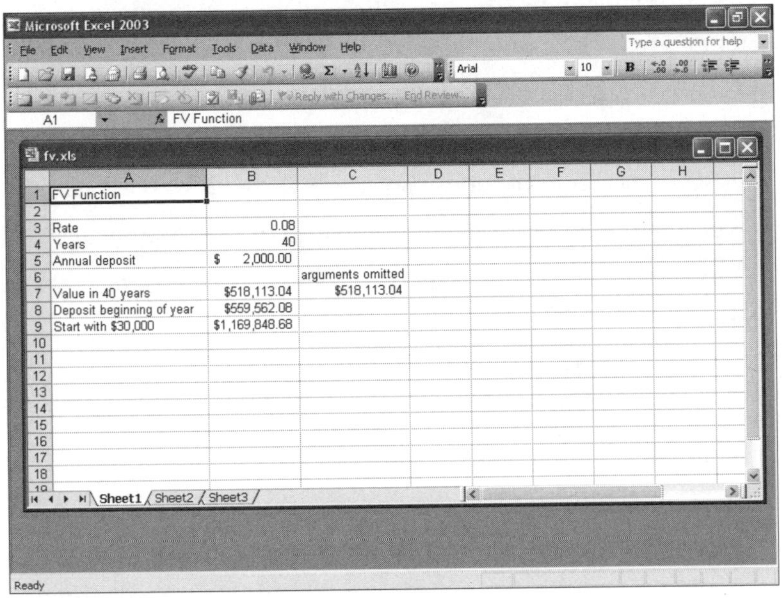

Figure 10-2   You can use the FV function to calculate the future value of investments.

Finally, suppose that in addition to investing $2,000 at the end of each of the next 40 years, we have $30,000 with which to invest initially. If we earn 8 percent per year on our investments, how much money will we have when we retire in 40 years? We can answer this question by setting *pv* equal to -$30,000 in the FV function. (The negative sign indicates that we have money rather than owe someone money.) In cell B9 the formula

```
FV(Rate,Years,-Annual_deposit,0,0)+FV(Rate,Years,0,-30000,1)
```

yields a future value of $1,169,848.68. The formula *FV(Rate,Years,0,-30000,1)* yields the future value (in 40 years) of $30,000 received today. The formula includes *type* = 1 because $30,000 is received today. I used a negative sign with the $30,000 because we are "owed" -$30,000. By the way, because our money is growing at 8 percent a year, *FV(Rate,Years,0,-30000,1)* simply yields $(1.08)^{40}(\$30,000)$.

I am borrowing $10,000 on a 10-month loan with an annual interest rate of 8 percent. What will my monthly payments be? How much principal and interest am I paying each month?

The Excel PMT function computes the periodic payments for a loan, assuming constant payments and a constant interest rate. The syntax of the PMT function is

```
PMT(rate,#per,pv,[fv],[type])
```

- *Rate* is the per-period interest rate on the loan. In our example, we'll use one month as a period, so *rate* = 0.08/12, or 0.006666667.

- *#per* is the number of payments made. In our case, *#per* = 10.

- *Pv* is the present value of all our payments. That is, *pv* is the amount of the loan. In our case, *pv* equals $10,000.

- *Fv* is an optional argument that indicates the cash balance you want after making the last payment. In our case, *fv* is 0. If *fv* is omitted, Excel assumes it is 0. If you want to have all but $1,000 of the loan paid off at the end of 10 months, *fv* would equal -1,000.

- *Type* is 0 or 1 and indicates when payments are due. If *type* equals 0 or is omitted, payments are made at the end of the period. In this example, we'll first assume end of month payment. If *type* is 1, payments are made (or money deposited) at beginning of the period.

You can find an example of the PMT function in the file PMT.xls, shown in Figure 10-3. In cell G1, I computed the monthly payment on a 10-month loan for $10,000, assuming an 8 percent annual rate and end-of-month payments. The formula is:

```
PMT(rate,months,loan_amount)
```

(Note that I used the names in cell range D1:D3 for the cell range E1:E3.) The monthly payment is $1,037.03.

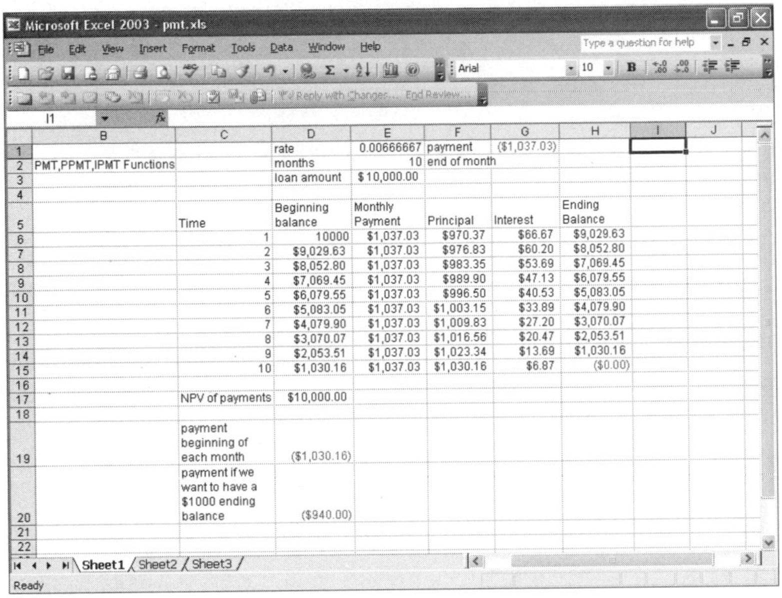

Row	B	C	D	E	F	G	H
1			rate	0.00666667	payment	($1,037.03)	
2	PMT,PPMT,IPMT Functions		months	10	end of month		
3			loan amount	$10,000.00			
4							
5		Time	Beginning balance	Monthly Payment	Principal	Interest	Ending Balance
6		1	10000	$1,037.03	$970.37	$66.67	$9,029.63
7		2	$9,029.63	$1,037.03	$976.83	$60.20	$8,052.80
8		3	$8,052.80	$1,037.03	$983.35	$53.69	$7,069.45
9		4	$7,069.45	$1,037.03	$989.90	$47.13	$6,079.55
10		5	$6,079.55	$1,037.03	$996.50	$40.53	$5,083.05
11		6	$5,083.05	$1,037.03	$1,003.15	$33.89	$4,079.90
12		7	$4,079.90	$1,037.03	$1,009.83	$27.20	$3,070.07
13		8	$3,070.07	$1,037.03	$1,016.56	$20.47	$2,053.51
14		9	$2,053.51	$1,037.03	$1,023.34	$13.69	$1,030.16
15		10	$1,030.16	$1,037.03	$1,030.16	$6.87	($0.00)
16							
17		NPV of payments	$10,000.00				
18							
19		payment beginning of each month	($1,030.16)				
20		payment if we want to have a $1000 ending balance	($940.00)				

Figure 10-3 Examples of the PMT, PPMT, and IPMT functions.

If you want, you can use the IPMT or the PPMT function to compute the amount of interest paid each month toward the loan and the amount of the balance paid down each month (called the *payment on the principal*).

To determine the interest paid each month, use the IPMT function. The syntax of the function is:

```
IPMT(rate, per, #per, pv, [fv],[type])
```

Except for the *per* argument, the arguments for the IPMT function are the same as for the PMT function. The *per* argument indicates the period number for which you're computing the interest.

Similarly, to determine the amount paid toward the principal each month, use the PPMT function. The syntax of the PPMT function is:

```
PPMT( rate, per, #per, pv, fv, type)
```

The meaning of each argument is the same as for the IPMT function.

By copying from F6 to F7:F15 the formula

```
-PPMT(rate,C6,months,loan_amount)
```

I compute each month's payment toward the principal. For example, during month 1, only $970.37 is paid toward principal. (As expected, the amount paid toward principal increases each month.) The minus sign is needed in the formula because Excel's natural convention is to label a payment as negative.

By copying from G6 to G7:G15 the formula

```
-IPMT(rate,C6,months,loan_amount)
```

I compute the amount of interest paid each month. For example, in month 1 we pay $66.67 in interest. Of course, the amount of interest we pay each month decreases. Note that each month *(Interest Paid) + (Payment Toward Principal) = (Total Payment)*. Sometimes the total is off by a penny because of rounding.

I can also create ending balances for each month in column H by using the relationship *(Ending Month t Balance) = (Beginning Month t Balance) − (Month t Payment toward Principal)*.

With a beginning balance of $10,000 in month 1, we create each month's beginning balance in column D by using the relationship *(Beginning Month t Balance) = (Ending Month t-1 Balance)*, where t = 2, 3, and so on up to 10. Of course, at the end of month 10, the balance is $0, as we'd expect.

Our interest each month can be computed as follows:

```
(Month t Interest) = (Interest rate)*(Beginning Month t Balance)
```

For example, for month 3 the interest is *(0.0066667)*($8,052.80) = $53.69*. Note, of course, that the net present value of all our payments is exactly $10,000. We checked this in cell D17 by using the formula *NPV(rate,E6:E15)*. (See Figure 10-4.)

If we make payments at the beginning of each month, the amount of each payment is computed in cell D19 with the formula:

```
PMT(rate,months,loan_amount,0,1)
```

Changing the last argument to 1 changes the timing of each payment to the beginning of the month. Because our lender is getting her money earlier, our monthly payments are less than in the end-of-the-month case. If we pay at the beginning of the month, our monthly payment is $1,030.16.

Finally, suppose that we want to leave $1,000 of our loan balance unpaid at the end of 10 months. If we make payments at the end of the month, the formula *PMT(rate,months,loan_amount,-1000)*, entered in cell D20, computes our monthly payment. Our monthly payment turns out to be $940.00. Because we are leaving $1,000 of our balance unpaid, it makes sense that our new monthly payment is less than the original end-of-month payment, $1,037.03.

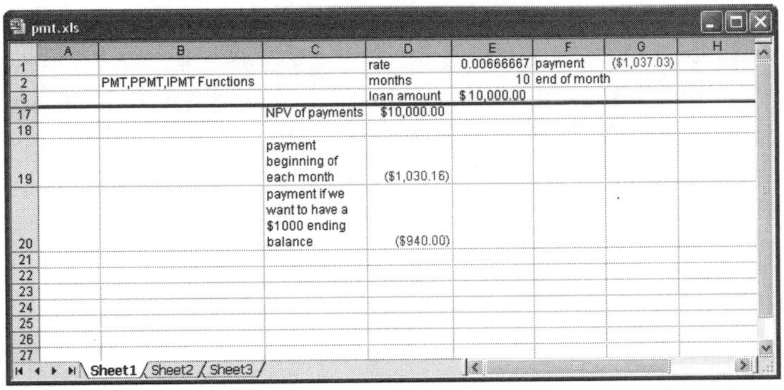

Figure 10-4   Calculations that use the PMT function to show payment amounts that occur at beginning of a month or with an ending balance.

Problems

1.   You have just won the lottery. At the end of each of the next 20 years, you'll receive a payment of $50,000. If the cost of capital is 10 percent per year, what's the present value of your lottery winnings?

2.   A *perpetuity* is an annuity that is received forever. If I rent my house and at the beginning of each year receive $14,000, what is the value of this perpetuity? Assume an annual cost of capital of 10 percent. (Hint: use the PV function and let the number of periods be large!)

3.   I now have $250,000 in the bank. At the end of each of the next 20 years, I withdraw $15,000 to live on. If I earn 8 percent per year on my investments, how much money will I have in 20 years?

4.   I deposit $1,000 per month (at the end of each month) over the next 10 years. My investments earn 0.8 percent per month. I would like to have $1,000,000 in 10 years. How much money should I deposit now?

5.   An NBA player is receiving $15 million at the end of each of the next 7 years. He can earn 6 percent per year on his investments. What is the present value of his future revenues?

6.   At the end of each of the next 20 years, I will receive the following amounts.

Years	Amounts
1-5	$200
6-10	$300
11-20	$400

Use the PV function to find the present value of these cash flows if the cost of capital is 10 percent. Hint: Begin by computing the value of receiving $400 a year for 20 years and then subtract the value of receiving $100 a year for 10 years, and so on.

7. We are borrowing $200,000 on a 30-year mortgage with an annual interest rate of 10 percent. Assuming end-of-month payments, determine the monthly payment, interest payment each month, and amount paid toward principal each month.

8. Answer each question in problem 7 assuming beginning-of-month payments.

9. Use the FV function to determine the value to which $100 accumulates in three years if you are earning 7 percent per year.

10. You have a liability of $1,000,000 due in 10 years. The cost of capital is 10 percent per year. What amount of money would you need to set aside at the end of each of the next 10 years to meet this liability?

11. You are going to buy a new car. The cost of the car is $50,000. You have been offered two payment plans:

    ❏   A 10 percent discount on the cost of the car followed by 60 monthly payments financed at 9 percent per year.

    ❏   There is no discount on the cost of the car, but the 60 monthly payments are financed at only 2 percent per year.

    If you believe your annual cost of capital is 9 percent, which payment plan is a better deal? Assume all payments occur at the end of the month.

12. I currently have $10,000 in the bank. At the beginning of each of the next 20 years, I am going to invest $4,000 and I expect to earn 6 percent per year on my investments. How much money will I have in 20 years?

13. A *balloon mortgage* requires you to pay off part of a loan during a specified time period and then make a lump sum payment to pay off the remaining portion of the loan. Suppose you borrow $400,000 on a 20-year balloon mortgage and the interest rate is .5 percent per month. Your end-of-month payments during the first 20 years are required to pay off $300,000 of your loan, and 20 years from now you will have to pay off the remaining $100,000. Determine your monthly payments for this loan.

11

Circular References

- I often get a circular reference message from Excel. Does this mean I've made an error?
- How can I resolve circular references?

When you receive a message from Excel that your workbook contains a circular reference, it means there is a "loop," or dependency, between two or more cells in a worksheet. For example, a circular reference occurs if the value in cell A1 influences the value in C2, the value in cell C2 influences the value in cell D2, and the value in cell D2 influences the value in cell A1. Figure 11-1 illustrates the pattern of a circular reference.

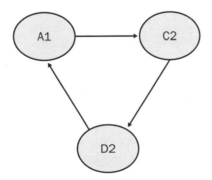

Figure 11-1 Example of a loop causing a circular reference.

As you'll soon see, you can resolve circular references by changing a setting in the Options dialog box. Click Tools, Options, select the Calculation tab, and then check the Iteration option.

I often get a circular reference message from Excel. Does this mean I've made an error?

A circular reference usually arises from a logically correct spreadsheet in which several cells exhibit a "looping" relationship similar to Figure 11-1. Let's look at a simple example of a problem that cannot easily be solved in Excel without creating a circular reference. A small company earns $1,500 in revenues and incurs $1,000 in costs. They want to give 10 percent of their after-tax profits to charity. The tax rate is 40 percent. How much money should they give to charity? The solution to this problem is in the file Circular.xls, shown in Figure 11-2.

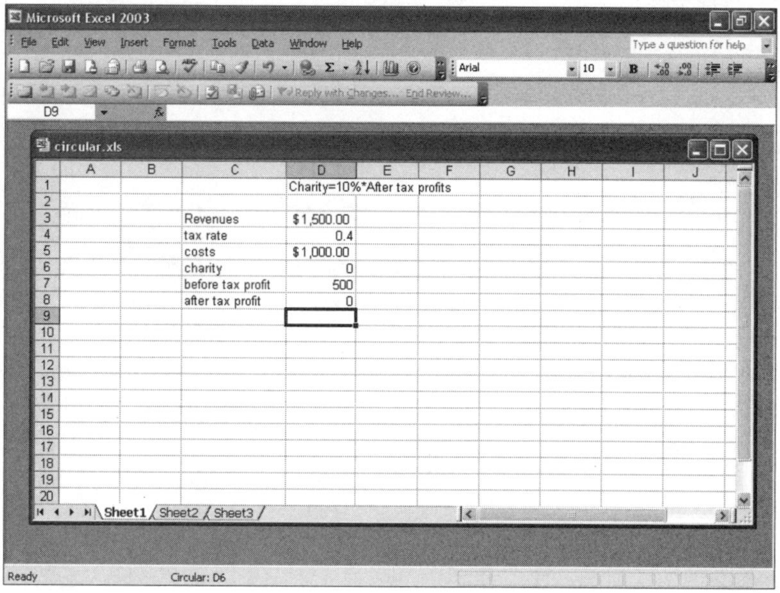

Figure 11-2   A circular reference can occur when you're calculating taxes.

We begin by naming the cells in D3:D8 with the corresponding names in cells C3:C8. Next we enter the firm's revenue, tax rate, and costs in D3:D5. To compute a contribution to charity as 10 percent of after-tax profit, we enter in cell D6 the formula *0.1*after_tax_profit*. Then we determine before-tax profit in cell D7 by subtracting costs and the charitable contribution from revenues. Our formula in cell D7 is Revenues-Costs-Charity. Finally, we compute after-tax profit in cell D8 as:

```
(1-tax_rate)*before_tax_profit
```

Excel indicates a circular reference in cell D6 (see the bottom of Figure 11-2). What's going on?

■   Charity (cell D6) influences before-tax profit (cell D7).

■   Before-tax profit (cell D7) influences after-tax profit (cell D8).

■   After-tax profit (cell D8) influences before-tax profit.

Thus we have a loop of the form D6-D7-D8-D6, which causes the circular reference message. Our spreadsheet is logically correct; we have done nothing wrong! Still, we see from Figure 11-2 that Excel is giving us a nonsensical answer for charitable contributions.

How can I resolve circular references?

Resolving a circular reference is easy. Simply click Options on the Tools menu, click the Calculation tab, and check the Iteration box, as shown in Figure 11-3.

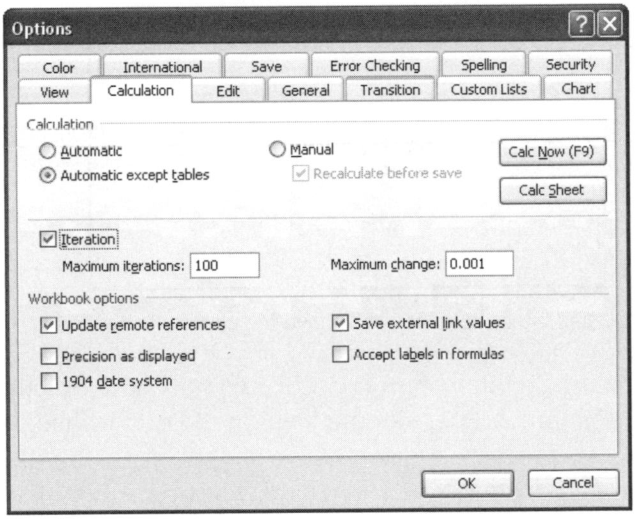

Figure 11-3   Use the Iteration option in the Options dialog box to resolve a circular reference.

When you check the Iteration option, Excel recognizes that your circular reference has generated the following system of three equations with three unknowns:

```
Charity = 0.1*(AfterTax profit)
BeforeTax Profit = Revenue - Charity - Costs
AfterTax Profit = (1 - Tax rate)*(BeforeTax Profit).
```

The three unknowns are *Charity*, *BeforeTax Profit*, and *AfterTax Profit*. When you check the Iteration box, Excel iterates (based on our limitation, 100 iterations will be used) to try and find a solution to all equations generated by the circular reference. From one iteration to the next, the values of the unknowns are changed by a complex mathematical procedure (Gauss-Seidel Iteration). Based on the value in the Maximum Change option (0.001 by default), Excel stops if the maximum change in any spreadsheet cell from one iteration to the next is at most 0.001. You should probably reduce the Maximum Change setting to a smaller number, such as 0.000001. Some complex spreadsheets might require more than 100 iterations before "converging" to a resolution of the circularity. For our example, however, the circularity is almost instantly resolved, and we see the solution given in Figure 11-4.

Figure 11-4   Excel runs the calculations to resolve the circular reference.

Note that our charitable contribution of $28.30 is now exactly 10 percent of our after-tax profit of $283.01. All other cells in the spreadsheet are now correctly computed.

Here's one more example of a circular reference. In any Excel formula, you can refer to the entire column with a range name. For example, the formula *AVERAGE(B:B)* will average all cells in column B. This shortcut is useful if you're continually dumping new data (such as monthly sales) into column B. Then our formula always computes average sales, and we do not need to ever change it. The problem is, of course, that if we enter this formula in column B, we'll create a circular reference. If you select Tools, Options, Calculation and then check the Iteration box, circular references such as these will be resolved quickly.

Problems

1. Before paying employee bonuses and state and federal taxes, a company earns profits of $60,000. The company pays employees a bonus equal to 5 percent of after-tax profits. State tax is 5 percent of profits (after bonuses are paid). Finally, federal tax is 40 percent of profits (after bonuses and state tax are paid). Determine the amount paid in bonuses, state tax, and federal tax.

2. On January 1, 2002, I have $500. At the end of each month I earn 2 percent interest. Each month's interest is based on the average of the month's beginning and ending balances. How much money will I have in 12 months—that is, after I've received 12 months of interest?

3. My airplane is flying the following route: Houston-Los Angeles-Seattle-Minneapolis-Houston. On each route the plane's miles-per-gallon is *40 - .02*(average fuel on route)*. Here, *average fuel on route* is equal to *.5*(initial fuel on route + final fuel on route)*. We begin in Houston with 1,000 gallons of fuel. The distance flown on each route is as follows. How many gallons of fuel will remain when I return to Houston?

Route	Miles
Houston-LA	1200
LA-Seattle	1100
Seattle-Minneapolis	1500
Minneapolis-Houston	1400

4. A common method used to allocate costs to support departments is the *reciprocal cost allocation method*. This method can easily be implemented by use of circular references. To illustrate, suppose Widgetco has two support departments: Accounting and Management Consulting. Widgetco also has two product divisions: Division 1 and Division 2. Widgetco has decided to allocate $600,000 of the cost for operating accounting to the two divisions and $116,000 of management consulting cost to the two divisions. The fraction of accounting and consulting time used by each part of the company is as follows.

	Accounting	Consulting	Division 1	Division 2
Percentage of accounting work done for other parts of company	0	20	30	50
Percentage of consulting work done for other parts of company	10	0	80	10

The question is how much of the cost for accounting and consulting should be allocated to other parts of the company? We need to determine two quantities: total cost allocated to accounting and total cost allocated to consulting. Total cost allocated to accounting equals *$600,000 + .1*(total cost allocated to management consulting)* because 10 percent of all consulting work was done for the accounting department. A similar equation can be written for the total cost allocated to management consulting. You should now be able to calculate the correct allocation of both accounting and management consulting costs to each other part of the company.

12

IF Statements

- If I order up to 500 units of a product, I pay $3.00 per unit. If I order between 501 and 1200 units, I pay $2.70 per unit. If I order between 1201 and 2000 units, I pay $2.30 per unit. If I order more than 2000 units, I pay $2.00 per unit. How can I write a formula that expresses the purchase cost as a function of the number of units purchased?

- I've just purchased 100 shares of stock at a cost of $55 per share. To hedge the risk that the stock might decline in value, I purchased 60 six-month European put options. Each option has an exercise price of $45 and costs $5. How can I develop a spreadsheet that indicates the six-month percentage return on my portfolio for a variety of possible future prices?

- Many stock market analysts believe that moving-average trading rules can outperform the market. A commonly suggested moving-average trading rule is to buy a stock when the stock's price moves above the average of the last 15 months and to sell a stock when the stock's price moves below the average of the last 15 months' price. How would this trading rule have performed against buying and holding the Standard and Poor's Index?

- In the game of craps, two dice are tossed. If the total of the dice on the first roll is 2, 3, or 12, you lose. If the total of the dice on the first roll is 7 or 11, you win. Otherwise, the game keeps going. How can I write a formula to determine the status of the game after the first roll?

- In most pro forma financial statements, cash is used as the plug to make assets and liabilities balance. I know that using debt as the plug would be more realistic. How can I set up a pro forma statement having debt as the plug?

The five situations listed above seem to have little, if anything, in common. However, setting up Excel models for each of these situations requires the use of an IF statement. I believe that the IF formula is the single most useful formula in Excel. IF formulas let you conduct conditional tests on values and formulas, mimicking (to a limited degree) the conditional logic provided by computing languages such as C, C++, and Java.

An IF formula begins with a condition, for example, *A1>10*. If the condition is true, the formula returns the first value listed in the formula; otherwise, we move on within the formula and repeat the process. The easiest way to show you the power and utility of IF formulas is to use them to help answer each of our five questions.

If I order up to 500 units of a product, I pay $3.00 per unit. If I order between 501 and 1200 units, I pay $2.70 per unit. If I order between 1201 and 2000 units, I pay $2.30 per unit. If I order more than 2000 units, I pay $2.00 per unit. How can I write a formula that expresses the purchase cost as a function of the number of units purchased?

You can find the solution to this question on the worksheet named Quantity Discount in the file IfStatement.xls. The worksheet is shown in Figure 12-1.

	A	B	C	D	E
1		cutoff	price		
2	cut1	500	$ 3.00	price1	
3	cut2	1200	$ 2.70	price2	
4	cut3	2000	$ 2.30	price3	
5			$ 2.00	price4	
6					
7					
8	order quantity	cost	per unit cost		
9	450	$1,350.00	$ 3.00		
10	900	$2,430.00	$ 2.70		
11	1450	$3,335.00	$ 2.30		
12	2100	$4,200.00	$ 2.00		
13					

Figure 12-1 You can use an IF formula to model quantity discounts.

Suppose cell A9 contains our order quantity. We can compute an order's cost as a function of the order quantity by implementing the following logic:

- If A9<=500, the cost is 3*A9.

- If A9 is between 501 and 1200, the cost is 2.70*A9.

- If A9 is between 1201 and 2000, the cost is 2.30*A9.

- If A9 is more than 2000, the cost is 2*A9.

We begin by linking the range names in A2:A4 to cells B2:B4, and linking the range names in cells D2:D5 to cells C2:C5. We can implement this logic in cell B9 with the formula:

```
IF(A9<=cut1,price1*A9,IF(A9<=cut2,price2*A9,IF(A9<=cut3,price3*A9,price4*A9)))
```

To understand how Excel computes a value from this formula, recall that IF statements are evaluated from left to right. If the order quantity is less than or equal to 500 (*cut1*), the cost is given by *price1*A9*. If the order quantity is not less than 500, the formula checks to see whether the order quantity is less than 1200. If this is the case, the order quantity is between 501 and 1200, and the formula computes a cost of *price2*A9*. Next we check whether the order quantity is less than or equal to 2000. If this is true, the order quantity is between 1201 and 2000, and our formula computes a cost of *price3*A9*. Finally, if the order cost has not yet been computed, our formula defaults to the value *price4*A9*. In each case, the IF formula returns the correct order cost. Note that I typed in three more order quantities in cells A10:A12 and copied our cost formula to B10:B12. For each order quantity, our formula returns the correct total cost.

An IF formula containing more than one IF statement is called a *nested IF formula*. A nested IF formula can contain up to seven IF statements and up to 256 characters. More complex formulas need to be broken into multiple cells.

I've just purchased 100 shares of stock at a cost of $55 per share. To hedge the risk that the stock might decline in value, I purchased 60 six-month European put options. Each option has an exercise price of $45 and costs $5. How can I develop a spreadsheet that indicates the six-month percentage return on my portfolio for a variety of possible future prices?

Before tackling this problem, I want to review some basic concepts from the world of finance. A European option allows you to sell at a given time in the future (in this case six months) a share of a stock for the exercise price (in this case $45). If our stock's price in 6 months is $45 or higher, the option has no value. Suppose, however, that the price of the stock in 6 months is below $45. Then you can make money by buying a share and immediately reselling the stock for $45. For example, if in 6 months our stock is selling for $37, you can make a profit of $45 - $37, or $8 per share, by buying a share for $37 and then using the put to resell the share for $45. You can see that put options protect you against downward moves in a stock price. In this case, whenever the stock's price in six months is below $45, the puts start kicking in some value. This cushions a portfolio against a decrease in value of the shares it owns. Note also that the percentage return on a portfolio is computed by taking the change in the portfolio's value (*final portfolio value – initial portfolio value*) and dividing that number by the portfolio's initial value.

With this background, let's look at how the six-month percentage return on our portfolio, consisting of 60 puts and 100 shares of our stock, varies as the share price varies between $20 and $65. You can find this solution on the sheet named Hedging in the file IfStatement.xls. The worksheet is shown in Figure 12-2.

	A	B	C	D	E
1					
2	Nputs	60			
3	Nshares	100			
4	exprice	$ 45.00			
5	pricenow	$ 55.00			
6	putcost	$ 5.00			
7	startvalue	$5,800.00			
8	final stock price	final put value	final share value	percentage return hedged	percentage return unhedged
9	$ 20.00	$1,500.00	$2,000.00	-39.7%	-63.6%
10	$ 25.00	$1,200.00	$2,500.00	-36.2%	-54.5%
11	$ 30.00	$ 900.00	$3,000.00	-32.8%	-45.5%
12	$ 35.00	$ 600.00	$3,500.00	-29.3%	-36.4%
13	$ 40.00	$ 300.00	$4,000.00	-25.9%	-27.3%
14	$ 45.00	$ -	$4,500.00	-22.4%	-18.2%
15	$ 50.00	$ -	$5,000.00	-13.8%	-9.1%
16	$ 55.00	$ -	$5,500.00	-5.2%	0.0%
17	$ 60.00	$ -	$6,000.00	3.4%	9.1%
18	$ 65.00	$ -	$6,500.00	12.1%	18.2%

Figure 12-2 Hedging example that uses IF statements.

The labels in A2:A7 are linked to the cells B2:B7. The initial portfolio value is equal to 100($55) + 60($5) = $5,800, shown in cell B7. By copying from B9 to B10:B18 the formula *IF(A9<exprice,exprice-A9,0)*Nputs*, we compute the final value of our puts. If the six-month price is less than our exercise price, we value each put as *exercise price-six-month price*. Otherwise, each put will in six months have a value of $0. Copying from C9 to C10:C18 the formula *Nshares*A9*, we compute the final value of our shares. Copying from D9 to D10:D18 the formula *((C9+B9)-startvalue)/startvalue)* computes the percentage return on our hedged portfolio. Copying from E9 to E10:E18 the formula *(C9-Nshares*pricenow)/(Nshares*pricenow)* computes the percentage return on our portfolio if we are unhedged (that is, buy no puts).

In Figure 12-2, you can see that if the stock price drops below $45, our hedged portfolio has a larger expected return than our unhedged portfolio. Also note that if the stock price does not decrease, the unhedged portfolio has a larger expected return. This is why the purchase of puts is often referred to as *portfolio insurance*.

Many stock market analysts believe that moving-average trading rules can outperform the market. A commonly suggested moving-average trading rule is to buy a stock when the stock's price moves above the average of the last 15 months and to sell a stock when the stock's price moves below the average of the last 15 months' price. How would this trading rule have performed against buying and holding the Standard and Poor's Index?

In this example, we'll compare the performance of the moving-average trading rule (in the absence of transaction costs for buying and selling stock) to a buy-and-hold strategy. The strength of a moving-average trading rule is that it helps you follow market trends. A moving-average trading rule lets you ride up with a bull market and sell before a bear market destroys you. Our data set contains the monthly value of the Standard and Poor's (S&P) Index for the time period January 1871 through October 2002. To track the performance of our moving-average trading strategy, we need to track the following information each month:

■   The average of the S&P Index over the last 15 months.

■   Do we own stock at the beginning of each month?

■   Do we buy stock during the month?

■   Do we sell stock during the month?

■   What is our cash flow for the month (positive if we sell stock, negative if we buy stock, and 0 otherwise)?

The file MaTradingRule.xls, shown in Figure 12-3, includes the work I did to answer this question. Tackling this problem requires several IF formulas, and some of the IF formulas will require an AND operator. For example, we'll buy the stock during a month if and only if we don't own the stock at the beginning of the month and the current month's price is larger than the 15-month moving average for the stock's price. The first month for which we can compute a 15-month moving average is April 1872, so we begin our calculations in row 24.

matradingrule.xls

	A	B	C	D	E	F	G	H
6		S&P				MA profit	$1,319.75	
7		Comp.				Buy and hold profit	$849.45	
8	Date	P	Own?	MA	Buy?	Sell?	Cash flow	
24	1872.04	5.18	Yes	4.739	no	no	0	
25	1872.05	5.18	Yes	4.788	no	no	0	
26	1872.06	5.13	Yes	4.833	no	no	0	
27	1872.07	5.1	Yes	4.868	no	no	0	
28	1872.08	5.04	Yes	4.892	no	no	0	
29	1872.09	4.95	Yes	4.904	no	no	0	
30	1872.1	4.97	Yes	4.913	no	no	0	
31	1872.11	4.95	Yes	4.929	no	no	0	
32	1872.12	5.07	Yes	4.939	no	no	0	
33	1873.01	5.11	Yes	4.955	no	no	0	
34	1873.02	5.15	Yes	4.989	no	no	0	
35	1873.03	5.11	Yes	5.023	no	no	0	
36	1873.04	5.04	Yes	5.048	no	yes	5.04	
37	1873.05	5.05	no	5.06	no	no	0	
38	1873.06	4.98	no	5.071	no	no	0	
39	1873.07	4.97	no	5.067	no	no	0	
40	1873.08	4.97	no	5.053	no	no	0	

Stock Data

Figure 12-3 Moving-average trading rule beats buy and hold!

- Let's assume we first owned the stock in April 1872, so we entered Yes in cell C24.
- By copying from D24 to D25:D1590 the formula *AVERAGE(B9:B23)*, we compute the 15-month moving average for each month.

> **Tip** An easy way to copy the formula from D24 to D25:D1590 is to point at the lower right corner of cell D24 (the pointer is displayed as a crosshair) and then double-click the left mouse button. Double-clicking copies the formula in a column to match the number of filled rows in the column to the left of the current column. This trick can also be used to copy formulas in multiple columns.

- By copying from E24 to E25:E1590 the formula *IF(AND(C24="No", B24>D24),"yes","no")*, we determine for each month whether our S&P share is purchased during the month. Remember that we purchase the share only if we did not own the stock at the beginning of the month and the current value of the S&P exceeds its 15-month moving average. Notice the AND portion of the formula. It contains two conditions (more than two are allowed) separated by a comma. If both conditions are satisfied, the formula returns Yes; otherwise, it returns No. For an IF formula to recognize text, you need to place quotation marks (" ") around the text.

- By copying from F24 to F25:F1590 the formula *IF(AND(C24="Yes", B24<D24),"yes","no")*, we determine for each month whether our S&P share is sold. The stock is sold if and only if we owned the S&P share at the beginning of the month and the current value of the S&P share is below the 15-month moving average. April 1873 is the first month in which we sell our S&P stock.

- During any month before October 2002, if we buy a share of the S&P during the month, our cash flow is negative the value of the S&P share we bought. If we sell a share of the S&P during the month, our cash flow equals the value of the S&P. Otherwise, the cash flow is 0. During October 2002, we sell any S&P share we own to get credit for its value. Therefore, by copying from G24 to G25:G1589 the formula *IF(E24="yes",-B24,IF(F24="yes",B24,0))*, we record our cash flow for all months before October 2002. Entering in cell G1590 the formula *IF(C1590="yes",B1590,0)* gives us credit for selling any stock we own at the beginning of October 2002.

- In cell G6 we compute our total profit from the moving-average trading strategy with the formula *SUM(G24:G1590)*. We find the 15-month moving average strategy earns a profit of $1319.75.

- The profit from buying and holding shares is simply the October 2002 S&P value minus the April 1872 S&P value. We compute the profit from the buy-and-hold strategy in cell G7 with the formula *B1590-B24*. We find that the buy and hold profit of $849.45 is far worse than the profit from the moving-average trading rule.

In the game of craps, two dice are tossed. If the total of the dice on the first roll is 2, 3, or 12, you lose. If the total of the dice on the first roll is 7 or 11, you win. Otherwise, the game keeps going. How can I write a formula to determine the status of the game after the first roll?

The fact that you lose in craps if you throw a 2, 3, or 12 can be conveniently modeled by placing an OR formula within an IF formula. In cell B5 of the worksheet Craps, shown in Figure 12-4 and found in the file IfStatement.xls, we enter the formula *IF(OR(A5=2,A5=3,A5=12),"Lose",IF(OR(A5=7,A5=11),"Win","Keep going"))*. This formula is then copied from B5 to B6:B7. The formula displays *Lose* if a 2, 3, or 12 is entered in cell A5. It displays *Win* if a 7 or 11 is entered, and it displays *Keep going* for any other value.

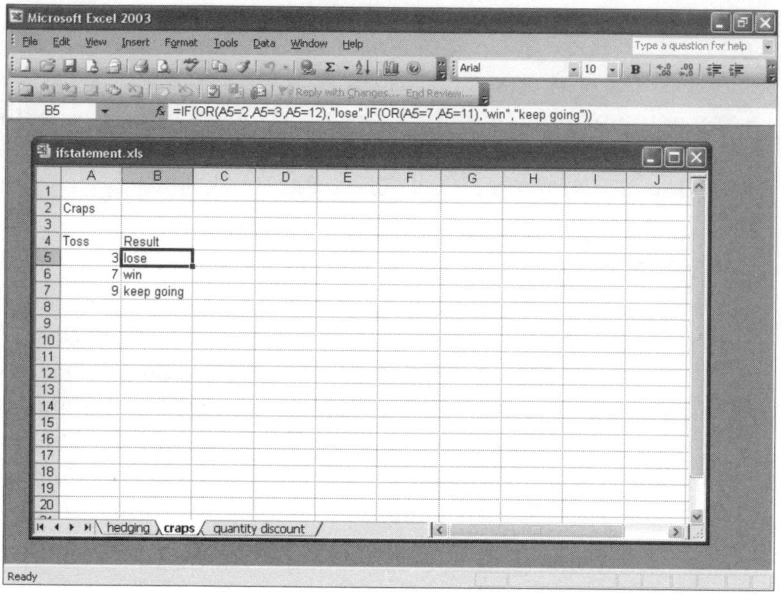

Figure 12-4   Using IF statements to model the first roll in craps.

In most pro forma financial statements, cash is used as the plug to make assets and liabilities balance. I know that using debt as the plug would be more realistic. How can I set up a pro forma statement having debt as the plug?

A pro forma is basically a prediction of a company's financial future. A pro forma requires construction of a company's future balance sheets and income statements. The balance sheet provides a snapshot of the company's assets and liabilities at any point in time. An income statement tells us how the company's financial status is changing at any point in time. Pro forma statements can help a company determine its future needs for debt and are also key parts of valuation models that stock analysts use to determine whether a stock is properly valued. In the file Proforma.xls, I've generated the free cash flows (FCFs) for the next four years for a firm. Figure 12-5 shows the balance sheet, and Figure 12-6 shows the income statement.

Figure 12-5   Pro forma assumptions and balance sheet.

The content of Figure 12-5 (spreadsheet) is as follows:

	A	B	C	D	E	F	G	H
3		Sales growth	SG	0.02		CA/Sales		0.15
4		Initial sales	IS	1,000.00		CL/Sales		0.07
5		Interest rate on debt	IRD	0.10		NFA/Sales		0.60
6		Dividend payout	DIV	0.05		GFA/Sales		0.90
7		Tax rate	TR	0.53				
8		COGS/Sales	COGS	0.75				
9		Depreciation rate	DEP	0.10				
10		Liquid asset interest rate	LAIR	0.09				
11		**Balance sheet**						
12				0.00	1.00	2.00	3.00	4.00
13		Cash and marketable securities			0.00	0.00	0.00	4.76
14		Current assets		150.00	153.00	156.06	159.18	162.36
15		Gross fixed assets		900.00	1,013.33	1,139.53	1,280.01	1,436.38
16		Acc. dep.		300.00	401.33	515.29	643.29	786.93
17		Net fixed assets		600.00	612.00	624.24	636.72	649.46
18		Total assets		750.00	765.00	780.30	795.91	816.59
19								
20		Current liabilities		70.00	71.40	72.83	74.28	75.77
21		Debt		180.00	130.83	83.16	37.69	0.00
22		Stock		400.00	400.00	400.00	400.00	400.00
23		Retained earnings		100.00	162.77	224.31	283.93	340.82
24		Equity		500.00	562.77	624.31	683.93	740.82
25		Total liabilities		750.00	765.00	780.30	795.91	816.59

Figure 12-6   Pro forma income statement.

The content of Figure 12-6 (spreadsheet) is as follows:

	A	B	C	D	E	F	G	H
27		**Income statement**		0.00	1.00	2.00	3.00	4.00
28		Sales		1,000.00	1,020.00	1,040.40	1,061.21	1,082.43
29		Cost of goods sold		700.00	765.00	780.30	795.91	811.82
30		Depreciation			101.33	113.95	128.00	143.64
31		Operating income			153.67	146.15	137.30	126.97
32		Interest income			0.00	0.00	0.00	0.43
33		Interest expense			13.08	8.32	3.77	0.00
34		Income before taxes			140.58	137.83	133.53	127.40
35		Taxes			74.51	73.05	70.77	67.52
36		Net income			66.07	64.78	62.76	59.88
37								
38		Beg. retained earnings			100.00	162.77	224.31	283.93
39		Dividends			3.30	3.24	3.14	2.99
40		Ending retained earnings			162.77	224.31	283.93	340.82

Column D contains information about the company's current status (during year 0). Our basic assumptions are as follows:

- Sales growth is 2 percent per year

- Initial sales are $1,000

- Interest rate on debt is 10 percent

- Dividend payout is 5 percent of net income

- The tax rate is 53 percent

- Cost of goods sold (COGS) are 75 percent of sales

- Depreciation is 10 percent of gross fixed assets

- Liquid assets earn 9 percent

- Current assets are 15 percent of sales

- Current liabilities are 7 percent of sales

- Net fixed assets are 60 percent of sales

I've assigned the names in the cell range C3:C10 to the cells in the range D3:D10. Then, during each year *t*, basic finance and accounting imply the following relationships, which are then implemented in a series of formulas.

- *Year t+1 sales = (Year t sales)*(1+SG)*. I've computed sales during each year by copying from E28 to F28:H28 the formula *D28*(1+SG)*. I'll refer to this formula as formula 12.1.

- *Year t COGS = COGS*(Year t sales)*. Each year's COGS are computed by copying from E29 to F29:H29 the formula *COGS*E28*. I'll refer to this formula as 12.2.

- If *Year t assets>Year t liabilities, Year t debt* must be set equal to *Year t total assets - Year t current liabilities - Year t equity*. Otherwise, *Year t debt = 0*. I've computed each year's debt in E21:H21 with the formula *IF((E18>E20+E24,E18-E20-E24,0)*. If Year *t* total assets are greater than Year *t* total liabilities, this formula sets Year *t* debt to *Year t total assets - Year t current liabilities - Year t equity*. This equalizes, or balances, assets and liabilities. Otherwise, we set Year *t* debt equal to 0. In this case, Year *t* cash and marketable securities will be used to balance assets and liabilities. (12.3)

- *Year t current liabilities = (CL/Sales ratio)*(Year t sales)*. In E20:H20, we use the formula *$H$4*E28* (formula 12.4) to compute current liabilities for each year (copying this formula from E20 to F20:H20).

- *Year t equity = Year t stock + Year t retained earnings.* In E24:H24, we compute equity by copying from E24 to F24:H24 the formula *SUM(E22:E23).* (12.5)

- If Year *t* debt is greater than 0, Year *t* cash and marketable securities equals 0. Otherwise, Year *t* cash and marketable securities equals *MAX(0, Year t total liabilities - Year t current assets - Year t net fixed assets).* In E13:H13, I compute cash and marketable securities for each year by copying from E13 to F13:H13 the formula *IF(E21>0,0,MAX(0,E25-E14-E17)).* If Year *t* debt is greater than 0, we need not use Year *t* cash and marketable securities to balance assets and liabilities. In this case we set Year *t* cash and marketable securities equal to 0. Otherwise, we set Year *t* cash and marketable securities equal to *Year t total assets - Year t current liabilities - Year t equity.* This balances assets and liabilities if Year *t* assets (without cash and marketable securities) are less than Year *t* liabilities. If debt does not balance assets and liabilities, this creates liquid assets as the plug that does balance assets and liabilities. (12.6)

- *Year t interest expense = (Year t Debt)*IRD.* In E33:H33, I compute interest expense by using the formula *IRD*E21,* copying this formula again to F33:H33. (12.7)

- *Year t interest income = (Year t cash and marketable securities)*LAIR.* In E32:H32, I compute interest income by copying from E32 to F32:H32 the formula *LAIR*E13.* (12.8)

- *Year t operating income = Year t sales - Year t COGS - Year t depreciation.* In E31:H31, operating income is computed by copying from E31 to F31:H31 the formula *E28-E29-E30.* (12.9)

- *Year t dividends = (Year t net income)*DIV.* In E39:H39, I copy from E39 to F39:H39 the formula *E36*DIV* to compute dividends for each year. (12.10)

- *Year t + 1 beginning retained earnings = Year t ending retained earnings.* I compute beginning retained earnings each year in F38:H38, copying from F38 to G38:H38 the formula *E40.* (12.11)

- *Year t end of year retained earnings = Year t beginning retained earnings + Year t net income - Year t dividends.* In E40:H40, I compute each year's ending retained earnings by copying from E40 to F40:H40 the formula *E38+E36-E39.* (12.12)

■ *Year t income before taxes = Year t operating income - Year t interest expense + Year t cash income.* By copying from E34 to F34:H34 the formula *E31-E33+E32*, I compute income before taxes. (12.13)

■ *Year t taxes = (Year t income before taxes)*TR.* I compute each year's taxes in E35:H35 by copying from E35 to F35:H35 the formula *TR*E34.* (12.14)

■ *Year t net income after taxes = (Year t income before taxes) - (Year t taxes).* In E36:H36, I compute each year's net income by copying from E36 to F36:H36 the formula *E34-E35.* (12.15)

■ *Year t net fixed assets = (Year t sales)*(NFA/Sales).* In E17:H17, I compute each year's net fixed assets by copying the formula *$H$5*E28* from E17 to F17:H17. (12.16)

■ *Year t gross fixed assets = Year t net fixed assets + Year t accumulated depreciation.* In cells E15:H15, I compute gross fixed assets for each year by copying the formula *E17+E16.* (12.17)

■ *Year t depreciation = (Year t net fixed assets)*DEP.* Each year I use the formula *DEP*E15* to compute depreciation, copying the formula from E30 to F30:H30. (12.18)

■ *Year t accumulated depreciation = Year t-1 accumulated depreciation + Year t depreciation.* Each year I use the formula *D16+E30* to compute accumulated depreciation by copying the formula from E16 to F16:H16. (12.19)

■ *Year t net fixed assets = Year t gross fixed assets - Year t accumulated depreciation.* In row 17, to compute net fixed assets, I copy from E16 to F16:H16 the formula *D15-D16.* (12.20)

■ *Year t total assets = Year t liquid assets + Year t net fixed assets + Year t cash and marketable securities.* By adding liquid assets, current assets, and net fixed assets, I compute our total assets by copying from E18 to F18:H18 the formula *SUM(E13,E14,E17).* (12.21)

■ *Year t total liabilities = Year t current liabilities + Year t debt + Year t equity.* By copying from E25 to F25:H25 the formula *SUM(E20,E21,E24)*, I compute total liabilities for each period. Each year will balance because of our debt and liquid asset statements.

Formulas 12.3 and 12.6 require the use of IF statements. This spreadsheet will also contain circular references. (For more information about solving circular references, see Chapter 11). For example, the following relationships create a circular reference:

- Year t cash affects Year t total assets.

- Year t total assets affect Year t debt.

- Year t debt affects Year t cash.

For this spreadsheet to return sensible results, we need to select the Iteration option on the Calculation tab of the Options dialog box. (Click Tools, Options to open the dialog box.) Note that for each year t, total assets in row 18 equal total liabilities in row 25. This shows the power of IF formulas and circular references.

Problems

1. Suppose the price of a product will change at dates in the future as follows:

Date	Price
On or before February 15, 2004	$8.00
Between February 16, 2004, and April 10, 2005	$9.00
Between April 11, 2005, and January 15, 2006	$10.00
After January 15, 2006	$12.00

    Write a formula that will compute the price of the product based on the date the product is sold.

2. The Flybynight Airline flight from Seattle to New York has a capacity of 250 people. 270 tickets have been sold for the flight at a price of $300 per ticket. Tickets are non-refundable. The variable cost of flying a passenger (mostly food costs and fuel costs) is $30 per passenger. If more than 250 people show up for the flight, the flight is overbooked and Flybynight must pay overbooking compensation of $350 per person to each overbooked passenger. Develop a spreadsheet that computes Flybynight's profit based on the number of customers who show up for the flight.

3. A major drug company is trying to determine the correct plant capacity for a new drug. A unit of annual capacity can be built for a cost of $10. Each unit of the drug sells for $12 and incurs variable costs of $2. The drug will be sold for 10 years. Develop a spreadsheet that computes the company's 10-year profit given the chosen annual capacity level and the annual demand for the drug. We will assume demand for the drug is the same each year. You may ignore the time value of money in this problem.

4. Our drug company is producing a new drug. They have made the following assumptions:

   ❑ 100,000 units will be sold during year 1.

   ❑ Sales will grow for 3 years and then decline for 7 years.

   ❑ During the growth portion of the product life cycle, sales will grow at 15 percent per year. During the decline part of the product life cycle, sales will drop at a rate of 10 percent per year.

   Develop a spreadsheet that takes values for year 1 sales, length of growth cycle, length of decline cycle, growth rate during growth cycle, and rate of decrease during decline cycle and computes units sales for years 1-11.

5. We are bidding on a construction project. The low bid will get the project. We estimate our project cost at $10,000. Four companies are bidding against us. It costs $400 to prepare the bid. Write a formula that (given the bids of our four competitors and our bid) computes our profit.

6. We are bidding on a valuable painting. The high bid will get the painting. We estimate the painting's value at $10,000. Four companies are bidding against us. It costs $400 to prepare the bid. Write a formula that (given the bids of our four competitors and our bid) determines whether we get the painting.

7. Our drug company believes a new drug will sell 10,000 units during 2004. They expect two competitors to enter the market. The year in which the first competitor enters, our company expects to lose 30 percent of their market share. The year in which the second competitor enters, they expect to lose 15 percent of their market share. The size of the market is growing at 10 percent per year. Given values of the years in which the two competitors enter, develop a spreadsheet that computes the annual sales for the years 2004-2013.

8. A clothing store has ordered 100,000 swimsuits. It costs $22 to produce a swimsuit. They plan to sell them until August 31 at a price of $40 and then mark the price down to $30. Given values for demand through August 31 and after August 31, develop a spreadsheet to compute the profit from this order.

9. In a game of craps, on each roll of the dice after the first roll, the rules are as follows: If the game has not ended and the current roll matches the first roll, we win the game. If the game has not ended and the current roll is a 7, we lose. Otherwise, the game continues. Develop a spreadsheet that tells us (given knowledge of the first four rolls) the status of the game after four dice rolls.

10. On our S&P moving-average example, suppose we still buy shares if the current price exceeds the 15-month moving average, but we sell if the current price is less than the 5-month moving average. Is this strategy more profitable than selling if the current price is less than the 15-month moving average?

11. A European call option gives us the right to *buy* at a specified future date a share of stock for a given exercise price. A *butterfly spread* involves buying one call option with a low exercise price, buying one call option with a high exercise price, and selling two call options with an exercise price midway between the low and high exercise prices. Here is an example of a butterfly spread. The current stock price is $60. We buy a $54 six-month European call option for $9, buy a $66 six-month European call option for $4, and sell two $60 European call options for the price of $6. Compute the profit (in dollars, not percentage) for this transaction as a function of six-month stock prices ranging from $40-$80. When a trader purchases a butterfly spread, which type of movement in the stock price during the next six months is the trader betting on?

12. Suppose a stock is currently selling for $32. We buy a six-month European call option with an exercise price of $30 for $2.50 and sell a six-month European call option with an exercise price of $35 for $1. Compute the profit of this strategy (in dollars) as a function of a six-month stock price ranging from $25-$45. Why is this strategy called a *bull spread*? How would you modify this strategy to create a *bear spread*?

13. Let's reconsider our pro forma example. Suppose the interest rate on our debt depends on our financial well-being. More specifically, suppose that if our earnings before interest and taxes (EBIT) is negative, our interest rate on debt is 16 percent. If our interest expense is more than 10 percent of EBIT and EBIT is positive, our interest rate on debt is 13 percent. Otherwise, our interest rate is 10 percent. Modify our pro forma to account for this variable interest rate.

14. Do this problem independently of problem 13. Suppose our firm wants a debt/equity ratio of 50 percent during each year. How would you modify our pro forma? Hint: You must keep each year's stock nonnegative and use stock and cash or marketable securities to balance assets and liabilities.

15. Martin Luther King Day occurs on the third Monday in January. Write a formula that computes (given the year) the date of Martin Luther King Day. Hint: First determine the day of the week for January 1 of the given year.

16. Thanksgiving occurs on the fourth Thursday in November. Write a formula that computes (given the year) the date of Thanksgiving. Hint: First determine the day of the week for November 1 of the given year.

17. The first quarter of the year is January-March; the second quarter, April-June; the third quarter, July-September; and the fourth quarter, October-December. Write a formula that returns (for any given date) the quarter of the year.

13

The Paste Special Command

- How can I move the results of calculations (not the formulas) to a different part of a worksheet?

- I have a list of names in a single column. How can I make the list appear in one row instead of one column?

- I've downloaded U.S. Treasury bill interest rates from a Web site into Excel. The data lists a 5 when the interest rate is 5 percent, 8 when the interest rate is 8 percent, and so on. How can I easily divide my results by 100 so that a 5 percent interest rate, for example, is listed as .05?

The Paste Special command in Excel enables you to easily perform certain manipulations of spreadsheet data. In this chapter, I'll show how you can use the Paste Special command to perform the following types of operations:

- Pasting only the values in cells (not the formulas) to a different part of a spreadsheet.

- Transposing data in columns to rows and vice versa.

- Transforming a range of numbers by adding, subtracting, dividing, or multiplying each number in the range by a given constant.

How can I move the results of calculations (not the formulas) to a different part of a worksheet?

In the worksheet named Paste Special Value in the file PasteSpecial.xls, the cell range E4:H9 contains the names, games, total points, and points per game for five 10–11-year-old basketball players from Bloomington, Indiana. In the cell range H5:H9, I've used the data in cells F5:G9 to compute each child's points per game, as shown in Figure 13-1. Suppose we want to copy this data and the calculated points per game—but not the formulas that perform the calculations—to a different cell range (E13:H18, for example). All you do is select the range E4:H9, choose Edit, Copy, and then move to the upper left corner of the range where you want to copy the data (cell E13 in this example). Next, select Edit, Paste Special, and then fill in the Paste Special dialog box as indicated in Figure 13-2. After clicking OK, the range E13:H18 contains the data but not the formulas from the cell range E4:H9. You can check this by going to cell H16. You will see a value (7) but not the formula that was used to compute Gregory's average points per game. Note that if you use the Paste Special command, select Values, and then paste the data into the same range from which you copied the data, your formulas will disappear from the spreadsheet.

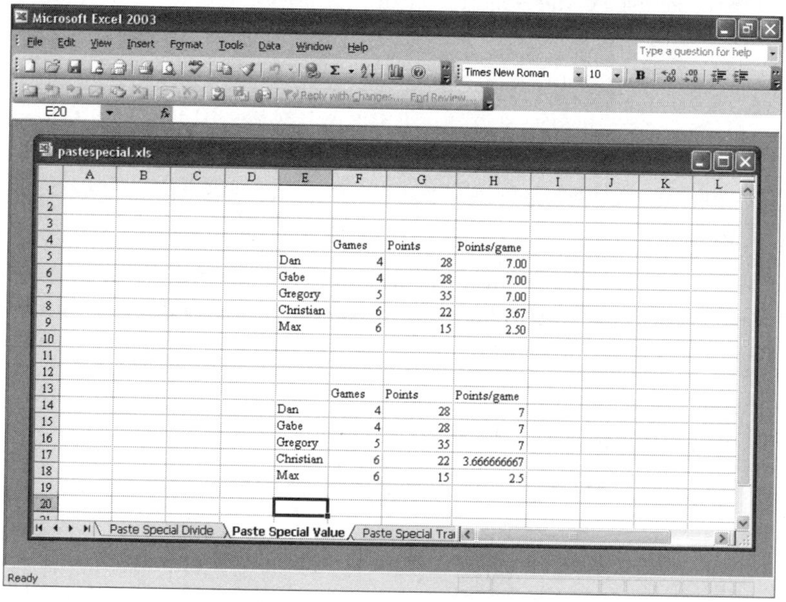

Figure 13-1   An example of using the Paste Special command to paste only values.

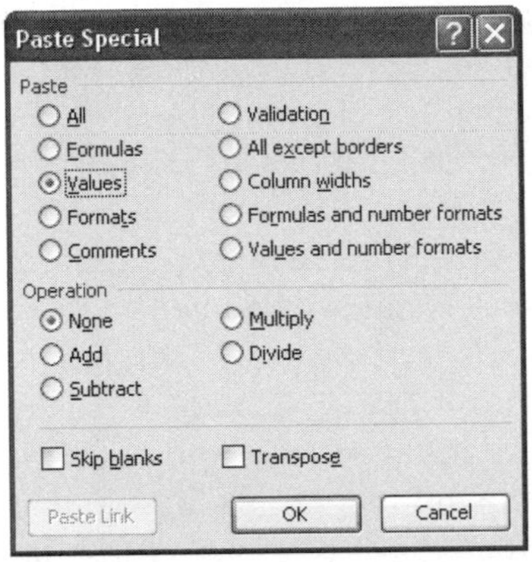

Figure 13-2   The Paste Special dialog box with Values selected. Selecting Values pastes only values and not any formulas.

I have a list of names in a single column. How can I make the list appear in one row instead of one column?

To realign data from a row to a column (or vice versa), the key is to use Edit, Copy and then Paste Special, Transpose. Essentially, the Transpose option in the Paste Special dialog box "flips" selected cells around so that the first row of the copied range becomes the first column of the range you paste data into, and so on. Look at the worksheet named Paste Special Transpose in the file PasteSpecial.xls, shown in Figure 13-3.

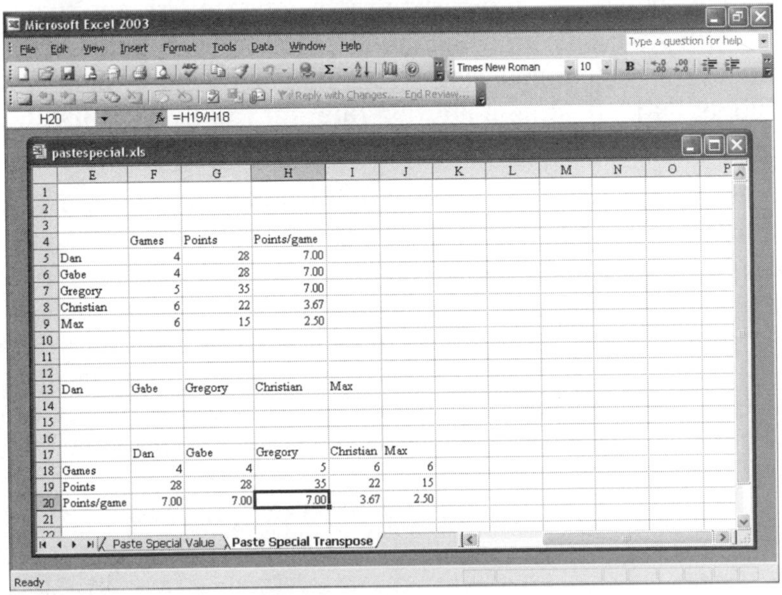

Figure 13-3   Use the Transpose option in the Paste Special dialog box to transpose a row of data into a column of data or a column into a row.

Suppose that you want to list the players' names in a single row (starting in cell E13). Simply select the range E5:E9, and then choose Edit, Copy. Move to cell E13, and then choose Edit, Paste Special and check Transpose in the Paste Special dialog box. After clicking OK, the players' names are transposed into a single row.

Suppose you want to transpose the spreadsheet content in E4:H9 to a range beginning in cell E17. Begin by selecting the range E4:H9. Next, choose Edit, Copy and then move to the upper left corner of the range where you want to put the transposed information (E17). Choose Edit, Paste Special, check Transpose, and then click OK. You'll see that the content of E4:H9 is transposed (turned on its side), as shown in Figure 13-3. Note that in F20:J20, Excel was smart enough to adjust the points-per-game formula so that the average for each player is now computed from data in the same column instead of the same row.

Note When you select Paste Special and click Paste Link instead of OK, the transposed cells are linked to the original cells, and changes you make to the original data are reflected in the copy. By changing the value in cell F5 to 7, the value in cell F18 becomes 7 as well, and cell F20 would display Dan's average as 4 points per game.

I've downloaded U.S. Treasury bill interest rates from a Web site into Excel. The data lists a 5 when the interest rate is 5 percent, 8 when the interest rate is 8 percent, and so on. How can I easily divide my results by 100 so that a 5 percent interest rate, for example, is listed as .05?

The worksheet Paste Special Divide in the file PasteSpecial.xls (see Figure 13-4) contains the annual rate of interest paid by three-month U.S. Treasury bills for each month between January 1970 and February 1987. In January 1970, the annual rate on a three-month Treasury bill was 8.01 percent. Suppose we want to earn annual interest on $1 invested at the current T-bill rate. The formula to calculate the rate is *(1 + (annual rate)/100)*. It would be easier to compute earned interest if our column of annual interest rates were divided by 100.

The Operations portion of the Paste Special dialog box lets you add, subtract, multiply, or divide each number in a range by a given number, providing an easy way to divide each interest rate by 100. Here we want to divide each number in column D. To begin, I entered our given number (100). You can enter it anywhere in the spreadsheet. I chose F5. With F5 selected, choose Edit, Copy. Next select the range of numbers you want to modify. To select all the data in column D, move the cursor to cell D10 and press Ctrl+Shift and then the down arrow. This shortcut is a useful trick for selecting a "tall" cell range. (By the way, to select a "wide" set of data listed in a single row, move to the first data point and then press Ctrl+Shift and the right arrow.) Next, select Edit, Paste Special, and then select Divide, as shown in Figure 13-5.

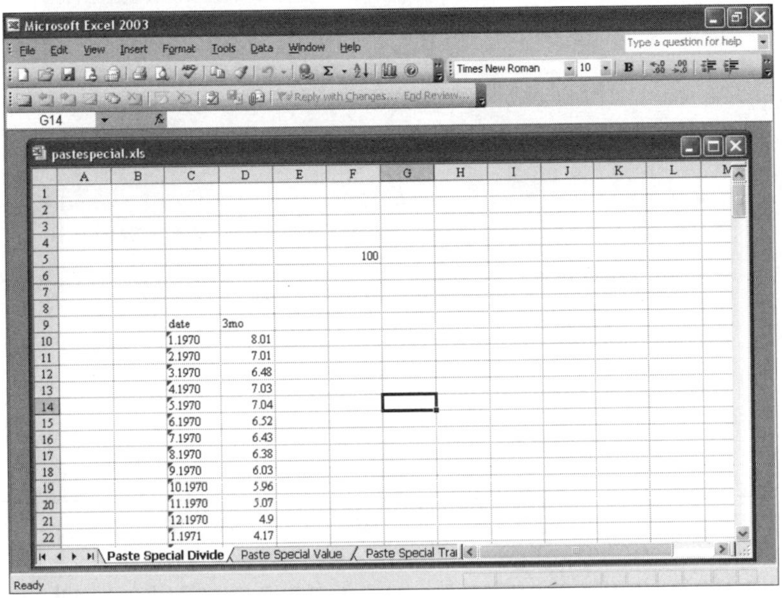

Figure 13-4   Use the Divide option in the Paste Special dialog box to divide a data range by a constant.

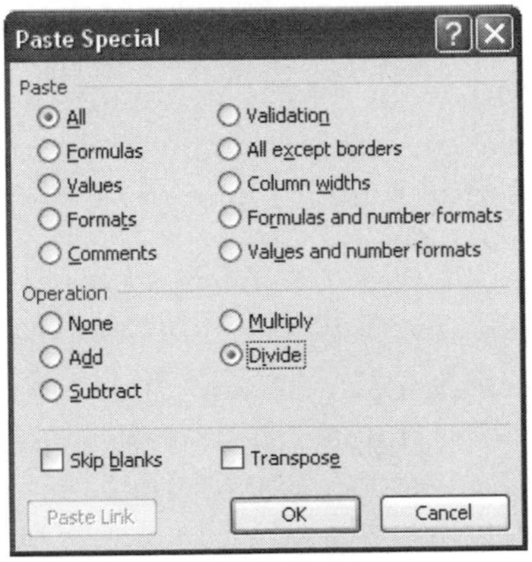

Figure 13-5   You can apply an option in the Operation area of the Paste Special dialog box to a range of cells.

After you click OK, Excel divides each selected number in column D by 100. The results are shown in Figure 13-6. If we had selected Add, D10 would have displayed 108.01; if we had selected Subtract, D10 would have displayed -91.99; and if we had selected Multiply, D10 would have displayed 801.

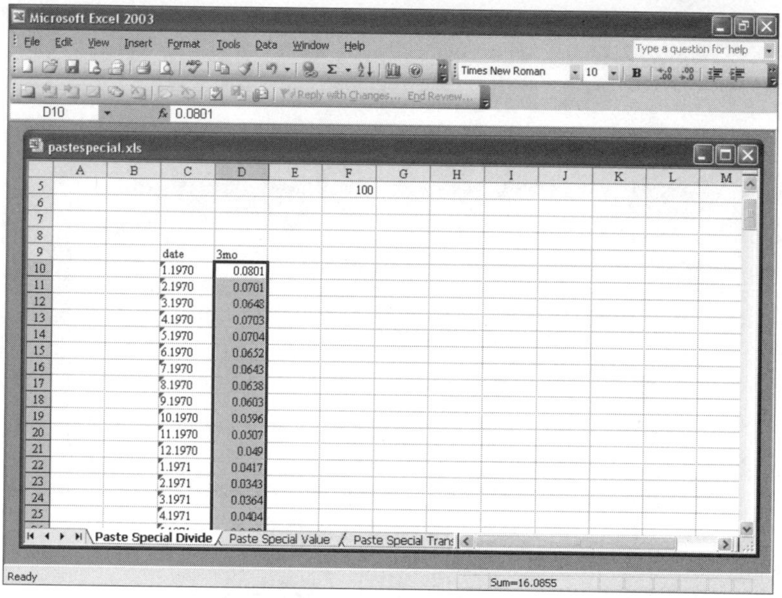

Figure 13-6   Results of using the Divide option in the Paste Special dialog box.

Problems

The workbook Mavs.xls contains statistics for the great 2002-2003 Dallas Mavericks basketball team. Player names are listed in column A, statistical categories are listed in row 3, and statistical results are listed in rows 4-20.

1.   Change the spreadsheet so that all player names are listed in the same row and all statistical categories are listed in the same column.

2.   Field goal percentage, free throw percentage, and three point percentage are listed as decimals. For example, Steve Nash makes 91.9 percent of his free throws, which is listed as .919. Change the spreadsheet so that all shooting percentages are listed as a number between 1 and 100.

3.   The file P13_3.xls, shown here, contains data on quarterly sales for four products.

Copy this data to another range so that quarterly sales are read across instead of down. Link your copied data to the original data so your computation of annual sales in the copied data range will reflect changes entered in rows 5–8.

14

The Auditing Tool

- I've just been handed a 5000-row spreadsheet that computes the net present value (NPV) for a new car. In the spreadsheet, my financial analyst made an assumption about the annual percentage of the growth in the product's price. What cells in the spreadsheet are affected by this assumption?

- I think my financial analyst made an error in computing year 1 before-tax profit. What cells in the spreadsheet model were used for this calculation?

- How does the auditing tool work when I'm working with data in more than one worksheet or workbook?

When we hear the word *structure*, we often think about how a building is built. The structure of a spreadsheet model refers to the way our input assumptions (data such as unit sales, price, and unit cost) are used to compute outputs of interest, such as NPV, profit, or cost. The Excel auditing tool provides an easy method for documenting the structure of a spreadsheet, which makes understanding the logic underlying complex spreadsheet models easier. To use the auditing tool (in Excel 2002 or later), select Tools, Formula Auditing and then choose Show Formula Auditing Toolbar. (In earlier versions of Excel, select Tools, Auditing and then choose Show Auditing Toolbar.) You'll see the toolbar displayed in Figure 14-1.

Note The Show Formula Auditing Toolbar command is a toggle switch. If you see the auditing toolbar and select Show Formula Auditing Toolbar, the toolbar disappears.

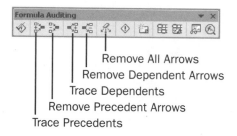

Remove All Arrows
Remove Dependent Arrows
Trace Dependents
Remove Precedent Arrows
Trace Precedents

Figure 14-1 The Formula Auditing toolbar.

In my experience teaching thousands of business analysts, I've found that most analysts use only the five commands labeled in Figure 14-1. These commands locate and display precedents and dependents for spreadsheet cells or formulas. A *precedent* is any cell whose value is needed to compute a selected formula's value. For example, if you were analyzing a direct mail campaign, you would make assumptions about the number of letters mailed and the response rate for the mailing. Then you could compute the number of responses as *response rate*letters mailed*. In this case, the response rate and total letters mailed are precedents of the cell containing the formula used to compute total responses. A *dependent* is any cell containing a formula whose values can't be computed without knowledge of a selected cell. In the previous example, the cell containing the total number of responses is a dependent of the cell containing the response rate. Excel marks precedents and dependents with blue arrows when you use the auditing tool.

Let's apply the auditing tool to some practical problems.

I've just been handed a 5000-row spreadsheet that computes the net present value (NPV) for a new car. In the spreadsheet, my financial analyst made an assumption about the annual percentage of the growth in the product's price. What cells in the spreadsheet are affected by this assumption?

The worksheet Original Model in the file NPVAudit.xls contains calculations that compute the NPV of after-tax profits for a car expected to sell for 5 years. (See Figure 14-2.) Price and cost are in thousands of dollars. The parameter values assumed for the analysis are given in cells C1:C8 (with associated range names listed in cells B1:B8). I've assumed that the price of the product will increase by 3 percent per year. What cells in the spreadsheet are dependents of this assumption?

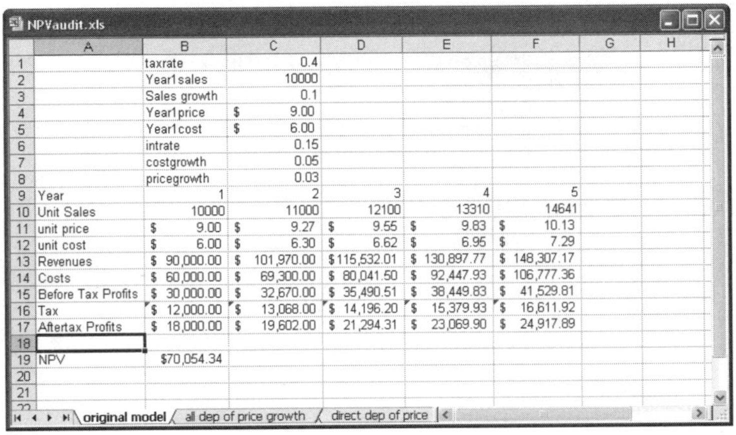

NPVaudit.xls

	A	B	C	D	E	F	G	H
1		taxrate	0.4					
2		Year1sales	10000					
3		Sales growth	0.1					
4		Year1price	$ 9.00					
5		Year1cost	$ 6.00					
6		intrate	0.15					
7		costgrowth	0.05					
8		pricegrowth	0.03					
9	Year	1	2	3	4	5		
10	Unit Sales	10000	11000	12100	13310	14641		
11	unit price	$ 9.00	$ 9.27	$ 9.55	$ 9.83	$ 10.13		
12	unit cost	$ 6.00	$ 6.30	$ 6.62	$ 6.95	$ 7.29		
13	Revenues	$ 90,000.00	$ 101,970.00	$115,532.01	$ 130,897.77	$ 148,307.17		
14	Costs	$ 60,000.00	$ 69,300.00	$ 80,041.50	$ 92,447.93	$ 106,777.36		
15	Before Tax Profits	$ 30,000.00	$ 32,670.00	$ 35,490.51	$ 38,449.83	$ 41,529.81		
16	Tax	$ 12,000.00	$ 13,068.00	$ 14,196.20	$ 15,379.93	$ 16,611.92		
17	Aftertax Profits	$ 18,000.00	$ 19,602.00	$ 21,294.31	$ 23,069.90	$ 24,917.89		
18								
19	NPV	$70,054.34						
20								
21								

original model / all dep of price growth / direct dep of price

Figure 14-2 You can use the auditing tool to trace formulas in complex spreadsheets such as this one.

To answer this question, select cell C8 (the cell containing the assumption of 3 percent price growth) and then click the Trace Dependents button on the Formula Auditing toolbar. Excel displays the set of arrows shown in Figure 14-3, pointing to dependent cells.

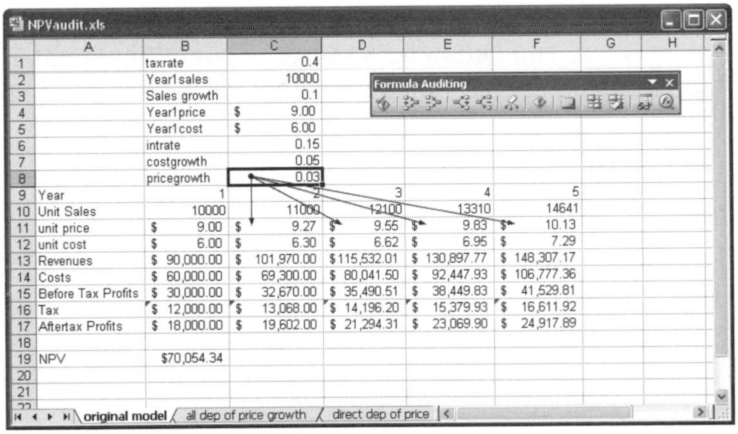

	A	B	C	D	E	F	G	H
1		taxrate	0.4					
2		Year1sales	10000					
3		Sales growth	0.1					
4		Year1price	$ 9.00					
5		Year1cost	$ 6.00					
6		intrate	0.15					
7		costgrowth	0.05					
8		pricegrowth	0.03					
9	Year	1	2	3	4	5		
10	Unit Sales	10000	11000	12100	13310	14641		
11	unit price	$ 9.00	$ 9.27	$ 9.55	$ 9.83	$ 10.13		
12	unit cost	$ 6.00	$ 6.30	$ 6.62	$ 6.95	$ 7.29		
13	Revenues	$ 90,000.00	$ 101,970.00	$115,532.01	$ 130,897.77	$ 148,307.17		
14	Costs	$ 60,000.00	$ 69,300.00	$ 80,041.50	$ 92,447.93	$ 106,777.36		
15	Before Tax Profits	$ 30,000.00	$ 32,670.00	$ 35,490.51	$ 38,449.83	$ 41,529.81		
16	Tax	$ 12,000.00	$ 13,068.00	$ 14,196.20	$ 15,379.93	$ 16,611.92		
17	Aftertax Profits	$ 18,000.00	$ 19,602.00	$ 21,294.31	$ 23,069.90	$ 24,917.89		
18								
19	NPV	$70,054.34						
20								
21								

Figure 14-3 Tracing dependent cells.

By clicking the Trace Dependents button once, Excel points to the cells that *directly* depend on our price growth assumption. In Figure 14-3, you can see that only the unit prices for years 2-5 depend directly on our price growth assumption. Clicking Trace Dependents repeatedly shows *all* formulas whose calculation requires the value for annual price growth, as shown in Figure 14-4.

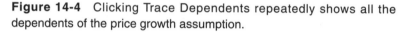

Figure 14-4 Clicking Trace Dependents repeatedly shows all the dependents of the price growth assumption.

You can see that in addition to unit price in years 2-5, our price growth assumption affects years 2–5 revenue, before-tax profits, tax paid, after-tax profits, and NPV. You can remove the arrows with the Remove Dependent Arrows button or the Remove All Arrows button.

I think my financial analyst made an error in computing year 1 before-tax profit. What cells in the spreadsheet model were used for this calculation?

Now we want to find the precedents for cell B15. These are the cells needed to compute year 1 before-tax profit. Select cell B15, and then click the Trace Precedents button once. You'll see the arrows shown in Figure 14-5.

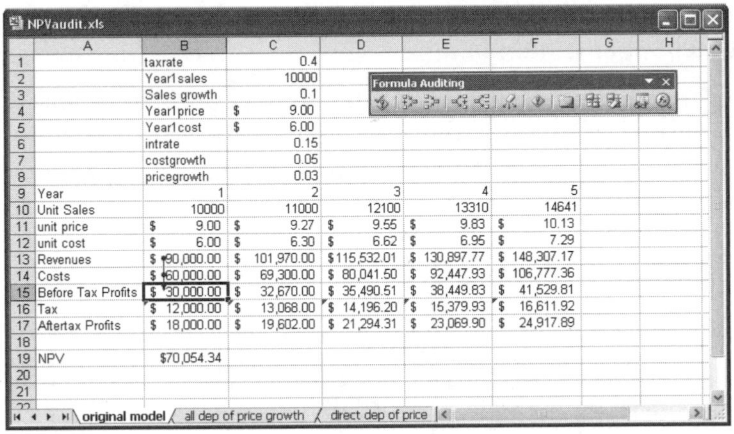

	A	B	C	D	E	F
1		taxrate	0.4			
2		Year1sales	10000			
3		Sales growth	0.1			
4		Year1price	$ 9.00			
5		Year1cost	$ 6.00			
6		intrate	0.15			
7		costgrowth	0.05			
8		pricegrowth	0.03			
9	Year	1	2	3	4	5
10	Unit Sales	10000	11000	12100	13310	14641
11	unit price	$ 9.00	$ 9.27	$ 9.55	$ 9.83	$ 10.13
12	unit cost	$ 6.00	$ 6.30	$ 6.62	$ 6.95	$ 7.29
13	Revenues	$ 90,000.00	$ 101,970.00	$115,532.01	$ 130,897.77	$ 148,307.17
14	Costs	$ 60,000.00	$ 69,300.00	$ 80,041.50	$ 92,447.93	$ 106,777.36
15	Before Tax Profits	$ 30,000.00	$ 32,670.00	$ 35,490.51	$ 38,449.83	$ 41,529.81
16	Tax	$ 12,000.00	$ 13,068.00	$ 14,196.20	$ 15,379.93	$ 16,611.92
17	Aftertax Profits	$ 18,000.00	$ 19,602.00	$ 21,294.31	$ 23,069.90	$ 24,917.89
18						
19	NPV	$70,054.34				

Figure 14-5 Direct precedents for year 1 before-tax profit.

We find that the cells directly needed to compute before-tax year 1 profit are year 1 revenues and year 1 cost. (Before-tax year 1 profit equals year 1 revenue minus year 1 cost.) Repeatedly clicking the Trace Precedents button yields all precedents of year 1 before-tax profit, as shown in Figure 14-6.

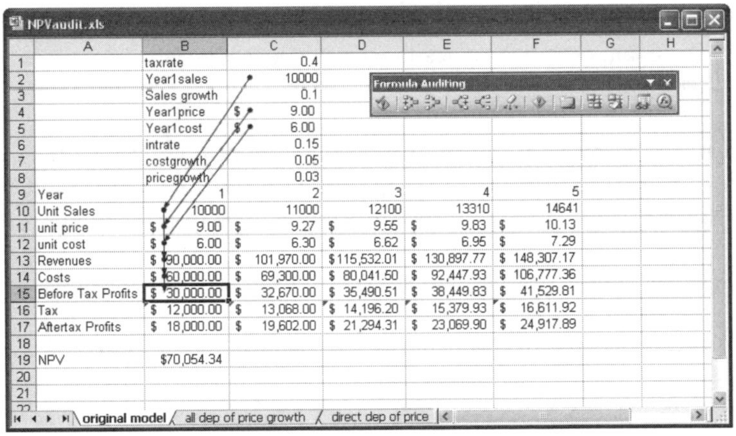

	A	B	C	D	E	F
1		taxrate	0.4			
2		Year1sales	10000			
3		Sales growth	0.1			
4		Year1price	$ 9.00			
5		Year1cost	$ 6.00			
6		intrate	0.15			
7		costgrowth	0.05			
8		pricegrowth	0.03			
9	Year	1	2	3	4	5
10	Unit Sales	10000	11000	12100	13310	14641
11	unit price	$ 9.00	$ 9.27	$ 9.55	$ 9.83	$ 10.13
12	unit cost	$ 6.00	$ 6.30	$ 6.62	$ 6.95	$ 7.29
13	Revenues	$ 90,000.00	$ 101,970.00	$115,532.01	$ 130,897.77	$ 148,307.17
14	Costs	$ 60,000.00	$ 69,300.00	$ 80,041.50	$ 92,447.93	$ 106,777.36
15	Before Tax Profits	$ 30,000.00	$ 32,670.00	$ 35,490.51	$ 38,449.83	$ 41,529.81
16	Tax	$ 12,000.00	$ 13,068.00	$ 14,196.20	$ 15,379.93	$ 16,611.92
17	Aftertax Profits	$ 18,000.00	$ 19,602.00	$ 21,294.31	$ 23,069.90	$ 24,917.89
18						
19	NPV	$70,054.34				

Figure 14-6 Click Trace Precedents repeatedly to show all precedents of year 1 before-tax profit.

We find that the only input assumptions that influence year 1 before-tax profit are year 1 sales, year 1 price, and year 1 cost.

How does the auditing tool work when I'm working with data in more than one worksheet or workbook?

Consider the simple spreadsheet model in the workbook AuditTwoSheets.xls, shown in Figure 14-7. The formula in the worksheet named Profit computes a company's profit (*unit sales*(price - variable cost) - fixed cost*) from information contained in the worksheet named Data.

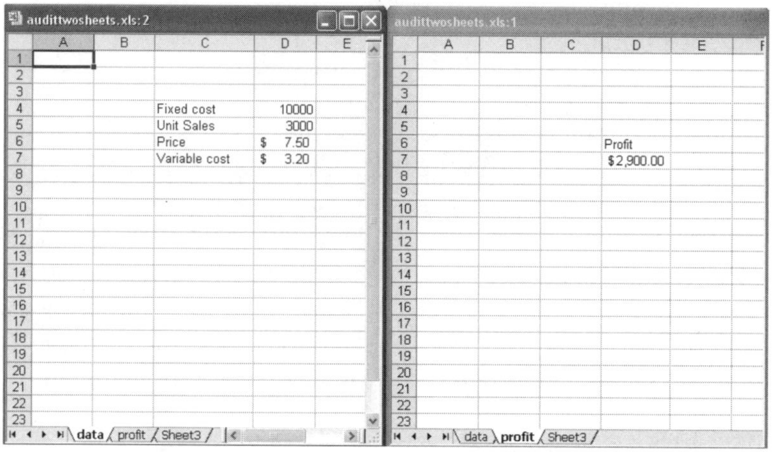

Figure 14-7   Example of how to use the auditing tool with data on multiple worksheets.

Suppose we want to know the precedents of the profit formula. Select cell D7 in the worksheet Profit, and then click Trace Precedents on the Formula Auditing toolbar. You'll see the arrow and spreadsheet icon shown in Figure 14-8.

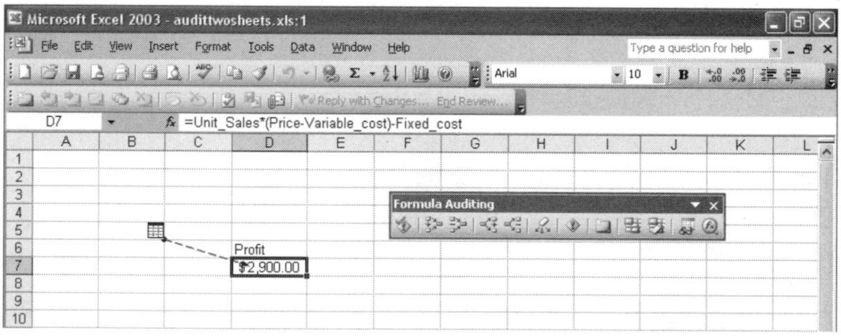

Figure 14-8   Results of applying trace precedents with multiple worksheets.

The spreadsheet icon indicates that the precedents of the profit formula lie in another worksheet. Clicking on the arrow displays the Go To dialog box, shown in Figure 14-9.

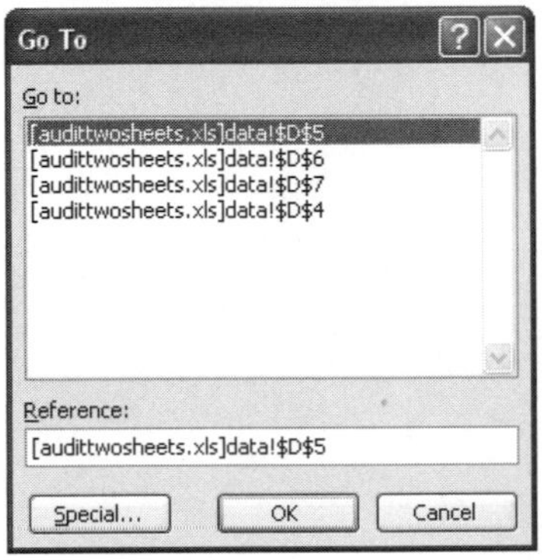

Figure 14-9 The Go To dialog box lets you audit data in multiple worksheets.

Now we can click on any of the listed precedents (cells D4:D7 in the worksheet Data), and Excel will send us to the precedent we selected.

Problems

In the car NPV example, determine the following:

- The direct dependents and all dependents of the interest rate.
- The direct dependents and all dependents of the tax rate.
- The direct precedents and all precedents for year 4 unit sales.
- The direct precedents and all precedents for year 3 costs.

15

Sensitivity Analysis with Data Tables

- ■ I'm thinking of starting a store to sell gourmet lemonade in the local mall. Before opening the store, I'm curious about how my profit, revenue, and variable costs will depend on the price I charge and the unit variable cost.

- ■ I am going to build a new house. The amount of money I need to borrow (with a 15-year repayment period) depends on the price I sell my current house for. I'm also unsure about the annual interest rate I'll receive when I close. Can I determine how my monthly payments will depend on the amount borrowed and the annual interest rate?

- ■ A major Internet company is thinking of purchasing another online retailer. The retailer's current annual revenues are $100 million, with expenses of $150 million. Current projections indicate that the retailer's revenues are growing at 25 percent per year and its expenses are growing at 5 percent per year. We know projections might be in error, however, and we would like to know, for a variety of assumptions about annual revenue and expense growth, the number of years before the retailer will show a profit.

Most spreadsheet models contain assumptions about certain parameters or inputs to the model. In our lemonade example, the inputs would include:

■   The price for which a glass of lemonade is sold

■   The variable cost of producing a glass of lemonade

■   The sensitivity of demand for lemonade to price charged

■   The annual fixed cost of running a lemonade stand

Based on input assumptions, we often compute outputs of interest. For the lemonade example, the outputs of interest might include:

■   Annual profit

■   Annual revenue

■   Annual variable cost

Despite best intentions, assumptions about input values can be in error. For example, our best guess about the variable cost of producing a glass of lemonade might be $0.45, but it's possible that our assumption will be in error. *Sensitivity analysis* determines how a spreadsheet's outputs vary in response to changes to the spreadsheet's inputs. For example, we might want to see how a change in product price affects yearly profit, revenue, and variable cost. A data table in Excel makes it easy to vary one or two inputs and perform a sensitivity analysis. A *one-way* data table enables you to determine how changing one input will change any number of outputs. A *two-way* data table allows you to determine how changing two inputs will change a single output. Our three examples will show how easy it is to use a data table and obtain meaningful sensitivity results.

I'm thinking of starting a store to sell gourmet lemonade in the local mall. Before opening the store, I'm curious about how my profit, revenue, and variable costs will depend on the price I charge and the unit variable cost.

The work required for this analysis is in the file Lemonade.xls. (See Figures 15-1, 15-2, and 15-4.) Our input assumptions are given in the range D1:D4. We're assuming that annual demand for lemonade (see the formula in cell D2) equals *65000-9000*price*. I've created the names in C1:C7 to correspond to cells D1:D7.

I computed annual revenue in cell D5 with the formula *demand*price*. In cell D6, I computed the annual variable cost with the formula *unit_cost*demand*. Finally, in cell D7, I computed profit by using the formula *revenue - fixed_cost - variable_cost*.

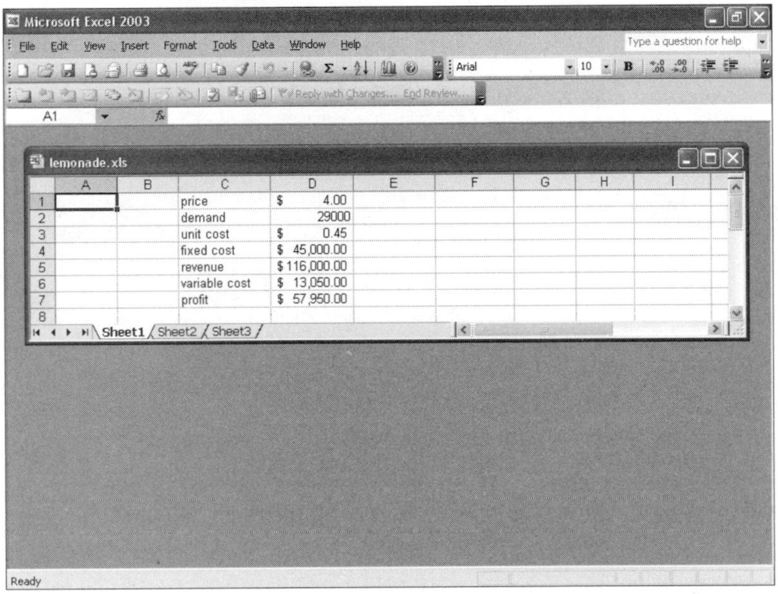

Figure 15-1   The inputs that change the profitability of a lemonade store.

Suppose that I want to know how changes in price (say, between $1.00 and $4.00 in $0.25 increments) affect annual profit, revenue, and variable cost. Because we're changing only one input, a one-way data table will solve our problem. The data table is shown in Figure 15-2.

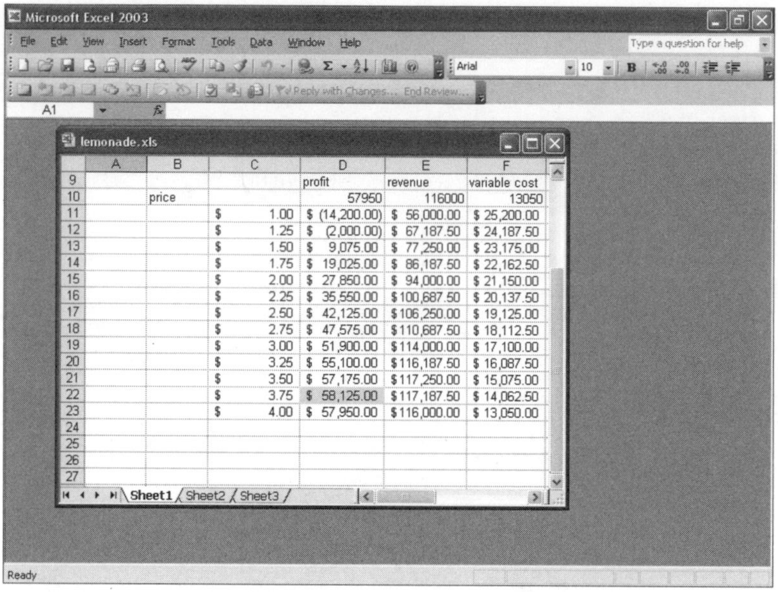

	A	B	C	D	E	F
9				profit	revenue	variable cost
10		price		57950	116000	13050
11			$ 1.00	$ (14,200.00)	$ 56,000.00	$ 25,200.00
12			$ 1.25	$ (2,000.00)	$ 67,187.50	$ 24,187.50
13			$ 1.50	$ 9,075.00	$ 77,250.00	$ 23,175.00
14			$ 1.75	$ 19,025.00	$ 86,187.50	$ 22,162.50
15			$ 2.00	$ 27,850.00	$ 94,000.00	$ 21,150.00
16			$ 2.25	$ 35,550.00	$100,687.50	$ 20,137.50
17			$ 2.50	$ 42,125.00	$106,250.00	$ 19,125.00
18			$ 2.75	$ 47,575.00	$110,687.50	$ 18,112.50
19			$ 3.00	$ 51,900.00	$114,000.00	$ 17,100.00
20			$ 3.25	$ 55,100.00	$116,187.50	$ 16,087.50
21			$ 3.50	$ 57,175.00	$117,250.00	$ 15,075.00
22			$ 3.75	$ 58,125.00	$117,187.50	$ 14,062.50
23			$ 4.00	$ 57,950.00	$116,000.00	$ 13,050.00

Figure 15-2 One-way data table with varying prices.

To set up a one-way data table, begin by listing input values down a single column. I listed the prices of interest (ranging from $1.00 to $4.00 in $0.25 increments) in the range C11:C23. Next I go over one column and up one row from the list of input values, and there I list the formulas we want a data table to calculate. I entered the formula for profit in cell D10, the formula for revenue in cell E10, and the formula for variable cost in cell F10. Now select the table range (C10:F23). The table range begins one row above the first input; its last row is the row containing the last input value. The first column in the table range is the column containing the inputs; its last column is the last column containing an output. After selecting the table range, select Data, Table and fill in the dialog box shown in Figure 15-3.

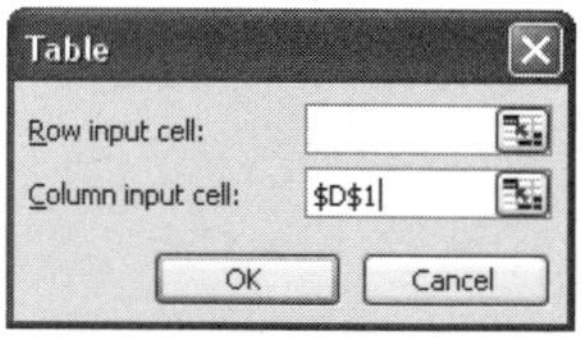

Figure 15-3 You fill in the Table dialog box to create a data table.

As the column input cell, use the cell in which you want the listed inputs—that is, the values listed in the first column of the data table range—to be assigned. Because the listed inputs are prices, I chose D1 as the column input cell. After clicking OK, Excel creates the one-way data table shown in Figure 15-4.

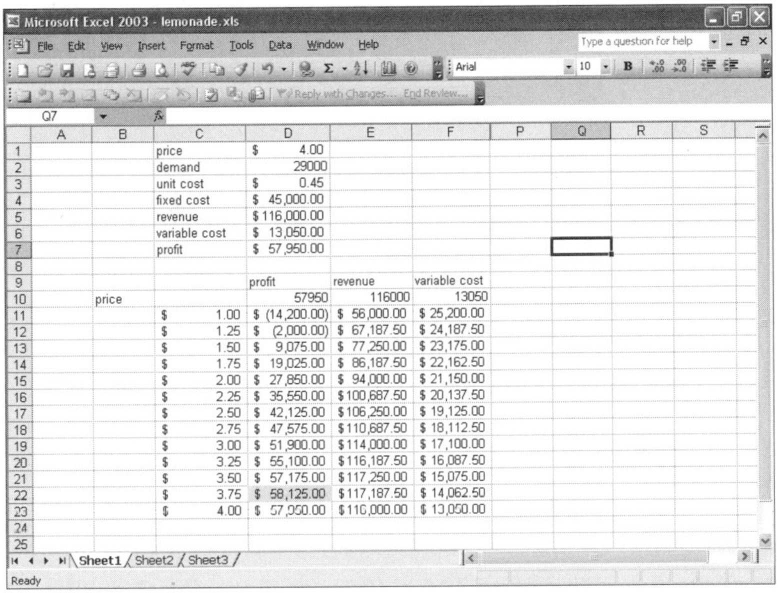

	A	B	C		D	E	F
1			price		$ 4.00		
2			demand		29000		
3			unit cost		$ 0.45		
4			fixed cost		$ 45,000.00		
5			revenue		$ 116,000.00		
6			variable cost		$ 13,050.00		
7			profit		$ 57,950.00		
8							
9					profit	revenue	variable cost
10		price			57950	116000	13050
11			$	1.00	$ (14,200.00)	$ 56,000.00	$ 25,200.00
12			$	1.25	$ (2,000.00)	$ 67,187.50	$ 24,187.50
13			$	1.50	$ 9,075.00	$ 77,250.00	$ 23,175.00
14			$	1.75	$ 19,025.00	$ 86,187.50	$ 22,162.50
15			$	2.00	$ 27,850.00	$ 94,000.00	$ 21,150.00
16			$	2.25	$ 35,550.00	$ 100,687.50	$ 20,137.50
17			$	2.50	$ 42,125.00	$ 106,250.00	$ 19,125.00
18			$	2.75	$ 47,575.00	$ 110,687.50	$ 18,112.50
19			$	3.00	$ 51,900.00	$ 114,000.00	$ 17,100.00
20			$	3.25	$ 55,100.00	$ 116,187.50	$ 16,087.50
21			$	3.50	$ 57,175.00	$ 117,250.00	$ 15,075.00
22			$	3.75	$ 58,125.00	$ 117,187.50	$ 14,062.50
23			$	4.00	$ 57,950.00	$ 116,000.00	$ 13,050.00
24							
25							

Figure 15-4 One-way data table with varying prices.

In the range D11:F11, profit, revenue, and variable cost are computed for a price of $1.00. In cells D12:F12, profit, revenue, and variable cost are computed for a price of $1.25, and on through the range of prices. The profit-maximizing price among all listed prices is $3.75. A price of $3.75 would produce an annual profit of $58,125, annual revenue of $117,187.50, and an annual variable cost of $14,062.50.

Suppose I want to determine how annual profit varies as price varies from $1.50 to $5.00 (in $0.25 increments) and unit variable cost varies from $0.30 to $0.60 (in $0.05 increments). Because we're changing two inputs, we need a *two-way* data table. (See Figure 15-5.) I list the values for one input down the first column of the table range (I'm using the range H11:H25 for the price values), and I list the values of the other input in the first column of the table range. (In this example, the range I10:O10 holds the list of variable cost values.)

A two-way data table can have only one output cell, and the formula for the output must be placed in the upper left corner of the table range. Therefore, I placed the formula for profit in cell H10.

	G	H	I	J	K	L	M	N	O	P
9			var cost							
10		57950	$ 0.30	$ 0.35	$ 0.40	$ 0.45	$ 0.50	$ 0.55	$ 0.60	
11		$ 1.50	$16,800.00	$14,225.00	$11,650.00	$ 9,075.00	$ 6,500.00	$ 3,925.00	$ 1,350.00	
12		$ 1.75	$26,412.50	$23,950.00	$21,487.50	$19,025.00	$16,562.50	$14,100.00	$11,637.50	
13		$ 2.00	$34,900.00	$32,550.00	$30,200.00	$27,850.00	$25,500.00	$23,150.00	$20,800.00	
14		$ 2.25	$42,262.50	$40,025.00	$37,787.50	$35,550.00	$33,312.50	$31,075.00	$28,837.50	
15		$ 2.50	$48,500.00	$46,375.00	$44,250.00	$42,125.00	$40,000.00	$37,875.00	$35,750.00	
16		$ 2.75	$53,612.50	$51,600.00	$49,587.50	$47,575.00	$45,562.50	$43,550.00	$41,537.50	
17		$ 3.00	$57,600.00	$55,700.00	$53,800.00	$51,900.00	$50,000.00	$48,100.00	$46,200.00	
18		$ 3.25	$60,462.50	$58,675.00	$56,887.50	$55,100.00	$53,312.50	$51,525.00	$49,737.50	
19		$ 3.50	$62,200.00	$60,525.00	$58,850.00	$57,175.00	$55,500.00	$53,825.00	$52,150.00	
20	price	$ 3.75	$62,812.50	$61,250.00	$59,687.50	$58,125.00	$56,562.50	$55,000.00	$53,437.50	
21		$ 4.00	$62,300.00	$60,850.00	$59,400.00	$57,950.00	$56,500.00	$55,050.00	$53,600.00	
22		$ 4.25	$60,662.50	$59,325.00	$57,987.50	$56,650.00	$55,312.50	$53,975.00	$52,637.50	
23		$ 4.50	$57,900.00	$56,675.00	$55,450.00	$54,225.00	$53,000.00	$51,775.00	$50,550.00	
24		$ 4.75	$54,012.50	$52,900.00	$51,787.50	$50,675.00	$49,562.50	$48,450.00	$47,337.50	
25		$ 5.00	$49,000.00	$48,000.00	$47,000.00	$46,000.00	$45,000.00	$44,000.00	$43,000.00	

Figure 15-5   A two-way data table showing profit as a function of price and unit variable cost.

I select the table range (cells H10:O25), and then choose Data, Table. Cell D1 (price) is the column input cell, and cell D3 (unit variable cost) is the row input cell. This ensures that the values in the first column of the table range are plugged in as prices, and the values in the first row of the table range are plugged in as unit variable costs. After clicking OK, we see the two-way data table shown in Figure 15-5. As an example, in cell K19, when we charge $3.50 and the unit variable cost is $0.40, our annual profit equals $58,850. For each unit cost, I've highlighted the profit-maximizing price. Note that as the unit cost increases, the profit-maximizing price increases as we pass on some of our cost increase to our customers. Of course, we can only guarantee that the profit-maximizing price in the data table is within $0.25 of the actual profit-maximizing price. When we study the Excel Solver in Chapters 24 and 25, you'll learn how to determine (to the penny) the exact profit-maximizing price.

Here are some other notes on this problem:

■   As you change input values in a spreadsheet, the values calculated by a data table change, too. For example, if we increased fixed cost by $10,000, all profit numbers in the data table would be reduced by $10,000.

■   You can't delete or edit a portion of a data table. If you want to save the values in a data table, select the table range, copy the values, and then choose Edit, Paste Special. Select Values in the Paste area of the dialog box. If you take this step, however, changes to your spreadsheet inputs will no longer cause the data table calculations to update.

■   When setting up a two-way data table, be careful not to mix up your row and column input cells. A mix-up will cause nonsensical results.

■   Most people set their spreadsheet calculation mode to Automatic. With this setting, any change in your spreadsheet will cause all your data tables to be recalculated. Usually, you want this, but if your data tables are large, automatic recalculation can be incredibly slow. If the constant recalculation of data tables is slowing your work down, select Tools, Options, and then click the Calculation tab. Select Automatic Except For Tables. When Automatic Except For Tables is selected, all your data tables recalculate only when you press the F9 (recalculation) key.

I am going to build a new house. The amount of money I need to borrow (with a 15-year repayment period) depends on the price I sell my current house for. I'm also unsure about the annual interest rate I'll receive when I close. Can I determine how my monthly payments will depend on the amount borrowed and the annual interest rate?

The real power of data tables becomes evident when you combine a data table with one of Excel's functions. In this example, we'll use a two-way data table to vary two inputs (the amount borrowed and the annual interest rate) to the Excel PMT function and determine how the monthly payment will vary as these inputs change. (The PMT function is discussed in detail in Chapter 10). Our work for this example is in the file Mortgagedt.xls, shown in Figure 15-6.

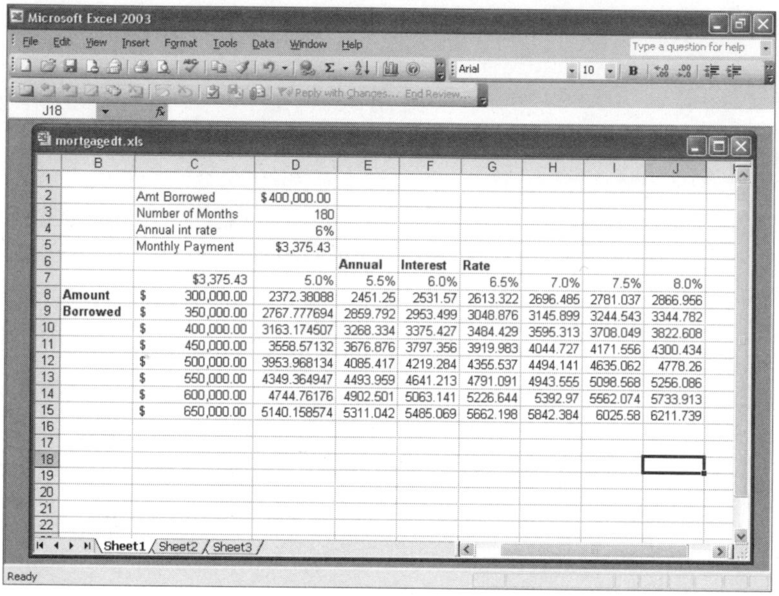

	B	C	D	E	F	G	H	I	J
1									
2		Amt Borrowed	$400,000.00						
3		Number of Months	180						
4		Annual int rate	6%						
5		Monthly Payment	$3,375.43						
6				**Annual**	**Interest**	**Rate**			
7		$3,375.43	5.0%	5.5%	6.0%	6.5%	7.0%	7.5%	8.0%
8	**Amount**	$ 300,000.00	2372.38088	2451.25	2531.57	2613.322	2696.485	2781.037	2866.956
9	**Borrowed**	$ 350,000.00	2767.777694	2859.792	2953.499	3048.876	3145.899	3244.543	3344.782
10		$ 400,000.00	3163.174507	3268.334	3375.427	3484.429	3595.313	3708.049	3822.608
11		$ 450,000.00	3558.57132	3676.876	3797.356	3919.983	4044.727	4171.556	4300.434
12		$ 500,000.00	3953.968134	4085.417	4219.284	4355.537	4494.141	4635.062	4778.26
13		$ 550,000.00	4349.364947	4493.959	4641.213	4791.091	4943.555	5098.568	5256.086
14		$ 600,000.00	4744.76176	4902.501	5063.141	5226.644	5392.97	5562.074	5733.913
15		$ 650,000.00	5140.158574	5311.042	5485.069	5662.198	5842.384	6025.58	6211.739

Figure 15-6 You can use a data table to determine how mortgage payments vary as the amount borrowed and the interest rate change.

Suppose we're borrowing money on a 15-year mortgage, where monthly payments are made at the end of each month. I've input the amount borrowed in cell D2, the number of months in the mortgage (180) in D3, and annual interest rate in D4. I've associated the range names in cells C2:C4 with the cells D2:D4. Based on these inputs, we compute our monthly payment in D5 with the formula:

```
-PMT(Annual_int_rate/12,Number_of_Months,Amt_Borrowed)
```

We think the amount borrowed will range (depending on the price we sell our current house for) between $300,000 and $650,000 and that our annual interest rate will range between 5 percent and 8 percent. In preparation for creating a data table, I entered the amounts borrowed in the range C8:C15 and possible interest rate values in the range D7:J7. Cell C7 contains the output we want to recalculate for various input combinations. Therefore, I set cell C7 equal to cell D5. Next I select the table range (C7:J15) and choose Data, Table. Because numbers in the first column of the table range are amounts borrowed, the column input cell is D2. Numbers in the first row of the table are annual interest rates, so our row input cell is D4. After clicking OK, we see the data table shown in Figure 15-6. This table shows us, for example, that if we borrow $400,000 at an annual rate of 6 percent, our monthly payments would be $3,375.43. Our data table also shows us that at a low interest rate (say 5 percent), an increase of $50,000 in the amount borrowed raises our monthly payment by around $395, while at a high interest rate (say 8 percent), an increase of $50,000 in the amount borrowed raises our monthly payment around $478.

A major Internet company is thinking of purchasing another online retailer. The retailer's current annual revenues are $100 million, with expenses of $150 million. Current projections indicate that the retailer's revenues are growing at 25 percent per year and its expenses are growing at 5 percent per year. We know projections might be in error, however, and we would like to know, for a variety of assumptions about annual revenue and expense growth, the number of years before the retailer will show a profit.

We want to determine the number of years needed to break even, using annual growth rates in revenue between 10 percent and 50 percent and annual expense growth rates between 2 percent and 20 percent. Let's also assume that if the firm cannot break even in 13 years, we'll say "cannot break even." Our work is in the file Bezos.xls, shown in Figures 15-7 and 15-8. (I used the Format, Rows Hide and Format, Columns Hide commands to hide some rows and columns of our spreadsheet. To display hidden rows, select the hidden rows and then choose Format, Rows Unhide or Format, Columns Unhide.)

In row 11, I project the firm's revenue out 13 years (based on the annual revenue growth rate assumed in E7) by copying from F11 to G11:R11 the formula *E11*(1+$E$7)*. In row 12, I project the firm's expenses out 13 years (based on the annual expense growth rate assumed in E8) by copying from F12 to G12:R12 the formula *E12*(1+$E$8)*.

	A	B	C	D	E	F	G	H	P	Q	R
6					growth						
7			Revenue	100000000	0.25						
8			Exp	1.50E+08	0.05						
9											
10					0	1	2	3	11	12	13
11				Rev	100000000	125000000	156250000	195312500	1164153218	1455191523	1818989404
12				Exp	150000000	157500000	165375000	173643750	256550904	269378449	282847371
13				Breakeven		0	0	3	0	0	0
14											
15				Total	3						

Figure 15-7   You can use a data table to calculate how many years it will take to break even.

We would like to use a two-way data table to determine how varying our growth rates for revenues and expenses affects the years needed to break even. We need a *single cell* whose value always tells us the number of years needed to break even. Because we can break even during any of the next 13 years, this might seem like a tall order.

I begin by using in row 13 an IF statement for each year to determine whether we break even during a year. The IF statement returns the number of the year if we break even during the year or 0 otherwise. I determine the year we break even in cell E15 by simply adding together all the numbers in row 13. Finally, I can use cell E15 as the output cell for our two-way data table.

I copy from cell F13 to G13:R13 the formula *IF(AND(E11<E12,F11>F12), F10,0)*. This formula reflects the fact that we break even for the first time during a year if, and only if, during the previous year, revenues are less than expenses *and* during the current year, revenues are greater than expenses. If this is the case, we enter the year number in row 13; otherwise, we enter 0.

Now, in cell E15, I can determine the breakeven year (if any) with the formula *IF(SUM(F13:R13)>0,SUM(F13:R13),"No BE")*. If we do not break even during the next 13 years, the formula enters the text string "No BE".

I now enter our annual revenue growth rates (10 percent to 50 percent) in the range E21:E61. I enter annual expense growth rates (2 percent to 20 percent) in the range F20:X20. I make sure that the year-of-breakeven formula is copied to cell E20 with the formula *=E15*. Next I select the table range E20:X61 and then choose Data, Table. I select cell E7 (revenue growth rate) as the column input cell and cell E8 (expense growth rate) as the row input cell. We obtain the two-way data table shown in Figure 15-8.

	D	E	F	G	H	P	Q	R	W	X
15	Total	3								
16										
17										
18										
19				Exp growth						
20		3	0.02	0.03	0.04	0.12	0.13	0.14	0.19	0.2
21		0.1	6	7	8	No BE	No BE	No BE	No BE	No BE
22	Rev	0.11	5	6	7	No BE	No BE	No BE	No BE	No BE
23	growth	0.12	5	5	6	No BE	No BE	No BE	No BE	No BE
24		0.13	4	5	5	No BE	No BE	No BE	No BE	No BE
25		0.14	4	4	5	No BE	No BE	No BE	No BE	No BE
55		0.44	2	2	2	2	2	2	3	3
56		0.45	2	2	2	2	2	2	3	3
57		0.46	2	2	2	2	2	2	2	3
58		0.47	2	2	2	2	2	2	2	2
59		0.48	2	2	2	2	2	2	2	2
60		0.49	2	2	2	2	2	2	2	2
61		0.5	2	2	2	2	2	2	2	2

Figure 15-8   Two-way data table for year of break even.

Note, for example, that if expenses grow at 4 percent a year, a 10-percent annual growth in revenue will result in breaking even in 8 years, while a 50-percent annual growth in revenue will result in breaking even in only 2 years! Also note that if expenses grow at 12 percent per year and revenues grow at 14 percent per year, we will not break even by the end of 13 years.

Problems

1. You've been assigned to analyze the profitability of Bill Clinton's new autobiography. The following assumptions have been made:

    ❏   Bill is receiving a $12-million royalty.

    ❏   The fixed cost of producing the hardcover version of the book is $1 million.

    ❏   The variable cost of producing each hardcover book is $4.

    ❏   The publisher's net from book sales per hardcover unit sold is $15.

    ❏   The publisher expects to sell 1 million hardcover copies.

    ❏   Paperback sales will be double hardcover sales.

    ❏   The fixed cost of producing the paperback is $100,000.

    ❏   The variable cost of producing each paperback book is $1.

    ❏   Publisher's net from book sales per paperback unit sold is $4.

    Use this information to answer the following questions.

    ❏   Determine how the publisher's before-tax profit will vary as hardcover sales vary between 100,000 and 1,000,000 copies.

    ❏   Determine how the publisher's before-tax profit varies as hardcover sales vary between 100,000 and 1,000,000 copies and the ratio of paperback to hardcover sales varies between 1 and 2.4.

2. The annual demand for a product equals

$$500 - 3p + 10\sqrt{a}$$

where p = price of product in dollars and a = hundreds of dollars spent on advertising the product. The annual fixed cost of selling the product is $10,000 and the unit variable cost of producing the product is $12. Determine a price (within $10) and amount of advertising (within $100) that maximizes profit.

3. Reconsider our hedging example in Chapter 12. For stock prices in six months that range from $20.00 to $65.00 and the number of puts purchased varying between 0 and 100 (in increments of 10), determine the percentage return on your portfolio.

4. For our mortgage example, suppose you know the annual interest rate will be 5.5 percent. Create a table that shows for amounts borrowed between $300,000 and $600,000 (in $50,000 increments) the difference in payments between a 15-year, 20-year, and 30-year mortgage.

5. Currently we sell 40,000 units of a product for $45. The unit variable cost of producing the product is $5. We are thinking of cutting the product price by 30 percent. We are sure this will increase sales by an amount between 10 percent and 50 percent. Perform a sensitivity analysis to show how profit will change as a function of the percentage increase in sales. Ignore fixed costs.

6. Let's assume that at the end of each of the next 40 years, we will put the same amount in our retirement fund and earn the same interest rate each year. Show how the amount of money we will have at retirement changes as we vary our annual contribution between $5,000 and $25,000 and the rate of interest varies between 3 percent and 15 percent.

7. The *payback period* for a project is the number of years needed for a project's future profits to pay back the project's initial investment. A project requires a $300 million investment at Time 0. The project yields profit for 10 years, and Time 1 cash flow will be between $30 million and $100 million. Annual cash flow growth will be between 5 percent and 25 percent a year. How does the project payback depend on the Year 1 cash flow and cash flow growth rates?

8. Microsoft is thinking of translating a software product into Swahili. Currently, 200,000 units per year of the product are sold at a price of $100. Unit variable cost is $20.00. The cost of translation is $5 million. Translating the product into Swahili will increase sales during each of the next three years by some unknown percentage over the current level of 200,000 units. Show how the change in profit resulting from the translation depends on the percentage increase in product sales. You can ignore the time value of money and taxes in your calculations.

16

The Goal Seek Command

■ For a given price, how many glasses of lemonade does a lemonade store need to sell per year to break even?

■ We want to pay off our mortgage in 15 years. The annual interest rate is 6 percent. The bank's told us we can afford monthly payments of $2,000. How much can we borrow?

■ I always had trouble with "story problems" in high-school algebra. Can Excel make solving story problems easier?

The Goal Seek feature in Excel enables you to compute a value for a spreadsheet input that makes the value of a given formula match the goal you specify. For example, in our lemonade store example from Chapter 15, suppose we charge $3.00 a glass. We want to know how many glasses we need to sell to break even. We can use Goal Seek to calculate this value. Essentially, Goal Seek embeds a powerful equation solver in your spreadsheet. To use Goal Seek, you need to provide Excel with three pieces of information:

■ **Set Cell** This cell contains the formula that calculates the information you're seeking. In the lemonade example, the set cell would contain the formula for profit.

■ **To Value** This cell includes the numerical value for the goal that's calculated in the set cell. In the lemonade example, because we want to determine a sales volume that lets us break even, To Value would equal 0.

■ **By Changing Cell** This is the input cell that Excel changes until the set cell calculates the goal defined in the To Value cell. In the lemonade example, the by-changing cell contains annual lemonade sales.

For a given price, how many glasses of lemonade does a lemonade store need to sell per year to break even?

Our work for this section is in the file Lemonadegs.xls, which is shown in Figure 16-1. As in Chapter 15, I've assumed an annual fixed cost of $45,000 and unit variable cost of $0.45. Let's assume a price of $3.00. The question is how many glasses do we need to sell in a year to break even.

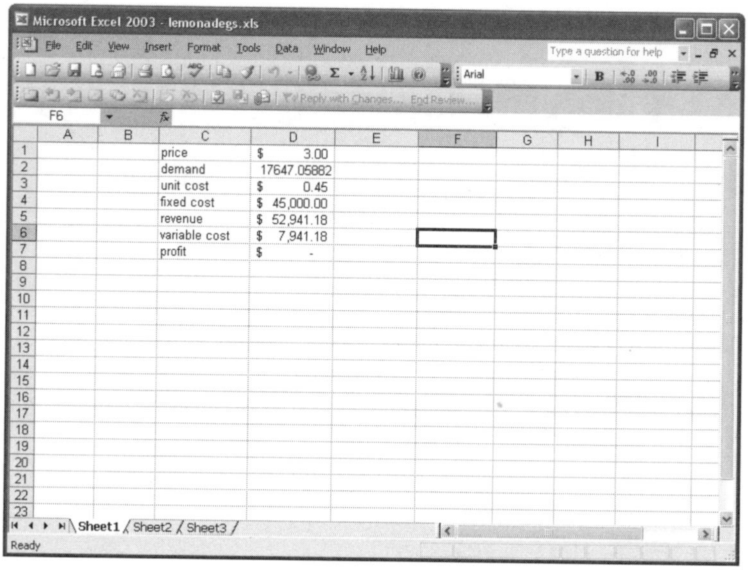

Figure 16-1   We'll use this data to set up the Goal Seek feature to perform a breakeven analysis.

To start, insert any number for demand in cell D2. Choose Tools, Goal Seek, and then fill in the dialog box shown in Figure 16-2.

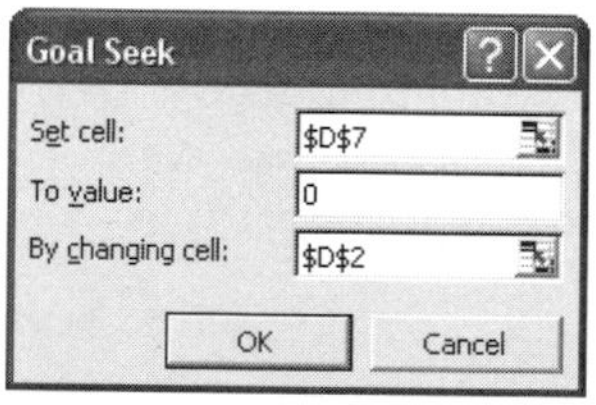

Figure 16-2   The Goal Seek dialog box filled in with entries for a breakeven analysis.

The dialog box indicates that we want to change cell D2 (annual demand, or sales) until cell D7 (profit) hits a value of 0. After clicking OK, we get the result that's shown in Figure 16-1. If we sell around 17,647 glasses of lemonade per year (about 48 glasses per day), we'll break even. To find the value we're seeking, Excel varies the demand in cell D2 (alternating between high and low values) until it finds a value that makes profit equal $0. If a problem has more than one solution, Goal Seek will still display only one answer.

Before using Goal Seek, you should choose Tools, Options and then click the Calculation tab. Set the Maximum Change option, shown below, to a very small number (say .000001). The default setting (.001) causes Goal Seek to stop when the set cell is within .001 of To Value, which means that Excel might stop when it finds a demand that yields a profit between -.001 and .001. Entering a smaller value (such as .000001) for Maximum Change ensures that Goal Seek returns a value for the by-changing cell that yields a set cell value within .000001 of the goal.

We want to pay off our mortgage in 15 years. The annual interest rate is 6 percent. The bank's told us we can afford monthly payments of $2000. How much can we borrow?

You can begin to answer this question by setting up a spreadsheet to compute the monthly payments on a 15-year loan (we'll assume payments at the end of the month) as a function of the annual interest rate and a trial loan amount. You can see the work I did in the file Paymentgs.xls and in Figure 16-3.

In cell E6, the formula *-PMT(annual_int_rate/12,years,amt._borrowed)* computes the monthly payment associated with the amount borrowed, which is listed in cell E5. Filling in the Goal Seek dialog box as shown in Figure 16-4 calculates the amount borrowed that results in monthly payments equal to $2000. With a limit of $2000 for monthly payments, we can borrow up to $237,007.03.

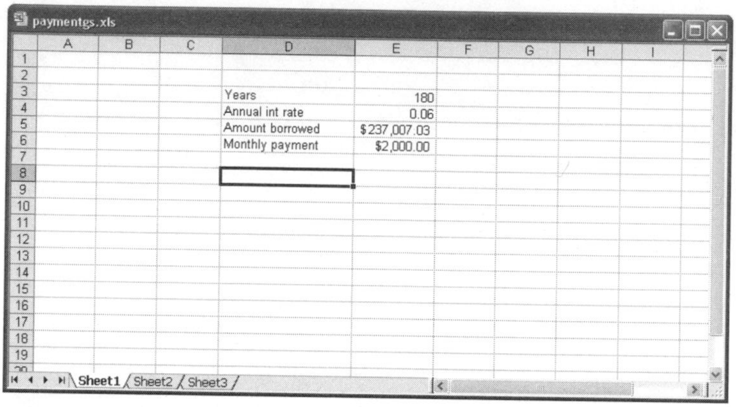

Figure 16-3   You can use data such as this with the Goal Seek feature to determine the amount you can borrow based on a set monthly payment.

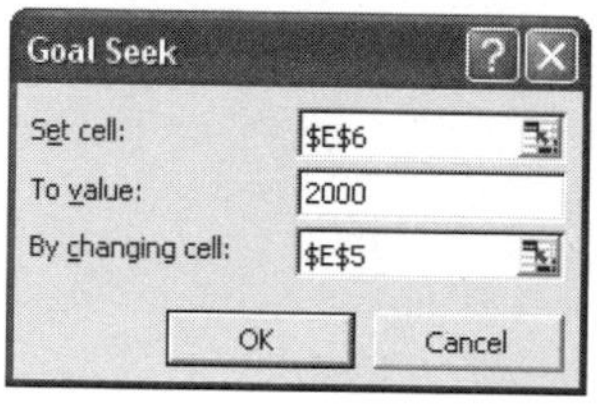

Figure 16-4   The Goal Seek dialog box set up to calculate the mortgage example.

I always had trouble with "story problems" in high-school algebra. Can Excel make solving story problems easier?

If you think back to high-school algebra, most story problems required you to choose a variable (most algebra teachers called it x) that solved a particular equation. Goal Seek is an equation solver, so solving story problems is made to order for Goal Seek. Here's a typical high-school algebra problem. You can find the Excel solution in the file Maria.xls, shown in Figure 16-5.

Maria and Edmund have a lover's quarrel while honeymooning in Seattle. Maria storms into her Mazda Miata and drives 64 miles per hour toward her mother's home in Los Angeles. Two hours after Maria leaves, Edmund jumps into his BMW in hot pursuit, driving 80 miles per hour. How many miles will each person have traveled when Edmund catches Maria?

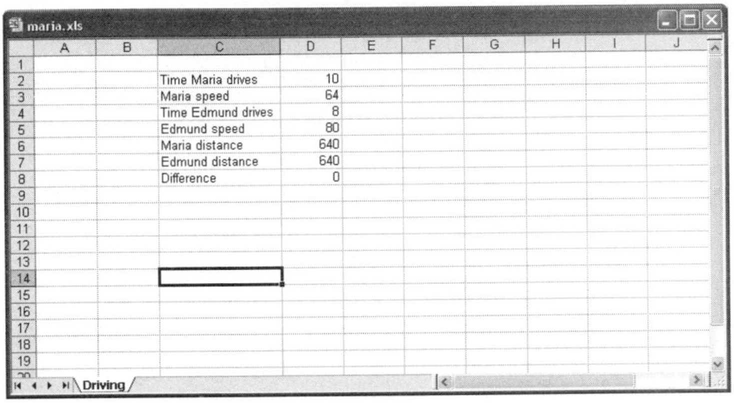

Figure 16-5   Goal Seek can help solve problems such as the Edmund and Maria algebra example.

Our set cell will be the difference between the distance Maria and Edmund have traveled. We will set this to a value of 0 by changing the number of hours Maria drives. Of course, Edmund drives two hours less than Maria drives.

I entered a trial number of hours that Maria drives in cell D2. Then I associated the range names in the cell range C2:C8 with the cells D2:D8. Because Edmund drives two fewer hours than Maria, in cell D4 I've entered the formula *Time_Maria_drives-2*. In cells D6 and D7, we use the fact that *distance – speed* time* to compute the total distance Maria and Edmund travel. The difference between the distances traveled by Edmund and Maria is computed in cell D8 with the formula *Maria_distance-Edmund_distance*. Now I can fill in the Goal Seek dialog box as shown in Figure 16-6.

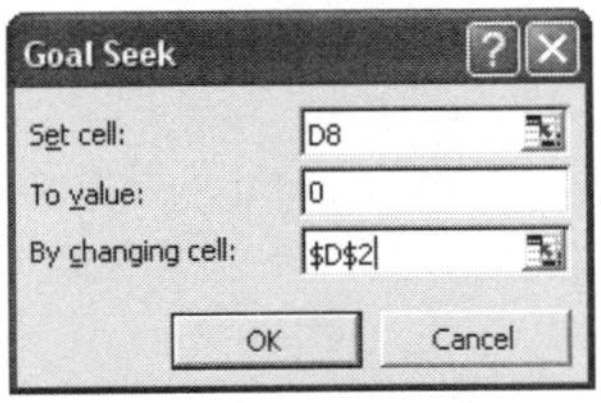

Figure 16-6   Goal Seek dialog box filled in to solve an algebra story problem.

We change Maria's hours of driving (cell D2) until the difference between the miles traveled by Edmund and Maria (cell D8) equals 0. We find that after Maria drives 10 hours and Edmund 8 hours, they both will have driven a distance of 640 miles.

Problems

1. For problem 1 in Chapter 15, determine how many hardcover books must be sold to break even.

2. For the car Net Present Value example in Chapter 14, by what rate do annual sales need to grow for total NPV to equal $100,000,000?

3. What value of year 1 unit cost would increase our NPV in the car example of Chapter 14 to $100,000,000?

4. In our mortgage example, suppose I need to borrow $200,000 for 15 years. If my maximum payments are limited to $2,000 per month, how high an annual interest rate can I tolerate?

5. How could I use Goal Seek to determine a project's IRR?

6. At the end of each of the next 40 years, I'm going to put $20,000 in my retirement fund. What rate of return on my investments do I need so that I will have $2,000,000 available for retirement when I retire in 40 years?

7. I expect to earn 10 percent per year on my retirement investments. At the end of each of the next 40 years, I want to put the same amount of money in my retirement portfolio. I am going to retire in 40 years. How much money do I need to put in each year if I want to have $2,000,000 in my account when I retire?

8. Consider two projects with the following cash flows:

	Year 1	Year 2	Year 3	Year 4
Project 1	-$1,000	$400	$350	$400
Project 2	-$900	$100	$100	$1,000

    For what rate of interest will project 1 have a larger NPV? (Hint: Find the interest rate that makes both projects have the same NPV.)

9. I am running a conference. My fixed costs are $15,000, and I must pay the college union $300 for food and lodging costs per conference participant. Each of 10 speakers must be paid $700. I am charging all participants who aren't speaking $900 for the conference, which includes their food and lodging costs. How many paid registrants need to attend for me to break even?

10. I am buying 40 pounds of candy. Some of the candy sells for $10 per pound and some sells for $6 per pound. How much of each type of candy should I buy to make the average cost per pound $7?

11. Three electricians are wiring my new home. Electrician 1 by himself will need 11 days to do the job. Electrician 2 by himself will need 5 days to do the job. Electrician 3 by herself will need 9 days to do the job. If all three electricians work on the job, how long will the job take to complete?

12. To celebrate the Lewis and Clark Expedition, I am traveling 40 miles upstream and then 40 miles downstream in a canoe. The speed of the river current is 5 miles per hour. If the trip takes me 5 hours total, how fast do I travel in the absence of the river's current?

17

Using the Scenario Manager for Sensitivity Analysis

- I'd like to create best, worst, and most-likely scenarios for the sales of an automobile by varying the values of year 1 sales, annual sales growth, and year 1 sales price. Data tables for sensitivity analysis allow me to vary only one or two inputs, so I can't use a data table. Does Excel have a tool that allows me to vary more than two inputs in a sensitivity analysis?

The Scenario Manager enables you to perform sensitivity analysis by varying as many as 32 input cells. With the Scenario Manager, you first define the set of input cells you want to vary. Next you name your scenario and enter for each scenario the value of each input cell. Finally, you select the output cells (also called *result cells*) that you want to track. The Scenario Manager then creates a beautiful report containing the inputs and the values of the output cells for each scenario.

I'd like to create best, worst, and most-likely scenarios for the sales of an automobile by varying the values of year 1 sales, annual sales growth, and year 1 sales price. Data tables for sensitivity analysis allow me to vary only one or two inputs, so I can't use a data table. Does Excel have a tool that allows me to vary more than two inputs in a sensitivity analysis?

Suppose we want to create the following three scenarios related to the net present value (NPV) of a car, using the example in Chapter 14.

Scenario	Year 1 Sales	Annual Sales Growth	Year 1 Sales Price
Best	20,000	20 percent	$10.00
Most likely	10,000	10 percent	$7.50
Worst	5,000	2 percent	$5.00

For each scenario, we want to look at the firm's NPV and each year's after-tax profit. Our work is in the file NPVAuditScenario.xls. Figure 17-1 shows the spreadsheet model (contained in the worksheet named Original Model), and Figure 17-2 shows the scenario report (contained in the worksheet Scenario Summary).

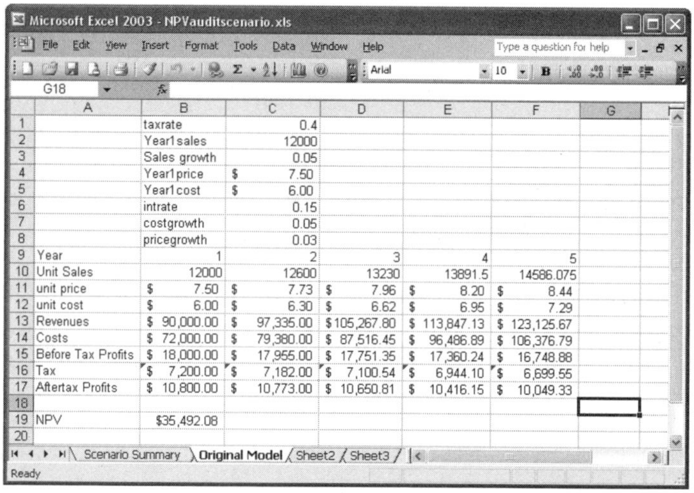

Figure 17-1   The data used to create scenarios with the Scenario Manager.

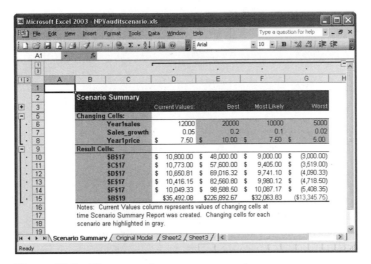

Figure 17-2   The scenario summary report.

To begin defining the best-case scenario, I choose Tools, Scenarios and then click the Add button. Next I fill in the Add Scenario dialog box as shown in Figure 17-3.

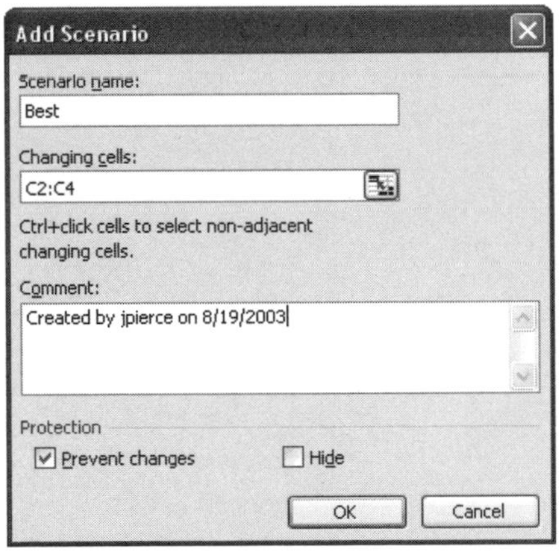

Figure 17-3   Data inputs for the best-case scenario.

I enter a name for the scenario (Best) and select C2:C4 as the input cells whose values will define the scenario. After I click OK in the Add Scenario dialog box, I fill in the Scenario Values dialog box with the input values that define the best case, as shown in Figure 17-4.

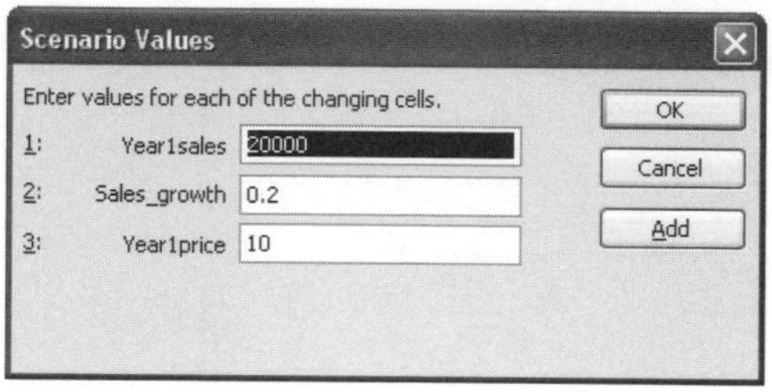

Figure 17-4 Defining the input values for best-case scenario.

By clicking Add in the Scenario Values dialog box, I can enter the data for the most-likely and then the worst-case scenarios. After I've entered data for all three scenarios, I click OK in the Scenario Values dialog box. In the Scenario Manager dialog box, shown in Figure 17-5, the scenarios I created are listed. When I click Summary in the Scenario Manager dialog box, I can choose the result cells that will be displayed in scenario reports. Figure 17-6 shows how I indicated in the Scenario Summary dialog box that I want the scenario summary report to track each year's after-tax profit (cells B17:F17) as well as total NPV (cell B19).

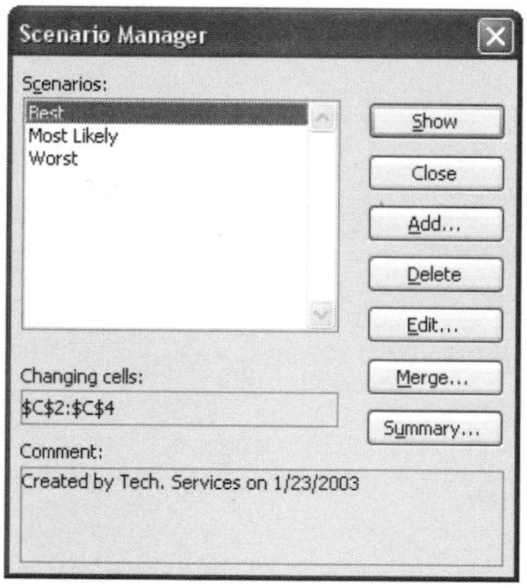

Figure 17-5 The Scenario Manager dialog box displays each scenario I defined.

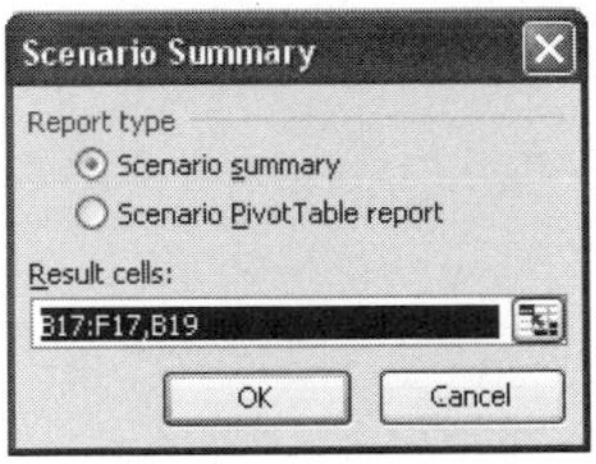

Figure 17-6   Use the Scenario Summary dialog box to select the result cells for the summary report.

Because the result cells come from more than one range, I've separated the ranges B17:F17 and B19 with a comma. (I could also have used the Ctrl key to select and enter multiple ranges.) After selecting Scenario Summary (instead of the Pivot Table option), I click OK, and Excel creates the beautiful Scenario Report pictured earlier in Figure 17-2. Notice that Excel includes a column, labeled Current Values, for the values that were originally placed in the spreadsheet. The worst case loses money ($13,345.75), while the best case is quite profitable (a profit of $226,892.67). Because the worst-case price is less than our variable cost, in each year the worst case loses money.

Remarks

- The option named Scenario PivotTable Report presents the scenario results in a PivotTable format. See Chapter 36 for a discussion of pivot tables.

- Suppose we select a scenario (say Worst) in the Scenario Manager dialog box and then click the Show button. The input cells' values for the Worst scenario then appear in the spreadsheet and all formulas are recalculated. This tool is great for presenting a "slide show" of your scenarios.

- It's hard to create many scenarios with the Scenario Manager because you need to input each individual scenario's values. Monte Carlo simulation (see Chapter 58) makes it easy to create many scenarios. Using Monte Carlo simulation, you can answer questions such as what is the probability that the NPV of a project's cash flows is nonnegative—an important measure because it is the probability that the project adds value to the firm.

Problems

1. Delete the best-case scenario and run another scenario report.

2. Add a scenario called High Price, in which year 1 price equals $15 and other two inputs remain at their most-likely values.

3. For the lemonade stand example in Chapter 15, use the Scenario Manager to display a report summarizing profit for the following scenarios:

Scenario	Price	Unit cost	Fixed cost
High cost and high price	$5	$1	$65,000
Medium cost and medium price	$4	$0.75	$45,000
Low cost and low price	$2.50	$0.40	$25,000

4. For the mortgage payment example in Chapter 15, use the Scenario Manager to create a report tabulating monthly payments for the following scenarios:

Scenario	Amount Borrowed	Annual Rate	Number of Monthly Payments
Lowest payment	$300,000	4 percent	360
Most-likely payment	$400,000	6 percent	240
Highest payment	$550,000	8 percent	180

18

Creating and Using Spinners for Sensitivity Analysis

■ I need to run a sensitivity analysis that has many key inputs, such as year 1 sales, annual sales growth, year 1 price, and year 1 unit cost. Is there a way I can quickly vary these inputs and see the effect of the variation on the calculation of net present value, for example?

The Scenario Manager lets you change a group of input cells and see how various spreadsheet outputs change. Unfortunately, the Scenario Manager requires you to enter each scenario individually, which makes it difficult to create more than a few scenarios. For example, suppose you believe that four key inputs to our car net present value (NPV) model are year 1 sales, sales growth, year 1 price, and year 1 cost. (See the file NPVAudit.xls.) We'd like to see how NPV changes as these inputs change in the following ranges:

Input	Low Value	High Value
Year 1 sales	5,000	30,000
Annual sales growth	0 percent	50 percent
Year 1 price	$6	$20
Year 1 cost	$2	$15

Using the Scenario Manager to generate the scenarios in which the input cells vary within the given ranges would be very time-consuming. By using *spinners*, however, a user can quickly generate a host of scenarios that vary each input between its low and high value. A spinner is a button that is linked to a given cell. As you click on the spinner button, the value of the linked cell changes and you can see how formulas of interest (such as a car's NPV) change in response to changes in the inputs.

I need to run a sensitivity analysis that has many key inputs, such as year 1 sales, annual sales growth, year 1 price, and year 1 unit cost. Is there a way I can quickly vary these inputs and see the effect of the variation on the calculation of net present value, for example?

Here's how to create spinners that allow us to vary year 1 sales, sales growth, year 1 price, and year 1 cost within the ranges we want. Our original spreadsheet (see the file NPVSpinners.xls) is shown in Figure 18-1.

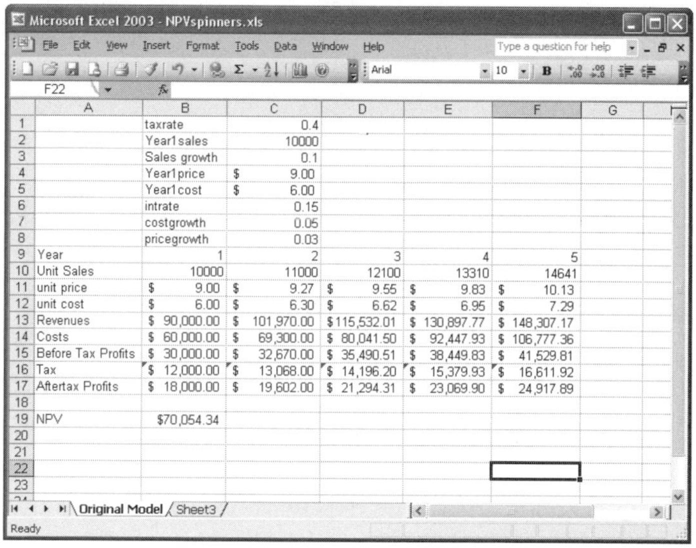

Figure 18-1   The automobile sales data spreadsheet without any spinners.

To create the spinners, I select the rows (I used 2–5 in this example) in which I want to insert buttons and then increase the height of the rows by selecting Format, Row and then Height. A row height of 25 is usually big enough.

Next I display the Forms toolbar, shown in Figure 18-2, by choosing View, Toolbar, Forms.

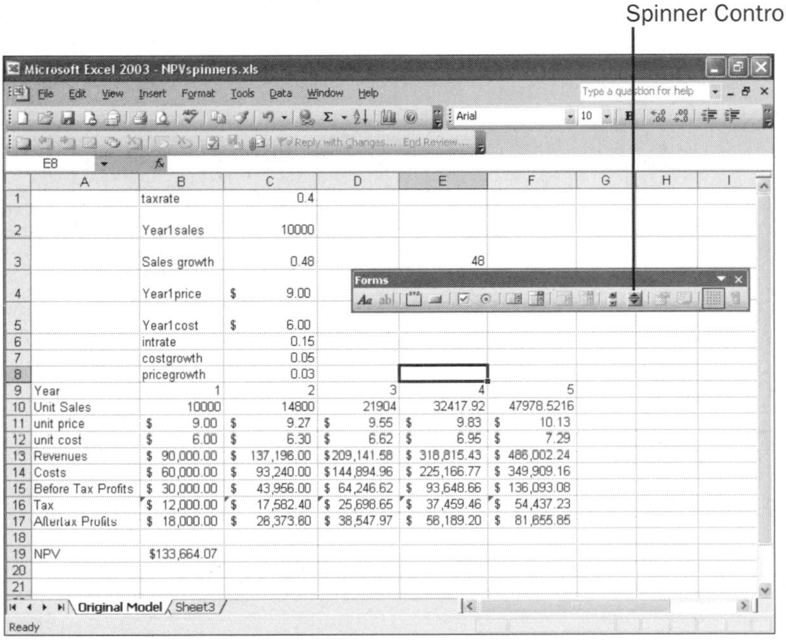

Figure 18-2   The Forms toolbar includes the spinner control.

I click on the spinner button and then draw a box for a spinner beginning at the top of cell D2 and ending at the bottom of cell D2. A spinner now appears in cell D2. We'll use this spinner to change the value of year 1 sales. Right-click on the spinner, and choose Copy from the shortcut menu. Right-click in cell D3, and then choose Paste. Also paste the spinner in cells D4 and D5. You should now see four spinners as displayed in Figure 18-3.

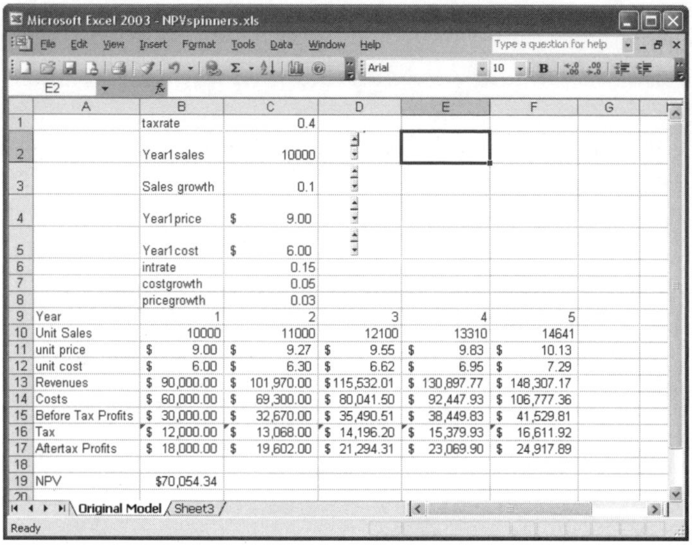

	A	B	C	D	E	F	G
1		taxrate	0.4				
2		Year1sales	10000				
3		Sales growth	0.1				
4		Year1price	$ 9.00				
5		Year1cost	$ 6.00				
6		intrate	0.15				
7		costgrowth	0.05				
8		pricegrowth	0.03				
9	Year	1	2	3	4	5	
10	Unit Sales	10000	11000	12100	13310	14641	
11	unit price	$ 9.00	$ 9.27	$ 9.55	$ 9.83	$ 10.13	
12	unit cost	$ 6.00	$ 6.30	$ 6.62	$ 6.95	$ 7.29	
13	Revenues	$ 90,000.00	$ 101,970.00	$115,532.01	$ 130,897.77	$ 148,307.17	
14	Costs	$ 60,000.00	$ 69,300.00	$ 80,041.50	$ 92,447.93	$ 106,777.36	
15	Before Tax Profits	$ 30,000.00	$ 32,670.00	$ 35,490.51	$ 38,449.83	$ 41,529.81	
16	Tax	$ 12,000.00	$ 13,068.00	$ 14,196.20	$ 15,379.93	$ 16,611.92	
17	Aftertax Profits	$ 18,000.00	$ 19,602.00	$ 21,294.31	$ 23,069.90	$ 24,917.89	
18							
19	NPV	$70,054.34					

Figure 18-3 Spinner buttons are placed in cells in the spreadsheet.

Now we need to link each spinner button to an input cell. To link the spinner in D2 to cell C2, right-click on the spinner in cell D2 and then choose Format Control from the shortcut menu. Fill in the Format Control dialog box as shown in Figure 18-4.

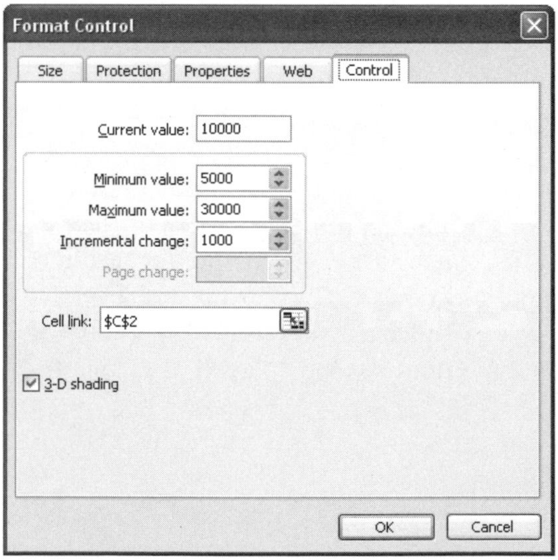

Figure 18-4 Use the Format Control dialog box to link a cell to a spinner.

The current value is not important. The rest of the settings tell Excel that this spinner is linked to the values in cell C2 (year 1 sales) and that each click on the upper spinner will increase the value in C2 by 1000, while each click on the lower spinner will decrease the value in C2 by 1,000. Once the value in C2 reaches 30,000, clicking the upper button will not increase it; once the value in C2 reaches 5,000, clicking the button will not decrease the value in cell C2.

Next we use the Format Control dialog box to link the spinner in D4 to year 1 price (cell C4). For current value, I used 9. The minimum value is 6, the maximum value is 20, and the incremental change is 1. Clicking the spinner in cell D4 will vary year 1 price between $6 and $20 in $1 increments.

To link the spinner in cell D5 to year 1 cost (cell D5), I used 6 for the current value, 2 as the minimum value, 15 for the maximum value, and 1 as the incremental change. Clicking the spinner in cell D5 will change year 1 cost from $2 to $15 in $1 increments.

Linking the spinner in cell D3 to sales growth is trickier. We would like the spinner to change sales growth to 0 percent, 1 percent, ... 50 percent. The problem is that the minimum increment allowed for a spinner is one. Therefore, we link our spinner to a dummy value in cell E3 and place the formula *E3/100* in cell C3. Now, as cell E3 varies from 1 to 50, our sales growth varies between 1 percent and 50 percent. Figures 18-5 and 18-6 show how I linked our spinner to cell E3. Remember that the sales growth in cell C3 is simply the number in cell E3 divided by 100.

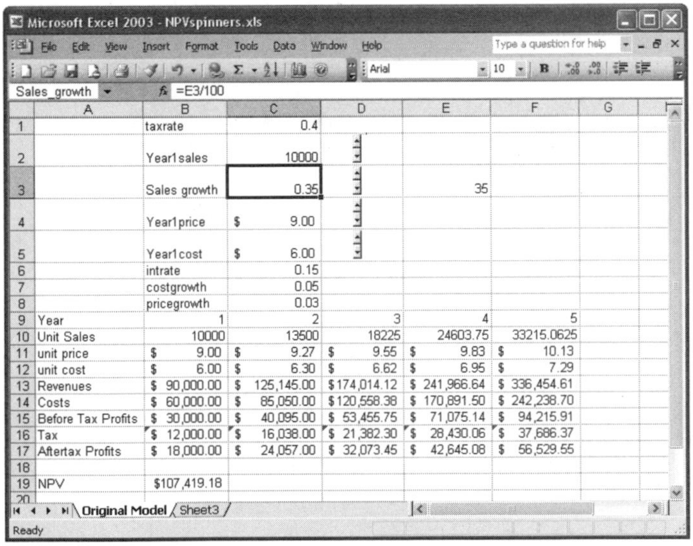

Figure 18-5   The spinner in cell D3 is linked to sales growth by using a formula that refers to cell E3.

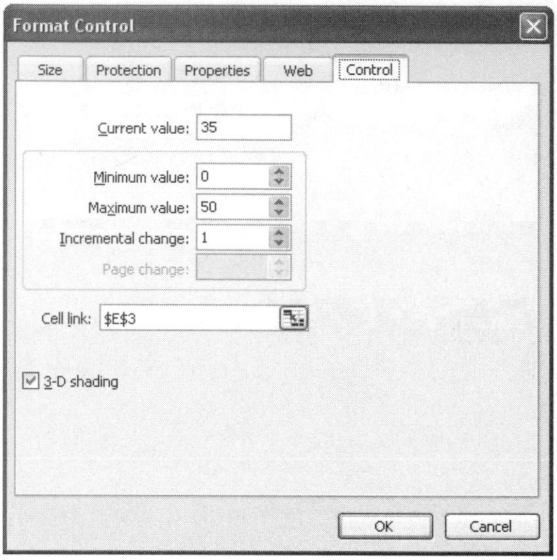

Figure 18-6   The Format Control dialog box settings that link the spinner in cell D3 to cell E3.

Now by clicking a spinner button, we can easily see how changing a single input cell—given the values for the other inputs listed in the spreadsheet—will change the car's NPV. To see the effect of the changes, you can select cell F9 and then choose Window, Freeze Panes. This command freezes the data above row 9 and to left of column F. You can now use the scroll bars to arrange the window as you see it in Figure 18-7.

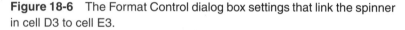

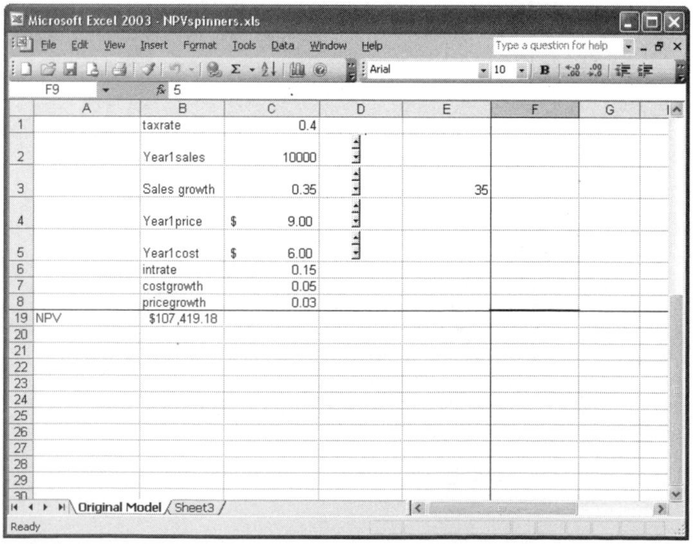

Figure 18-7   You can freeze panes to see the results of calculations in other parts of a spreadsheet.

Given the values of our other inputs, clicking the spinner for sales growth shows us that a 1 percent increase in sales growth is worth about $2,000! (Choosing Window, Unfreeze Panes will return the spreadsheet to its normal state.)

Problems

1. Add a spinner for the car NPV example that allows the tax rate to vary between 30 percent and 50 percent.

2. Add a spinner for the car NPV example that allows the interest rate to vary between 5 percent and 20 percent.

3. The Format Control dialog box allows a minimum value of 0. Despite this limitation, can you figure out a way to use a spinner to vary sales growth between -10 percent and 20 percent?

4. Using our lemonade example in Chapter 15, create spinners that allow our inputs to vary within the following ranges.

Input	Low Value	High Value
Price	$2.00	$5.00
Unit cost	$0.20	$1.00
Fixed cost	$20,000	$100,000

5. Using the mortgage payment example in Chapter 15, create spinners that allow our inputs to vary within the following ranges.

Input	Low Value	High Value
Amount borrowed	$250,000	$800,000
Number of months of payments	120	360
Annual interest rate	4 percent	10 percent

19

The COUNTIF, COUNT, COUNTA, and COUNTBLANK Functions

Suppose I have a list of songs that are played on the radio. For each song, I know the singer, the date the song was played, and the length of the song. How can I answer questions such as

■ How many songs were sung by each singer?

■ How many songs were not sung by Eminem?

■ How many songs lasted at least 4 minutes?

■ How many songs were longer than average?

■ How many songs were sung by a singer whose last name begins with S?

■ How many songs were sung by a singer whose last name contains six letters?

■ How many songs were sung after June 15, 2005?

■ How many songs were sung before the beginning of 2009?

■ How many songs lasted exactly 4 minutes?

In a more general context, how do I perform operations such as

- Count the number of cells in a range containing numbers?

- Count the number of blank cells in a range?

- Count the number of nonblank cells in a range?

We often want to count the number of cells in a range that meet a given criterion. For example, if a spreadsheet contains information about makeup sales, we might want to count how many sales transactions were made by the salesperson named Jennifer or how many sales transactions occurred after June 10. The COUNTIF function lets you count the number of cells in a range that meet criteria that are defined on the basis of a single row or column of the spreadsheet.

The syntax of the COUNTIF function is *COUNTIF(range, criteria)*.

- *Range* is the range of cells in which you want to count cells meeting a given criterion.

- *Criteria* is a number, date, or expression that determines whether a given cell in the range is counted.

The key to using the COUNTIF function (and other similar functions) successfully is understanding the wide variety of criteria that Excel will accept. The types of criteria you can use are best explained through the use of examples. In addition to examples of the COUNTIF function, I'll provide examples of the COUNT, COUNTA, and COUNTBLANK functions. The COUNT function counts the number of cells in a range containing numbers. The COUNTA function counts the number of nonblank cells in a range. The COUNTBLANK function counts the number of blank cells in a range.

To illustrate how to use these functions, consider a database that gives the following information for each song played on radio station WKRP:

- Singer

- The date the song was played

- The length of the song

The file Rock.xls, shown in Figure 19-1, shows a subset of the data.

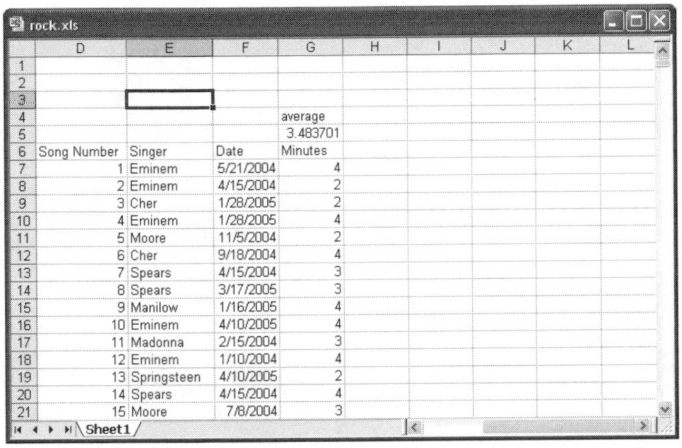

Figure 19-1   A song database that we'll use for COUNTIF examples.

How many songs were sung by each singer?

To begin, I select the first row of the database, the range D6:G6. Then I select the whole database by pressing Ctrl+Shift+Down Arrow. Next I choose Insert, Name, Create, and then choose Top Row. We have now named the range D7:D957 Song Numb, the range E7:E957 Singer, the range F7:F957 Date, and the range G7:G957 Minutes. To determine how many songs were sung by each singer, we copy from C5 to C6:C12 the formula *COUNTIF(Singer,B5)*. In cell C5, this formula now displays the number of cells in the range Singer that match the value in B5 (Eminem). The database contains 114 songs sung by Eminem. Similarly, Cher sang 112 songs, and so on, as you can see in Figure 19-2. I could have also found the number of songs sung by Eminem with the formula *COUNTIF("Singer,eminem")*. Note that you must enclose text such as *eminem* in quotation marks (" ")and that criteria are not case sensitive.

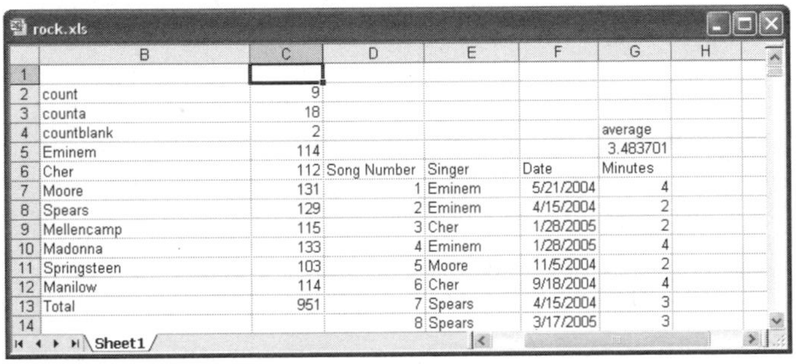

Figure 19-2   Using COUNTIF to determine how many songs were sung by each singer.

How many songs were not sung by Eminem?

To solve this problem, you need to know that Excel interprets the character combination <> as "not equal to." The formula *COUNTIF(Singer, "<>Eminem")*, entered in cell C15, tells us that 837 songs in the database were not sung by Eminem, as you can see in Figure 19-3. I need to enclose <>*Eminem* in quotation marks because Excel treats the character combination <> as text and *Eminem* is, of course, text. You could obtain the same result by using the formula *COUNTIF(Singer, "<>"&B5)*, which uses the & symbol to concatenate the reference to cell B5 and the <> operator.

	B	C	D	E	F	G	H	I
4	countblank	2				average		
5	Eminem	114				3.483701		
6	Cher	112	Song Number	Singer	Date	Minutes		
7	Moore	131	1	Eminem	5/21/2004	4		
8	Spears	129	2	Eminem	4/15/2004	2		
9	Mellencamp	115	3	Cher	1/28/2005	2		
10	Madonna	133	4	Eminem	1/28/2005	4		
11	Springsteen	103	5	Moore	11/5/2004	2		
12	Manilow	114	6	Cher	9/18/2004	4		
13	Total	951	7	Spears	4/15/2004	3		
14			8	Spears	3/17/2005	3		
15	Not by Eminem	837	9	Manilow	1/16/2005	4		
16	Songs >= 4 minutes	477	10	Eminem	4/10/2005	4		
17	Songs longer than average	477	11	Madonna	2/15/2004	3		
18	Singer begins with S	232	12	Eminem	1/10/2004	4		
19	Singer has six letters in name	243	13	Springsteen	4/10/2005	2		
20	Songs after 6/15/2005	98	14	Spears	4/15/2004	4		
21	Songs Before 2009	951	15	Moore	7/8/2004	3		
22	Songs exactly 4 minutes	247	16	Madonna	6/26/2004	4		
23	Songs exactly 5 minutes	230	17	Spears	5/28/2005	3		
24			18	Mellencamp	7/27/2005	5		
25			19	Spears	9/18/2004	5		

Figure 19-3   You can combine the COUNTIF function with the not-equal-to operator (<>).

How many songs lasted at least 4 minutes?

In cell C16, I've computed the number of songs played that lasted at least 4 minutes by using the formula *COUNTIF(Minutes, ">=4")*. You need to enclose >=4 in quotation marks because >=, like <>, is treated as text. We find that 477 songs lasted at least 4 minutes.

How many songs were longer than average?

To answer this question, I first computed in cell G5 the average length of a song with the formula *AVERAGE(Minutes)*. Then, in cell C17, I compute the number of songs that last longer than the average with the formula *COUNTIF(Minutes, ">"&G5)*. I can refer to another cell (in this case G5) in the criteria by using the & sign. You can see that 477 songs lasted longer than average, which matches the number of songs lasting at least 4 minutes. The reason these numbers match is that I assumed the length of each song was an integer. For a song to last at least 3.48 minutes, it has to last at least 4 minutes.

How many songs were sung by a singer whose last name begins with S?

To answer this question, I use a wildcard character, the asterisk (*), in the criteria. An asterisk represents any sequence of characters. Thus the formula *COUNTIF(Singer, "S*")* in cell C18 picks up any song sung by a singer whose last name begins with S. (The criteria are not case sensitive.) Two hundred thirty-two songs were sung by singers with a last name that begins with S. This number is simply the total of the songs sung by either Bruce Springsteen or Britney Spears (103 + 129 = 232).

How many songs were sung by a singer whose last name contains six letters?

In this example, I used the question mark (?) wildcard character. The question mark matches any character. Therefore, entering the formula *COUNTIF(Singer, "??????")* in cell C19 counts the number of songs sung by singers having six letters in their last name. The result is 243. (Two singers have last names with six characters, Britney Spears and Eminem, who together sang a total of 129 + 114 = 243 songs.)

How many songs were sung after June 15, 2005?

The criteria you use with COUNT functions handle dates on the basis of a date's serial number. (A later date is considered larger than an earlier date.) The formula *COUNTIF(Date, ">6/15/2005")* in cell C20 tells us that 98 songs were sung after June 15, 2005.

How many songs were sung before the beginning of 2009?

We want our criteria to pick up all dates on or before December 31, 2008. I've entered in cell C21 the formula *COUNTIF(Date, "<=12/31/2008")*. We find that 951 songs (which turns out to be all the songs) were sung before the start of 2009.

How many songs lasted exactly 4 minutes?

In cell C22, I compute the number of songs lasting exactly 4 minutes with the formula *COUNTIF(Minutes, 4)*. This formula counts the number of cells in the range G7:G957 containing a 4. We find that 247 songs lasted exactly 4 minutes. In a similar fashion, we found in cell C23 that 230 songs lasted exactly 5 minutes.

How do I count the number of cells in a range containing numbers?

The COUNT function counts the number of cells in a range containing a numeric value. For example, the formula *COUNT(B5:C14)* in cell C2 displays 9 because nine cells (the cells in C5:C13) in the range B5:C14 contain numbers. (See Figure 19-2.)

How do I count the number of blank cells in a range?

The COUNTBLANK function counts the number of blank cells in a range. For example, the formula *COUNTBLANK(B5:C14)* entered in cell C4 returns a value of 2 because two cells (B14 and C14) in the range B5:C14 contain blanks.

How do I count the number of nonblank cells in a range?

The COUNTA function returns the number of nonblank cells in a range. For example, the formula COUNTA(B5:C14) in cell C3 returns 18 because 18 cells in the range B5:C14 are not blank.

Remarks

Unless you use array functions (see Chapter 72), the COUNTIF function can handle only a single criterion. For example, without using an array function, you cannot use COUNTIF to answer a question that depends on two or more criteria, such as how many Britney Spears songs were played before June 10, 2005. The easiest way to answer questions involving multiple criteria is to use *database statistical functions*. See Chapter 37 for a discussion of database statistical functions.

Problems

The following questions refer to the file Rock.xls.

1. How many songs were not sung by Britney Spears?

2. How many songs were sung before June 15, 2004?

3. How many songs were sung between June 1, 2004, and July 4, 2006? Hint: Take the difference between two COUNTIF functions.

4. How many songs were sung by singers whose last name begins with *M*?

5. How many songs were sung by singers whose names contain an *e*?

6. Create a formula that will always yield the number of songs played today. Hint: Use the TODAY() function.

7. For the cell range D4:G15, count the cells containing a numeric value. Count the number of blank cells. Count the number of nonblank cells.

8.   The file NBA.xls contains the following information:

❏   In columns A and B, the name of each NBA team and a code number for each team. For example, Team 1 is Atlanta.

❏   Column C contains the home team for each game.

❏   Column D contains the visiting team for each game.

❏   Column E contains points scored by the home team.

❏   Column F contains points scored by the visiting team.

From this data, compute for each team the number of games played by each team.

20

The SUMIF Function

- I'm a sales manager for a makeup company and have summarized for each sales transaction the following information: salesperson, date of sale, units sold (or returned), total price received (or paid out for returns). How can I answer the following questions?

  - ❏ What was the total dollar amount of merchandise sold by each salesperson?

  - ❏ How many units were returned?

  - ❏ What was the total dollar volume sold in 2005 or later?

  - ❏ How many units of lip gloss were sold?

  - ❏ How much revenue did lip gloss sales bring in?

  - ❏ What dollar amount of sales were not made by Jen?

  If you want to sum all the entries in one column (or row) that match criteria that depend on another column (or row), the SUMIF function gets the job done. The syntax of the SUMIF function is *SUMIF(range, criteria, [sum range])*.

- *Range* is the range of cells that you want to evaluate with a criterion.

- *Criteria* is a number, date, or expression that determines whether a given cell in the sum range is added.

- *Sum* range is the range of cells that are added. If *sum range* is omitted, it is assumed to be the same as *range*.

  The rules for criteria you can use with the SUMIF function are identical to the rules used with the COUNTIF function. For information about the COUNTIF function, see Chapter 19.

What was the total dollar amount of merchandise sold by each salesperson?

Our work for the problems in this chapter is in the file Makeup.xls. Figure 20-1 shows a subset of the data.

makeup.xls

	G	H	I	J	K	L
3						
4	Trans Number	Name	Date	Product	Units	Dollars
5	1	Betsy	4/1/2004	lip gloss	45	$ 137.20
6	2	Hallagan	3/10/2004	foundation	50	$ 152.01
7	3	Ashley	2/25/2005	lipstick	9	$ 28.72
8	4	Hallagan	5/22/2006	lip gloss	55	$ 167.08
9	5	Zaret	6/17/2004	lip gloss	43	$ 130.60
10	6	Colleen	11/27/2005	eye liner	58	$ 175.99
11	7	Cristina	3/21/2004	eye liner	8	$ 25.80
12	8	Colleen	12/17/2006	lip gloss	72	$ 217.84
13	9	Ashley	7/5/2006	eye liner	75	$ 226.64
14	10	Betsy	8/7/2006	lip gloss	24	$ 73.50
15	11	Ashley	11/29/2004	mascara	43	$ 130.84
16	12	Ashley	11/18/2004	lip gloss	23	$ 71.03
17	13	Emilee	8/31/2005	lip gloss	49	$ 149.59
18	14	Hallagan	1/1/2005	eye liner	18	$ 56.47
19	15	Zaret	9/20/2006	foundation	-8	$ (21.99)
20	16	Emilee	4/12/2004	mascara	45	$ 137.39
21	17	Colleen	4/30/2006	mascara	66	$ 199.65
22	18	Jen	8/31/2005	lip gloss	88	$ 265.19
23	19	Jen	10/27/2004	eye liner	78	$ 236.15
24	20	Zaret	11/27/2005	lip gloss	57	$ 173.12

data / sumif rows

Figure 20-1 Data about makeup sales we'll use for SUMIF examples.

As usual, we begin by naming the data in columns G through L with the corresponding names in cells G4:L4. For example, the range name Product corresponds to the range J5:J1904. To compute the total amount sold by each salesperson, I simply copy from cell B5 to B6:B13 the formula *SUMIF(Name,A5,Dollars)*. This formula adds up every entry in the Dollars column that has the name *Emilee* in the Name column. We find that Emilee sold $25,258.87 worth of makeup, as you can see in Figure 20-2.

makeup.xls

	A	B
3		
4	Name	Dollar Volume
5	Emilee	$ 25,258.87
6	Hallagan	$ 28,705.16
7	Ashley	$ 25,947.24
8	Zaret	$ 26,741.31
9	Colleen	$ 24,890.66
10	Cristina	$ 23,849.56
11	Betsy	$ 28,803.15
12	Jen	$ 29,050.53
13	Cici	$ 27,590.57
14		
15		
16	Units returned	922
17	Total dollars sold 2005 or later	$ 157,854.32
18	Units of lip gloss sold	16333
19	$s of lip gloss sold	$ 49,834.64
20	$s sold not by Jen	$ 211,786.51
21		
22		
23		

data / sumif rows

Figure 20-2 Results of SUMIF computations for makeup sales.

How many units were returned?

In cell B16, the formula *SUMIF(Units,"<0",Units)* adds up every cell in the Units column (column K) that has a number less than 0. The result is -922. After inserting a minus sign in front of the *SUMIF* formula, we see that 922 units were returned. (Recall that when the *sum range* argument is omitted from a SUMIF function, Excel assumes that *sum range* equals *range*. Therefore, the formula *-SUMIF(Units,"<0")* would yield 922 as well.)

What was the total dollar volume sold in 2005 or later?

In cell B17, the formula *SUMIF(Date,">= 1/1/2005",Dollars)* adds up every cell in the Dollar column (column L) that has a date on or after 1/1/2005. We find that $157,854.32 worth of makeup was sold in 2005 or later.

How many units of lip gloss were sold? How much revenue did lip gloss sales bring in?

In cell B18, the formula *SUMIF(Product,"lip gloss",Units)* adds up every cell in the Units column that has the text "lip gloss" in the Product column (column J). You can see that 16,333 units of lip gloss were sold. Transactions in which units of lip gloss were returned are counted as negative sales.

In similar fashion, in cell B19 the formula *SUMIF(Product,"lip gloss",Dollars)* tells us that $49,834.64 worth of lip gloss was sold. This calculation counts refunds associated with returns as negative revenue.

What dollar amount of sales were not made by Jen?

In cell B20, the formula *SUMIF(Name,"<>Jen",Dollars)* sums up the dollar amount of each transaction that does not include *Jen* in the Name column. We find that saleswomen other than Jen sold $211,786.51 worth of makeup.

Remarks

Unless you use array functions (see Chapter 72), the SUMIF function can handle only a single criteria. For example, if you do not use array functions, you cannot use SUMIF to answer a question that depends on two or more criteria, such as how many units of lip gloss Jen sold before June 10, 2005? The easiest way to answer questions involving multiple criteria is to use database statistical functions. See Chapter 37 for a discussion of database statistical functions.

Problems

1. Determine the total number of units and dollar volume sold for each product.

2. Determine the total revenue earned before December 10, 2005.

3. Determine the total units sold by salespeople whose last name begins with C.

4. Determine total revenue earned by people having five letters in their name.

5. How many units were sold by people other than Colleen?

6. How many units of makeup were sold between January 15, 2004, and February 15, 2005?

7. The file NBA.xls contains the following information:

❑ In columns A and B, the name of each NBA team and a code number for each team. For example, team 1 is Atlanta, and so on.

❑ Column C lists the home team for each game.

❑ Column D lists the visiting team for each game.

❑ Column E lists points scored by the home team.

❑ Column F lists points scored by the visiting team.

From this data, compute for each team the average number of points the team scored per game and the average of how many points the team gave up.

8. The file Toysrus.xls contains sales revenue (in millions) during each quarter for the years 1997–2001 and the first two quarters of 2002. Use this data to compute a *seasonal index* for each quarter of the year. For example, the first quarter would have a seasonal index of .8 if average sales during the first quarter were 80 percent of the overall average sales per quarter.

9. How much revenue was made on sales transactions involving at least 100 units of makeup?

10. The file SumIfRows.xls contains sales data during several winter, summer, spring, and fall quarters. Determine average sales during the winter, summer, spring, and fall quarters.

21

The OFFSET Function

- How can I create a reference to a rectangular range of cells that is a specified number of rows and columns from a cell or another range of cells?

- How can I perform a lookup operation by keying off the right-most column instead of the left-most column in a table range?

- I often download sales of a software product listed by country. I need to track revenues from Iran as well as costs and units sold, but the data about Iran isn't always in the same location in the spreadsheet. Can I create a formula that will always pick up Iran's revenues, costs, and units sold?

- Each drug developed by my company goes through three stages of development. I have a list of the cost by month for each drug, and I also know how many months each development stage took for each drug. Can I create formulas that compute for each drug the total cost incurred during each stage of development?

- I run a small video store. In a spreadsheet, my accountant has listed the name of each movie in stock and the number of copies in stock. Unfortunately, for each movie this information is in a single cell. How can I extract the number of copies of each movie in stock to a separate cell?

- I am charting my company's monthly unit sales. Each month I download the most recent month's unit sales. I would like my chart to automatically update. Is there an easy way to accomplish this?

The OFFSET function is used to create a reference to a rectangular range that is a specified number of rows and columns away from a cell or range of cells. Basically, to create a reference to a range of cells, you first specify a reference cell. You then indicate to Excel the number of rows and column away from the reference cell that you want to create your rectangular range. For example, by using the OFFSET function I can create a reference to a cell range that contains two rows and three columns and begins two columns to the right and one row above the current cell. The OFFSET function is very useful because you can copy it as you can any other Excel function, and the specified number of rows and columns you move from a reference cell can be calculated by using other Excel functions.

The syntax of the OFFSET function is

```
OFFSET(reference, rows moved, columns moved, [height], [width])
```

- *Reference* is a cell or range of cells from which the offset begins. If you specify a range of cells, the cells must be adjacent.

- *Rows moved* is the number of rows away from the reference that you want the range reference to start (the upper left cell in the offset range). A negative number of rows moves you up from the reference; a positive number of rows moves you down. For example, if *reference* equals C5 and *rows moved* equals -1, you move to row 4. If *rows moved* equals +1, you move to row 6. If *rows moved* equals 0, you stay at row 5.

- *Columns moved* is the number of columns away from the reference that you want the range reference to start (the upper left cell in the offset range). A negative number of columns moves you left from the reference; a positive number of columns moves you right. For example, if *reference* equals C5 and *columns moved* equals -1, you move to column B. If *columns moved* equals +1, you move to column D. If *columns moved* equals 0, you stay at column C.

- *Height* is an optional argument that gives the number of rows in the offset range. *Width* is an optional argument that gives the number of columns in the offset range. If *height* or *width* is omitted, the OFFSET function creates a range for which the value of *height* or *width* equals the height or width of *reference*.

How can I create a reference to a rectangular range of cells that is a specified number of rows and columns from a cell or another range of cells?

The file OffsetExample.xls, shown in Figure 21-1, provides some examples of the OFFSET function in action.

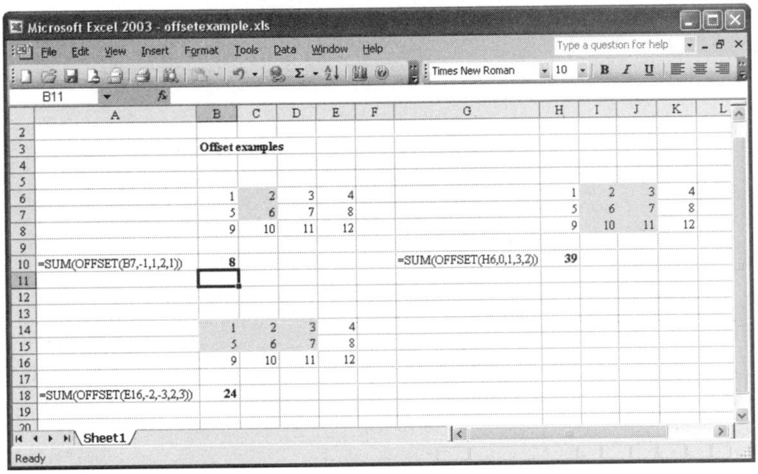

Figure 21-1   Examples of using the OFFSET function.

For example, in cell B10 I entered the formula *SUM(OFFSET(B7,-1,1,2,1))*. This formula begins in cell B7. We move up one row and one column to the right, which brings us to cell C6. We now pick out a range consisting of 2 rows and 1 column, which yields the range C6:C7. The SUM function adds the numbers in this range, which yields 2 + 6 = 8. The other two examples shown in Figure 21-1 work the same way. In the following sections, we'll apply the OFFSET function to solve some problems that were sent to me by MBAs working at major U.S. companies.

How can I perform a lookup operation keying off the right-most column instead of the left-most column in a table range?

In Figure 21-2, I've listed the members of the Dallas Mavericks NBA team and their field goal percentages. If I'm asked to "look up" the player with a given field goal percentage, I could easily solve that problem by using a VLOOKUP function. But what I really want to do is a "left-hand lookup," which involves finding the field goal percentage for a player by using his name. A VLOOKUP function can't perform a left-hand lookup, but a left-hand lookup is a snap if you combine the MATCH and OFFSET functions.

	A	B	C	D	E
1					
2					
3					
4					
5			**Left-hand lookup**		
6				Name	FG %age
7		FG%	Player	Walt Williams	0.397
8		45.8%	Dirk Nowitzki		
9		41.8%	Michael Finley		
10		46.3%	Steve Nash		
11		39.5%	Nick Van Exel		
12		53.5%	Raef LaFrentz		
13		60.2%	Eduardo Najera		
14		51.2%	Shawn Bradley		
15		39.7%	Walt Williams		
16		44.4%	Adrian Griffin		
17		48.4%	Avery Johnson		
18		47.6%	Raja Bell		
19		66.7%	Evan Eschmeyer		
20		41.0%	Popeye Jones		
21		40.0%	Mark Strickland		
22		23.5%	Adam Harrington		

Figure 21-2   You can do a left-hand lookup by using the MATCH and OFFSET functions.

I enter the player's name in cell D7. Then I use a reference cell of B7 in the OFFSET function. To find the player's field goal percentage, we need to move down to the row below row 7 where the player's name appears. This is a job for the MATCH function. The portion *MATCH(D7,$C$8:$C$22,0)* of the formula *OFFSET(B7,MATCH(D7,$C$8:$C$22,0),0)* picks up the number of rows below row 7 where our player's name occurs. Then we move that many rows below row 7 and move over no columns from column B. Because the reference consists of a single cell, omitting the *height* and *width* arguments of the OFFSET function ensures that the range returned by this formula consists of one row and column (a single cell). Thus we pick up the player's field goal percentage.

I often download sales of a software product listed by country. I need to track revenues from Iran as well as costs and units sold, but the data about Iran isn't always in the same location in the spreadsheet. Can I create a formula that will always pick up Iran's revenues, costs, and units sold?

The file AsianSales.xls (see Figure 21-3) contains data for the units sold, sales revenue, and variable cost for software sold to several countries in Asia and the Middle East. Each month, when we download the monthly financials, the location of each country in the spreadsheet changes, so we want formulas that will always return (for a given country) the correct units sold, revenue, and variable cost.

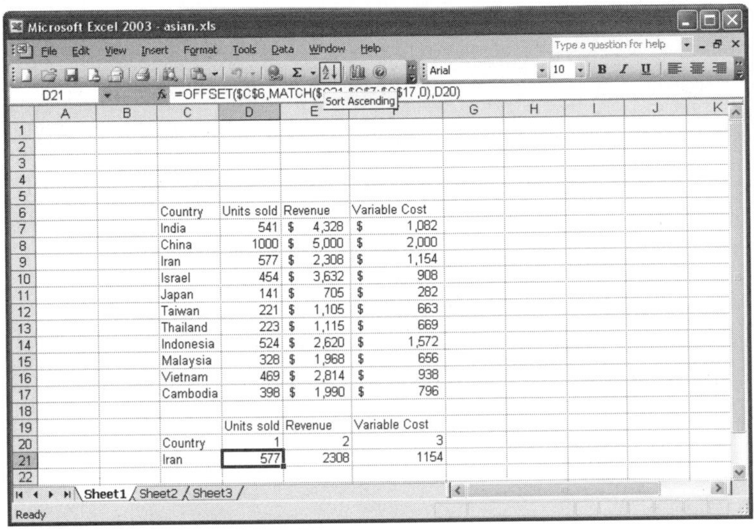

Row	C	D	E	F
6	Country	Units sold	Revenue	Variable Cost
7	India	541	$ 4,328	$ 1,082
8	China	1000	$ 5,000	$ 2,000
9	Iran	577	$ 2,308	$ 1,154
10	Israel	454	$ 3,632	$ 908
11	Japan	141	$ 705	$ 282
12	Taiwan	221	$ 1,105	$ 663
13	Thailand	223	$ 1,115	$ 669
14	Indonesia	524	$ 2,620	$ 1,572
15	Malaysia	328	$ 1,968	$ 656
16	Vietnam	469	$ 2,814	$ 938
17	Cambodia	398	$ 1,990	$ 796
18				
19		Units sold	Revenue	Variable Cost
20	Country	1	2	3
21	Iran	577	2308	1154

Figure 21-3 You can use the OFFSET function in calculations when you're working with data that isn't in a fixed location in a spreadsheet.

By copying from D21 to E21:F21 the formula *OFFSET($C$6,MATCH($C21,$C$7:$C$17,0),D20)* we compute the result we want. This formula sets *reference* equal to cell C6 (which contains the word *Country*). Then it moves over one column (the value in cell D20) to pick up units sold and down the number of rows that match the number of rows below row 6 in which the country listed in C21 is found. In cell E21, the reference to D20 now refers to E20 and becomes a 2, so we move over two columns to the right of column C and pick up revenue. In cell E21, the reference to D20 now refers to F20 and becomes a 3, so we move three columns to the right of column C and pick up variable cost.

Each drug developed by my company goes through three stages of development. I have a list of the cost by month for each drug, and I also know how many months each development stage took for each drug. Can I create formulas that compute for each drug the total cost incurred during each stage of development?

The file OffsetCost.xls contains the monthly costs incurred in developing five drugs. Each drug goes through three stages of development. For each drug, the data also includes the number of months required to complete each phase. A subset of the data is shown in Figure 21-4.

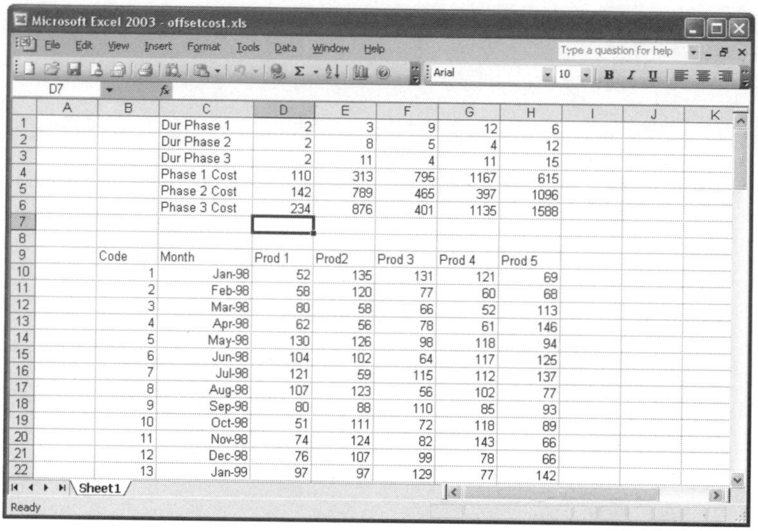

	A	B	C	D	E	F	G	H
1			Dur Phase 1	2	3	9	12	6
2			Dur Phase 2	2	8	5	4	12
3			Dur Phase 3	2	11	4	11	15
4			Phase 1 Cost	110	313	795	1167	615
5			Phase 2 Cost	142	789	465	397	1096
6			Phase 3 Cost	234	876	401	1135	1588
7								
8								
9		Code	Month	Prod 1	Prod2	Prod 3	Prod 4	Prod 5
10		1	Jan-98	52	135	131	121	69
11		2	Feb-98	58	120	77	60	68
12		3	Mar-98	80	58	66	52	113
13		4	Apr-98	62	56	78	61	146
14		5	May-98	130	126	98	118	94
15		6	Jun-98	104	102	64	117	125
16		7	Jul-98	121	59	115	112	137
17		8	Aug-98	107	123	56	102	77
18		9	Sep-98	80	88	110	85	93
19		10	Oct-98	51	111	72	118	89
20		11	Nov-98	74	124	82	143	66
21		12	Dec-98	76	107	99	78	66
22		13	Jan-99	97	97	129	77	142

Figure 21-4 Using the OFFSET function to compute development costs for phases 1–3.

The goal is to determine for each drug the total cost incurred during each development phase. In cells D4:D6, I compute the total development costs for phases 1–3 for drug 1. I compute phase 1 costs for drug 1 by using a cell reference of D10, with *rows moved* and *columns moved* equal to 0. Setting *height* equal to the number of months in phase 1 and *width* equal to 1 captures all first-phase costs. I compute phase 1 costs for drug 1 in cell D4 with the formula *SUM(OFFSET(D10,0,0,D1,1))*. Next, in cell D5, I compute phase 2 total costs for drug 1 by using the formula *SUM(OFFSET(D10,D1,0,D2,1))*. Note that I start with a cell reference of D10 (the first month of costs) and move down the number of rows equal to the length of phase 1. This brings me to the beginning of phase 2. Setting *height* equal to the value in cell D2 ensures that we pick up all phase 2 costs. Finally, in cell D6, I pick up the phase 3 development costs for drug 1 with the formula *SUM(OFFSET(D10,D1+D2,0,D3,1))*. In this formula, I start from the first month of sales and move down the number of rows equal to the total time needed for phases 1 and 2. This brings us to the beginning of phase 3, and we add up the number of rows in cell D3 to capture phase 3 costs. Then, by copying the formulas in D4:D6 to E4:H6, I can compute total costs for phases 1–3 for drugs 2 through 5. For example, we find that for drug 2, total phase 1 costs equal $313, total phase 2 costs equal $789, and total phase 3 costs equal $876.

I run a small video store. In a spreadsheet, my accountant has listed the name of each movie in stock and the number of copies in stock. Unfortunately, for each movie this information is in a single cell. How can I extract the number of copies of each movie in stock to a separate cell?

The file Movies.xls, shown in Figure 21-5, contains the movies in stock and the number of copies of each movie in stock.

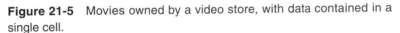

	C
1	Movie and Number of Copies
2	Seabiscuit 40
3	Laura Croft Tombraider 12
4	Raiders of the Lost Ark 36
5	Annie Hall 5
6	Manhattan 4
7	Star Wars 112
8	How to Deal 128
9	The Matrix Reloaded 1
10	Johnny English 1040
11	Rosemary's Baby 12
12	High Noon 1002

Figure 21-5   Movies owned by a video store, with data contained in a single cell.

We want to extract the number of copies owned of each movie to a separate cell. If the number of copies were listed to the left of a movie's title, this problem would be easy. We could use the FIND function to locate the first space and then use the LEFT function to pick up all the data to the left of the first space. (See Chapter 6 for a discussion of how to use the LEFT and FIND functions as well as other functions you can use to work with text.) Unfortunately, this technique doesn't work when the number of copies is listed to the right of the movie title. For a one-word movie title, for example, the number of copies is to the right of the first space, but for a four-word movie title, the number of copies is to the right of the fourth space.

One way to solve this problem is to use the Data, Text To Columns command to place each word in a title and the number of copies in separate columns. We can then use the COUNTA function to count the total number of words in a title, including the number of items as a word, for each movie. We can then use the OFFSET function to "pick off" the number of items.

To begin, insert enough columns to the right of the data to allow each word in the movies' titles and the number of items to be extracted to a separate column. I used six columns (*Raiders of the Lost Ark* requires 6 columns), as you can see in Figure 21-6. Then I select the cell range C2:C12 and chose Data, Text To Columns. I select Delimited in the Convert Text To Columns Wizard and use the space character as the delimiting character. After selecting cell D2 as the destination cell, I have the results shown in Figure 21-6.

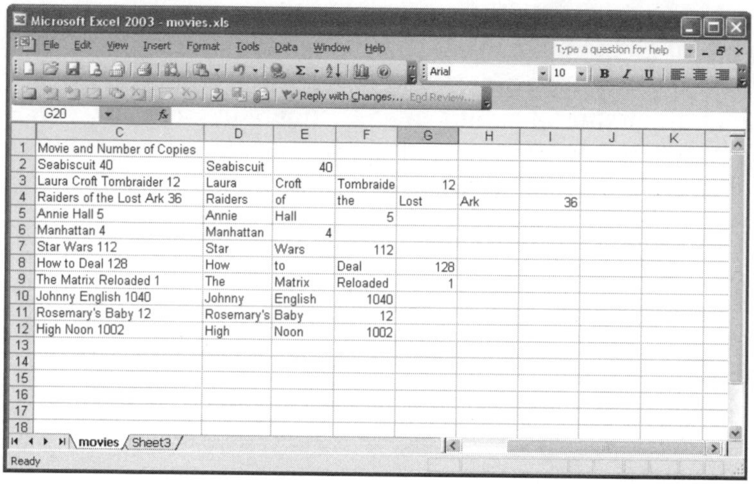

Figure 21-6   The Data To Text command extracts data in a single cell to multiple cells.

Now we count the number of words, including the number of items as one word, for each movie by copying from A2 to A3:A12 the formula *COUNTA(D2:I2)*. The results are shown in Figure 21-7.

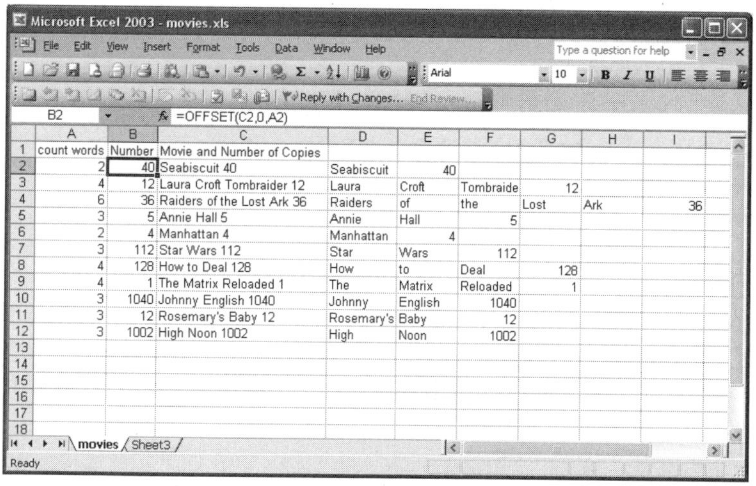

Figure 21-7   Final result for the movie example.

Finally, copying from B2 to B3:B12 the formula *OFFSET(C2,0,A2)*, I can pick up the number of copies of each movie in stock. This formula begins at the cell reference containing the movie title and moves over the number of columns equal to the number of "words" in the title cell. Because the cell reference contains only one cell, we can omit the last two arguments of the OFFSET function so that the function picks up only the single cell containing the last "word" (which is the number of copies) of the title cell.

I am charting my company's monthly unit sales. Each month I download the most recent month's unit sales. I would like my chart to update automatically. Is there an easy way to accomplish this?

The workbook DynamicRange.xls (see Figure 21-8) contains units sold for our company's product. As you can see, the units sold have been charted using an XY (Scatter) chart.

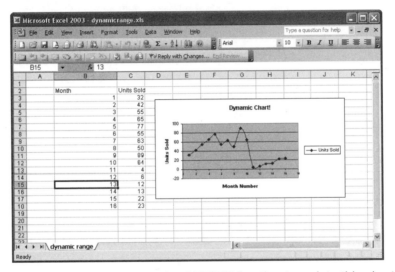

Figure 21-8 We can use the OFFSET function to update this chart dynamically.

Beginning in row 19, we will download new sales data. Is there an easy way to ensure that the chart automatically includes the new data?

The key to updating the chart is to use the OFFSET function to create a dynamic range name for both the Months column and the Units Sold column. As new data is entered, the dynamic range for unit sales will automatically include all sales data and the dynamic range for months will include each month number. After creating these ranges, I modify the chart, replacing the data ranges used in the chart with the dynamic ranges. The chart will now be updated as new data is entered.

To begin, select Insert, Name Define and create a range named Units by filling in the dialog box as shown in Figure 21-9.

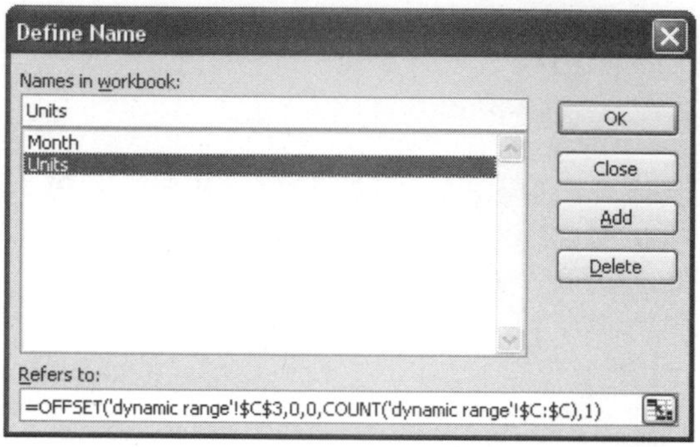

Figure 21-9 Creating dynamic range name for the units sold.

Entering *=OFFSET('dynamic range'!$C$3,0,0,COUNT('dynamic range' !$C:$C),1)* in the Refers To area of the dialog box creates a range one column wide beginning in cell C3, which contains the first units sales data point. The range will contain as many numbers as there are in column C, which is derived by the portion of the formula that reads *COUNT('dynamic range'!$C:$C)*. As new data is entered into column C, the data is automatically included in the range named Units.

Next we create a dynamic range named Months for the months entered in column B. The formula is shown in Figure 21-10.

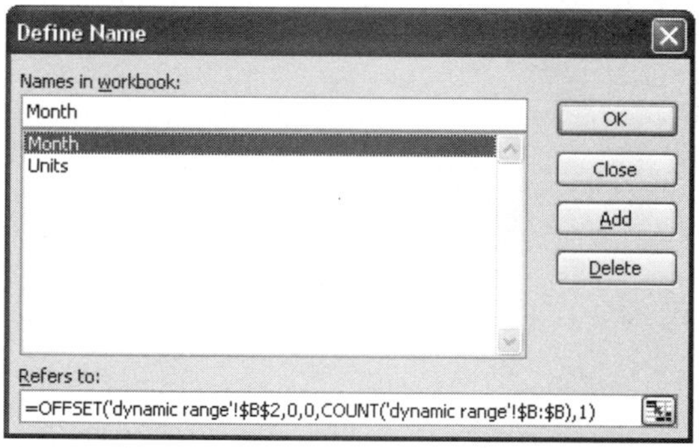

Figure 21-10 The formula used to define a dynamic range named Month.

Now we go to our chart and click on any selected point. In the formula box you'll see the formula *SERIES('dynamic range'!$C$2,'dynamic range'!$B$3:$B$18,'dynamic range'!$C$3:$C$18,1)*. This formula is Excel's version of the data used to originally set up the chart. Replace the ranges $B$3:$B$18 and $C$3:$C18 with our dynamic range names as follows: *SERIES('dynamic range'!$C$2,dynamicrange.xls!Month,dynamicrange.xls!Units,1)*. Of course, if a blank space is listed above any new data, this method won't work. Enter some new data and you'll see that the data is included in the chart.

Problems

1. The file C21p1.xls supplies data about the units sold for 11 products during the years 1999–2003. Write a formula using the MATCH and OFFSET functions that picks up the sales of a given product during a given year. Can you think of another way to solve this problem without using the MATCH and OFFSET functions?

2. A commonly suggested moving average trading rule is to buy a stock when the stock's price moves above the average of the last D months and to sell a stock when the stock's price moves below the average of the last D month's price. In Chapter 12, we showed that for $D = 15$, this trading rule outperformed the S&P by a substantial amount. By combining a one-way data table with the OFFSET function, determine the value of D that maximizes trading profit (excluding transactions costs). You can find data in the file MaTradingRule.xls.

3. A commonly suggested moving average trading rule is to buy a stock when the stock's price moves above the average of the last B months and to sell a stock when the stock's price moves below the average of the last S month's price. In Chapter 12, we showed that for $B = S = 15$, this trading rule outperformed the S&P by a substantial amount. By combining a two-way data table with the OFFSET function, determine the values of B and S that maximize trading profit (excluding transactions costs). Data is in the file MaTradingRule.xls.

4. The file Lagged.xls contains data about the number of magazine ads placed by Army recruiting during each of 60 consecutive months. For each month, we define the k month lagged number of ads to equal the number of ads placed k months ago. For months 7–60, we would like to compute the 1-month lagged, 2-month lagged… 6-month lagged values of the number of ads. Use the OFFSET function to efficiently compute these lagged values.

5. Suppose you are continually entering monthly sales in column C of a spreadsheet. The first month's sales is entered in cell C2. Assume that as data is entered, no rows are left blank. Thus, if the last month of sales is in cell C50, the next month's sales will be entered in cell C51, and so on. Write a formula that will always return sales during the most recent month. Hint: The expression *COUNTA(C:C)* will always yield the number of nonblank entries in column C.

22

The INDIRECT Function

- My spreadsheet formulas often contain references to cells or ranges or both. Rather than change these references in my formulas, I'd like to know how I can place the references in their own cells so that I can easily change my cell or range references without changing my underlying formulas.

- Each worksheet in a workbook lists monthly sales of a product in cell D1. Is there an easy way to write and copy a formula that lists each month's product sales in a single worksheet?

- Suppose I'm adding up the values in the range A5:A10 with the formula *SUM(A5:A10)*. If I insert a blank row somewhere between row 5 and row 10, my formula updates itself to read *SUM(A5:A11)*. Can I write a formula so that when I insert a blank row between row 5 and row 10, my formula still adds the values in the range A5:A10?

The INDIRECT function is probably one of the most difficult functions to master in Excel. Knowing how to use the INDIRECT function, however, enables you to solve many seemingly unsolvable problems. Essentially any reference to a cell within the INDIRECT portion of a formula results in the cell reference being immediately evaluated to equal the content of the cell. To illustrate the use of the INDIRECT function, look at the file IndirectSimpleEx.xls, which is shown in Figure 22-1.

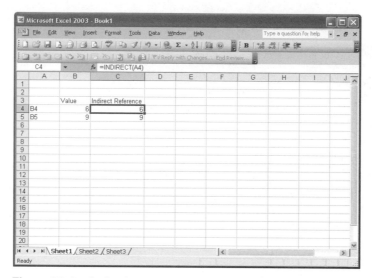

Figure 22-1   A simple example of the INDIRECT function.

In cell C4, I've entered the formula *=INDIRECT(A4)*, and Excel returns a value of 6. Excel returns this value because the reference to A4 is immediately replaced by the text string *B4*. Therefore, the formula is evaluated as *=B4*, which yields a value of 6. Similarly, entering in cell C5 the formula *=INDIRECT(A5)* returns the value in cell B5, which is 9.

My spreadsheet formulas often contain references to cells or ranges or both. Rather than change these references in my formulas, I'd like to know how I can place the references in their own cells so that I can easily change my cell or range references without changing my underlying formulas.

In this example, the data we'll use is contained in the file SumIndirect.xls, shown in Figure 22-2. The cell range B4:H16 lists monthly sales data for six products during a 12-month period.

I currently compute total sales of each product during months 2–12. An easy way to make this calculation is to copy from C18 to D18:H18 the formula *SUM(C6:C16)*. Suppose, however, that you want to be able to change which months are totaled. For example, you might want to total sales for months 3–12. You could change the formula in cell C18 to *SUM(C7:C16)* and then copy this formula to D18:H18, but using this approach is a pain because you have to copy the formula in C18 to D18:H18 and, without looking at the formulas, nobody knows which rows are being added.

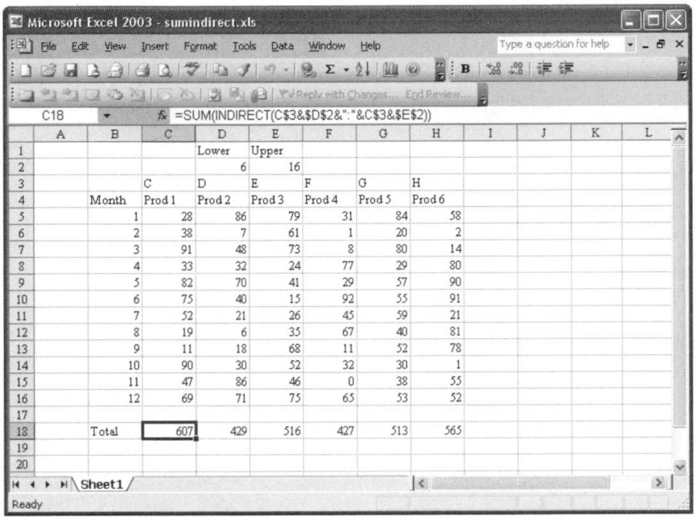

	A	B	C	D	E	F	G	H
1				Lower	Upper			
2				6	16			
3			C	D	E	F	G	H
4		Month	Prod 1	Prod 2	Prod 3	Prod 4	Prod 5	Prod 6
5		1	28	86	79	31	84	58
6		2	38	7	61	1	20	2
7		3	91	48	73	8	80	14
8		4	33	32	24	77	29	80
9		5	82	70	41	29	57	90
10		6	75	40	15	92	55	91
11		7	52	21	26	45	59	21
12		8	19	6	35	67	40	81
13		9	11	18	68	11	52	78
14		10	90	30	52	32	30	1
15		11	47	86	46	0	38	55
16		12	69	71	75	65	53	52
17								
18		Total	607	429	516	427	513	565

Figure 22-2 You can use the INDIRECT function to change cell references in formulas without changing the formulas themselves.

The INDIRECT function provides another approach. I've placed in cells D2 and E2 the starting and ending rows of our summation. Then, using the INDIRECT function, all I need to do is change the starting and ending row references in D2 and E2 and the sums are updated to include the rows we want. Also, by looking at the values in D2 and E2, it is obvious which rows (months) are being added! All I need to do is copy from C18 to D18:H18 the formula *SUM(INDIRECT(C$3&$D$2&":"&C$3&$E$2))*. Every cell reference within the INDIRECT portion of this formula is evaluated to equal the contents of the cell. *C$3* is evaluated as C, *$D$2* is evaluated as 6, and *$E$2* is evaluated as 16. Using the concatenation symbol (&), Excel evaluates this formula as *SUM(C6:C16)*, which is exactly want we want. The formula in C18 returns the value 38 + 91 + ... 69 = 607. In cell D18, our formula evaluates as *SUM(D6:D16)*, which is the result we want. Of course, if we want to add up sales during, say, months 4 through 6, we simply enter 8 in D2 and 10 in cell E2. Then the formula in C18 returns 33 + 82 + 75 = 190. (For information about using the ampersand to concatenate values, see Chapter 6.)

Each worksheet in a workbook lists monthly sales of a product in cell D1. Is there an easy way to write and copy a formula that lists each month's product sales in a single worksheet?

The file IndirectMultiSheet.xls (see Figure 22-3) contains seven worksheets. In each worksheet, cell D1 contains data about the sales of a product during a particular month. Let's suppose Sheet1 contains month 1 sales, Sheet 2 contains month 2 sales, and so on. For instance, sales in month 1 equals 1.

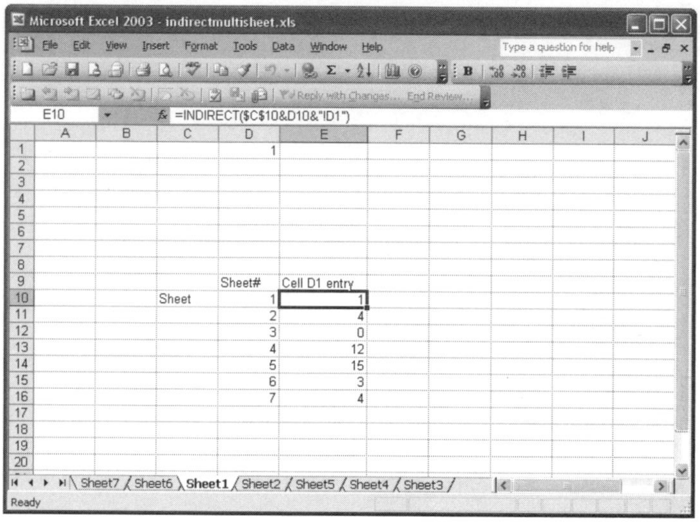

Figure 22-3   Monthly sales (months 1–7) of a product listed by using the INDIRECT function.

Suppose you want to list each month's sales in a single worksheet. A tedious approach would be to list month 1 sales with the formula *=Sheet1!D1*, list month 2 sales with the formula *=Sheet2!D1*, and so on until you've listed month 7 sales with the formula *=Sheet7!D1*. If you have 100 months of data, this approach would be a royal pain! A much more elegant approach is to list month 1 sales in cell E10 of Sheet1 with the formula *INDI-RECT($C$10&D10&"!D1")*. Excel evaluates C10 as "Sheet", D10 as 1, and "!D1" as the text string *!D1*. The whole formula is evaluated as *=Sheet1!D1*, which, of course, yields month 1 sales, located in cell D1 of Sheet1. Copying this formula to the range E11:E16 lists the entries in cell D1 of sheets 2 through 7. Note that when the formula in cell E10 is copied to cell E11, the reference to D10 changes to D11, and cell E11 returns the value located at Sheet2!D1 and so on.

Suppose I'm adding up the values in the range A5:A10 with the formula *SUM(A5:A10)*. If I insert a blank row somewhere between row 5 and row 10, my formula updates itself to read *SUM(A5:A11)*. Can I write a formula so that when I insert a blank row between row 5 and row 10, my formula still adds the values in the range A5:A10?

The worksheet named Sum(A5A10) in the file IndirectInsertRow.xls (shown in Figure 22-4) illustrates several ways to add up the numbers in the cell range

A5:A10. In cell A12, I've entered the traditional formula *SUM(A5:A10)*. This formula yields 6 + 7 + 8 + 9 + 1 + 2 = 33.

Similarly, the formula *SUM($A$5:$A$10)* in cell E9 yields a value of 33. As you'll soon see, however, if we insert a row between rows 5 and 10, both formulas will attempt to add up the cells in the range A5:A11.

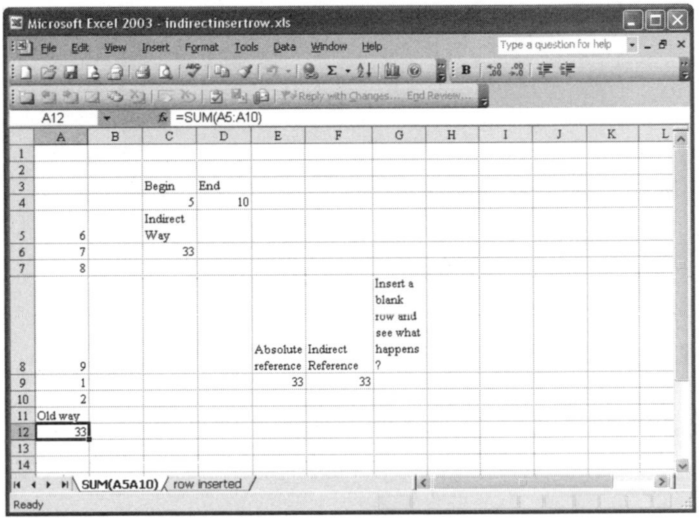

Figure 22-4   This spreadsheet shows several ways to sum the values in the cell range A5:A10.

With the INDIRECT function, you have at least two ways to sum the values in the range A5:A10. In cell F9, I've entered the formula *SUM(INDIRECT("A5:A10"))*. Because Excel treats *INDIRECT("A5:A10")* as the text string "A5:A10", if I insert a row in the spreadsheet, this formula still adds up the entries in the cell range A5:A10!

Another way to use the INDIRECT function to add up the entries in the range A5:A10 is the formula *SUM(INDIRECT("A"&C4&":A"&D4))*, which is the formula entered in cell C6. Excel treats the reference to C4 as a 5 and the reference to D4 as a 10, so this formula becomes *SUM(A5:A10)*. Inserting a blank row between row 5 and row 10 has no effect on this formula because the reference to C4 will still be treated as a 5 and the reference to D4 will still be treated as a 10. In Figure 22-5, you can see the sums computed by our four formulas after a blank row is inserted below row 7. You can find this data on the worksheet Row Inserted in the file IndirectInsertRow.xls.

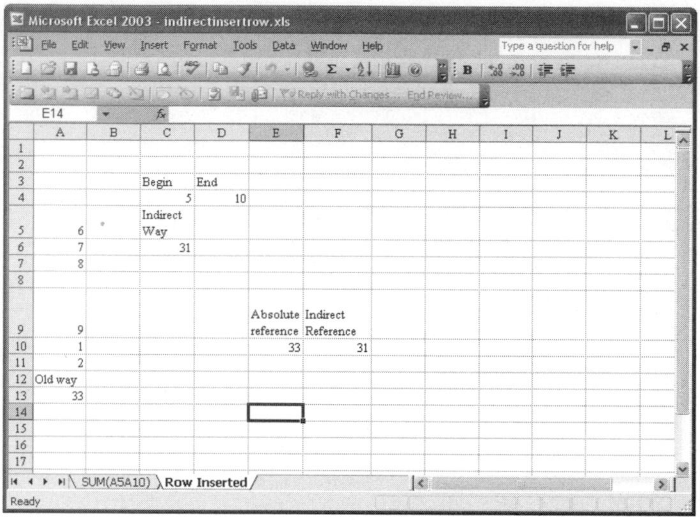

Figure 22-5   Results of SUM formulas after a blank row is inserted below row 7.

Note that the classic SUM formulas that do not involve the INDIRECT function have changed to add up the entries in the range A5:A11, so these formulas still yield a value of 33. The two SUM formulas involving the INDIRECT function continue to add up the entries in the range A5:A10, so we lose the value of 2 (now in cell A11) when we compute our sum. The SUM formulas that use the INDIRECT function yield a value of 31.

Problems

1. The ADDRESS function yields the actual cell address associated with a row and column. For example, the formula *ADDRESS(3,4)* yields $D$3. What result would be obtained if you entered the formula *=INDIRECT(ADDRESS(3,4))*?

2. The workbook P22_2.xls contains data for the sales of five products in four regions (East, West, North, and South). Use the INDIRECT function to create formulas that enable you to easily add up the total sales of any combination of consecutively numbered products, such as Products 1–3, Products 2–5, and the like.

3. The file P22_3.xls contains six worksheets. Sheet1 contains month 1 sales for products 1–4. These sales are always listed in the range E5:H5. Use the INDIRECT function to efficiently tabulate the sales of each product by month in a separate worksheet.

4. Write a formula that will add up the entries in the cell range G2:K2 even if one or more columns are inserted between columns G and K.

23

Conditional Formatting

- How can I highlight monthly stock returns so that every good month is highlighted in one color and every bad month is highlighted in another?

- Given quarterly corporate revenues, how can I highlight quarters in which revenues increased over the previous quarter in one color and quarters in which revenues decreased from the previous quarter in another?

- Given a list of dates, how can I highlight the weekend dates in a specific color?

- Our basketball coach has given each player a rating between 1 and 10 for her ability to play guard, forward, or center. Can I set up a spreadsheet that highlights the ability of each player to play the position to which she's assigned?

Conditional formatting lets you specify formatting for a cell range depending on the contents of the cell range. For example, given exam scores for students, you can use conditional formatting to highlight in red the names of students who have a final average of at least 90. For any cell, conditional formatting allows you to create up to three conditions and define formatting for each condition. Basically, when you set up conditions to format a range of cells, Excel checks each cell in the range to see whether any of the conditions you created (such as *exam score > 90*) is satisfied. The format you link to that condition is applied to all cells in the range that satisfy the condition. If the content of the cell does not satisfy any of the conditions, the formatting of the cell is unchanged.

How can I highlight monthly stock returns so that every good month is highlighted in one color and every bad month is highlighted in another?

The file SandP.xls, shown in Figure 23-1, contains monthly values and returns on the Standard and Poor's stock index. Suppose that you want to highlight in purple each month in which the S&P index went up more than 3 percent and highlight in red each month in which the S&P went down more than 3 percent.

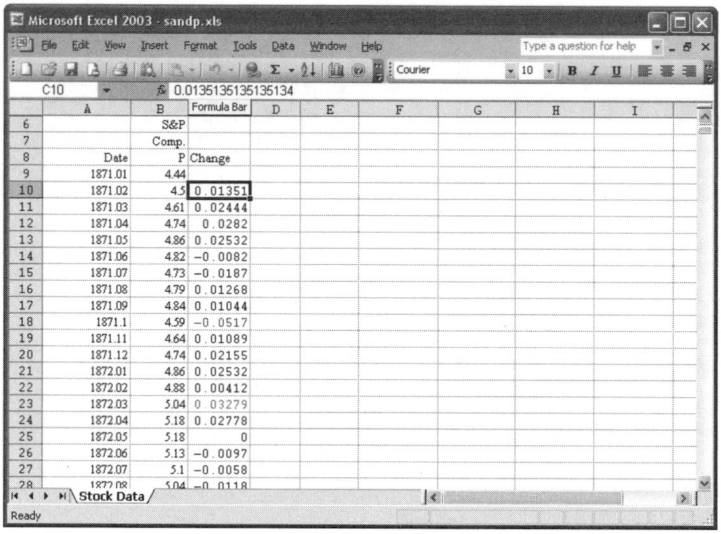

Figure 23-1 Conditional formatting highlights returns in the S&P stock index.

In this example, I begin by moving to cell C10 (the first month containing an S&P return) and select all monthly returns by pressing Ctrl+Shift+Down Arrow. Next I choose Conditional Formatting from the Format menu. In the Conditional Formatting dialog box, shown in Figure 23-2, I select Cell Value Is and then Greater Than and then fill in .03. These settings mean that the formatting we select will be applied to all cells in the range that contain a value greater than .03.

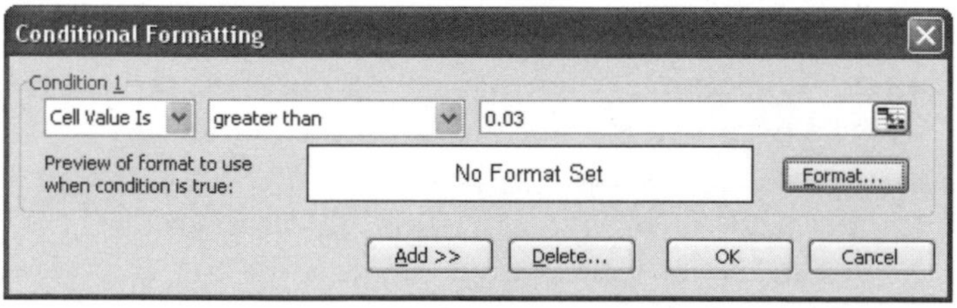

Figure 23-2 Setting up the condition that will apply special formatting to S&P returns greater than .03.

Now click the Format button, and then select purple (or whatever color or other formatting you'd like) in the Format Cells dialog box, shown in Figure 23-3.

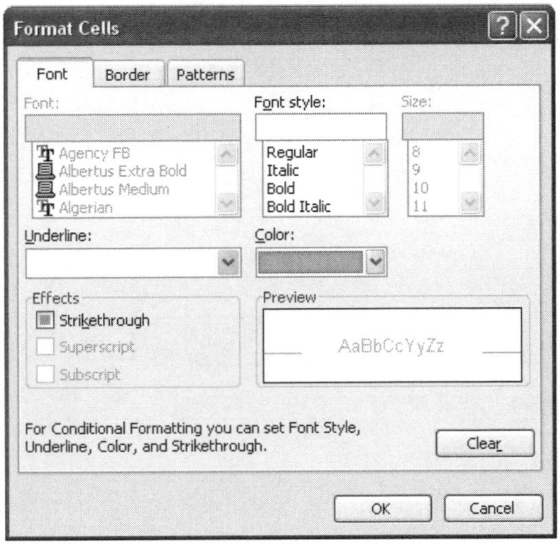

Figure 23-3 You use the Format Cells dialog box to select the formatting that's applied to the cells that meet the condition you defined.

Notice that the lists for fonts and font size aren't available, so your choice of formatting can't change the font or font size. The Patterns tab provides the option to shade cells in a color you choose, while the Borders tab lets you create a border for cells that satisfy your conditional criteria. After clicking OK in the Format Cells dialog box, you're returned to the Conditional Formatting dialog box, which now appears as it's shown in Figure 23-4.

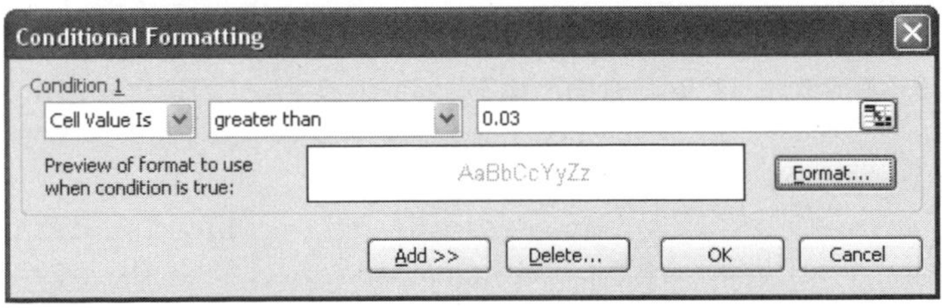

Figure 23-4 All months with S&P return greater than 3 percent will be colored in purple.

We could stop here, click OK, and months meeting our condition would be highlighted in purple. To define a second condition (in a fashion similar to the first), click Add and then specify that all months in which the S&P return is less than -3 percent will be colored red. The Conditional Formatting dialog box should now appear as it's shown in Figure 23-5.

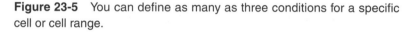

Figure 23-5 You can define as many as three conditions for a specific cell or cell range.

When you now click OK, all months with an S&P return that's greater than 3 percent (see cell C23, for example) are displayed in purple, and all months with an S&P return less than -3 percent (see cell C18) are displayed in red. Cells in which the monthly returns don't meet either of our conditions maintain their original formatting.

By the way, to delete conditional formatting (or any format) applied to a range of cells, simply select the range of cells and choose Edit, Clear Formats. To select all the cells in a spreadsheet to which conditional formatting applies, press F5 to open the Go To dialog box. In the dialog box, click the Special button, select Conditional Formats, and then click OK.

Given quarterly corporate revenues, how can I highlight quarters in which revenues increased over the previous quarter in one color and quarters in which revenues decreased from the previous quarter in another?

The file ToysrusFormat.xls contains quarterly revenues (in millions) for Toys "R" Us during the years 1997–2002. (See Figure 23-6.) We'd like to highlight quarters in which revenues increased over the previous quarter in one color and highlight quarters in which revenues decreased over the previous quarter in another.

The Formula Is option in the Conditional Formatting dialog box enables you to use a formula to define conditions that Excel checks before it applies formatting to a cell. We'll use this option in this example, but before we work with the Formula Is option, let's look at how Excel evaluates some logical functions.

What happens when we type a formula such as *=B3<2* in cell B4? If the value in B3 is a number smaller than 2, Excel returns the value True in cell B4; otherwise, Excel returns False. You can refer to the file LogicalExamples.xls, shown in Figure 23-7, for other examples like this. As you can see in Figure 23-7, you can also use combinations of AND, OR, and NOT in formulas.

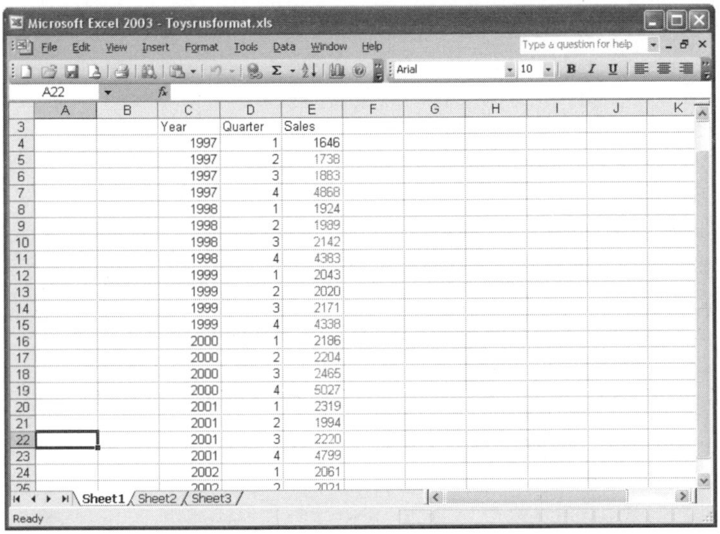

Figure 23-6 In this spreadsheet, we've highlighted increased sales in purple and decreased sales in red.

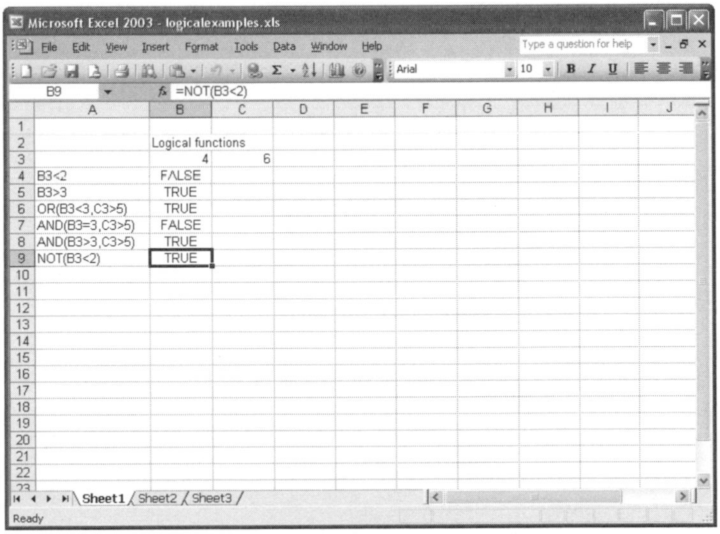

Figure 23-7 Examples of logical functions.

■   In cell B6, the formula *=OR(B3<3, C3>5)* returns the value True if either of the conditions B3<3 or C3>5 is true. Since the value of C3 is greater than 5, Excel returns True.

■   In cell B7, the formula =*AND(B3=3,C3>5)* returns True if B3=3 and C3>5. Because B3 is not equal to 3, Excel returns False. In cell B8, however, the formula =*AND(B3>3,C3>5)* returns True because B3>3 and C3>5 are both true.

■   In cell B9, the formula =*NOT(B3<2)* returns True because B3<2 would return False, and Not False becomes True.

Now let's look at how to use the Formula Is feature to create a conditional format in a range of cells. Begin by selecting the range of cells to which the conditional format should be applied. Open the Conditional Formatting dialog box, select Formula Is, and then enter the formula that defines the condition (it must start with an equals sign). The formula should be relative to the cell that's selected in the range. Click Format, and then enter the formatting you want. Click OK. After clicking OK in the Conditional Formatting dialog box, your formula and formatting are copied to the whole cell range. The format will be applied to any cell in the selected range that satisfies the condition defined in the formula.

Returning to the file ToysrusFormat.xls, let's focus on highlighting in purple the quarters in which revenues increase. Basically, what we want to do is select the range E5:E25 (there is no prior quarter to which we can compare the revenue figure in cell E4) and then instruct Excel that if a cell's value is larger than the cell above it, highlight the cell in purple. Figure 23-8 shows how to fill in the Conditional Formatting dialog box.

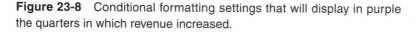

Figure 23-8   Conditional formatting settings that will display in purple the quarters in which revenue increased.

If you enter =*E5>E4* by pointing to the appropriate cells, be sure you remove the $ signs from the formula in the Conditional Formatting dialog box or the formula won't be copied. The formula in this example ensures that cell E5 is colored purple if and only if sales in that quarter exceed the previous quarter. After clicking OK, you'll find that all quarters in which revenue increased are colored purple. Notice that in cell E6, for example, the formula was copied in the usual way, as =*E6>E5*.

To add the condition for formatting cells in which revenue decreased, select the range E5:E25 again, open the Conditional Formatting dialog box, and then select Formula Is. Enter the formula =*E5<E4* and change the color to red. The Conditional Formatting dialog box will now appear as it's shown in Figure 23-9.

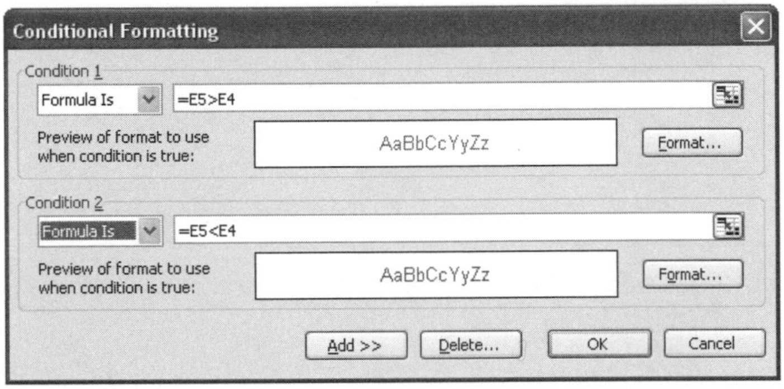

Figure 23-9   These conditions will display quarters in which revenue increased in purple and quarters in which revenue decreased in red.

Given a list of dates, how can I highlight the weekend dates in a specific color?

The file WeekendFormatting.xls (see Figure 23-10) contains several dates. We want to highlight all Saturdays and Sundays in red. To do this, I first copied the formula *WEEKDAY(C6,2)* from cell D6 to D7:D69. Choosing *Type = 2* for the WEEKDAY function returns a 1 for each Monday, 2 for each Tuesday, and so on, so that the function returns 6 for each Saturday and 7 for each Sunday.

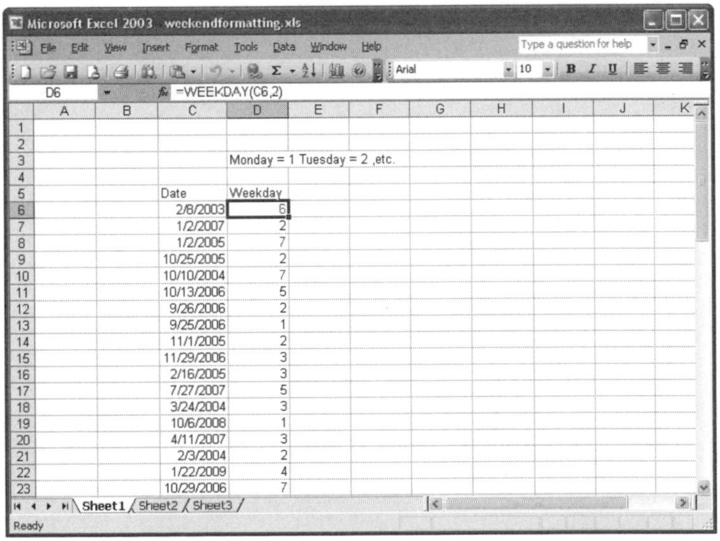

Figure 23-10   In this spreadsheet, we've used the WEEKDAY function to help highlight weekend days in red.

I now select the range D6:D69 and then choose Format, Conditional Formatting. After selecting Formula Is, I fill in the dialog box as shown in Figure 23-11.

Conditional Formatting	✕
Condition 1	
Formula Is ▼ =OR(D6=6,D6=7) ▦	
Preview of format to use when condition is true: AaBbCcYyZz Format...	
Add >> Delete... OK Cancel	

Figure 23-11   The Conditional Formatting dialog box set up to display weekend days in red.

After clicking OK, each date having its weekday equal to 6 (for Saturday) or 7 (for Sunday) is colored red.

Our basketball coach has given each player a rating between 1 and 10 for her ability to play guard, forward, or center. Can I set up a spreadsheet that highlights the ability of each player to play the position to which she's assigned?

The file Basketball.xls, shown in Figure 23-12, contains ratings given to 20 players for each position and the position (1 = guard, 2 = forward, 3 = center) played by each player. We would like to display in bold type the rating for each player for the position to which she's assigned.

	A	B	C	D	E	F	G	H	I
1			1	2	3				
2	Position played	Player	Guard rating	Forward rating	Center rating				
3	1	1	**1**	9	2	1=Guard			
4	1	2	**4**	3	9	2=Forward			
5	2	3	7	**3**	7	3=Center			
6	2	4	9	**8**	8				
7	2	5	5	**8**	9				
8	3	6	2	7	**2**				
9	3	7	7	6	**6**				
10	3	8	4	4	**3**				
11	3	9	3	8	**10**				
12	3	10	6	1	**4**				
13	2	11	6	**7**	5				
14	2	12	2	**6**	5				
15	2	13	8	**6**	9				
16	1	14	**1**	1	3				
17	1	15	**3**	6	8				
18	2	16	4	**10**	1				
19	2	17	8	**5**	1				
20	2	18	1	**7**	7				
21	3	19	9	2	**7**				
22	3	20	10	3	**10**				
23									

Figure 23-12   This spreadsheet rates each player's ability to play a position.

Begin by selecting the range C3:E22, which contains the players' ratings. Choose Format, Conditional Formatting and then fill in the dialog box as shown Figure 23-13.

Figure 23-13   The Conditional Formatting dialog box set up to show player ratings in bold type.

The formula *=$A3=C$1* compares the player's assigned position to the column heading (1, 2, or 3) in row 1. If the player's assigned position equals 1 (guard), her rating in column C, which is her guard rating, appears in bold. Similarly, if the player's assigned position equals 2, the rating in column D, her forward rating, appears in bold. Finally, if the assigned position equals 3, the rating in column E appears in bold.

Problems

1. Using the data in the file SandP.xls, use conditional formatting in the following situations:

    ❑ Format in bold each month in which the value of the S&P increased and underline each month in which the value of the S&P decreased.

    ❑ Highlight in green each month in which the S&P changed by at most 2 percent.

    ❑ Highlight the largest S&P value in red and the smallest value in purple.

2. Using the data in the file Toysrus.xls, highlight in red all quarters for which revenue has increased over at least the last two quarters. Highlight all fourth-quarter revenues in blue and first-quarter revenues in red.

3. The file Test.xls contains exam scores for students. The top 10 students receive an A, the next 20 students receive a B, and all other students receive a C. Highlight the A grades in red, the B grades in

green, and C grades in blue. Hint: The function *LARGE(D4:D63,10)* gives you the tenth highest grade on the test.

4. In the file WeekendFormatting.xls, highlight all weekdays in red. Highlight all days that occur in the first 10 days of the month.

5. Suppose each worker in Microsoft's finance department has been assigned to one of four groups. The supervisor of each group has rated each worker on a 0–10 scale, and each worker has rated his satisfaction with each of the four groups. (See the file SatisSuper.xls.) Based on the group to which each worker is assigned, highlight the supervisor rating and worker satisfaction rating for each worker.

6. The file VarianceAnalysis.xls contains monthly profit forecasts and monthly actual sales. The sales variance for a month equals

$$\frac{actual\ sales - forecasted\ sales}{forecasted\ sales}$$

Highlight in red all months with a favorable variance of at least 20 percent and highlight in green all months with an unfavorable variance of more than 20 percent.

7. For our drug cost example from Chapter 21, format the worksheet so that all phase 1 costs are displayed in red, all phase 2 costs are displayed in green, and all phase 3 costs are displayed in purple.

24

An Introduction to Optimization with the Excel Solver

- How can a large drug company determine the monthly product mix at their Indianapolis plant that maximizes corporate profitability?

- If Microsoft produces Xbox consoles at three locations, how can they minimize the cost of meeting demand for Xbox consoles?

- What price for Xbox consoles and games will maximize Microsoft's profit from Xbox sales?

- Microsoft would like to undertake 20 strategic initiatives that will tie up money and skilled programmers for the next five years. They do not have enough resources to undertake all 20 projects. Which projects should they undertake?

- How do bookmakers find the best set of "ratings" for NFL teams to set accurate point spreads?

- How should I allocate my retirement portfolio among high-tech stocks, value stocks, bonds, cash, and gold?

In all these situations, we want to find the best way to do something. More formally, we want to find the values of certain cells in a spreadsheet that *optimize* (maximize or minimize) a certain objective. The Excel Solver helps you answer optimization problems.

191

An optimization model has three parts: the target cell, the changing cells, and the constraints. The *target cell* represents the objective or goal. We want to either minimize or maximize the target cell. In the example of a drug company's product mix, the plant manager would presumably want to maximize the profitability of the plant during each month. The cell that measures profitability would be the target cell. The target cells for each situation described at the beginning of the chapter are listed in Table 24-1.

Table 24-1   List of Target Cells

Model	Maximize or Minimize	Target cell
Drug company product mix	Maximize	Monthly profit
Xbox shipping	Minimize	Distribution costs
Xbox pricing	Maximize	Profit from Xbox consoles and games
Microsoft project initiatives	Maximize	Net present value (NPV) contributed by selected projects
NFL ratings	Minimize	Difference between scores predicted by ratings and actual game scores
Retirement portfolio	Minimize	Riskiness of portfolio

Keep in mind that in some situations, you might have multiple target cells. For example, Microsoft might have a secondary goal to maximize Xbox market share.

Changing cells are the spreadsheet cells that we can change or adjust to optimize the target cell. In the drug company example, the plant manager can adjust the amount produced for each product during a month. The cells in which these amounts are recorded are the changing cells in this model. Table 24-2 lists the appropriate changing cell definitions for the models described at the beginning of the chapter.

Table 24-2   List of Changing Cells

Model	Changing Cells
Drug company product mix	Amount of each product produced during the month
Xbox shipping	Amount produced at each plant each month that is shipped to each customer

Table 24-2   List of Changing Cells

Model	Changing Cells
Xbox pricing	Console and game prices
Microsoft program initiatives	Which projects are selected
NFL ratings	Team ratings
Retirement portfolio	Fraction of money invested in each asset class

are restrictions you place on the changing cells. In our product mix example, the product mix can't use more of any available resource (for example, raw material and labor) than the amount of the available resource. Also, we should not produce more of a product than people are willing to buy. In most Solver models, there is an implicit constraint that all changing cells must be nonnegative. I'll discuss nonnegativity constraints in more detail in later chapters. Remember that a Solver model does not need to have any constraints. Table 24-3 lists the constraints for the problems presented at the start of the chapter.

Table 24-3   List of Problem Constraints

Model	Constraints
Drug company product mix	Product mix uses no more resources than are available
	Do not produce more of a product than can be sold
Xbox shipping	Do not ship more units each month from a plant than plant capacity
	Make sure that each customer receives the number of Xboxes they need
Xbox pricing	Prices can't be too far out of line with competitors' prices
Microsoft project initiatives	Projects selected can't use more money or skilled programmers than are available
NFL ratings	None
Retirement portfolio	Invest all our money somewhere (cash is a possibility)
	Obtain an expected return of at least 10 percent on our investments

The best way to understand how to use the Excel Solver is by looking at some detailed examples. In later chapters, you'll learn how to use the Solver to address each of the problems presented in this chapter as well as several other important business problems.

To install the Excel Solver, click Tools, Add-Ins, and then check Solver-Add In. Click OK, and Excel will install the Solver. Once Solver is installed, you can run Solver by selecting Tools, Solver. Figure 24-1 shows the Solver Parameters dialog box. In the next few chapters, you'll see how to use this dialog box to input the target cell, changing cells, and constraints for a Solver model.

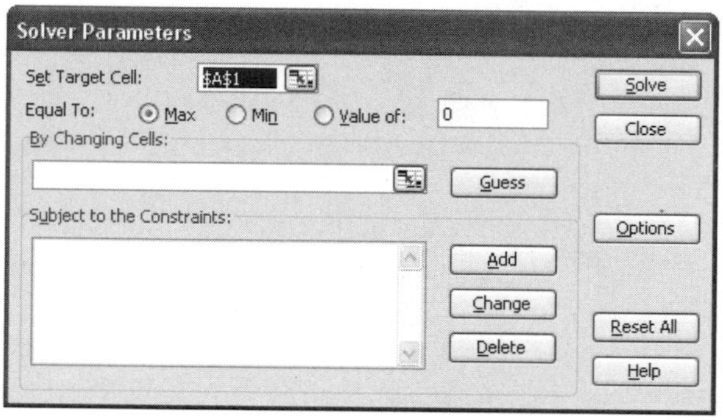

Figure 24-1   The Solver Parameters dialog box.

After you have input the target cell, changing cells, and constraints, what does Solver do? To answer this question, you need some background in Solver terminology. Any specification of the changing cells that satisfies the model's constraints is known as a *feasible solution*. For instance, in our product mix example, any product mix that satisfies the following three conditions would be a feasible solution:

- Mix does not use more raw material and labor than is available.

- Mix produces no more of each product than is demanded.

- Amount produced of each product is nonnegative.

Essentially, Solver searches over all feasible solutions and finds the feasible solution that has the "best" target cell value (the largest value for maximum optimization, the smallest for minimum optimization). Such a solution is called an *optimal solution*. As you'll see in Chapter 25, some Solver models have no optimal solution and some have a unique solution. Other Solver models have multiple (actually an infinite number of) optimal solutions. In the next chapter, we'll begin our study of Solver examples by examining the drug company product mix problem.

Problems

For each situation described below, identify the target cell, changing cells, and constraints.

1. I am borrowing $100,000 for a 15-year mortgage. The annual rate of interest is 8 percent. I make monthly payments. How can I determine my monthly mortgage payment?

2. How should an auto company allocate its advertising budget between different advertising formats?

3. How should cities bus students to obtain racial balance?

4. Where should a city locate a single hospital?

5. How should a drug company allocate sales-force effort to their products?

6. A drug company has $2 billion to allocate to purchasing biotech companies. Which companies should they buy?

7. The tax rate charged to a drug company depends on the country in which a product is produced. How can a drug company determine where each drug should be made?

25

Using Solver to Determine the Optimal Product Mix

- How can I determine the monthly product mix for our plant that maximizes corporate profitability?

- Does a Solver model always have a solution?

- What does it mean if a Solver model yields the result Set Values Do Not Converge?

How can I determine the monthly product mix for our plant that maximizes corporate profitability?

Companies often need to determine the monthly (or weekly) production schedule that gives the quantity of each product that must be produced. In its simplest incarnation, the *product mix* problem involves how to determine the amount of each product that should be produced during a month to maximize profits. Product mix must often satisfy the following constraints:

- Product mix can't use more resources than are available.

- There is a limited demand for each product. We can't produce more of a product during a month than is demanded because the excess production is wasted (consider a perishable drug, for example).

Let's now solve the following example of the product mix problem. You can find the solution to this problem in the file ProdMix.xls, shown in Figure 25-1.

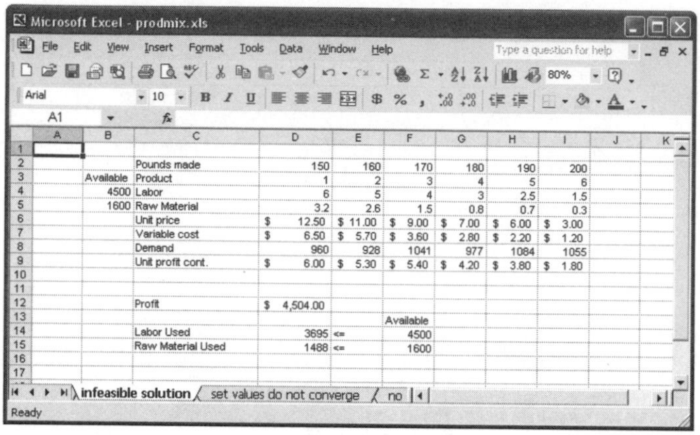

Figure 25-1 The product mix example.

Let's say we work for a drug company that can produce six products at their plant. Production of each product requires labor and raw material. Row 4 in Figure 25-1 gives the hours of labor needed to produce a pound of each product, and row 5 gives the pounds of raw material needed to produce a pound of each product. For example, producing a pound of product 1 requires 6 hours of labor and 3.2 pounds of raw material. For each drug, the price per pound is given in row 6, the unit cost per pound is given in row 7, and the profit contribution per pound is given in row 9. For example, product 2 sells for $11.00 per pound, incurs a unit cost of $5.70 per pound, and contributes $5.30 profit per pound. This month's demand for each drug is given in row 8. For example, demand for product 3 is 1041 pounds. This month, 4500 hours of labor and 1600 pounds of raw material are available. How can this company maximize its monthly profit?

If we knew nothing about the Excel Solver, we would attack this problem by constructing a spreadsheet in which we track for each product mix the profit and resource usage associated with the product mix. Then we would use trial and error to vary the product mix to optimize profit without using more labor or raw material than is available and without producing more of any drug than there is demand. We use Solver in this process only at the trial-and-error stage. Essentially, Solver is an optimization engine that flawlessly performs the trial-and-error search.

A key to solving the product mix problem is efficiently computing the resource usage and profit associated with any given product mix. An important tool that we can use to make this computation is the SUMPRODUCT function. The SUMPRODUCT function multiplies corresponding values in cell ranges and returns the sum of those values. Each cell range used in a SUM-PRODUCT evaluation must have the same dimensions, which implies that you can use SUMPRODUCT with two rows or two columns but not with a column and a row.

As an example of how we can use the SUMPRODUCT function in our product mix example, let's try to compute our resource usage. Our labor usage is given by

```
(Labor used per pound of drug 1)*(Drug 1 pounds produced)+(Labor used per pound
 of drug 2)*(Drug 2 pounds produced) + …(Labor used per pound of drug 6)*(Drug
6 pounds produced)
```

We could compute labor usage in a tedious fashion as $D2*D4 + E2*E4 + F2*F4 + G2*G4 + H2*H4 + I2*I4$. Similarly, raw material usage could be computed as $D2*D5 + E2*E5 + F2*F5 + G2*G5 + H2*H5 + I2*I5$. Entering these formulas in a spreadsheet is time-consuming with six products. Imagine how long it would take if you were working with a company that produced, say, 50 products at their plant. A much easier way to compute labor and raw material usage is to copy from D14 to D15 the formula $SUMPRODUCT(\$D\$2:\$I\$2,D4:I4)$. This formula computes $D2*D4 + E2*E4 + F2*F4 + G2*G4 + H2*H4 + I2*I4$ (which is our labor usage) and is much easier to enter! Notice that I use the $ sign with the range D2:I2 so that when I copy the formula I still pull the product mix from row 2. The formula in cell D15 computes raw material usage.

In a similar fashion, our profit is given by

```
(Drug 1 profit per pound)*(Drug 1 pounds produced) + (Drug 2 profit per pound)*
(Drug 2 pounds produced) + …(Drug 6 profit per pound)*(Drug 6 pounds produced).
```

Profit is easily computed in cell D12 with the formula $SUMPRODUCT(D9:I9,\$D\$2:\$I\$2)$.

We now can identify the three parts of our product mix Solver model.

- **Target cell**   Our goal is to maximize profit (computed in cell D12).

- **Changing cells**   The number of pounds produced of each product (listed in the cell range D2:I2).

- **Constraints**   We have the following constraints:

    ❑   Do not use more labor and raw material than are available. That is, the values in cells D14:D15 (resources used) must be less than or equal to the values in cells F14:F15 (the available resources).

❑   Do not produce more of a drug than is in demand. That is, the values in the cells D2:I2 (pounds produced of each drug) must be less than or equal to the demand for each drug (listed in cells D8:I8).

❑   We can't produce a negative amount of any drug.

I'll now show you how to input the target cell, changing cells, and constraints into Solver. Then, all you need to do is click the Solve button and Solver will find a profit-maximizing product mix!

To begin, select Tools, Solver. (See Chapter 24 for instructions on how to install Solver.) The Solver Parameters dialog box will appear, as shown in Figure 25-2.

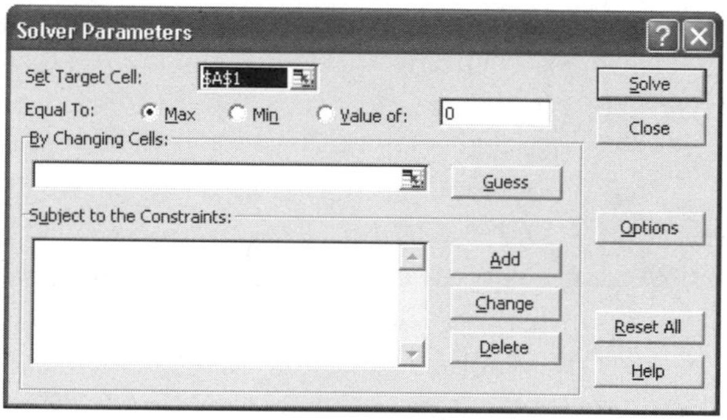

Figure 25-2   The Solver Parameters dialog box.

To input the target cell, click in the Set Target Cell box and then select our profit cell (cell D12). To input our changing cells, click in the By Changing Cells box and then point to the range D2:I2, which contains the pounds produced of each drug. The dialog box should now look Figure 25-3.

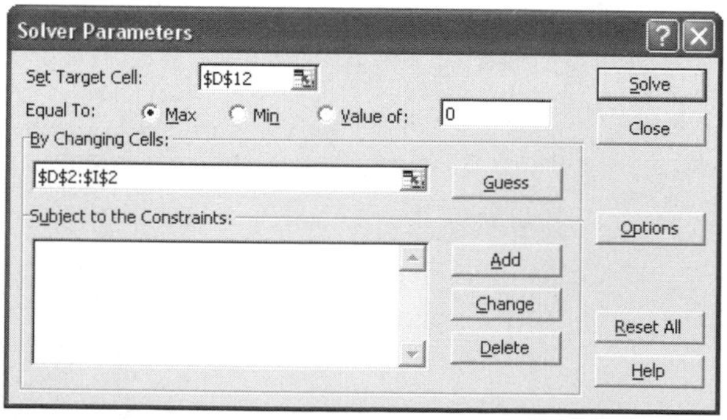

Figure 25-3   The Solver Parameters dialog box with the target cell and changing cells defined.

We're now ready to add constraints to the model. Click the Add button. You'll see the Add Constraint dialog box, shown in Figure 25-4.

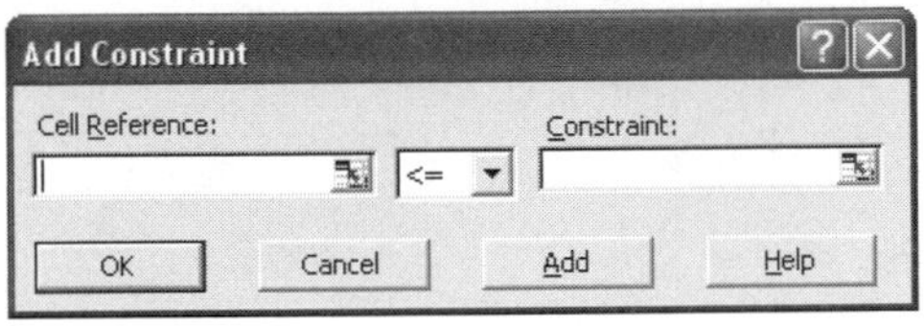

Figure 25-4   The Add Constraint dialog box.

To add the resource usage constraints, click in the box labeled Cell Reference and then select the range D14:D15. Select <= from the drop-down list in the middle of the dialog box. Click in the box labeled Constraint, and then select the cell range F14:F15. The Add Constraint dialog box should now look like Figure 25-5.

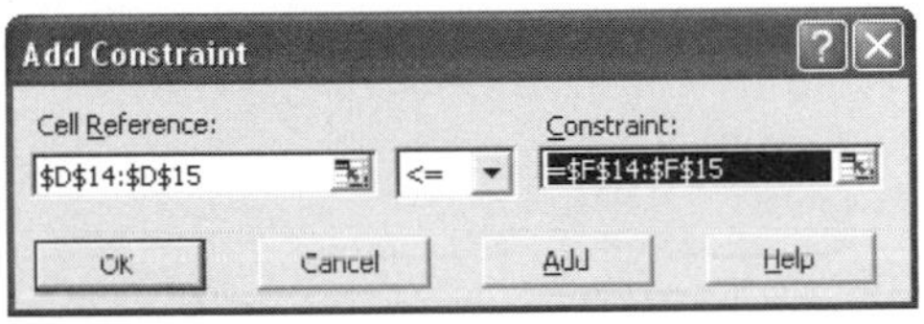

Figure 25-5   The Add Constraint dialog box with the resource usage constraints entered.

We have now ensured that when Solver tries different values for the changing cells, Solver will consider only combinations that satisfy both *D14<=F14* (labor used is less than or equal to labor available) and *D15<=F15* (raw material used is less than or equal to raw material available). Now click Add in the Add Constraint dialog box to enter the demand constraints. Simply fill in the Add Constraint dialog box as shown in Figure 25-6.

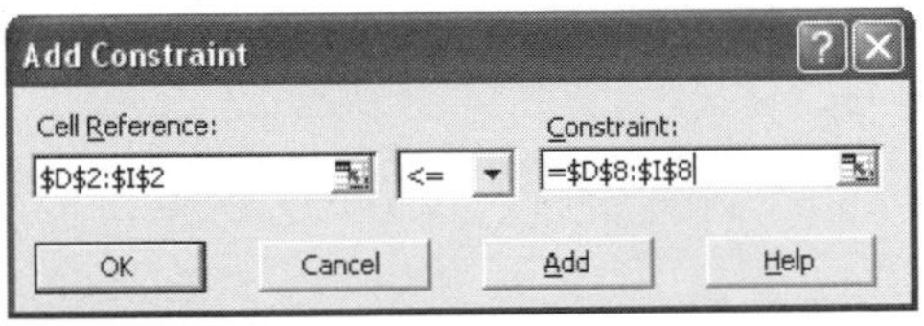

Figure 25-6   The Add Constraint dialog box with the demand constraints entered.

Adding these constraints ensures that when Solver tries different combinations for the changing cell values, Solver will consider only combinations that satisfy the following:

- *D2<=D8* (the amount of drug 1 made is less than or equal to the demand for drug 1)

- *E2<=E8* (the amount of drug 2 made is less than or equal to the demand for drug 2)

- *F2<=F8* (the amount of drug 3 made is less than or equal to the demand for drug 3)

- *G2<=G8* (the amount of drug 4 made is less than or equal to the demand for drug 4)

- *H2<=H8* (the amount of drug 5 made is less than or equal to the demand for drug 5)

- *I2<=I8* (the amount of drug 6 made is less than or equal to the demand for drug 6)

Click OK in the Add Constraint dialog box. The Solver window should look like Figure 25-7.

Figure 25-7 The final Solver window for the product mix problem.

We enter the constraint that all changing cells be nonnegative in the Solver Options dialog box. Click the Options button in the Solver Parameters dialog box. Select the options Assume Linear Model and Assume Non-Negative, as shown in Figure 25-8. Click OK.

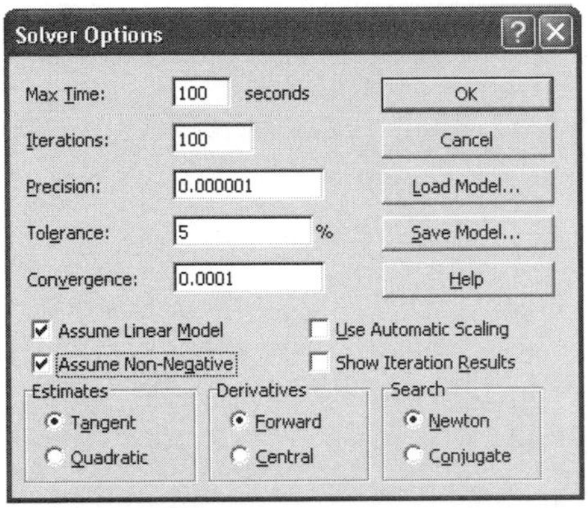

Figure 25-8   Solver options settings.

Selecting the Assume Non-Negative option ensures that Solver considers only combinations of changing cells in which each changing cell assumes a nonnegative value. We selected Assume Linear Model because the product mix problem is a special type of Solver problem called a *linear model*. Essentially, a Solver model is linear under the following conditions:

■   The target cell is computed by adding together terms of the form *(changing cell)*(constant)*.

■   Each constraint satisfies the "linear model requirement." This means that each constraint is evaluated by adding together terms of the form *(changing cell)*(constant)* and comparing such sums to a constant.

Why is this Solver problem linear? Our target cell (profit) is computed as

```
(Drug 1 profit per pound)*(Drug 1 pounds produced) + (Drug 2 profit per pound)*
(Drug 2 pounds produced) + …(Drug 6 profit per pound)*(Drug 6 pounds produced)
```

This computation follows a pattern in which the target cell's value is derived by adding together terms of the form *(changing cell)*(constant)*.

Our labor constraint is evaluated by comparing the value derived from *(Labor used per pound of drug 1)*(Drug 1 pounds produced) + (Labor used per pound of drug 2)*(Drug 2 pounds produced) + … (Labor used per pound of drug 6)*(Drug 6 pounds produced)* to the labor available.

Therefore, the labor constraint is evaluated by adding together terms of the form *(changing cell)*(constant)* and comparing such sums to a constant. Both the labor constraint and the raw material constraint satisfy the linear model requirement.

Our demand constraints take the form

```
(Drug 1 produced)<=(Drug 1 Demand)
(Drug 2 produced)<=(Drug 2 Demand)
⋮
(Drug 6 produced)<=(Drug 6 Demand)
```

Each demand constraint also satisfies the linear model requirement because each is evaluated by adding together terms of the form *(changing cell)*(constant)* and comparing such sums to a constant.

Having shown that our product mix model is a linear model, why should we care?

- If a Solver model is linear and we select Assume Linear Model, Solver is guaranteed to find the optimal solution to the Solver model. If a Solver model is not linear, Solver may or may not find the optimal solution.

- If a Solver model is linear and we select Assume Linear Model, Solver uses a very efficient algorithm (the simplex method) to find the model's optimal solution. If a Solver model is linear and we do not select Assume Linear Model, Solver uses a very inefficient algorithm (the GRG2 method) and might have difficulty finding the model's optimal solution.

After clicking OK in the Solver Options dialog box, we're returned to the main Solver dialog box, shown earlier in Figure 25-7. When we click Solve, Solver calculates an optimal solution (if one exists) for our product mix model. As I stated in Chapter 24, an optimal solution to the product mix model would be a set of changing cell values (pounds produced of each drug) that maximizes profit over the set of all feasible solutions. Again, a feasible solution is a set of changing cell values satisfying all constraints. The changing cell values shown in Figure 25-9 are a feasible solution because all production levels are nonnegative, no production levels exceed demand, and resource usage does not exceed available resources.

	A	B	C	D	E	F	G	H	I
1									
2			Pounds made	150	160	170	180	190	200
3		Available	Product	1	2	3	4	5	6
4		4500	Labor	6	5	4	3	2.5	1.5
5		1600	Raw Material	3.2	2.6	1.5	0.8	0.7	0.3
6			Unit price	$ 12.50	$ 11.00	$ 9.00	$ 7.00	$ 6.00	$ 3.00
7			Variable cost	$ 6.50	$ 5.70	$ 3.60	$ 2.80	$ 2.20	$ 1.20
8			Demand	960	928	1041	977	1084	1055
9			Unit profit cont.	$ 6.00	$ 5.30	$ 5.40	$ 4.20	$ 3.80	$ 1.80
10									
11									
12			Profit	$ 4,504.00					
13						Available			
14			Labor Used	3695	<=	4500			
15			Raw Material Used	1488	<=	1600			

Figure 25-9   A feasible solution to the product mix problem fits within constraints.

The changing cell values shown in Figure 25-10 represent an *infeasible solution* for the following reasons:

■   We produce more of drug 5 than is demanded.

■   We use more labor than labor available.

■   We use more raw material than raw material available.

	B	C	D	E	F	G	H	I
1								
2		Pounds made	300	0	0	0	1085	1000
3	Available	Product	1	2	3	4	5	6
4	4500	Labor	6	5	4	3	2.5	1.5
5	1600	Raw Material	3.2	2.6	1.5	0.8	0.7	0.3
6		Unit price	$ 12.50	$ 11.00	$ 9.00	$ 7.00	$ 6.00	$ 3.00
7		Variable cost	$ 6.50	$ 5.70	$ 3.60	$ 2.80	$ 2.20	$ 1.20
8		Demand	960	928	1041	977	1084	1055
9		Unit profit cont.	$ 6.00	$ 5.30	$ 5.40	$ 4.20	$ 3.80	$ 1.80
10								
11								
12		Profit	$ 7,723.00					
13					Available			
14		Labor Used	6012.5	<=	4500			
15		Raw Material Used	2019.5	<=	1600			

Figure 25-10   An infeasible solution to the product mix problem doesn't fit within the constraints we defined.

After clicking Solve, Solver quickly finds the optimal solution shown in Figure 25-11. You need to select Keep Solver Solution to preserve the optimal solution values in the spreadsheet.

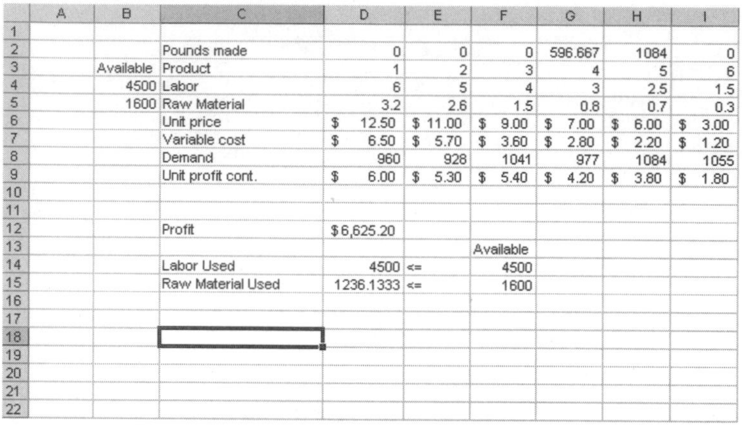

	A	B	C	D	E	F	G	H	I
1									
2			Pounds made	0	0	0	596.667	1084	0
3		Available	Product	1	2	3	4	5	6
4		4500	Labor	6	5	4	3	2.5	1.5
5		1600	Raw Material	3.2	2.6	1.5	0.8	0.7	0.3
6			Unit price	$ 12.50	$ 11.00	$ 9.00	$ 7.00	$ 6.00	$ 3.00
7			Variable cost	$ 6.50	$ 5.70	$ 3.60	$ 2.80	$ 2.20	$ 1.20
8			Demand	960	928	1041	977	1084	1055
9			Unit profit cont.	$ 6.00	$ 5.30	$ 5.40	$ 4.20	$ 3.80	$ 1.80
10									
11									
12			Profit	$6,625.20					
13						Available			
14			Labor Used	4500	<=	4500			
15			Raw Material Used	1236.1333	<=	1600			
16									
17									
18									
19									
20									
21									
22									

Figure 25-11   The optimal solution to the product mix problem.

Our drug company can maximize its monthly profit at a level of $6,625.20 by producing 596.67 pounds of drug 4, 1084 pounds of drug 5, and none of the other drugs! We can't determine if we can achieve the maximum profit of $6,625.20 in other ways. All we can be sure of is that with our limited resources and demand, there is no way to make more than $6,625.20 this month.

Does a Solver model always have a solution?

Suppose that demand for each product *must* be met. (See the worksheet named No Feasible Solution in the file ProdMix.xls.) We then have to change our demand constraints from *D2:I2<=D8:I8* to *D2:I2>=D8:I8*. To do this, open Solver, select the D2:I2<=D8:I8 constraint, and then click Change. The Change Constraint dialog box, shown in Figure 25-12, appears.

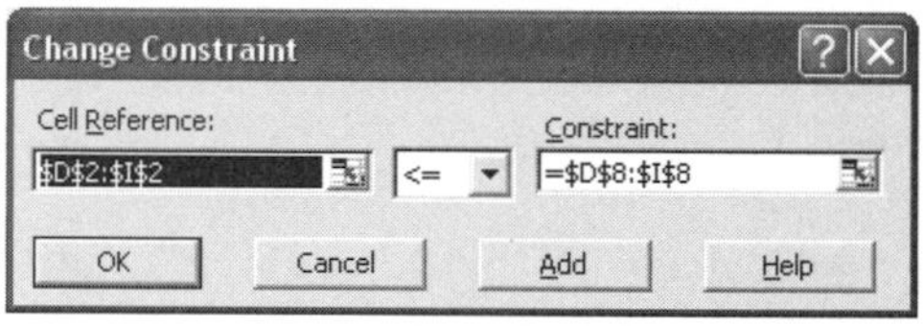

Figure 25-12   The Change Constraint dialog box.

Select >=, and then click OK. We've now ensured that Solver will consider only changing cell values that meet all demands. When you click Solve, you'll see the message "Solver could not find a feasible solution." This message means that with our limited resources, we can't meet demand for all products. We have not made a mistake in our model! Solver is simply telling us that if we want to meet demand for each product, we need to add more labor, more raw material, or more of both.

What does is mean if a Solver model yields the result Set Values Do Not Converge?

Let's see what happens if we allow unlimited demand for each product and we allow negative quantities to be produced of each drug. (You can see this Solver problem on the worksheet named Set Values Do Not Converge in the file Prod-Mix.xls.) To find the optimal solution for this situation, open Solver, click the Options button, and clear the option Assume Non-Negative. In the Solver Parameters dialog box, select the demand constraint D2:I2<=D8:I8 and then click Delete to remove the constraint. When you click Solve, Solver returns the message "The Set Cell values do not converge." This message means that if the target cell is to be maximized (as in our example), there are feasible solutions with arbitrarily large target cell values. (If the target cell is to be minimized, the message "Set values do not converge" means there are feasible solutions with arbitrarily small target cell values.) In our situation, by allowing negative production of a drug, we in effect "create" resources that can be used to produce arbitrarily large amounts of other drugs. Given our unlimited demand, this allows us to make unlimited profits. In a real situation, we can't make an infinite amount of money. In short, if you see "Set values do not converge," your model does have an error.

Problems

1. Suppose our drug company could buy up to 500 hours of labor at $1 per hour. Would they take advantage of this opportunity?

2. At a chip manufacturing plant, four technicians (A, B, C, and D) produce three products (products 1, 2, and 3). The chip manufacturer can sell 80 units of product 1 this month, 50 units of product 2, and at most 50 units of product 3. Technician A can make only products 1 and 3. Technician B can make only products 1 and 2. Technician C can make only product 3. Technician D can make only product 2. For each unit produced, the products contribute the following profit: product 1, $6; product 2, $7; product 3, $10. The time (in hours) each technician needs to manufacture a product is as follows:

Product	Technician A	Technician B	Technician C	Technician D
1	2	2.5	Cannot do	Cannot do
2	Cannot do	3	Cannot do	3.5
3	3	Cannot do	4	Cannot do

Each technician can work up to 120 hours per month. How can the chip manufacturer maximize its monthly profit?

3. A computer manufacturing plant produces mice, keyboards, and video game joysticks. The per-unit profit, per-unit labor usage, monthly demand, and per-unit machine-time usage are given in the following table:

	Mice	**Keyboards**	**Joysticks**
Profit/unit	$8	$11	$9
Labor usage/unit	.2 hour	.3 hour	.24 hour
Machine time/unit	.04 hour	.055 hour	.04 hour
Monthly demand	15,000	25,000	11,000

Each month, a total of 13,000 labor hours and 3000 hours of machine time are available. How can the manufacturer maximize its monthly profit contribution from the plant?

4. Resolve our drug example assuming a minimum demand of 200 units for each drug must be met.

5. Jason the jeweler makes diamond bracelets, necklaces, and earrings. He wants to work at most 160 hours per month. He has 800 ounces of diamonds. The profit, labor time, and ounces of diamonds required to produce each product are given below. If demand for each product is unlimited, how can Jason maximize his profit?

Product	Unit Profit	Labor Hours Per Unit	Ounces of Diamonds Per Unit
Bracelet	$300	.35	1.2
Necklace	$200	.15	.75
Earrings	$100	.05	.5

Using Solver to Solve Transportation or Distribution Problems

- How can a drug company determine the locations at which they should produce drugs and from which they should ship drugs to customers?

Many companies manufacture products at locations (often called *supply points*) and ship their products to customers (often called *demand points*). A natural question is what is the least expensive way to produce and ship products to customers and meet customer demand? This type of problem is called a *transportation problem*. A transportation problem can be set up as a linear Solver model with the following specifications:

- **Target cell**   Minimize total production and shipping cost.

- **Changing cells**   The amount produced at each supply point that is shipped to each demand point.

- **Constraints**   The amount shipped from each supply point can't exceed plant capacity. Each demand point must receive its required demand. Also, each changing cell must be nonnegative.

How can a drug company determine the locations at which they should produce drugs and from which they should ship drugs to customers?

You can follow along with this problem by looking at the file Transport.xls. Let's suppose a drug company produces a drug in Los Angeles, Atlanta, and New York. The Los Angeles plant can produce up to 10,000 pounds of the drug per month. Atlanta can produce up to 12,000 pounds of the drug per month, and New York can produce up to 14,000 pounds per month. Each month, the company must ship to the four regions of the United States—East, Midwest, South, and West—the number of pounds listed in cells B2:E2, as shown in Figure 26-1. For example, the West region must receive at least 13,000 pounds of the drug each month. The cost per pound of producing a drug at each plant and shipping the drug to each region of the country are given in cells B4:E6. For example, it costs $3.50 to produce a pound of the drug in Los Angeles and ship it to the Midwest region. What is the cheapest way to get each region the quantity of the drug they need?

Figure 26-1   Data for a transportation problem that we'll set up to be resolved by Solver.

To express our target cell, we need to track total shipping cost. After entering in the cell range B10:E12 trial values for our shipments from each supply point to each region, we can compute total shipping cost as the following:

```
(Amount sent from LA to East)*(Cost per pound of sending drug from LA to East)
+ (Amount sent from LA to Midwest)*(Cost per pound of sending drug from LA to
Midwest) + (Amount sent from LA to South)*(Cost per pound of sending drug from
LA to South) + (Amount sent from LA to West)*(Cost per pound of sending drug
from LA to West) + ...(Amount sent from New York City to West)*(Cost per pound
of sending drug from New York City to West)
```

The SUMPRODUCT function can multiply corresponding elements in two separate rectangles (as long as the rectangles are the same size) and add together the products. I've named the cell range B4:E6 as *costs* and the changing-cells range (B10:E12) as *shipped*. Therefore, our total shipping and production cost is computed in cell B18 with the formula *SUMPRODUCT(costs,shipped)*.

To express our constraints, we first compute the total shipped from each supply point. By entering the formula *SUM(B10:E10)* in cell F10, we compute the total number of pounds shipped from Los Angeles as *(LA shipped to East) + (LA shipped to Midwest) + (LA shipped to South) + (LA shipped to West)*. Copying this formula to F11:F12 computes the total shipped from Atlanta and New York City. Later I'll add constraints (called *supply constraints*) that ensure the amount shipped from each location does not exceed the plant's capacity.

Next I compute the total received by each demand point. I begin by entering in cell B13 the formula *SUM(B10:B12)*. This formula computes the total number of pounds received in the East as *(Pounds shipped from LA to East) + (Pounds shipped from Atlanta to East) + (Pounds shipped from New York City to East)*. By copying this formula from B13 to C13:E13, I compute the pounds of the drug received by the Midwest, South, and West regions. Later, I'll add constraints (called *demand constraints*) that ensure that each region receives the amount of the drug it requires.

We now open the Solver Parameters dialog box (click Tools, Solver) and fill it in as shown in Figure 26-2.

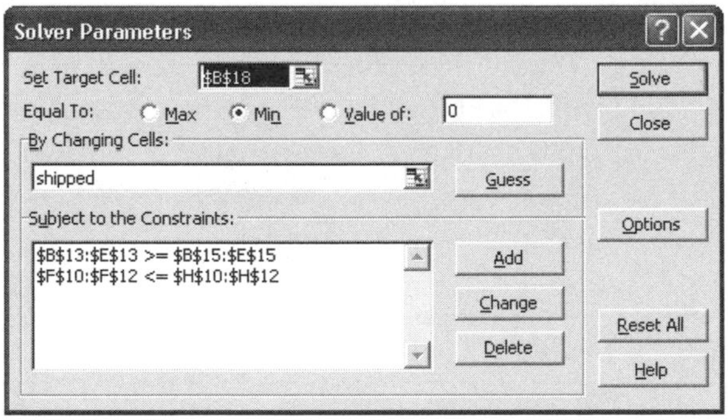

Figure 26-2   The Solver set up to answer our transportation example.

We want to minimize total shipping cost (computed in cell B18). Our changing cells are the number of pounds shipped from each plant to each region of the country. (These amounts are listed in the range named *shipped*, consisting of cells B10:E12.) The constraint *F10:F12<=H10:H12* (the supply constraint) ensures that the amount sent from each plant does not exceed its capacity. The constraint *B13:E13>=B15:E15* (the demand constraint) ensures that each region receives at least the amount of the drug it needs.

Our model is a linear Solver model because our target cell is created by adding together terms of the form *(changing cell)*(constant)* and both our supply and demand constraints are created by comparing the sum of changing cells to a constant.

I now click Options in the Solver Parameters dialog box and check the Assume Linear Model and Assume Non-Negative options. After clicking Solve in the Solver Parameters dialog box, we're presented with the optimal solution shown earlier in Figure 26-1. The minimum cost of meeting customer demand is $86,800. This minimum cost can be achieved if the company uses the following production and shipping schedule:

- Ship 10,000 pounds from Los Angeles to the West region.

- Ship 3000 pounds from Atlanta to the West region and from Atlanta to the Midwest region. Ship 6000 pounds from Atlanta to the South region.

- Ship 9000 pounds from New York City to the East region and 3000 pounds from New York City to the Midwest region.

Problems

1. The distances between Boston, Chicago, Dallas, Los Angeles, and Miami are given in the following table. Each city needs 40,000 kilowatt hours (kwh) of power, and Chicago, Dallas, and Miami are capable of producing 70,000 kwh. Assume that shipping 1000 kwh over 100 miles costs $4.00. From where should power be sent to minimize the cost of meeting each city's demand?

	Boston	**Chicago**	**Dallas**	**LA**	**Miami**
Chicago	983	0	1205	2112	1390
Dallas	1815	1205	0	801	1332
Miami	1539	1390	1332	2757	0

2. What would be the optimal solution to our drug company example if New York's capacity were 5000 pounds?

3. We produce drugs at several locations and sell them at several locations. The decision of where to produce goods for each sales location can have a huge impact on profitability. Our model is similar to the model used in this chapter to determine where drugs should be produced. We're using the following assumptions:

❑ We produce drugs at six locations and sell to customers in six different areas.

❑ Tax rate and variable production cost depend on the location where the drug is produced. For example, any units produced at Location 3 cost $6.00 per unit to produce and profits from these goods are taxed at 20 percent.

❑ The sales price of each good depends on the place where the good is sold. For example, each product sold in Location 2 is sold for $40.00.

Production Location	1	2	3	4	5	6
Sales price	$45	$40	$38	$36	$39	$34
Tax rate	30%	40%	20%	40%	35%	18%
Variable production cost	$8	$7	$6	$9	$7.	$7

❑ Each of our six plants can produce up to 6,000,000 units per year.

❑ The annual demand (in millions) for our product in each location is as follows:

Sales Location	1	2	3	4	5	6
Demand	1	2	3	4	5	6

❑ The unit shipping cost depends on the plant where the product is produced and the location where the product is sold.

	Sold 1	Sold 2	Sold 3	Sold 4	Sold 5	Sold 6
Made 1	$3	$4	$5	$6	$7	$8
Made 2	$5	$2	$6	$9	$10	$11
Made 3	$4	$3	$1	$6	$8	$6
Made 4	$5	$5	$7	$2	$5	$5
Made 5	$6	$9	$6	$5	$3	$7
Made 6	$7	$7	$8	$9	$10	$4

For example, if we produce a unit at Plant 1 and sell it in Location 3, it costs $5 to ship it.

How can we maximize after-tax profit with our limited production capacity?

4. Suppose that each day, northern, central, and southern California each use 100 billion gallons of water. Also assume that northern California and central California have available 120 billion gallons of water, while southern California has 40 billion gallons of water available. The cost of shipping one billion gallons of water between the three regions is as follows:

	Northern	**Central**	**Southern**
Northern	$5,000	$7,000	$10,000
Central	$7,000	$5,000	$6,000
Southern	$10,0000	$6,000	$5,000

We will not be able to meet all demand for water, so we assume that each billion gallons of unmet demand incurs the following shortage costs:

	Northern	**Central**	**Southern**
Shortage cost/billion gallons short	$6,000	$5,500	$9,000

How should California's water be distributed to minimize the sum of shipping and shortage costs?

27

Using Solver to Schedule Your Workforce

■ How can I efficiently schedule my workforce to meet labor demands?

Many organizations (banks, restaurants, postal services) know what their labor requirements will be at different times and need a method to efficiently schedule their workforce to meet their labor requirements. You can use the Excel Solver to easily address a problem such as this. Here's an example.

How can I efficiently schedule my workforce to meet labor demands?
Bank 24 processes checks 7 days a week. The number of workers needed each day to process checks is given in row 14 of the file Bank24.xls, which is shown in Figure 27-1. For example, 13 workers are needed on Tuesday, 15 workers are needed on Wednesday, and so on. All bank employees work five consecutive days. What is the minimum number of employees Bank 24 can have and still meet its labor requirements?

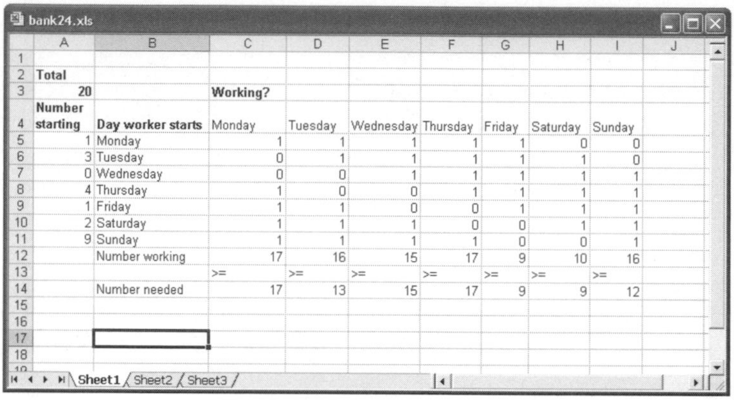

	A	B	C	D	E	F	G	H	I	J
1										
2	**Total**									
3	**20**		**Working?**							
4	**Number starting**	**Day worker starts**	Monday	Tuesday	Wednesday	Thursday	Friday	Saturday	Sunday	
5	1	Monday	1	1	1	1	1	0	0	
6	3	Tuesday	0	1	1	1	1	1	0	
7	0	Wednesday	0	0	1	1	1	1	1	
8	4	Thursday	1	0	0	1	1	1	1	
9	1	Friday	1	1	0	0	1	1	1	
10	2	Saturday	1	1	1	0	0	1	1	
11	9	Sunday	1	1	1	1	0	0	1	
12		Number working	17	16	15	17	9	10	16	
13			>=	>=	>=	>=	>=	>=	>=	
14		Number needed	17	13	15	17	9	9	12	
15										
16										
17										
18										

Figure 27-1 The data we'll use to work through the bank workforce scheduling problem.

We begin by identifying the target cell, changing cells, and constraints for our Solver model.

- **Target cell** Minimize total number of employees.
- **Changing cells** Number of employees who start work (the first of five consecutive days) each day of the week. Each changing cell must be a nonnegative integer.
- **Constraints** For each day of the week, the number of employees who are working must be greater than or equal to the number of employees required. *(Number of employees working)>=(Needed employees.)*

To set up our model, we need to track the number of employees working each day. I began by entering trial values for the number of employees who start their five-day shift each day in the cell range A5:A11. For example, in A5, I entered 1, indicating that 1 employee begins work on Monday and works Monday through Friday. I entered each day's required workers in the range C14:I14.

To track the number of employees working each day, I entered in each cell in the range C5:I11 a 1 or a 0. The value 1 in a cell indicates that the employees who started working on the day designated in the cell's row are working on the day associated with the cell's column. For example, the 1 in cell G5 indicates that employees who started working on Monday are working on Friday; the 0 in cell H5 indicates that the employees who started working on Monday are not working on Saturday.

By copying from C12 to D12:I12 the formula *SUMPRODUCT($A$5:$A$11, C5:C11)*, I compute the number of employees working each day. For example, in cell C12 this formula evaluates to *A5+A8+A9+A10+A11*, which equals *(Number starting on Monday) + (Number starting on Thursday) + (Number starting on Friday) + (Number starting on Saturday) + (Number starting on Sunday)*. This total is indeed the number of people working on Monday.

After computing the total number of employees in cell A3 with the formula *SUM(A5:A11)*, I can enter our model in Solver as shown in Figure 27-2.

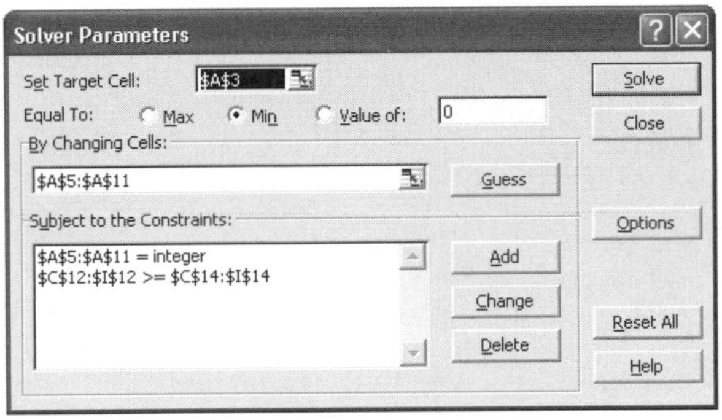

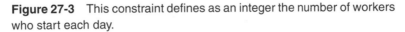

Figure 27-2   The Solver Parameters dialog box filled in to solve the bank workforce problem.

In the target cell (A3), we want to minimize the number of total employees. The constraint *C12:I12>=C14:I14* ensures that the number of employees working each day is at least as large as the number needed each day. The constraint *A5:A11 = integer* ensures that the number of employees beginning work each day is an integer. To add this constraint, I clicked Add in the Solver Parameters dialog box and filled in the Add Constraint dialog box as shown in Figure 27-3.

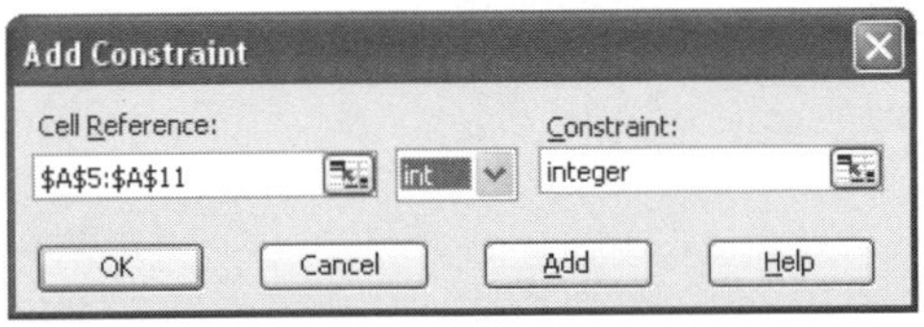

Figure 27-3   This constraint defines as an integer the number of workers who start each day.

I also selected the options Assume Linear Model and Assume Non-Negative for the changing cells by clicking Options in the Solver Parameters dialog box and then checking these options in the Solver Options dialog box. After clicking Solve, we find the optimal solution that's shown earlier in Figure 27-1.

A total of 20 employees is needed. One employee starts on Monday, 3 start on Tuesday, 0 start on Wednesday, 4 start on Thursday, 1 starts on Friday, 2 start on Saturday, and 9 start on Sunday.

Note that this model is linear because the target cell is created by adding together changing cells and the constraint is created by comparing the result obtained by adding together the product of each changing cell times a constant (either 1 or 0) to the required number of workers.

Problems

1. Suppose our bank had 22 employees and that their goal was to schedule employees so that they would have the maximum number of weekend days off. How should the workers be scheduled?

2. Suppose Bank 24 employees are paid $150 per day the first 5 days they work and can work a day of overtime at a cost of $350. How should the bank schedule its employees?

3. The number of telephone reservation operators needed by an airline during each time of day is as follows:

Time	Operators Needed
Midnight–4 A.M.	12
4 A.M.–8 A.M.	16
8 A.M.–Noon	22
Noon–4 P.M.	27
4 P.M.–8 P.M.	31
8 P.M.–Midnight	22

Each operator works one of the following 6-hour shifts: midnight–6 A.M., 6 A.M.–noon, noon–6 P.M., 6 P.M.–midnight. What is the minimum number of operators needed?

4. Shown below are the number of people in different demographic groups who watch various TV shows and the cost (in thousands of dollars) of placing a 30-second ad with each show. For example, it costs $160,000 to place a 30-second ad on *Friends*. The show is watched by 6 million males between the ages 18 and 35, 3 million males between 36 and 55, 1 million males over 55, 9 million women between 18 and 35, 4 million women between 36 and 55,

and 2 million women over 55. The data also includes the number of people in each group (in millions) that we want to see the ad. For example, the advertiser wants at least 60 million 18 to 35 year old males to see its ads. What is the cheapest way to meet our goals?

	D	E	F	G	H	I	J	K
1								
2	000	Needed	60	60	28	60	60	28
3	Cost		Male 18-35	Male 36-55	Male >55	Women 18-35	Women 36-55	Women >55
4	160	Friends	6	3	1	9	4	2
5	100	MNF	6	5	3	1	1	1
6	80	Malcolm in Middle	5	2	0	4	2	0
7	9	Sports Center	0.5	0.5	0.3	0.1	0.1	0
8	13	MTV	0.7	0.2	0	0.9	0.1	0
9	15	Lifetime	0.1	0.1	0	0.6	1.3	0.4
10	8	CNN	0.1	0.2	0.3	0.1	0.2	0.3
11	85	JAG	1	2	4	1	3	4

28

Using Solver for Capital Budgeting

■ How can a company use Solver to determine which projects it should undertake?

Each year, a company such as Eli Lilly needs to determine which drugs to develop; a company like Microsoft, which software programs to develop; a company like Proctor and Gamble, which new consumer products to develop. Excel's Solver can help a company make these decisions.

How can a company use Solver to determine which projects it should undertake?

Most corporations want to undertake projects that contribute the greatest net present value (NPV), subject to limited resources (usually capital and labor). Let's say that Microsoft is trying to determine which of 20 software projects it should undertake. The NPV (in millions of dollars) contributed by each project as well as the capital (in millions of dollars) and the number of programmers needed during each of the next three years is given on the worksheet named Basic Model in the file CapBudget.xls, which is shown in Figure 28-1. For example, project 2 yields $908 million. It requires $151 million during year 1, $269 million during year 2, and $248 million during year 3. Project 2 requires 139 programmers during year 1, 86 programmers during year 2, and 83 programmers during year 3. (In the file CapBudget.xls, I've hidden the information for projects 14–18 by selecting rows 19–23 and then choosing Format, Row Hide. To display these rows again, select rows 19–23 and then choose Format, Row Unhide.) Cells E4:G4 show the capital (in millions of dollars) available during each of the next three years, and cells H4:J4 indicate how many programmers are available. For example, during year 1 up to $2.5 billion in capital and 900 programmers are available.

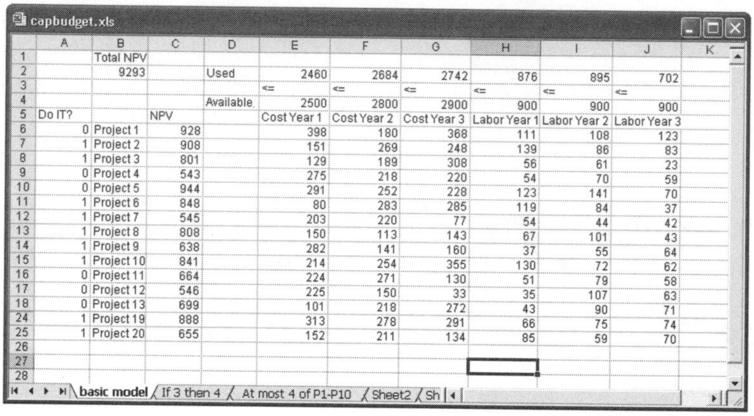

	A	B	C	D	E	F	G	H	I	J	K
1		Total NPV									
2		9293		Used	2460	2684	2742	876	895	702	
3					<=	<=	<=	<=	<=	<=	
4				Available	2500	2800	2900	900	900	900	
5	Do IT?		NPV		Cost Year 1	Cost Year 2	Cost Year 3	Labor Year 1	Labor Year 2	Labor Year 3	
6	0	Project 1	928		398	180	368	111	108	123	
7	1	Project 2	908		151	269	248	139	86	83	
8	1	Project 3	801		129	189	308	56	61	23	
9	0	Project 4	543		275	218	220	54	70	59	
10	0	Project 5	944		291	252	228	123	141	70	
11	1	Project 6	848		80	283	285	119	84	37	
12	1	Project 7	545		203	220	77	54	44	42	
13	1	Project 8	808		150	113	143	67	101	43	
14	1	Project 9	638		282	141	160	37	55	64	
15	1	Project 10	841		214	254	355	130	72	62	
16	0	Project 11	664		224	271	130	51	79	58	
17	0	Project 12	546		225	150	33	35	107	63	
18	0	Project 13	699		101	218	272	43	90	71	
24	1	Project 19	888		313	278	291	66	75	74	
25	1	Project 20	655		152	211	134	85	59	70	
26											
27											
28											

Figure 28-1 Data we will use with Solver to determine which projects Microsoft should select.

For each project, Microsoft must decide whether it should undertake the project. Let's assume that we can't undertake a fraction of a software project; if we allocate .5 of the needed resources, for example, we would have a non-working program that would bring us $0 revenue!

The trick in modeling situations in which you either do or don't do something is to use *binary changing cells*. A binary changing cell always equals 0 or 1. When a binary changing cell that corresponds to a project equals 1, we do the project. If a binary changing cell that corresponds to a project equals 0, we don't do the project. You set up Solver to use a range of binary changing cells by adding a constraint—select the changing cells you want to use and then choose Bin from the drop-down list in the Add Constraint dialog box.

With this background, we're ready to solve Microsoft's project selection problem. As always with a Solver model, we begin by identifying our target cell, changing cells, and constraints.

- **Target cell** Maximize the NPV generated by selected projects.
- **Changing cells** A 0 or 1 binary changing cell for each project. I've located these cells in the range A6:A25 (and named the range *doit*). For example, a 1 in cell A6 indicates that we undertake project 1; a 0 in cell C6 indicates that we don't undertake project 1.
- **Constraints** We need to ensure that for each year t (t = 1, 2, 3), year t capital used is less than or equal to year t capital available, and year t labor used is less than or equal to year t labor available.

As you can see, our spreadsheet must compute for any selection of projects the NPV, the capital used annually, and the programmers used each year. In cell B2, I use the formula *SUMPRODUCT(doit,NPV)* to compute the total NPV generated by selected projects. (The range name *NPV* refers to the range C6:C25.) For every project with a 1 in column A, this formula picks up the NPV of the project, and for every project with a 0 in column A, this formula does not pick up the NPV of the project. Therefore, we're able to compute the NPV of all projects and our target cell is linear because it is computed by summing terms that follow the form *(changing cell)*(constant)*. In a similar fashion, I compute the capital used each year and the labor used each year by copying from E2 to F2:J2 the formula *SUMPRODUCT(doit,E6:E25)*.

I now fill in the Solver Parameters dialog box as shown in Figure 28-2.

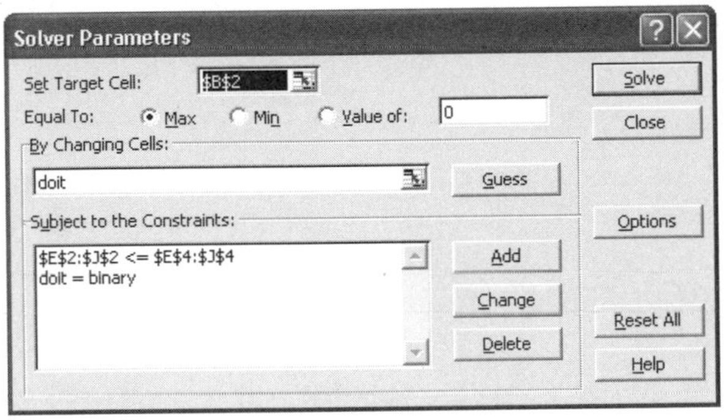

Figure 28-2   The Solver Parameters dialog box set up for the project selection model.

Our goal is to maximize NPV of selected projects (cell B2). Our changing cells (the range named *doit*) are the binary changing cells for each project. The constraint *E2:J2<=E4:J4* ensures that during each year the capital and labor used are less than or equal to the capital and labor available. To add the constraint that makes the changing cells binary, I click Add in the Solver Parameters dialog box and then select Bin from the drop-down list in the middle of the dialog box. The Add Constraint dialog box should appear as it's shown in Figure 28-3.

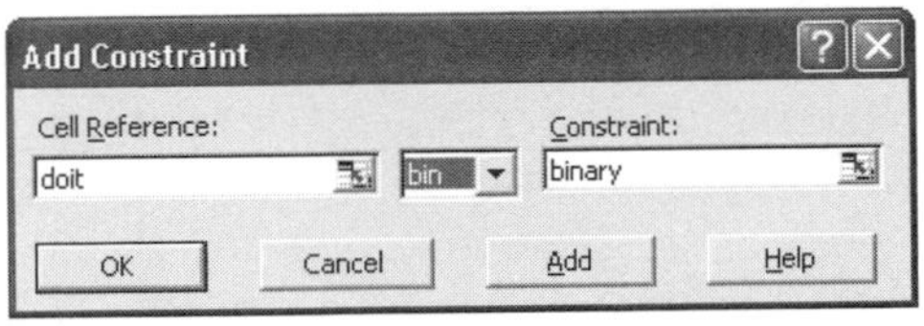

Figure 28-3   Use the Bin option in the Add Constraint dialog box to set up binary changing cells—cells that will display either a 0 or a 1.

Our model is linear because the target cell is computed as the sum of terms that have the form *(changing cell)*(constant)* and because the resource usage constraints are computed by comparing the sum of *(changing cells)*(constants)* to a constant.

With the Solver Parameters dialog box filled in, click Solve and we have the results shown earlier in Figure 28-1. Microsoft can obtain a maximum NPV of $9,293 million ($9.293 billion) by choosing projects 2, 3, 6–10, 14–16, 19, and 20.

Handling Other Constraints

Sometimes project-selection models have other constraints. For example, suppose that if we select project 3, we must also select project 4. Because our current optimal solution selects project 3 but not project 4, we know that our current solution can't remain optimal. To solve this problem, simply add the constraint that the binary changing cell for project 3 is less than or equal to the binary changing cell for project 4.

You can find this example on the worksheet named IF 3 Then 4 in the file CapBudget.xls, which is shown in Figure 28-4. Cell L9 refers to the binary value related to project 3, and cell L12 to the binary value related to project 4. By adding the constraint *L9<=L12*, if we choose project 3, L9 equals 1 and our constraint forces L12 (the project 4 binary) to equal 1. Our constraint must also leave the binary value in project 4's changing cell unrestricted if we do not select project 3. If we do not select project 3, L9 equals 0 and our constraint allows the project 4 binary to equal 0 or 1, which is what we want. The new optimal solution is shown in Figure 28-4.

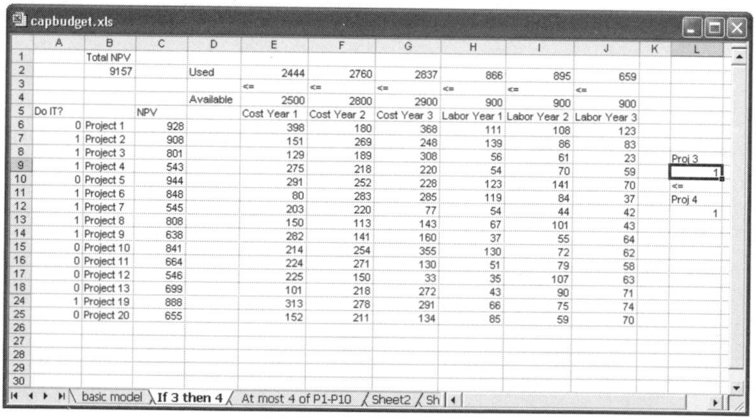

	A	B	C	D	E	F	G	H	I	J	K	L
1		Total NPV										
2		9157		Used	2444	2760	2837	866	895	659		
3					<=	<=	<=	<=	<=	<=		
4				Available	2500	2800	2900	900	900	900		
5	Do IT?		NPV		Cost Year 1	Cost Year 2	Cost Year 3	Labor Year 1	Labor Year 2	Labor Year 3		
6	0	Project 1	928		398	180	368	111	108	123		
7	1	Project 2	908		151	269	248	139	86	83		
8	1	Project 3	801		129	189	308	56	61	23		Proj 3
9	1	Project 4	543		275	218	220	54	70	59		1
10	0	Project 5	944		291	252	228	123	141	70		<=
11	1	Project 6	848		80	283	285	119	84	37		Proj 4
12	1	Project 7	545		203	220	77	54	44	42		1
13	1	Project 8	808		150	113	143	67	101	43		
14	1	Project 9	638		282	141	160	37	55	64		
15	0	Project 10	841		214	254	355	130	72	62		
16	0	Project 11	664		224	271	130	51	79	58		
17	0	Project 12	546		225	150	33	35	107	63		
18	0	Project 13	699		101	218	272	43	90	71		
24	1	Project 19	888		313	278	291	66	75	74		
25	0	Project 20	655		152	211	134	85	59	70		
26												
27												
28												
29												
30												

Figure 28-4 A new optimal solution is calculated if selecting project 3 means we must also select project 4.

Now suppose that we can do only four projects from among projects 1 through 10. (See the worksheet titled At Most 4 Of P1-P10, shown in Figure 28-5.) In cell L8, we compute the sum of the binary values associated with projects 1 through 10 with the formula *SUM(A6:A15)*. Then we add the constraint *L8<=L10*, which ensures that at most 4 of the first 10 projects are selected. The new optimal solution is shown in Figure 28-5. The NPV has dropped to $9.014 billion.

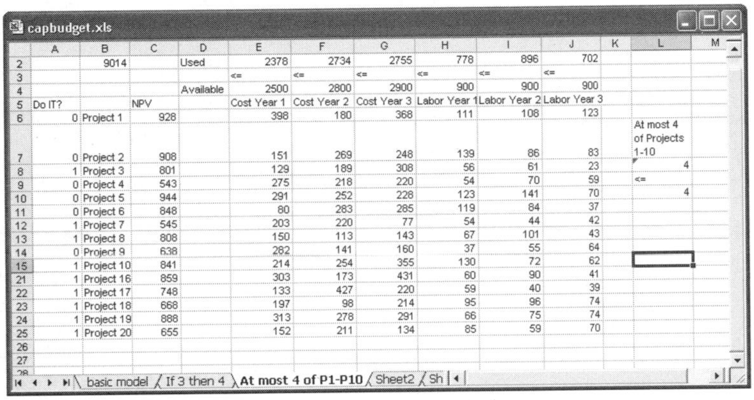
capbudget.xls

	A	B	C	D	E	F	G	H	I	J	K	L	M
2		9014		Used	2378	2734	2755	778	896	702			
3					<=	<=	<=	<=	<=	<=			
4				Available	2500	2800	2900	900	900	900			
5	Do IT?		NPV		Cost Year 1	Cost Year 2	Cost Year 3	Labor Year 1	Labor Year 2	Labor Year 3			
6	0	Project 1	928		398	180	368	111	108	123			
7	0	Project 2	908		151	269	248	139	86	83		At most 4 of Projects 1-10	
8	1	Project 3	801		129	189	308	56	61	23		4	
9	0	Project 4	543		275	218	220	54	70	59		<=	
10	0	Project 5	944		291	252	228	123	141	70		4	
11	0	Project 6	848		80	283	285	119	84	37			
12	1	Project 7	545		203	220	77	54	44	42			
13	1	Project 8	808		150	113	143	67	101	43			
14	0	Project 9	638		282	141	160	37	55	64			
15	1	Project 10	841		214	254	355	130	72	62			
21	1	Project 16	859		303	173	431	60	90	41			
22	1	Project 17	748		133	427	220	59	40	39			
23	1	Project 18	668		197	98	214	95	96	74			
24	1	Project 19	888		313	278	291	66	75	74			
25	1	Project 20	655		152	211	134	85	59	70			
26													
27													

basic model / If 3 then 4 / At most 4 of P1-P10 / Sheet2 / Sh

Figure 28-5 The optimal solution when we can select only four projects from projects 1–10.

Problems

1. A company has nine projects under consideration. The NPV added by each project and the capital required by each project during the next two years is shown in the following table. (All numbers are in millions.) For example, project 1 will add $14 million in NPV and require expenditures of $12 million during year 1 and $3 million during year 2. $50 million is available for projects during year 1, and $20 million is available during year 2.

	NPV	Year 1 Expenditure	Year 2 Expenditure
Project 1	14	12	3
Project 2	17	54	7
Project 3	17	6	6
Project 4	15	6	2
Project 5	40	30	35

	NPV	Year 1 Expenditure	Year 2 Expenditure
Project 6	12	6	6
Project 7	14	48	4
Project 8	10	36	3
Project 9	12	18	3

❑   If we can't undertake a fraction of a project but must undertake all of a project or none of a project, how can we maximize NPV?

❑   Suppose that if project 4 is undertaken, project 5 must be undertaken. How can we maximize NPV?

2.   Microsoft Press is trying to determine which of 36 books it should publish this year. The file PressData.xls gives the following information about each book:

❑   Projected revenue and development costs (in thousands of dollars)

❑   Pages in each book

❑   Whether book is geared toward audience of software developers (indicated by a 1 in column E)

Microsoft Press can publish books totaling up to 8500 pages this year and must publish at least 4 books geared toward software developers. How can Microsoft Press maximize its profit?

Using Solver for Financial Planning

- Can I use Solver to check out the accuracy of the Excel PMT function or to determine mortgage payments for a variable interest rate?

- Can I use Solver to determine how much money I need to save for retirement?

The Excel Solver can be a powerful tool for analyzing financial planning problems. In many financial planning problems, a quantity such as the unpaid balance on a loan or the amount of money needed for retirement changes over time. For example, consider a situation in which you borrow money. Because only the noninterest portion of each monthly payment reduces the unpaid loan balance, we know that the following equation (which I'll refer to as equation 1) is true.

```
(Unpaid loan balance at end  of period t) = (Unpaid loan balance at beginning
of period t) - [(Month t payment)-(Month t interest paid)]
```

Now suppose that you are saving for retirement. Until you retire, you deposit at the beginning of each period (let's say periods equal years) an amount of money in your retirement account, and during the year, your retirement fund is invested and receives a return of some percentage. During retirement, you withdraw money at the beginning of each year and your retirement fund still receives an investment return. We know that the following equation (equation 2) describes the relationship between contributions, withdrawals, and return.

```
(Retirement savings at end of year t + 1) = (Retirement savings at end of year
t + retirement contribution at beginning of year t+1 -
 Year t + 1 retirement withdrawal)*(Investment return earned during year t + 1)
```

Combining basic relationships such as these with Solver enables you to answer a myriad of interesting financial planning problems.

Can I use Solver to check out the accuracy of the Excel PMT function or to determine mortgage payments for a variable interest rate?

Recall that in Chapter 10, we found the monthly payment (assuming payments occur at the end of a month) on a 10-month loan for $8000 at an annual interest rate of 10 percent to be $1,037.03. Could we have used Solver to determine our monthly payment? You'll find the answer in the worksheet named PMT By Solver in the file FinMathSolver.xls, which is shown in Figure 29-1.

	A	B	C	D	E	F	G	H	I
1			rate	0.006667					
2									
3		From PMT function	$1,037.03						
4	Month	Beginning Balance	Payment	Interest Owed	Ending Balance				
5	1	$ 10,000.00	$ 1,037.03	$ 66.67	$9,029.63				
6	2	$ 9,029.63	$ 1,037.03	$ 60.20	$8,052.80				
7	3	$ 8,052.80	$ 1,037.03	$ 53.69	$7,069.45				
8	4	$ 7,069.45	$ 1,037.03	$ 47.13	$6,079.55				
9	5	$ 6,079.55	$ 1,037.03	$ 40.53	$5,083.05				
10	6	$ 5,083.05	$ 1,037.03	$ 33.89	$4,079.90				
11	7	$ 4,079.90	$ 1,037.03	$ 27.20	$3,070.07				
12	8	$ 3,070.07	$ 1,037.03	$ 20.47	$2,053.51				
13	9	$ 2,053.51	$ 1,037.03	$ 13.69	$1,030.16				
14	10	$ 1,030.16	$ 1,037.03	$ 6.87	$ 0.00				
15									
16									
17									

Figure 29-1 The Solver model for calculating the monthly payment for a loan.

The key to our model is to use equation 1 to track the monthly beginning balance. Our Solver target cell is to minimize our monthly payment. The changing cell is the monthly payment. The only constraint is that the ending balance in month 10 equal 0.

I entered the beginning balance in cell B5. I entered a trial monthly payment in cell C5. Then I copied the monthly payment to the range C6:C14. Because we've assumed that the payments occur at the end of each month, interest is incurred on the balance at the beginning of the month. Our monthly interest rate (I've named cell D1 *rate*) is computed in D1 by dividing the annual rate of .08 by 12. The interest paid each month is computed by copying from cell D5 to D6:D14 the formula *rate*B5*. Each month, this formula computes the interest as *.006666 *(month's beginning balance)*. By copying the formula *(B5-(Payment-D5))* from cell E5 to the range E6:E14, we use equation 1 to compute each month's ending balance. Because *(Month t + 1 beginning balance)* = *(Month t ending balance)*, we compute each month's beginning balance by copying from cell B6 to B7:B14 the formula *=E5*.

We are now ready to use Solver to determine our monthly payment. To see how I've set up the Solver window, take a look at Figure 29-2.

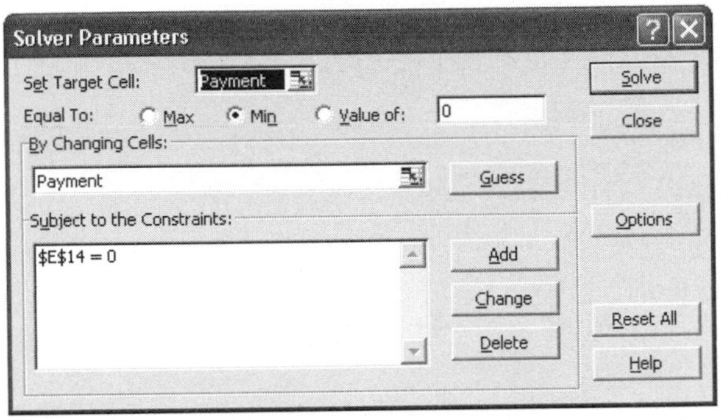

Figure 29-2   The Solver window set up to determine mortgage payments.

Our goal is to minimize the monthly payment (cell C5). Note that the changing cell is the same as the target cell. The only constraint is that the ending balance for month 10 equal 0. Adding this constraint ensures that the loan is paid off. After we check the Assume Linear Model option and the Assume Non-Negative changing cells option (these options appear in the Solver Options dialog box; click Options in the Solver Parameters dialog box to select these options), the Solver calculates a payment of $1,037.03, which matches the amount calculated by the Excel PMT function.

This model is linear because the target cell equals the changing cell and the constraint is created by adding multiples of changing cells.

Can I use Solver to determine how much money I need to save for retirement?

By using equation 2 (shown earlier in the chapter), we can easily determine how much money a person needs to save for retirement. Here's an example.

I am planning for my retirement, and at the beginning of this year and each of the next 39 years, I'm going to contribute some money to my retirement fund. Each year I plan to increase my retirement contribution by $500. When I retire in 40 years, I plan to withdraw (at the beginning of each year) $100,000 per year for 20 years. I've made the following assumptions about the yields for my retirement investment portfolio:

- During the first 20 years of my investing, the investments will earn 10 percent per year.

- During all other years, my investments will earn 5 percent per year.

I've assumed that all contributions and withdrawals occur at the beginning of the year. Given these assumptions, what is the least amount of money I can contribute this year and still have enough to make my retirement withdrawals?

You can find the solution to this question on the worksheet named Retire in the file FinMathSolver.xls, shown in Figure 29-3. Note that I've hidden many rows in the model.

	A	B	C	D	E	F	G	H	I	J
1										
2										
3										
4										
5	Year	Initial balance	Contribution	Return	Withdrawal	Ending Balance				
6	1	0	1387.86809	10%	0	1526.655				
7	2	1526.655	1887.86809	10%	0	3755.975				
8	3	3755.975	2387.86809	10%	0	6758.228				
44	39	1146596	20387.8681	5%	0	1225333				
45	40	1225333	20887.8681	5%	0	1308532				
46	41	1308532		5%	100000	1268959				
47	42	1268959		5%	100000	1227407				
62	57	372324.8		5%	100000	285941				
63	58	285941		5%	100000	195238.1				
64	59	195238.1		5%	100000	100000				
65	60	100000		5%	100000	6.87E-07				
66										

Figure 29-3 Retirement planning data that can be set up for analysis with Solver.

This worksheet simply tracks my retirement balance during each of the next 60 years. Each year I earn the indicated interest rate on the retirement balance. I begin by entering a trial value for my year 1 payment in cell C6. Copying the formula $C6+500$ from cell C7 to C8:C45 ensures that the retirement contribution increases by $500 per year during years 2–40. I've entered in column D the assumed return on my investments for each of the next 60 years. In cells E46:E65, I've entered the annual $100,000 withdrawal for years 41–60. Copying the formula $(B6+C6-E6)*(1+D6)$ from F6 to F7:F65 uses equation 2 to compute each year's ending retirement account balance. Copying the formula =F6 from cell B7 to B8:B65 computes the beginning balance for years 2–60. Of course, the year 1 initial balance is 0.

The Solver Parameters dialog box for this model is shown in Figure 29-4. We want to minimize our year 1 contribution (cell C6). The changing cell is also our year 1 contribution (cell C6). We make sure that we never run out of money during retirement by adding the constraint $F46:F65>=0$. This formula ensures that the ending balance for years 41–60 is nonnegative.

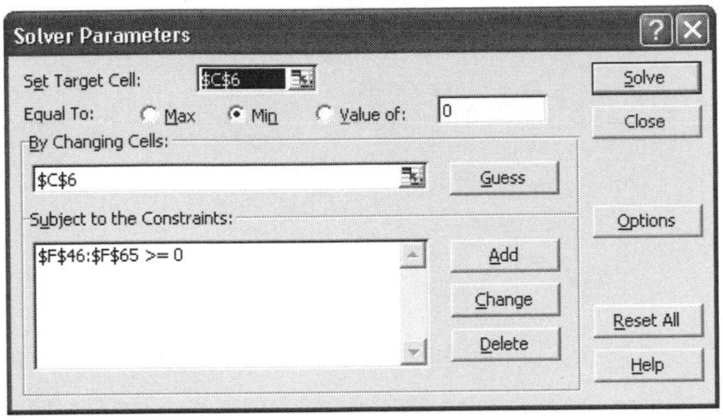

Figure 29-4   Solver Parameters dialog box set up for the retirement problem.

After checking the Assume Linear Model and Assume Non-Negative options and clicking Solve, we find that our first year's contribution should equal $1,387.87.

This model is linear because the target cell equals the changing cell and our constraint is created by adding multiples of changing cells. Note that because the return on the investments is not the same each year, there is no easy way to use Excel financial functions to solve this problem. Solver provides a general framework that can be used to analyze financial planning problems when mortgage rates or investment returns are not constant.

Problems

1. I am borrowing $15,000 for a new car. I am going to make 60 end-of-month payments. The annual interest rate on the loan is 10 percent. The car dealer is a friend of mine, and he will allow me to make the monthly payment for months 1–30 equal one-half the payment for months 31–60. What is the payment during each month?

2. Solve the retirement planning problem assuming that withdrawals occur at the end of each year and contributions occur at the beginning of each year.

3. Solve our mortgage example assuming that payments are made at the beginning of each month.

4. In the retirement planning example, suppose that during year 1, our salary is $40,000 and our salary increases 5 percent per year until retirement. We want to save the same percentage of our salary each year we work. What percentage of our salary should we save?

5. In the mortgage example, suppose that we want our monthly payment to increase by $50 each month. What should each month's payment be?

30

Using Solver to Rate Sports Teams

■ Can I use Excel to set NFL point spreads?

Many of us follow basketball, football, hockey, and baseball. Bookmakers set point spreads on games in all these sports and others. For example, the bookmakers' best guess was that the Oakland Raiders would win the 2003 Super Bowl by 3 points. How can you use Excel to come up with team "ratings" that generate reasonable point spreads?

Using a simple Solver model, you can generate reasonable point spreads. The changing cells for the Solver model will be a rating for each team and the size of the home field advantage. For example, if the Indianapolis Colts have a rating of +5 and the New York Jets have a rating of +7, the Jets are considered 2 points better than the Colts.

With regard to the home field edge, in most years, professional football teams tend to win by an average of 3 points (while home college basketball teams tend to win by an average of 5 points). We can define the outcome of an NFL game to be the number of points by which the home team outscores the visitors. We can predict the outcome of each game by using the following equation (which I'll refer to as equation 1).

```
(Predicted points by which home team outscores visitors) = (Home team rating) -
  (Visiting team rating) + (Home field edge)
```

For example, if the home field edge equals 3 points, when the Colts host the Jets, the Colts will be a 1 point favorite (5 + 3 − 7). If the Jets host the Colts, the Jets will be a 5 point favorite (7 − 5 + 3).

What target cell will yield "good" ratings? Our goal is to find the set of values for team ratings and home field edge that best predict the outcome of all games. In short, we want the prediction for each game to be as close as possible to the outcome of each game. This suggests that we want to minimize the sum over all games of *(Actual outcome) – (Predicted outcome)*. The problem with using this target is that positive and negative prediction errors cancel each other out. For example, if we overpredict the home team margin by 50 points in one game and underpredict the home team margin by 50 points in another game, our target cell would yield a value of 0, indicating perfect accuracy when in fact we were off by 50 points a game. We can remedy this problem by minimizing the sum over all games by using *[(Actual Outcome) – (Predicted Outcome)]²*. Now positive and negative errors will not cancel each other out.

Can I use Excel to set NFL point spreads?

Let's now see how to determine accurate ratings for NFL teams by using the scores from the 2002–2003 regular season. You can find the data for this problem in the file NFL2002Ratings.xls, which is shown in Figure 30-1. Note that I've hidden the ratings of some teams so that the ratings and model would fit in a single screen.

	B	C	D	E	F	G	H	I	J	K
1		Rating			Home edge					
2	1	Ari	-9.88976		2.246094					
3	2	Atl	5.058158							
4	3	Balt	-2.11788							
5	4	Buff	-0.27413							
6	5	Carolina	-3.27205							
11	10	Den	4.890103							
12	11	Det	-9.17275							
24	23	Oak	10.63524		Oakland by 2. We all make					
30	29	Seattle	-1.25121							
31	30	Tampa	8.801907							
32	31	Tenn	1.764062							
33	32	Wash	-4.45295						SSE	
34		mean	-1E-06						35330.58	
35	game#	H	A	HS	AS	Home Marg	Prediction	Error	Sq Err	
36	1	21	28	13	16	-3	2.438107	-5.43811	29.57301	
37	2	4	22	31	37	-6	-1.19696	-4.80304	23.06918	
38	3	5	3	10	7	3	1.091926	1.908074	3.640745	
39	4	6	18	27	23	4	-0.01016	4.010158	16.08136	
40	5	7	27	6	34	-28	-7.5369	-20.4631	418.7386	

Figure 30-1 The data rating NFL teams that we'll use with Solver.

To begin, I named the range D2:D33, which contains each team's rating, *rating*. I also named (for reasons that will soon become apparent) the range B2:D33 *lookup* and the cell F2 *home_edge*. I placed a trial home-edge value in that cell.

Starting in row 36, columns C and D contain the team code number (listed in B2:B33) for the home and away team for each game. For example, the first game (listed in row 36) is the San Francisco 49ers (team 28) playing at the New York Giants (team 21). Column E contains the home team's score, and column F contains the visiting team's score. As you can see, the 49ers beat the Giants 16-13. I can now compute the outcome of each game (the number of points by which the home team beats the visiting team) by entering the formula *=E36-F36* in cell G36. By pointing to the lower-right portion of this cell and double-clicking the left mouse button, you can copy this formula down to the last game, which appears in row 291. (By the way, an easy way to find the last row of the data is to press Ctrl+Shift +Down Arrow. This key combination takes you to the last row filled with data—row 291 in this case.)

In column H, I use equation 1 to generate the prediction for each game. The prediction for the first game is computed in cell H36 with the formula *Home_edge+VLOOKUP(C36,lookup,3)-VLOOKUP(D36,lookup,3)*. This formula creates a prediction for the first game by adding the home edge to the home team rating and then subtracting the visiting team rating. Note that *VLOOKUP(C36,lookup,3)* locates the home team rating by using the home team code number in column C, while *VLOOKUP(D36,lookup,3)* looks up the visiting team's rating by using the visiting team's code number in column D. (For more information about using lookup functions, see Chapter 3.)

In column I, I compute the error (*actual score – predicted score*) for each game. Our error for the first game is computed in cell I36 with the formula *=G36-H36*. In column J, I compute the squared error for each game. The squared error for the first game is computed in cell J36 with the formula *=I36^2*. After selecting the cell range H36:J36, I copied the formulas down to the bottom of our spreadsheet (H291:J291).

In cell J34, I've computed our target cell by summing all the squared errors with the formula *SUM(J36:J291)*. (You can enter a formula for a large column of numbers such as this by typing *=SUM(* and then selecting the first cell in the range you want to add together. Press Ctrl+Shift+Down Arrow to enter the range from the cell you've selected to the bottom row in the column and then add the closing parenthesis.)

It is convenient to make our average team rating equal to 0. A team with a positive rating is better than average and a team with a negative rating is worse than average. I've computed the average team rating in cell D34 with the formula *AVERAGE(rating)*.

I can now fill in the Solver window as shown in Figure 30-2.

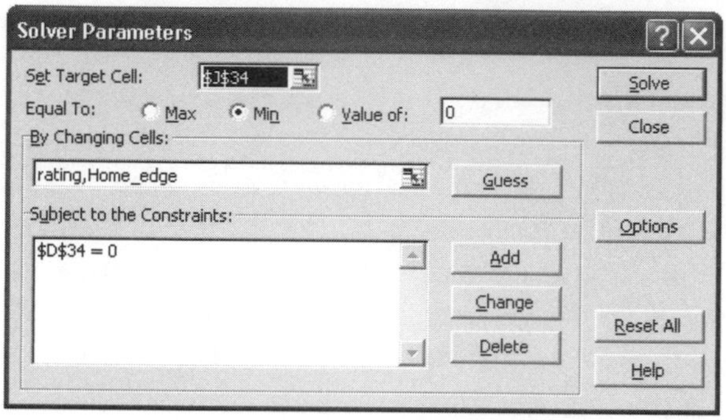

Figure 30-2 The Solver window set up for NFL ratings.

We minimize the sum of our squared prediction errors for all games (computed in cell J34) by changing each team's rating and the home edge. The constraint *D34=0* ensures that the average team rating is 0. From Figure 30-1, we find that the home team has an advantage of 2.25 points over the visiting team. Our 10 highest-rated teams are shown in Figure 30-3.

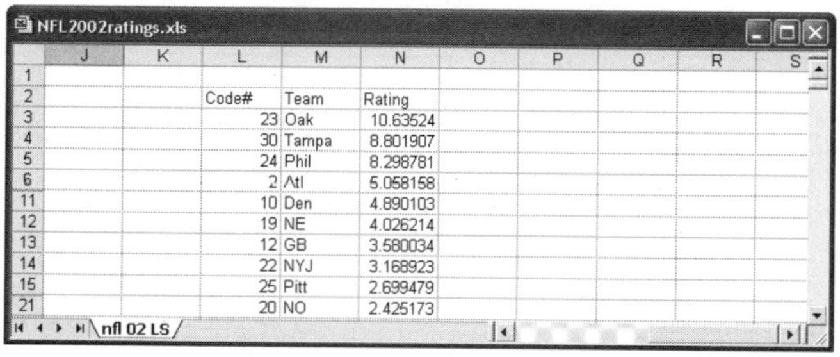

	Code#	Team	Rating
3	23	Oak	10.63524
4	30	Tampa	8.801907
5	24	Phil	8.298781
6	2	Atl	5.058158
11	10	Den	4.890103
12	19	NE	4.026214
13	12	GB	3.580034
14	22	NYJ	3.168923
15	25	Pitt	2.699479
21	20	NO	2.425173

Figure 30-3 Top 10 teams for the NFL 2002 season.

Note that we would have predicted that Oakland would play Tampa Bay in the Super Bowl. Unfortunately, our predicted Super Bowl outcome was Oakland by about 2 points (10.64 – 8.8 = 1.84 points). There's no home team in the Super Bowl!

Our model is not linear because the target cell adds together terms of the form *(Home Team Rating + Home Field Edge – Visiting Team Rating)*^{2}. Recall that for a Solver model to be linear, the target cell must be created by adding together terms with the form *(changing cell)*(constant)*. This relationship doesn't exist in this case, so our model is not linear. Solver does obtain the correct answer, however, for any sports rating model in which the target cell minimizes the sum of squared errors.

Problems

1. The file NBA02_03.xls contains scores for every regular season game during the 2002–2003 NBA season. Rate the teams.

2. The file NBA01_02.xls contains scores for every game during the 2001-2002 NBA season. Rate the teams.

3. The file NFL01.xls contains scores for every regular season game during the 2001 NFL season. Rate the teams. Who would you have forecasted to make the Super Bowl?

4. True or False? An NFL team could lose every game and be an above average team.

5. Our method of rating teams works fine for basketball. What problems arise if we apply our method to hockey or baseball?

31

Importing Text or Microsoft Word Data into Excel

■ Jeff Sagarin, the creator of the *USA Today* basketball and football ratings, and I have developed a system to rate NBA players for the Dallas Mavericks team and its owner Mark Cuban. Every day during the season, Jeff's FORTRAN program produces a multitude of information, including ratings for each Dallas Maverick lineup during each game. Unfortunately, Jeff's program produces this information in the form of a text file. How can I import the data into Excel so that I can analyze the data?

We often receive data in a Microsoft Word document or in a text file (a file with the .txt extension) that we need to import into Excel for numerical analysis. To import a Word file into Excel, you should first save it as a text file. You can then use the Text Import Wizard to import the text file into Excel. The Text Import Wizard allows you to break data in a text file into columns by using one of the following approaches.

■ If you choose the *fixed-width* option, Excel guesses where the data should be broken into columns. You can easily modify Excel's assumptions.

■ If you choose the *delimited* option, you pick a character (common choices are a comma, a space, or a plus sign), and Excel breaks the data into columns wherever it spots the character you chose.

As an example, the file LineupSch31.doc (a sample of the data is shown below) contains the length of time each lineup played for Dallas in several games during the 2002–2003 season. The file also contains the "rating" of the lineup. For example, the first two lines tell us that against Sacramento, the lineup of Bell, Finley, LaFrentz, Nash, and Nowitzki were on the court together for 9.05 minutes and that the lineup played at a level of 19.79 points (per 48 minutes), worse than an average NBA lineup.

```
Bell        Finley      LaFrentz    Nash        Nowitzki    -19.79
695#  9.05m  SAC  DAL*
Finley      Nash        Nowitzki    Van Exel    Williams    -11.63
695#  8.86m  SAC  DAL*
Finley      LaFrentz    Nash        Nowitzki    Van Exel    102.98
695#  4.44m  SAC  DAL*
Bradley     Finley      Nash        Nowitzki    Van Exel    -44.26
695#  4.38m  SAC  DAL*
Bradley     Nash        Nowitzki    Van Exel    Williams    9.71
695#  3.05m  SAC  DAL*
Bell        Finley      LaFrentz    Nowitzki    Van Exel    -121.50
695#  2.73m  SAC  DAL*
Bell        LaFrentz    Nowitzki    Van Exel    Williams    39.35
695#  2.70m  SAC  DAL*
Bradley     Finley      Nowitzki    Van Exel    Williams    86.87
695#  2.45m  SAC  DAL*
Bradley     Nash        Van Exel    Williams    Rigaudeau   -54.55
695#  2.32m  SAC  DAL*
```

We'd like to import this lineup information into Excel so that for each lineup we would have the following information listed in different columns.

- Each player's name

- Minutes played by lineup

- Rating of the lineup

The player Van Exel (actually Nick Van Exel) raises a problem. If we choose the delimited option and use a space character to break the data into columns, Van Exel will occupy two columns. For lineups that include Van Exel, the numerical data will be located in a different column from the column in which the data is located for lineups that don't include Van Exel. To remedy this problem, I've used the Edit, Replace command in Word and changed each occurrence of Van Exel to Exel. Now, when we break up the data where a space occurs, Van Exel will require only one column. The first few rows of our data now look like the following.

```
Bell        Finley      LaFrentz     Nash         Nowitzki      -
19.79   695#  9.05m  SAC  DAL*
Finley      Nash         Nowitzki     Exel     Williams     -
11.63   695#  8.86m  SAC  DAL*
Finley      LaFrentz     Nash         Nowitzki     Exel     102.98    695#  4.44m
SAC   DAL*
Bradley      Finley       Nash         Nowitzki     Exel     -
44.26   695#  4.38m  SAC  DAL*
Bradley     Nash         Nowitzki     Exel     Williams     9.71    695#  3.05m
SAC   DAL*
Bell        Finley      LaFrentz     Nowitzki     Exel     -
121.50    695#  2.73m  SAC  DAL*
Bell        LaFrentz     Nowitzki     Exel     Williams     39.35    695#  2.70m
SAC   DAL*
Bradley      Finley       Nowitzki     Exel     Williams     86.87    695#  2.45m
SAC   DAL*
Bradley     Nash         Exel     Williams     Rigaudeau     -
54.55   695#  2.32m  SAC  DAL*
```

The trick in importing data from a Word file or text file into Excel is to utilize Excel's Text Import Wizard. As I mentioned earlier, I first need to save the Word file (LineupSch31.doc in this example) as a text file. To do this, simply open the file in Word, select File Save As, and then select Plain Text in the Files Of Type list. In the File Conversion dialog box, select the Windows (Default) option and then click OK. Your file will now be saved with the name LineupSch31.txt. Close the file in Word. In Excel, open the file LineupSch31.txt. You'll see step 1 of the Text Import Wizard, which is shown in Figure 31-1.

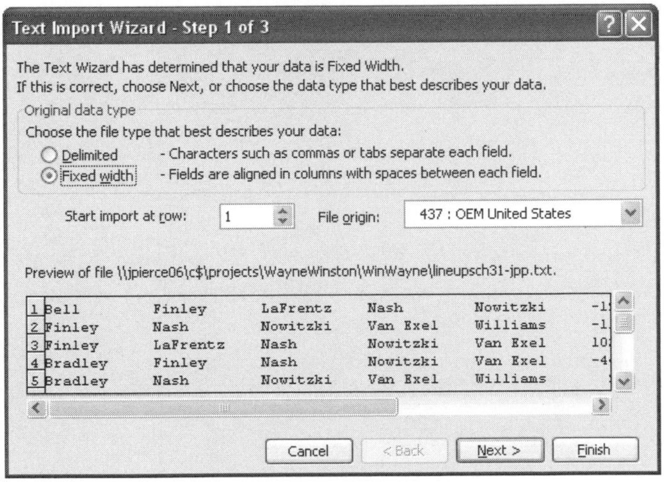

Figure 31-1   Step 1 of the Text Import Wizard.

Clearly, we want to select the Delimited option and break the data at each space. However, let's suppose that we choose Fixed Width. Then step 2 of the

Text Import Wizard appears, shown in Figure 31-2. As you can see, you can create, move, or delete a break line. For many data import operations, changing column breaks can be a hit-or-miss adventure.

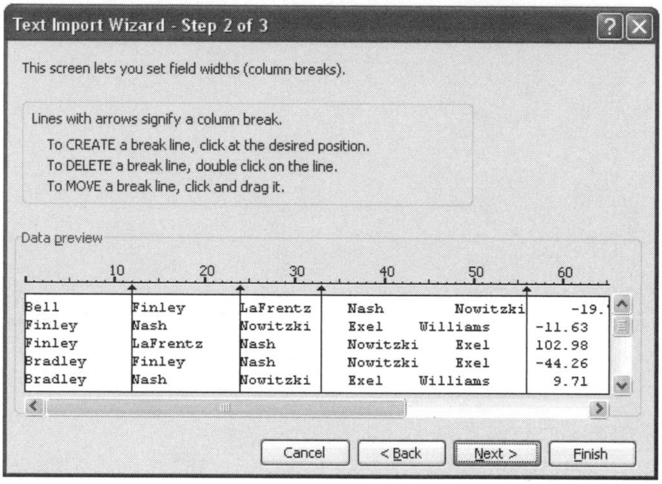

Figure 31-2   Step 2 of the Text Import Wizard after selecting the Fixed Width option.

If we select Delimited in step 1, you'll see the second step of the Text Import Wizard that's shown in Figure 31-3. In this example, I've selected Space as the delimiter. Selecting the option Treat Consecutive Delimiters As One ensures that consecutive spaces will result in only a single column break.

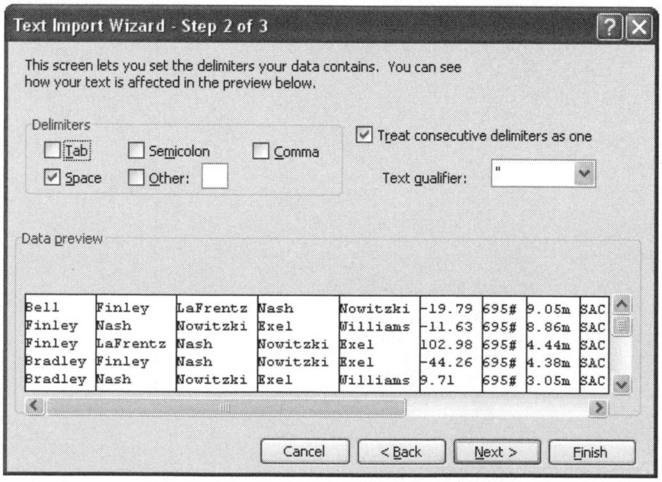

Figure 31-3   After choosing the Delimited option, select the character that indicates where the data should be broken into columns.

When you click Next, you're sent to the third step in the wizard, which is shown in Figure 31-4. By selecting the General option as the format, we have Excel treat numerical data as numbers and other values as text.

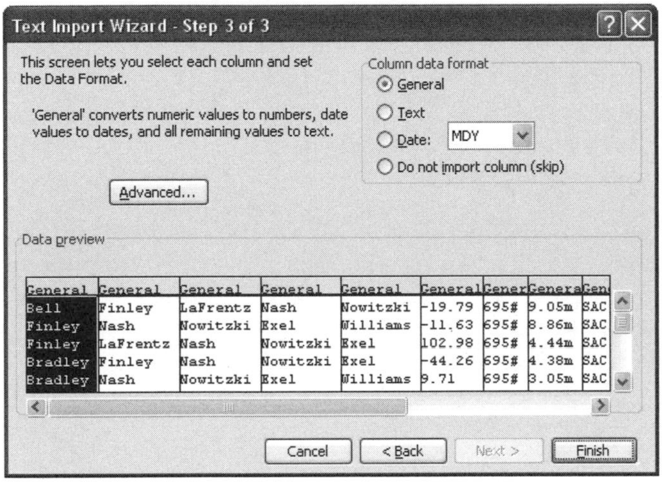

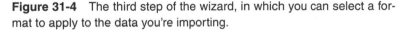

Figure 31-4   The third step of the wizard, in which you can select a format to apply to the data you're importing.

When you click Finish, the wizard imports the data into Excel, as you can in Figure 31-5.

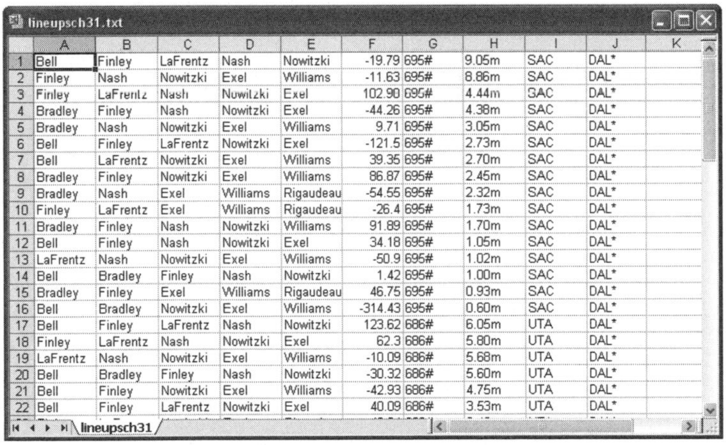

Figure 31-5   The Excel file with lineup information.

Each player is listed in a separate column (columns A-E), column F contains the rating of each lineup, and column H contains the minutes played by each lineup. After saving the file as an Excel workbook (.xls), you can use all of Excel's analytic capabilities to analyze the performance of Dallas's lineups. For example, we could calculate the average performance of the team when Dirk Nowitzki is on or off the court.

Problems

1. The file KingsLineups.doc contains performance ratings for some of the Sacramento Kings lineups. Import this data into Excel.

2. In our example, the time each lineup played (column H) ends with an *m*. Modify the file so that the time played by each lineup is an actual number.

32

Importing Data from the Web into Excel

- The Web site for MSN Money Central provides analyst ratings (buy, sell, and hold) for stocks. How can I import this information into Excel?

- I need to gather data about monthly price changes in the U.S. over the past 80 years. I know this data is available on the Web. How can I import this data into Excel so that I can incorporate it into other business analyses?

- Is there a way I can download current stock prices into Excel?

We all know that the World Wide Web contains useful data on just about everything. However, we can't really do any sort of analysis of this data while it's on the Web. We need to import the data into Excel. Excel 2002 and Excel 2003 make importing data from the Web very easy. After you have found the URL where the data you want is located, copy the URL to the Windows Clipboard. Then open an Excel spreadsheet and choose Data, Import External Data, New Web Query. Paste the URL into the New Web Query dialog box, and then click Go. The Web page appears, and you can select the data you want to import into Excel. Our first example will show you how to implement this easy procedure!

The Web site for MSN Money Central provides analyst ratings (buy, sell, and hold) for stocks. How can I import this information into Excel?

The URL *http://moneycentral.msn.com/investor/invsub/analyst/recomnd.asp?Symbol=MSFT* contains information about analysts' forecasts for the future price of Microsoft stock. For example, in Figure 32-1, we find that on September 23,

2003, 17 of 27 analysts rated Microsoft a strong buy, while a month before 16 of 27 analysts rated Microsoft a strong buy. It would be useful to import this data into Excel so that we could better understand the data.

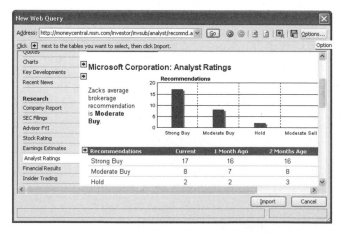

Figure 32-1 Analyst forecast for Microsoft in September 2003. The Web contains a lot of useful data, but it isn't easy to analyze the data on a Web site.

To import the data into Excel, copy the URL and then open a blank worksheet. Now choose Data, Import External Data, New Web Query. After pasting the URL into the Address box and clicking Go, the New Web Query dialog box will display the data shown in Figure 32-2.

Figure 32-2 The New Web Query dialog box after choosing a URL.

You now click on the arrow that points to the data you want to download and import. In our case, we would click on the arrow directly to the left of Recommendations. The arrow changes to a check mark. After clicking Import, you'll see the Import Data dialog box, in which you indicate to Excel where you want to place the data. I chose cell C2 of the current worksheet for this example. After clicking OK, the analysts' ratings are imported into the spreadsheet. (See Figure 32-3.) Note that the numbers are beautifully separated into different columns!

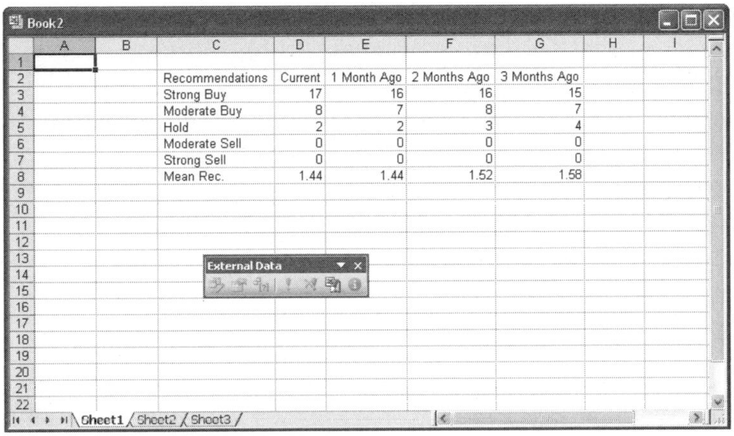

Figure 32-3   Analyst forecasts imported into Excel.

You can easily save a Web query and call it up again later. For example, to save the Web query we just created, click the Save Query button, located directly to left of the Options button in the upper-right corner of the New Web Query dialog box. Name the query using the .iqy extension (I used msft.iqy), and then click Save. To retrieve and run this Web query later, choose Data, Import External Data, Import Data, and select your Web query from the list of data sources. Of course, when you run this Web query again, you'll probably see different information because analysts are constantly changing their views of Microsoft's future stock price.

Unfortunately the New Web Query import process does not always go smoothly. On rare occasions I have encountered the following problems:

■   When I paste the URL into the Address box, Excel cannot find the Web page.

■   After completing the import process, two or more data fields are located in a single column, several blank rows may be interspersed among the data, and column headings may be misplaced.

When these problems occur, probably the best thing to do is to select the data from your Web page, copy it into Microsoft Word, and then save the data as a .txt file. You can then use the Text Import Wizard (described in Chapter 31) to import the data into Excel. Sometimes you'll need to clean up some of the data to ensure that it comes into Excel the way you want. The following example illustrates some of the steps you might need to take.

I need to gather data about monthly price changes in the U.S. over the past 80 years. I know this data is available on the Web. How can I import this data into Excel so that I can incorporate it into other business analyses?

The Bureau of Labor Statistics Web site (*ftp://ftp.bls.gov/pub/special.requests/cpi /cpiai.txt*) contains monthly changes in the Consumer Price Index (CPI). How can I download this data into Excel? When I go to this Web site, I see data that appears in Figure 32-4 (some columns would not fit on the screen).

3-21-2003

U.S. Department Of Labor
Bureau of Labor Statistics
Washington, D.C. 20212

Consumer Price Index

All Urban Consumers - (CPI-U)

U.S. city average

All items

1982-84=100

YEAR	JAN.	FEB.	MAR.	APR.	MAY	JUNE	JULY	AUG.	SEP.	OCT.	NOV.
1913	9.8	9.8	9.8	9.8	9.7	9.8	9.9	9.9	10.0	10.0	10.1
1914	10.0	9.9	9.9	9.8	9.9	9.9	10.0	10.2	10.2	10.1	10.2
1915	10.1	10.0	9.9	10.0	10.1	10.1	10.1	10.1	10.1	10.2	10.3
1916	10.4	10.4	10.5	10.6	10.7	10.8	10.8	10.9	11.1	11.3	11.5
1917	11.7	12.0	12.0	12.6	12.8	13.0	12.8	13.0	13.3	13.5	13.5
1918	14.0	14.1	14.0	14.2	14.5	14.7	15.1	15.4	15.7	16.0	16.3
1919	16.5	16.2	16.4	16.7	16.9	16.9	17.4	17.7	17.8	18.1	18.5

Figure 32-4 CPI data from the U.S. Bureau of Labor Statistics Web site.

When I copy the URL into the New Web Query dialog box (see the previous example for detail instructions), Excel indicates that it can't find the Web page. Therefore, I select the data I want to import, copy it into Word, and save the results as a text file (with the name CpiText.txt). After running the Text Import Wizard in Excel, using a space as the delimiting character, I obtain the results shown in the worksheet named Original Import in the file CpiText.xls, shown in Figure 32-5.

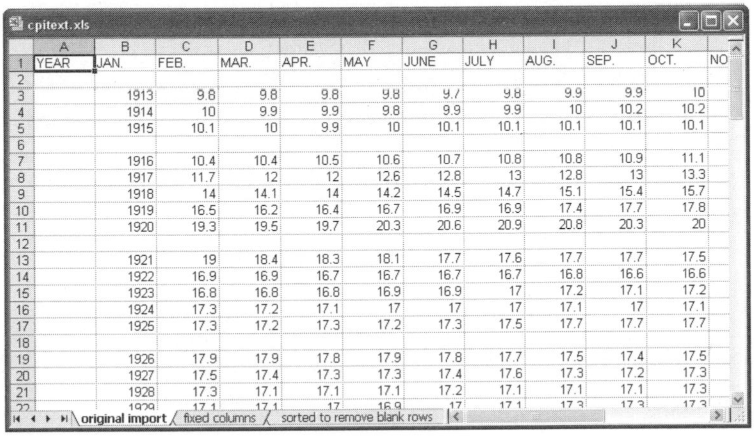

Figure 32-5   CPI data.

Note that the column headings need to be moved one column to the right and that we need to delete blank rows. Before I move the column headings, I want to make a copy of the worksheet. To do this, I can simply point to the worksheet tab, hold down the Ctrl key while I press the left mouse button and drag the sheet name to another worksheet tab. After renaming the copied sheet *Fixed Columns* (to rename a worksheet, double-click the worksheet name and then enter the name you want), we cut the cell range A1:R1 and paste the results to the range B1:S1. The result is shown in Figure 32-6.

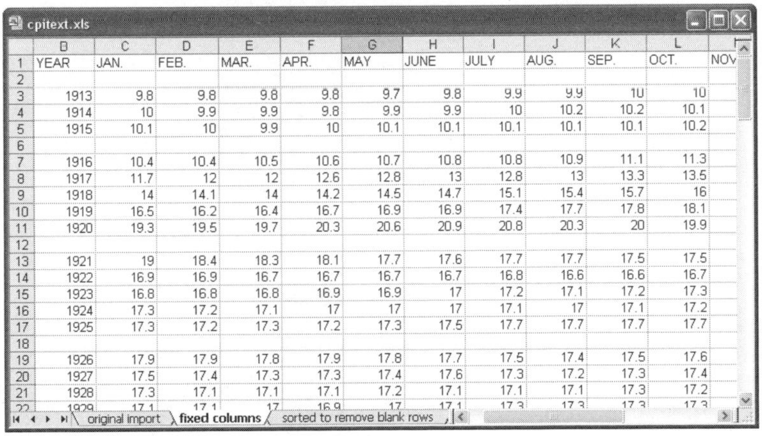

Figure 32-6   CPI data with the column headings fixed.

To eliminate the blank rows, I copied the Fixed Columns worksheet to another worksheet and named it Sorted to Remove Blank Rows. You can now sort on the Year (using ascending values), which will place all the blank rows at the bottom of the spreadsheet. To perform this sort, select the cell range containing the data (B1:S112) and then choose Sort on the Data menu. Select the Header Row option, and then select Year from the first Sort By list, as shown in Figure 32-7.

Figure 32-7   The Sort dialog box set up to eliminate blank rows.

After hiding the rows that contain data for the years 1921-1996, the results appear as shown in Figure 32-8. Now our data is in Excel and is amenable to any form of analysis we need to perform.

	B	C	D	E	F	G	H	I	J	K	L	
1	YEAR	JAN.	FEB.	MAR.	APR.	MAY	JUNE	JULY	AUG.	SEP.	OCT.	
2	1913	9.8	9.8	9.8	9.8	9.7	9.8	9.9	9.9	10	10	
3	1914	10	9.9	9.9	9.8	9.9	9.9	10	10.2	10.2	10.1	
4	1915	10.1	10	9.9	10	10.1	10.1	10.1	10.1	10.1	10.2	
5	1916	10.4	10.4	10.5	10.6	10.7	10.8	10.8	10.9	11.1	11.3	
6	1917	11.7	12	12	12.6	12.8	13	12.8	13	13.3	13.5	
7	1918	14	14.1	14	14.2	14.5	14.7	15.1	15.4	15.7	16	
8	1919	16.5	16.2	16.4	16.7	16.9	16.9	17.4	17.7	17.8	18.1	
9	1920	19.3	19.5	19.7	20.3	20.6	20.9	20.8	20.3	20	19.9	
86	1997	159.1	159.6	160	160.2	160.1	160.3	160.5	160.8	161.2	161.6	
87	1998	161.6	161.9	162.2	162.5	162.8	163	163.2	163.4	163.6	164	
88	1999	164.3	164.5	165	166.2	166.2	166.2	166.7	167.1	167.9	168.2	
89	2000	168.8	169.8	171.2	171.3	171.5	172.4	172.8	172.8	173.7	174	
90	2001	175.1	175.8	176.2	176.9	177.7	178	177.5	177.5	178.3	177.7	
91	2002	177.1	177.8	178.8	179.8	179.8	179.9	180.1	180.7	181	181.3	
92												
93												
94												

fixed columns \ sorted to remove blank rows

Figure 32-8   Cleaned up CPI data.

Is there a way I can download current stock prices into Excel?

Excel comes with a built-in Web query that can be used to download current information about stocks. This Web query is a *dynamic Web query*, which means that you can set the query to update stock information as it changes in real time. All you have to do is select the data you want to update and choose

Data, Refresh Data. Let's see how to download real-time stock information about Microsoft (ticker symbol MSFT) and General Motors (ticker symbol GM) into Excel.

Open a worksheet in Excel. Choose Data, Import External Data, Import Data and then select the Web query named MSN MoneyCentral Investor Stock Quotes.iqy. Click Open, and then use the Import Data dialog box to indicate where you want to place the data in the worksheet. Click OK, and then fill in the Enter Parameter Value dialog box as shown in Figure 32-9. The query will download information about Microsoft and GM into Excel. Figure 32-10 (and the file MsftGMQuotes.xls) shows a sample of the downloaded information. Checking the options in the Enter Parameter Value dialog box shown in Figure 32-9 ensures that when you choose Data, Refresh Data, the spreadsheet changes to reflect the most current information.

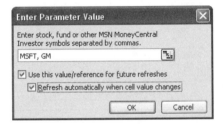

Figure 32-9   Use the Enter Parameter Value dialog box to designate the stocks for which you want the dynamic Web query to download information.

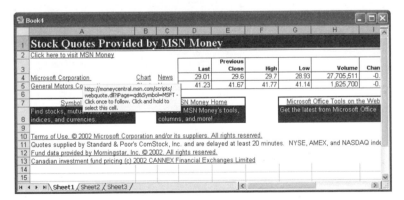

Figure 32-10   Downloaded information about Microsoft and General Motors stocks.

Excel also comes with Web queries designed to download currency exchange rates and information about major stock indexes. These Web queries are static, however, and will not update information in real-time unless you rerun the query.

Of course, you can create your own Web queries. The steps to create the queries are beyond the scope of this book. See Chapter 4 of *Data Analysis for Managers with Microsoft Excel* by S. Christian Albright, Wayne L. Winston, and Christopher Zappe (Duxbury Press, 2004) for an introduction to creating Web queries.

Problems

1.   The URL *http://www.bea.gov/bea/dn/nipaweb/TableViewFixed.asp? SelectedTable=1&FirstYear=2001&LastYear=2002&Freq=Qtr* contains recent data about the gross domestic product (GDP) in the United States. Import this data into Excel.

2.   The URL *http://www.nascar.com/races/wc/2003/1/data/results_ official.html* contains the results of the 2003 Daytona 500. Import this data into Excel.

3.   The URL *http://www.nba.com/pacers/stats/* contains player statistics for the Indiana Pacers NBA team. Import this data into Excel.

4.   The URL *http://www.baseball-reference.com/b/bondsba01.shtml* contains Barry Bond's major league baseball statistics. Import this data into Excel.

5.   Download real-time information about Disney (ticker symbol Walt) and the Gap (ticker symbol GPS) into Excel.

6.   Use the built-in Web query designed to download current foreign exchange rate information into Excel.

33

Validating Data

- I'm entering scores of professional basketball games into Excel. I know that a team scores between 50 and 200 points a game. I once entered 1000 points instead of 100 points, which messed up my analysis. Is there a way to have Excel prevent me from making this type of error?

- I'm entering the date and amount of my business expenses for a new year. Early in the year, I often enter the previous year in the date by mistake. Is there a way I can set up Excel to prevent me from making this type of error?

- I'm entering a long list of numbers. Can I have Excel warn me if I enter a nonnumeric value?

- My assistant needs to enter state abbreviations as she enters dozens and dozens of sales transactions. Can we set up a list of state abbreviations to minimize the chance that she'll enter an incorrect abbreviation?

Our work often involves mind-numbing data entry. When you're entering a lot of information into Excel, it's easy to make an error. Excel's data validation feature can greatly lessen the chances that you'll commit a costly error. To set up data validation, you begin by selecting the cell range that you want to apply data validation to. Choose Data, Validation, and then specify the criteria (as you'll see in this chapter's examples) that Excel uses to flag any invalid data that's entered.

I'm entering scores of professional basketball games into Excel. I know that a team scores between 50 and 200 points a game. I once entered 1000 points instead of 100 points, which messed up my analysis. Is there a way to have Excel prevent me from making this type of error?

Let's suppose that you're going to enter into cells A2:A11 the number of points scored by the home team, and in cells B2:B11, you'll enter the number of points scored by the visiting team. (You'll find the work I did to solve this problem in the file NbaDvl.xls.) You want to ensure that each value entered in the range A2:B11 is a whole number between 50 and 200.

Begin by selecting the range A2:B11, and then choose Data, Validation. Select the Settings tab. Select Whole Number from the Allow list, and then fill in the Data Validation dialog box as shown in Figure 33-1.

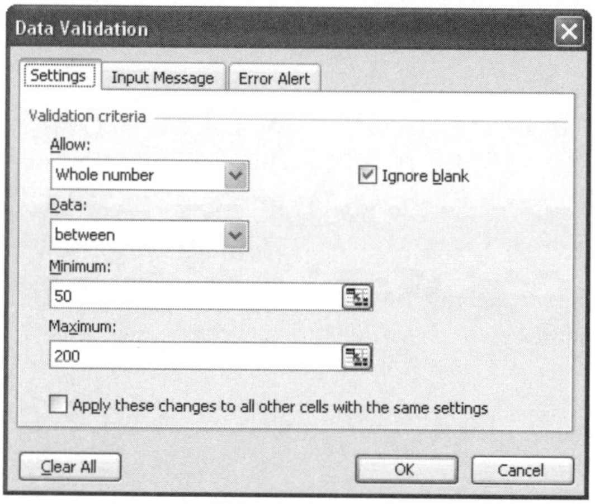

Figure 33-1   Use the Settings tab on the Data Validation dialog box to set up data validation criteria.

Now any entry in cells A2:B11 that is not a whole number between 50 and 200 will be greeted by the error alert shown in Figure 33-2. Clicking Retry lets you enter another value in the cell. Clicking Cancel retains the cell's previous contents.

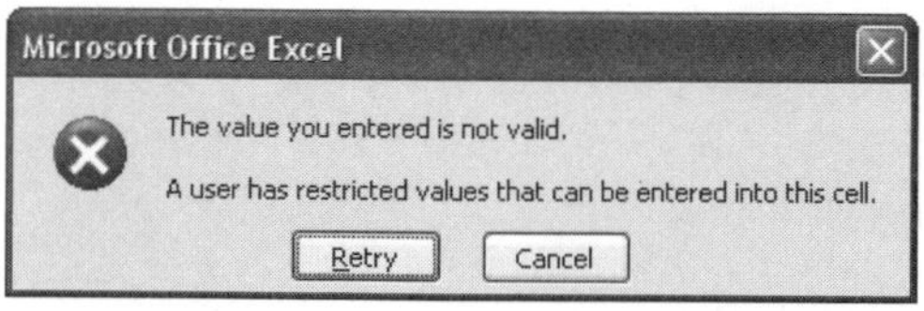

Figure 33-2   The warning message Excel displays when invalid data is entered.

You can use the Error Alert tab in the Data Validation dialog box (the dialog box shown in Figure 33-1) to change the nature of the error alert, including the icon, the title for the message box, and the text of the message itself. On the Input Message tab, you can create a prompt that informs a user about the type of data that can be safely entered. The message is displayed as a comment in the selected cell. For example, in cell E5 I created the prompt shown in Figure 33-3.

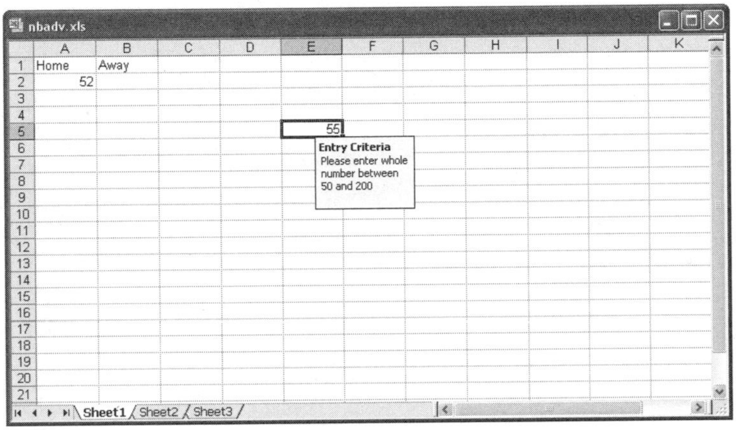

Figure 33-3   Add a data validation input prompt so that users know what data they can enter.

I'm entering the date and amount of my business expenses for a new year. Early in the year, I often enter the previous year in the date by mistake. Is there a way I can set up Excel to prevent me from making this type of error?

Suppose you're entering the year in the cell range A2:A20. (See the file DateDv.xls.) Simply select the A2:A20, and then choose Data, Validation. On the Settings tab, complete the dialog box as shown in Figure 33-4.

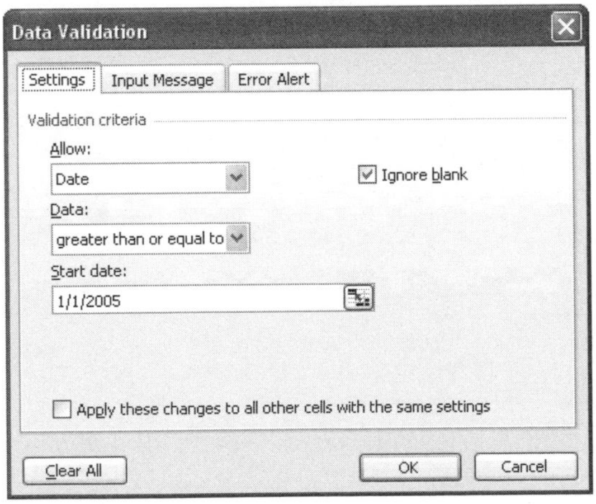

Figure 33-4   Use settings such as these to ensure the validity of dates you enter.

If you enter a date in this range that occurs earlier than January 1, 2005, you'll be warned about the error. For example, entering 1/15/2004 in cell A3 will bring up the error alert shown earlier in Figure 33-2.

I'm entering a long list of numbers. Can I have Excel warn me if I enter a nonnumeric value?

To unleash the power of data validation, you need to utilize the Custom setting. When you select Custom in the Allow list on the Settings tab of the Data Validation dialog box (see Figure 33-1), you use a formula to define valid data. A formula you enter for data validation works the same as a formula used for conditional formatting, which is described in Chapter 23. You enter a formula that is true if and only if the content of the first cell in the selected range is valid. When you click OK in the Data Validation dialog box, the formula is copied to the remaining cells in the range. When you enter a value in a cell in the selected range, Excel will display an error alert if the formula you entered returns False for that value.

To illustrate the use of the Custom setting, let's suppose we want to ensure that each entry in the cell range B2:B20 is a number. (See the workbook NumberDv.xls.) The key to solving this problem is using the Excel ISNUMBER function. The ISNUMBER function returns True if the function refers to a cell that contains numeric data. The function returns False if the function refers to a cell that contains a nonnumeric value.

After selecting the cell range B2:B20, choose Data, Validation, and then fill in the Settings tab of the Data Validation dialog box as shown in Figure 33-5.

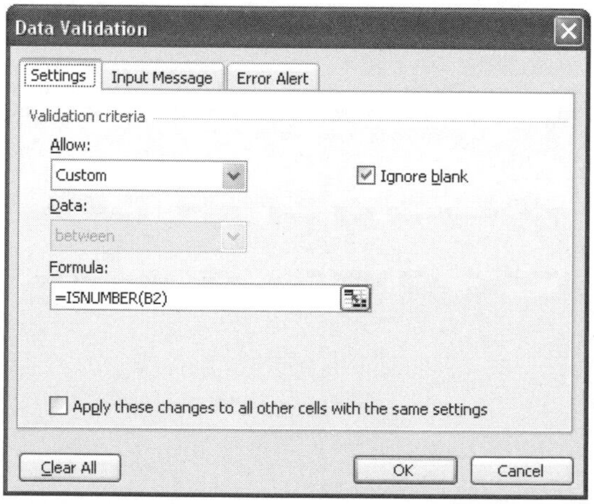

Figure 33-5   Use the ISNUMBER function to ensure that the data in a range is numeric.

After clicking OK, we'll receive an error prompt if we try to enter any non-numeric value in B2:B20. For example, if we type *John* in cell B3, we receive an error prompt.

If you choose Data, Validation while in cell B3, the formula shown in Figure 33-5 is displayed as *=ISNUMBER(B3)*. This demonstrates that the formula entered in cell B2 is copied in the correct fashion. Entering *John* in cell B3 causes *=ISNUMBER(B3)* to return False, so we receive the error alert.

My assistant needs to enter state abbreviations as she enters dozens and dozens of sales transactions. Can we set up a list of state abbreviations to minimize the chance that she'll enter an incorrect abbreviation?

The key to this data validation problem is to use the List validation criteria. Begin by entering a list of state abbreviations. In this example, I've used the range I6:I55 and named the range *abbrev*. Next, select the range in which you'll enter state abbreviations. (The example uses D5:D156.) After choosing Data, Validation, fill in the Data Validation dialog box as shown in Figure 33-6.

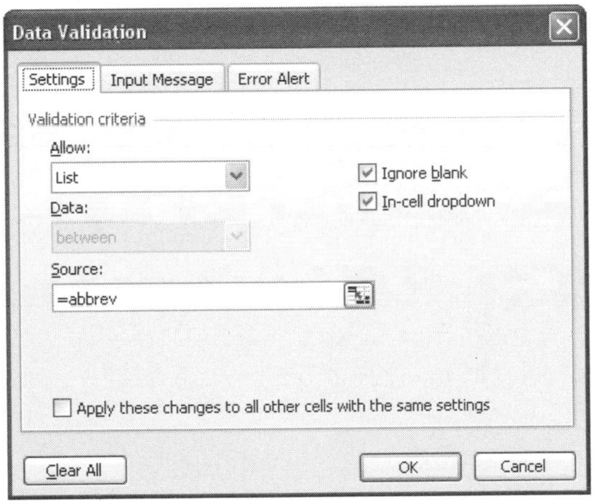

Figure 33-6   The Data Validation dialog box can be used to define a list of valid values.

Now, whenever you select a cell in the range D6:D156, a drop-down list appears, as shown in Figure 33-7. The list contains the state abbreviations. Only abbreviations that appear on the list are valid values in this range.

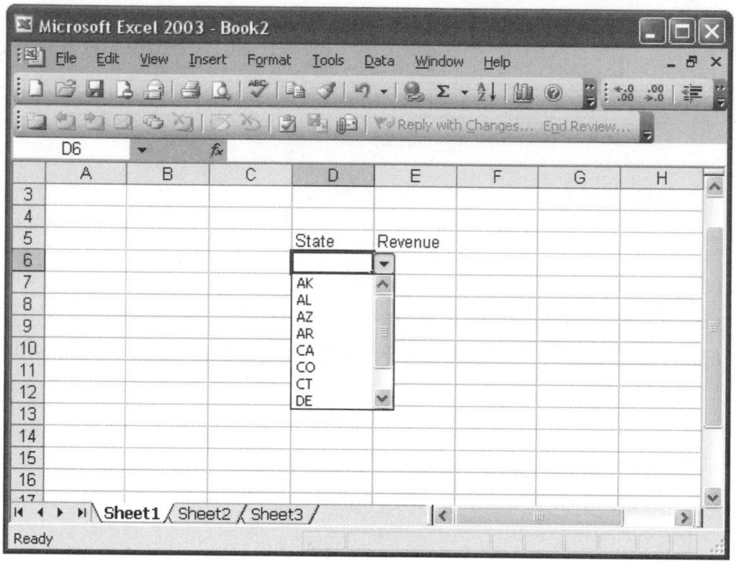

Figure 33-7   Drop-down box for state abbreviations.

If you do not use the drop-down list and instead type in a state abbreviation, should you enter an incorrect abbreviation (such as ALK for Alaska), you'll receive an error message.

Problems

1. You are entering nonnegative whole numbers into the cell range C1:C20. Enter a data validation setting that ensures that each entry is a nonnegative whole number.

2. You are entering in the cell range C1:C15 the dates of transactions that occur during July 2004. Enter a data validation setting that ensures that each date entered occurs in July 2004.

3. The List option in the group of data validation settings enables you to generate an error message if a value that is not included in a list is entered in the cell range you're validating. Suppose you are entering employee first names in the cell range A1:A10. The only employees of the company are Jen, Greg, Vivian, Jon, and John. Use the List option to ensure that no one misspells a first name.

4.   The Text Length option in the group of data validation settings enables you to generate an error message when the number of characters in a cell does not match the number you define. Use the Text Length option to ensure that each cell in the range C1:C10 will contain at most 5 characters (including blanks).

5.   You are entering employee names in the cell range A1:A10. Use data validation to ensure that no employee's name is entered more than twice. (Hint: Use the Custom setting and the COUNTIF function.)

6.   You are entering product ID codes in the cell range A1:A15. Product ID codes must always end with the characters *xyz*. Use data validation to ensure that each product ID code entered ends with *xyz*. (Hint: Use the Custom settings and the RIGHT function.)

7.   Suppose you want every entry in the cell range B2:B15 to contain text and not a numerical value. Use data validation to ensure that entering a numerical value will return an error. (Hint: Use the ISTEXT function.)

34

Summarizing Data with Histograms

■ Wise people often say that a picture is worth a thousand words. Can I use Excel to create a picture (called a *histogram*) that summarizes the values in a data set?

■ What are some common shapes of histograms?

■ What can I learn by comparing histograms from different data sets?

The ability to summarize a large data set is important. The three tools used most often to summarize data in Excel are *histograms, descriptive statistics*, and *PivotTables*. In this chapter, I'll discuss the use of histograms for summarizing data. I'll cover descriptive statistics in Chapter 35 and PivotTables in Chapter 36.

Wise people often say that a picture is worth a thousand words. Can I use Excel to create a picture (called a *histogram*) that summarizes the values in a data set?

A *histogram* is a commonly used tool to summarize data. Essentially, a histogram tells us how many observations (another term for data points) fall in various ranges of values. For example, a histogram created from monthly Cisco stock returns might show how many monthly returns on Cisco were between 0 and 10 percent, 10 and 20 percent, and so on. The ranges in which you group data are known as *bin ranges*.

Let's look at how to construct and interpret histograms that summarize the values of monthly returns on Cisco and GM stock for the years 1990–2000. You'll find this data (and returns for other stocks) in the file Stock.xls. Figure 34-1 shows a subset of the data. During March 1990, for example, Cisco stock increased in value by 1.075 percent.

	A	B	C	D	E	F	G
							stock.xls
51	Date	MSFT	GE	INTC	GM	CSCO	
52	30-Mar-90	0.121518984	0.040485829	0.037267081	0.022284122	0.01075	
53	30-Apr-90	0.047404062	-0.00389105	-0.05389221	-0.03542234	0.01064	
54	31-May-90	0.258620679	0.083515622	0.221518993	0.115819208	0.04211	
55	29-Jun-90	0.04109589	0.005444646	-0.02590674	-0.02056555	0.07071	
56	31-Jul-90	-0.125	0.034296028	-0.05319149	-0.02099738	-0.0377	
57	31-Aug-90	-0.07518797	-0.13438046	-0.25	-0.1313673	-0.0294	
58	28-Sep-90	0.024390243	-0.11338709	-0.00374532	-0.08805031	-0.0909	
59	31-Oct-90	0.011904762	-0.04587156	0.007518797	0.013793103	0.31111	
60	30-Nov-90	0.13333334	0.052884616	0.119402982	0.013605442	0.33898	
61	31-Dec-90	0.041522492	0.057260275	0.026666667	-0.05821918	0.13608	
62	31-Jan-91	0.303986698	0.115468413	0.188311681	0.054545455	0.30362	
63	28-Feb-91	0.057324842	0.070468754	0.043715846	0.100689657	-0.0427	
64	28-Mar-91	0.022891566	0.023897059	-0.02094241	-0.0443038	-0.1295	
65	30-Apr-91	-0.06713781	0.016157989	0.053475935	-0.05298013	0.22051	
66	31-May-91	0.108585857	0.09908127	0.131979689	0.217482507	0.08403	
67	28-Jun-91	-0.06890661	-0.0420712	-0.16591929	-0.05507246	-0.0543	
68	31-Jul-91	0.078899086	-0.01013514	0.010752688	-0.02453988	0.28689	
69	30-Aug-91	0.159863949	0.022184301	0.053191491	-0.03396227	0.15605	
70	30-Sep-91	0.043988269	-0.06664441	-0.14646465	-0.01644737	-0.0964	
71	31-Oct-91	0.054775283	-0.00540541	-0.03846154	-0.06020067	0.18902	

Figure 34-1 Monthly stock returns.

When constructing histograms with Excel, you can let Excel define the bin ranges or you can define the bin ranges yourself. If Excel defines the bin ranges, you could end up with weird looking bin ranges, such as -12.53 to 4.52 percent. For this reason, I prefer to define the ranges myself.

A good way to start defining bin ranges for a histogram (you can think of defining bin ranges as setting boundaries) is to divide the range of values (between the smallest and largest) into 8 to 15 equally spaced categories. All the monthly returns for Cisco are between -30 percent and 40 percent, so I chose bin range boundaries of -30 percent, -20 percent, -10 percent, 0 percent, and so on up to 40 percent.

To create our bin ranges, I first enter CSCO, .4, .3, .2, …, -.2, -.3 (the boundaries of the bin ranges) in cells H54:H62. Next I choose Tools, Data Analysis to open the Analysis Toolpak. The Analysis Toolpak contains many of Excel's statistical capabilities.

Note If the Data Analysis command doesn't appear on the Tools menu, choose Tools, Add-Ins, select the check boxes for Analysis Toolpak and Analysis Toolpak VBA, and then click OK. Now when you choose Tools, Data Analysis, the Analysis Toolpak will be ready to use.

By selecting the Histogram option in the Data Analysis dialog box, we open the Histogram dialog box, shown in Figure 34-2.

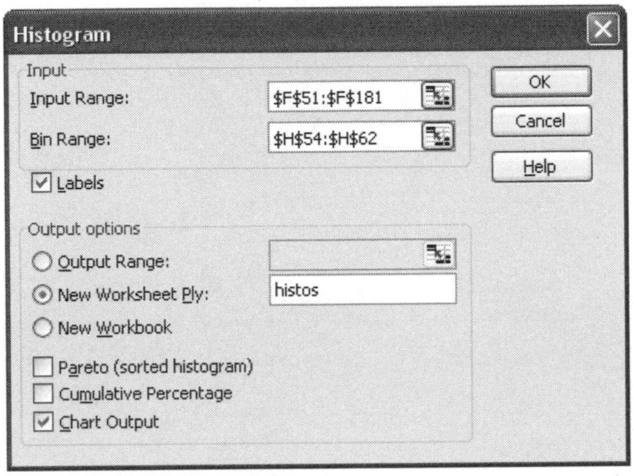

Figure 34-2   Dialog box for the Cisco histogram.

Here's how to fill in the dialog box as it's shown:

- Select the Input Range (F51:F181). (To select the range F51:F181, you can select cell F51 and then press Ctrl+Shift+Down Arrow. This takes you to the bottom of the column.) This range includes all the data we want to use to create our histogram. I included the label CSCO from cell F51 because when you do not include a label in the first row, the x-axis of the histogram is often labeled with a number, which is confusing.

- Bin Range (H54:H62) includes the boundaries of our bin ranges. Excel will create bins of -30 to -20 percent, -20 to -10 percent, and so on up to 30–40 percent.

- I checked the Labels option because the first rows of both our bin range and input range contain labels.

- I chose to create the histogram in a new worksheet (named Histo).

- Select Chart Output, or you will not create a histogram.

Click OK in the Histogram dialog box, and our Cisco histogram will look like the one shown in Figure 34-3.

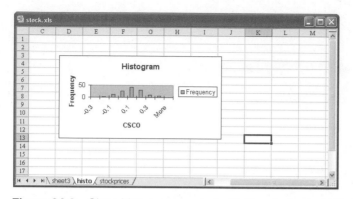

Figure 34-3 Cisco histogram created with Excel's Analysis Toolpak.

When you create the histogram, you'll see gaps between the bars. To remove these gaps, select any bar on the graph and choose Format, Data Series. On the Options tab, set Gap Width to 0. You will also see that a label does not show for each bar. To show a label for each bar, you must reduce the font size. To reduce the font size, right-click on the graph axis and choose Format Axis. Change the font size to 5 points. You can also change the title of the chart by selecting the text and entering the title you want. After making these changes, the histogram appears as its shown in Figure 34-4.

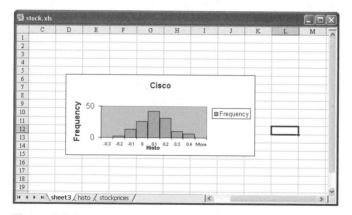

Figure 34-4 You can change the format of different elements in the chart.

Notice that Cisco returns are most likely between 0 and 10 percent per month, and the height of the bars drops off as the graph moves away from the tallest bar. When we create the histogram, we also obtain the bin range frequency summary shown in Figure 34-5.

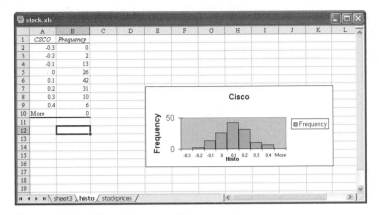

Figure 34-5 Cisco bin range frequencies.

From the bin range frequencies, we learn, for example, that for two months Cisco's return was greater than -30 percent and less than or equal to -20 percent; in 13 months, the monthly return was greater than -20 percent and less than or equal to -10 percent.

What are some common shapes of histograms?

For most data sets, a histogram created from the data will be classified as one of the following:

■ Symmetric

■ Skewed right (positively skewed)

■ Skewed left (negatively skewed)

■ Multiple peaks

Let's look at each type in more detail.

■ **Symmetric distribution** A histogram is symmetric if it has a single peak and looks approximately the same to the left of the peak as to the right of the peak. Test scores (such as IQ tests) are often symmetric. For example, the histograms of IQs might look like Figure 34-6. Notice that the height of the bars one bar away from the peak bar are approximately the same, the height of the bars two bars away from the peak bar are approximately the same, and so on. The bar labeled 105 represents all people with an IQ greater than 95 and less than or equal to 105, the bar labeled 65 represents all people having an IQ less than or equal to 65, and so on. Also note that Cisco monthly returns are approximately symmetric.

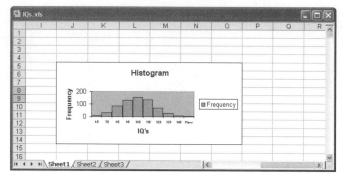

Figure 34-6   Symmetric histogram.

■ **Skewed right (positively skewed)**   A histogram is skewed right (positively skewed) if it has a single peak and the values of the data set extend much farther to the right of the peak bar than to the left of the peak. Many economic data sets (such as family or individual income) exhibit positive skewness. Figure 34-7 shows an example of a positively skewed histogram created from a sample of family incomes.

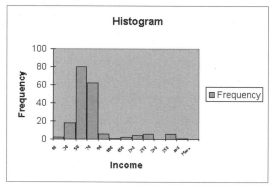

Figure 34-7   A positively skewed histogram created from data about family income.

■ **Skewed left (negatively skewed)**   A histogram is skewed left (negatively skewed) if it has a single peak and the values of the data set extend much farther to the left of the peak than to the right of the peak. Days from conception to birth are negatively skewed. An example is shown in Figure 34-8.

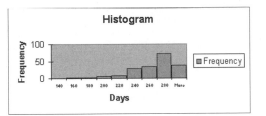

Figure 34-8   A histogram of data that plots days from conception to birth is negatively skewed.

■   **Multiple peaks**   When a histogram exhibits multiple peaks, it usually means that data from two or more populations are being graphed together. For example, suppose the diameter of elevator rails produced by two machines yields the histogram shown in Figure 34-9.

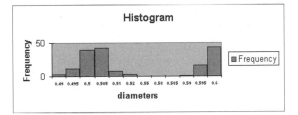

Figure 34-9   A multiple peak histogram.

In this histogram, the data clusters into two separate groups. In all likelihood, each group of data corresponds to the elevator rails produced by one of the machines. If we assume that the diameter we want for an elevator rail is .55 inches, we can conclude that one machine is producing elevator rails that are too short, while the other machine is producing elevator rails that are too long. We should follow up with our interpretation of this histogram by constructing a histogram charting the elevator rails produced by each machine. This example shows why histograms are a powerful tool in quality control.

What can I learn by comparing histograms from different data sets?

We're often asked to compare different data sets. For example, we might wonder how the monthly returns on GM and Cisco stock differ. To answer a question such as this, you can construct a histogram for GM using the same bin ranges as for Cisco and then lay the histograms on top of each other, as shown in Figure 34-10.

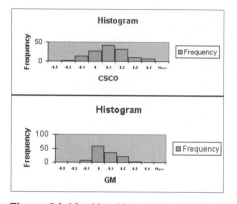

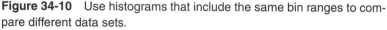

Figure 34-10   Use histograms that include the same bin ranges to compare different data sets.

By comparing these two histograms, we can draw two important conclusions:

■   Typically, Cisco performed better than GM. We know this because the highest bar for Cisco is one bar to the right of the highest bar for GM. Also, the Cisco bars extend farther to the right than the GM bars.

■   Cisco had more variability, or spread about the mean, than GM. Note that GM's peak bar contains 59 months, while Cisco's peak bar contains only 41 months. This shows that for Cisco, more of the returns are outside the bin that represents the most likely Cisco return. Cisco returns are more "spread out" than GM returns.

In the next chapter, we'll look at more details about the differences between the monthly returns on Cisco and GM.

Problems

1.   Use the data in Stock.xls to construct histograms for monthly returns on GE and Intel.

2.   Use the data in file HistoricalInvest.xls to create histograms for annual returns on stocks and bonds. Then compare the annual returns on stocks and bonds.

3.   You are given (in the file Deming.xls) the measured diameter (in inches) reported by the production foreman for 500 rods produced by Rodco. A rod is considered acceptable if it is at least 1 inch in diameter. In the past, the diameter of the rods produced by Rodco has followed a symmetric histogram.

❑   Construct a histogram of these measurements.

❑   Comment on any unusual aspects of the histogram.

❑   Can you guess what might have caused any unusual aspects of the histogram? (Hint: One of quality guru Deming's 14 points is to "Drive Out Fear.")

35

Summarizing Data with Descriptive Statistics

- What defines a typical value for a data set?

- How can I measure how much a data set spreads out from its typical value?

- Together, what do the mean and standard deviation of a data set tell me about the data?

- How can I use descriptive statistics to compare data sets?

- How can I find the 90th percentile of a data set? For a given data point, can I easily find its percentile ranking within the data set?

In Chapter 34, I showed how you can describe data sets by using histograms. In this chapter, I'll show how to describe a data set by using particular properties of the data, such as the mean, median, standard deviation, and variance—measures that Excel groups together as *descriptive statistics*. You can obtain the descriptive statistics for a set of data by choosing Tools, Data Analysis, and then selecting the Descriptive Statistics option. After entering the relevant data and clicking OK, you'll have all the descriptive statistics of interest (and some of little interest!) for your data.

What defines a typical value for a data set?
To illustrate the use of descriptive statistics, let's return to the Cisco and GM monthly stock return data in the file Stock.xls. To create a set of descriptive statistics for this data, choose Tools, Data Analysis, and then select Descriptive Statistics. Fill in the dialog box as shown in Figure 35-1.

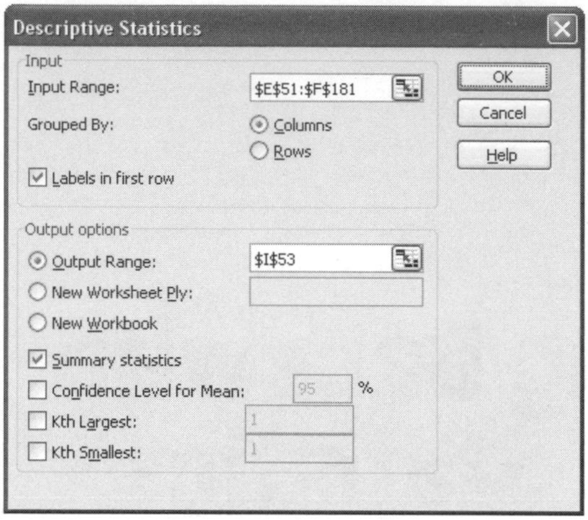

Figure 35-1 The Descriptive Statistics dialog box.

■ The Input Range is the monthly Cisco and GM returns located in the range E51:F181 (including the labels in row 51).

■ I selected Columns because each data set is listed in a different column.

■ I checked the Labels In First Row option because the first row of the data range contains labels and not data.

■ I selected cell I53 of the current worksheet as the upper-left corner of the output range.

■ By selecting Summary Statistics, I ensure that we get the most commonly used descriptive statistics measures for both GM and Cisco monthly returns.

When you click OK, Excel calculates the descriptive statistics shown in Figure 35-2.

GM		CSCO	
Mean	0.009276966	Mean	0.055573
Standard Error	0.007864031	Standard Error	0.010701
Median	-0.005420048	Median	0.05007
Mode	#N/A	Mode	0.051429
Standard Deviation	0.089663746	Standard Deviation	0.12201
Sample Variance	0.008039587	Sample Variance	0.014887
Kurtosis	0.474825023	Kurtosis	-0.31952
Skewness	0.223940162	Skewness	0.10465
Range	0.516939536	Range	0.541492
Minimum	-0.240320429	Minimum	-0.20251
Maximum	0.276619107	Maximum	0.338983
Sum	1.20600562	Sum	7.224442
Count	130	Count	130

Figure 35-2 Descriptive statistics results for Cisco and GM stocks.

Let's interpret the descriptive statistics that define a typical value (or a central location) for Cisco's monthly stock returns. The Descriptive Statistics output contains three measures of central location: mean (or average), median, and mode.

- **Mean**   The mean of a data set is written as $\bar{x}$. The mean of a data set is simply the average of all observations in the sample. Thus, if the data values are x^1, x^2, ... x^n, the following equation calculates the mean.

$$\bar{x} = \frac{1}{n} \sum_{i=1}^{i=n} x_i$$

  Here, n equals the number of observations in the sample, and xi is the ith observation in the sample. We find that the mean monthly return on Cisco was 5.6 percent per month.

  It is always true that the sum of the deviations of all values from the mean will equal 0. Thus, you can think of a data set's mean as a "balancing point" for the data. Of course, without using the Descriptive Statistics option, we can obtain a sample's mean in Excel by applying the AVERAGE function to the appropriate cell range.

- **Median**   The median of a sample is the "middle" observation, when the data is listed from smallest to largest. If a sample contains an odd number of observations, the median is the observation that has as many observations below it as above it. Thus, for a sample of size 9, the median would be the fifth smallest (or fifth largest) observation. When a sample includes an even number of observations, you can simply average the two middle observations. Essentially, the median is the 50th percentile of the data. The median monthly return on Cisco was 5.0 percent. We could also obtain this information by using the MEDIAN function.

- **Mode**   The mode is the most frequently occurring value in the sample. If no value occurs more than once, the mode does not exist. For GM, no monthly return occurred more than once for the years 1990–2000, so the mode does not exist. For Cisco, the mode was around 5.14 percent. You can also use the MODE function to compute the mode. If no data value occurs more than once, the MODE function returns #NA.

  The mode is almost never used as a measure of central location. It is interesting to note, however, that for a symmetric data set, the mean, median, and mode are equal.

A natural question is whether the mean or median is a better measure of central location. Essentially, we use the mean as the best measure of central location if the data set does not exhibit excessive skewness. Otherwise, we use the median as the measure of central location. If a data set is highly skewed, extreme values distort the mean. In this case, the median is a better measure of a typical data set value. For example, the U.S. government reports median family income in lieu of mean family income because family income is highly positively skewed.

The skewness measure reported by the Descriptive Statistics output lets us know whether a data set is highly skewed.

- Skewness greater than +1 indicates a high degree of positive skewness.

- Skewness less than -1 indicates a high degree of negative skewness.

- Skewness between -1 and +1 indicates a relatively symmetric data set.

Thus, monthly returns of GM and Cisco exhibit a slight degree of positive skewness. Because the skewness measure for each data set is less than +1, the mean is a better measure of a typical return than the median. You can also use the SKEW function to compute skewness for a data set.

Kurtosis Kurtosis, which sounds like a disease, is not a very important measure. Kurtosis near 0 means a data set exhibits "peakedness" close to the normal (or standard Bell-shaped) curve. (I'll discuss the normal curve in Chapter 56.) Positive kurtosis means that a data set is more peaked than a normal random variable, while negative kurtosis means that data is less peaked than a normal random variable. GM monthly returns are more peaked than a normal curve, while Cisco monthly returns are less peaked than a normal curve.

How can I measure how much a data set spreads out from its typical value?

Consider two investments that yield an average of 20 percent per year. Before deciding which investment we prefer, we'd like to know about the spread, or riskiness, of the investment. The most important measures of the spread (or dispersion) of a data set about its mean are sample variance, sample standard deviation, and range.

- **Sample variance and sample standard deviation** The sample variance s^2 is defined by the following formula:

$$s^2 = \frac{1}{n-1} \sum_{i=1}^{i=n} (x_i - \bar{x})^2$$

You can think of the sample variance as the average squared deviation of the data about its mean. Intuitively, it seems like we should divide by n to compute a true average squared deviation, but technical reasons[1] require us to divide by n -1. The sample standard

---

1. Dividing the sum of the squared deviations by $n - 1$ ensures that our sample variance will be an unbiased measure of the true variance of the population from which the sampled data was drawn.

deviation s is just the square root of s^2.

Here's an example of these computations. For the data set 1, 3, and 5 we find that

$$s^2 = \frac{1}{2}\left[(1-3)^2 + (3-3)^2 + (5-3)^2\right] = 4$$

Then we find that

$$s = \sqrt{4} = 2.$$

We find that the sample standard deviation of monthly returns on Cisco is 12.2 percent with a sample variance of .015%2. Naturally, %2 is hard to interpret, so we usually look at the sample standard deviation. For GM, the sample standard deviation is 8.97 percent.

■ **Range**   The range of a data set is the largest number in the data set minus the smallest number. We find the range in the monthly Cisco returns is equal to 54 percent and the range for GM monthly returns is 52 percent.

Together, what do the mean and standard deviation of a data set tell me about the data?

Assuming that a histogram is symmetric, the rule of thumb tells us the following:

■ Approximately 68 percent of all observations are between $\overline{x} - s$ and + s.

■ Approximately 95 percent of all observations are between $\overline{x}$ – 2s and + 2s.

■ Approximately 99.7 percent of all observations are between $\overline{x}$ – 3s and +3s.

For example, we would expect around 95 percent of all Cisco monthly returns to be between -19 percent and 30 percent.[2] Any observation more than two standard deviations away from the mean is called an outlier. For the Cisco data, 9 of 130 observations (or roughly 7 percent of all returns) are outliers. In general, the rule of thumb is less accurate for highly skewed data sets than it is for relatively symmetric data sets.

Many valuable insights can be obtained by finding causes of outliers. Any company should try and ensure that the causes of "good outliers" occur more frequently and the causes of "bad" outliers occur less frequently.

---

2. Mean – 2s = .056-2*(.122) = -19% and Mean + 2s = .056 + 2*(.122) = 30%

Using Conditional Formatting to Highlight Outliers We can use the cool conditional formatting feature described in Chapter 23 to highlight outliers. Figure 35-3 shows an example.

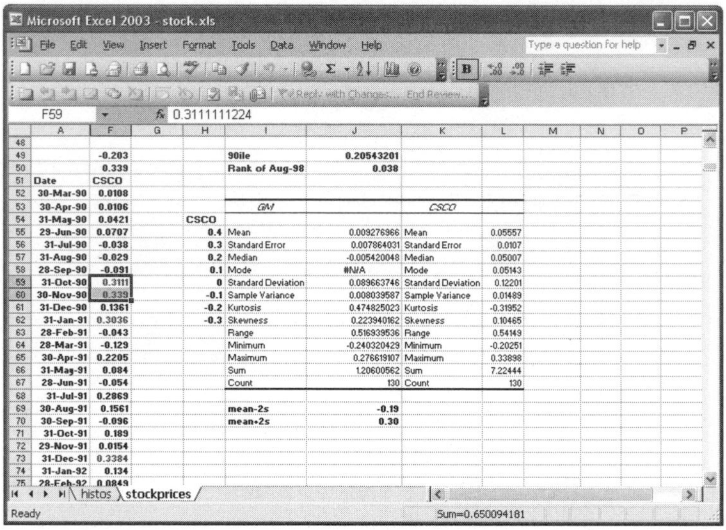

Figure 35-3 Outliers for Cisco highlighted with conditional formatting.

To begin, I computed the lower cutoff for an outlier (*mean – 2s*) in cell J69 and the upper cutoff for an outlier (*mean + 2s*) in cell J70. Next I selected the entire range of Cisco returns (cells F52:F181). I then go to the first cell in the range (F52), select Format, Conditional Formatting, and fill in the dialog box as shown in Figure 35-4.

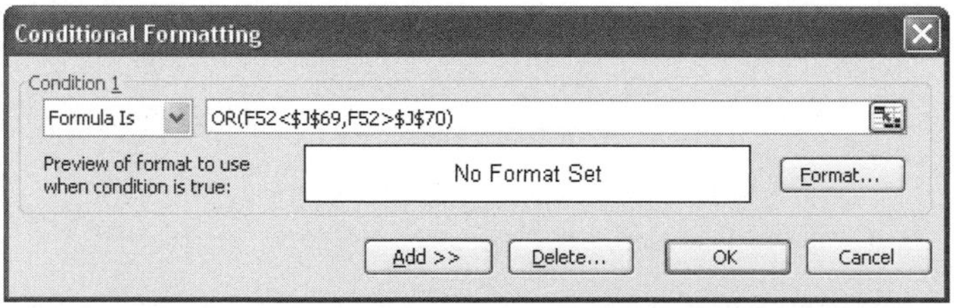

Figure 35-4 Conditional formatting condition to select outliers.

This condition ensures that if cell F52 is either more than 2*s* above the mean monthly Cisco return or more than 2*s* below the mean monthly return, the format we select (a red font color in this case) will be applied to cell F52. Of course, this formatting condition is automatically copied to our selected range. Note that all outliers show up in red.

How can I use descriptive statistics to compare data sets?

You can use descriptive statistics to summarize the differences between Cisco and GM monthly returns. Looking at the measures of typical value, shape, and spread about a typical value, we can conclude the following:

- Typically (looking at either mean or median), Cisco monthly returns are higher than GM.

- Cisco monthly returns are more variable (looking at standard deviation, variance, and range) than monthly GM returns.

- Both Cisco and GM monthly returns exhibit slight positive skewness. GM monthly returns are more peaked than a normal curve, while Cisco monthly returns are less peaked than a normal curve.

How can I find the 90th percentile of a data set? For a given data point, can I easily find its percentile ranking within the data set?

The PERCENTRANK and PERCENTILE functions are useful when you want to determine an observation's relative position in a data set. The PERCENTILE function returns the percentile of a data set that you specify. The syntax of the PERCENTILE function is *PERCENTILE(data, k)*, which returns the kth percentile of the information in the cell range specified by *data*. For example, $k = .9$ returns a value such that 90 percent of all data points are below the returned value, and $k = .10$ returns a value such that 10 percent of all data points are below the returned value. To find the 90th percentile of the monthly Cisco returns, I entered in cell J49 the formula *PERCENTILE(CSCO,0.9)*. (The range B52:B181, where Cisco returns are recorded, is named *CSCO*.) As you can see in Figure 35-3, during 10 percent of all months, monthly returns on Cisco exceeded 20.5 percent.[3]

The PERCENTRANK function returns the ranking of an observation relative to all values in a data set. The syntax of this function is *PERCENTRANK(data,value)*. For example, in cell J50, we obtain the percentage rank for August 1998 with the formula *PERCENTRANK(CSCO,F153)*. As shown in Figure 35-3, only 3.8 percent of all months yielded a return lower than August 1998.

> **Note** It is easy to confuse the PERCENTILE and PERCENTRANK functions. PERCENTILE yields a value of the data, while PERCENTRANK yields a percentage.

---

3. The PERCENTILE function will yield the exact k^{th} percentile only if k is an exact multiple of $1/(n-1)$. Thus, we would obtain the exact percentile for 1/129, 2/129, … 128/129. Otherwise, Excel interpolates in a complex fashion to obtain an approximation for the percentile specified.

Problems

1. Use the data in Stock.xls to generate descriptive statistics for Intel and GE stock.

2. Use your answer to problem 1 to compare the monthly returns on Intel and GE stock.

3. Electro produces voltage regulating equipment in New York and ships the equipment to Chicago. The voltage held by each unit is measured in New York before each unit is shipped to Chicago. The voltage held by each unit is also measured when the unit arrives in Chicago. A sample of voltage measurements at each city is given in the file Electro.xls. A voltage regulator is considered acceptable if it can hold a voltage of between 25 and 75 volts.

❑ Using descriptive statistics, comment on what you have learned about the voltage held by units before shipment and after shipment.

❑ What percentage of units are acceptable before and after shipping?

❑ Do you have any suggestions about how to improve the quality of Electro's regulators?

❑ Ten percent of all New York regulators have a voltage exceeding what value?

❑ Five percent of all New York regulators have a voltage less than or equal to what value?

4. In the file DecadeIncome.xls, you are given a sample of family incomes (in thousands of 1980 dollars) for a set of families sampled in 1980 and 1990. Assume that these families are representative of the whole United States. Republicans claim that the country was better off in 1990 than in 1980 because average income increased. Do you agree?

5. Use descriptive statistics to compare the annual returns on stocks, bonds, and T-bills. Use the data contained in the file Historical-Invest.xls.

6. In 1970 and 1971, eligibility for the Vietnam draft was determined on the basis of a draft lottery number that was determined by your birthday. Three hundred and sixty-six (366) balls, one for each possible birth date, were placed in a container and were shaken up. The first ball selected was given the number 1 in the lottery and so on. Men whose birthdays corresponded to the lowest numbers were drafted first. The file DraftLottery.xls contains the actual results of the 1970 and 1971 drawings. For example, in the 1970 drawing, January 1 received the number 305. Use descriptive statistics to demonstrate that the 1970 draft lottery was unfair and the 1971 lottery was fair. Hint: Use the AVERAGE and MEDIAN functions to compute the mean and median lottery number for each month.

7. The file Jordan.xls gives the starting salaries (hypothetical) of all 1984 geography graduates from the University of North Carolina (UNC)? What is your best estimate of a "typical" starting salary for a geography major? In reality, the major at UNC having the highest average starting salary in 1984 was actually geography. This was because Michael Jordan was a geography major!

36

Using PivotTables to Describe Data

■ I work for a small travel agency, and I'm about to do a mass mailing of a travel brochure. My funds are limited, so I want to mail the brochure to people who spend the most money on travel. For a random sample of 925 people, I have the gender, age, and the amount they spent on travel last year. How can I use this data to determine how gender and age influence a person's travel expenditures? What recommendations can I make about the type of person to whom I should mail the brochure?

■ Suppose that you're doing market research about Volvo Cross Country Wagons. Your goal is to determine what factors influence the likelihood that a family will purchase a station wagon. For a large sample of families, you're given the family size (large or small) and the family income (high or low). Can you determine how family size and income influence the likelihood that a family purchases a station wagon?

■ You work for a microchip manufacturer and are given monthly actual and predicted sales during 1997 for chip 1, chip 2, and chip 3 in Canada, France, and the United States. You are also given the variance, or difference, between actual revenues and budgeted revenues. For each month and each combination of country and product, you'd like to display the following data: actual revenue, budgeted revenue, actual variance, actual revenue as percentage of annual revenue, variance as percentage of budgeted revenue.

■   I often have to pull data such as April sales of chip 1 in France from a PivotTable in order to use the data in determining profit. Unfortunately, this data moves around as new fields are added to my PivotTable. Does Excel have a function that enables me to always pull April chip 1 sales in France from the PivotTable?

In numerous business situations, you need to slice and dice your data to gain important business insights. In the travel agency example, for instance, you would like to slice the data so that you can determine whether the average amount spent on travel is influenced by age or gender or both factors. In the station wagon example, we'd like to compare the fraction of large families that buy a station wagon to the fraction of small families that purchase a station wagon. In the microchip example, we'd like to determine our total chip 1 sales in France during April, and so on. An Excel PivotTable is an incredibly powerful tool that can be used to slice and dice data. The easiest way to understand how a PivotTable works is to walk through some carefully constructed examples, so let's get started!

I work for a small travel agency, and I'm about to do a mass mailing of a travel brochure. My funds are limited, so I want to mail the brochure to people who spend the most money on travel. For a random sample of 925 people, I have the gender, age, and the amount they spent on travel last year. How can I use this data to determine how gender and age influence a person's travel expenditures? What recommendations can I make about the type of person to whom I should mail the brochure?

To understand this data, we need a breakdown of

■   Average amount spent on travel by gender

■   Average amount spent on travel for each age group

■   Average amount spent on travel by gender for each age group

Our data is included on the worksheet named Data in the file Travel-Data.xls. A sample of the data is shown in Figure 36-1. For example, our first person is a 44-year-old male who spent $997 on travel.

To determine the average amount spent on travel by men and women, we begin by selecting a cell anywhere in the range that contains our data. When you create a PivotTable, the data must have headings in the first row of the range that defines the data. Then choose Data, Pivot Table And PivotChart Report. Excel displays the dialog box shown in Figure 36-2.

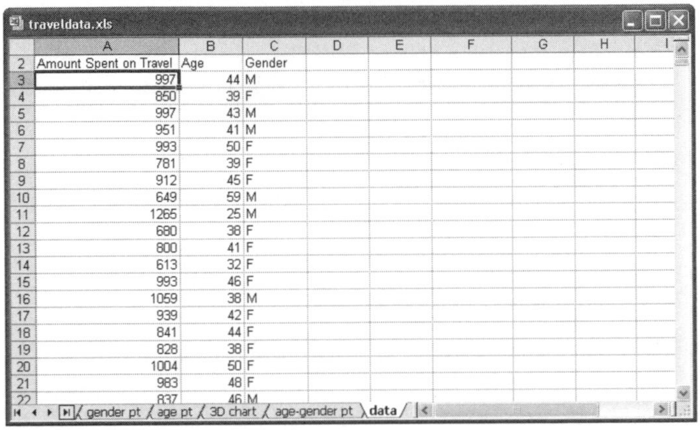

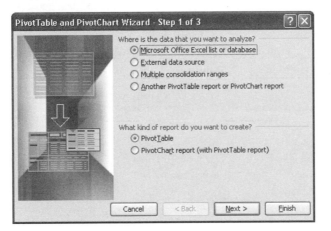

Figure 36-1   Travel agency data showing amount spent on travel, age, and gender.

Figure 36-2   The first step in the PivotTable and PivotChart Wizard.

Because we're basing our PivotTable on data from a spreadsheet, we'll select the option Microsoft Excel List Or Database. Here's a recap of situations in which you'd use a different option:

■ **External Data Source**   Use this option if the PivotTable will be formed using data from a database created in Microsoft Access, dBASE, or Microsoft SQL Server.

■ **Multiple Consolidation Ranges**   Use this option if your PivotTable is to be based on data from multiple ranges and/or multiple worksheets.

- **Another PivotTable Report Or PivotChart Report**   Use this option if you're creating a PivotTable based on a set of data that has previously been used to create a PivotTable. If applicable, this procedure is more efficient than creating a PivotTable from the actual data.

After selecting PivotTable as the type of report to create, we click Next and see the dialog box shown in Figure 36-3.

Figure 36-3   Use this dialog box to indicate the location of the data you want to use as the basis of a PivotTable.

Excel usually finds all your data (in our case, the data is in the range A2:C927). If Excel doesn't select the correct data range, you can enter it yourself. Remember that the first row of your data range must contain a heading for each column. After clicking Next, the dialog box shown in Figure 36-4 shows up.

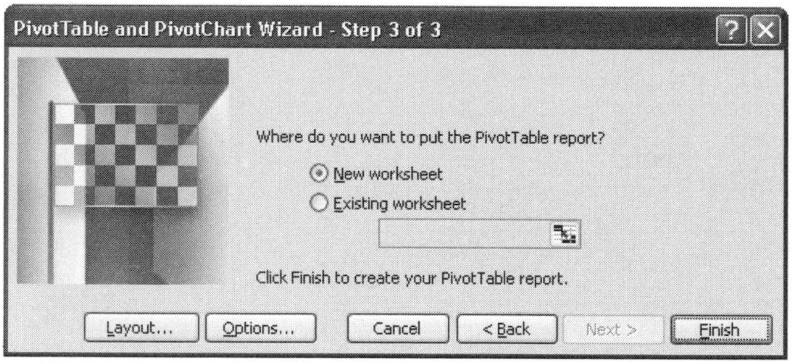

Figure 36-4   Dialog box for locating the PivotTable.

Here we've selected New Worksheet. If you want the PivotTable to be in an existing worksheet, select Existing Worksheet and then point to the cell where you want the upper left corner of the PivotTable to appear. When you click Finish, you'll see the PivotTable design area and the field list, shown in Figure 36-5. The field list enables you to determine how the PivotTable will summarize the data.

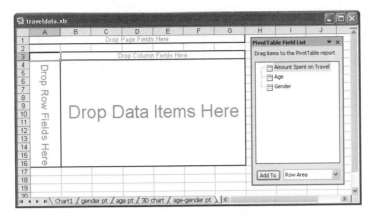

Figure 36-5   You can use the PivotTable field list to create a PivotTable.

For now, we'll ignore page fields. We first want a breakdown of the amount spent on travel by gender. To organize the PivotTable to display this data, we drag Gender from the field list to the area labeled Drop Row Fields Here, and drag Amount Spent On Travel to the area labeled Drop Data Items Here. This yields the PivotTable results shown in Figure 36-6.

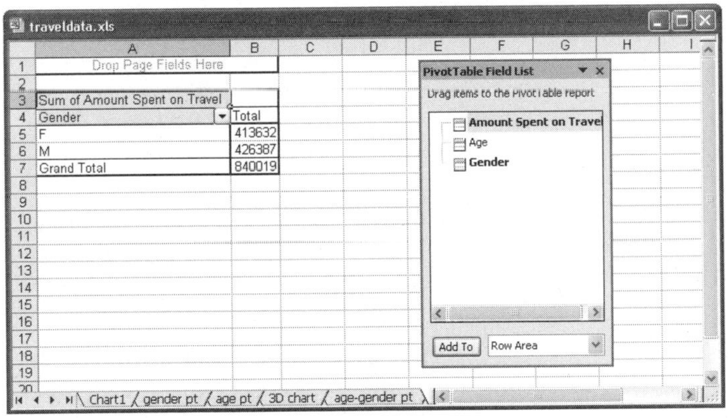

Figure 36-6   This PivotTable summarizes total travel expenditures by gender.

We can tell from the heading Sum of Amount Spent on Travel that we are summarizing the total amount spent on travel, but we actually want the average amount spent on travel by men and women. To calculate these quantities, we double-click on Sum of Amount Spent on Travel and then select Average from the PivotTable Field dialog box, shown in Figure 36-7.

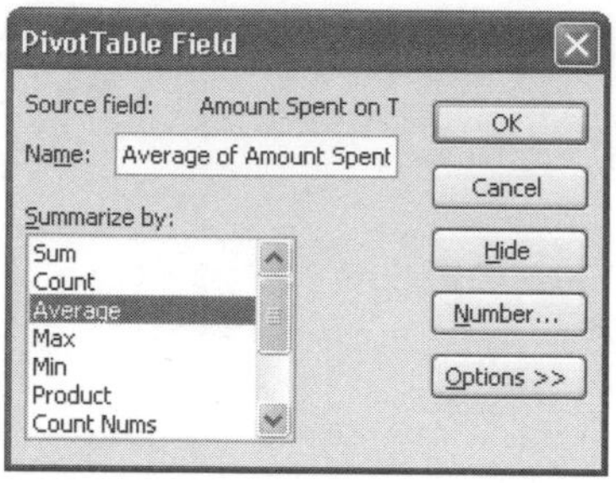

Figure 36-7 You can select a different summary function in the PivotTable Field dialog box.

We now obtain the results shown in Figure 36-8.

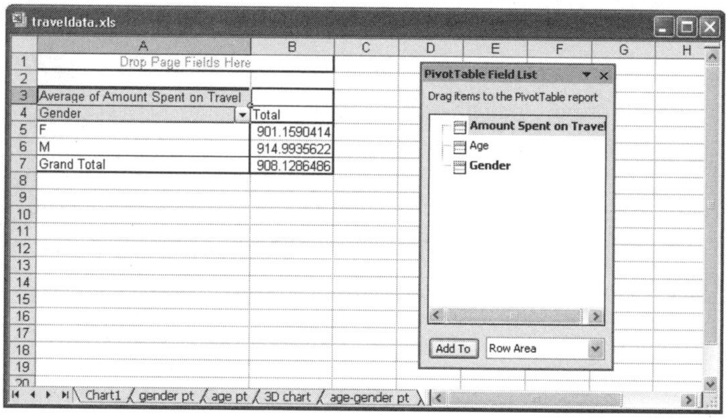

Figure 36-8 Average travel expenditures by gender.

We find that on average, people spend $908.13 on travel. Women spend $901.16 on average, while men spend $914.99. This PivotTable indicates that gender has little influence on the propensity to travel. By the way, we could "pivot" Gender to the column field area (shown in Figure 36-5) and obtain the PivotTable shown in Figure 36-9. PivotTables get their name from the fact that you can easily switch the layout from a row to a column view. By clicking on the drop-down arrow next to Gender, you can show just male or female results if you want.

Now we want to see how age influences travel spending. To remove Gender from the PivotTable, just drag Gender off the PivotTable. Then, to get a spending breakdown by age, drag Age to the row area. The PivotTable now appears as it's shown in Figure 36-10. (Some rows are hidden.)

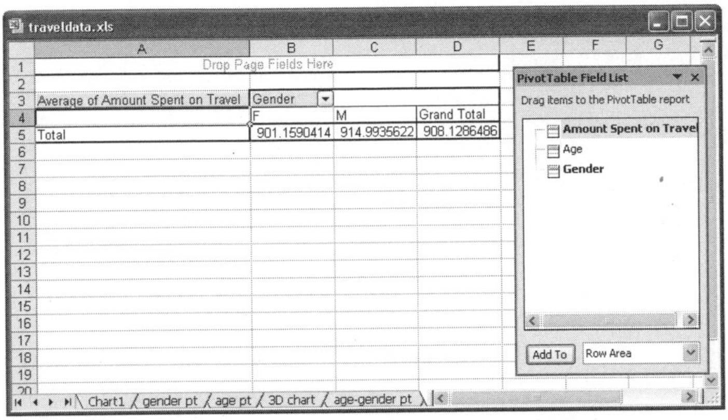

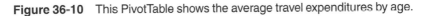

Figure 36-9   Column view of the travel-by-gender PivotTable.

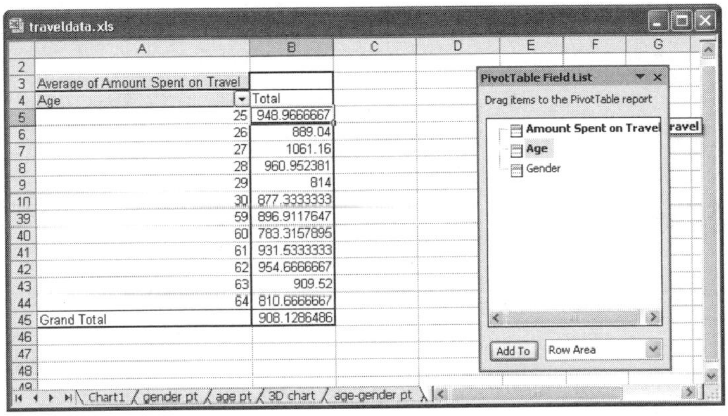

Figure 36-10   This PivotTable shows the average travel expenditures by age.

We find that age seems to have little effect on travel expenditures. In fact, this PivotTable is pretty useless in its present state. We need to group data by age to see any trends. To group our results by age, right-click anywhere in the Age column, choose Group And Show Detail, and then choose Group. In the Grouping dialog box, you can designate the interval by which to define an age group. Using 10 year increments, we obtain the PivotTable shown in Figure 36-11.

We now find that 25–34 year olds on average spend $935.84 on travel, 55–64 year olds on average spend $903.57 on travel, and so on. This information is more useful, but it still indicates that people of all ages tend to spend about the same amount on travel. This view of our data does not help determine who we should mail our brochure to.

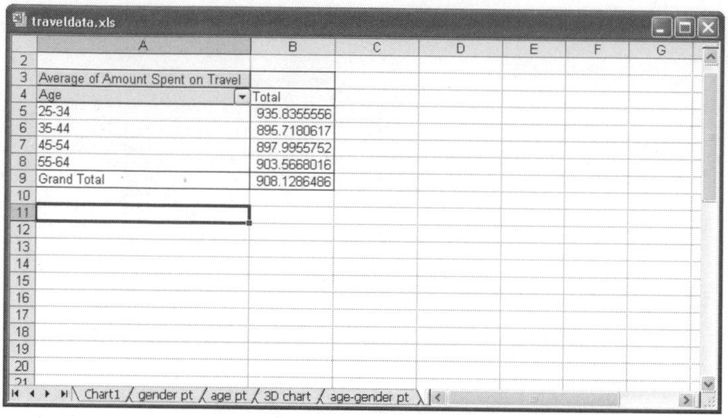

Figure 36-11   Use the Group And Show Detail command to group detailed records.

Finally, let's get a breakdown of average travel spending by age, for men and women separately. All we have to do is drag Gender to the Column area of the PivotTable (above the label Total in Figure 36-11) and we obtain the Pivot-Table shown in Figure 36-12.

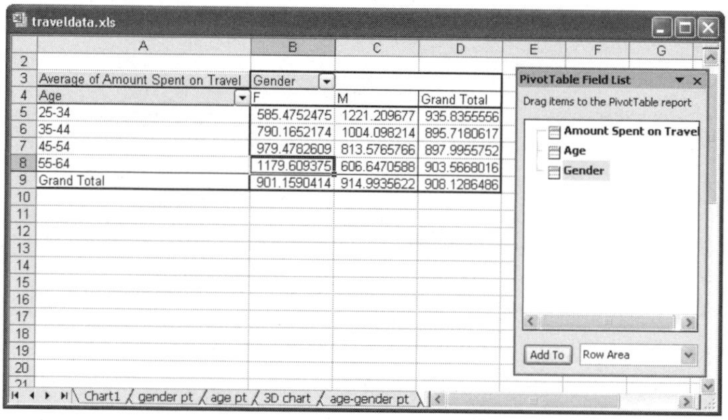

Figure 36-12   Age/gender breakdown of travel spending.

Now we're cooking! We see that as age increases, women spend more on travel and men spend less. Now we know who should get the brochure: older women and younger men. As one of my students said, "That would be some kind of cruise!"

A graph provides a nice summary of our analysis. By right-clicking on the PivotTable and choosing PivotChart, we can display the chart shown in Figure 36-13.

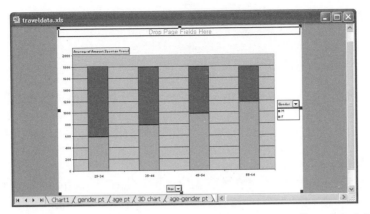

Figure 36-13 PivotChart for age/gender travel expenditure breakdown.

We see that each age group spends around the same on travel, but as age increases, women spend more than men. If you want to use a different type of chart, you can change the chart type by right-clicking the PivotChart and then choosing Chart Type. For example, if we select the chart type described as Clustered Column With A 3-D Visual Effect (the fourth option under Column), we obtain the chart shown in Figure 36-14.

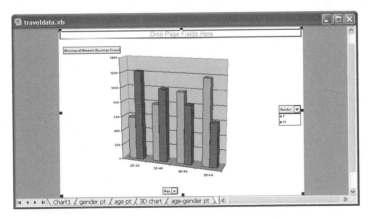

Figure 36-14 A 3-D PivotChart for travel expenditures.

Notice that the bars showing expenditures by males decrease with age, and the bars representing the amount spent by women increase with age. We can see why the PivotTables that showed only gender and age data failed to unmask this pattern. Because half our sample population are men and half are women, we found that the average amount spent by people does not depend on the age. (Notice that the average height of the two bars for each age is about the same.) We also found that the average amount spent for men and women was approximately the same. We can see this because averaged over all ages, the blue and red bars have approximately equal heights. Slicing and dicing our data simultaneously along age and gender does a much better job of showing us the real scoop.

Suppose that you're doing market research about Volvo Cross Country Wagons. Your goal is to determine what factors influence the likelihood that a family will purchase a station wagon. For a large sample of families, you're given the family size (large or small) and the family income (high or low). Can you determine how family size and income influence the likelihood that a family purchases a station wagon?

In the file Station.xls, you can find the following information.

■ Family size, large or small.

■ Income, high or low.

■ Did family buy station wagon? Yes or No.

A sample of the data is shown in Figure 36-15. For example, the first family listed is a small, high-income family that did not buy a station wagon.

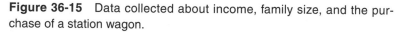

	A	B	C	D	E	F	G	H	I	J	K
1											
2		Station Wagon?	Family Size	Salary							
3		No	Small	High							
4		Yes	Large	High							
5		Yes	Large	High							
6		Yes	Large	High							
7		Yes	Large	High							
8		No	Small	High							
9		Yes	Large	High							
10		Yes	Large	High							
11		Yes	Large	Low							
12		Yes	Large	High							
13		Yes	Large	Low							
14		No	Small	Low							
15		No	Small	Low							
16		No	Small	High							
17		Yes	Large	High							
18		Yes	Large	High							
19		No	Small	High							
20		Yes	Large	High							

Figure 36-15   Data collected about income, family size, and the purchase of a station wagon.

We want to determine how family size and income influence the likelihood that a family purchases a station wagon. The trick is to look at how income affects purchases for each family size and how family size affects purchases for each income level.

To begin, we choose Data, PivotTable And PivotChart Report, and then select our data (the cell range B2:D345). Using the PivotTable field list, we drag Salary and then Family Size to the Row area, Station Wagon to the Column area, and any of the three fields to the Data area. You'll obtain the PivotTable shown in Figure 36-16. Notice that Excel has chosen to summarize the data appropriately by counting the number of observations in each category. For example, 34 high-salary, large families did not buy a station wagon, while 100 high-salary, large families did buy one.

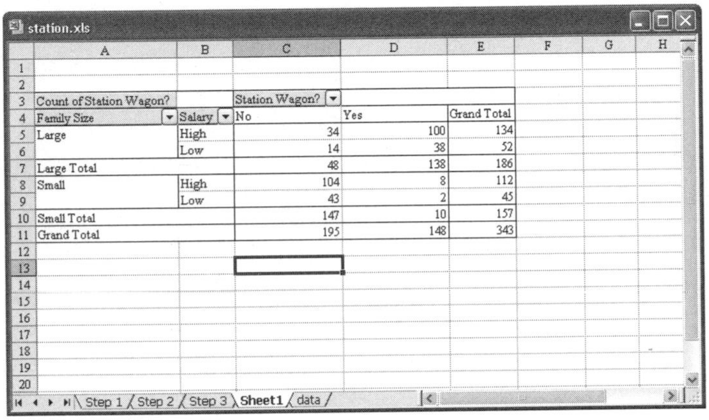

Count of Station Wagon?		Station Wagon?		
Family Size	Salary	No	Yes	Grand Total
Large	High	34	100	134
	Low	14	38	52
Large Total		48	138	186
Small	High	104	8	112
	Low	43	2	45
Small Total		147	10	157
Grand Total		195	148	343

Figure 36-16 Summary of station wagon ownership by family size and salary.

We would like to know, for each row in the PivotTable, the percentage of families that purchased a station wagon. To display the data in this format, we right-click anywhere in the PivotTable and then choose Field Settings, which displays the PivotTable Field dialog box. In the dialog box, click Options and then select % Of Row in the Show Data As list. We now obtain the PivotTable shown in Figure 36-17.

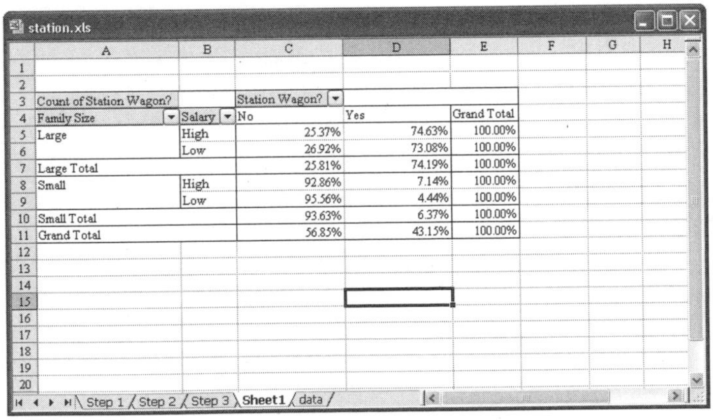

Count of Station Wagon?		Station Wagon?		
Family Size	Salary	No	Yes	Grand Total
Large	High	25.37%	74.63%	100.00%
	Low	26.92%	73.08%	100.00%
Large Total		25.81%	74.19%	100.00%
Small	High	92.86%	7.14%	100.00%
	Low	95.56%	4.44%	100.00%
Small Total		93.63%	6.37%	100.00%
Grand Total		56.85%	43.15%	100.00%

Figure 36-17 Percentage breakdown of station wagon ownership by income for large and small families.

From Figure 36-17 we learn that for both large and small families, income has little effect on whether the family purchases a station wagon. Now we try to determine how family size affects the propensity to buy a station wagon for high- and low-income families. To do this, we move Family Size to the right of Salary and obtain the PivotTable shown in Figure 36-18.

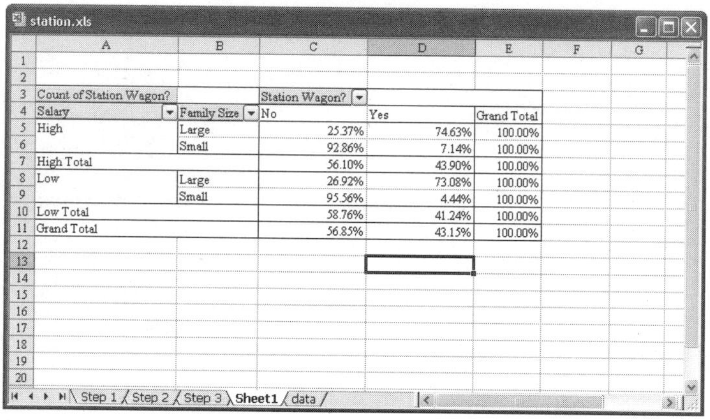

Count of Station Wagon?		Station Wagon?		
Salary	Family Size	No	Yes	Grand Total
High	Large	25.37%	74.63%	100.00%
	Small	92.86%	7.14%	100.00%
High Total		56.10%	43.90%	100.00%
Low	Large	26.92%	73.08%	100.00%
	Small	95.56%	4.44%	100.00%
Low Total		58.76%	41.24%	100.00%
Grand Total		56.85%	43.15%	100.00%

Figure 36-18 Breakdown of station wagon ownership by family size for high and low salaries.

From this table we learn that for high-income families, a large family is much more likely to buy a station wagon than is a small family. Similarly, for low-income families, a large family is also more likely to purchase a wagon than is a small family. The bottom line is that family size has a much greater effect on the likelihood that a family purchases a station wagon than does income.

You work for a microchip manufacturer and are given monthly actual and predicted sales during 1997 for chip 1, chip 2, and chip 3 in Canada, France, and the United States. You are also given the variance, or difference, between actual revenues and budgeted revenues. For each month and each combination of country and product, you'd like to display the following data: actual revenue, budgeted revenue, actual variance, actual revenue as percentage of annual revenue, variance as percentage of budgeted revenue.

Suppose you are a finance manager for a microchip manufacturer. You sell your products in different countries and at different times. PivotTables can help you summarize your data in a format in which it's easily understood.

The file PTableExample.xls includes monthly actual and predicted sales during 1997 of chip 1, chip 2, and chip 3 in Canada, France, and the United States. The file also contains the variance, or difference, between actual revenues and budgeted revenues. A sample of the data is shown in Figure 36-19. For example, in January in the U.S., chip 1 sold $4,000, although sales of $5,454 were predicted. This yielded a variance of -$1,454.

	A	B	C	D	E	F
1	Month	Product	Country	Revenue	Budget	Var
2	January	Chip 1	US	4000	5454	-1454
3	January	Chip 1	Canada	3424	5341	-1917
4	January	Chip 1	US	8324	1232	7092
5	January	Chip 1	France	5555	3424	2131
6	January	Chip 1	Canada	5341	8324	-2983
7	January	Chip 1	US	1232	5555	-4323
8	January	Chip 1	France	3424	5341	-1917
9	January	Chip 1	Canada	8324	1232	7092
10	January	Chip 1	US	5555	3424	2131
11	January	Chip 1	France	5341	8324	-2983
12	January	Chip 1	Canada	1232	5555	-4323
13	January	Chip 1	US	3424	5341	-1917
14	January	Chip 1	Canada	8383	5454	2929
15	January	Chip 1	France	8324	1232	7092
16	January	Chip 1	Canada	5555	3424	2131
17	January	Chip 1	US	5341	8324	-2983
18	January	Chip 1	France	1232	5555	-4323
19	January	Chip 1	France	3523	9295	-5772

Figure 36-19   Chip data from different countries for different months showing actual, budget, and variance.

For each month and each combination of country and product, we would like to display the following data:

- Actual revenue

- Budgeted revenue

- Actual variance

- Each month's actual revenue as a percentage of annual revenue

- Variance as a percentage of budgeted revenue

To begin, select a cell within the range of data we're working with (remember that the first row must include headings) and then choose Data, PivotTable And PivotChart Report. Select Microsoft Excel List or Database and PivotTable (rather than PivotChart). Click Next, and Excel automatically determines that our data is in the range A1:F208. After clicking Next again and indicating that we want the PivotTable to appear in a new worksheet, we click Finish and see the PivotTable layout area and the field list.

If we drag Month to the Row area, Country to the Column area, and Revenue to the Data area, for example, we obtain total revenue each month by country. A field you add to the Page Field area (Product, for example) lets you filter your PivotTable using values in that field. By adding Product to the Page Field area, we can view sales of only chip 1 by month for each country. Given that we want to be able to show data for any combination of country and product, we should add Month to the Row area of the PivotTable and both Country and Product to the Page Field area. Next we drag Var, Revenue, and Budget to the Data area. We have now created the PivotTable that is shown in Figure 36-20.

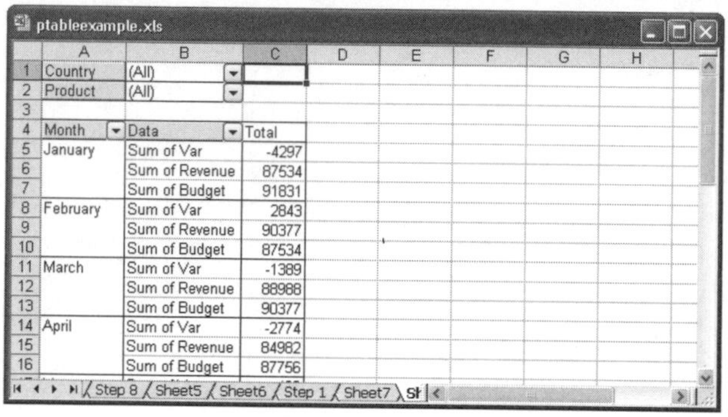

ptableexample.xls

	A	B	C
1	Country	(All)	
2	Product	(All)	
3			
4	Month	Data	Total
5	January	Sum of Var	-4297
6		Sum of Revenue	87534
7		Sum of Budget	91831
8	February	Sum of Var	2843
9		Sum of Revenue	90377
10		Sum of Budget	87534
11	March	Sum of Var	-1389
12		Sum of Revenue	88988
13		Sum of Budget	90377
14	April	Sum of Var	-2774
15		Sum of Revenue	84982
16		Sum of Budget	87756

Figure 36-20 The first of our microchip finance PivotTables.

The PivotTable would be more aesthetically pleasing if our data were displayed across columns rather than down rows. If we drag the Data button onto the label Total, our data is now listed across columns rather down a single row, as is shown in Figure 36-21. For example, in January, total revenue was $87,534, total budgeted sales were $91,831, so our actual sales fell $4,297 short of forecast.

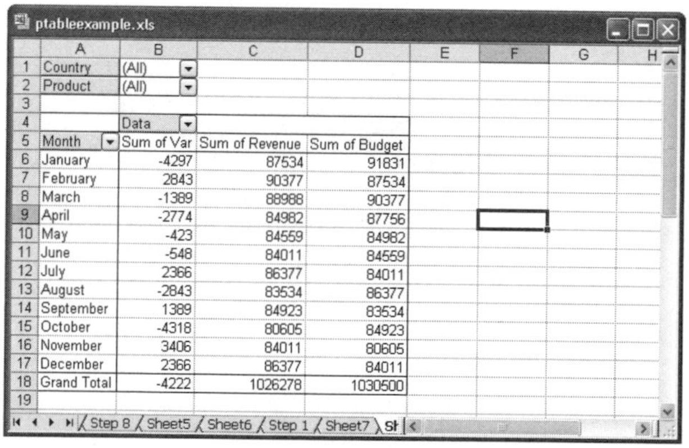

ptableexample.xls

	A	B	C	D
1	Country	(All)		
2	Product	(All)		
3				
4		Data		
5	Month	Sum of Var	Sum of Revenue	Sum of Budget
6	January	-4297	87534	91831
7	February	2843	90377	87534
8	March	-1389	88988	90377
9	April	-2774	84982	87756
10	May	-423	84559	84982
11	June	-548	84011	84559
12	July	2366	86377	84011
13	August	-2843	83534	86377
14	September	1389	84923	83534
15	October	-4318	80605	84923
16	November	3406	84011	80605
17	December	2366	86377	84011
18	Grand Total	-4222	1026278	1030500
19				

Figure 36-21 Monthly summary of revenue, budget, and variances.

We want to determine the percentage of revenue earned during each month. We again drag Revenue from the field list to the Data area of the PivotTable table. Right-click in this data column, and then choose Field Settings. In the PivotTable Field dialog box, click Options. In the Show Data As list, select % Of Column and rename this field as % of Revenue, as shown in Figure 36-22.

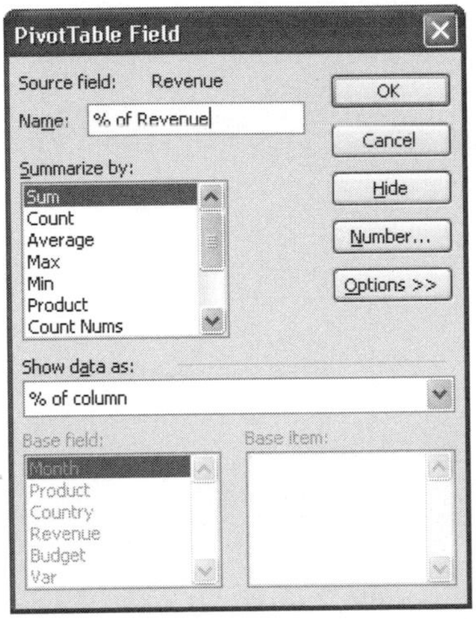

Figure 36-22 Creating each month's percentage of annual revenue.

We now obtain the PivotTable shown in Figure 36-23. January sales provided 8.53 percent of revenue. Total revenue for the year was $1,026,278.

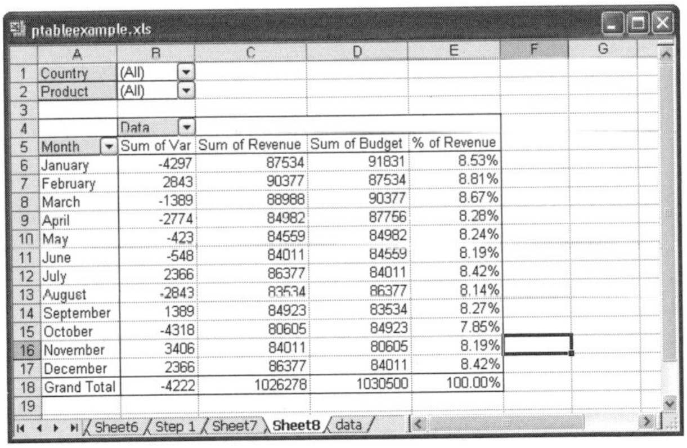
ptableexample.xls

	A	B	C	D	E
1	Country	(All)			
2	Product	(All)			
3					
4		Data			
5	Month	Sum of Var	Sum of Revenue	Sum of Budget	% of Revenue
6	January	-4297	87534	91831	8.53%
7	February	2843	90377	87534	8.81%
8	March	-1389	88988	90377	8.67%
9	April	-2774	84982	87756	8.28%
10	May	-423	84559	84982	8.24%
11	June	-548	84011	84559	8.19%
12	July	2366	86377	84011	8.42%
13	August	-2843	83534	86377	8.14%
14	September	1389	84923	83534	8.27%
15	October	-4318	80605	84923	7.85%
16	November	3406	84011	80605	8.19%
17	December	2366	86377	84011	8.42%
18	Grand Total	-4222	1026278	1030500	100.00%
19					

Sheet6 / Step 1 / Sheet7 / Sheet8 / data

Figure 36-23 PivotTable with monthly revenue percentages.

Creating a Calculated Field Now we want to determine for each month the variance as a percentage of total sales. To do this, we will create a *calculated field*. Select a cell anywhere within the data area of the PivotTable, and then choose Formulas from the PivotTable menu on the PivotTable toolbar (in Office XP or later). Choose Calculated Field, and you'll see the Insert Calculated Field dialog box. As shown in Figure 36-24, enter a name for your field, and then enter your formula. The formula we're using in this example is *=Var/Budget*. You can enter the formula yourself or use the list of fields and the Insert Field button to add a field to the formula. After clicking Add and then OK, we obtain the PivotTable shown in Figure 36-25.

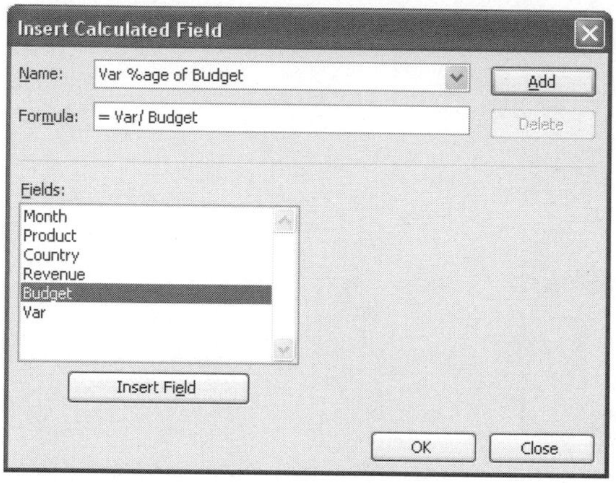

Figure 36-24 Creating a calculated field.

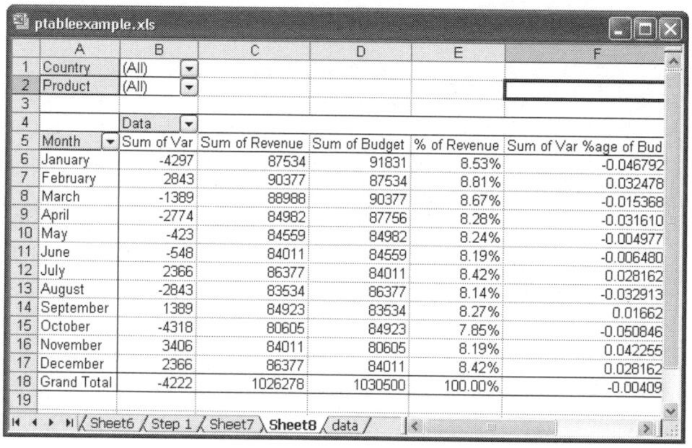

ptableexample.xls

	A	B	C	D	E	F
1	Country	(All)				
2	Product	(All)				
3						
4		Data				
5	Month	Sum of Var	Sum of Revenue	Sum of Budget	% of Revenue	Sum of Var %age of Bud
6	January	-4297	87534	91831	8.53%	-0.046792
7	February	2843	90377	87534	8.81%	0.032478
8	March	-1389	88988	90377	8.67%	-0.015368
9	April	-2774	84982	87756	8.28%	-0.031610
10	May	-423	84559	84982	8.24%	-0.004977
11	June	-548	84011	84559	8.19%	-0.006480
12	July	2366	86377	84011	8.42%	0.028162
13	August	-2843	83534	86377	8.14%	-0.032913
14	September	1389	84923	83534	8.27%	0.01662
15	October	-4318	80605	84923	7.85%	-0.050846
16	November	3406	84011	80605	8.19%	0.042255
17	December	2366	86377	84011	8.42%	0.028162
18	Grand Total	-4222	1026278	1030500	100.00%	-0.00409
19						

Sheet6 / Step 1 / Sheet7 / Sheet8 / data

Figure 36-25 PivotTable with calculated field for variance percentage.

Thus in January, our sales were 4.7 percent lower than budgeted. By opening the Insert Calculated Field dialog box again, you can modify or delete a calculated field.

Using Page Fields To see sales of chip 2 in France, for example, you can select the appropriate values from the Product and Country fields in the Page Fields area. With Chip 2 and France selected, we would see the PivotTable shown in Figure 36-26.

Country	France				
Product	Chip 2				
	Data				
Month	Sum of Var	Sum of Revenue	Sum of Budget	% of Revenue	Sum of Var %age of Budget
February	-3846	29108	32954	23.90%	-0.116708139
May	3318	35363	32045	29.04%	0.103541894
August	2769	33432	30663	27.45%	0.090304276
November	0	23876	23876	19.61%	0
Grand Total	2241	121779	119538	100.00%	0.018747177

Figure 36-26 Sales of chip 2 in France.

If we drag, say, Country to the Row area, we can select which countries we want to view. For example, we could select only France and the U.S. to obtain the PivotTable shown in Figure 36-27.

Product	Chip 2					
		Data				
Month	Country	Sum of Var	Sum of Revenue	Sum of Budget	% of Revenue	Sum of Var %age of Budget
February	France	-3846	29108	32954	13.10%	-0.116708139
	US	3371	25906	22535	11.66%	0.149589527
February Total		-475	55014	55489	24.76%	-0.008560255
May	France	3318	35363	32045	15.91%	0.103541894
	US	-12073	20521	32594	9.23%	-0.370405596
May Total		-8755	55884	64639	25.15%	-0.135444546
August	France	2769	33432	30663	15.05%	0.090304276
	US	-1757	26127	27884	11.76%	-0.063011046
August Total		1012	59559	58547	26.80%	0.017285258
November	France	0	23876	23876	10.74%	0
	US	477	27876	27399	12.54%	0.017409395
November Total		477	51752	51275	23.29%	0.009302779
Grand Total		-7741	222209	229950	100.00%	-0.03366384

Figure 36-27 France and U.S. sales data.

Grouping Items Often we want to group headings in a PivotTable. For example, we might want to combine sales for January through March. To create a group, select the items you want to group, right-click the selection, and then choose Group And Show Detail, Group. An additional column is displayed with a group heading, and you'll obtain the PivotTable shown in Figure 36-28.

You can now drag the Month button away from the PivotTable and rename Group 1 *January-March* to obtain the PivotTable shown in Figure 36-29.

ptableexample.xls

Product	(All)					
Country	(All)					
		Data				
Month2	Month	Sum of Var	Sum of Revenue	Sum of Budget	% age of revenue	Sum of Var % of Budegt
Group1	January	-4297	87534	91831	8.53%	-0.046792477
	February	2843	90377	87534	8.81%	0.032478808
	March	-1389	88988	90377	8.67%	-0.015368954
April	April	-2774	84982	87756	8.28%	-0.031610374
May	May	-423	84559	84982	8.24%	-0.004977525
June	June	-548	84011	84559	8.19%	-0.006480682
July	July	2366	86377	84011	8.42%	0.028162979
August	August	-2843	83534	86377	8.14%	-0.032913854
September	September	1389	84923	83534	8.27%	0.01662796
October	October	-4318	80605	84923	7.85%	-0.050846061
November	November	3406	84011	80605	8.19%	0.042255443
December	December	2366	86377	84011	8.42%	0.028162979
Grand Total		-4222	1026278	1030500	100.00%	-0.00409704

get pivotdata / Step 5 / Step 6 / Step 7 / Step 8 / Sheet5 / Sl

Figure 36-28 Grouping items together for January, February, and March.

ptableexample.xls

Product	(All)				
Country	(All)				
	Data				
Month2	Sum of Var	Sum of Revenue	Sum of Budget	% age of revenue	Sum of Var % of Budegt
January-March	-2843	266899	269742	26.01%	-0.010539701
April	-2774	84982	87756	8.28%	-0.031610374
May	-423	84559	84982	8.24%	-0.004977525
June	-548	84011	84559	8.19%	-0.006480682
July	2366	86377	84011	8.42%	0.028162979
August	-2843	83534	86377	8.14%	-0.032913854
September	1389	84923	83534	8.27%	0.01662796
October	-4318	80605	84923	7.85%	-0.050846061
November	3406	84011	80605	8.19%	0.042255443
December	2366	86377	84011	8.42%	0.028162979
Grand Total	-4222	1026278	1030500	100.00%	-0.00409704

get pivotdata / Step 5 / Step 6 / Step 7 / Step 8 / Sh

Figure 36-29 Final grouping of data for sales in January, February, and March.

Remarks about Grouping

1. You can disband a group by selecting Group And Show Detail and then Ungroup.
2. You can group nonadjacent selections by holding down the Ctrl key while you select nonadjacent rows or columns.
3. With numerical values or dates in a row field, you can group by number or dates in arbitrary intervals. For example, you can create groups for age ranges and then find the average income for all 25-34 year olds.

Calculated Item   We could also have created the January-March group by creating a *calculated item*. A calculated item works just like a calculated field except that you are creating a single row rather than a column. To create a calculated item, you should select an item in the Row area of the PivotTable, not an item in the body of the PivotTable.

Drilling Down   If you double-click on a cell in a PivotTable, you see all the detailed data that's summarized in that field. For example, double-clicking on any March entry will display the data that's related to March sales.

Layout Option   In Excel 97 and earlier versions, you had to create a PivotTable with the layout feature. In our current example, the layout feature displays the field and page layout as shown in Figure 36-30. In Excel 2000 and later versions, you can use the layout option by clicking Layout during step 3 of the PivotTable Wizard (shown earlier in Figure 36-4). In a completed PivotTable, you can display the Layout window by right-clicking in the PivotTable, selecting PivotTable Wizard, and then clicking Layout.

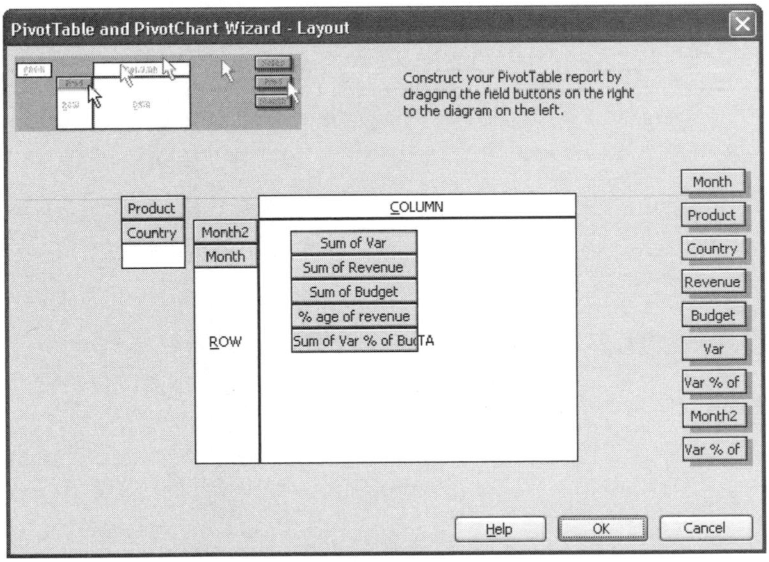

Figure 36-30   Layout window for the microchip PivotTable.

For me, at least, the layout approach makes it easier to modify the Data area of a PivotTable.

Refreshing a Pivot Table   To refresh the data in a PivotTable so that it shows any changes in the source data, right-click the PivotTable and then choose Refresh Data. You can also click the Refresh Data button on the PivotTable tool bar. (It's the button with an exclamation point.)

Table Options By right-clicking in the PivotTable and selecting Table Options, you'll display the PivotTable Options dialog box, shown in Figure 36-31.

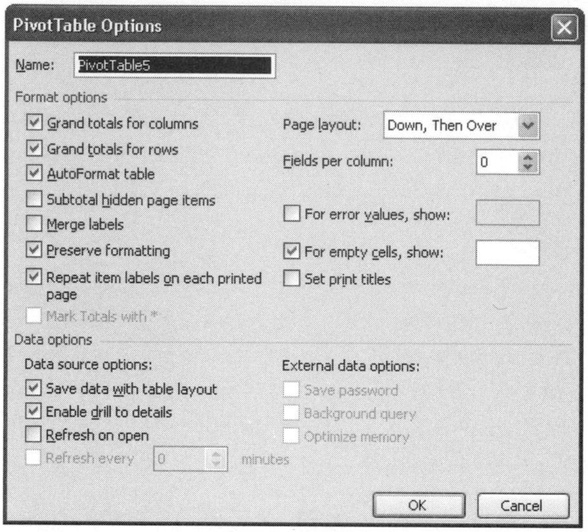

Figure 36-31 PivotTable Options dialog box.

This dialog box provides options that enable you to suppress row or column totals, for example, or to refresh the table each time you open the file.

AutoFormat By selecting Format Report from the PivotTable toolbar, you can format your PivotTable with one of the many formats. A sample of the available formats is shown in Figure 36-32.

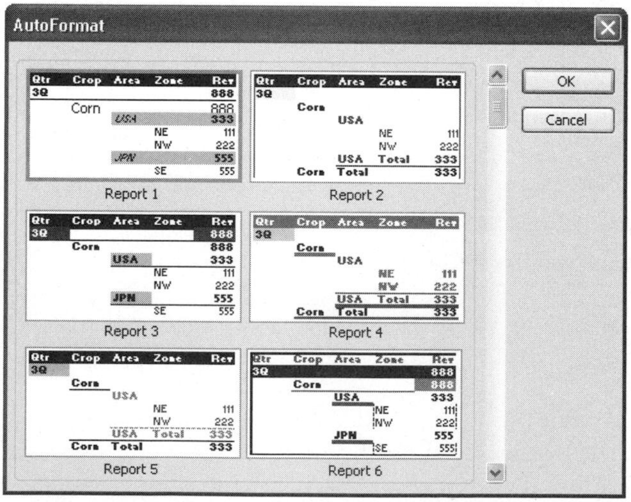

Figure 36-32 A sampling of autoformat options.

I often have to pull data such as April sales of chip 1 in France from a PivotTable in order to use the data in determining profit. Unfortunately, this data moves around as new fields are added to my PivotTable. Does Excel have a function that enables me to always pull April chip 1 sales in France from the PivotTable?

Yes Virginia, there is such a function. The GETPIVOTDATA function fills the bill. Suppose that you want to extract sales of chip 1 in France during April from the PivotTable contained on the worksheet GetPivotData in the file ChipPTable.xls. (See Figure 36-33.) Entering in cell E2 the formula *GETPIVOTDATA(A4,"April France Chip 1 Sum of Revenue")* yields the correct value ($37,600) even if additional products, countries, and months are added to the PivotTable later.

The first argument for this function is the upper left corner of the PivotTable (cell A4). Then we enclose in quotation marks (separated by spaces) the PivotTable headings that define the entry we want. The last entry must specify the data field, but other headings can be listed in any order. Thus our formula means "For the PivotTable whose upper left corner is in cell A4, find the Sum of Revenue for chip 1 in France during April." This formula will return the correct answer even if the sales data for chip 1 in France in April moves to a different location in the PivotTable.

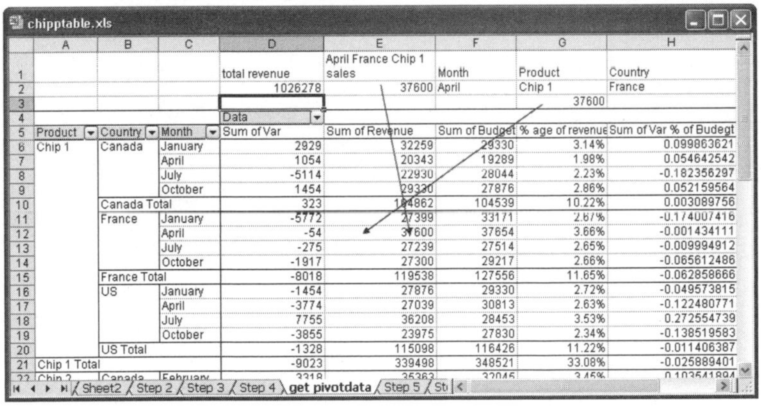

	A	B	C	D	E	F	G	H
1				total revenue	April France Chip 1 sales	Month	Product	Country
2				1026278	37600	April	Chip 1	France
3							37600	
4				Data				
5	Product	Country	Month	Sum of Var	Sum of Revenue	Sum of Budget	% age of revenue	Sum of Var % of Budegt
6	Chip 1	Canada	January	2929	32259	29330	3.14%	0.099863621
7			April	1054	20343	19289	1.98%	0.054642542
8			July	-5114	22930	28044	2.23%	-0.182356297
9			October	1454	29330	27876	2.86%	0.052159564
10		Canada Total		323	104862	104539	10.22%	0.003089756
11		France	January	-5772	27399	33171	2.67%	-0.174007416
12			April	-54	37600	37654	3.66%	-0.001434111
13			July	-275	27239	27514	2.65%	-0.009994912
14			October	-1917	27300	29217	2.66%	-0.065612486
15		France Total		-8018	119538	127556	11.65%	-0.062858666
16		US	January	-1454	27876	29330	2.72%	-0.049573815
17			April	-3774	27039	30813	2.63%	-0.122480771
18			July	7755	36208	28453	3.53%	0.272554739
19			October	-3855	23975	27830	2.34%	-0.138519583
20		US Total		-1328	115098	116426	11.22%	-0.011406387
21	Chip 1 Total			-9023	339498	348521	33.08%	-0.025889401
22	Chip 2	Canada	February	3318	35363	32045	3.45%	0.103541894

Figure 36-33 Use the GETPIVOTDATA function to locate data in a PivotTable.

Another way to obtain the chip1 April sales in France is by entering the following formula in cell G3: *GETPIVOTDATA(A4,F2&" "&G2&" "&H2&" "&I2)*. The double quotation marks (" ") insert a space. Recall that the ampersand (&) is used to combine text values. The advantage of this approach is that the formula can be easily copied and used again to efficiently retrieve multiple PivotTable entries.

If you want to simply return total revenue, you could enter the following formula (see cell D2): *GETPIVOTDATA(A4,"Sum of Revenue")*.

In Office XP or later, the easiest way to create a GETPIVOTDATA function reference is to select a blank cell, enter an equal sign, and then point to the cell whose value you want to retrieve. Excel automatically creates the appropriate GETPIVOTDATA function! Try this and see how easy it is.

You can also combine the MATCH and OFFSET functions (explained in Chapter 5 and Chapter 21, respectively) to "pick off" various PivotTable entries.

Problems

1. Chandler Enterprises produces microchips. Five types of defects (labeled 1–5) have been known to occur. Chips are manufactured by two operators (A and B). Four machines (1–4) are used to manufacture chips. You are given data about a sample of defective chips, including the type of defect, the operator, machine number, and day of the week. Use this data to chart a course of action that would lead, as quickly as possible, to improved product quality. You should use the PivotTable Wizard to "stratify" the defects with respect to type of defect, day of the week, machine used, and operator working. You might even want to break down the data by machine, operator, and so on. Assume that each operator and machine made an equal number of products. You'll find this data in the file Chandler.xls.

2. You own a fast food restaurant and have done some market research in an attempt to better understand your customers. For a random sample of customers, you are given the income, gender, and number of days per week that residents go out for fast food. Use this information to determine how gender and income influence the frequency with which a person goes out to eat fast food. Data is in the file Macdonald.xls.

3. Students at Faber College apply to study either English or Science. You have been assigned to determine whether Faber College discriminates against women in admitting students to the school of their choice. You are given the following data on Faber's students:

   ❑   Female or male.

   ❑   Major applied for, English (Eng) or Science (Sci).

   ❑   Admit? Yes or No.

   Assuming that women are as well qualified for each major as are men, does this data indicate that the college discriminated against women? Make sure you use all available information! The data is in the file Faber.xls.

4. You have been assigned to evaluate the quality of care given to heart attack patients at Emergency Room (ER) and Chicago Hope (CH). For the last month you are given the following patient data:

❑   Hospital. Where a patient was admitted, ER or CH.

❑   Risk category (high or low). High-risk people are less likely to survive than low-risk people.

❑   Patient outcome (live or die).

Use this data to determine which hospital is doing a better job of caring for heart attack patients. Hint: Use all the data! The data is in the file Hospital.xls.

5. You are given the monthly level of the Dow Jones Index for the years 1947–1992. Does this data indicate any unusual seasonal patterns in stock returns? Hint: You can extract the month (January, February, and so on) by using the formula TEXT(A4, "mmm") copied down any column. The data is in the file Dow.xls.

6. The file MakeupDb.xls contains information about the sales of makeup products. For each transaction you are given the following information:

❑   Name of salesperson

❑   Date of sale

❑   Product sold

❑   Units sold

❑   Transaction revenue

Create a PivotTable to compile the following information:

❑   The number of sales transactions for each salesperson.

❑   For each salesperson, the total revenue by product.

❑   Use your answer to the previous question to create a function that always yields Jen's lipstick sales.

❑   Total revenue generated by each salesperson broken down by location.

❑   Total revenue by salesperson and year. (Hint: You will need to do group data by year.)

7. For the years 1985–1992, you are given monthly interest rates on bonds that pay money one year after the day they're bought. It is often suggested that interest rates are more volatile—tend to change more—when interest rates are high. Does the data in the file Intrate-Volatility.xls support this statement? Hint: PivotTables can display standard deviations.

37

Summarizing Data with Database Statistical Functions

Joolas is a small makeup company. In an Excel spreadsheet they track each sales transaction. Often they want to answer questions such as:

■ How many dollars worth of lip gloss did Jen sell?

■ What was the average number of units of lipstick sold each time Jen made a sale in the East region?

■ How many dollars of sales were made by Emilee or in the East region?

■ How many dollars worth of lipstick were sold by Colleen or Zaret in the East region?

■ How many lipstick transactions were not in the East?

■ How many dollars worth of lipstick did Jen sell during 2004?

■ How many units of makeup were sold for a price of at least $3.20?

■ What is the total dollar amount each salesperson sold of each product?

■ What cute tricks can I use to set up criteria ranges?

■ I have a database that lists for each sales transaction the revenue, date, and product ID code. Given the date and ID code for a transaction, is there an easy way to pick off the transaction's revenue?

As you saw in Chapter 36, PivotTables are a great tool for summarizing data. Often, however, a PivotTable gives us much more information than we need. *Database statistical functions* make it easy to answer any "reporting" question without having to create a PivotTable.

You are already familiar with functions such as SUM, AVERAGE, COUNT, MAX, and MIN. By prefixing a *D* (which stands for *database*) to these (and other functions), you create a database statistical function. But what does the DSUM function do, for example, that the SUM function can't? While the SUM function adds up every cell in a cell range, the DSUM function allows you to specify (using criteria) a subset of rows to add together in a cell range. Suppose we have a sales database for a small makeup company that contains the following information about each sales transaction:

- Salesperson
- Transaction date
- Product sold
- Units sold
- Dollars of revenue generated by transaction
- Region of country where transaction took place

You can find this data in the file MakeupDb.xls, which is shown in Figure 37-1.

makeupdb.xls

	G	H	I	J	K	L	M	Z	AA
1									
2					78707				
3									
4	Trans Number	Name	Date	Product	Units	Dollars	Location		
5	1	Betsy	4/1/2004	lip gloss	45	$ 137.20	south		
6	2	Hallagan	3/10/2004	foundation	50	$ 152.01	midwest		
7	3	Ashley	2/25/2005	lipstick	9	$ 28.72	midwest		
8	4	Hallagan	5/22/2006	lip gloss	55	$ 167.08	west		
9	5	Zaret	6/17/2004	lip gloss	43	$ 130.60	midwest		
10	6	Colleen	11/27/2005	eye liner	58	$ 175.99	midwest		
11	7	Cristina	3/21/2004	eye liner	8	$ 25.80	midwest		
12	8	Colleen	12/17/2006	lip gloss	72	$ 217.84	midwest		
13	9	Ashley	7/5/2006	eye liner	75	$ 226.64	south		
14	10	Betsy	8/7/2006	lip gloss	24	$ 73.50	east		
15	11	Ashley	11/29/2004	mascara	43	$ 130.84	east		
16	12	Ashley	11/18/2004	lip gloss	23	$ 71.03	west		
17	13	Emilee	8/31/2005	lip gloss	49	$ 149.59	west		
18	14	Hallagan	1/1/2005	eye liner	18	$ 56.47	south		
19	15	Zaret	9/20/2006	foundation	-8	$ (21.99)	east		
20	16	Emilee	4/12/2004	mascara	45	$ 137.39	east		
21	17	Colleen	4/30/2006	mascara	66	$ 199.65	south		
22	18	Jen	8/31/2005	lip gloss	88	$ 265.19	midwest		

data

Figure 37-1 We'll use this data to describe how to work with database statistical functions.

Using the DSUM function with appropriate criteria, we could, for example, add up the revenue generated only by transactions involving lip gloss sales in the East during 2004. Essentially, the criteria we set up flags those rows that we want to include in the total sum. Within these rows, the DSUM function acts like the ordinary SUM function.

The syntax of the DSUM function is:

```
DSUM(database, field, criteria)
```

- *Database* is the cell range that makes up the database. The first row of the list contains labels for each column.

- *Field* is the column containing the values you want the function to add. You can define the field by enclosing the column label in quotation marks. (For example, we would designate the Dollars column by entering "Dollars".) The field can also be specified using the position of the column in the database, measured left to right. For example, if our database uses columns H through M, we could specify column H as field 1 and column M as field 6.

- *Criteria* refers to a cell range that specifies the rows on which the function should operate. The first row of a criteria range must include one or more column labels. (The only exception to this rule is computed criteria, which I'll discuss in the last two examples in this chapter.) As our examples illustrate, the key to creating a criteria range is to understand that multiple criteria in the same row are joined by AND, while criteria in different rows are joined by OR.

Now let's go on to some examples that illustrate the power and versatility of database statistical functions.

How many dollars worth of lip gloss did Jen sell?

Here we want to apply DSUM to column 5 of the database. Column 5 contains the dollar volume for each transaction. (I gave the name *data* to our database, which consists of the range H4:M1896.) Our criteria range in O4:P5 flags all rows in the database in which Name equals Jen *and* Product equals lip gloss. Thus, entering in cell N5 (see Figure 37-2) the formula *DSUM(data,5,O4:P5)* calculates the total dollar amount of lip gloss sold by Jen. We could have also entered the formula as *DSUM(data,"Dollars",O4:P5)*. We find that Jen sold $5,461.61 of lip gloss.

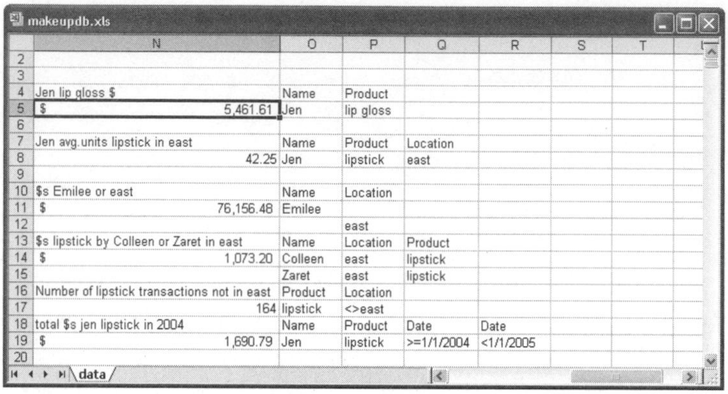

makeupdb.xls

	N		O	P	Q	R
2						
3						
4	Jen lip gloss $		Name	Product		
5	$	5,461.61	Jen	lip gloss		
6						
7	Jen avg.units lipstick in east		Name	Product	Location	
8		42.25	Jen	lipstick	east	
9						
10	$s Emilee or east		Name	Location		
11	$	76,156.48	Emilee			
12				east		
13	$s lipstick by Colleen or Zaret in east		Name	Location	Product	
14	$	1,073.20	Colleen	east	lipstick	
15			Zaret	east	lipstick	
16	Number of lipstick transactions not in east		Product	Location		
17		164	lipstick	<>east		
18	total $s jen lipstick in 2004		Name	Product	Date	Date
19	$	1,690.79	Jen	lipstick	>=1/1/2004	<1/1/2005
20						

data

Figure 37-2 Examples of database statistical functions.

What was the average number of units of lipstick sold each time Jen made a sale in the East region?

We can compute this number by entering in cell N8 the formula *DAVERAGE(data,4,O7:Q8)*. Using *4* as the value for *field* specifies the Units column, and the criteria range O7:Q8 flags all rows in the database in which Name equals *Jen*, Product equals *lipstick*, and Region equals *East*. Using DAVERAGE ensures that we average the units sold for the flagged rows. We find that on average, Jen sold 42.25 units of lipstick in transactions in the East region.

How many dollars of sales were made by Emilee or in the East region?

In cell N11, we can compute the total dollars ($76,156.48) of sales made by Emilee or in the East by using the formula *DSUM(data,5,O10:P12)*. The criteria in O10:P12 flags sales in the East *or* by Emilee. The great programmers at Microsoft have ensured that this formula will not double-count sales by Emilee in the East.

How many dollars worth of lipstick were sold by Colleen or Zaret in the East region?

The formula *DSUM(data,5,O13:Q15)* in cell N14 computes the total lipstick revenue generated through sales by Colleen and Zaret ($1,073.20) in the East. Notice that O14:Q14 specifies criteria that selects lipstick sales by Colleen in the East, and O15:Q15 specifies criteria that selects lipstick sales by Zaret in the East. Remember that criteria in different rows are treated as "or".

How many lipstick transactions were not in the East?

In cell N17, we compute the total number of lipstick transactions (164) outside the East region with the formula *DCOUNT(data,4,O16:P17)*. I use DCOUNT in this problem because we want to specify criteria by which the function will count the number of rows involving lipstick sales and regions other than the East. Excel treats the expression *<>East* in the criteria range as "not East".

Because the COUNT function counts numbers, we need to refer to a column containing numerical values. Column 4, the Units column, contains numbers, so I designated that column in the formula. The formula *DCOUNT(data,3,O16:P17)* would return 0 because there are no numbers in the database's third column (which is column J in the spreadsheet). Of course, the formula *DCOUNTA(data,3,O16:P17)* would return the correct answer because COUNTA counts text as well as numbers.

How many dollars worth of lipstick did Jen sell during 2004?

The trick here is how to flag only sales that occurred in 2004. By including in a single row of our criteria range a reference to the Date field, using the expressions *>=1/1/2004* and *<1/1/2005*, we capture only 2004 sales. Thus, entering in cell N19 the formula *DSUM(data,5,O18:R19)* computes the total lipstick sales by Jen ($1,690.79) after January 1, 2004, and before January 1, 2005.

How many units of makeup were sold for a price of at least $3.20?

This example involves *computed criteria*. Basically, computed criteria flags rows of the database on the basis of whether a computed condition is true or false for that row. For this question, we want to flag each row having *Dollars/Units >=$3.20*. When setting up a computed criteria (see Figure 37-3), the label in the first row above the computed criteria *must not* be a column label. For example, you can't use Name, Product, or another label from row 4 of this spreadsheet. If you do repeat a column label, the computed criteria is set up to be a formula that returns True based on the first row of information in the database. Thus, to specify rows in which the average price is greater than or equal to $3.20, we need to enter *=(L5/K5)>=3.2* in our criteria range below a heading that is not a column label. If the first row of data does not satisfy this condition, you will see FALSE in the spreadsheet, but Excel will still flag all rows having a unit price that's greater than or equal to $3.20. Entering in N22 the formula *DSUM(data,4,O21:O22)* computes the total number of units of makeup sold (1127) in orders for which the unit price was greater than or equal to $3.20. Note that cell O22 contains the formula *=(L5/K5)>=3.2*.

makeupdb.xls

	N		O	P	Q	R
4	Jen lip gloss $		Name	Product		
5	$	5,461.61	Jen	lip gloss		
7	Jen avg.units lipstick in east		Name	Product	Location	
8		42.25	Jen	lipstick	east	
10	$s Emilee or east		Name	Location		
11	$	76,156.48	Emilee			
12				east		
13	$s lipstick by Colleen or Zaret in east		Name	Location	Product	
14	$	1,073.20	Colleen	east	lipstick	
15			Zaret	east	lipstick	
16	Number of lipstick transactions not in east		Product	Location		
17		164	lipstick	<>east		
18	total $s jen lipstick in 2004		Name	Product	Date	Date
19	$	1,690.79	Jen	lipstick	>=1/1/2004	<1/1/2005
21	Units sold for >=$3.20		Big price			
22		1127	FALSE			

data

Figure 37-3 An example of computed criteria.

What is the total dollar amount each salesperson sold of each product?

For this problem, I'd like to use a DSUM function whose criteria range keys off both the Name and Product columns. Using a data table, I can easily "loop through" all possible combinations of name and product in the criteria range and compute the total revenue for each Name and Product combination.

I begin by entering any name in cell X26 and any product in cell Y26. Then I enter in cell Q25 the formula *DSUM(data,5,X25:Y26)*, which computes total sales revenue for (in this case) Betsy and eye liner. Now I enter each salesperson's name in the cell range Q26:Q33 and each product in the cell range R25:V25. Now highlight the data table range (Q25:V33) and choose Data, Table. Choose cell X26 as the Column Input Cell and Y26 as the Row Input Cell. We then obtain the results shown in Figure 37-4. Each entry in the data table computes the revenue generated for a different name/product combination because the data table causes the names to be placed in cell X26 and the products to be placed in cell Y26. For example, we find that Ashley sold $3,245.44 worth of lipstick.

makeupdb.xls

	Q	R	S	T	U	V	W	X	Y
25	6046.53428	lip gloss	foundation	lipstick	mascara	eye liner		Name	Product
26	Betsy	5675.65005	8043.486	3968.605	4827.254	6046.534		Betsy	eye liner
27	Hallagan	5603.11938	6985.734	3177.871	5703.347	6964.621			
28	Zaret	5670.32933	6451.65	2448.707	3879.95	8166.749			
29	Colleen	5573.32373	6834.768	2346.414	6746.525	3389.625			
30	Cristina	5297.97981	5290.99	2401.668	5461.647	5397.274			
31	Jen	5461.61479	5628.648	3953.3	6887.175	7010.441			
32	Ashley	6053.68456	4186.059	3245.443	6617.1	5844.949			
33	Emilee	5270.25031	5313.788	2189.138	4719.3	7587.389			

data

Figure 37-4 Combining data tables with a DSUM function.

This example shows how combining data tables with database statistical functions can quickly generate many statistics of interest.

What cute tricks can I use to set up criteria ranges?

Here are some examples of little tricks that might help you set up an appropriate criteria range. Suppose the column label in the first row of the criteria range refers to a column containing text (say column H).

- *Allie* will flag records containing the text string Allie in column H.

- A?X will flag a record if the record's column H entry begins with *A* and has the character *X* as its third character. (The second character can be anything!)

- <>*B* will flag a record if column H's entry does not contain any Bs.

  If a column (say column I) contains numerical values,

- >100 will flag a record if column I contains a value greater than 100.

- <>100 will flag a record if column I contains a value not equal to 100.

- >=1000 will flag a record if column I contains a value greater than or equal to 1000.

I have a database that lists for each sales transaction the revenue, date, and product ID code. Given the date and ID code for a transaction, is there an easy way to pick off the transaction's revenue?

The file Dget.xls (see Figure 37-5) contains a database that lists revenue, date, and product ID code for a series of sales transactions. If you know the date and the product ID code for a transaction, how can you find the transaction's revenue? The DGET function makes this a snap. The syntax of the DGET function is *DGET(database, field#, criteria)*. Given a database (a cell range) and a *field#* in the database (counting columns from left to right across the range) the DGET function returns the entry in column *field#* from the database record satisfying the criteria. If no record satisfies the criteria, the DGET function returns the #VALUE error message. If more than one record satisfies the criteria, the DGET function returns the #NUM! error message.

Suppose that we want to know the revenue for a transaction involving product ID 62426 that occurred on 1/9/2006. Assuming that the transaction involving this product on the given date is unique, the formula (entered in cell G9) *DGET(B7:D32,1,G5:H6)* yields the transaction's revenue of $299. Note we used 1 for the *field#* argument because Revenue is listed in the first column of the database. (Our database is contained in the cell range B7:D32). The criteria range G5:H6 ensures we find a transaction involving product 62426 on 1/9/2006.

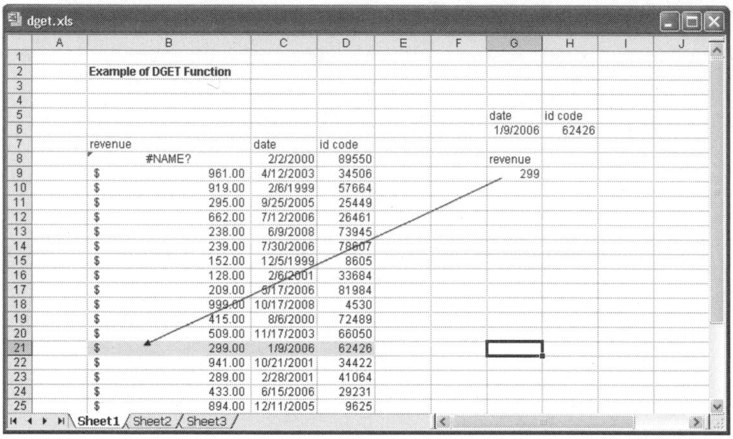

Figure 37-5 Example of DGET function.

Problems

1. How many units of lip gloss did Zaret sell during 2004 and 2005?

2. Create a data table that contains each person's total revenue and units sold.

3. How many units of lip gloss did Colleen sell outside the West region?

4. Create a data table that shows the average per unit revenue generated by each person on sales for which the average per unit price exceeded $3.30.

5. Use the data in the file Sales.xls to determine the following:

   ❑ Total dollar sales in the Midwest

   ❑ Total dollars sold by Heather in the East

   ❑ Total dollars sold by Heather or sold in the East

   ❑ Total dollars sold by Heather or John in the East

   ❑ Number of transactions in the East region

   ❑ Number of transactions with greater than average sales

   ❑ Total dollar sales not in the Midwest

6. The file HousePriceData.xls contains for selected homes the following information:

❏   Square footage

❏   Price

❏   Number of bathrooms

❏   Number of bedrooms

Use this information to answer the following questions:

a. What is the average price of all homes having bathrooms + bedrooms >= 6?

b. How many homes sell for over $300,000 and have bedrooms + bathrooms <=5?

c. How many homes have at least 3 bathrooms but bedrooms + bathrooms <=6?

d. What is the highest price of a home having at most 3000 square feet and bedrooms + bathroom <=6? (Hint: Use the DMAX function to solve this problem.)

38

Filtering Data

Joolas is a small makeup company. In an Excel spreadsheet, they track each sales transaction. They often want to extract, or "filter out," a subset of their sales data. For example, they often want to identify sales transactions that satisfy the following conditions:

■ All transactions in which Jen sold lip gloss.

■ The ten largest transactions (by revenue).

■ The bottom 5 percent of transactions (by revenue) in which Colleen was the salesperson.

■ All 2005 lipstick transactions in which Ashley was the salesperson.

■ All foundation transactions in the first six months of 2005 in which Emilee or Jen was the salesperson and the average per unit price was more than $3.20.

Excel's filtering capabilities make identifying the subset of data you need a snap. Our work for this chapter is in the file MakeupFilter.xls. For the 1891 sales transactions listed in this file, we have the following information. (Figure 38-1 shows a subset of the data.)

■ Transaction code number

■ Name of the salesperson

■ Date of the transaction

■ Product sold

■ Units sold

- Dollar amount of the transaction
- Transaction location

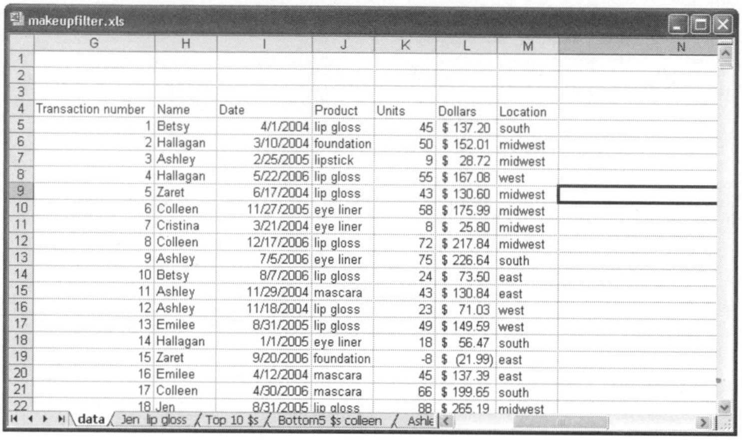

	G	H	I	J	K	L	M	N
1								
2								
3								
4	Transaction number	Name	Date	Product	Units	Dollars	Location	
5	1	Betsy	4/1/2004	lip gloss	45	$ 137.20	south	
6	2	Hallagan	3/10/2004	foundation	50	$ 152.01	midwest	
7	3	Ashley	2/25/2005	lipstick	9	$ 28.72	midwest	
8	4	Hallagan	5/22/2006	lip gloss	55	$ 167.08	west	
9	5	Zaret	6/17/2004	lip gloss	43	$ 130.60	midwest	
10	6	Colleen	11/27/2005	eye liner	58	$ 175.99	midwest	
11	7	Cristina	3/21/2004	eye liner	8	$ 25.80	midwest	
12	8	Colleen	12/17/2006	lip gloss	72	$ 217.84	midwest	
13	9	Ashley	7/5/2006	eye liner	75	$ 226.64	south	
14	10	Betsy	8/7/2006	lip gloss	24	$ 73.50	east	
15	11	Ashley	11/29/2004	mascara	43	$ 130.84	east	
16	12	Ashley	11/18/2004	lip gloss	23	$ 71.03	west	
17	13	Emilee	8/31/2005	lip gloss	49	$ 149.59	west	
18	14	Hallagan	1/1/2005	eye liner	18	$ 56.47	south	
19	15	Zaret	9/20/2006	foundation	-8	$ (21.99)	east	
20	16	Emilee	4/12/2004	mascara	45	$ 137.39	east	
21	17	Colleen	4/30/2006	mascara	66	$ 199.65	south	
22	18	Jen	8/31/2005	lip gloss	88	$ 265.19	midwest	

Figure 38-1 Makeup sales data.

Each column (G through M) of our "database" (cell range G4:M1895) is called a *field*. Each row of the database that contains data is called a *record*. (Thus the records in our database are contained in the cell range G5:M1895.) The first row of each field must contain a field name. For example, the name of the field in column J is Product. By using Excel's AutoFilter capabilities, you can "query" a database using AND criteria to identify a subset of records you need. This means that you can use queries of the form "Find all records where Field 1 satisfies certain conditions, *and* Field 2 satisfies certain conditions, *and* Field 3 satisfies certain conditions, and so on." Our next four examples illustrate the capabilities of the Excel AutoFilter.

Locate all transactions in which Jen sold lip gloss.

We want to locate all sales transactions in which the salesperson was Jen and the product sold was lip gloss. Begin by selecting a cell in the database (see the worksheet named Data) and then choosing Data, Filter, AutoFilter. You will see a drop-down arrow for each column, as shown in Figure 38-2.

After clicking the drop-down arrow for a column, you can select any entry that occurs in the column. (You can also select All, Top 10, or Custom. I'll explain these options later in the chapter.) Click the drop-down arrow for Name in column H and select Jen. Now click on the drop-down arrow for Product in column J and select Lip Gloss. Excel displays each record in which the salesperson is Jen *and* the product was lip gloss. (See Figure 38-3 and the worksheet Jen Lip Gloss.) Notice that the buttons for Name and Product have now turned green because we have selected a particular record value for those fields.

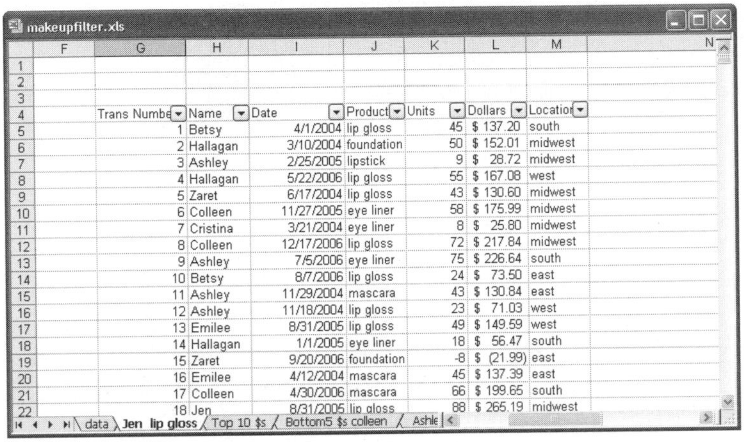

Row	Trans Number	Name	Date	Product	Units	Dollars	Location
5	1	Betsy	4/1/2004	lip gloss	45	$ 137.20	south
6	2	Hallagan	3/10/2004	foundation	50	$ 152.01	midwest
7	3	Ashley	2/25/2005	lipstick	9	$ 28.72	midwest
8	4	Hallagan	5/22/2006	lip gloss	55	$ 167.08	west
9	5	Zaret	6/17/2004	lip gloss	43	$ 130.60	midwest
10	6	Colleen	11/27/2005	eye liner	58	$ 175.99	midwest
11	7	Cristina	3/21/2004	eye liner	8	$ 25.80	midwest
12	8	Colleen	12/17/2006	lip gloss	72	$ 217.84	midwest
13	9	Ashley	7/5/2006	eye liner	75	$ 226.64	south
14	10	Betsy	8/7/2006	lip gloss	24	$ 73.50	east
15	11	Ashley	11/29/2004	mascara	43	$ 130.84	east
16	12	Ashley	11/18/2004	lip gloss	23	$ 71.03	west
17	13	Emilee	8/31/2005	lip gloss	49	$ 149.59	west
18	14	Hallagan	1/1/2005	eye liner	18	$ 56.47	south
19	15	Zaret	9/20/2006	foundation	-8	$ (21.99)	east
20	16	Emilee	4/12/2004	mascara	45	$ 137.39	east
21	17	Colleen	4/30/2006	mascara	66	$ 199.65	south
22	18	Jen	8/31/2005	lip gloss	88	$ 265.19	midwest

Figure 38-2 AutoFilter drop-down arrows.

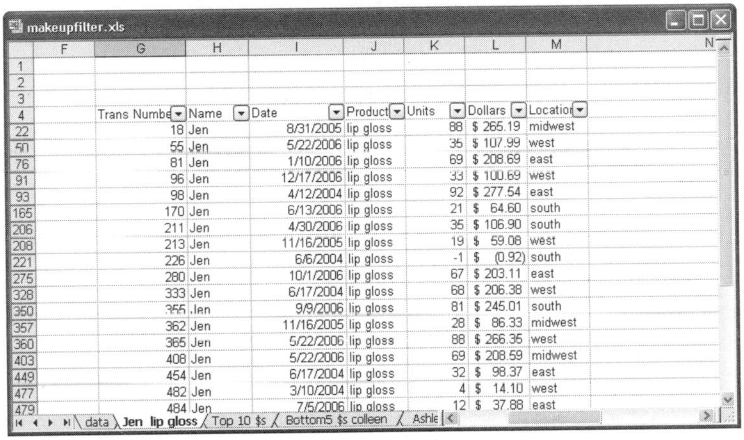

Row	Trans Number	Name	Date	Product	Units	Dollars	Location
22	18	Jen	8/31/2005	lip gloss	88	$ 265.19	midwest
50	55	Jen	5/22/2006	lip gloss	35	$ 107.99	west
76	81	Jen	1/10/2006	lip gloss	69	$ 208.69	east
91	96	Jen	12/17/2006	lip gloss	33	$ 100.69	west
93	98	Jen	4/12/2004	lip gloss	92	$ 277.54	east
165	170	Jen	6/13/2006	lip gloss	21	$ 64.60	south
206	211	Jen	4/30/2006	lip gloss	35	$ 106.90	south
208	213	Jen	11/16/2005	lip gloss	19	$ 59.08	west
221	226	Jen	6/6/2004	lip gloss	-1	$ (0.92)	south
275	280	Jen	10/1/2006	lip gloss	67	$ 203.11	east
328	333	Jen	6/17/2004	lip gloss	68	$ 206.38	west
350	355	Jen	9/9/2006	lip gloss	81	$ 245.01	south
357	362	Jen	11/16/2005	lip gloss	28	$ 86.33	midwest
360	365	Jen	5/22/2006	lip gloss	88	$ 266.35	west
403	408	Jen	5/22/2006	lip gloss	69	$ 208.59	midwest
449	454	Jen	6/17/2004	lip gloss	32	$ 98.37	east
477	482	Jen	3/10/2004	lip gloss	4	$ 14.10	west
479	484	Jen	7/5/2006	lip gloss	12	$ 37.88	east

Figure 38-3 All records for which Jen sold lip gloss.

By selecting All from the Name drop-down box, we clear the AutoFilter from the Name column and would then see all lip gloss sales, regardless of who the salesperson was. To display the original database, choose Data, Filter, Show All. To remove the AutoFilter drop-down lists, choose Data, Filter, AutoFilter. The AutoFilter check box is cleared, and the drop-down arrows disappear. (You are limited to one AutoFilter per worksheet.)

Locate the ten largest transactions (by revenue).

To find this data, select the drop-down arrow for column L and then select the Top 10 option. The dialog box shown in Figure 38-4 appears.

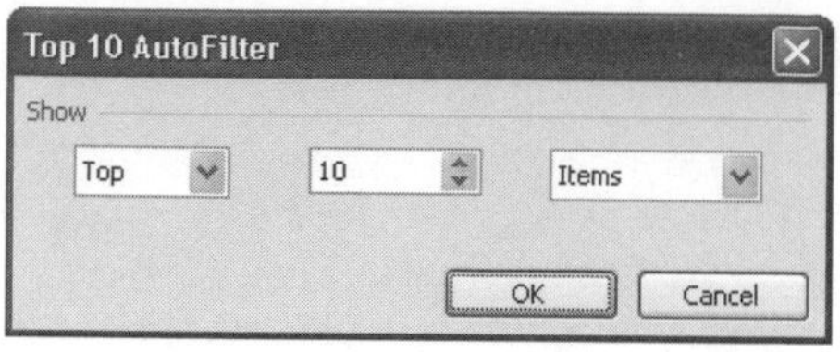

Figure 38-4 The Top 10 AutoFilter dialog box.

In the drop-down box at the left, you can select either Top or Bottom; in the middle drop-down box, you can use any positive integer. In the drop-down box at the right, select either Items or Percent. With the Top 10 AutoFilter dialog box set up as shown above, we'll select the records with the 10 largest dollar amounts. (See Figure 38-5.) We could also use this dialog box to extract subsets of records such as

- Top 10 percent of all dollar amounts

- Bottom 6 of all dollar amounts

- Bottom 7 percent of all dollar amounts

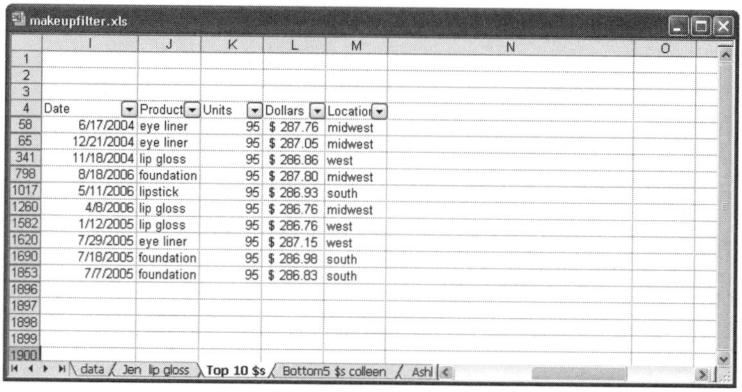

Figure 38-5 Top 10 dollar amounts.

Locate the bottom 5 percent of transactions (by revenue) in which Colleen was the salesperson.

To answer this question we need to select Colleen from the Name drop-down list and use the Top 10 option (see Figure 38-6) in the Dollar column. The results are shown in Figure 38-7.

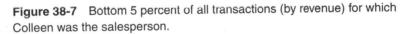

Figure 38-6   Selecting bottom 5 percent of all dollar values.

makeupfilter.xls

	E	F	G	H	I	J	K	L	M
4			Trans Numbe	Name	Date	Product	Units	Dollars	Location
192			197	Colleen	2/6/2004	mascara	-5	$ (12.90)	east
308			313	Colleen	12/30/2005	eye liner	-9	$ (24.97)	midwest
496			501	Colleen	10/12/2006	lip gloss	-10	$ (28.51)	east
618			623	Colleen	4/1/2004	mascara	-8	$ (22.23)	west
622			627	Colleen	5/22/2006	foundation	-8	$ (21.53)	south
747			752	Colleen	10/25/2005	lip gloss	-5	$ (12.57)	east
860			865	Colleen	2/17/2004	foundation	-10	$ (27.72)	midwest
935			940	Colleen	1/1/2005	lipstick	-9	$ (24.56)	west
976			981	Colleen	8/20/2005	foundation	-6	$ (15.85)	midwest
997			1002	Colleen	10/5/2004	lip gloss	-10	$ (28.33)	south
1102			1107	Colleen	3/10/2004	lipstick	-9	$ (24.90)	midwest
1255			1260	Colleen	2/6/2004	foundation	-6	$ (16.24)	west
1385			1390	Colleen	2/6/2004	mascara	-7	$ (19.44)	east
1572			1577	Colleen	5/13/2005	lip gloss	-7	$ (18.81)	south
1723			1728	Colleen	7/9/2004	mascara	-7	$ (19.35)	south
1768			1773	Colleen	7/20/2004	foundation	-10	$ (27.45)	midwest
1854			1859	Colleen	8/22/2004	lipstick	-6	$ (16.59)	south
1896									

data / Jen lip gloss / Top 10 $s \ Bottom5 $s colleen / Ashl

Figure 38-7   Bottom 5 percent of all transactions (by revenue) for which Colleen was the salesperson.

Note that we are not seeing the lowest 5 percent of Colleen's transactions. We are seeing the bottom 5 percent of all transactions in which Colleen happened to be the salesperson.

Locate all 2005 lipstick transactions in which Ashley was the salesperson.

The question here is how we select all records in the year 2005. We need to use the AutoFilter's Custom option to solve this problem. The Custom option allows you to enter as many as two conditions per data field. The conditions can be joined with AND or OR. An AND condition returns records that satisfy both criteria, while an OR condition returns records that satisfy either criteria. The available conditions include greater than, less than or equal to, and so on. After selecting Ashley from the Name column and Lipstick from the Product column, we use the Custom option to select all records from the Date field that are *>=1/1/2005* and *<=12/31/2005*, as you can see in Figure 38-8. These conditions give us all sales transactions by Ashley during 2005.

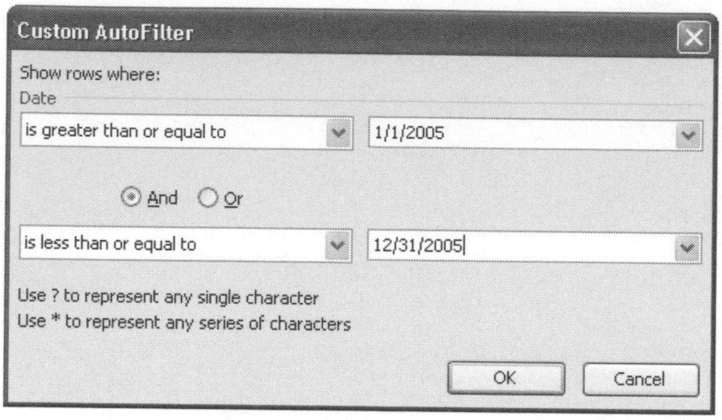

Figure 38-8 Selecting 2005 transactions with the Custom AutoFilter.

Excel now returns the records shown in Figure 38-9. Ashley completed only eight lipstick transactions during 2005.

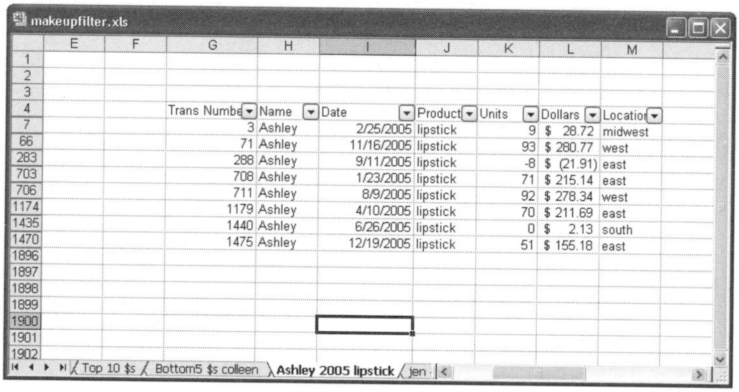

Row	Trans Numbe	Name	Date	Product	Units	Dollars	Locatio
7	3	Ashley	2/25/2005	lipstick	9	$ 28.72	midwest
66	71	Ashley	11/16/2005	lipstick	93	$ 280.77	west
283	288	Ashley	9/11/2005	lipstick	-8	$ (21.91)	east
703	708	Ashley	1/23/2005	lipstick	71	$ 215.14	east
706	711	Ashley	8/9/2005	lipstick	92	$ 278.34	west
1174	1179	Ashley	4/10/2005	lipstick	70	$ 211.69	east
1435	1440	Ashley	6/26/2005	lipstick	0	$ 2.13	south
1470	1475	Ashley	12/19/2005	lipstick	51	$ 155.18	east

Figure 38-9 Ashley's lipstick transactions during 2005.

Locate all foundation transactions in the first six months of 2005 for which Emilee or Jen was the salesperson and the average per unit price was more than $3.20.

The AutoFilter feature (even with the Custom option) is limited to AND queries across columns. That means, for example, we cannot find all transactions for lipstick sales by Jen during 2005 *OR* foundation sales by Zaret during 2004. To perform more complex queries such as this one, we need to use Advanced Filter. To use Advanced Filter, we set up a criteria range (this process is described in detail in Chapter 37) that specifies the records we want to extract. After specifying the criteria range, we tell Excel whether we want the records extracted to the current location or to a different location. To identify all foundation transactions in the first six months of 2005 for which Emilee or Jen was the salesperson and the average per unit price was more than \$3.20, we use the criteria range shown in cell range O4:S6 in Figure 38-10.

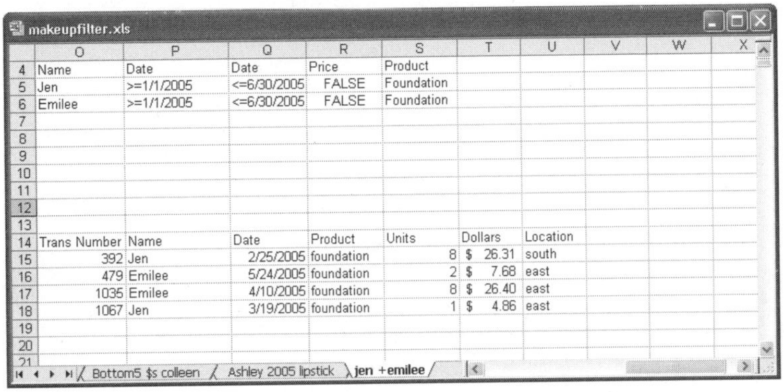

makeupfilter.xls

	O	P	Q	R	S	T	U
4	Name	Date	Date	Price	Product		
5	Jen	>=1/1/2005	<=6/30/2005	FALSE	Foundation		
6	Emilee	>=1/1/2005	<=6/30/2005	FALSE	Foundation		
7							
8							
9							
10							
11							
12							
13							
14	Trans Number	Name	Date	Product	Units	Dollars	Location
15	392	Jen	2/25/2005	foundation	8	\$ 26.31	south
16	479	Emilee	5/24/2005	foundation	2	\$ 7.68	east
17	1035	Emilee	4/10/2005	foundation	8	\$ 26.40	east
18	1067	Jen	3/19/2005	foundation	1	\$ 4.86	east
19							
20							

Bottom5 \$s colleen / Ashley 2005 lipstick / jen +emilee

Figure 38-10 Setting up criteria range to use with an advanced filter.

In cells R5 and R6, I entered the formula *=(L5/K5)>3.2*. Recall from Chapter 37 that this formula creates computed criteria that flags each row in which the per unit price is more than \$3.20. Also remember that our heading for a computed criteria must not be a field name, so I used Price as the field heading. Our criteria in O5:S5 flags all records in which Jen is the salesperson, the date is between 1/1/2005 and 6/30/2005, the product sold is foundation, and the per unit price is more than \$3.20. Our criteria in O6:S6 flags all records in which Emilee is the salesperson, the date is between 1/1/2005 and 6/30/2005, the product sold is Foundation, and the per unit price is more than \$3.20. The criteria range of O4:S6 flags exactly the records we want. Remember that criteria in different rows are joined by OR.

We can now select any cell within the database range and choose Data, Filter, Advanced Filter. We fill in the dialog box as shown in Figure 38-11.

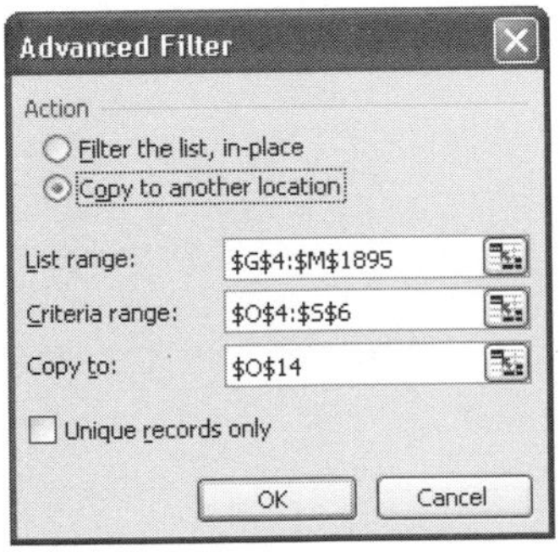

Figure 38-11 Advanced Filter dialog box settings.

We are telling Excel to extract all records in the database (cell range G4:M1895) that satisfy the criteria specified in O4:S6. These records should be copied to a range whose upper left corner is in cell O14. The records extracted are shown in the cell range O14:U18. Only four records meet the criteria we defined.

If we check the Unique Records Only option in the Advanced Filter dialog box, no duplicate records are returned. For example, if Jen had another foundation transaction in the East on 3/19/2005 for 1 unit for $4.88, only one of these transactions would be extracted.

Problems

1. Find all transactions in which Hallagan sold eye liner in the West.

2. Find all transactions that rank in the top 5 percent with regards to units sold.

3. Find the top 20 revenue-generating transactions that involve foundation sales.

4. Find all transactions involving sales of at least 60 units during 2004 for which the per unit price was at most $3.10.

5. Find all foundation transactions during the first three months of 2004 for which the unit price was larger than the average price received for foundation during the whole time period.

6. Find all transactions in which Zaret or Betsy sold lipstick or foundation.

39

Consolidating Data

- My company sells products in several regions of the United States. Each region keeps records of the number of units of each product sold during the months of January, February, and March. Is there an easy way to create a "master workbook" that always combines each region's sales and gives a tally of the total amount sold in the U.S. of each product during each month?

A business analyst often receives worksheets that tally the same information (such as monthly product sales) from different affiliates or regions. To determine the company's overall profitability, the analyst usually needs to combine or consolidate this information in a single workbook. PivotTables built from multiple consolidation ranges can be used to accomplish this goal, but the little known Data, Consolidate command makes it easy to accomplish this goal as well. With Data, Consolidate, you can ensure that changes in the individual worksheets will be automatically reflected in the consolidated worksheet.

My company sells products in several regions of the United States. Each region keeps records of the number of units of each product sold during the months of January, February, and March. Is there an easy way to create a "master workbook" that always combines each region's sales and gives a tally of the total amount sold in the U.S. of each product during each month?

The file East.xls (shown in Figure 39-1) displays monthly unit sales of products A–H in the eastern U.S. during January, February, and March. Similarly, the file West.xls (shown in Figure 39-2) gives monthly unit sales of products A–H in the western U.S. from January through March. We'd like to create a consolidated worksheet that tabulates each product's total sales by month.

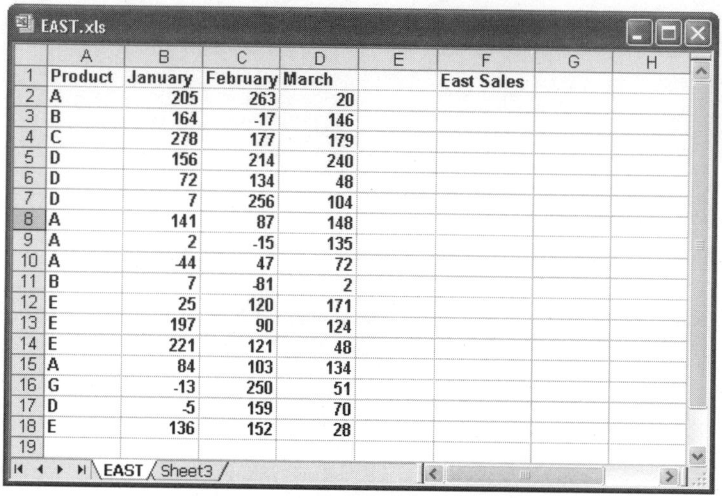

EAST.xls

	A	B	C	D	E	F
1	Product	January	February	March		East Sales
2	A	205	263	20		
3	B	164	-17	146		
4	C	278	177	179		
5	D	156	214	240		
6	D	72	134	48		
7	D	7	256	104		
8	A	141	87	148		
9	A	2	-15	135		
10	A	-44	47	72		
11	B	7	-81	2		
12	E	25	120	171		
13	E	197	90	124		
14	E	221	121	48		
15	A	84	103	134		
16	G	-13	250	51		
17	D	-5	159	70		
18	E	136	152	28		

Figure 39-1 East region sales during January–March.

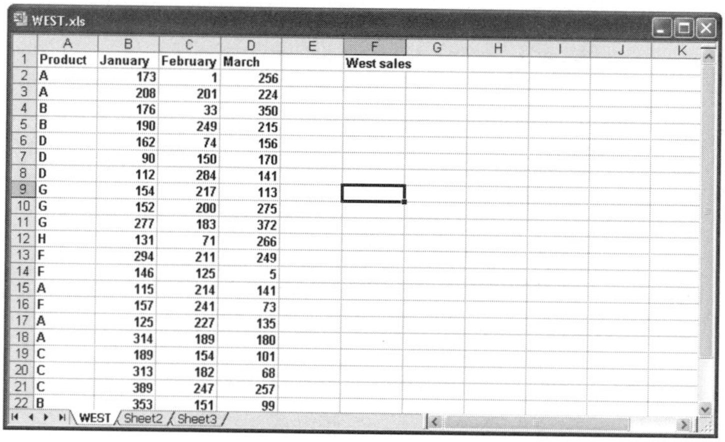

WEST.xls

	A	B	C	D	E	F
1	Product	January	February	March		West sales
2	A	173	1	256		
3	A	208	201	224		
4	B	176	33	350		
5	B	190	249	215		
6	D	162	74	156		
7	D	90	150	170		
8	D	112	284	141		
9	G	154	217	113		
10	G	152	200	275		
11	G	277	183	372		
12	H	131	71	266		
13	F	294	211	249		
14	F	146	125	5		
15	A	115	214	141		
16	F	157	241	73		
17	A	125	227	135		
18	A	314	189	180		
19	C	189	154	101		
20	C	313	182	68		
21	C	389	247	257		
22	B	353	151	99		

Figure 39-2 West region sales during January–March.

Before using Data, Consolidate, it's helpful to see both spreadsheets together on the same screen. To see both spreadsheets on the same screen, open both workbooks and then select Window, Arrange, Tiled. Your screen should now look like Figure 39-3.

Now open a blank worksheet and choose Window, Arrange, Tiled again. In the blank spreadsheet, select Data, Consolidate, and you'll see the Consolidate dialog box, shown in Figure 39-4.

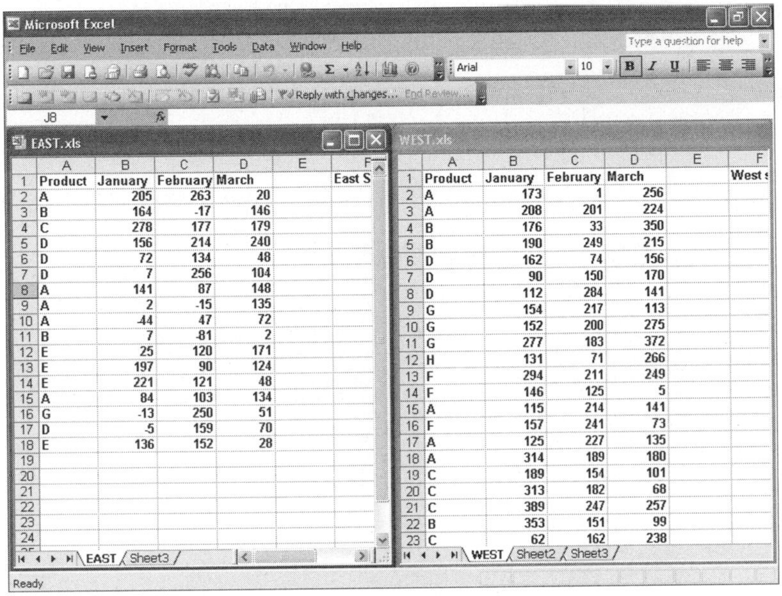

Figure 39-3   East and West sales arranged on the same screen.

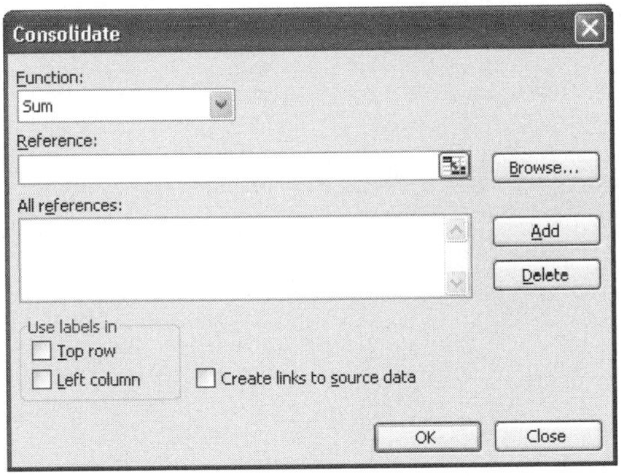

Figure 39-4   The Consolidate dialog box.

To consolidate the data from the East and West regions in our blank workbook, we enter the ranges we want to consolidate in the Reference area of the Consolidate dialog box, clicking add after selecting each range. By checking Top Row and Left Column in the Use Labels In area, we ensure that Excel will consolidate the selected ranges by looking at labels in the top row and left column of the ranges we select. The option Create Links To Source Data enables changes in our selected ranges to be reflected in the consolidated worksheet. We select Sum because we want Excel to add up the total sales of each product by month. Selecting Count, for instance, would count the number of transactions for each product during each month. Selecting Max would compute the largest sales transaction for each product during each month. The Consolidate dialog box should be filled out as shown in Figure 39-5.

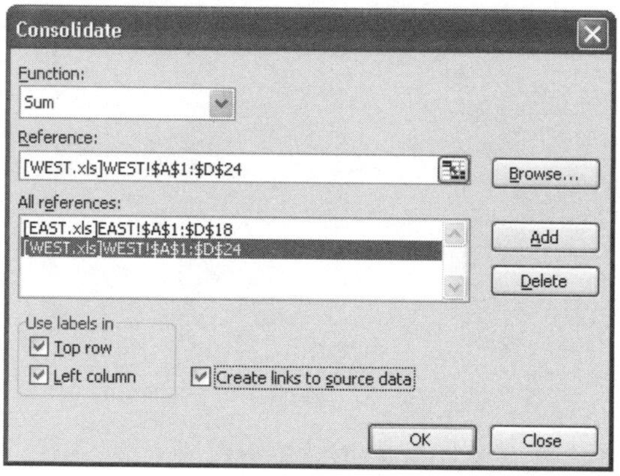

Figure 39-5 The completed Consolidate dialog box.

After clicking OK, our new worksheet looks like the one shown in Figure 39-6.

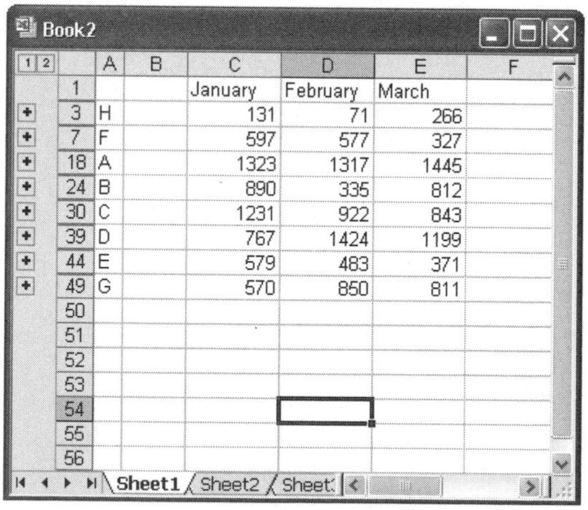

Figure 39-6 Total sales after consolidation.

We find, for example, that 1317 units of product A were sold in February, 597 units of product F were sold in January, and so on.

Now go to the cell C2 of East.xls and change the February product A sales from 263 to 363. Note that in the consolidated worksheet, our entry for February product A sales has increased by 100 as well (from 1317 to 1417). This change occurs because we checked the Create Links To Source Data option. (By the way, if you click on the 2 right below the workbook name in the consolidated worksheet, you'll see how Excel grouped the data to perform the consolidation.)

If you are frequently downloading new data to your source spreadsheets (in this case East.xls and West.xls), it's a good idea to select cell ranges that will include all data you will eventually download. For example, if you know that you'll have at most 100 transactions in a month and at most 6 months of data, you could select the cell range for data consolidation from East sales to be $A$1:$G$601. Then, as new data is downloaded from the East region, the consolidated worksheet automatically includes the data in the consolidation.

Problems

The following problems refer to the data in files JanCon.xls and FebCon.xls. Each file contains the unit sales, dollar revenues, and product sold for each transaction during the month.

1. Create a consolidated worksheet that gives by region the total unit sales and dollar revenue for each product.

2. Create a consolidated worksheet that gives by region the largest first-quarter transaction for each product from the standpoint of revenue and units sold.

40

Creating Subtotals

- Joolas is a small makeup company. For each transaction, they track in an Excel spreadsheet the name of the salesperson, the location of the transaction, the product sold, units sold, and transaction revenue. Is there an easy way to create (within the worksheet) the total revenue and units sold by region?

We know that PivotTables can be used to "slice and dice" data in Excel. Often, however, we'd like an easy way to summarize a list or a database within the list. In a sales database, for example, we might want to create a summary of sales revenue by region, a summary of sales revenue by product, and a summary of sales revenue by salesperson. If you sort a list by the column in which specific data is listed, the Excel Subtotals command lets you create a subtotal in a list on the basis of the values in the column. For example, if we sort our makeup database by location, we can calculate total revenue and units sold for each region and place the totals just below the last row for that region. As another example, after sorting our database by product, we could use the Subtotals command to calculate total revenue and units sold for each product and display the totals below the row in which the product changes. In the next section, we'll look at some specific examples.

Joolas is a small makeup company. For each transaction, they track in an Excel spreadsheet the name of the salesperson, the location of the transaction, the product sold, units sold, and transaction revenue. Is there an easy way to create (within the worksheet) the total revenue and units sold by region?

Our work is in file MakeupSubtotals.xls. In Figure 40-1, you can see a subset of the data as it appears after sorting the list by the Location column.

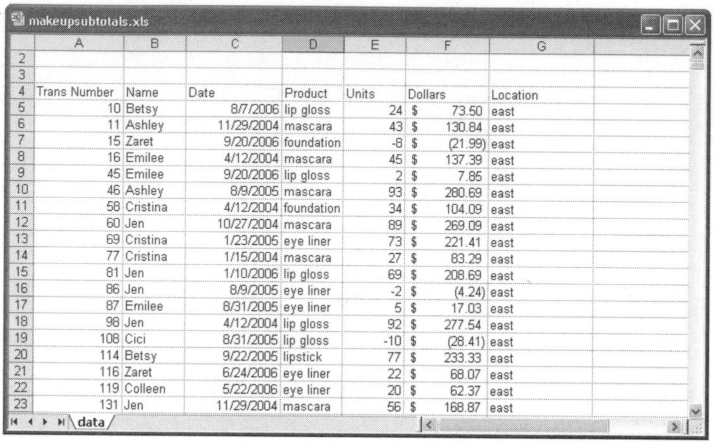

	A	B	C	D	E	F	G
2							
3							
4	Trans Number	Name	Date	Product	Units	Dollars	Location
5	10	Betsy	8/7/2006	lip gloss	24	$ 73.50	east
6	11	Ashley	11/29/2004	mascara	43	$ 130.84	east
7	15	Zaret	9/20/2006	foundation	-8	$ (21.99)	east
8	16	Emilee	4/12/2004	mascara	45	$ 137.39	east
9	45	Emilee	9/20/2006	lip gloss	2	$ 7.85	east
10	46	Ashley	8/9/2005	mascara	93	$ 280.69	east
11	58	Cristina	4/12/2004	foundation	34	$ 104.09	east
12	60	Jen	10/27/2004	mascara	89	$ 269.09	east
13	69	Cristina	1/23/2005	eye liner	73	$ 221.41	east
14	77	Cristina	1/15/2004	mascara	27	$ 83.29	east
15	81	Jen	1/10/2006	lip gloss	69	$ 208.69	east
16	86	Jen	8/9/2005	eye liner	-2	$ (4.24)	east
17	87	Emilee	8/31/2005	eye liner	5	$ 17.03	east
18	98	Jen	4/12/2004	lip gloss	92	$ 277.54	east
19	108	Cici	8/31/2005	lip gloss	-10	$ (28.41)	east
20	114	Betsy	9/22/2005	lipstick	77	$ 233.33	east
21	116	Zaret	6/24/2006	eye liner	22	$ 68.07	east
22	119	Colleen	5/22/2006	eye liner	20	$ 62.37	east
23	131	Jen	11/29/2004	mascara	56	$ 168.87	east

Figure 40-1 After sorting a list by the values in a specific column, you can easily create subtotals for that data.

To total revenue and units sold by region, place the cursor anywhere in the database and then select Data, Subtotals. In the Subtotal dialog box, we fill in the values as shown in Figure 40-2.

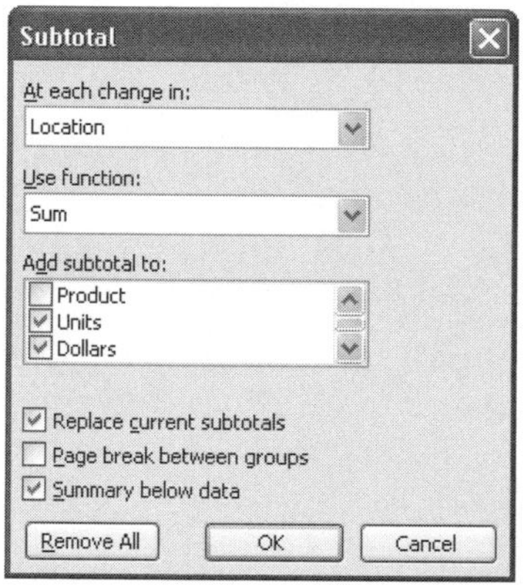

Figure 40-2 Filling in the Subtotal dialog box.

By selecting Location from the At Each Change In list, we ensure that subtotals are created at each point in which the value in the Location column changes. This corresponds to the different regions. Selecting Sum from the Use Function box tells Excel to sum the units and dollars for each different region. By choosing Units and Dollars from the Add Subtotal To box, we indicate that subtotals should be created on the basis of the values in these columns. The Replace Current Subtotals option causes Excel to remove any previously computed subtotals. Because we haven't created any subtotals, it doesn't matter whether or not this option is checked in this example. With the Page Break Between Groups option selected, Excel inserts a page break after each subtotal. Checking Summary Below Data causes Excel to place subtotals below the data. If this box is not checked, the subtotals are created above the data used for the computation. Clicking the Remove All button removes subtotals from the list.

A sample of our subtotals results is shown in Figure 40-3. We find that 18,818 units were sold in the East, earning revenue of $57,372.09.

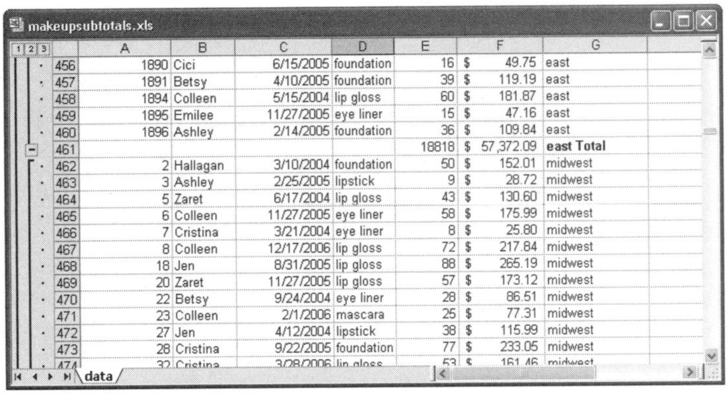

	A	B	C	D	E	F	G
456	1890	Cici	6/15/2005	foundation	16	$ 49.75	east
457	1891	Betsy	4/10/2005	foundation	39	$ 119.19	east
458	1894	Colleen	5/15/2004	lip gloss	60	$ 181.87	east
459	1895	Emilee	11/27/2005	eye liner	15	$ 47.16	east
460	1896	Ashley	2/14/2005	foundation	36	$ 109.84	east
461					18818	$ 57,372.09	**east Total**
462	2	Hallagan	3/10/2004	foundation	50	$ 152.01	midwest
463	3	Ashley	2/25/2005	lipstick	9	$ 28.72	midwest
464	5	Zaret	6/17/2004	lip gloss	43	$ 130.60	midwest
465	6	Colleen	11/27/2005	eye liner	58	$ 175.99	midwest
466	7	Cristina	3/21/2004	eye liner	8	$ 25.80	midwest
467	8	Colleen	12/17/2006	lip gloss	72	$ 217.84	midwest
468	18	Jen	8/31/2005	lip gloss	88	$ 265.19	midwest
469	20	Zaret	11/27/2005	lip gloss	57	$ 173.12	midwest
470	22	Betsy	9/24/2004	eye liner	28	$ 86.51	midwest
471	23	Colleen	2/1/2006	mascara	25	$ 77.31	midwest
472	27	Jen	4/12/2004	lipstick	38	$ 115.99	midwest
473	28	Cristina	9/22/2005	foundation	77	$ 233.05	midwest

Figure 40-3 Subtotals are added for each region.

Notice in the left-hand corner of the screen, below the Name Box, buttons with the numbers 1, 2, and 3 appear. Clicking the largest number (in this case 3) yields the data and subtotals. If we click on the 2, we see just the subtotals by region, shown in Figure 40-4. Clicking on the 1 yields the grand total, as shown in Figure 40-5. In short, clicking on a lower number reduces the level of detail shown.

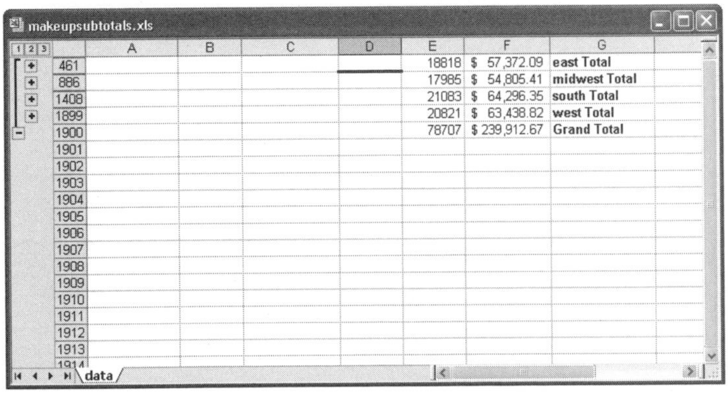

	A	B	C	D	E	F	G
461					18818	$ 57,372.09	**east Total**
886					17985	$ 54,805.41	**midwest Total**
1408					21083	$ 64,296.35	**south Total**
1899					20821	$ 63,438.82	**west Total**
1900					78707	$ 239,912.67	**Grand Total**

Figure 40-4 When you create subtotals, Excel creates buttons that display subtotals only or both subtotals and details.

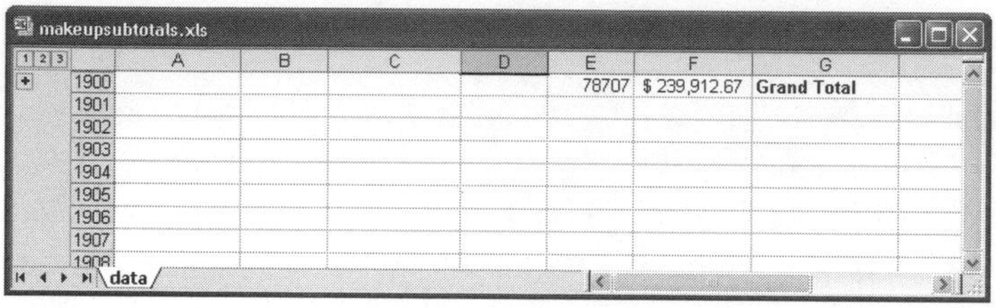

Figure 40-5 You can also see just the overall total without any detail.

Problems

You can find the data for this chapter's problems in the file MakeupSubtotals.xls.

- Use the Subtotals command to compute the following:
  - ❑ Units sold and revenue for each salesperson
  - ❑ Number of sales transactions involving each product
  - ❑ Largest transaction (in terms of revenue) for each product
  - ❑ Average dollar amount per transaction by region

41

Estimating Straight Line Relationships

- I manage a plant that produces small refrigerators. National headquarters tells me how many refrigerators to produce each month. For budgeting purposes, I want to forecast my monthly operating costs. How can I determine the relationship between monthly production and monthly operating costs?

- How well does my relationship explain the monthly variation in plant operating cost?

- How accurate are my predictions likely to be?

- When estimating a straight line relationship, which Excel functions can I use to give me the slope and intercept of the line that best fits the data?

Every business analyst should have the ability to estimate the relationship between important business variables. The Excel trend curve, which we'll discuss in this chapter as well as in Chapter 42 and Chapter 43, is often helpful in determining the relationship between two variables. The variable we're trying to predict is called the *dependent variable*. The variable we use for prediction is called the *independent variable*. Here are some examples of business relationships we might want to estimate.

Independent Variable	Dependent Variable
Units produced by plant during month	Monthly cost of operating plant
Dollars spent on advertising during month	Monthly sales
Number of employees	Annual travel expenses
Company revenue	Number of employees (headcount)
Monthly return on the stock market	Monthly return on a stock (for example, Dell)
Square feet in home	Value of home

The first step in determining how two variables are related is to graph the data points (using the Chart Wizard) so that the independent variable is on the x-axis and the dependent variable is on the y-axis. With the chart selected, you click on a data point (they are then all displayed in gold) and then choose Chart, Add Trendline (or right-click and select Add Trendline). You'll see the Add Trendline dialog box, which is shown in Figure 41-1.

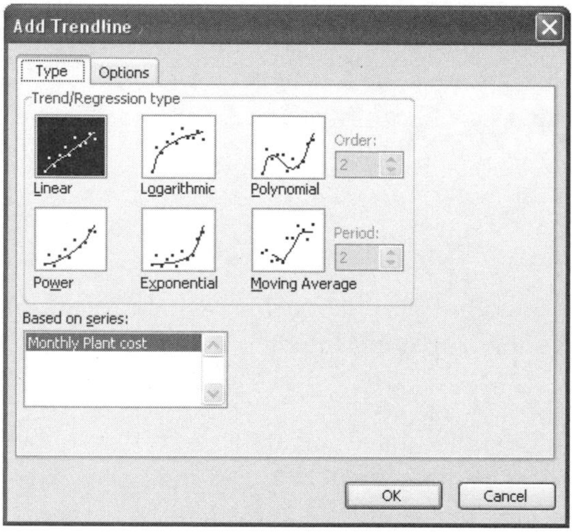

Figure 41-1 Add Trendline options.

If your graph indicates that a straight line is a reasonable fit to the points, choose the Linear option. If the graph indicates that the dependent variable increases at an increasing rate, the Exponential (and perhaps Power) option probably fits the relationship. If the graph shows that the dependent variable increases at a decreasing rate, or that the dependent variable decreases at a decreasing rate, the power curve is probably relevant.

In this chapter, I'll focus on the Linear option. In Chapter 42, I'll discuss the Exponential option. In Chapter 43, I'll cover the Power option. In Chapter 50, I'll discuss the moving average curve, and in Chapter 69, I'll discuss the polynomial curve. (The logarithmic curve is of little interest, so I won't discuss it.)

I manage a plant that produces small refrigerators. National headquarters tells me how many refrigerators to produce each month. For budgeting purposes, I want to forecast my monthly operating costs. How can I determine the relationship between monthly production and monthly operating costs?

The file CostEstimate.xls, shown in Figure 41-2, contains data about the units produced and the monthly plant operating cost for 14 months. We are interested in predicting monthly operating costs from units produced, which will help the plant manager determine her operating budget and better understand the cost to produce refrigerators.

	A	B	C	D	E	F
1					sum errors	-0.0304
2		Month	Units Produced	Monthly Plant cost	Predicted cost	Error
3		1	1260	123118	118872.66	4245.342
4		2	1007	99601	102612.68	-3011.68
5		3	1296	132000	121186.33	10813.67
6		4	873	80000	94000.671	-14000.7
7		5	532	52000	72085.044	-20085
8		6	476	58625	68485.997	-9861
9		7	482	74624	68871.609	5752.391
10		8	1273	110000	119708.15	-9708.15
11		9	692	81000	82368.036	-1368.04
12		10	690	73507	82239.499	-8732.5
13		11	564	95024	74141.642	20882.36
14		12	470	88004	68100.385	19903.62
15		13	675	70000	81275.468	-11275.5
16		14	870	110253	93807.865	16445.14

Figure 41-2   Plant operating data.

We begin by creating an XY chart (or a scatter plot) that displays our independent variable (units produced) on the x-axis and our dependent variable (monthly plant cost) on the y-axis. The column of data that you want to display on the x-axis must be located to the left of the column of data you want to display on the y-axis. To create the graph, we select the data in the range C2:D16 (including the labels in cells C2 and D2). Then we click the Chart Wizard button on the toolbar, select the XY (Scatter) option as the chart type, and then click Finish. You'll see the graph shown in Figure 41-3.

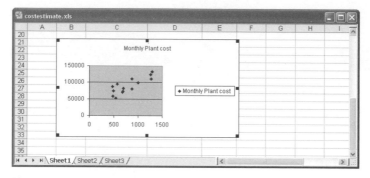

Figure 41-3   Scatter plot of operating cost vs. units produced.

Looking at our scatter plot, it seems reasonable that there is a straight line (or linear relationship) between units produced and monthly operating costs. We can see the straight line that "best fits" the points by adding a trendline to the chart. Click on the chart to select it, and then click on a data point. All the data points are displayed in gold. Choose Chart, Add Trendline. In the Add Trendline dialog box, select the Linear option. Click the Options tab, and then select the options Display Equation On Chart and Display R-Squared Value On Chart, as shown in Figure 41-4.

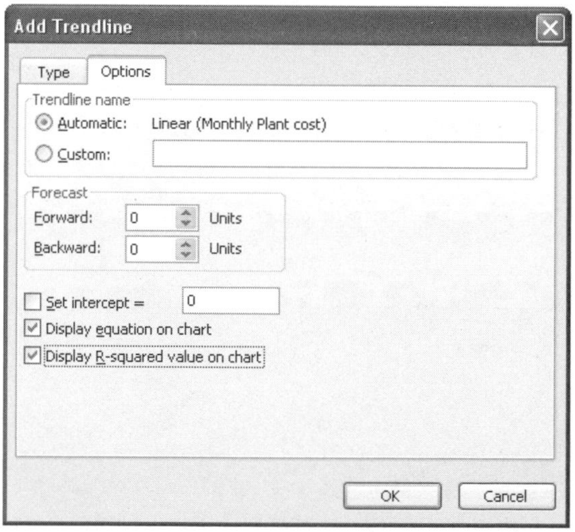

Figure 41-4   Selecting trendline options.

After clicking OK, you'll see the results shown in Figure 41-5. Notice that I added a title to the chart and labels for the x and y axes by choosing Chart, Options and then filling in the Chart Options dialog box. I also added another decimal point to the equation by double-clicking on the equation, clicking the

Number tab in the Format Data Labels dialog box, selecting Number as the category, and choosing four decimal places.

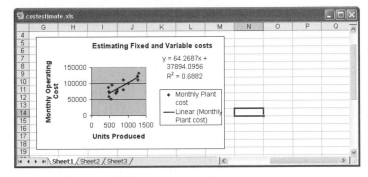

Figure 41-5   The completed trend curve.

How does Excel determine the "best fitting" line? Excel chooses the line that minimizes (over all lines that could be drawn) the sum of the squared vertical distance from each point to the line. The vertical distance from each point to our line is called an *error*, or *residual*. The line created by Excel is called the *least-squares line*. We minimize the sum of squared errors rather than the sum of the errors because in simply summing the errors, positive and negative errors can cancel each other out. For example, a point 100 units above the line and a point 100 units below the line will cancel each other if we add errors. If we square errors, however, the fact that our predictions for each point were wrong will be used by Excel to find the best fitting line.

Thus Excel calculates that the best fitting straight line for predicting monthly operating cost from monthly units produced is

`(Monthly operating cost) = 37,894.10 + 64.2687(Units produced)`

By copying from cell E3 to the cell range E4:E16 the formula *64.2687*C3+37894.0956*, we compute the predicted cost for each observed data point. For example, when 1260 units are produced, the predicted cost (see Figure 41-2) is $123,118.

You should not use a least-squares line to predict values of an independent variable that lie outside the range for which you have data. Thus our line should be used only to predict monthly plant operating costs during months in which production is between approximately 450 and 1300 units.

The intercept of this line is $37,894.10, which can be interpreted as the *monthly fixed cost*. So, even if the plant produces no refrigerators during a month, we estimate the plant will incur costs of $37,894.10. The slope of this line (64.2687) indicates that each extra refrigerator we produce increases monthly cost by $64.27. Thus we estimate the *variable cost* of producing a refrigerator is $64.27.

In cells F3:F16, I've computed the errors (or residuals) for each data point. We define the error for each data point to be the amount by which the point varies from the least-squares line. For each month, error equals the observed cost minus the predicted cost. Copying from F3 to F4:F16 the formula *D3-E3* computes the error for each data point. A positive error indicates a point is above the least-squares line, and a negative error indicates that the point is below the least-squares line. In cell F1, I computed the sum of the errors and obtained –0.03. In reality, for any least-squares line, the sum of the errors should equal 0. (I obtained –0.03 because I rounded the equation to four decimal points.) Errors summing to 0 implies that the least-squares line has the intuitively satisfying property of splitting the points in half.

How well does my relationship explain the monthly variation in plant operating cost?

Clearly, each month both the operating cost and the units produced vary. A natural question is what percentage of the monthly variation in operating cost is explained by the monthly variation in units produced? The answer to this question is the R^2 value (.6882) shown in Figure 41-5. We can state that our linear relationship explains 68.82 percent of the variation in monthly operating costs. This implies that 31.18 percent of the variation in monthly operating costs is explained by other factors. Using *multiple regression* (see Chapters 45–47), we can try to determine other factors that influence operating costs.

People always ask what is a good R^2 value. There is really no definitive answer to this question. With one independent variable, of course, a larger R^2 value indicates a better fit of the data than a smaller R^2 value. A better measure of the accuracy of your predictions is the *standard error of the regression*, which I'll describe in the next section.

How accurate are my predictions likely to be?

When we fit a line to points, we obtain a standard error of the regression that measures the "spread" of the points about the least-squares line. The standard error associated with a least-squares line can be computed with the STEYX function. The syntax of this function is STEYX(*yrange, xrange*), where *yrange* contains the values of the dependent variable, and *xrange* contains the values of the independent variable. In cell K1, I computed the standard error of our cost estimate line with the formula *STEYX(D3:D16,C3:C16)*. The result is shown in Figure 41-6.

costestimate.xls

	D	E	F	G	H	I	J	K	L	M
1		sum errors	-0.0304		slope	64.2687	std err	13771.85		
2	Monthly Plant cost	Predicted cost	Error		intercept	37894.1				
3	123118	118872.66	4245.342		RSq	0.688203				
4	99601	102612.68	-3011.68							
5	132000	121186.33	10813.67							
6	80000	94000.671	-14000.7							
7	52000	72085.044	-20085							
8	58625	68485.997	-9861							
9	74624	68871.609	5752.391							
10	110000	119708.15	-9708.15							
11	81000	82368.036	-1368.04							
12	73507	82239.499	-8732.5							
13	95024	74141.642	20882.36							
14	88004	68100.385	19903.62							
15	70000	81275.468	-11275.5							
16	110253	93807.865	16445.14							
17		108589.67								

Chart: **Estimating Fixed and Variable costs**

$y = 64.2687x + 37894.0956$
$R^2 = 0.6882$

Monthly Operating Cost (vertical axis): 0, 50000, 100000, 150000
Units Produced (horizontal axis): 0, 500, 1000, 1500

Legend: ♦ Monthly Plant cost; — Linear (Monthly Plant cost)

Sheet1 / Sheet2 / Sheet3

Figure 41-6 Computation of slope, intercept, RSQ, and standard error of regression.

Approximately 68 percent of our points should be within one standard error of regression (SER) of the least-squares line, and about 95 percent of our points should be within two SER of the least-squares line. These measures are reminiscent of the descriptive statistics rule of thumb that I described in Chapter 35. In our example, the absolute value of around 68 percent of the errors should be $13,772 or smaller, and the absolute value of around 95 percent of the errors should be $27,544, or 2*13,772, or smaller. Looking at the errors in column F, we find that 10 of 14, or 71 percent, of our points are within one SER of the least-squares line and all (100 percent) of our points are within two standard SER of the least-squares line. Any point that is more than two SER from the least-squares line is called an *outlier*. Looking for causes of outliers can often help you to improve the operation of your business. For example, a month in which actual operating costs were $30,000 higher than anticipated would be a cost outlier on the high side. If we could ascertain the cause of this high cost outlier and prevent it from recurring, we would clearly improve plant efficiency. Similarly, consider a month in which actual costs are $30,000 less than expected. If we could ascertain the cause of this low cost outlier and make sure it occurred more often, we would also improve plant efficiency.

When estimating a straight line relationship, which Excel functions can I use to give me the slope and intercept of the line that best fits the data?

The Excel SLOPE(*yrange*, *xrange*) and INTERCEPT(*yrange*, *xrange*) functions return the slope and intercept, respectively, of the least-squares line. Thus, entering in cell I1 the formula *SLOPE(D3:D16,C3:C16)* (see Figure 41-6) returns the slope (64.27) of the least-squares line. Entering in cell I2 the formula

INTERCEPT(D3:D16,C3:C16) returns the intercept (37,894.1) of the least-squares line. By the way, the RSQ(*yrange, xrange*) function returns the R^2 value associated with a least-squares line. So, entering in cell I3 the formula RSQ(D3:D16,C3:C16) returns the R^2 value of .688 for our least-squares line.

Problems

1. The file DellData.xls contains monthly returns for the S&P (Standard and Poor's) stock index and Dell. The *beta* of a stock is defined to be the slope of the least-squares line used to predict monthly return for a stock from monthly return for the market.

   a. Estimate the beta of Dell.

   b. Interpret the meaning of Dell's beta.

   c. If you believe a recession is coming, would you rather invest in a high beta or low beta stock?

   d. During a month in which the market goes up 5 percent, you are 95 percent sure that Dell's stock price will increase by between which range of values?

2. The file HouseData.xls gives the square footage and sales prices for several houses in Bellevue, Washington.

   a. You are going to build a 500-square-foot addition to your house. By how much do you think your home value will increase?

   b. What percentage of the variation in home value is explained by variation in house size?

   c. A 3000-square-foot house is selling for $500,000. Is this price out of line with typical real estate values in Bellevue? What might cause this discrepancy?

3. We all know that 32 degrees Fahrenheit is equivalent to 0 degrees Centigrade and that 212 degrees Fahrenheit is equivalent to 100 degrees Centigrade. Use the trend curve to determine the relationship between Fahrenheit and Centigrade temperatures. When you create your initial chart, before clicking Finish, you must indicate to Excel that data is in columns and not rows because with only two data points, Excel assumes different variables are in different rows.

42

Modeling Exponential Growth

■ How can I model the growth of a company's revenue over time?

If you want to value a company, it's important to have some idea about its future revenues. Although the future may not be like the past, we often begin a valuation analysis of a corporation by studying the company's revenue growth during the recent past. Many analysts like to fit a trend curve to recent revenue growth. To fit a trend curve, you plot on the x-axis the year. (For example, the first year of data is year 1, the second year of data is year 2, and so on.) On the y-axis, you plot the company's revenue.

Usually, the relationship between time and revenue will not be a straight line. Recall that a straight line always has the same slope, which implies that when the independent variable (in this case, year) is increased by 1, our prediction for the dependent variable (revenue) increases by the same amount. For most companies, revenue grows by a fairly constant percentage each year. If this is the case, as revenue increases, the annual increase in revenue will also increase. After all, revenue growth of 10 percent of $1 million means revenue grows by $100,000. Revenue growth of 10 percent of $100 million means revenue grows by $10 million. This analysis implies that a trend curve for forecasting revenue should grow more steeply and have an increasing slope. The *exponential function* has the property that whenever the independent variable increases by 1, the dependent variable increases by the same percentage. This relationship is exactly what we need to model revenue growth.

The equation for the exponential function is $y = ae^{bx}$. Here x is the value of the independent variable (in this example, the year), while y is the value of the dependent variable (in this case, annual revenue). The value e (approximately 2.7182) is the base of natural logarithms. If we select Exponential from the Excel trend line options, Excel calculates the values of a and b that best fit the data. Let's look at an example.

How can I model the growth of a company's revenue over time?

The file CiscoExpo.xls, shown in Figure 42-1, contains the revenues for Cisco for the years 1990–1999. All revenues are in millions of dollars. In 1990, for example, Cisco's revenues were $103.47 million.

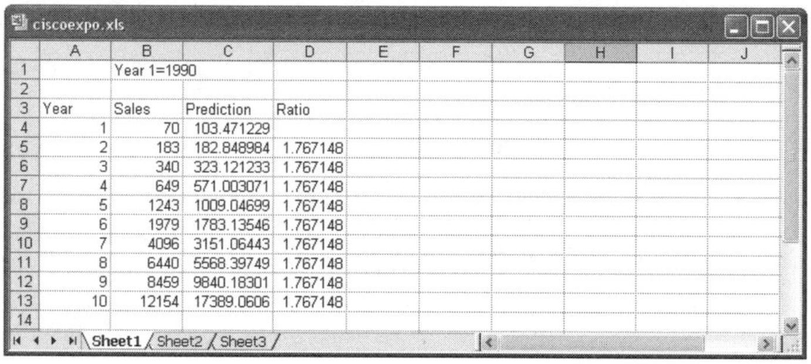

	A	B	C	D
1		Year 1=1990		
2				
3	Year	Sales	Prediction	Ratio
4	1	70	103.471229	
5	2	183	182.848984	1.767148
6	3	340	323.121233	1.767148
7	4	649	571.003071	1.767148
8	5	1243	1009.04699	1.767148
9	6	1979	1783.13546	1.767148
10	7	4096	3151.06443	1.767148
11	8	6440	5568.39749	1.767148
12	9	8459	9840.18301	1.767148
13	10	12154	17389.0606	1.767148
14				

Figure 42-1 Cisco's annual revenues for the years 1990 through 1999.

To fit an exponential curve to this data, begin by selecting the cell range A3:B13. Next choose Insert, Chart (or click the Chart Wizard button). To create the scatter plot shown in Figure 42-2, I selected the first chart sub-type option for the X-Y (Scatter) chart type.

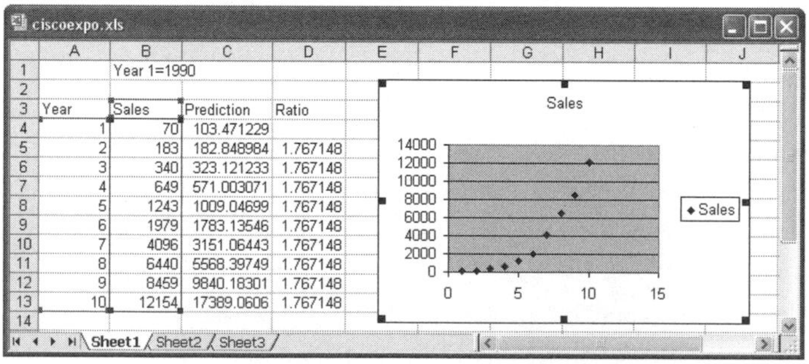

	A	B	C	D
1		Year 1=1990		
2				
3	Year	Sales	Prediction	Ratio
4	1	70	103.471229	
5	2	183	182.848984	1.767148
6	3	340	323.121233	1.767148
7	4	649	571.003071	1.767148
8	5	1243	1009.04699	1.767148
9	6	1979	1783.13546	1.767148
10	7	4096	3151.06443	1.767148
11	8	6440	5568.39749	1.767148
12	9	8459	9840.18301	1.767148
13	10	12154	17389.0606	1.767148
14				

Figure 42-2 Scatter plot for the Cisco trend curve.

Fitting a straight line to this data would be ridiculous. The slope of the graph is rapidly increasing. In this situation, exponential growth will usually provide a good fit to the data.

To obtain the exponential curve that best fits this data, right-click on a data point (all the points turn gold) and then select Add Trendline. In the Add Trendline dialog box, select the Exponential option on the Type tab, and then click the Options tab. Select the options Display Equation On Chart and Display R-Squared Value On Chart. After you click OK, you'll see the trend curve shown in Figure 42-3.

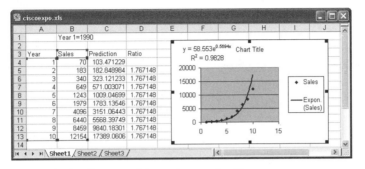

Figure 42-3 Exponential trend curve for Cisco revenues.

Our estimate of Cisco's revenue in year x (remember that $x = 1$ is the year 1990) is computed from the formula

```
Estimated Revenue = 58.552664*e.569367x
```

I computed predicted revenue in the cell range C4:C13 by copying from C4 to C5:C13 the formula *=58.552664*EXP(0.569367*A4)*. For example, our estimate of Cisco's revenue in 1999 (year 10) is $17.389 billion.

Notice that most of the data points are very close to the fitted exponential curve. This pattern indicates that exponential growth does a good job of explaining Cisco's revenue growth during the 1990s. The fact that the R^2 value (.98) is very close to 1 is also consistent with the visual evidence of a good fit.

Remember that whenever x increases by 1, the estimate from an exponential curve increases by the same percentage. We can verify this fact by computing the ratio of each year's estimated revenue to the previous year's estimated revenue. To compute this ratio, copy from D5 to D6:D13 the formula *=C5/C4*. We find that our estimate of Cisco's growth rate is 76.4 percent per year, which is the best estimate of Cisco's annual growth rate for the years 1990–1999.

Of course, to use this estimated annual revenue growth rate in a valuation analysis, we need to ask ourselves whether it's likely that this growth rate can be maintained. Be forewarned that exponential growth cannot continue forever. For example, if we use our exponential trend curve to forecast revenues for 2005 (year 16), we would predict Cisco's 2005 revenues to be $530 billion. If this estimate were realized, Cisco's revenues would triple the 2002 revenues of the world's largest company (Wal-Mart). This seems highly unrealistic. The moral is that during its early years, the revenue growth for a technology company follows exponential growth. After a while, however, the growth rate slows down. If Wall Street analysts had understood this fact during the late 1990s, the Internet stock bubble might have been avoided.

Note that during 1999, Cisco's actual revenue fell well short of the trend curve's esimated revenue. This fact may well have indicated the start of the technology slowdown, which began during late 2000.

By the way, why must you use $x = 1$ instead of x = 1990? If we used x = 1990, Excel would have to juggle numbers around the size of e^{1990}. A number this large causes Excel a great deal of difficulty.

Problems

The file ExponentialData.xls contains annual sales revenue for Staples, Wal-Mart, and Intel. Use this data to work through the following problems.

1. For each company, fit an exponential trend curve to their sales data.

2. For which company does exponential growth best fit its revenue growth?

3. For which company does exponential growth have the worst fit to its revenue growth?

4. For each company, estimate the annual percentage growth rate for revenues.

5. For each company, use your trend curve to predict 2003 revenues.

43

The Power Curve

■ As a company produces more of a product, it learns how to make the product more efficiently. Can we model the relationship between units produced and the time needed to produce a unit?

A power curve is calculated with the equation $y = ax^b$. In the equation, a and b are constants. Using a trend curve, we can determine the values of a and b that make the power curve best fit a scatter plot diagram. In most situations, a is greater than 0. When this is the case, the slope of the power curve depends on the value of b as follows:

■ For $b > 1$, y increases as x increases, and the slope of the power curve will be increasing as x increases.

■ For $0 < b < 1$, y increases as x increases, and the slope of the power curve decreases as x increases.

■ For $b = 1$, the power curve is a straight line.

■ For $b < 0$, y decreases as x increases, and the power curve flattens out as x increases.

Here are some examples of different relationships that can be modeled by the power curve.

■ If we are trying to predict total production cost as a function of units produced, we might find a relationship similar to that shown in Figure 43-1.

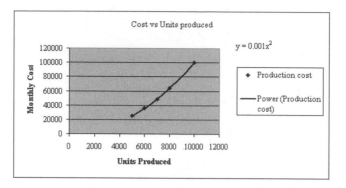

Figure 43-1 The curve created by predicting cost as a function of the number of units produced.

Notice that b equals 2. As I mentioned previously, with this value of b, the cost of production increases with the number of units produced. The slope becomes steeper, which indicates that each additional unit costs more to produce. This relationship might occur because increased production requires more overtime labor, which costs more than regular labor.

■   If we are trying to predict sales as a function of advertising expenditures, we might find a curve similar to that shown in Figure 43-2.

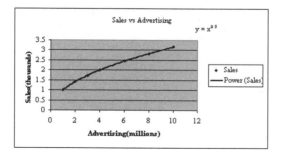

Figure 43-2 Plotting sales as a function of advertising.

Here b equals 0.5, which is between 0 and 1. When b has a value in this range, sales increase with increased advertising but at a decreasing rate. Thus the power curve enables us to model the idea of diminishing return—that each additional dollar spent on advertising will provide less benefit.

■   If we are trying to predict the time needed to produce the last unit of a product based on the number of units produced to date, we often find a scatter plot similar to Figure 43-3.

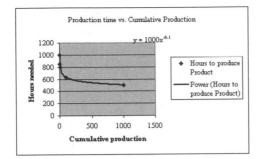

Figure 43-3   A plot of the time needed to produce a unit based on cumulative production.

Here we find that *b* equals –0.1. Because *b* is less than 0, the time needed to produce each unit decreases, but the rate of decrease—that is, the rate of "learning"—slows down. This relationship means that during the early stages of a product's life cycle, huge savings in labor time occur. As we make more of a product, however, savings in labor time occur at a slower rate. The relationship between cumulative units produced and time needed to produce the last unit is called the *learning* or *experience* curve.

A power curve has the following properties:

- **Property 1**   If *x* increases by 1 percent, *y* increases by approximately *b* percent.

- **Property 2**   Whenever *x* doubles, *y* increases by the same percentage.

Suppose that demand for a product as a function of price can be modeled as *1000(Price)*$^{-2}$. Property 1 then implies that a 1 percent increase in price will lower demand (for any price!) by 2 percent. In this case, the exponent *b* (without the negative sign) is called the *elasticity* of product demand. (I'll discuss demand elasticity in more detail in Chapter 69.) With this background, let's take a look at how to fit a power curve to data.

As a company produces more of a product, it learns how to make the product more efficiently. Can we model the relationship between units produced and the time needed to produce a unit?

The file Fax.xls contains data about the number of fax machines produced and the unit cost (in 1982 dollars) of producing the "last" fax machine made during each year. In 1983, for example, 70,000 fax machines were produced and the cost of producing the last fax machine was $3,416. The data is shown in Figure 43-4.

	A	B	C	D	E	F	G	H	I
1	Learning curve FAX data								
2									
3	Year	Production	Cumulative Production	Unit Cost	Forecast				
4	1982	64000	64000	$3,700.00	3955.81				
5	1983	70000	134000	$3,416.00	3280.54				
6	1984	100000	234000	$3,125.00	2848.51				
7	1985	150000	384000	$2,583.00	2512.63				
8	1986	175000	559000	$2,166.00	2284.66				
9	1987	400000	959000	$1,833.00	1992.72				
10	1988	785000	1744000	$1,788.00	1712.60				
11	1989	1000000	2744000		1526.85		learning		
12		double	3488000		1436.83		percentage		
13		cumulative production					0.83897516		

Figure 43-4   The data we'll use to plot the learning curve for producing fax machines.

Because a learning curve tries to predict cost or the time needed to produce a unit from data about cumulative production, I've calculated in column C the cumulative number of fax machines produced by the end of each year. In cell C4, I refer to cell B4 to show the number of fax machines produced in 1982. By copying from C5 to C6:C10 the formula *C4+B5*, I compute cumulative fax machine production for the end of each year.

We can now use the Chart Wizard to create a scatter plot that shows cumulative units produced on the x-axis and unit cost on the y-axis. After creating the chart, click on one of the data points (the data points will be displayed in gold) and then choose Chart, Add Trendline. In the Add Trendline dialog box, select the Power option on the Type tab and then select the options Display Equation On Chart and Display R-Squared Value On Chart on the Options tab. With these settings, we obtain the chart shown in Figure 43-5. The curve drawn represents the power curve that best fits the data.

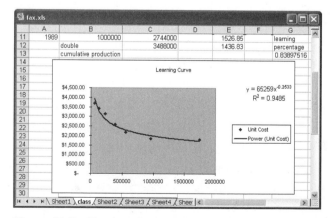

Figure 43-5   The learning curve for producing fax machines.

Our best-fitting power curve predicts the cost of producing a fax machine as follows:

```
Cost of producing fax machine = 65,259(cumulative units produced)-.2533
```

Notice that most data points are near the fitted power curve and that the R^2 value is nearly 1, indicating that the power curve fits the data well.

By copying from cell E4 to E5:E10 the formula *65259*C4^–0.2533*, we compute the predicted cost for the last fax machine produced during each year. (The carat symbol [^], which is located over the 6 key, is used to raise a number to a power.)

If we suppose that 1,000,000 fax machines are going to be produced in 1989, after computing total production by end of 1989 (2,744,000) in cell C11, we can copy our forecast equation to cell E11 to predict that the last fax machine produced in 1989 will cost $1,526.85 to produce.

Remember that property 2 of the power curve states that whenever *x* doubles, *y* increases by the same percentage. By entering twice cumulative 1988 production in cell C12 and copying our forecast formula in E10 to cell E12, we find that doubling cumulative units produced reduces our predicted cost to 83.8 percent of its previous value (1,436.83/1,712.60). For this reason, the current learning curve is known as an 84 percent learning curve. Each time we double units produced, the labor needed to make a fax machine drops by 16.2 percent.

If a curve gets steeper, the exponential curve (as well as the power curve) might fit the data well. A natural question is which curve fits the data better? In most cases, this question can be answered simply by eyeballing the curves and choosing the curve that looks like it fits the data better.

Problems

1. Use the fax machine data to model the relationship between cumulative fax machines produced and total production cost. Predict the total cost of making the first 3,000,000 fax machines.

2. Use the fax machine data to model the relationship between cumulative fax machines produced and average production cost per fax machine. Predict the average cost per unit assuming that a total of 5,000,000 fax machines will be produced.

3. A marketing director estimates that total sales of a product as a function of price will be as follows. Estimate the relationship between price and demand and predict demand for a $46 price. A 1 percent increase in price will reduce demand by what percentage?

Price	Demand
$30.00	300
$40.00	200
$50.00	110
$60.00	60

4. The brand manager for a new drug believes that the annual sales of the drug as a function of the number of sales calls on doctors will be as follows. Estimate sales of the drug if 80,000 sales calls are made on doctors.

Sales Calls	Units Sold
50,000	25,000
100,000	52,000
150,000	68,000
200,000	77,000

44

Using Correlations to Summarize Relationships

■ How are monthly stock returns on Microsoft, GE, Intel, GM, and Cisco related?

Trend curves are a great help in understanding how two variables are related. Often, however, we need to understand how more than two variables are related. Looking at the correlation between any pair of variables can provide insights into how multiple variables move up and down in value together.

The correlation (usually denoted by r) between two variables (call them x and y) is a unit-free measure of the strength of the linear relationship between x and y. The correlation between any two variables is always between -1 and $+1$. While the exact formula used to compute the correlation between two variables isn't very important, being able to interpret the correlation between the variables is.

A correlation near $+1$ means that x and y have a strong positive linear relationship. That is, when x is larger than average, y tends to be larger than average, and when x is smaller than average, y also tends to be smaller than average. When a straight line is fit to the data, there will be a straight line with a positive slope that does a good job of fitting the points. As an example, for the data shown in Figure 44-1 (x equals units produced and y equals monthly production cost), x and y have a correlation of $+0.90$.

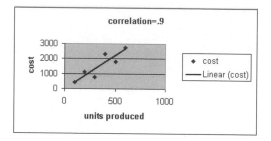

Figure 44-1   Example of a correlation near +1. This correlation indicates that two variables have a strong positive linear relationship.

On the other hand, a correlation near −1 means that there is a strong negative linear relationship between x and y. That is, when x is larger than average, y tends to be smaller than average, and when x is smaller than average, y tends to be larger than average. When a straight line is fit to the data, the line will have a negative slope that does a good job of fitting the points. As an example, for the data shown in Figure 44-2 (here x equals the price charged for a product and y equals product demand), x and y have a correlation of −0.94.

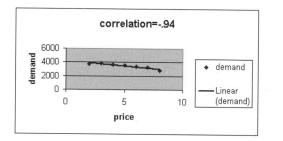
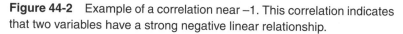

Figure 44-2   Example of a correlation near −1. This correlation indicates that two variables have a strong negative linear relationship.

A correlation near 0 means that x and y have a weak linear relationship. That is, knowing whether x is larger or smaller than its mean tells you little about whether y will be larger or smaller than its mean. Figure 44-3 shows a graph of the dependence of unit sales (y) on years of sales experience (x). Years of experience and unit sales have a correlation of 0.003. In our data set, the average experience is 10 years. We see that when a person has more than 10 years of sales experience, his or her sales can be either low or high. We also see that when a person has less than 10 years of sales experience, sales can be low or high. Although experience and sales have little or no linear relationship, there is a strong nonlinear relationship (see the fitted curve) between years of experience and sales. Correlation does not measure the strength of nonlinear relationships.

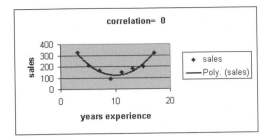

Figure 44-3 Example of a correlation near zero. This correlation shows a weak linear relationship between two variables.

How are monthly stock returns on Microsoft, GE, Intel, GM, and Cisco related?

The file StockCorrel.xls (see Figure 44-4) shows monthly returns on Microsoft, GE, Intel, GM, and Cisco during the 1990s. We can use correlations to try to understand how movements in these stocks are related.

	A	B	C	D	E	F	G
48							
49							
50							
51	Date	MSFT	GE	INTC	GM	CSCO	
52	3/30/1990	0.121518984	0.040485829	0.037267081	0.022284122	0.010753	
53	4/30/1990	0.047404062	-0.003891051	-0.053892214	-0.035422344	0.010638	
54	5/31/1990	0.258620679	0.083515622	0.221518993	0.115819208	0.042105	
55	6/29/1990	0.04109589	0.005444646	-0.025906736	-0.020565553	0.070707	
56	7/31/1990	-0.125	0.034296028	-0.05319149	-0.020997375	-0.037736	
57	8/31/1990	-0.075187966	-0.13438046	-0.25	-0.131367296	-0.029412	
58	9/28/1990	0.024390243	-0.113387093	-0.003745318	-0.088050313	-0.090909	
59	10/31/1990	0.011904762	-0.04587156	0.007518797	0.013793103	0.311111	
60	11/30/1990	0.13333334	0.052884616	0.119402982	0.013605442	0.338983	
61	12/31/1990	0.041522492	0.057260275	0.026666667	-0.05821918	0.136076	
62	1/31/1991	0.303986698	0.115468413	0.188311681	0.054545455	0.303621	
63	2/28/1991	0.057324842	0.070468754	0.043715846	0.100689657	-0.042735	
64	3/28/1991	0.022891566	0.023897059	-0.020942409	-0.044303797	-0.129464	
65	4/30/1991	-0.067137808	0.016157989	0.053475935	-0.052980132	0.220513	
66	5/31/1991	0.108585857	0.09908127	0.131979689	0.217482507	0.084034	
67	6/28/1991	-0.068906605	-0.042071197	-0.165919289	-0.055072464	-0.054264	
68	7/31/1991	0.078899086	-0.010135135	0.010752688	-0.024539877	0.286885	
69	8/30/1991	0.159863949	0.022184301	0.053191491	-0.033962265	0.156051	

stockcorrel.xls

stockprices / full matrix and correl function

Figure 44-4 Monthly stock returns during 1990s. We'll use this data to see what correlations exist between the stocks.

To find the correlations between each pair of stocks, choose Tools, Data Analysis, and then select the Correlation option. Click OK, and then fill in the Correlation dialog box as shown in Figure 44-5.

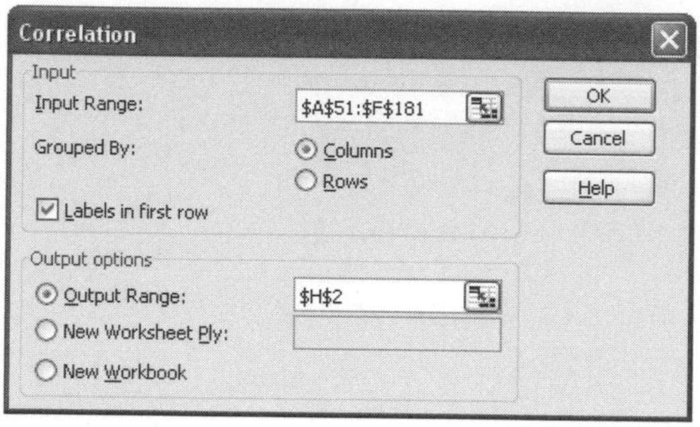

Figure 44-5 The Correlation dialog box.

The easiest way to enter the input range is to select the cell at the upper left corner of the data range (A51) and then press Ctrl+Shift+Right Arrow followed by Ctrl+Shift+Down Arrow. Check the Labels In First Row option if the first row of the input range contains labels. I entered cell H52 as the upper left corner of our output range. After clicking OK, we see the results shown in Figure 44-6.

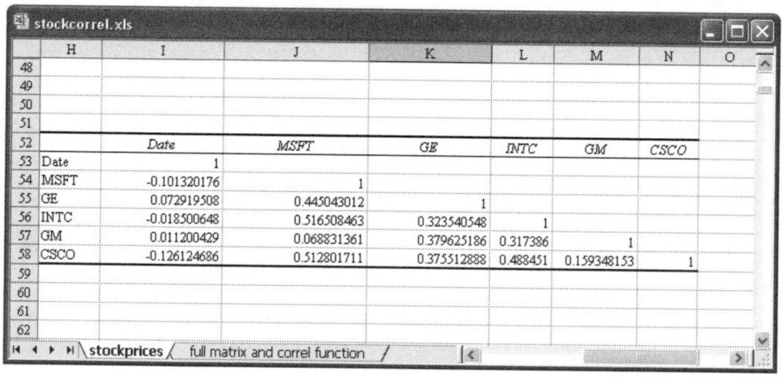

	Date	MSFT	GE	INTC	GM	CSCO
Date	1					
MSFT	-0.101320176	1				
GE	0.072919508	0.445043012	1			
INTC	-0.018500648	0.516508463	0.323540548	1		
GM	0.011200429	0.068831361	0.379625186	0.317386	1	
CSCO	-0.126124686	0.512801711	0.375512888	0.488451	0.159348153	1

Figure 44-6 Stock return correlations.

We find, for example, that the correlation between CISCO and Microsoft is .513, while the correlation between GM and Microsoft is .07. The analysis shows that returns on Cisco, Intel, and Microsoft are most closely tied together. Because the correlation between each pair of these stocks is around .5, these stocks exhibit a moderate positive relationship. In other words, if one stock does better than average, it is likely (but not certain) that the other stocks will do better than average. Because Cisco, Intel, and Microsoft stock returns are closely tied to technology spending, their fairly strong correlation is not surprising. We find also that the monthly returns on Microsoft and GM are virtually uncorrelated. This relationship indicates that when Microsoft does better than average, we really can't tell whether GM stock will do better or worse than average. Again, this trend is not surprising because GM is not really a high-tech company and is more susceptible to the vagaries of the business cycle.

Filling in the correlation matrix As you can see in this example, Excel was lazy and left some entries in the correlation matrix blank. For example, the correlation between Microsoft and GE (which is equal to the correlation between GE and Microsoft) is omitted. If you want to fill in the entire correlation matrix, select the matrix and then choose Edit, Copy. Move to a blank portion of the worksheet, and then choose Edit, Paste Special. In the Paste Special dialog box, select Transpose. This flips the data on its side. Now select the flipped data and choose Edit, Copy. Select the original correlation matrix, and choose Edit, Paste Special again. In the Paste Special dialog box, select Skip Blanks and then click OK. This copies the transposed data to the original matrix but does not copy the blanks from the transposed data. The full correlation matrix is shown in Figure 44-7.

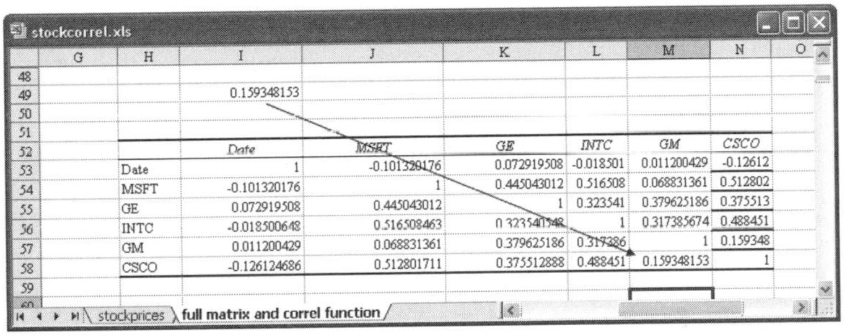

	G	H	I	J	K	L	M	N
48								
49			0.159348153					
50								
51								
52			*Date*	*MSFT*	*GE*	*INTC*	*GM*	*CSCO*
53		Date	1	-0.101320176	0.072919508	-0.018501	0.011200429	-0.12612
54		MSFT	-0.101320176	1	0.445043012	0.516508	0.068831361	0.512802
55		GE	0.072919508	0.445043012	1	0.323541	0.379625186	0.375513
56		INTC	-0.018500648	0.516508463	0.323540548	1	0.317385674	0.488451
57		GM	0.011200429	0.068831361	0.379625186	0.317386	1	0.159348
58		CSCO	-0.126124686	0.512801711	0.375512888	0.488451	0.159348153	1
59								

Figure 44-7 The complete correlation matrix and an example of CORREL function.

Using the CORREL function As an alternative to using the Correlation option of the Analysis Toolpak, you can use the CORREL function. For example, entering in cell I49 the formula *CORREL(E52:E181,F52:F181)* confirms that the correlation between monthly returns on Cisco (shown in column F) and GM (shown in column E) is .159.

The relationship between correlation and R^2 In Chapter 41, we found an R^2 value for units produced and monthly operating cost of .688. How is this value related to the correlation between units produced and monthly operating costs? The correlation between two sets of data is simply $\sqrt{R^2\ value}$ for the trend line, where we choose the sign for the square root to be the same as the sign of the slope of the trend line. Thus the correlation between units produced and monthly operating cost for our Chapter 41 data is $\sqrt{.688} = .829$.

Problems

The data for the following problems is in file Ch44Data.xls.

1. The worksheet Problem 1 contains the number of cars parked each day in the outdoor lot and parking garage near the Indiana University Kelley School of Business. Find and interpret the correlation between the number of cars parked in the outdoor lot and the parking garage.

2. The worksheet Problem 2 contains daily sales volume (in dollars) of laser printers, printer cartridges, and school supplies. Find and interpret the correlations between these quantities.

3. The worksheet Problem 3 contains annual returns on stocks, T-bills, and bonds. Find and interpret the correlations between the annual returns on these three classes of investments.

45

Introduction to Multiple Regression

- A factory produces three products (A, B, and C). How can we predict the cost of running the factory based on knowing the number of units produced?

- How accurate are our forecasts for predicting monthly cost from units produced?

- I know how to use the Data Analysis command to run a multiple regression. Is there a way to "run the regression" without using this command and place the regression's results in the same worksheet as the data?

In Chapters 41, 42, and 43, I described how to use Excel's trend curve to predict one variable (called y, or the dependent variable) from another variable (called x, or the independent variable). However, we often want to use more than one independent variable (called the independent variables $x1$, $x2$, … xn) to predict the value of a dependent variable. In these cases, we can use the multiple regression option in Excel's data analysis feature or the LINEST function to estimate the relationship we want.

Multiple regression assumes that the relationship between y and $x1$, $x2$, … xn has the form

```
Y = Constant + B1X1 + B2X2 + … BnXn
```

Excel calculates the values of *Constant*, *B*1, *B*2, … *B*n to make the predictions from this equation as accurate (in the sense of minimizing the sum of squared errors) as possible. The following example illustrates how multiple regression works.

A factory produces three products (A, B, and C). How can we predict the cost of running the factory based on knowing the number of units produced?

The worksheet named Data in the workbook Mrcostest.xls (see Figure 45-1) contains the cost of running a plant over 19 months as well as the number of units of product A, B, and C produced during each month.

Month	Cost	A Made	B Made	C Made
1	44439	515	541	928
2	43936	929	692	711
3	44464	800	710	824
4	41533	979	675	758
5	46343	1165	1147	635
6	44922	651	939	901
7	43203	847	755	580
8	43000	942	908	589
9	40967	630	738	682
10	48582	1113	1175	1050
11	45003	1086	1075	984
12	44303	843	640	828
13	42070	500	752	708
14	44353	813	989	804
15	45968	1190	823	904
16	47781	1200	1108	1120
17	43202	731	590	1065
18	44074	1089	607	1132
19	44610	786	513	839

Figure 45-1 Data for predicting monthly operating costs.

We would like to find the best forecast for monthly operating cost that has the form (which I'll refer to as Form 1)

```
Monthly operating cost = Constant + B1*(Units A produced) + B2*(Units B
produced) + B3*(Units C produced)
```

Excel's Data Analysis feature can find the equation for this form that best fits our data. Click Tools, Data Analysis, and then select Regression. Fill in the Regression dialog box as shown in Figure 45-2.

> **Note** If you haven't previously installed the Analysis Toolpak, choose Tools, Add-Ins, and then select Analysis ToolPak and Analysis ToolPak-VBA.

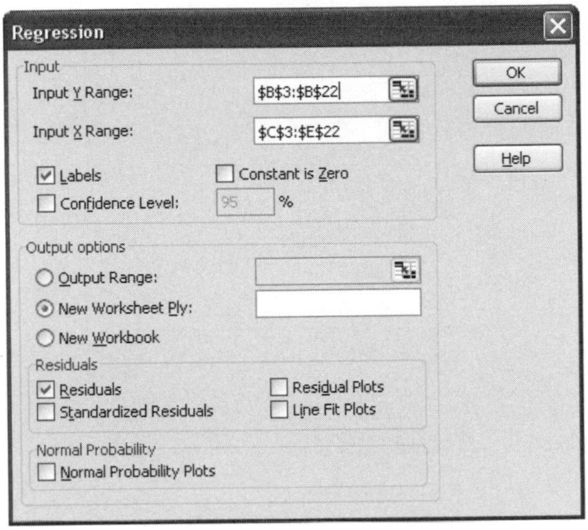

Figure 45-2   Multiple regression dialog box.

■   The Input Y range, B3:B22, contains the dependent variable or data (including the label Cost) that we want to predict.

■   The Input X range, C3:E22, contains the data or independent variables (including the labels AMade, BMade, CMade) that we want to use in the prediction. Excel has a limit of 15 independent variables, and they must be in adjacent columns.

■   Since both the Input X and Input Y ranges include labels, I've checked the Labels box.

■   I chose to place the output in a worksheet named Regression.

■   Checking the Residuals option causes Excel to list for each observation the prediction from Form 1 and the residual, which equals the observed cost minus the predicted cost.

After clicking OK in the Regression dialog box, we obtain the output shown in Figures 45-3 and 45-4.

mrcostest.xls

	A	B	C	D	E	F	G	H
1	SUMMARY OUTPUT							
2								
3	*Regression Statistics*							
4	Multiple R	0.803398744						
5	R Square	0.645449542						
6	Adjusted R Square	0.57453945						
7	Standard Error	1252.763898						
8	Observations	19						
9								
10	ANOVA							
11		*df*	*SS*	*MS*	*F*	*Significance F*		
12	Regression	3	42856229.89	14285409.96	9.102365067	0.001126532		
13	Residual	15	23541260.74	1569417.383				
14	Total	18	66397490.63					
15								
16		*Coefficients*	*Standard Error*	*t Stat*	*P-value*	*Lower 95%*	*Upper 95%*	*Lower 9*
17	Intercept	35102.90045	1837.226911	19.10645889	6.11198E-12	31186.94158	39018.85932	31186.
18	A Made	2.065953296	1.664981779	1.240826369	0.23372682	-1.482873542	5.614780134	-1.4828
19	B Made	4.176355531	1.681252566	2.484073849	0.025287785	0.592848311	7.759862751	0.5928
20	C Made	4.790641037	1.789316107	2.677358695	0.017222643	0.97680169	8.604480385	0.976

Regression / Data / NoA / A removed / Sheet2 / Sheet3

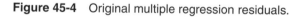

Figure 45-3 Original multiple regression output.

mrcostest.xls

	A	B	C
24	RESIDUAL OUTPUT		
25			
26	*Observation*	*Predicted Cost*	*Residuals*
27	1	42871.98962	1567.01
28	2	43318.35487	617.6451
29	3	43668.36373	795.6363
30	4	43575.81462	-2042.815
31	5	45342.07289	1000.927
32	6	44685.80146	236.1985
33	7	42784.48312	418.5169
34	8	43662.84685	-662.8468
35	9	42753.81859	-1786.819
36	10	47339.69731	1242.303
37	11	46550.0987	-1547.099
38	12	43484.0174	818.9826
39	13	42668.27031	-598.2703
40	14	44764.61149	-411.6115
41	15	45329.26497	638.735
42	16	47574.96429	206.0357
43	17	44179.19478	-977.1948
44	18	45310.77705	-1236.777
45	19	42888.55796	1721.442

regression / data / noa / A removed / Sheet2

Figure 45-4 Original multiple regression residuals.

What is the best prediction equation? We find in the Coefficients column (column B in the output) that the best equation of Form 1 that can be used to predict monthly cost is

```
Predicted monthly cost = 35,102.90 + 2.07(AMade) + 4.18(BMade) + 4.79(CMade)
```

A natural question is which of our independent variables are useful for predicting monthly cost? After all, if we had chosen the number of games won by the Seattle Mariners during a month as an independent variable, we would expect that this variable would have little effect on predicting monthly operating cost. Any independent variable with a p-value (see column E) of less than or equal to .15 is considered to be useful for predicting the dependent variable. Thus, the smaller the p-value, the higher the predictive power of the independent variable. Our three independent variables have p-values of .23 (for AMade), .025 (for BMade), and .017 (for CMade). These p-values may be interpreted as follows:

- When we use BMade and CMade to predict monthly operating cost, we have a 77 percent chance (1 – .23) that AMade adds predictive power.
- When we use AMade and CMade to predict monthly operating cost, there is a 97.5 percent chance (1 – .025) that BMade adds predictive power.
- When we use AMade and BMade to predict monthly operating cost, there is a 98.3 percent chance (1 – .017) that CMade adds predictive power.

Our p-values indicate that AMade does not add much predictive power to BMade and CMade, which means that if we know BMade and CMade, we can predict monthly operating cost about as well as we can if we include AMade as an independent variable. Therefore, we can opt to delete AMade as an independent variable and use just BMade and CMade in our prediction. I copied our data to the worksheet named A Removed and deleted the column containing A (column C). I then adjusted the Input X range to be C3:D22. In the worksheet named NoA, you can see the regression output shown in Figure 45-5 and Figure 45-6.

mrcostest.xls

	A	B	C	D	E	F	G	H
1	SUMMARY OUTPUT							
2								
3	*Regression Statistics*							
4	Multiple R	0.780421232						
5	R Square	0.609057299						
6	Adjusted R Squar	0.560189461						
7	Standard Error	1273.715391						
8	Observations	19						
9								
10	ANOVA							
11		*df*	*SS*	*MS*	*F*	*Significance F*		
12	Regression	2	40439876.29	20219938.14	12.46335684	0.000545638		
13	Residual	16	25957614.34	1622350.896				
14	Total	18	66397490.63					
15								
16		*Coefficients*	*Standard Error*	*t Stat*	*P-value*	*Lower 95%*	*Upper 95%*	*Lower 95.0*
17	Intercept	35475.30255	1842.860853	19.25012543	1.72346E-12	31568.61295	39381.99216	31568.612
18	B Made	5.320968077	1.429095476	3.72331182	0.001849065	2.291421689	8.350514465	2.2914216
19	C Made	5.417137848	1.745311646	3.103822668	0.006825007	1.717243277	9.117032419	1.7172432
20								
21								

Regression / Data / NoA / A removed / Sheet2 / Sheet3

Figure 45-5 Multiple regression output with AMade data removed as an independent variable.

	A	B	C	D	E	F	G
23	RESIDUAL OUTPUT						
24							
25	Observation	Predicted Cost	Residuals				
26	1	43381.05021	1057.949794				
27	2	43008.99747	927.002527				
28	3	43716.91148	747.0885248				
29	4	43173.14649	-1640.146495				
30	5	45018.33547	1324.664528				
31	6	45352.53278	-430.5327792				
32	7	42634.5734	568.4265963				
33	8	43497.43576	-497.4357601				
34	9	43096.66501	-2129.665007				
35	10	47415.43478	1166.565215				
36	11	46525.80688	-1522.806879				
37	12	43366.11226	936.8877388				
38	13	43312.00414	-1242.004144				
39	14	45093.11881	-740.1188117				
40	15	44751.5519	1216.448104				
41	16	47438.12957	342.8704271				
42	17	44383.92553	-1181.925527				
43	18	44837.33022	-763.3302206				
44	19	42749.93783	1860.062168				

Figure 45-6 Residuals calculated when AMade data is removed as an independent variable.

We see that AMade and BMade each have very low p-values (.002 and .007, respectively). These values tell us that both these independent variables have useful predictive power. Using the new coefficients in column B, we can now predict monthly operating cost using the equation

```
Predicted monthly operating cost = 35,475.3 + 5.32(BMade) + 5.42(CMade)
```

How accurate are our forecasts for predicting monthly cost from units produced?

In the regression output in cell B5 of the worksheet NoA (see Figure 45-5), we find that R^2 equals .61. An R^2 value such as this means that together, BMade and CMade explain 61 percent of the variation in monthly operating costs. Notice that in our original regression, which included AMade as an independent variable, R2 equals .65. This indicates that the addition of AMade as an independent variable explains only 4 percent more variation in monthly operating costs. Having such a minor difference is consistent with deleting AMade as an independent variable.

In the regression output in cell B7 in the worksheet NoA, we find that the standard error for the regression with BMade and CMade as independent variables is 1274. We expect about 68 percent of our multiple regression forecasts to be accurate within one standard error, and 95 percent of our multiple regression forecasts to be accurate within two standard errors. Any forecast that differs from the actual value by more than two standard errors is considered an outlier. Thus, if our forecasted operating cost is in error by more than $2,548 (2*1274), we consider that observation to be an outlier.

In the Residual portion of our output, shown above in Figure 45-6, we are given for each observation the predicted cost and the residual, which equals the actual cost less the predicted cost. For the first observation, for example, we predict a cost of $43,381.10 and our residual of $1,057.95 indicates that we under-predicted actual cost by $1,057.95.

I know how to use the Data Analysis command to run a multiple regression. Is there a way to "run the regression" without using this command and place the regression's results in the same worksheet as the data?

The Excel LINEST function can be used to insert the results of a regression analysis directly in a workbook. To use the LINEST function when there are *m* independent variables, begin by selecting a blank cell range, consisting of five rows and *m*+1 columns, where you want LINEST to deposit the results. In the worksheet A Removed, I used the range F5:H9. The syntax of the LINEST function is

```
LINEST (Known Ys, Known Xs, True, True)
```

If the third argument is changed to False, Excel will estimate the equation with no constant term. Changing the fourth argument to False causes the LINEST function to omit many regression computations and only return the multiple regression equation.

With the cell at the upper left corner of the target range selected (F5 in this example), enter the formula *=LINEST(B4:B22,C4:D22,TRUE,TRUE)*. At this point, *do not* press Enter! LINEST is an array function, so you must hold down Ctrl+Shift and then press Enter for the function to work correctly. After using this key combination, we obtain the results shown in Figure 45-7.

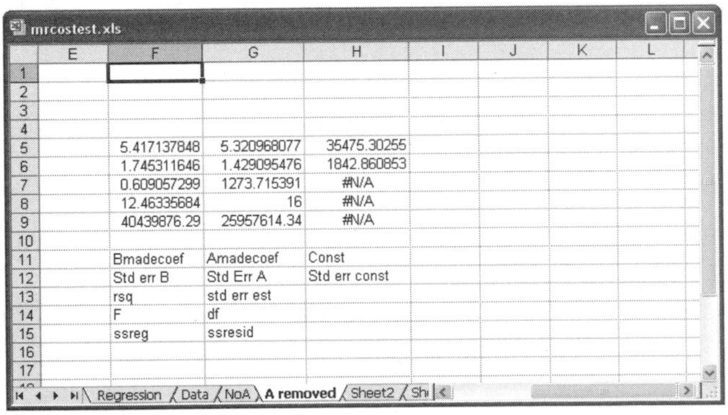

Figure 45-7   Results of using the LINEST function to calculate a multiple regression.

From row 5 we find our prediction equation (coefficients read right to left, starting with the intercept) of *Predicted monthly cost = 35,475.3 + 5.32(BMade) + 5.43(CMade)*. Row 6 contains standard errors for each coefficient estimate, but these are not too important. Cell F7 contains our R^2 value of .61, and cell G7 contains the regression standard error of 1274. Rows 8 and 9 contain information (F statistic, degrees of freedom, sum of squares regression, and sum of squares residual) that is also not very important.

Note   Problems that you can work with to learn more about multiple regression are available at the end of Chapter 47.

46

Incorporating Qualitative Factors into Multiple Regression

■ How can I predict quarterly U.S. auto sales?

■ How can I predict U.S. presidential elections?

■ Is there an Excel function I can use to easily make forecasts from a multiple regression equation?

In our first example of multiple regression in Chapter 45, we forecast the monthly cost of plant operations by using the number of units of each product manufactured at the plant. Because we can quantify exactly the amount of a product produced at a plant, we can refer to the units produced of products A, B, and C as *quantitative independent variables*. In many situations, however, independent variables can't be easily quantified. In this chapter, we'll look at ways to incorporate qualitative factors such as seasonality, gender, or the party of a presidential candidate into a multiple regression analysis.

How can I predict quarterly U.S. auto sales?

Suppose we want to predict quarterly U.S. auto sales to know how the quarter of the year influences auto sales. We'll use the data in the file Auto.xls, shown in Figure 46-1. (I've hidden some rows. Sales are listed in thousands of cars.)

	A	B	C	D	E	F	M	N	O	P
9	Historical data									
10	Year	Quarter	Sales	GNP	Unemp	Int				
11	79	1	Sales	2541	5.9	9.4				
12	79	2	2910	2640	5.7	9.4				
13	79	3	2562	2595	5.9	9.7				
14	79	4	2385	2701	6	11.9				
15	80	1	2520	2785	6.2	13.4				
16	80	2	2142	2509	7.3	9.6				
17	80	3	2130	2570	7.7	9.2				
18	80	4	2190	2667	7.4	13.6				
19	81	1	2370	2878	7.4	14.4				
20	81	2	2208	2835	7.4	15.3				
21	81	3	2196	2897	7.4	15.1				
22	81	4	1758	2744	8.3	11.8				
23	82	1	1944	2582	8.8	12.8				
24	82	2	2094	2613	9.4	12.4				
25	82	3	1911	2529	10	9.3				
26	82	4	2031	2544	10.7	7.9				
27	83	1	2046	2633	10.4	7.8				
28	83	2	2502	2878	10.1	8.4				
29	83	3	2238	3051	9.4	9.1				
30	83	4	2394	3274	8.5	8.8				

Figure 46-1 Auto sales data.

You might be tempted to define an independent variable that equals 1 during the first quarter, 2 during the second quarter, and so on. Unfortunately, this approach would force the fourth quarter to have four times the effect of the first quarter, which might not be true. The quarter of the year is a *qualitative independent variable*. To model a qualitative independent variable, we create an independent variable (called a *dummy variable*) for all but one of the qualitative variable's possible values. (It is arbitrary which value you leave out. In this example, I chose to leave out Quarter 4.) The dummy variables tell you which value of the qualitative variable occurs. Thus, we'll have a dummy variable for Quarter 1, Quarter 2, and Quarter 3 with the following properties:

- Quarter 1 dummy variable equals 1 if the quarter is Quarter 1 and 0 otherwise.

- Quarter 2 dummy variable equals 1 if the quarter is Quarter 2 and 0 otherwise.

- Quarter 3 dummy variable equals 1 if the quarter is Quarter 3 and 0 otherwise.

A Quarter 4 observation will be identified by the fact that the dummy variables for Quarters 1 through 3 equal 0. You can see why we don't need a dummy variable for Quarter 4. In fact, if we include a dummy variable for Quarter 4 as an independent variable in our regression, Excel returns an error message. The reason we get an error is that if an exact linear relationship[1] exists between any set

---

1. An exact linear relationship occurs if there exists constants $c_0, c_1, \ldots c_N$, such that for each data point $c_0 + c_1 x_1 + c_2 x_2 + \cdots c_N x_N = 0$. Here $x_1, \ldots x_N$ are the values of the independent variables.

of independent variables, Excel must perform the mathematical equivalent of dividing by 0 (an impossibility) when running a multiple regression. In our situation, if we include a Quarter 4 dummy variable, every data point satisfies the following exact linear relationship:

```
(Quarter 1 Dummy) + (Quarter 2 Dummy) + (Quarter 3 Dummy) + (Quarter 4 Dummy) = 1
```

To create our dummy variable for Quarter 1, I copied from G12 to G13:G42 the formula *IF(B12=1,1,0)*. This formula places a 1 in column G whenever a quarter is the first quarter and places a 0 in column G whenever the quarter is not the first quarter. In a similar fashion, I created dummy variables for Quarter 2 (in H12:H42) and Quarter 3 (in I12:I42). You can see the results of the formulas in Figure 46-2.

9	Historical data												
	A	B	C	D	E	F	G	H	I	J	K	L	M
10	Year	Quarter	Sales	GNP	Unemp	Int	Q1	Q2	Q3	LagGNP	LagUnemp	LagInt	
11	79	1	Sales	2541	5.9	9.4	Q1	Q2	Q3	LagGNP	LagUnemp	LagInt	
12	79	2	2910	2640	5.7	9.4	0	1	0	2541	5.9	9.4	
13	79	3	2562	2595	5.9	9.7	0	0	1	2640	5.7	9.4	
14	79	4	2385	2701	6	11.9	0	0	0	2595	5.9	9.7	
15	80	1	2520	2785	6.2	13.4	1	0	0	2701	6	11.9	
16	80	2	2142	2509	7.3	9.6	0	1	0	2705	6.2	13.4	
17	80	3	2130	2570	7.7	9.2	0	0	1	2509	7.3	9.6	
18	80	4	2190	2667	7.4	13.6	0	0	0	2570	7.7	9.2	
19	81	1	2370	2878	7.4	14.4	1	0	0	2667	7.4	13.6	
20	81	2	2208	2835	7.4	15.3	0	1	0	2878	7.4	14.4	
21	81	3	2196	2897	7.4	15.1	0	0	1	2835	7.4	15.3	
22	81	4	1758	2744	8.3	11.8	0	0	0	2897	7.4	15.1	
23	82	1	1944	2582	8.8	12.8	1	0	0	2744	8.3	11.8	
24	82	2	2094	2613	9.4	12.4	0	1	0	2582	8.8	12.8	
25	82	3	1911	2529	10	9.3	0	0	1	2613	9.4	12.4	
26	82	4	2031	2544	10.7	7.9	0	0	0	2529	10	9.3	
27	83	1	2046	2633	10.4	7.8	1	0	0	2544	10.7	7.9	
28	83	2	2502	2878	10.1	8.4	0	1	0	2633	10.4	7.8	
29	83	3	2238	3051	9.4	9.1	0	0	1	2878	10.1	8.4	
30	83	4	2394	3274	8.5	8.8	0	0	0	3051	9.4	9.1	
31	84	1	2586	3594	7.9	9.2	1	0	0	3274	8.5	8.8	
32	84	2	2898	3774	7.5	9.8	0	1	0	3594	7.9	9.2	
33	84	3	2448	3861	7.5	10.3	0	0	1	3774	7.5	9.8	

Figure 46-2 Using dummy variables, this data tracks the quarter in which a sale occurs.

In addition to seasonality, we'd like to use macroeconomic variables such as gross national product (GNP, in billions of 1986 dollars), interest rates, and unemployment rates to predict car sales. Suppose, for example, that we are trying to predict sales for the second quarter of 1979. Because values for GNP, interest rate, and unemployment rate aren't known at the beginning of the second quarter 1979, we can't use second quarter 1979 GNP, interest rate, and unemployment to predict Quarter 2 1979 auto sales. Instead, we'll use the values for GNP, interest rate, and unemployment rate *lagged one quarter* to forecast auto sales. By copying from J12 to J12:L42 the formula *=D11*, we create the lagged value for GNP, the first of our macroeconomic independent variables. For example, the range J12:L12 contains GNP, unemployment rate, and interest rate for the first quarter of 1979.

We can now run our multiple regression by choosing Tools, Data Analysis, and then selecting Regression in the Data Analysis dialog box. We use C11:C42 as the Input Y Range, G11:L42 as the Input X Range, select the Labels option (row 11 contains labels), and also select the Residuals option. After clicking OK, we obtain the output, which you can see on the worksheet named Regression and in Figures 46-3 through 46-5.

auto.xls

	A	B	C	D	E	F	G	H
1	SUMMARY OUTPUT							
2								
3	*Regression Statistics*							
4	Multiple R	0.884139126						
5	R Square	0.781701994						
6	Adjusted R Square	0.727127492						
7	Standard Error	190.5240756						
8	Observations	31						
9								
10	ANOVA							
11		*df*	*SS*	*MS*	*F*	*Significance F*		
12	Regression	6	3119625	519937.5	14.32358	6.79746E-07		
13	Residual	24	871186.2	36299.42				
14	Total	30	3990811					

Regression / Data

Figure 46-3 Summary output and ANOVA table for auto sales data.

In Figure 46-4, you can see that the equation (equation 1) used to predict quarterly auto sales is as follows:

```
Predicted quarterly sales =  3154.7 + 156.833Q1 + 379.784Q2 + 203.036Q3
+ .174(LAGGNP in billions) - 93.83(LAGUNEMP) - 73.91(LAGINT)
```

Also in Figure 46-4, we see that each independent variable has a p-value less than or equal to .15. We can conclude that all independent variables have a significant effect on quarterly auto sales. We interpret all coefficients in our regression equation *ceteris paribus* (which means that each coefficient gives the effect of the independent variable after adjusting for effects of all other variables in the regression).

auto.xls

	A	B	C	D	E	F	G	H
16		*Coefficients*	*Standard Error*	*t Stat*	*P-value*	*Lower 95%*	*Upper 95%*	*Lower 95.0%*
17	Intercept	3154.700285	462.6530922	6.818716525	4.7214E-07	2199.83143	4109.56914	2199.83143
18	Q1	156.833091	98.87110703	1.586237838	0.125774521	-47.22680256	360.8929846	-47.22680256
19	Q2	379.7835116	96.08921514	3.95240518	0.000594196	181.4651595	578.1018637	181.4651595
20	Q3	203.035501	95.40891864	2.128055783	0.043800625	6.12121161	399.9497905	6.12121161
21	LagGNP	0.174156906	0.05842	2.981117865	0.006490201	0.053583977	0.294729835	0.053583977
22	LagUnemp	-93.83233214	28.32328716	-3.312904029	0.002918487	-152.2887117	-35.37595254	-152.2887117
23	LagInt	-73.9167147	17.78851573	-4.155305356	0.000355622	-110.6303992	-37.20303022	-110.6303992
24								
25								

Regression / Data

Figure 46-4 Coefficient information for auto sales regression.

Here's an interpretation of each coefficient:

- A one billion dollar increase in last quarter's GNP increases quarterly car sales by 174.

- An increase of 1 percent in last quarter's unemployment rate decreases quarterly car sales by 93,832.

- An increase of 1 percent in last quarter's interest rate will decrease quarterly car sales by 73,917.

To interpret the coefficients of the dummy variables, we must realize that they tell us the effect of seasonality relative to the value left out of the qualitative variables. Therefore,

- In Quarter 1, car sales exceed Quarter 4 car sales by 156,833.

- In Quarter 2, car sales exceed Quarter 4 car sales by 379,784.

- In Quarter 3, car sales exceed Quarter 4 car sales by 203,036.

We find that car sales are highest during the second quarter (April–June; tax refunds and summer is coming) and lowest during the third quarter (October–December; why buy a new car when winter salting will ruin it?).

Interpreting the Summary Output   From the Summary Output shown in Figure 46-3, we can learn the following:

- The variation in our independent variables (macroeconomic factors and seasonality) explains 78 percent of the variation in our dependent variable (quarterly car sales).

- The standard error of our regression is 190,524 cars. We can expect around 68 percent of our forecasts to be accurate within 190,524 cars and about 95 percent of our forecasts to be accurate within 381,048 cars (2*190,524).

- There are 31 observations used to fit the regression.

Interpreting the ANOVA Table   The only quantity of interest to us in the ANOVA table is the significance (.00000068). This measure implies that there are only 6.8 chances in 10,000,000 that our independent variables are useless in forecasting car sales.

Interpreting the Residuals   Figure 46-5 gives for each observation the predicted sales and residual. For example, for the second quarter of 1979 (observation 1), predicted sales from equation 1 are 2728.6 thousand and our residual is 181,400 cars (2910 - 2728.6). Note that no residual exceeds 381,000 in absolute value, so we have no outliers.

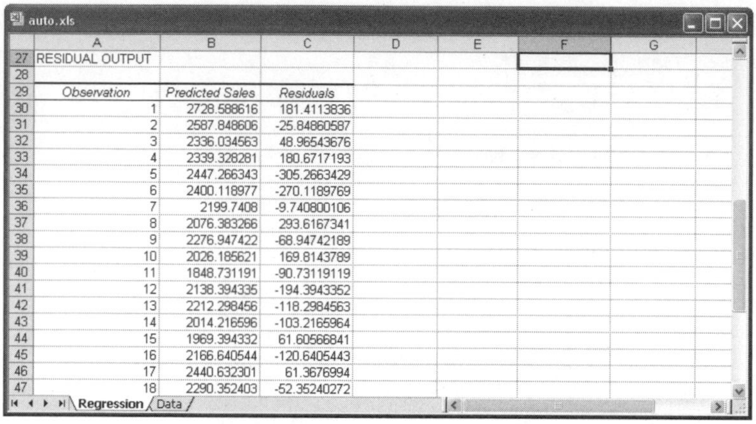

auto.xls

	A	B	C
27	RESIDUAL OUTPUT		
28			
29	*Observation*	*Predicted Sales*	*Residuals*
30	1	2728.588616	181.4113836
31	2	2587.848606	-25.84860587
32	3	2336.034563	48.96543676
33	4	2339.328281	180.6717193
34	5	2447.266343	-305.2663429
35	6	2400.118977	-270.1189769
36	7	2199.7408	-9.740800106
37	8	2076.383266	293.6167341
38	9	2276.947422	-68.94742189
39	10	2026.185621	169.8143789
40	11	1848.731191	-90.73119119
41	12	2138.394335	-194.3943352
42	13	2212.298456	-118.2984563
43	14	2014.216596	-103.2165964
44	15	1969.394332	61.60566841
45	16	2166.640544	-120.6405443
46	17	2440.632301	61.3676994
47	18	2290.352403	-52.35240272

Regression / Data

Figure 46-5 Residuals for the auto sales example.

How can I predict U.S. presidential elections?

Presidential advisor James Carville said "It's the economy, stupid," when asked about which factors drive presidential elections. Yale economist Roy Fair[2] showed that Carville was right in thinking that the state of the economy has a large influence on the results of presidential elections. Fair's dependent variable (see the file President.xls, shown in Figure 46-6) for each election (1916–2000) was the percentage of the two party vote (ignoring votes received by third party candidates) that went to the incumbent party. He tried to predict the incumbent party's percentage of the two party vote by using the following independent variables:

- Party in power. In our data, we use a 1 to denote that the Republican party is in power and a 0 to denote that the Democratic party is in power.
- Percentage growth in GNP during the first nine months of the election year.
- Absolute value of the inflation rate during the first nine months of the election year. We use the absolute value because either a positive or a negative inflation rate is bad.
- Number of quarters during the last four years in which economic growth has been strong. Strong economic growth is defined as growth at an annual level of 3.2 percent or more.

2. Our data comes from Roy Fair's excellent book *Predicting Presidential Elections and Other Things* (Stanford University Press, 2002).

	A	B	C	D	E	F	G	H	I	J	K	L
1	Presidential Elections							0=1 term				
2								1=2 terms				
3								1.25=3 terms				
4								1.5=4 terms				
5								1.75=5 terms				
6	Candidates	Year	Incumbent Share	Party in Power	Growth rate in election year	Abs. Value Inflation rate in election year	Quarters Growth>3.2 %	Time Incumbent in Office	Incumbent Party 1 = Republican	War	President Running?	Prediction
7	Wilson-Hughes	1916	51.7	D	2.2	4.3	3	0	0	0	1	50.7156536
8	Harding-Cox	1920	36.1	D	-11.5	0	0	1	0	1	0	38.862535
9	Coolidge-Davis	1924	58.2	R	-3.9	5.2	10	0	1	0	1	57.7981626
10	Hoover-Smith	1928	58.8	R	4.6	0.2	7	1	1	0	0	57.2814143
11	Hoover-FDR	1932	40.8	R	-14.9	7.1	4	1.25	1	0	1	39.1412859
12	FDR-Landon	1936	62.5	D	11.9	2.4	9	0	0	0	1	64.2935414
13	FDR-Wilkie	1940	55	D	3.7	0	8	1	0	0	1	56.019
14	FDR-Dewey	1944	53.8	D	4.1	0	0	1.25	0	1	1	52.9411966
15	Truman-Dewey	1948	52.4	D	1.8	0	0	1.5	0	1	1	50.4962684
16	Ike-Stevenson	1952	44.6	D	0.6	2.3	6	1.75	0	0	0	43.9146735
17	Ike-Stevenson	1956	57.8	R	-1.5	1.9	5	0	1	0	1	57.3057142
18	Kennedy-Nixon	1960	49.9	R	0.1	1.9	5	1	1	0	0	51.1083145
19	Johnson-Goldw	1964	61.3	D	5.1	1.2	10	0	0	0	1	61.2893759
20	Nixon-Humphre	1968	49.6	D	4.8	3.2	7	1	0	0	0	49.6217695
21	Nixon-McCgover	1972	61.8	R	6.3	4.8	4	0	1	0	1	59.7995525
22	Ford-Carter	1976	48.9	R	3.7	7.7	4	1	1	0	0	48.5942045
23	Carter-Reagan	1980	44.7	D	-3.8	8.1	5	0	0	0	1	45.6153782

Figure 46-6 Presidential election data.

- Time incumbent party has been in office. Fair used 0 to denote one term in office, 1 for two terms, 1.25 for three terms, 1.5 for four terms, and 1.75 for at least five terms. This definition implies that each term after the first term in office has less influence on the election results than the first term in office.

- Is the election during wartime? The elections in 1920 (World War I), 1944 (World War II), and 1948 (World War II was still underway in 1945) were defined as wartime elections. Elections held during the Vietnam war were not considered wartime elections. During wartime years, the variables related to quarters of good growth and inflation were deemed irrelevant and were set to 0.

- Is the current president running for re-election? If so, this variable is set to 1; otherwise, this variable is set to 0. In 1976, Gerald Ford was not considered a president running for re-election because he was not elected as either president or vice-president.

I've attempted to use the data from the elections in 1916 through 1996 to develop a multiple regression equation that can be used to forecast future presidential elections. I saved the infamous 2000 election as a "validation point." When fitting a regression to data, it's always a good idea to hold back some of your data for use in validating your regression equation. Holding back data enables you to determine whether your regression equation can do a good job of forecasting data it hasn't seen. Any forecasting tool that poorly forecasts data it hasn't seen should not be used to predict the future.

To run the regression, select Tools, Data Analysis, and then select the Regression item in the Data Analysis dialog box. I used C6:C27 as the Input Y Range and E6:K27 as the Input X Range. I also selected the Labels option (row 6 contains labels) and the Residuals option. I've placed the output in the worksheet named Results, which you can see in Figures 46-7 and 46-8.

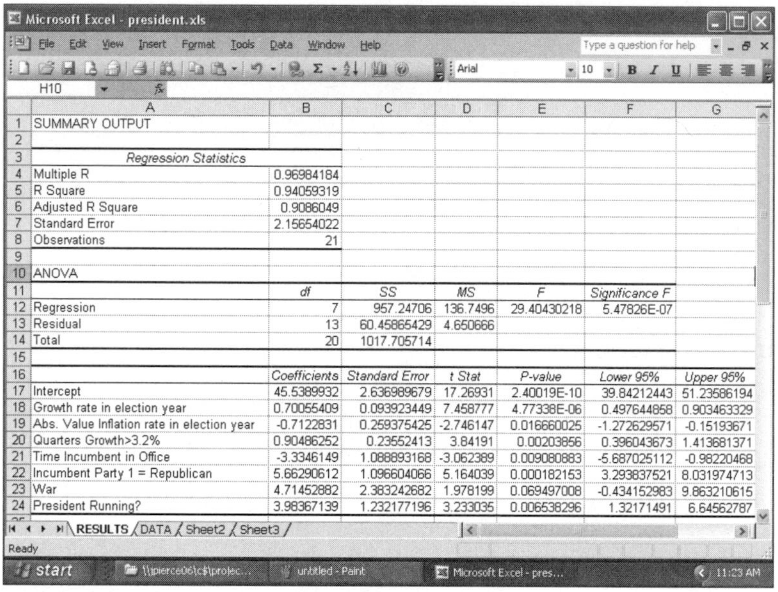

	A	B	C	D	E	F	G
1	SUMMARY OUTPUT						
2							
3	*Regression Statistics*						
4	Multiple R	0.96984184					
5	R Square	0.94059319					
6	Adjusted R Square	0.9086049					
7	Standard Error	2.15654022					
8	Observations	21					
9							
10	ANOVA						
11		*df*	*SS*	*MS*	*F*	*Significance F*	
12	Regression	7	957.24706	136.7496	29.40430218	5.47826E-07	
13	Residual	13	60.45865429	4.650666			
14	Total	20	1017.705714				
15							
16		*Coefficients*	*Standard Error*	*t Stat*	*P-value*	*Lower 95%*	*Upper 95%*
17	Intercept	45.5389932	2.636989679	17.26931	2.40019E-10	39.84212443	51.23586194
18	Growth rate in election year	0.70055409	0.093923449	7.458777	4.77338E-06	0.497644858	0.903463329
19	Abs. Value Inflation rate in election year	-0.7122831	0.259375425	-2.746147	0.016660025	-1.272629571	-0.15193671
20	Quarters Growth>3.2%	0.90486252	0.23552413	3.84191	0.00203856	0.396043673	1.413681371
21	Time Incumbent in Office	-3.3346149	1.088893168	-3.062389	0.009080883	-5.687025112	-0.98220468
22	Incumbent Party 1 = Republican	5.66290612	1.096604066	5.164039	0.000182153	3.293837521	8.031974713
23	War	4.71452882	2.383242682	1.978199	0.069497008	-0.434152983	9.863210615
24	President Running?	3.98367139	1.232177196	3.233035	0.006538296	1.32171491	6.64562787

Figure 46-7 Regression output for predicting presidential elections.

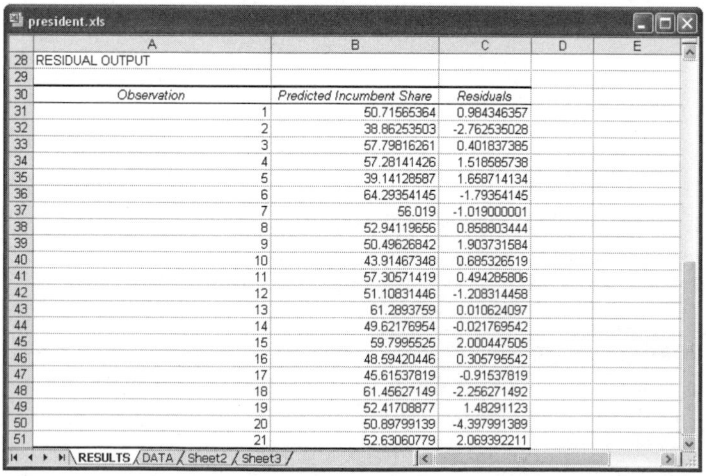

	A	B	C
28	RESIDUAL OUTPUT		
29			
30	*Observation*	*Predicted Incumbent Share*	*Residuals*
31	1	50.71565364	0.984346357
32	2	38.86253503	-2.762535028
33	3	57.79816261	0.401837385
34	4	57.28141426	1.518585738
35	5	39.14128587	1.658714134
36	6	64.29354145	-1.79354145
37	7	56.019	-1.019000001
38	8	52.94119656	0.858803444
39	9	50.49626842	1.903731584
40	10	43.91467348	0.685326519
41	11	57.30571419	0.494285806
42	12	51.10831446	-1.208314458
43	13	61.2893759	0.010624097
44	14	49.62176954	-0.021769542
45	15	59.7995525	2.000447505
46	16	48.59420446	0.305795542
47	17	45.61537819	-0.91537819
48	18	61.45627149	-2.256271492
49	19	52.41708877	1.48291123
50	20	50.89799139	-4.397991389
51	21	52.63060779	2.069392211

Figure 46-8 Presidential election residuals.

In Figure 46-7, you can see that the p-value for each independent variable is much less than .15, which indicates that each of our independent variables is helpful in predicting presidential elections. We can predict elections using an equation such as the following (equation 2):

```
Predicted presidential election percentage =  45.53 + .70GROWTH -.71ABSINF
+ .90GOODQUARTERS -3.33TIMEINCUMB + 5.66REP +4.71WAR+3.99PRESRUNNING
```

The coefficients of the independent variables can be interpreted as follows (after adjusting for all other independent variables used in equation 2):

■   A 1 percent increase in the annual GNP growth rate during an election year is worth .7 percent to the incumbent party.

■   A 1 percent deviation from the ideal (0 percent inflation) costs the incumbent party .71 percent of the vote.

■   Every good quarter of growth during an incumbent's term increases his (maybe her someday soon!) vote by .90 percent.

■   Relative to having one term in office, the second term in office decreases the incumbent's vote by 3.33 percent, and each later term decreases the incumbent's vote by .25*(3.33 percent) = .83 percent.

■   A Republican has a 5.66 percent edge over a Democrat.

■   A wartime incumbent president has a 4.71 percent edge over his opponent.

■   A sitting president running for re-election has a 3.99 percent edge over his opponent.

We find that 94 percent of the variation in the percentage received by an incumbent in a presidential election is explained by our independent variables. This is amazing! We have made no mention whether the candidates are "good or bad" candidates. Our standard error of 2.16 percent indicates that about 95 percent of our forecasts will be accurate within 4.32 percent. From our residuals, shown in Figure 46-8, we find the only election outlier to be the 1992 Clinton-Bush (senior) election. George Bush Sr. received 4.39 percent less than our model predicted, which probably indicates that Bill Clinton was a great campaigner!

Is there an Excel function I can use to easily make forecasts from a multiple regression equation?

It's tedious to make forecasts using an equation such as equation 2, but the Excel TREND function makes it easy to generate forecasts from a multiple regression. You don't even have to run a regression with the Data Analysis command.

To illustrate the use of the TREND function, I'll describe how to generate forecasts for the 1916–2000 elections using data from only the 1916–1996 elections. Begin by selecting the cell range (in our example, L7:L28 on the worksheet Data) where you want your forecasts to go. With the pointer in the first cell of this range (cell L7 in our example), enter the formula *TREND(C7:C27,E7:K27,E7:K28)*. Next press Ctrl+Shift+Enter. You'll now see the forecast for each election generated in cells L7:L28. Note that the forecast for the 2000 election (using data only through 1996) was that Gore would receive 52.2 percent of the vote. This is very close to the actual 50 percent of the two party vote that Gore received.

The TREND function is an example of an *array function*. I'll provide a more complete discussion of array functions in Chapter 72. For now, here is some background about array functions:

- Before entering an array function, you must always select the cell range in which you want the results of the array function to be located.

- Instead of pressing Enter to perform the calculation, you need to press Ctrl+Shift+Enter to complete the entry of an array function.

- After entering an array function, you'll see a curly bracket in the formula bar when you select a cell in which the array function's results are located. This bracket indicates that the results in the cell were computed with an array function.

- You can't modify data in any part of the range created by an array function.

Note   Problems that you can work with to learn more about multiple regression are available at the end of Chapter 47.

47

Modeling Nonlinearities and Interactions

- What does it mean when we say that an independent variable has a nonlinear effect on a dependent variable?

- What does it mean when we say that the effects of two independent variables on a dependent variable interact?

- How can we test for the presence of nonlinearity and interaction in a regression?

What does it mean when we say that an independent variable has a nonlinear effect on a dependent variable?

An independent variable will often influence a dependent variable through a nonlinear relationship. For example, if we try to predict product sales using an equation such as *Sales = 500 - 10*Price,* Price influences Sales linearly. This equation indicates that a unit increase in Price will (at any price level) reduce sales by 10 units. If the relationship between Sales and Price were governed by an equation such as *Sales = 5000 - 4*Price - .40*Price^2*, Price and Sales are related nonlinearly. As shown in Figure 47-1, larger increases in price result in larger decreases in demand. In short, if the change in the dependent variable caused by a unit change in the independent variable is not constant, there is a nonlinear relationship between the independent and dependent variables.

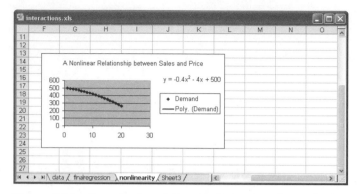

Figure 47-1 A nonlinear relationship between sales and price.

What does it mean when we say that the effects of two independent variables on a dependent variable interact?

If the effect of one independent variable on a dependent variable depends on the value of another independent variable, we say that the two independent variables exhibit *interaction*. For example, suppose we try to predict sales using price and the amount spent on advertising. If the effect of changing the level of advertising dollars is large when the price is small, and small when the price is high, price and advertising exhibit interaction. If the effect of changing the level of advertising dollars is the same for any price level, sales and price do not exhibit any interaction.

How can we test for the presence of nonlinearity and interaction in a regression?

To see whether an independent variable has a nonlinear effect on a dependent variable, we simply add an independent variable to the regression that equals the square of the independent variable. If the squared term has a low p-value (less than .15), we have evidence of a nonlinear relationship.

To check whether two independent variables exhibit interaction, we simply add a term to the regression that equals the product of the independent variables. If the term has a low p-value (less than .15), we have evidence of interaction.

To illustrate these ideas, let's try and determine how gender and experience influence salaries at a small manufacturing company. For each employee we are given the following set of data. You can find the data on the worksheet named Data in the file Interactions.xls, shown in Figure 47-2.

- Annual salary (in thousands of dollars)

- Years of experience working in the manufacturing business

- Gender (1 = female, 0 = male)

Figure 47-2   Data used for predicting salary from gender and experience.

We'll use this data to try and predict salary (the dependent variable) from years of experience and gender. To test whether years of experience has a non-linear effect on salary, I added the term Experience Squared by copying from D2 to D3:D98 the formula *B2^2*. To test whether experience and gender have a significant interaction, I added the term Experience*Gender by copying from E2 to E3:E98 the formula *B2*C2*. I ran a regression with an Input Y Range of A1:A98 and an Input X Range of B1:E98. After selecting the Labels option in the Regression dialog box and clicking OK, I got the results shown in Figure 47-3.

Figure 47-3   Regression results that test for nonlinearity and interaction.

We find that gender is insignificant (its p-value is greater than .15). All other independent variables are significant (meaning they have a p-value less than or equal to .15). We can delete the insignificant variable gender as an independent variable. To do this, I copied the data to another worksheet using the Move Or Copy Sheet command on the Edit menu. (Be sure to check Create A Copy.) After deleting the Gender column, we obtain the regression results included in the worksheet FinalRegression and shown in Figure 47-4.

	H	I	J	K	L	M	N	
1								
2	SUMMARY OUTPUT							
3								
4	*Regression Statistics*							
5	Multiple R	0.930385789						
6	R Square	0.865617717						
7	Adjusted R Square	0.861282805						
8	Standard Error	4.513993788						
9	Observations	97						
10								
11	ANOVA							
12		df	SS	MS	F	Significance F		
13	Regression	3	12206.43899	4068.812995	199.6851716	2.12292E-40		
14	Residual	93	1894.981012	20.37613992				
15	Total	96	14101.42					
16								
17		Coefficients	Standard Error	t Stat	P-value	Lower 95%	Upper 95%	Low
18	Intercept	59.05744235	1.455412135	40.57781363	6.05677E-61	56.16728518	61.94759951	56.
19	Exp	0.781117168	0.354623849	2.202663952	0.030089718	0.076905191	1.485329146	0.07
20	Exp^2	-0.033594184	0.017492209	-1.920522609	0.057855662	-0.06833021	0.001141843	-0.0
21	Exp*Gender	-2.073394532	0.087774433	-23.62185052	4.49201E-41	-2.247696986	-1.899092079	-2.24

Figure 47-4   Regression results after deleting insignificant gender variable.

All independent variables are now significant (have a p-value less than or equal to .15). Therefore, we can predict salary (in thousands of dollars) from the following equation (equation 1):

```
Predicted salary = 59.06 + .78(EXP) - .03EXP² - 2.07(EXP*GENDER)
```

The negative EXP^2 term indicates that each additional year of experience has less impact on salary, which means that experience has a nonlinear effect on salary. In fact, our model shows that after 13 years of experience, each additional year of experience reduces salary.

Remember that gender equals 1 for a woman and 0 for a man. After substituting 1 for gender in equation 1, we find that for a woman:

```
Predicted salary = 59.06 + 78EXP - .03EXP² - 2.07(EXP*1)
= 59.06 - .03EXP² - 1.29EXP
```

For a man, (substituting gender = 0), we find that:

```
Predicted salary = 59.06 + .78EXP - .03EXP² - 2.07(EXP*0)
= 59.06 + .78EXP - .03EXP²
```

Thus, the interaction between gender and experience shows that each additional year of experience benefits a woman an average of .78 - (-1.29) = $2,070 less than a man. This indicates that women are not being treated fairly.

Problems for Chapters 45–47

1. Fizzy Drugs wants to optimize the yield from an important chemical process. The company thinks that the number of pounds yielded each time the process is run depends on the size of the container used, the pressure, and the temperature. The scientists involved believe the effect of changing one variable might depend on the values of other variables. The size of the process container must be between 1.3 and 1.5 cubic meters, pressure must be between 4 and 4.5 mm, and temperature must be between 22 and 30 degrees Centigrade. The scientists patiently set up experiments at the lower and upper levels of the three control variables and obtain the data in file Fizzy.xls.

❑ Determine the relationship between yield, size, temperature, and pressure.

❑ Discuss the interactions between pressure, size, and temperature.

❑ What settings for temperature, size, and pressure would you recommend?

2. For 12 straight weeks you have observed the sales (in number of cases) of canned tomatoes at Mr. D's Supermarket. (See the file Grocery.xls.) Each week you keep track of the following:

❑ Was a promotional notice for canned tomatoes placed in all shopping carts?

❑ Was a coupon given for canned tomatoes?

❑ Was a price reduction (none, 1, or 2 cents off) given?

Use this data to determine how the above factors influence sales. Predict sales of canned tomatoes during a week in which we use a shopping cart notice, a coupon, and reduce price by 1 cent.

3. The file Countries.xls contains the following data for several underdeveloped countries:

❑ Infant mortality rate

❑ Adult literacy rate

❑ Percentage of students finishing primary school

❑ Per capita GNP

Use this data to develop an equation that can be used to predict infant mortality. Are there any outliers in this set of data? Interpret the coefficients in your equation. Ninety-five percent of our predictions for infant mortality should be accurate within what value?

4. The file Baseball96.xls gives runs scored, singles, doubles, triples, home runs, and stolen bases for each major league baseball team during the 1996 season. Use this data to determine the effects of singles, doubles, and other categories on run production.

Analysis of Variance: One-Way ANOVA

- Microsoft Press wants to know whether the position of its books in the computer book section of bookstores influences sales. More specifically, does it really matter whether the books are placed in the front, back, or middle of the computer book section?

- If we are determining whether populations have significantly different means, why is the technique called *analysis of variance?*

- How can we use the results of one-way ANOVA for forecasting?

We often have several different groups of people or items and want to determine whether data about the groups differs significantly. Here are some examples:

- Is there a significant difference in the length of time that four doctors keep mothers in the hospital after they give birth?

- Does production yield for a new drug depend on whether the size of the container in which the drug is produced is large, small, or medium?

- Does the drop in blood pressure attained after taking one of four drugs depend on the drug taken?

When you're trying to determine whether the means in several sets of data that depend on one factor are significantly different, one-way analysis of variance, or ANOVA, is the correct tool to use. In the examples given above, the factors are the doctors, the container size, and the drug, respectively. In analyzing the data, we can choose between two hypotheses:

■ Null hypothesis, which indicates that the means of all groups are identical.

■ Alternative hypothesis, which indicates that there is a statistically significant difference between the groups' means.

To test these hypotheses in Excel, we can use the Anova: Single Factor option in the Data Analysis dialog box. If the p-value computed by Excel is small (usually less than or equal to .15), we can conclude that the alternative hypothesis is true (that means are significantly different). If the p-value is greater than .15, the null hypothesis is true (the populations have identical means). Let's look at an example.

Microsoft Press wants to know whether the position of its books in the computer book section of bookstores influences sales. More specifically, does it really matter whether the books are placed in the front, back, or middle of the computer book section?

Microsoft Press wants to know whether its books sell better when a display is set up in the front, back, or middle of the computer book section. Weekly sales (in 100s) were monitored at 12 different stores. At 5 stores the books were placed in the front, at 4 stores the books were placed in the back, and at 3 stores the books were placed in the middle. Resulting sales are contained in the worksheet named Signif in the file OnewayAnova.xls, which is shown in Figure 48-1. Does the data indicate that the location of the books has a significant affect on sales?

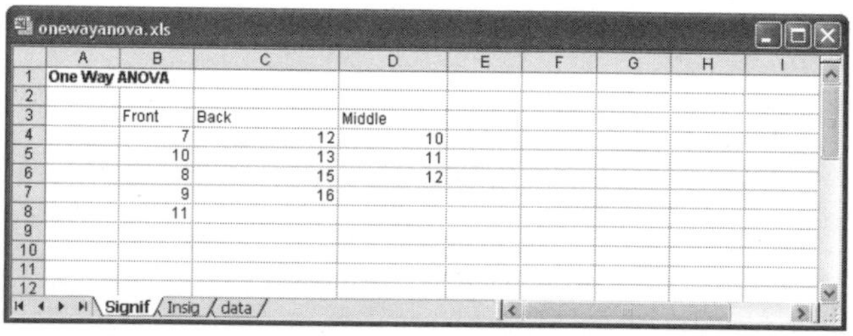

Figure 48-1 Book sales data.

We assume that the 12 stores have similar sales patterns and are approximately the same size. This assumption allows us to use one-way ANOVA because we believe that at most one factor (the position of the display in the computer book section) is affecting sales. (If the stores were different sizes, we would need to analyze our data with two-way ANOVA, which I'll discuss in Chapter 49.)

To analyze the data, choose Tools, Data Analysis, and then select Anova: Single Factor. Fill in the dialog box as shown in Figure 48-2.

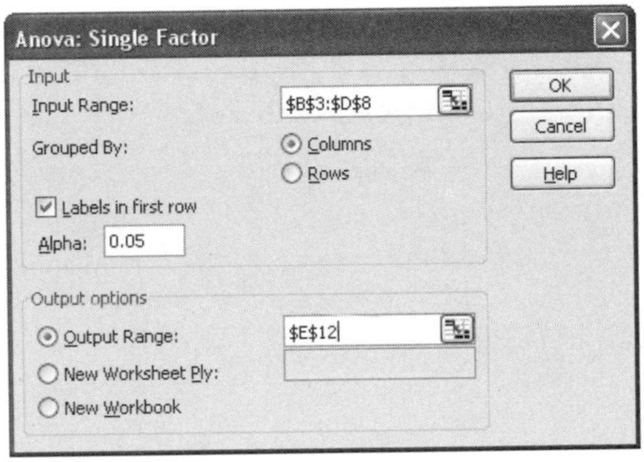

Figure 48-2   Anova: Single Factor dialog box.

- The data for our input range, including labels, is in cells B3:D8.

- Select the Labels option because the first row of our input range contains labels.

- I've selected the Columns option because the data is organized in columns.

- I've selected cell E12 as the upper-left corner of the output range.

- The selected alpha value is not important. You can use the default value.

After clicking OK, we obtain the results shown in Figure 48-3.

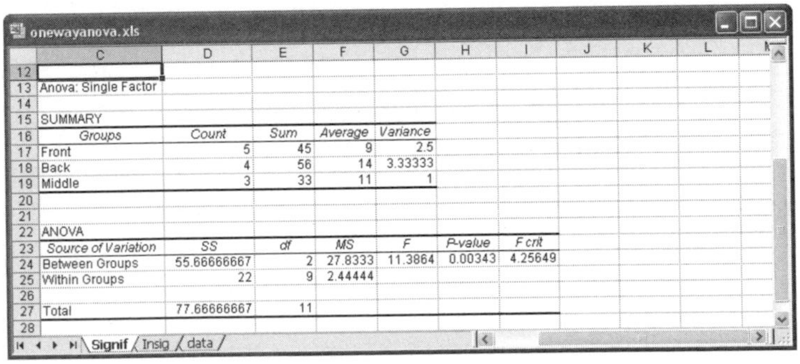

Figure 48-3   One-way ANOVA results.

In cells F17:F19, we see average sales depending on the location of the display. When the display is at the front of the computer book section, average sales are 900; when the display is at the back of the section, sales average 1,400; and when the display is in the middle, sales average 1,100. Because our p-value of .003 (in cell H24) is less than .15, we can conclude that these means are significantly different.

If we are determining whether populations have significantly different means, why is the technique called *analysis of variance*?

Suppose that the data in our book sales study is the data shown in the worksheet named Insig, shown in Figure 48-4. (Also in the file Onewayanova.xls.) If we run a one-way ANOVA on this data, we obtain the results shown in Figure 48-5.

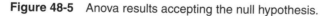

Figure 48-4 Book store data for which the null hypothesis is accepted.

	D	E	F	G	H	I	J	K	L	M
11										
12		Anova: Single Factor		Overall mean						
13				11.1666667						
14		SUMMARY								
15		*Groups*	*Count*	*Sum*	*Average*	*Variance*				
16		Front	5	45	9	44				
17		Back	4	56	14	90				
18		Middle	3	33	11	64				
19										
20										
21		ANOVA								
22		*Source of Variation*	*SS*	*df*	*MS*	*F*	*P-value*	*F crit*		
23		Between Groups	55.66667	2	27.83333	0.436411	0.659334	4.256492		
24		Within Groups	574	9	63.77778					
25										
26		Total	629.6667	11						

Figure 48-5 Anova results accepting the null hypothesis.

Note that the mean sales for each part of the store are exactly as before, yet our p-value of .66 indicates that we should accept the null hypothesis and conclude that the position of the display in the computer book section doesn't affect sales. The reason for this strange result is that in our second data set, we have much more variation in sales when the display is at each position in the computer book section. In our first data set, for example, the variation in sales when the display is at the front is between 700 and 1100, while in the second data set, the variation in sales is between 200 and 2000. The variation of sales within each store position is measured by the sum of the squares of data within a group. This measure is shown in cell D25 in the first data set and in cell F24 in the second. In our first data set, the sum of squares of data within groups is only 22, while in the second data set, the sum of squares within groups is 574! This large variation within the data points at each store position masks the variation between the groups (store positions) themselves and makes it impossible to conclude for the second data set that the difference between sales in different store positions is significant.

How can we use the results of a one-way ANOVA for forecasting?

If there is a significant difference between group means, our best forecast for each group is simply the group's mean. Therefore, in the first data set we predict the following:

■   Sales when the display is at the front of the computer book section will be 900 books per week.

■   Sales when the display is at the back will be 1400 books per week.

■   Sales when the display is in the middle will be 1100 books per week.

If there is no significant difference between the group means, our best forecast for each observation is simply the overall mean. Thus, in the second data set we predict weekly sales of 1167, independent of where the books are placed.

We can also estimate the accuracy of our forecasts. The square root of the Within Groups MS (mean square) is the standard deviation of our forecasts from a one-way ANOVA. As shown in Figure 48-6, our standard deviation of forecasts for the first data set is 156. By the rule of thumb, this means that we would expect, for example:

■   During 68 percent of all the weeks in which books are placed at the front of the computer section, sales will be between 900 - 156 = 744 and 900 + 156 = 1056 books.

■   During 95 percent of all weeks in which books are placed at the front of the computer book section, sales will be between 900 - 2(156) = 588 books and 900 + 2(156) = 1212 books.

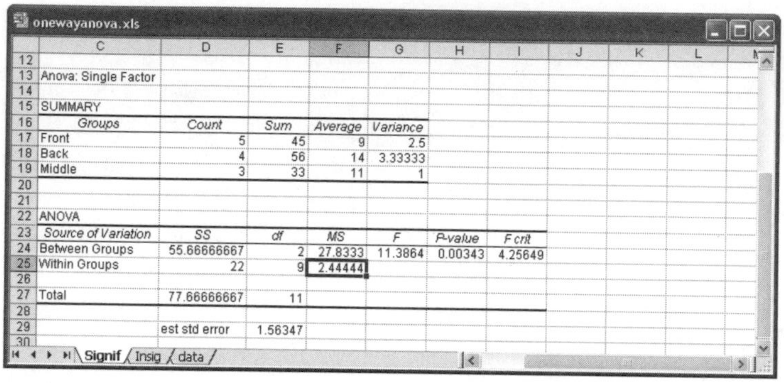

onewayanova.xls

	C	D	E	F	G	H	I
12							
13	Anova: Single Factor						
14							
15	SUMMARY						
16	Groups	Count	Sum	Average	Variance		
17	Front	5	45	9	2.5		
18	Back	4	56	14	3.33333		
19	Middle	3	33	11	1		
20							
21							
22	ANOVA						
23	Source of Variation	SS	df	MS	F	P-value	F crit
24	Between Groups	55.66666667	2	27.8333	11.3864	0.00343	4.25649
25	Within Groups	22	9	2.44444			
26							
27	Total	77.66666667	11				
28							
29		est std error	1.56347				
30							

Signif / Insig / data

Figure 48-6 Computation of forecast standard deviation.

Problems

You can find the data for these problems in the file Chapter48data.xls.

1. For patients of four cardiologists, we are given the number of days the patients stayed in the hospital after open heart surgery.
   - Is there evidence that the doctors have different discharge policies?
   - You are 95 percent sure that a patient of doctor 1 will stay in the hospital between what range of days?
2. A drug can be produced using a 400, 300, or 200 degree oven. You are given the pounds of the drug yielded when various batches are baked at different temperatures.
   - Does temperature appear to influence the process yield?
   - What is the range of pounds of the product that you are 95 percent sure will be produced with a 200 degree oven?
   - If you believe that pressure within the container also influences process yield, does this analysis remain valid?

Randomized Blocks and Two-Way ANOVA

■ I am trying to analyze the effectiveness of my sales force. The problem is that in addition to a salesperson's effectiveness, the amount that a salesperson sells depends on the district to which he or she is assigned. How can I incorporate the district assignments of my sales-people into my analysis?

■ Based on a knowledge of sales rep and district, how can I forecast sales? How accurate are my sales forecasts?

■ How can I determine whether varying the price and the amount of advertising affects the sales of a video game? How can I determine whether price and advertising interact significantly?

■ How can I interpret the effects of price and advertising on sales when there is a significant interaction between price and advertising?

In many sets of data, two factors can influence a dependent variable. Here are some examples.

Factors	Dependent Variable
Sales person and district assignment	Sales
Product price and advertising expenditure	Sales
Temperature and pressure	Production yield
Surgeon and brand of stent used	Health of patient after open heart surgery

When two factors might influence a dependent variable, randomized blocks or two-way ANOVA (analysis of variance) can easily be used to determine which, if any, of the factors have a significant influence on the dependent variable. With two-way ANOVA, you can also determine whether two factors exhibit a significant interaction. For example, suppose we are trying to predict sales by using product price and advertising budget. Price and advertising interact significantly if the effect of advertising depends on the product price.

In a randomized block model, we observe each possible combination of factors exactly once. You can't test for interactions in a randomized block design. In a two-way ANOVA model, we observe each combination of factors the same number of times (call it *k*). In this case, *k* must be greater than 1. In a two-way ANOVA model, you can easily test for interactions.

I am trying to analyze the effectiveness of my sales force. The problem is that in addition to a salesperson's effectiveness, the amount that a salesperson sells depends on the district to which he or she is assigned. How can I incorporate the district assignments of my salespeople into my analysis?

Suppose we want to determine how a sales representative and the sales district to which the representative is assigned influence product sales. To answer the question in this example, we can have each of our four sales reps spend a month selling in each of our five sales districts. The resulting sales are given in the worksheet named Randomized Blocks in the file TwowayAnova.xls, shown in Figure 49-1. For example, sales rep 1 sold 20 units during the month she was assigned to district 4.

	Rep 1	Rep 2	Rep 3	Rep 4
Dist 1	1	3	10	12
Dist 2	17	12	16	14
Dist 3	17	21	22	25
Dist 4	20	10	17	23
Dist 5	22	21	37	32

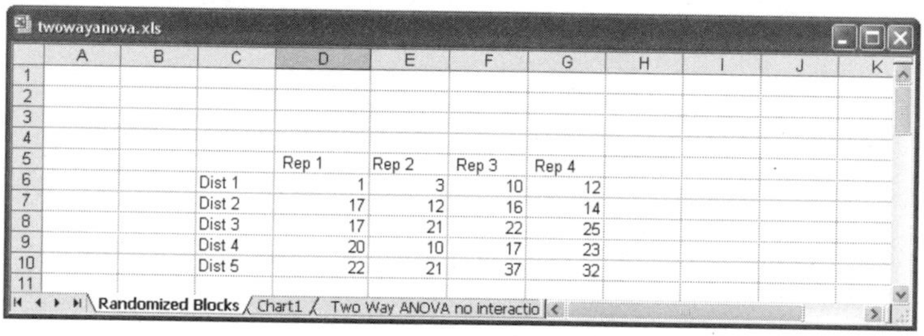

Figure 49-1 Data for the randomized blocks example.

This model is called a *two-way ANOVA without replication* because two factors (district and salesperson) can potentially influence sales and we have only a single instance pairing each salesperson with each district. This model is also called a *randomized block* design because we'd like to randomize (chronologically) the assignment of representatives to districts. In other words, we'd like to ensure that the month during which sales rep 1 is assigned to district 1 is equally likely to be the first, second, third, fourth, or fifth month. This randomization hopefully lessens the effect of time (a salesperson presumably becomes better over time) on our analysis; in a sense, we are "blocking" the effect of districts when we try to compare sales reps.

To analyze this data in Excel, click Tools, Data Analysis, and then select the option Anova: Two-Factor Without Replication. Then fill in the dialog box as shown in Figure 49-2.

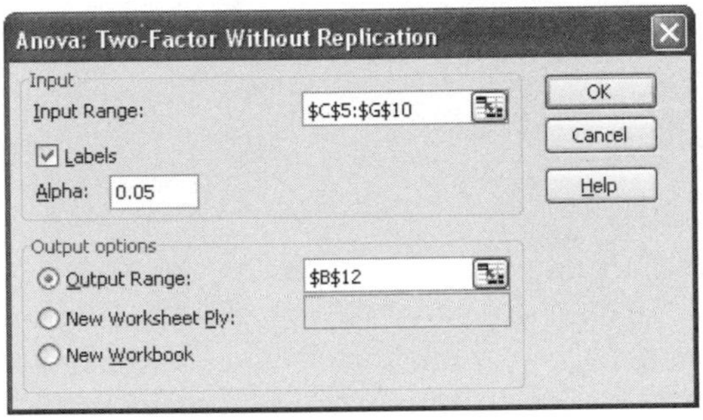

Figure 49-2 Dialog box for setting up a randomized blocks model.

- Our input range data is in cells C5:G10.
- I've checked Labels because the first row of the input range contains labels.
- I entered cell B12 as the upper-left corner of our output range.
- The alpha value is not important. You can use the default value.

The output we obtain is shown in Figure 49-3. (The results in cells G12:G24 were not created by Excel's data analysis feature. I entered formulas in these cells as I'll explain later in the chapter.)

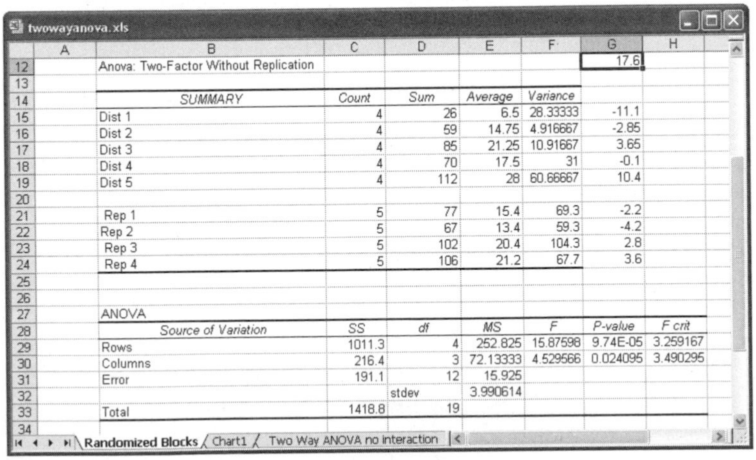

	A	B	C	D	E	F	G	H
12		Anova: Two-Factor Without Replication					17.6	
13								
14		SUMMARY	Count	Sum	Average	Variance		
15		Dist 1	4	26	6.5	28.33333	-11.1	
16		Dist 2	4	59	14.75	4.916667	-2.85	
17		Dist 3	4	85	21.25	10.91667	3.65	
18		Dist 4	4	70	17.5	31	-0.1	
19		Dist 5	4	112	28	60.66667	10.4	
20								
21		Rep 1	5	77	15.4	69.3	-2.2	
22		Rep 2	5	67	13.4	59.3	-4.2	
23		Rep 3	5	102	20.4	104.3	2.8	
24		Rep 4	5	106	21.2	67.7	3.6	
25								
26								
27		ANOVA						
28		Source of Variation	SS	df	MS	F	P-value	F crit
29		Rows	1011.3	4	252.825	15.87598	9.74E-05	3.259167
30		Columns	216.4	3	72.13333	4.529566	0.024095	3.490295
31		Error	191.1	12	15.925			
32				stdev	3.990614			
33		Total	1418.8	19				
34								

Figure 49-3 Randomized blocks output.

To determine whether the row factor (districts) or column factor (sales rep) has a significant effect on sales, just look at the p-value. If the p-value for a factor is low (less than .15), the factor has a significant effect on sales. The row p-value (.0000974) and column p-value (.024) are both less than .15, so both district and sales rep have a significant effect on sales.

Based on a knowledge of sales rep and district, how can I forecast sales? How accurate are my sales forecasts?

How should we predict product sales? We can predict sales during a month by using equation 1, shown here:

```
Predicted sales = Overall average + (Rep effect) + (District effect)
```

In this equation, *rep effect* equals 0 if the sales rep factor is not significant. If the sales rep factor is significant, *rep effect* equals the mean for the given rep minus the overall average. Likewise, *district effect* equals 0 if the district factor is not significant. If the district factor is significant, *district effect* equals the mean for the given district minus the overall average.

I computed the overall average (17.6) in cell G12 by using the formula *AVERAGE(D6:G10)*. The rep and district effects are computed by copying from cell G15 to G16:G24 the formula *E15-$G$12*. As an example, you can compute predicted sales by rep 4 in district 2 as 17.6 - 2.85 + 3.6 = 18.35. This value is computed in cell D38 (see Figure 49-4) with the formula *G12+G16+G24*. If the district effect was significant and the sales rep effect was not significant, our predicted sales for rep 4 in district 2 would be 17.6 - 2.85 = 14.75.

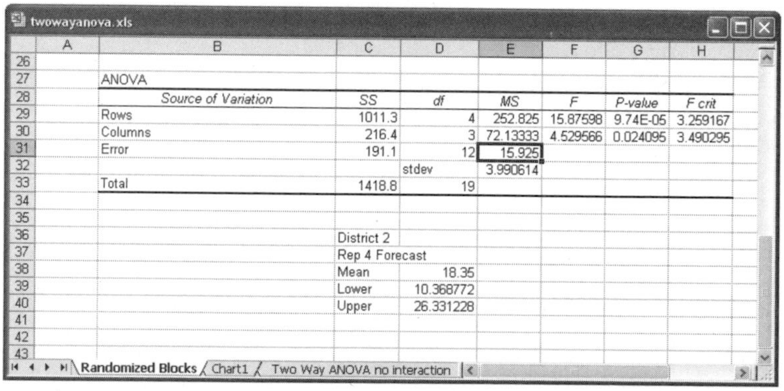

ANOVA

Source of Variation	SS	df	MS	F	P-value	F crit
Rows	1011.3	4	252.825	15.87598	9.74E-05	3.259167
Columns	216.4	3	72.13333	4.529566	0.024095	3.490295
Error	191.1	12	15.925			
		stdev	3.990614			
Total	1418.8	19				

District 2	
Rep 4 Forecast	
Mean	18.35
Lower	10.368772
Upper	26.331228

Figure 49-4 Forecast for sales in district 2 by sales rep 4.

As in one-way ANOVA, the standard deviation of our forecast errors is the square root of the mean square error shown in cell E31. I computed this standard deviation ($\sqrt{15.92} = 3.99$) in cell E32 with the formula *SQRT(E31)*.

Thus, we are 95 percent sure that if sales rep 4 is assigned to district 2, monthly sales will be between 18.35 - 2(3.99) = 10.37 and 18.35 + 2(3.99) = 26.33. These limits are computed in cell D39 and D40 with the formulas *D38 - 2*E32* and *D38 + 2*E32*, respectively.

How can I determine whether varying the price and the amount of advertising affects the sales of a video game? How can I determine whether price and advertising interact significantly?

When you have more than one observation for each combination of the row and column factors, you have a *two-factor ANOVA with replication*. To perform this sort of analysis, Excel requires that you have the same number of observations for each row-and-column combination.

In addition to testing for the significance of the row and column factors, we can also test for significant interaction between the row and column factors. For example, if we want to understand how price and advertising affect sales, an interaction between price and advertising would indicate that the effect of an advertising change would depend on the price level (or equivalently, the effect of a price change would depend on the advertising level). A lack of interaction between price and advertising would mean that the effect of a price change would not depend on the level of advertising.

As an example of two-factor ANOVA with replication, suppose we want to determine how price and advertising level affect the monthly sales of a video game. In the worksheet named Two Way ANOVA No Interaction in the file TwoWayAnova.xls, we have the data shown in Figure 49-5. During the three months in which we had low advertising and a medium price, for example, we sold 21, 20, and 16 units.

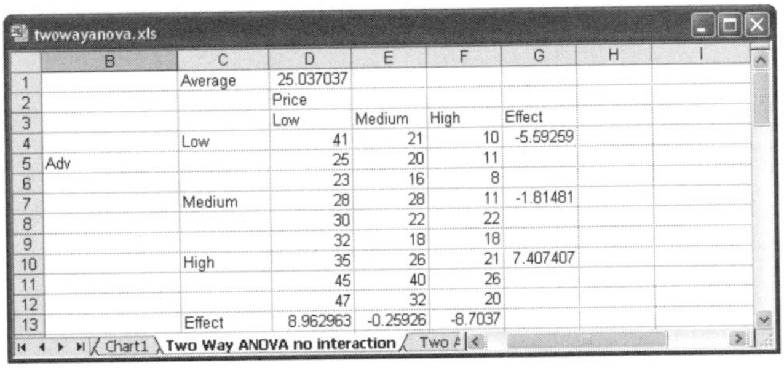

	B	C	D	E	F	G
1		Average	25.037037			
2			Price			
3			Low	Medium	High	Effect
4		Low	41	21	10	-5.59259
5	Adv		25	20	11	
6			23	16	8	
7		Medium	28	28	11	-1.81481
8			30	22	22	
9			32	18	18	
10		High	35	26	21	7.407407
11			45	40	26	
12			47	32	20	
13		Effect	8.962963	-0.25926	-8.7037	

Figure 49-5 Video game sales data: no interaction.

Notice that for each price/advertising combination, we have exactly three observations. In cell D1, I've computed the overall average (25.037) of all observations with the formula *AVERAGE(D4:F12)*. In cells G4, G7, and G10, I computed the effect for each level of advertising. For example, the effect of having a low level of advertising equals the average for low advertising minus the overall average. In cell G4, I computed the low advertising effect of -5.59 with the formula *AVERAGE(D4:F6) - $D$1*. In a similar fashion, I computed the effect of each price level by copying from D13 to E13:F13 the formula *AVERAGE(D4:D12) - $D$1*.

To analyze this data, choose Tools, Data Analysis, and then select Anova: Two-Factor With Replication in the Data Analysis dialog box. Fill in the dialog box as shown in Figure 49-6.

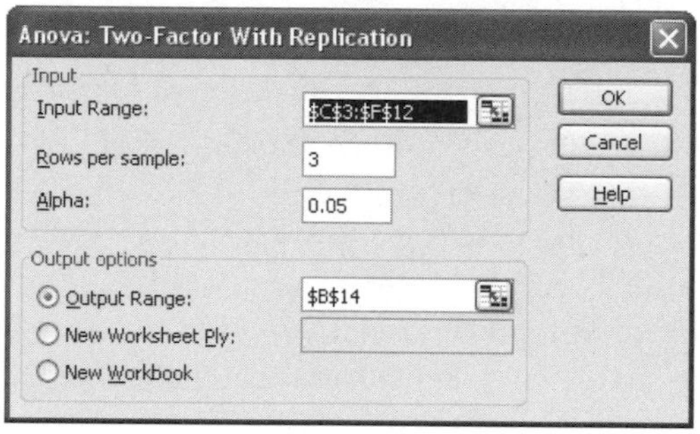

Figure 49-6   Dialog box for running a two-factor ANOVA with replication.

■   Our input range data, including labels, is in C3:F12. In two-way ANOVA with replication, Excel requires a label for each level of the column effect in the first row of each column in the input range. Thus, we entered Low, Medium, and High in cells D3:F3 to indicate the possible price levels. Excel also requires a label for each level of the row effect in the first column of the input range. These labels must appear in the row that marks the beginning of the data for each level. Thus we placed labels corresponding to low, medium and high levels of advertising in cells C4, C7, and C10.

■   In the Rows Per Sample box, I've entered 3 because we have three replications for each combination of price and advertising level.

■   The upper-left corner of our output range is B14.

The only important portion of the output is the ANOVA table, which is shown in Figure 49-7.

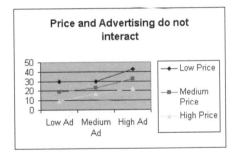

	B	C	D	E	F	G	H	I	J
42	ANOVA								
43	Source of Variation	SS	df	MS	F	P-value	F crit	F crit	
44	Sample	804.962963	2	402.4815	13.51617	0.00026	3.554557	3.55456109	
45	Columns	1405.40741	2	702.7037	23.59826	9.32E-06	3.554557	3.55456109	
46	Interaction	50.5925926	4	12.64815	0.424751	0.788777	2.927744	2.92774871	
47	Within	536	18	29.77778					
48									
49	Total	2796.96296	26						
50									

Figure 49-7   Two-way ANOVA with replication output. The factors have no interaction.

As with randomized blocks, an effect (including interactions) is significant if it has a p-value that's less than .15. We find that Sample (this is the row for advertising effect) and Price (shown in the row labeled Columns) are highly significant and also that there is no significant interaction. (The interaction p-value is .79!) Therefore, we can conclude that price and advertising influence sales and that the effect of advertising on sales does not depend on the price level. Figure 49-8 graphically demonstrates the fact that price and advertising do not exhibit a significant interaction.

Figure 49-8   Price and advertising do not interact in this data set.

Notice that as advertising increases, sales increase at roughly the same rate, whether the price level is low, medium, or high.

Forecasting Sales in the Absence of Interaction   In the absence of a significant interaction, we can forecast sales in a two-factor ANOVA with replication in the same way that we do in a two-factor ANOVA without replication. Here's the equation we use (equation 2):

```
Predicted sales = Overall average + [Row or advertising effect (if significant)]
+ [Column or price effect (if significant)]
```

For example, when price is high and advertising is low, our predicted sales are given by 25.04 + (-1.814) + (-8.7) = 14.52. (See cell E54 in Figure 49-9.) In Figure 49-5, shown earlier, you can see that we found the overall average is equal to 25.037, the medium advertising effect equals -1.814, and the high price effect = -8.704.

	A	B	C	D	E	F	G	H	I
41									
42		ANOVA							
43		Source of Variation	SS	df	MS	F	P-value	F crit	F crit
44		Sample	804.962963	2	402.4815	13.51617	0.00026	3.554557	3.55456109
45		Columns	1405.40741	2	702.7037	23.59826	9.32E-06	3.554557	3.55456109
46		Interaction	50.5925926	4	12.64815	0.424751	0.788777	2.927744	2.92774871
47		Within	536	18	29.77778				
48									
49		Total	2796.96296	26					
50									
51					Stdev	5.456902			
52					Medium Ad				
53					High Price				
54					Mean	14.51852			
55					Lower	3.604715			
56					Upper	25.43232			
57									

Two Way ANOVA no interaction / Two ANOVA with Inte

Figure 49-9   Forecasts for sales with high price and medium advertising.

The standard deviation of our forecast errors equals the square root of our mean squared within error ($\sqrt{29.78} = 5.46$). We are 95 percent sure that our forecast is accurate within 10.92 units. In other words, we are 95 percent sure that sales during a month with high price and medium advertising will be between 3.60 and 25.43 units.

Our analysis assumes that price and advertising are the only factors that affect sales. If sales are highly seasonal, seasonality would need to be incorporated into the analysis. Seasonality will be discussed in Chapters 51 through 53.

How can I interpret the effects of price and advertising on sales when there is a significant interaction between price and advertising?

In the worksheet named Two ANOVA with Interaction, I've changed the data from the previous example to the data shown in Figure 49-10. After running our analysis for a two-factor ANOVA with replication, we obtain the results shown in Figure 49-11.

	C	D	E	F	G	H	I	J	K
1									
2				Price					
3									
4			Low	Medium	High				
5		Low	41	21	15				
6	Adv		25	20	14				
7			23	16	13				
8		Medium	28	28	14				
9			30	22	13				
10			32	18	12				
11		High	50	34	13				
12			51	40	13				
13			52	32	13				
14									

Two ANOVA with Interaction / graph no interaction

Figure 49-10   Sales data with interaction between price and advertising.

twowayanova.xls

	C	D	E	F	G	H	I	J
41								
42								
43	ANOVA							
44	*Source of Variation*	*SS*	*df*	*MS*	*F*	*P-value*	*F crit*	
45	Sample	828.963	2	414.4815	24.22294	7.85669E-06	3.5545611	
46	Columns	2498.741	2	1249.37	73.01515	2.30747E-09	3.5545611	
47	Interaction	509.9259	4	127.4815	7.450216	0.001006454	2.9277487	
48	Within	308	18	17.11111				
49								
50	Total	4145.63	26					
51		Std dev	4.136558					
52								
53								

Two ANOVA with Interaction / graph no interaction /

Figure 49-11   Output for the two-factor ANOVA with interaction.

In this data set, we find the p-value for Interaction is .001. When we see a low p-value (less than .15) for interactions, *we do not even check p-values for row and column factors!* We simply forecast sales for any price and advertising combination to equal the mean of the three observations involving that price and advertising combination. For example, our best forecast for sales during a month with high advertising and medium price is:

$$\frac{34 + 40 + 32}{3} = \frac{106}{3} = 35.33 \, units.$$

The standard deviation of our forecast errors is again the square root of the mean square within ($\sqrt{17.11} = 4.13$). Thus we are 95 percent sure that our sales forecast is accurate within 8.26 units.

Figure 49-12 illustrates why this data exhibits a significant interaction between price and advertising. For a low and medium price, increased advertising increases sales, but if price is high, increased advertising has no effect on sales. This explains why we cannot use equation 2 to forecast sales when a significant interaction is present. After all, how can we talk about an advertising effect when the effect of advertising depends on the price!

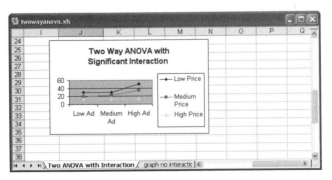

Figure 49-12   Price and advertising exhibit a significant interaction in this set of data.

Problems

All data for problems is in file CH49.xls.

1. We believe that pressure (high, medium, or low) and temperature (high, medium, or low) influence the yield of a production process.

    ❑   Use the data in the worksheet Problem 1 to determine how temperature and/or pressure influence the yield of the process.

    ❑   With high pressure and low temperature, we're 95 percent sure that process yield will be in what range?

2. We are trying to determine how the particular sales rep and the number of sales calls (either one, three, or five) made on a doctor influence the amount (in $1,000s) that each doctor prescribes of our drug.

    ❑   Use the data in the worksheet Problem 2 to determine how the sales rep and number of sales calls influence our sales volume.

    ❑   If sales rep 3 makes five sales calls on a doctor, we're 95 percent sure she will generate prescriptions within what range of dollars?

3. Answer the same questions given in Problem 2 using the data in the worksheet named Problem 3.

50

Using Moving Averages to Understand Time Series

■ I'm trying to analyze the upward trend in quarterly revenues of toy sales since 1993. Fourth quarter sales are always larger (because of the Christmas holidays) than sales during the first quarter of the following year. This pattern obscures the upward trend in sales. Is there any way that I can graphically show the upward trend in revenues?

Time series data simply displays the same quantity measured at different points in time. For example, the worksheet named Data and Chart in the file Toysrusma.xls, shown in Figure 50-1, displays the time series for quarterly revenues in thousands of dollars. Our data covers the time interval from the first quarter of 1993 through the fourth quarter of 2003. (The figure does not show all the data.)

Toysrusma.xls

	A	B	C	D	E
1					
2					
3		Quarter of Year	Year	Quarter#	Sales
4		1	1993	1	1172
5		2	1993	2	1249
6		3	1993	3	1346
7		4	1993	4	3402
8		1	1994	5	1296
9		2	1994	6	1317
10		3	1994	7	1449
11		4	1994	8	3893
12		1	1995	9	1462
13		2	1995	10	1462
14		3	1995	11	1681
15		4	1995	12	4200
16		1	1996	13	1498
17		2	1996	14	1614
18		3	1996	15	1715
19		4	1996	16	4605
20		1	1997	17	1646
21		2	1997	18	1738

data and chart / forecast sophisticated / forecast easy / Sheet

Figure 50-1 Quarterly revenues for toy sales.

To graph this time series, select the range D3:E47, which contains the quarter number (the first quarter is quarter 1, and the last quarter is quarter 44) and each quarter's revenue. Then choose Insert, Chart and choose the second option under the XY (Scatter) chart type. The time series plot is shown in Figure 50-2.

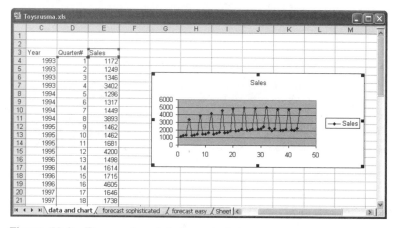

Figure 50-2   Time series plot of quarterly toy revenues.

There is an upward trend in revenues, but the fact that fourth quarter revenues dwarf revenues during the first three quarters of each year makes it hard to spot the trend. Because there are four quarters per year, it would be nice to graph an average of revenues during the last four quarters. Using an average washes out the seasonal influence because each average will contain a data point for the first, second, third, and fourth quarter. Such a graph is called a *moving average graph* because the plotted average "moves" over time.

To create a moving average graph of quarterly revenues, we can modify the chart created by the Chart Wizard. (The Chart Wizard is discussed in detail in Chapters 41–43.) Select the graph, and then click on a data point until all the data points are displayed in gold. Right-click, choose Add Trendline, and then select the Moving Average option. Set the period equal to 4. Excel now creates the four-quarter moving average trend curve that's shown in Figure 50-3.

For each quarter, Excel plots the average of the current quarter and the last three quarters. Of course, for a four-quarter moving average, our moving average curve starts with the fourth data point. The moving average curve makes it clear that toy sales had a steady upward trend through quarter 33. Beginning in quarter 34 (the second quarter of 2001), the trend curve dips, indicating that revenue began to slow during late 2000, which was the start of our current recession, of course.

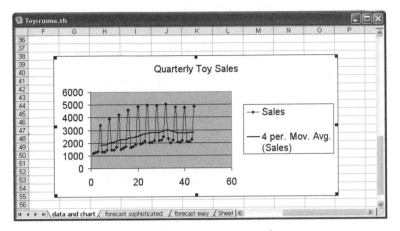

Figure 50-3   Four quarter moving average trend curve.

In the next chapter, I'll describe how to use moving averages to derive good forecasts for future values of a time series. It is harder than you think!

Problem

The file CH50data.xls contains quarterly revenues for GM, Ford, and GE. Construct a four-quarter moving average trend curve for each company's revenues. Describe what you learn from each trend curve.

51

Forecasting with Moving Averages

- What are the shortcomings of using moving averages in forecasting?

- How can I optimize moving average forecasts?

- Can I modify moving average forecasting to incorporate trend and seasonality?

Consider a department store that sells thousands of products. (The products are often referred to as SKUs, or stock keeping units.) The department store needs an easy, efficient method to forecast demand for each SKU. For example, it needs to predict next week's demand for baseball bats.

A commonly used approach is to predict demand for next week using the average of, say, the demand for each of the last three weeks. This approach is known as a three-week moving average forecast. The data points used in the forecast "move" each week, with the most current week's demand replacing the demand from three weeks ago. Many companies also use the approach that next week's demand will equal last week's demand. In effect, this method is a one-week moving average forecast. A multiple-period moving average forecast is usually more accurate than a one-week moving average because multiple weeks tends to smooth out the noise inherent in any demand process. Of course, in an industry in which demand is rapidly changing, if you use a long interval, say a 52-week moving average, to forecast next week's sales, your forecasts will be poor because you'll be using obsolete data to forecast the future. As you'll soon see, moving average forecasts can be implemented in Excel very easily.

What are the shortcomings of using moving averages in forecasting?

Moving averages often provide poor forecasts for two reasons.

- If there is an upward trend in the data, a moving average will lag behind this trend. For example, if sales are increasing by exactly 1000 units per week, a three-week moving average would always forecast 2000 units below demand.

- If the data exhibits a lot of seasonality, a moving average forecast may be inaccurate. For example, consider the effects of using a three-quarter moving average to forecast toy store revenues. If you are forecasting fourth quarter revenues, the forecast will be much too low because the three-quarter moving average does not include the previous fourth quarter, and historically, fourth quarter sales at the toy store are much higher than sales during other quarters.

How can I optimize moving average forecasts?

Despite the shortcomings of moving average forecasts, they are widely used. A key question when using a moving average forecast is how to determine the "best number of periods" to use in the forecast. In this section, I'll show how to find the number of periods that minimizes the average absolute percentage forecasting error. The discussion makes heavy use of the OFFSET function (covered in detail in Chapter 21) and data tables (which are described in Chapter 15).

Let's suppose we want to use a moving average to forecast quarterly revenues for a toy store. The data we'll use is on the worksheet named Forecast Easy in the file Toysrusma.xls, shown in Figure 51-1. Let's find the optimal number of quarters (ranging between 1 and 8) to use in forecasting future quarterly revenues.

	B	C	D	E	F	G	H	I	J
1					periods	4			
2					MAPE	0.358			
3	Quarter of Year	Year	Quarter#	Sales	Forecast	abs %age error			
4	1	1993	1	1172					
5	2	1993	2	1249					
6	3	1993	3	1346					
7	4	1993	4	3402					
8	1	1994	5	1296					
9	2	1994	6	1317					
10	3	1994	7	1449					
11	4	1994	8	3893					
12	1	1995	9	1462	1988.75	0.360294		Quarters	0.358000224
13	2	1995	10	1462	2030.25	0.38868		1	0.541677702
14	3	1995	11	1681	2066.5	0.229328		2	0.541151376
15	4	1995	12	4200	2124.5	0.494167		3	0.487185375
16	1	1996	13	1498	2201.25	0.469459		4	0.358000224
17	2	1996	14	1614	2210.25	0.369424		5	0.37582698
18	3	1996	15	1715	2248.25	0.310933		6	0.390812454
19	4	1996	16	4605	2256.75	0.509935		7	0.395309196
20	1	1997	17	1646	2358	0.432564		8	0.338579322

Figure 51-1 Optimizing moving average forecasts.

We begin by entering in cell G1 a trial number of quarters to use in a moving average forecast. Because we can include as many as eight quarters in the average, the first quarter we will forecast will be the ninth quarter (quarter 1 of 1995). To create a moving average forecast for each quarter, copy from F12 to F13:F47 the formula *AVERAGE(OFFSET(E12,-$G$1,0,$G$1,1))*.

Suppose that cell G1 contains the value 4 (for a four-quarter moving average). The OFFSET formula selects the current quarter's revenues (cell E12) and then moves up four rows (-$G$1) and over zero (0) columns. Then the OFFSET function picks out an array consisting of four rows and one column. The array contains sales figures for the last four quarters. These quarters are then averaged to yield the four-quarter moving average forecast for the current quarter. If we change the value in G1 to 2, we obtain a two-quarter moving average forecast, and so on.

We now compute the absolute percentage error for each forecast by copying from G12 to G13:G47 the formula *ABS(E12-F12)/E12*. In cell G2, we compute our Mean Absolute Percentage Error (MAPE) with the formula *AVERAGE(G12:G47)*. We calculate the average of the absolute percentage errors to prevent positive and negative errors from canceling each other.

As shown in Figure 51-1, a four-quarter moving average is off by an average of 35.8 percent. Is there any other number of quarters that we can use in the moving average that yields a lower MAPE? This question is easily answered by using a data table.

Enter the numbers 1 through 8 in the cell range I13:I20. Next, compute the MAPE by entering =G2 in cell J12. Now select the table range (I12:J20) and choose Data, Table. After choosing G1 as the Column Input Cell, we obtain in cells J13:J20 the MAPE for moving averages that use one to eight quarters as the moving time period. We find that an eight-quarter moving average (yielding a MAPE of 33.9 percent) is best.

Clearly, being off by an average of 33.9 percent is pretty poor forecasting. We have this level of error because the moving average forecast lags behind the upward trend in the toy store's revenues. However, by using an eight-quarter moving average forecast (eight is a multiple of four), we do account for seasonality because each of our forecasts contains two first quarters, two second quarters, and so on.

Can I modify moving average forecasting to incorporate trend and seasonality?

A technique called modified moving average (MMA) remedies the shortcomings with the traditional moving average approach that I discussed earlier. The way to use this technique is demonstrated on the worksheet named Forecast Sophisticated in the file Toyrsusma.xls, shown in Figure 51-2.

	B	C	D	E	F	G	H	I
					Quarters in MA	4		
1								
2								
3	Quarter of Year	Year	Quarter#	Sales	Deseasonalized	Percent Growth	Mean growth	Deseaonalized Mean
4	1	1993	1	1172	1795.515397			
5	2	1993	2	1249	1840.401013	0.024998736		
6	3	1993	3	1346	1820.8322	-0.010632907		
7	4	1993	4	3402	1763.2573	-0.031620103		
8	1	1994	5	1296	1985.484603	0.126032261		
9	2	1994	6	1317	1940.598987	-0.022606882		
10	3	1994	7	1449	1960.1678	0.010083903		
11	4	1994	8	3893	2017.7427	0.029372435		
12	1	1995	9	1462	2239.798217	0.110051453	0.035720429	1975.998522
13	2	1995	10	1462	2195.563913	-0.019749236	0.031725227	2039.576926
14	3	1995	11	1681	2349.641055	0.070176569	0.032439639	2103.318158
15	4	1995	12	4200	2297.477724	-0.022200553	0.047462805	2200.686471
16	1	1996	13	1498	2275.786802	-0.009441189	0.034569558	2270.620227
17	2	1996	14	1614	2462.816481	0.082182425	0.004696398	2279.617374
18	3	1996	15	1715	2364.152157	-0.040061582	0.030179313	2346.430516
19	4	1996	16	4605	2492.976183	0.054490582	0.002619775	2350.058291
20	1	1997	17	1646	2535.312669	0.016982307	0.021792559	2398.932906

data and chart \ **forecast sophisticated** \ forecast easy \ Sheet

Figure 51-2   Modified moving average forecasts. A much better approach.

The procedure for using MMA is a little involved, so here is a step-by-step description of how the technique works.

1. Begin by computing seasonal indices for each quarter. For example, if the average quarterly sales are $300 million and the average fourth quarter sales are $600 million, the fourth quarter has a seasonal index of 600/300 = 2. In this example, I used the last two years of data to obtain a current estimate of the seasonal indices.

2. Next compute deseasonalized sales for each quarter by dividing each quarter's sales by the quarter's seasonal index. This operation lowers sales during the fourth quarter and raises them during the other quarters.

3. Supposing that you are using a four-quarter moving average, you would now determine the average percentage growth in the deseasonalized sales during the last four quarters. This calculation gives us an idea of the current trend in sales growth.

4. Figure out a "guess" at where the deseasonalized process was two quarters ago (4/2) by averaging the last four quarters of deseasonalized revenue.

5. Compute a forecast for the current quarter using an expression such as *(Current guess for deseasonalized process)*(Mean growth percentage)$^{4/2}$*(Seasonal index for forecasted quarter)*.

The term *(Current guess for deseasonalized process)*(Mean growth percentage)$^{4/2}$* brings our estimate of where deseasonalized sales were two quarters ago to the present. Multiplying by the seasonal index for the forecasted quarter gives us a forecast for the current quarter that incorporates seasonality.

6.   Finally, use a data table to determine the number of quarters that yields the lowest MAPE.

Let's see how MMA is used to forecast quarterly toy store revenue. We begin by computing seasonal indices for the first two years (1993 and 1994) by copying from J4 to J5:J7 the formula *AVERAGE(E4,E8)/AVERAGE($E$4:$E$11)*. Then we copy these values to J8:J11. Next we compute our seasonal indices for all other years based on the last eight quarters of data by copying from J12 to J13:J47 the formula *AVERAGE(E4,E8)/AVERAGE(OFFSET(E12,-8,0,8,1))*. This formula takes the average of the last two observations that occurred in the same quarter as the current quarter and divides that average by the average of the last eight quarters. The results are shown in Figure 51-3.

	C	D	E	J	K	L	M
1							
2					MAPE	0.043951	
3	Year	Quarter#	Sales	seasonal index	Forecast	abs %age error	
4	1993	1	1172	0.652737371			
5	1993	2	1249	0.67865644			
6	1993	3	1346	0.739222428			
7	1993	4	3402	1.929383761			
8	1994	5	1296	0.652737371			
9	1994	6	1317	0.67865644			
10	1994	7	1449	0.739222428			
11	1994	8	3893	1.929383761			
12	1995	9	1462	0.652737371	1383.599	0.053626	
13	1995	10	1462	0.665888154	1445.671	0.011169	
14	1995	11	1681	0.715428425	1603.986	0.045815	
15	1995	12	4200	1.828091718	4414.011	0.050955	
16	1996	13	1498	0.65823389	1599.721	0.067904	
17	1996	14	1614	0.655347247	1508.006	0.065671	
18	1996	15	1715	0.725418622	1806.434	0.053314	
19	1996	16	4605	1.847189729	4363.778	0.052383	
20	1997	17	1646	0.649229588	1626.08	0.012102	

Figure 51-3   Computation of seasonal indices.

By copying from F4:F47 the formula *E4/J4*, we compute the deseasonalized sales for each quarter. Note that each fourth quarter sales value is lowered and each sales value during the first three quarters of a year is increased.

Copying from cell G5 to G6:G47 the formula *F5/F4-1* computes the percentage growth during each quarter. For example, during the second quarter of 1993, deseasonalized sales grew by 2.5 percent. Copying from H12 to H13:H47 the formula *AVERAGE(OFFSET(G12,-$G$1,0,$G$1,1))* computes the average growth percentage for deseasonalized revenue during the last four quarters. For example, during the first quarter of 1995, average growth during the last four quarters in deseasonalized revenue was 3.6 percent.

By copying from I12 to I13:I47 the formula *AVERAGE(OFFSET(F12,-$G$1,0,$G$1,1)),* we obtain the average of the last four quarters of deseasonalized revenue for each quarter. For example, during the first quarter of 1995, our best guess of where the deseasonalized revenues were two quarters ago is $1.976 billion.

Finally, copying from K12 to K13:K47 the formula *(1+H12)^($G$1/2)*I12*J12* computes our actual forecast for each quarter. The expression *(1+H12)^($G$1/2)*I12* brings our average deseasonalized revenue estimate from two quarters to the present quarter. Multiplying by the value in J12 reseasonalizes our forecast. In each fourth quarter, we bump up our deseasonalized estimate of where the series is now. In all other quarters, we reduce our deseasonalized estimate to obtain a forecast for the quarter's revenues.

Using the same technique we used for moving average forecasts, we compute MAPE and absolute percentage errors for our MMA forecasts in column L. As described earlier in the discussion of traditional moving average forecasts, we can now use a one-way data table (see Figure 51-4) to determine how our MAPE depends on the number of quarters used to generate our MMA forecast.

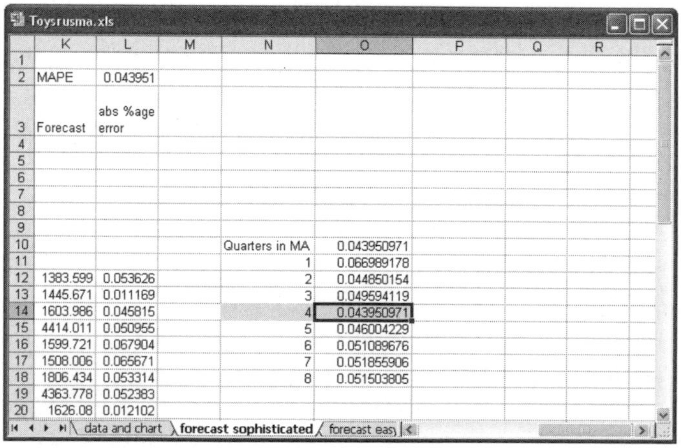
Toysrusma.xls

	K	L	M	N	O
1					
2	MAPE	0.043951			
3	Forecast	abs %age error			
4					
5					
6					
7					
8					
9					
10				Quarters in MA	0.043950971
11				1	0.066989178
12	1383.599	0.053626		2	0.044850154
13	1445.671	0.011169		3	0.049594119
14	1603.986	0.045815		4	0.043950971
15	4414.011	0.050955		5	0.046004229
16	1599.721	0.067904		6	0.051089676
17	1508.006	0.065671		7	0.051855906
18	1806.434	0.053314		8	0.051503805
19	4363.778	0.052383			
20	1626.08	0.012102			

data and chart / forecast sophisticated / forecast eas

Figure 51-4 Data table computations of MAPE for the modified moving average technique.

We find that a four-quarter MMA yields the best MAPE: 4.4 percent. Compare this percentage error with the poor performance of an ordinary moving average, which had a MAPE of over 33 percent.

In summary, we should forecast the toy store's next quarter's revenue using the form as *(Average of last four quarter's deseasonalized sales)*(Average percentage growth last 4 quarters)^2*(Seasonal index for quarter being forecasted).*

Problems

1. Use the Ford, GE, and GM quarterly revenues in file CH50data.xls to develop optimal moving average forecasts for quarterly revenue.

2. Use the Ford, GE, and GM quarterly revenues in file CH50data.xls to develop optimal MMA forecasts for quarterly revenue.

3. How would you modify the MMA forecast procedure if your goal was to forecast revenues two quarters into the future?

52

Forecasting in the Presence of Special Events

■ When predicting the number of customers who enter a bank each day, customer traffic is influenced by seasonality (in the form of the month of the year or the day of the week). Special factors such as whether the day is a staff or faculty payday, whether the day is before or after a holiday, and so on also affect customer traffic. How can I determine how these factors influence customer traffic?

■ How can I check whether my forecast errors are random?

For a student project, we attempted to forecast the number of customers visiting the Eastland Plaza Branch of the Indiana University (IU) Credit Union each day. Interviews with the branch manager made clear that the following factors affected the number of customers:

■ Month of the year

■ Day of the week

■ Was the day a faculty or staff payday?

■ Was the day before or after a holiday?

When predicting the number of customers who enter a bank each day, customer traffic is influenced by seasonality (in the form of the month of the year or the day of the week). How can I determine how this influences customer traffic?

The data collected is contained in the worksheet named Original in the file CreditUnion.xls, shown in Figure 52-1. If we try and run a regression on this data using dummy variables (as described in Chapter 46), the dependent variable would be the number of customers arriving each day (the data in column E). We would need 19 independent variables: 11 to account for the month (12-1), 4 to account for the day of the week (5-1), and 2 each to account for the paydays and whether a particular day follows or precedes a holiday. Excel allows only 15 independent variables, so it appears that we're in trouble.

	A	B	C	D	E	F
2						
3		MONTH	DAYMON	DAYWEEK	CUST	SPECIAL
4		1	2	2	1825	SP,FAC,AH
5		1	3	3	1257	0
6		1	4	4	969	0
7		1	5	5	1672	SP
8		1	8	1	1098	0
9		1	9	2	691	0
10		1	10	3	672	0
11		1	11	4	754	0
12		1	12	5	972	0
13		1	15	1	816	0
14		1	16	2	717	0
15		1	17	3	728	0
16		1	18	4	711	0
17		1	19	5	1545	SP
18		1	22	1	873	0
19		1	23	2	713	0
20		1	24	3	626	0
21		1	25	4	653	0
22		1	26	5	1080	0

original / 1st three days / christr

Figure 52-1 Data for predicting credit union customer traffic.

When a regression forecasting model requires more than 15 independent variables, we can use Excel's Solver to estimate the coefficients of the independent variables. We can also use Excel to compute the R-squared values between forecasts and actual customer traffic and the standard deviation for the forecast errors. To analyze this data, I created a forecasting equation by using a lookup table to "look up" the day of week, the month, and other factors. Then I used Solver to choose the coefficients for each level of each factor that yields the minimum sum of squared errors. (Each day's error equals actual customers less forecasted customers.) Here are the particulars.

I began by creating indicator variables (in Columns G–J) for whether the day is a staff payday (SP), faculty payday (FAC), before a holiday (BH), or after a holiday (AH). (See Figure 52-2.) For example, in cells G4, H4, and J4, I entered 1 to indicate that January 2 was a staff payday, faculty payday, and after a holiday. Cell I4 contains a 0 to indicate that January 2 was not before a holiday.

	A	B	C	D	E	F	G	H	I	J
2										
3		MONTH	DAYMON	DAYWEEK	CUST	SPECIAL	SP	FAC	BH	AH
4		1	2	2	1825	SP,FAC,AH	1	1	0	1
5		1	3	3	1257	0	0	0	0	0
6		1	4	4	969	0	0	0	0	0
7		1	5	5	1672	SP	1	0	0	0
8		1	8	1	1098	0	0	0	0	0
9		1	9	2	691	0	0	0	0	0
10		1	10	3	672	0	0	0	0	0
11		1	11	4	754	0	0	0	0	0
12		1	12	5	972	0	0	0	0	0
13		1	15	1	816	0	0	0	0	0
14		1	16	2	717	0	0	0	0	0
15		1	17	3	728	0	0	0	0	0
16		1	18	4	711	0	0	0	0	0
17		1	19	5	1545	SP	1	0	0	0
18		1	22	1	873	0	0	0	0	0
19		1	23	2	713	0	0	0	0	0
20		1	24	3	626	0	0	0	0	0
21		1	25	4	653	0	0	0	0	0
22		1	26	5	1080	0	0	0	0	0

original / 1st three days / christmas week / changes in sign /

Figure 52-2   Dummy variables for paydays and holidays.

Our forecast is defined by a constant (which helps to center the forecasts so that they will be more accurate), an effect for each day of the week, an effect for each month, an effect for a staff payday, an effect for a faculty payday, an effect for a day occurring before a holiday, and an effect for a day occurring after a holiday. I inserted trial values for all these parameters (the Solver changing cells) in the cell range O4:O26, shown in Figure 52-3. Solver will then choose values that make our model best fit the data. For each day, our forecast of customer count will be generated by the following:

```
Predicted customer count = Constant + (Month effect) + (Day of week effect) + (
Staff payday effect, if any) + (Faculty payday effect, if any) + (Before holida
y effect, if any) + (After holiday effect, if any)
```

Using this model, we compute a forecast for each day's customer count by copying from K4 to K5:K257 the formula

```
$O$26+VLOOKUP(B4,$N$14:$O$25,2)+VLOOKUP(D4,$N$4:$O$8,2)
+G4*$O$9+H4*$O$10+I4*$O$11+J4*$O$12
```

Cell O26 picks up the constant term. *VLOOKUP(B4,$N$14:$O$25,2)* picks up the month coefficient for the current month, and *VLOOKUP(D4,$N$4:$O$8,2)* picks up the day of the week coefficient for the current week. *G4*$O$9+H4*$O$10+I4*$O$11+J4*$O$12* picks up the effects (if any) when the current day is SP, FAC, BH, or AH.

By copying from L4 to L5:L257 the formula *(E4-K4)^2*, I compute the squared error for each day. Then, in cell L2, I compute the sum of squared errors with the formula *SUM(L4:L257)*.

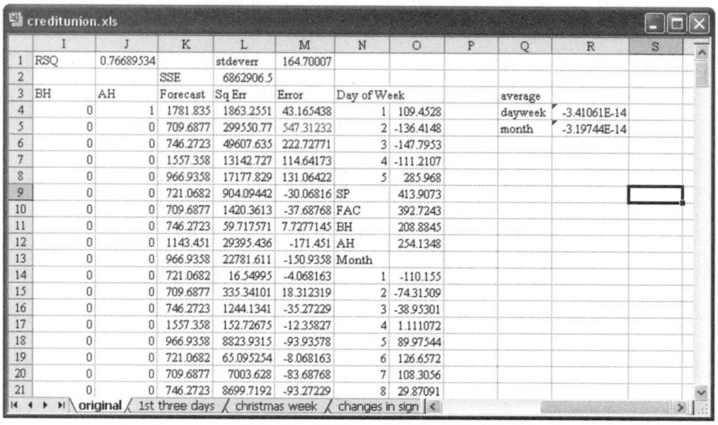

	I	J	K	L	M	N	O	P	Q	R	S
1	RSQ	0.76689534		stdeverr	164.70007						
2			SSE	6862906.5							
3	BH	AH	Forecast	Sq Err	Error	Day of Week			average		
4	0	1	1781.835	1863.2551	43.165438	1	109.4528		dayweek	-3.41061E-14	
5	0	0	709.6877	299550.77	547.31232	2	-136.4148		month	-3.19744E-14	
6	0	0	746.2723	49607.635	222.72771	3	-147.7953				
7	0	0	1557.358	13142.727	114.64173	4	-111.2107				
8	0	0	966.9358	17177.829	131.06422	5	285.968				
9	0	0	721.0682	904.09442	-30.06816	SP	413.9073				
10	0	0	709.6877	1420.3613	-37.68768	FAC	392.7243				
11	0	0	746.2723	59.717571	7.7277145	BH	208.8845				
12	0	0	1143.451	29395.436	-171.451	AH	254.1348				
13	0	0	966.9358	22781.611	-150.9358	Month					
14	0	0	721.0682	16.54995	-4.068163	1	-110.155				
15	0	0	709.6877	335.34101	18.312319	2	-74.31509				
16	0	0	746.2723	1244.1341	-35.27229	3	-38.95301				
17	0	0	1557.358	152.72675	-12.35827	4	1.111072				
18	0	0	966.9358	8823.9315	-93.93578	5	89.97544				
19	0	0	721.0682	65.095254	-8.068163	6	126.6572				
20	0	0	709.6877	7003.628	-83.68768	7	108.3056				
21	0	0	746.2723	8699.7192	-93.27229	8	29.87091				

Figure 52-3 Changing cells and customer forecasts.

In cell R4, I average the day of the week changing cells with the formula *AVERAGE(O4:O8)*, and in cell R5, I average the month changing cells with formula *AVERAGE(O14:O25)*. Later, we'll constrain the average month and day of the week effects to equal 0, which ensures that a month or day of the week with a positive effect has a higher than average customer count, and a month or day of the week with a negative effect has a lower than average customer count.

We can use the Solver settings shown in Figure 52-4 to choose our forecast parameters to minimize the sum of squared errors.

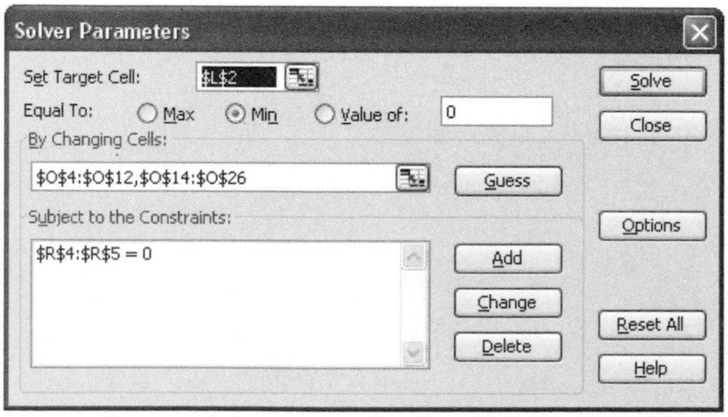

Figure 52-4 Solver window for determining forecast parameters.

Our Solver model changes the coefficients for the month, day of the week, BH, AH, SP, FAC, and the constant to minimize sum of square errors. We also constrain the average day of the week and month effect to equal 0. Using the Solver, we obtain the results shown in Figure 52-3. For example, we find that Friday is the busiest day of the week and June is the busiest month. A staff pay-day raises our forecast (all else being equal—in the Latin, *ceteris paribus*) by 414 customers.

Evaluating Forecast Accuracy   To evaluate the accuracy of the forecast, we compute the R-squared value between the forecasts and the actual customer count in cell J1. The formula we use is *RSQ(E4:E257,K4:K257)*. This formula computes the percentage of the actual variation in customer count that is explained by our forecasting model. We find that our independent variables explain 77 percent of the daily variation in customer count.

We compute the error for each day in column M by copying from M4 to M5:M257 the formula *E4–K4*. A close approximation to the standard error of the forecast is given by the standard deviation of the errors. This value is computed in cell M1 by using the formula *STDEV(M4:M257)*. Thus, approximately 68 percent of our forecasts should be accurate within 165 customers, 95 percent accurate within 329 customers, and so on.

Let's try and spot any outliers. Recall that an observation is an outlier if the absolute value of our forecast error exceeds two times the standard error of the regression. Select the range M4:M257, and then select Format, Conditional Formatting. Fill in the Conditional Formatting dialog box as shown in Figure 52-5. (For more information about conditional formatting, see Chapter 23.)

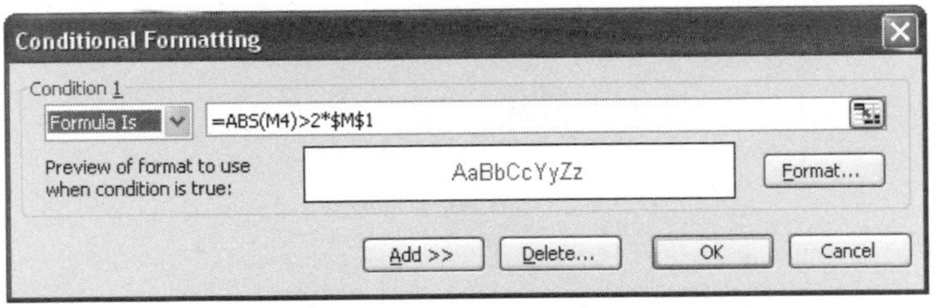

Figure 52-5   Use conditional formatting to spot forecast outliers.

After choosing a format with a red font, our conditional formatting settings will display in red any error that exceeds *2*(standard deviation of errors)* in absolute error. Looking at the outliers, we find that we often under forecast the customer count for the first thee days of the month. Also, during the second week in March (spring break), we overforecast, and the day before spring break, we greatly underforecast.

To remedy this problem, in the worksheet 1st Three Days, we add changing cells for each of the first three days of the month and changing cells for spring break and the day before spring break. We added trial values for these new effects in cells O26:O30. By copying from K4 to K5:K257 the formula

```
$O$25+VLOOKUP(B4,$N$13:$O$24,2)+VLOOKUP(D4,$N$4:$O$8,2)+G4*$O$9+H4*$O$10+I4*$O$
11+J4*$O$12+IF(C4=1,$O$26,IF(C4=2,$O$27,IF(C4=3,$O$28,0)))
```

we include the effects of the first three days of the month. (The term *IF(C4=1,$O$26,IF(C4=2,$O$27,IF(C4=3,$O$28,0)))* picks up the effect of the first three days of the month.) We manually entered the spring break coefficients in cells K52:K57. For example, in cell K52 we add *+O29* to the formula, and in cells K53:K57, we add *+O30*.

After including our new changing cells in the Solver window, we find the results shown in Figure 52-6. Notice that the first three days of the month greatly increase customer count (probably because of government support and Social Security checks) and that spring break reduces customer count. Figure 52-6 also shows the improvement in our forecasting accuracy. We have improved our RSQ to 87 percent and reduced our standard error to 123 customers.

G	H	I	J	K	L	M	N		O
		RSQ	0.86807		stdeverr	123.907			
				SSE	3884302				
SP	FAC	BH	AH	Forecas	Sq Err	Error	Day of Week		
1	1	0	1	1891.9	4480.59	-66.937		1	112.51
0	0	0	0	995.14	68569.2	261.857		2	-136.2
0	0	0	0	723.6	60219	245.396		3	-150.9
1	0	0	0	1555.4	13598	116.611		4	-112.2
0	0	0	0	948.32	22403.2	149.677		5	286.73
0	0	0	0	699.64	74.7058	-8.6432	SP		432.85
0	0	0	0	684.95	167.573	-12.945	FAC		91.909
0	0	0	0	723.6	923.89	30.3956	BH		199.32
0	0	0	0	1122.5	22660.9	-150.54	AH		299.98
0	0	0	0	948.32	17509.4	-132.32		1	-104.8
0	0	0	0	699.64	301.257	17.3568		2	-80.41
0	0	0	0	684.95	1853.73	43.055		3	-26.79
0	0	0	0	723.6	158.872	-12.604		4	-6.046
1	0	0	0	1555.4	107.939	-10.389		5	85.995
0	0	0	0	948.32	5673.54	-75.323		6	123.82
0	0	0	0	699.64	178.403	13.3568		7	99.372
0	0	0	0	684.95	3474.51	-58.945		8	14.352
0	0	0	0	723.6	4984.99	-70.604		9	-63.21
0	0	0	0	1122.5	1809.24	-42.535		10	-67.15
0	0	0	0	948.32	88996.6	-298.32		11	-30.9
0	0	0	0	699.64	3096.17	-55.643		12	55.718
0	0	0	0	684.95	13937	118.055	constant		940.57
0	1	0	0	1398.4	13555.8	-116.43	d1		558.56
1	0	0	0	1947.3	3160.15	95.7087	d2		367.55
0	0	0	0	972.68	30041.2	173.324	d3		310.2
0	0	0	0	724	256.121	16.0038	day before sp bre		238.49
0	0	0	0	709.3	127.644	-11.298	sp break		-58.36

Figure 52-6 Forecast parameters and forecasts including spring break and the first three days of the month.

By looking at the forecast errors for the week 12/24 through 12/31 (see Figure 52-7), we see that we've greatly overforecasted the customer counts for the days in this week.

creditunion.xls

	A	B	K	L	M	N	O	P
1				stdeverr	123.90711			
2			SSE	3884301.8				
3		MONTH	Forecast	Sq Err	Error	Day of Week		
253		12	1308.12	134777.29	-367.1203			
254		12	1145.406	21434.72	-146.406			
255		12	884.0836	70269.332	-265.0836			
256		12	1283.014	119725.93	-346.0144			
257		12	1308.12	26282.981	-162.1203			
258								
259								
260								
261								
262								

Figure 52-7 Errors for Christmas week.

In the worksheet named Christmas Week, I've added a changing cell representing the effect of Christmas week and run the Solver model again. The results are shown in Figure 52-8. Note that Christmas week reduced our daily customer count by 410.

creditunion.xls

	I	J	K	L	M	N	O	P
1	RSQ	0.88598353		stdeverr	115.18664			
2			SSE	3356794.11				
3	BH	AH	Forecast	Sq Err	Error	Day of Week		
21	0	0	726.44978	5394.87089	-73.44978	9	-177.2682	
22	0	U	1128.2576	2328.79698	-48.25761	10	-176.6509	
23	0	0	953.81741	92305.0169	-303.8174	11	-150.3414	
24	0	0	692.30297	2333.17672	-48.30297	12	32.770951	
25	0	0	685.22058	13871.9907	117.77942	constant	1052.8509	
26	U	0	1396.4323	13094.7538	-114.4323	d1	572.99305	
27	0	0	1939.4067	10731.5661	103.59327	d2	367.62499	
28	0	0	978.41387	28085.1106	167.58613	d3	284.80864	
29	0	0	716.89943	533.636239	23.100568	day before sp break	230.98327	
30	0	0	709.81705	139.642632	-11.81705	sp break	-58.75403	
31	0	0	751.04625	3141.18201	-56.04625	christmas week	-409.9546	
32	0	0	1152.8541	37.7723993	6.1459254			
33	0	0	978.41387	9489.46228	-97.41387			
34	0	0	716.89943	2611.26804	51.100568			
35	0	0	709.81705	3115.54289	-55.81705			
36	0	0	751.04625	11439.1049	106.95375			

original / 1st three days / christmas week

Figure 52-8 Final Forecast Parameters.

Our RSQ is now up to 89 percent, and the standard deviation of our errors is down to 115! Notice how we've improved our forecasting model by using outliers. If your outliers have something in common (like being the first three days of the month), include the common factor as an independent variable and your forecasting error will drop.

How can I check if my forecast errors are random?

A good forecasting method should create forecast errors or residuals that are random. By random errors, I mean that our errors exhibit no discernible pattern. If forecast errors are random, the sign of your errors should change (from plus to minus or minus to plus) around half the time. Therefore, a commonly used test to evaluate the randomness of forecast errors is to look at the number of sign changes in the errors. If you have *n* observations, nonrandomness of the errors is indicated if you find either fewer than

$$\frac{n-1}{2}-\sqrt{n}$$

or more than

$$\frac{n-1}{2}+\sqrt{n}$$

changes in sign. In the worksheet named Changes in Sign, shown in Figure 52-9, I determined the number of sign changes in our residuals by copying from cell N5 to N6:N257 the formula *IF(M5*M4<0,1,0)*. A sign change in the residuals occurs if and only if the product of two consecutive residuals is negative. Therefore, our formula yields a 1 whenever a change in the sign of the residuals occurs. There were 111 changes in sign. In cell P1, I computed

$$\frac{254-1}{2}-\sqrt{254}=110.6$$

changes in sign as the cutoff for nonrandom residuals. Therefore we have (borderline) random residuals. Perhaps the inclusion of some omitted variables might improve the randomness of the residuals.

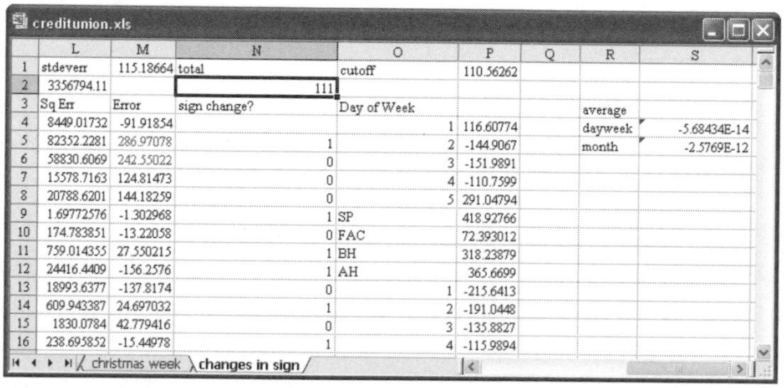

creditunion.xls

	L	M	N	O	P	Q	R	S
1	stdeverr	115.18664	total	cutoff	110.56262			
2	3356794.11		111					
3	Sq Err	Error	sign change?	Day of Week			average	
4	8449.01732	-91.91854		1	116.60774		dayweek	-5.68434E-14
5	82352.2281	286.97078	1	2	-144.9067		month	-2.5769E-12
6	58830.6069	242.55022	0	3	-151.9891			
7	15578.7163	124.81473	0	4	-110.7599			
8	20788.6201	144.18259	0	5	291.04794			
9	1.69772576	-1.302968	1	SP	418.92766			
10	174.783851	-13.22058	0	FAC	72.393012			
11	759.014355	27.550215	1	BH	318.23879			
12	24416.4409	-156.2576	1	AH	365.6699			
13	18993.6377	-137.8174	0	1	-215.6413			
14	609.943387	24.697032	1	2	-191.0448			
15	1830.0784	42.779416	0	3	-135.8827			
16	238.695852	-15.44978	1	4	-115.9894			

christmas week | changes in sign

Figure 52-9 Are residuals random?

Problems

1. How could you use the techniques outlined in this chapter to predict daily sales of pens at Staples?

2. Test the residuals from our MA and MMA forecasts of toy store quarterly revenue in Chapter 51 for randomness. (The data is in the file Toysrusma.xls.)

53

An Introduction to Random Variables

- What is a random variable?
- What is a discrete random variable?
- What are the mean, variance, and standard deviation of a random variable?
- What is a continuous random variable?
- What is a probability density function?
- What are independent random variables?

In today's world, the only thing that's certain is that we face a great deal of uncertainty. In the next nine chapters, I'll give you some powerful techniques that enable you to incorporate uncertainty in business models. The key building block in modeling uncertainty is an understanding of how to use random variables.

What is a random variable?

Any situation whose outcome is uncertain is called an *experiment*. A *random variable* is a function that associates a value with each possible experimental outcome. For example, tossing a pair of dice is an experiment, and a random variable might be defined as the sum of the values showing on each die. In this case, the random variable could assume any of the values 2, 3, and so on up to 12. As another example, consider the "experiment" of selling a new video game console. A random variable of interest might be the market share for this new product.

What is a discrete random variable?

A random variable is discrete if it can assume a finite number of possible values. Here are some examples of discrete random variables:

- Number of potential competitors for your product

- Number of aces drawn in a five-card poker hand

- Number of car accidents you have (hopefully zero!) in a year

- Number of dots showing on a die

- Number of free throws Steve Nash makes when he shoots 12 free throws during a basketball game

What are the mean, variance, and standard deviation of a random variable?

In Chapter 35, I discussed the mean, variance, and standard deviation for a data set. In essence, the mean of a random variable (often denoted by μ) is the average value of the random variable we would expect if we performed an experiment many times. The mean of a random variable is often referred to as the random variable's *expected* value. The variance of a random variable (often denoted by σ^2) is the average value of the squared deviation from the mean of a random variable that we would expect if we performed our experiment many times. The standard deviation of a random variable (often denoted by σ) is simply the square root of its variance. As with data sets, the mean of a random variable is a summary measure for a typical value of the random variable, whereas the variance and standard deviation measure the spread of the random variable about its mean.

As an example of how to compute the mean, variance, and standard deviation of a random variable, suppose we feel that the return on the stock market during the next year is governed by the following probabilities:

Probability	Market Return
.40	+20 percent
.30	0 percent
.30	-20 percent

Hand calculations show the following:

μ = .40(.20) + .30(.00) + .30(-.20) = .02 or 2 percent

σ^2 = .4*(.20-.02)2 + .30*(.0 - .02)2 + .30*(-.20 - .02)2 = .0275

$$\sigma = \sqrt{.0275} = .166 \text{ or } 16.6 \text{ percent.}$$

In the file MeanVariance.xls (shown in Figure 53-1), I've verified these computations.

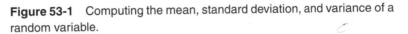

Figure 53-1   Computing the mean, standard deviation, and variance of a random variable.

I computed the mean of our market return in cell C9 with the formula *SUMPRODUCT(B4:B6,C4:C6)*. This formula multiplies each value of the random variable by its probability and sums up the products.

To compute the variance of our market return, I determine the squared deviation of each value of the random variable from its mean by copying from D4 to D5:D6 the formula *(B4-$C$9)^2*. Then, in cell C10, I compute the variance of the market return as the average squared deviation from the mean with the formula *SUMPRODUCT(C4:C6,D4:D6)*. Finally, I compute the standard deviation of the market return in cell C11 with the formula *SQRT(C10)*.

What is a continuous random variable?

A continuous random variable is a random variable that can assume a very large number or, to all intents and purposes, an infinite number of values. Here are some examples of continuous random variables:

- Price of Microsoft stock a year from now
- Market share for a new product
- Market size for a new product
- Cost of developing a new product
- Newborn baby's weight
- Person's IQ
- Dirk Nowitzki's three-point shooting percentage during next season

What is a probability density function?

A discrete random variable can be specified by a list of values and the probability of occurrence for each value of the random variable. Because a continuous random variable can assume an infinite number of values, we can't list the probability of occurrence for each value of a continuous random variable. A continuous random variable is completely described by its *probability density function*. For example, the probability density function for a randomly chosen person's IQ is shown in Figure 53-2.

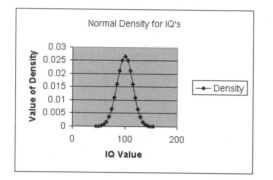

Figure 53-2 Probability density function for IQs.

A probability density function (PDF) has the following properties.

■ The value of the PDF is always greater than or equal to 0.

■ The area under the PDF equals 1.

■ The height of the density function for a value x of a random variable is proportional to the likelihood that the random variable assumes a value near x. For example, the height of our density for IQs at 83 is roughly half the height of the density for an IQ of 100. This tells us that IQs near 83 are around half as likely as IQs around 100. Also, because the density peaks at 100, IQs around 100 are most likely.

■ The probability that a continuous random variable assumes a range of values equals the corresponding area under the density function. For example, the fraction of people having IQs between 80 and 100 is simply the area under the density between 80 and 100.

What are independent random variables?

A set of random variables are independent if knowledge of the value of any subset of the random variables tells you nothing about the values of the other random variables. For example, the number of games won by the Indiana University football team during a year is independent of the percentage return on Microsoft during the same year. Knowing that Indiana did very well would not change your view of how Microsoft stock did during the year.

On the other hand, the return on Microsoft stock and Intel stock are not independent. If we are told that Microsoft stock had a high return in one year, in all likelihood PC sales were high, which tells us that Intel probably had a good year as well.

Problems

1. Identify the following random variables as discrete or continuous:

    ❑   Number of games Kerry Wood wins for the Chicago Cubs next season

    ❑   Number that comes up when the roulette wheel is spun

    ❑   Unit sales of Tablet PCs next year

    ❑   Length of time that a light bulb lasts before it burns out

2. Compute the mean, variance, and standard deviation of the number of dots showing when a die is tossed.

3. Discuss whether or not you feel the following random variables are independent

    ❑   Daily temperature and sales at an ice cream store

    ❑   Suit and number of a card drawn from a deck of playing cards

    ❑   Inflation and return on stock market

    ❑   Price charged for a car and units sold of car

4. The current price of a stock is $20. The stock is a takeover target. If the takeover is successful, the stock's price will increase to $30. If the takeover is unsuccessful, the stock's price will drop to $12. Determine the range of values for the probability of a successful takeover that would make it worthwhile to purchase the stock today. Assume your goal is to maximize your expected profit. Hint: Use Excel's Goal Seek command, which is discussed in detail in Chapter 16.

54

The Binomial and Hypergeometric Random Variables

- What is the binomial random variable?

- How do we use the BINOMDIST function to compute binomial probabilities?

- Assume that equal numbers of people prefer Coke to Pepsi and Pepsi to Coke. We ask 100 people whether they prefer Coke to Pepsi. We're interested in the probability that exactly 60 people prefer Coke to Pepsi and the probability that between 40 and 60 people (inclusive) prefer Coke to Pepsi.

- Three percent of all elevator rails we produce are considered defective. Suppose we ship a batch of 10,000 elevator rails to a customer. To determine whether the batch is acceptable, the customer will randomly choose a sample of 100 rails and determine whether each sampled rail is defective. If 2 or fewer sampled rails are defective, the customer will accept the batch. We want to determine the probability that the batch will be accepted.

- Airlines do not like to fly flights with empty seats. Suppose that on average, 95 percent of all ticket purchasers show up for a flight. If the airline sells 105 tickets for a 100-seat flight, what is the probability that the flight will be overbooked?

- What is the hypergeometric random variable?

What is the binomial random variable?

The binomial random variable is a discrete random variable used to calculate probabilities in the following situation:

■ n independent trials occur.

■   Each trial results in one of two outcomes: success or failure.

■   In each trial, the probability of success (p) remains constant.

In such a situation, the binomial random variable can be used to calculate probabilities related to the number of successes in a given number of trials. We let x be the random variable denoting the number of successes occurring in n independent trials when the probability of success on each trial is p. Here are some examples in which the binomial random variable is relevant.

Coke or Pepsi   Assume that equal numbers of people prefer Coke to Pepsi and Pepsi to Coke. We ask 100 people whether they prefer Coke to Pepsi and are interested in the probability that exactly 60 people prefer Coke to Pepsi and the probability that between 40 and 60 people (inclusive) prefer Coke to Pepsi. In this situation, we have a binomial random variable defined by the following:

■   Trial: survey individuals

■   Success: prefer Coke

■ p equals .50

■ n equals 100

Let x equal the number of people sampled who prefer Coke. We want to determine the probability that $x = 60$ and also the probability that $40 \leq x \leq 60$.

Elevator Rails   Three percent of all elevator rails produced by our company are considered defective. Suppose we ship a batch of 10,000 elevator rails to a customer. To determine whether the batch is acceptable, the customer will randomly choose a sample of 100 rails and determine whether each sampled rail is defective. If two or fewer sampled rails are defective, the customer will accept the batch. We want to determine the probability that the batch will be accepted.

We have a binomial random variable defined by the following:

■   Trial: look at a sampled rail

■   Success: rail is defective

■ p equals .03

■ n equals 100

Let x equal the number of defective rails in the sample. We want to find the probability that $x \leq 2$.

Airline Overbooking   Airlines don't like to fly flights with empty seats. Suppose that on average, 95 percent of all ticket purchasers show up for a flight. If the airline sells 105 tickets for a 100-seat flight, what is the probability that the flight will be overbooked?

We have a binomial random variable defined by the following

- Trial: individual ticket holders

- Success: ticket holder shows up

- p equals .95

- n equals 105

Let x equal number of ticket holders who show up. Then we want to find the probability that $x \geq 101$.

How do we use the BINOMDIST function to compute binomial probabilities?

Excel includes the BINOMDIST function with which you can compute binomial probabilities. If you want to compute the probability of x or fewer successes for a binomial random variable having n trials with probability of success p, simply enter *BINOMDIST(x, n, p, 1)*. If you want to compute the probability of exactly x successes for a binomial random variable having n trials with probability of success of p, enter *BINOMDIST(x, n, p, 0)*. Entering 1 as the last argument of BINOMDIST yields a "cumulative" probability; entering 0 yields the "probability mass function" for any particular value. Let's use the BINOMDIST function to calculate some probabilities of interest. Our work is in the file Binomialexamples.xls, which is shown in Figure 54-1.

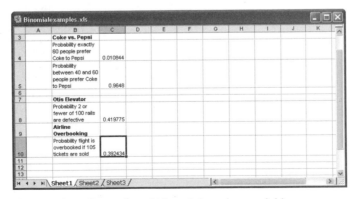

Figure 54-1   Examples of binomial random variable.

Assume that equal numbers of people prefer Coke to Pepsi and Pepsi to Coke. We ask 100 people whether they prefer Coke to Pepsi. We're interested in the probability that exactly 60 people prefer Coke to Pepsi and the probability that between 40 and 60 people (inclusive) prefer Coke to Pepsi.

We have $n = 100$ and $p = .5$ and seek the probability that $x = 60$ and the probability that $40 \leq x \leq 60$ where x equals the number of people who prefer Coke to Pepsi. First we find the probability that $x = 60$ by entering the formula *BINOMDIST(60,100,.5,0)*. Excel returns the value .011.

To use the BINOMDIST function to compute the probability that $40 \leq x \leq 60$, we note that the probability that $40 \leq x \leq 60$ equals the (*probability that* $x \leq 60$) – (*the probability that* $x \leq 39$). Thus, we can obtain the probability that between 40 and 60 people prefer Coke by entering the formula *BINOMDIST(60,100,.5,1) - BINOMDIST(39,100,.5,1)*. Excel returns the value .9648. So, if Coke and Pepsi are equally preferred, it is very unlikely that in a sample of 100 people, Coke or Pepsi would be more than 10 percent ahead. If a sample of 100 people shows Coke or Pepsi to be more than 10 percent ahead, we would probably doubt that Coke and Pepsi are equally preferred.

Three percent of all elevator rails we produce are considered defective. Suppose we ship a batch of 10,000 elevator rails to a customer. To determine whether the batch is acceptable, the customer will randomly choose a sample of 100 rails and determine whether each sampled rail is defective. If 2 or fewer sampled rails are defective, the customer will accept the batch. We want to determine the probability that the batch will be accepted.

If we let x equal the number of defective rails in a batch, we have a binomial random variable with $n = 100$ and $p = .03$. We seek the probability that $x \leq 2$. We simply enter the formula *BINOMDIST(2, 100, .03, 1)*. Excel returns the value .419. Thus the batch will be accepted 41.9 percent of the time.

Really, our chance of success is not exactly 3 percent on each trial. For example, if the first 10 rails are defective, the chance the next rail is defective has dropped to 290/9990; if the first 10 rails are not defective, the chance the next rail is defective is 300/9990. Therefore, the probability of success on the 11th trial is not independent of the probability of success on one of the first 10 trials. Despite this fact, the binomial random variable is used as an approximation when a sample is drawn and the sample size is less than 10 percent of the total population. Here our population size equals 10,000 and our sample size is 100. Exact probabilities involving sampling from a finite population can be calculated with the hypergeometric random variable, which I'll discuss later in this chapter.

Airlines do not like to fly planes with empty seats. Suppose that on average 95 percent of all ticket purchasers show up for a flight. If the airline sells 105 tickets for a 100-seat flight, what is the probability that the flight will be overbooked?

Let x equal the number of ticket holders who show up for the flight. We have n = 105 and p = .95 and seek the probability that $x \geq 101$. We note that the probability that $x \geq 101$ equals $1 -$ probability that $x \leq 100$. So, to compute the probability that the flight is overbooked, we enter the formula *1 - BINOM-DIST(100, 105, .95, 1)*. Excel yields .392, which means there is a 39.2 percent chance that the flight will be overbooked.

What is the hypergeometric random variable?

The hypergeometric random variable governs situations such as the following:

- An urn contains N balls.

- Each ball is one of two types (called success or failure).

- There are s successes in the urn.

- A sample of size n is drawn from the urn.

Let's look at an example in the file Hypergeo.xls, which is shown in Figure 54-2. The Excel function *HYPGEOMDIST(x,n,s,N)* gives the probability of x successes. For example, suppose that 40 of the Fortune 500 companies have a woman CEO. If we randomly select 10 Fortune 500 companies, the probability that our sample will contain 0, 1 ... 2 women CEOs is obtained by copying from D8 to D9:D18 the formula *HYPGEOMDIST(C8,Sample_Size, Population_women,Population_size)*. (I assigned the names in C3:C5 to the cells in D3:D5.)

We consider finding a woman CEO a success. In our sample of 10, we find, for example, a probability of .431 that no women CEOs will be in the sample. By the way, we could have approximated this probability with the formula *BINOMDIST(0,10,0.08,0)*, which yields .434, which is very close to the true probability of .4309.

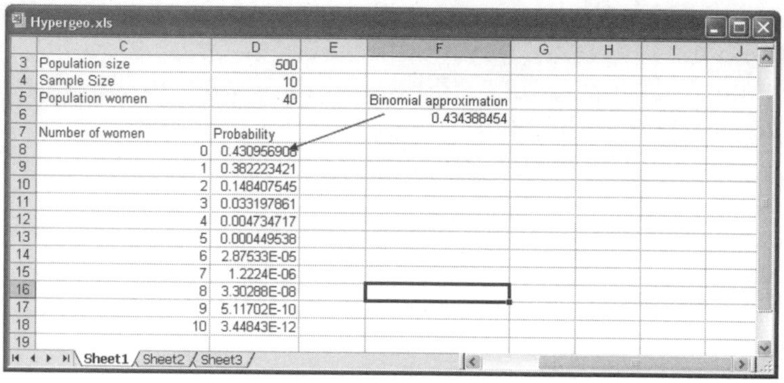

Figure 54-2   Example of using the hypergeometric random variable.

Problems

1. Suppose that, on average, 4 percent of all floppy disk drives received by Dell Computer are defective. Dell has adopted the following policy: sample 50 disk drives in each shipment and accept the shipment if all disk drives in the sample are nondefective.

    ❑   What fraction of batches will be accepted?

    ❑   Suppose the batch is accepted if at most one disk drive in the sample is defective. What fraction of batches will be accepted?

    ❑   What is the probability that a sample of size 50 will contain at least 10 defective disks?

2. In our airline overbooking example, determine how the probability of overbooking varies as the number of tickets sold varies between 100 and 115. Hint: use a one-way data table.

3. In our airline overbooking example, show how the probability of overbooking varies as the number of tickets sold varies between 100 and 115 and the probability that a ticket holder shows up varies between 80 percent and 95 percent. Hint: Use a two-way data table.

4. Suppose that during each year, a given mutual fund has a 50 percent chance of beating the Standard and Poor's (S&P) index. In a group of 100 mutual funds, what is the probability that at least 10 funds will beat the S&P index during at least 8 out of 10 years?

5.   Steve Nash is a 90 percent foul shooter. If he shoots 100 free throws, what is the probability that he will miss more than 15 shots?

6.   In being tested for extra sensory perception (ESP), participants are asked to identify the shape of a card from a 25-card deck. The deck consists of five cards of each of five shapes. If a person identifies 12 cards correctly, what would you conclude?

7.   Suppose that in a group of 100 people, 20 have the flu and 80 do not. If we randomly select 30 people, what is the chance that at least 10 people have the flu?

55

The Poisson and Exponential Random Variable

- What is the Poisson random variable?

- How do I use Excel to compute probabilities for the Poisson random variable?

- Suppose that the number of customers arriving at a bank is governed by a Poisson random variable. What random variable governs the time between arrivals?

What is the Poisson random variable?

The Poisson random variable is a discrete random variable that is useful for describing probabilities for situations in which events (such as customer arrivals at a bank or orders placed for a product) have a small probability of occurring during a small time interval. More specifically, during a small time interval Δt, either zero or one event will occur, and the probability of one event occurring during a small interval of length Δt is (for some λ) given by $\lambda \Delta t$. Here, λ is the mean number of occurrences per time unit. Situations in which the Poisson random variable have been applied include the following:

- Number of units of a product demanded during a month.

- Number of deaths per year by horse kick in Prussian army.

- Number of car accidents you have during a year.

- Number of copies of *Seat of the Soul* ordered today at Amazon.com.

- Number of workers' compensation claims filed at Microsoft this month.

- Number of defects in 100 yards of string. (Here, 1 yard of string plays the role of time.)

How do I use Excel to compute probabilities for the Poisson random variable?

The Excel POISSON function is used to compute probabilities involving the Poisson random variable. Just remember that in a length of time t, the mean of a Poisson random variable is λt. The syntax of the POISSON function is as follows:

- *POISSON(x, Lambda, True)* calculates the probability that a Poisson random variable with a mean equal to *Lambda* is less than or equal to *x*.

- *POISSON(x, Lambda, False)* calculates the probability that a Poisson random variable with a mean equal to *Lambda* is equal to *x*.

Here are some examples of how to compute probabilities for Poisson random variables. You can find these examples in the file Poisson.xls, shown in Figure 55-1.

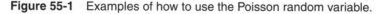

Figure 55-1 Examples of how to use the Poisson random variable.

Suppose that my consulting business receives an average of 30 phone calls per hour. During a 2-hour period, I want to determine the following:

- The probability that exactly 60 calls will be received in the next 2 hours.

- The probability that the number of calls received in the next 2 hours will be less than or equal to 60.

- The probability that between 50 and 100 calls (inclusive) will be received in the next 2 hours.

During a 2-hour period, the mean number of calls is 60. In cell C4, we find the probability (.05) that exactly 60 calls will be received in next 2 hours by using the formula *POISSON(60,C2,FALSE)*. In cell C5, we find the probability (.53) that at most 60 calls are received in 2 hours with the formula *POISSON(60,C2,TRUE)*. In cell C6, we find the probability (.915) that between 50 and 100 calls are received in 2 hours with the formula *POISSON(100,C2,TRUE)-POISSON(49,C2,TRUE)*.

Suppose the number of customers arriving at a bank is governed by a Poisson random variable. What random variable governs the time between arrivals?

The time between arrivals can be any value, which means that the time between arrivals is a continuous random variable. If an average of λ arrivals occur per time unit, the time between arrivals follows an exponential random variable having the probability density function (PDF) of $f(t) = \lambda e^{-\lambda t}$, $t \geq 0$. This random variable has a mean, or average, value equal to $1/\lambda$. For $\lambda = 30$, a graph of the exponential PDF is shown in Figure 55-2. You can find this chart and the data for this example in the file Exponentialdist.xls.

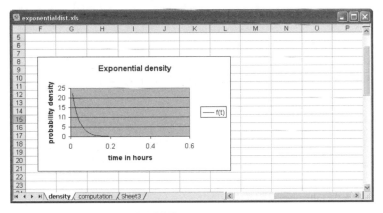

Figure 55-2   Exponential PDF.

Recall from Chapter 53 that for a continuous random variable, the height of the PDF for a number *x* reflects the likelihood that the random variable assumes a value near *x*. Thus, we see in Figure 55-2 that extremely short times between bank arrivals (say, less than .05 hours) are very likely, but after that the PDF drops off sharply.

Even though the average time between arrivals is 1/30 = .033 hours, there's a reasonable chance that the time between arrivals will be as much as .20 hours. The Excel function *EXPONDIST(x, 1/mean, TRUE)* will give the probability that an exponential random variable with a given *mean* will assume a value less than or equal to *x*. Thus, the second argument to the EXPONDIST function is the rate per time unit at which events occur. For example, to compute the probability that the time between arrivals is at least 5, 10, or 15 minutes, I copied from cell D5 to D7 the formula *1-EXPONDIST(C5,$D$2,TRUE)*.

Note that I first converted minutes to hours (5 minutes = 1/12 hour, and so on). Also, the mean time between arrivals is .033 hours, so I entered into our formula *1/Mean = 1/.033 = 30*. In short, I input the arrival rate per time unit, as you can see in Figure 55-3.

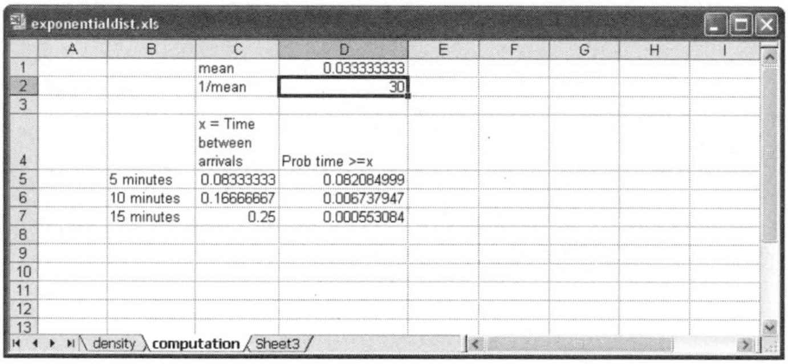

	A	B	C	D
1			mean	0.033333333
2			1/mean	30
3				
4			x = Time between arrivals	Prob time >=x
5		5 minutes	0.08333333	0.082084999
6		10 minutes	0.16666667	0.006737947
7		15 minutes	0.25	0.000553084

Figure 55-3 Computations of exponential probabilities.

Problems

1. An average of 40 pitchers of beer are ordered per hour at Nick's Pub in Bloomington, Indiana.
   - What is the probability that at least 100 pitchers are ordered in a 2-hour period?
   - What is the chance that the time between pitchers being ordered will be 30 seconds or less?
2. Suppose that teenage drivers have an average of 0.3 accidents per year.
   - What is the probability that a teenager will have no more than one accident during a year?
   - What is the probability that the time between accidents will be 6 months or less?

56

The Normal Random Variable

■ What are the properties of the normal random variable?

■ How do I use Excel to find probabilities for the normal random variable?

■ Can I use Excel to find percentiles for normal random variables?

■ Why is the normal random variable appropriate in many real-world situations?

In Chapter 53, you learned that continuous random variables can be used to model quantities such as the following:

■ Price of Microsoft stock a year from now

■ Market share for a new product

■ Market size for a new product

■ Cost of developing a new product

■ Newborn baby's weight

■ A person's IQ

Remember that if a discrete random variable (such as sales of blazers during 2006) can assume many possible values, we can approximate the value by using a continuous random variable as well. As I described in Chapter 53, any continuous random variable X has a probability density function (PDF). The PDF for a continuous random variable is a nonnegative function with the following properties. (In what follows, *a* and *b* are arbitrary numbers.)

■   The area under the PDF is 1.

■   The probability that $X < a$ equals the probability that $X \leq a$. This probability is represented by the area under the PDF to the left of a.

■   The probability that $X > b$ equals the probability that $X \geq b$. This probability is shown in the area under the PDF to the right of b.

■   The probability that $a < X < b$ equals the probability that $a \leq X \leq b$. This probability is the area under the PDF between a and b.

Thus, the area under a continuous random variable's PDF represents probability. Also, the larger the value of the density function at X, the more likely the random variable will take on a value near X. For example, if the density function of a random variable at 20 is twice the density function of the random variable at 5, then the random variable is twice as likely to take on a value near 20 than near 5. For a continuous random variable, the probability that X equals a will always equal 0. For example, some people are between 5.99999' and 6.00001' tall, but no person can be exactly 6 feet tall. This explains why we can replace the less than sign ($<$) with the less than but equal to sign ($\leq$) in our probability statements.

Figure 56-1 displays the PDF for $X =$ IQ of a randomly chosen person. The area under this PDF is 1. If we wanted to find the probability that a person's IQ is less than or equal to 90, we would just find the area to the left of 90. If we wanted to find the probability that a person's IQ is between 95 and 120, we would find the area under the PDF between 95 and 120. If we wanted to find the probability that a person's IQ is more than 130, we would find the area under the density function to the right of 130.

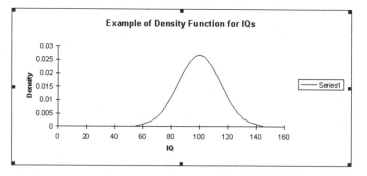

Figure 56-1   PDF for IQs.

Actually, the density sketched in Figure 56-1 is an example of the normal random variable. The normal random variable is specified by its mean μ and standard deviation σ. IQs follow a normal random variable with μ = 100 and σ = 15. This is the PDF displayed in Figure 56-1. The normal random variable has the following properties:

- The most likely value of a normal random variable is μ (as indicated by the PDF peaking at 100 in Figure 56-1.)

- As the value x of the random variable moves away from μ, the probability that the random variable is near x sharply decreases.

- The normal random variable is symmetric about its mean. For example, IQs near 80 are as likely as IQs near 120.

- A normal random variable has 68 percent of its probability within σ of its mean, 95 percent of its probability within 2σ of its mean, and 99.7 percent of its probability within 3σ of its mean. These measures should remind you of the rule of thumb I described in Chapter 35 when we covered descriptive statistics. In fact, the rule of thumb is based on the assumption that data is "sampled" from a normal distribution, which explains why the rule of thumb does not work as well when the data fails to exhibit a symmetric histogram.

For a larger σ, the more spread out a normal random variable will be about its mean. This pattern is illustrated in Figures 56-2 and 56-3.

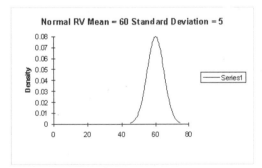

Figure 56-2   A normal random variable PDF with a mean equal to 60 and a standard deviation equal to 5.

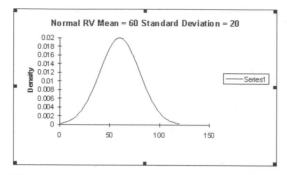

Figure 56-3 A normal random variable PDF with a mean equal to 60 and a standard deviation equal to 20.

How do I use Excel to find probabilities for the normal random variable?

Consider a normal random variable X with a mean µ and standard deviation σ. Suppose for any number x, we want to find the probability that $X \leq x$, which is called the normal cumulative function. To find the probability that $X \leq$ x, simply enter the function NORMDIST(x, µ, σ, 1) in Excel.

The argument 1 tells Excel to compute the normal cumulative. If the last argument of the function is 0, Excel returns the actual value of the normal random variable's PDF.

We can use the NORMDIST function to answer many questions concerning normal probabilities. You can find examples in the file NormalExamples.xls, which is shown in Figure 56-4.

	A	B	C	D	E	F	G	H	I	J
1										
2			Prob							
3		IQ<90	0.25249254							
4		95<IQ<120	0.53934744							
5		IQ>130	0.02275013							
6										
7		99 %ile Prozac	71.6317394							
8		10% Bloomington income	19747.5875							
9										
10										
11										
12										
13										

Figure 56-4 Normal probability examples.

What fraction of people have an IQ less than 90?

Let X equal the IQ of a randomly chosen person. Then we seek the probability that $X < 90$, which is equal to the probability that $X \leq 90$. Therefore, we can enter into cell C3 the formula

NORMDIST(90,100,15,1), and Excel returns .252. Thus 25.2 percent of all people have an IQ less than 90.

What fraction of all people have IQs between 95 and 120?   In finding the probability that a $\leq X \leq$ b, note that this probability can be determined using the form *(Area under the normal density function to the left of b) - (Area under normal density function to the left of a)*. Thus, we can find the probability that a $\leq X \leq$ b by entering the formula *NORMDIST(b, Ϥ,σ,1) - NORMDIST(a, Ϥ,σ,1)*. This fact is illustrated in Figure 56-5, where clearly the shaded area is *(area to left of b) - (area to left of a)*.

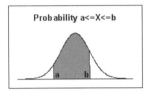

Figure 56-5   The probability that a random variable is between *a* and *b*.

You can answer the question about IQs between 95 and 120 by entering into cell C4 the formula *NORMDIST(120,100,15,1) - NORMDIST(95,100,15,1)*. Excel returns the probability .539. So, 53.9 percent of all people have an IQ between 95 and 120.

What fraction of all people have IQs of at least 130?   To find the probability that $X \geq$ b, we note from Figure 56-6 that the probability that $X \geq$ b equals *1- probability X < b*. We can compute the probability that $X \geq$ b by entering the formula *1 - NORMDIST(b, Ϥ, σ, 1)*.

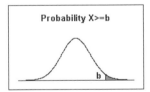

Figure 56-6   Probability random variable is greater than or equal to *b*.

We seek the probability that $X \geq 130$. This equals 1- probability $X \leq 130$. We enter in cell C5 the formula *1 - NORMDIST(130,100, 15,1)*. Excel returns .023, so we know that 2.3 percent of people have an IQ of at least 130.

Can I use Excel to find percentiles for the normal random variable?

Consider a given normal random variable X with mean Ϥ and standard deviation σ. In many situations, we want to answer questions such as the following:

- A drug manufacturer believes that next year's demand for its popular antidepressant will be normally distributed, with μ equal to 60 million days of therapy (DOT) and σ equal to 5 million DOT. How many units of the drug should be produced this year if the company wants to have only a 1 percent chance of running out of the drug?

- Family income in Bloomington, Indiana, is normally distributed, with μ equal to $30,000 and σ equal to $8,000. The poorest 10 percent of all families in Bloomington are eligible for federal aid. What should the aid cutoff be?

In our first example, we want to determine the 99th percentile of demand for the antidepressant. That is, we seek the number x such that there is only a 1 percent chance that demand will exceed x and a 99 percent chance that demand will be less than x. In our second example, we want the 10th percentile of family income in Bloomington. That is, we seek the number x such that there is only a 10 percent chance that family income will be less than x and a 90 percent chance that family income will exceed x.

Suppose we want to find the pth percentile (expressed as a decimal) of a normal random variable X with a mean μ and a standard deviation σ. Simply enter the following formula into Excel:

`NORMINV(p, μ, σ)`

This formula will return the number x having the property that the probability that $X \leq x$ equals the percentile, as we want. We now can solve our examples. You'll find these exercises in the file NormalExamples.xls.

For the drug manufacturing example, let X equal annual demand for the drug. We want a value x such that the probability that $X \geq x$ equals .01 or the probability that $X \leq x$ equals .99. Again, we seek the 99th percentile of demand, which we find (in millions) by entering in cell C7 the formula *NORMINV(.99,60,5)*. Excel returns 71.63, so the company must produce 71,630,000 DOT. This assumes, of course, that the company begins the year with no supply of the drug on hand. If, say, they had a beginning inventory of 10 million DOT, they would need to produce 61,630,000 DOT during the current year.

To determine the cutoff for federal aid, if X equals the income of a Bloomington family, we seek a value of x such that the probability that $X \leq x$ equals .10, or the 10th percentile of Bloomington family income. We find this value with the formula *NORMINV(.10,30000,8000)*. Excel returns $19,747.59, so aid should be given to all families with incomes smaller than $19,749.59.

Why is the normal random variable appropriate in many real-world situations?

A well-known mathematical result called the *Central Limit Theorem* tells us that if we add together many (usually at least 30 is sufficient) independent random variables, their sum is normally distributed. This result holds even if the individual random variables are not normally distributed. Many quantities (such as measurement errors) are created by adding together many independent random variables, which explains why the normal random variable occurs often in the real world. Here are some other situations in which we can use the Central Limit Theorem.

■   The total demand for pizzas during a month at a supermarket is normally distributed, even if the daily demand for pizzas is not.

■   The amount of money we win if we play craps 1000 times is normally distributed, even though the amount of money we win on each individual play is not normally distributed.

Another mathematical result tells us how to find the mean, variance, and standard deviations of sums of independent random variables. If we are adding together independent random variables $X_1, X_2, \ldots X_n$, where mean $X_i = \mu_i$, variance $X_i = \sigma_i^2$, and standard deviation $X_i = \sigma_i$, then the following are true:

1.   Mean $(X_1 + X_2 + \ldots X_n) = \mu_1 + \mu_2 + \ldots \mu_n$

2.   Variance $(X_1 + X_2 + \ldots X_n) = \sigma_1^2 + \sigma_2^2 + \ldots \sigma_n^2$

3.   Standard deviation $((X_1 + X_2 + \ldots X_n) = \sqrt{\text{Variance } (X_1 + X_2 + \ldots X_n)}$)

We note that 1 is true even when the random variables are not independent. By combining 1 through 3 with the Central Limit Theorem, we can solve many complex probability problems, such as those concerning the demand for pizza. Our solution is in the worksheet Central Limit in the file NormalExamples.xls, which is shown in Figure 56-7.

	A	B	C	D	E	F	G	H
1								
2			Daily frozen pizza demand					
3			mean	45				
4			sigma	12				
5								
6			30 day					
7			mean	1350				
8			variance	4320				
9			sigma	65.72671				
10								
11			Probability more than 1400 sold	0.225689				
12			1% chance of running out	1502.903				
13								
14								
15								

Figure 56-7   Example of the Central Limit Theorem.

Even though the daily demand for frozen pizzas is not normally distributed, we know from the Central Limit Theorem that the 30-day demand for frozen pizzas will be normally distributed. Given this, 1–3 above imply the following:

- From 1, mean of 30-day demand = 30(45) = 1350

- From 2, variance of 30-day demand = $30(12)^2 = 4320$.

- From 3, standard deviation of 30-day demand = $\sqrt{4320} = 65.73$.

Thus, 30-day demand for pizzas can be modeled following a normal random variable with a mean of 1350 and a standard deviation of 65.73. In cell D11, I compute the probability that at least 1400 pizzas are sold as the probability that our normal approximation is at least 1399.5 (note that a demand of, say, 1399.6 would round up to 1400) with the formula *1-NORMDIST(1399.5,D7,D9,TRUE)*. We find the probability that demand in a 30-day period is for at least 1400 pizzas to be 22.6 percent.

The number of pizzas that we must stock to have only a 1 percent chance of running out of pizzas is just the 99th percentile of our demand distribution. We determine the 99th percentile of our demand distribution (1503) in cell D12 with the formula *NORMINV(0.99,D7,D9)*. Therefore, at the beginning of a month, we should bring our stock of pizzas up to 1503 if we want to have only a 1 percent chance of running out of pizzas.

Problems

1. Suppose we can set the mean number of ounces of soda that is put into a can of soda. The actual number of ounces in a can has a standard deviation of .05 ounces.

    ❑ If we set the mean at 12.03 ounces, and a soda can is acceptable if it contains at least 12 ounces, what fraction of our cans are acceptable?

    ❑ What fraction of cans have less than 12.1 ounces?

    ❑ What should we set the mean to if we want at most 1 percent of our cans to contain at most 12 ounces? Hint: Use the Goal Seek command.

2. Annual demand for a drug is normally distributed with a mean of 40,000 units and a standard deviation of 10,000 units.

    ❑ What is the probability that annual demand is between 35,000 and 49,000 units?

❏   If we want to have only a 5 percent chance of running out of the drug, to what level should we set annual production?

3.   The probability of winning a game of craps is .493. If I play 10,000 games of craps, what is the probability that I'm ahead? Begin by determining the mean and standard deviation of the profit on a single game of craps. Then use the Central Limit Theorem.

4.   Weekly sales of Volvo's Cross Country wagons are normally distributed with a mean of 1000 and standard deviation of 250.

❏   What is the probability that during a week, between 400 and 1100 wagons are sold?

❏   There is a 1 percent chance that fewer than what number of wagons are sold during a week?

57

Weibull and Beta Distributions: Modeling Machine Life and Duration of a Project

- ■ I want to know the probability that a machine will work without failing for at least 20 hours. How would I estimate this probability?

- ■ I want to know the probability that installing dry wall on a building will take more than 200 hours. How would I estimate this probability?

The Weibull random variable is a continuous random variable that is often used to model the lifetime of a machine. If we have data about how long similar machines have lasted in the past, we can estimate the two parameters (*alpha* and *beta*) that define a Weibull random variable. You can then use the WEIBULL function in Excel to determine probabilities of interest, such as an estimate of how long a machine will run without failing.

The Beta random variable is a continuous random variable that's often used to model the duration of an activity. Given estimates of the minimum duration, maximum duration, mean duration, and the standard deviation of the duration, you can use the BETADIST function in Excel to determine probabilities of interest.

I want to know the probability that a machine will work without failing for at least 20 hours. How would I estimate this probability?

Suppose we have observed the lifetime of seven similar machines. The data we've collected about the machines is contained in the file Weibullest.xls, shown in Figure 57-1.

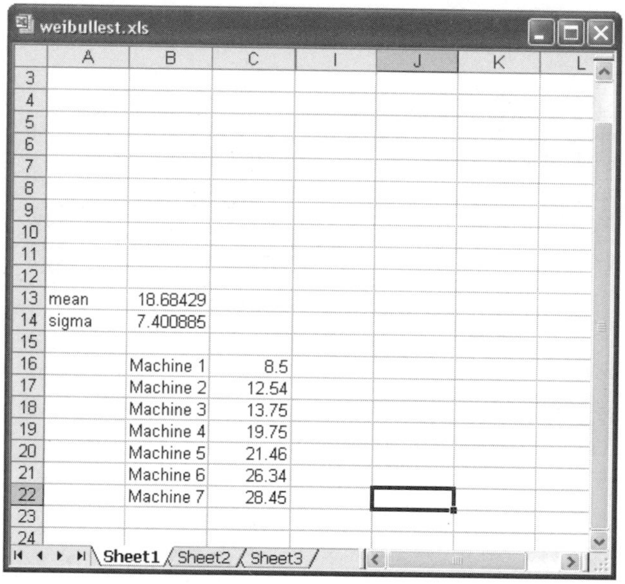

Figure 57-1 Machine lifetime data.

Reliability engineers have found that the Weibull random variable is usually appropriate for modeling machine lifetimes. The Weibull random variable is specified by two parameters: *alpha* and *beta*. Based on our data, we find (using the AVERAGE and STDEV functions in cells B13 and B14) that on average, a machine lasts 18.68 hours, with a standard deviation of 7.40 hours. After copying these values into cells G6 and G11 and running the Solver, we find estimates of *alpha* and *beta* that ensure that the Weibull random variable will have a mean and standard deviation matching our data. In our case, we find that *alpha* equals 2.725 and *beta* equals 21.003, as you can see in Figure 57-2. Any value you enter for *alpha* and *beta* in cells E2 and E3 for a Weibull random variable yields a mean (computed in cell E6) and standard deviation (computed in cell E11). Our Solver model varies *alpha* and *beta* until the mean and standard deviation of the Weibull distribution equal the mean and standard deviation of machine lifetime computed from our data.

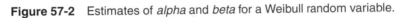

	A	B	C	D	E	F	G	H	I
1									
2				alpha	2.725264				
3				beta	21.00372				
4									
5							assumed	Sq Err	
6				mean	18.68428	=	18.68429	2.51E-12	
7				variance parts	441.1563				
8					0.915493				
9					0.88957				
10				variance	54.77318				
11				sigma	7.400891	=	7.400885	3.6E-11	
12									
13	mean	18.68429							
14	sigma	7.400885							
15									
16		Machine 1	8.5			Prob>=20 hours	0.416832		
17		Machine 2	12.54						
18		Machine 3	13.75			Prob between 15 and 30 hours	0.599417		
19		Machine 4	19.75						
20		Machine 5	21.46						
21		Machine 6	26.34						
22		Machine 7	28.45						

Also present: cell F13 "SSE", G13 "3.85E-11".

Sheet1 / Sheet2 / Sheet3

Figure 57-2   Estimates of *alpha* and *beta* for a Weibull random variable.

Here's the syntax of the WEIBULL function:

```
WEIBULL(x, alpha, beta, True)
```

This function gives the probability that a Weibull random variable with parameters *alpha* and *beta* is less than or equal to *x*. Changing *True* to *False* yields the height of the Weibull probability density function (PDF). Remember from Chapter 53 that the height of a PDF for any value x of a continuous random variable indicates the likelihood that the random variable assumes a value near x. Thus, if the Weibull density for 20 hours were twice the Weibull density for 10 hours, we would know that our machine was twice as likely to work for 20 hours before failing than to work for 10 hours before failing. We can now answer some questions involving probabilities of interest.

What is the probability that a machine will last at least 20 hours?   This probability (41.6 percent) is computed in cell G16 with the formula *1-WEIBULL(20,alpha,beta,1)*. Essentially, this formula computes the area under the Weibull PDF to the right of 20 hours by taking 1 minus the area to the left of 20 hours.

What is the probability that a machine will last between 15 and 30 hours?   This probability (59.9 percent) is computed in cell G18 with the formula *WEIBULL(30,alpha,beta,TRUE)-WEIBULL(15,alpha,beta,TRUE)*. This formula finds the area under the Weibull PDF between 15 and 30 hours by computing the area to the left of 30 hours less the area to the left of 15 hours. After we subtract the probability of a machine working without failure for less than 15 hours from the probability of a machine working without failure for less than or equal to 30 hours, we are left with the probability that a machine will work without failure for between 15 and 30 hours.

I want to know the probability that installing dry wall on a building will take more than 200 hours. How would I estimate this probability?

Since the development of the Polaris missile in the 1950s, project managers have modeled activity durations with the Beta random variable. To specify a Beta random variable, you need to specify a minimum value, a maximum value, and two parameters (*alpha* and *beta*). The data in the file Beta.xls (see Figure 57-3) can be used to estimate the parameters of a Beta distribution.

	B	C	D	E	F	G	H
1							
2							
3	Fit a beta						
4							
5	alpha	2.196262		mean	78.48647118		
6	beta	14.59335		sigma	47.96749188		
7	lower	0			Data		
8	upper	600			26.25660896		
9	mean	78.48647			91.84026718		
10	sigma	47.96749			66.54324532		
11	transformed mean	0.130811			53.89266014		
12	transformed var	0.006391			222.4365234		
13					72.0543623		
14					75.35727024		
15	Probability>=200 hours	0.020502			78.27422619		
16	Probability <=80 hours	0.583238			99.04375076		
17	Probability between 30 and 150 hours	0.771058			90.47598839		
18					47.00031281		
19					16.21513367		
20					117.2774076		
21					69.93505955		
22					50.69425106		

Figure 57-3   Determining probabilities with the Beta random variable.

Let's suppose that we think that the time needed to install dry wall in a building will be between 0 and 600 hours. These are our minimum and maximum values, entered in cells C7 and C8. The cell range F8:F19 contain the lengths of time needed to hang dry wall in 12 buildings of a similar size. In cell F5, I used the AVERAGE function to compute the mean time (78.49 hours) needed to drywall these 12 buildings. In cell F6, I used the STDEV function to determine the standard deviation (47.97 hours) of the time needed to drywall these buildings. Any choice of values of *alpha* and *beta* determine the shape of the Beta distribution's PDF and the mean and standard deviation for the corresponding Beta random variable. If we can choose values of *alpha* and *beta* to match the mean and standard deviation of the dry-wall installation times computed from our data, it seems reasonable that these values of *alpha* and *beta* will yield probabilities consistent with the observed data. After entering the mean and standard deviation of the dry-wall installation from our data in cells C9 and C10, our spreadsheet computes values for *alpha* (2.20) in cell C5 and *beta* (14.59) in cell C6 that ensure that the mean and standard deviation of the Beta random variable match the mean and standard deviation of our data.

The function *BETADIST(x, alpha, beta, lower, upper)* determines the probability that a Beta random variable ranging between *lower* and *upper*, with parameters *alpha* and *beta*, assumes a value less than or equal to *x*. We can now use the BETADIST function to determine probabilities of interest.

To compute the probability that hanging dry wall will take at least 200 hours, we can use the formula in cell C15, *1-BETADIST(200,alpha,beta,lower,upper)*. The result is 2.1 percent. This formula simply computes the probability that installing dry wall will take at least 200 hours as *1 – probability drywalling takes less than or equal to 200 hours*.

The probability that dry-wall installation will take at most 80 hours (58.3 percent) can be computed with the formula in cell C16, *BETADIST(80,alpha,beta,lower,upper)*. And to compute the probability that the task will take between 30 and 150 hours (77.1 percent), in cell C17 we use the formula *BETADIST(150,alpha,beta,lower,upper)-BETADIST(30,alpha,beta,lower,upper)*. This formula computes the probability that drywalling takes between 30 and 150 hours as the probability that drywalling takes less than or equal to 150 hours minus the probability that drywalling takes less than or equal to 30 hours. The difference between these probabilities counts only instances when drywalling takes between 30 and 150 hours.

Problems

The data for this chapter's problems is contained in the file CH57data.xls.

1. In the worksheet Problem 1, you are given data about the duration of a machine's lifetime.

    ❑   What is the probability that the machine will last at least 10 hours?

    ❑   What is the probability that the machine will last between 1 and 5 hours?

    ❑   What is the probability that the machine will fail within 6 hours?

2. You need to clean your house today. In the worksheet Problem 2, you are given data about how long it has taken to clean your house in the past. If you start cleaning at noon, what are the chances that you'll be finished in time to leave at 7 P.M. for a movie?

Introduction to Monte Carlo Simulation

- Who uses Monte Carlo simulation?

- What happens when I enter *=RAND()* in a cell?

- How can I simulate values of a discrete random variable?

- How can I simulate values of a normal random variable?

- How should a greeting card company determine how many cards to produce?

We would like to be able to accurately estimate the probabilities of uncertain events. For example, what is the probability that a new product's cash flows will have a positive net present value (NPV)? What is the riskiness of our investment portfolio? Monte Carlo simulation enables us to model situations that present uncertainty and play them out thousands of times on a computer.

Note The name *Monte Carlo simulation* comes from the fact that during the 1930s and 1940s, many computer simulations were performed to estimate the probability that the chain reaction needed for the atom bomb would work successfully. The physicists involved in this work were big fans of gambling, so they gave the simulations the code name Monte Carlo.

In the next five chapters, I'll provide some examples of how you can use Excel to perform Monte Carlo simulations.

Who uses Monte Carlo simulation?

Many companies use Monte Carlo simulation as an important tool for decision-making. Here are some examples.

- General Motors, Proctor and Gamble, and Eli Lilly use simulation to estimate both the average return and the riskiness of new products. At GM, this information is used by CEO Rick Waggoner to determine the products that come to market.

- GM uses simulation for activities such as forecasting net income for the corporation, predicting structural costs and purchasing costs, determining its susceptibility to different kinds of risk (such as interest rate changes and exchange rate fluctuations).

- Lilly uses simulation to determine the optimal plant capacity that should be built for each drug.

- Wall Street firms use simulation to price complex financial derivatives and determine the *Value at RISK* (VAR) of their investment portfolios.

- Proctor and Gamble uses simulation to model and optimally hedge foreign exchange risk.

- Sears uses simulation to determine how many units of each product line should be ordered from suppliers—for example, how many pairs of Dockers should be ordered this year.

- Simulation can be used to value "real options," such as the value of an option to expand, contract, or postpone a project.

- Financial planners use Monte Carlo simulation to determine optimal investment strategies for their clients' retirement.

What happens when I enter =RAND() in a cell?

When you enter the formula =RAND() in a cell, you get a number that is equally likely to assume any value between 0 and 1. Thus, around 25 percent of the time, you should get a number less than or equal to .25; around 10 percent of the time you should get a number that is at least .90, and so on. To demonstrate how the RAND function works, take a look at the file RandDemo.xls, shown in Figure 58-1.

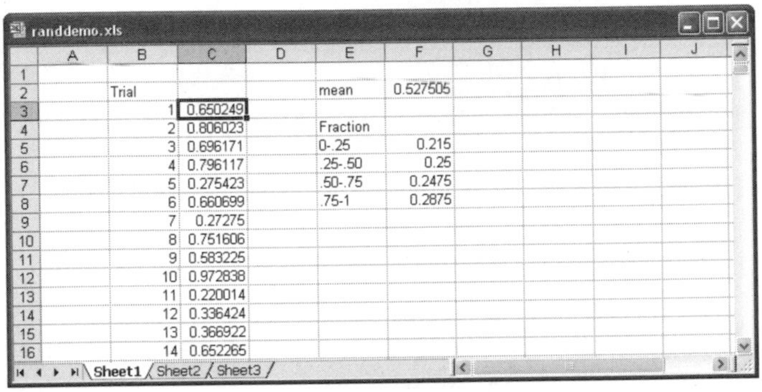

randdemo.xls

	A	B	C	D	E	F	G	H	I	J
1										
2		Trial			mean	0.527505				
3		1	0.650249							
4		2	0.806023		Fraction					
5		3	0.696171		0-.25	0.215				
6		4	0.796117		.25-.50	0.25				
7		5	0.275423		.50-.75	0.2475				
8		6	0.660699		.75-1	0.2875				
9		7	0.27275							
10		8	0.751606							
11		9	0.583225							
12		10	0.972838							
13		11	0.220014							
14		12	0.336424							
15		13	0.366922							
16		14	0.652265							

Sheet1 / Sheet2 / Sheet3

Figure 58-1 Demonstrating the *RAND* function.

> **Note** When, you open the file RandDemo.xls, you will not see the same random numbers shown in Figure 58-1. The RAND function always recalculates the numbers it generates when a spreadsheet is opened or new information is entered in the spreadsheet.

I copied from cell C3 to C4:C402 the formula *=RAND()*. I named the range C3:C402 *Data*. Then, in column F, I tracked the average of the 400 random numbers (cell F2) and used the COUNTIF function to determine the fractions that are between 0 and .25, .25 and .50, .50 and .75, and .75 and 1. When you press the F9 key, the random numbers are recalculated. Notice that the average of the 400 numbers is always near .5 and that around 25 percent of the results are in each interval of .25. These results are consistent with the definition of a random number. Also note that the values generated by RAND in different cells are independent. For example, if the random number generated in cell C3 is a large number (say .99), this tells us nothing about the values of the other random numbers generated.

How can I simulate values of a discrete random variable?

Suppose the demand for a calendar is governed by the following discrete random variable:

Demand	Probability
10,000	.10
20,000	.35
40,000	.3
60,000	.25

How can we have Excel play out, or simulate, this demand for calendars many times? The trick is to associate each possible value of the RAND function with a possible demand for calendars. The following assignment ensures that a demand of 10,000 will occur 10 percent of the time, and so on.

Demand	Random Number Assigned
10,000	Less than .10
20,000	Greater than or equal to .10, and less than .45
40,000	Greater than or equal to .45, and less than .75
60,000	Greater than or equal to .75

To demonstrate the simulation of demand, look at the file Discretesim.xls, shown in Figure 58-2.

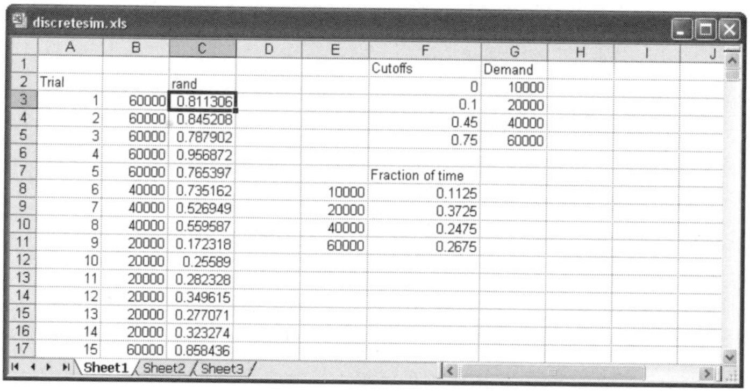

Figure 58-2 Demonstration of simulating a discrete random variable.

The key to our simulation is to use a random number to key a lookup from the table range F2:G5 (named *lookup*). Random numbers greater than or equal to 0 and less than .10 will yield a demand of 10,000; random numbers greater than or equal to .10 and less than .45 will yield a demand of 20,000; random numbers greater than or equal to .45 and less than .75 will yield a demand of 40,000; and random numbers greater than or equal to .75 will yield a demand of 60,000. I generated 400 random numbers by copying from C3 to C4:C402 the formula RAND(). Then I generated 400 trials or iterations of calendar demand by copying from B3 to B4:B402 the formula *VLOOKUP(C3,lookup,2)*. This formula ensures that any random number less than .10 generates a demand of 10,000; any random number between .10 and .45 generates a demand of 20,000, and so on. In the cell range F8:F11, I used the COUNTIF function to determine the fraction of our 400 iterations yielding each demand. Note that whenever you press F9 to recalculate the random numbers, the simulated probabilities are close to our assumed demand probabilities.

How can I simulate values of a normal random variable?

If you enter into any cell the formula *NORMINV(rand(), mu, sigma)*, you will generate a simulated value of a normal random variable having a mean *mu* and standard deviation *sigma*. I've illustrated this procedure in the file NormalSim.xls, shown in Figure 58-3

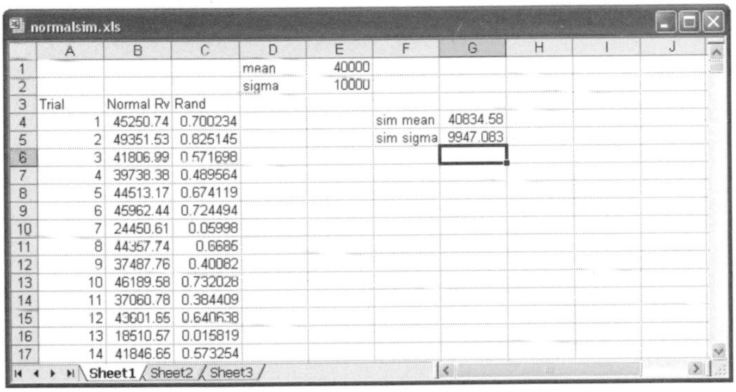
normalsim.xls

	A	B	C	D	E	F	G	H	I	J
1				mean	40000					
2				sigma	10000					
3	Trial	Normal Rv	Rand							
4	1	45250.74	0.700234			sim mean	40834.58			
5	2	49351.53	0.825145			sim sigma	9947.083			
6	3	41806.99	0.571698							
7	4	39738.38	0.489564							
8	5	44513.17	0.674119							
9	6	45962.44	0.724494							
10	7	24450.61	0.05998							
11	8	44357.74	0.6686							
12	9	37487.76	0.40082							
13	10	46189.58	0.732028							
14	11	37060.78	0.384409							
15	12	43601.65	0.640638							
16	13	18510.57	0.015819							
17	14	41846.65	0.573254							

Sheet1 / Sheet2 / Sheet3

Figure 58-3 Simulating a normal random variable.

Let's suppose we want to simulate 400 trials or iterations for a normal random variable with a mean of 40,000 and a standard deviation of 10,000. (I entered these values in cells E1 and E2 and named these cells *mean* and *sigma*, respectively.) Copying the formula *=RAND()* from C4 to C5:C403 generates 400 different random numbers. Copying from B4 to B5:B403 the formula *NORMINV(C4,mean,sigma)* generates 400 different trial values from a normal random variable with a mean of 40,000 and a standard deviation of 10,000. When we press the F9 key to recalculate the random numbers, the mean remains close to 40,000 and the standard deviation close to 10,000.

Essentially, for a random number *x*, the formula *NORMINV(p, mu, sigma)* generates the pth percentile of a normal random variable with a mean *mu* and a standard deviation *sigma*. For example, the random number .73 in cell C13 (see Figure 58-3) generates in cell B13 approximately the 73rd percentile of a normal random variable with a mean of 40,000 and a standard deviation of 10,000.

How should a greeting card company determine how many cards to produce?

In this section, I'll show how Monte Carlo simulation can be used as a tool to help businesses make better decisions. Suppose that the demand for a Valentine's Day card is governed by the following discrete random variable:

Demand	Probability
10,000	.10
20,000	.35
40,000	.3
60,000	.25

The greeting card sells for $4.00, and the variable cost of producing each card is $1.50. Leftover cards must be disposed of at a cost of $0.20 per card. How many cards should be printed?

Basically, we simulate each possible production quantity (10,000, 20,000, 40,000, or 60,000) many times (say, 1,000 iterations). Then we determine which order quantity yields the maximum average profit over the 1000 iterations. You can find the work for this section in the file Valentine.xls, shown in Figure 58-4. I've assigned the range names in cells B1:B11 to cells C1:C11. I've assigned the cell range G3:H6 the name *lookup*. Our sales price and cost parameters are entered in cells C4:C6.

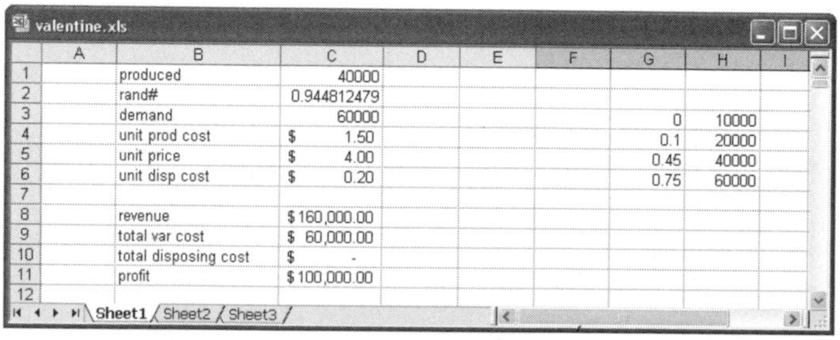

valentine.xls

	A	B	C	D	E	F	G	H
1		produced	40000					
2		rand#	0.944812479					
3		demand	60000				0	10000
4		unit prod cost	$ 1.50				0.1	20000
5		unit price	$ 4.00				0.45	40000
6		unit disp cost	$ 0.20				0.75	60000
7								
8		revenue	$ 160,000.00					
9		total var cost	$ 60,000.00					
10		total disposing cost	$ -					
11		profit	$ 100,000.00					
12								

Sheet1 / Sheet2 / Sheet3

Figure 58-4 Valentine's Day card simulation.

I then enter a trial production quantity (40,000 in this example) in cell C1. Next I create a random number in cell C2 with the formula *=RAND()*. As previously described, I simulate demand for the card in cell C3 with the formula

VLOOKUP(rand,lookup,2). (In the VLOOKUP formula, *rand* is the cell name assigned to cell C3, not the RAND function.)

The number of units sold is the smaller of our production quantity and demand. In cell C8, I compute our revenue with the formula *MIN(produced,demand)*unit_price*. In cell C9, I compute total production cost with the formula *produced*unit_prod_cost*.

If we produce more cards than are demanded, the number of units left over equals production minus demand; otherwise no units are left over. We compute our disposal cost in cell C10 with the formula *unit_disp_cost*IF(produced>demand,produced-demand,0)*. Finally, in cell C11, we compute our profit as *revenue-total_var_cost-total_disposing_cost*.

We would like an efficient way to press F9 many (say, 1,000 times) for each production quantity and tally up our expected profit for each production quantity. This situation is one in which a two-way data table comes to our rescue. (See Chapter 15 for details about data tables.) The data table I used in this example is shown in Figure 58-5.

	A	B	C	D	E
13	mean	25000	44960	58866	42312
14	st dev	0	13655.21383	48602.36	72270.09
15	100000	10000	20000	40000	60000
16	1	25000	50000	16000	66000
17	2	25000	50000	-26000	66000
18	3	25000	8000	100000	-18000
19	4	25000	50000	100000	-18000
20	5	25000	50000	100000	150000
21	6	25000	50000	100000	-18000
22	7	25000	50000	100000	-18000
23	8	25000	50000	100000	66000
24	9	25000	50000	100000	-18000
25	10	25000	50000	100000	66000
26	11	25000	50000	100000	66000
27	12	25000	50000	100000	-18000
28	13	25000	50000	16000	-60000
29	14	25000	50000	16000	-60000
30	15	25000	50000	16000	-18000
31	16	25000	50000	100000	66000
32	17	25000	8000	100000	150000

Figure 58-5   Two-way data table for greeting card simulation.

In the cell range A16:A1015, I entered the numbers 1-1000 (corresponding to our 1000 trials). One easy way to create these values is to enter a 1 in cell A16, select the cell, and then click Edit, Fill Series. In the Series dialog box, shown in Figure 58-6, enter a step value of 1 and a stop value of 1000. Select Columns, and then click OK. The numbers 1 through 1000 will be entered in column A starting in cell A16.

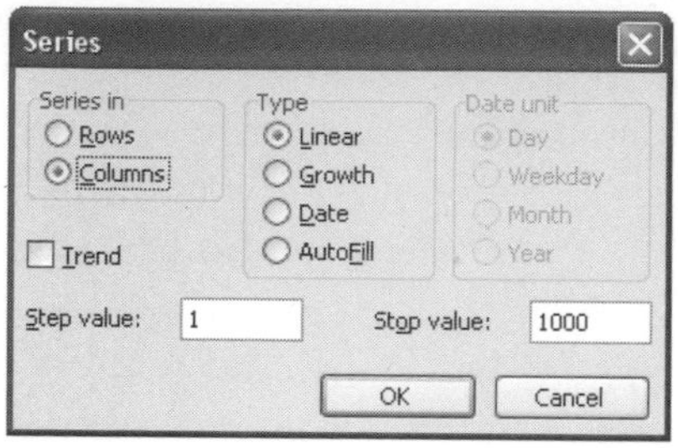

Figure 58-6 Use the Series dialog box to fill in the trial numbers 1 through 1000.

Next we enter our possible production quantities (10,000, 20,000, 40,000, 60,000) in cells B15:E15. We want to calculate profit for each trial number (1 through 1000) and each production quantity. We refer to the formula for profit (calculated in cell C11) in the upper left cell of our data table (A15) by entering *=C11*.

We are now ready to trick Excel into simulating 1000 iterations of demand for each production quantity. Select the table range (A15:E1014), and then choose Data, Table. To set up a two-way data table, we select any blank cell (we chose cell I14) as our column input cell and choose our production quantity (cell C1) as the row input cell. After clicking OK, Excel simulates 1000 demand values for each order quantity.

To illustrate why this works, consider the values placed by the data table in the cell range C16:C1015. For each of these cells, Excel will use a value of 20,000 in cell C1. In C16, the column input cell value of 1 is placed in a blank cell and the random number in cell C2 recalculates. The corresponding profit is then recorded in cell C16. Then the column cell input value of 2 is placed in a blank cell, and the random number in C2 again recalculates. The corresponding profit is entered in cell C17.

By copying from cell B13 to C13:E13 the formula *AVERAGE(B16:B1015)*, we compute average simulated profit for each production quantity. By copying the formula *STDEV (B16:B1015)* from cell B14 to C14:E14, we compute the standard deviation of our simulated profits for each order quantity. Each time we press F9, 1000 iterations of demand are simulated for each order quantity. Producing 40,000 cards always yields the largest expected profit. Therefore, it appears as if producing 40,000 cards is the proper decision.

The Impact of Risk on Our Decision   If we produced 20,000 cards instead of 40,000 cards, our expected profit drops approximately 22 percent, but our risk (as measured by the standard deviation of profit) drops almost 73 percent. Therefore, if we are extremely risk averse, producing 20,000 cards might be the right decision. By the way, producing 10,000 cards always has a standard deviation of zero cards because if we produce 10,000 cards, we will always sell all of them and have none left over.

Note   In this worksheet, I set the Calculation option to Automatic Except For Tables. (See the Calculation tab on the Options dialog box.) This setting ensures that our data table will not recalculate unless we press F9, which is a good idea because a large data table will slow down your work if it recalculates every time you type something into your spreadsheet. Note that in this example, whenever you press F9, the mean profit will change. This happens because each time you press F9, a different sequence of 1000 random numbers is used to generate demands for each order quantity.

Confidence Interval for Mean Profit   A natural question to ask in this situation is Into what interval are we 95 percent sure the true mean profit will fall? This interval is called the *95 percent confidence interval for mean profit.* A 95 percent confidence interval for the mean of any simulation output is computed by the following formula:

$$Mean\,Profit \pm \frac{1.96 * profit\,std.dev.}{\sqrt{number\,iterations}}$$

In cell J11, I computed the lower limit for the 95 percent confidence interval on mean profit when 40,000 calendars are produced with the formula *D13-1.96*D14/SQRT(1000)*. In cell J12, I computed the upper limit for our 95 percent confidence interval with the formula *D13+1.96*D14/SQRT(1000)*. These calculations are shown in Figure 58-7.

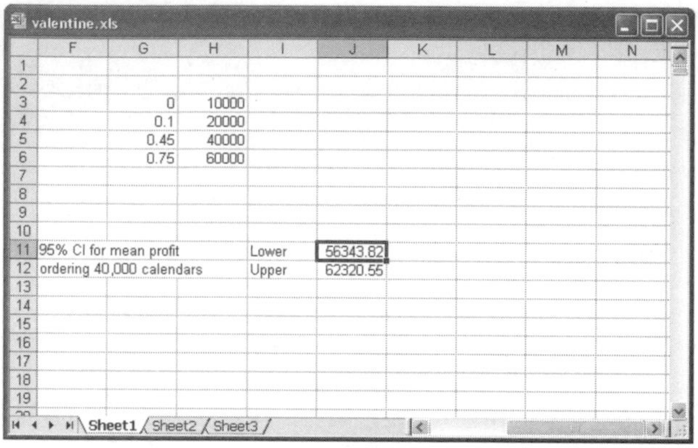

Figure 58-7   95 percent confidence interval for mean profit when 40,000 calendars are ordered.

We are 95 percent sure that our mean profit when 40,000 calendars are ordered is between $56,344 and $62,321.

Problems

1. A GMC dealer believes that demand for 2005 Envoys will be nor-mally distributed with a mean of 200 and standard deviation of 30. His cost of receiving an Envoy is $25,000, and he sells an Envoy for $40,000. Half of all leftover Envoys can be sold for $30,000. She is considering ordering 200, 220, 240, 260, 280, or 300 Envoys. How many should she order?

2. A small supermarket is trying to determine how many copies of *People* magazine they should order each week. They believe their demand for *People* is governed by the following discrete random variable:

Demand	Probability
15	.10
20	.20
25	.30
30	.25
35	.15

The supermarket pays $1.00 for each copy of *People* and sells each copy for $1.95. They can return each unsold copy of *People* for $0.50. How many copies of *People* should the store order?

59

Calculating an Optimal Bid

- How do I simulate a binomial random variable?
- How can I determine whether a continuous random variable should be modeled as a normal random variable?
- How can I use simulation to determine the optimal bid for a construction project?

When bidding against competitors on a project, the two major sources of uncertainty are the number of competitors and the bid submitted by each competitor. If you bid too high, you'll make a lot of money on each project but you'll get very few projects. If you bid too low, you'll work on lots of projects but make very little money on each. The optimal bid is somewhere in the middle. Monte Carlo simulation provides a useful tool for determining the bid that maximizes expected profit.

How do I simulate a binomial random variable?
The function *CRITBINOM(n, p, rand())* simulates the number of successes in *n* trials, each of which has a probability of success equal to *p*. As shown in the file Binomialsim.xls (see Figure 59-1), when you press F9, the formula *CRITBINOM(100,0.9,D3)* entered in cell C3 simulates the number of free throws that Steve Nash (a 90-percent foul shooter) makes in 100 attempts. The formula *CRITBINOM(100,0.5,D4)* in cell C4 simulates the number of heads tossed in 100 tosses of a fair coin. In cell C5, the formula *CRITBINOM(3,0.4,D5)* simulates the number of competitors entering the market during a year in which there are three possible entrants and each competitor is assumed to have a 40 percent chance of entering the market. Of course, in D3:D5, I've entered the formula *=RAND()*.

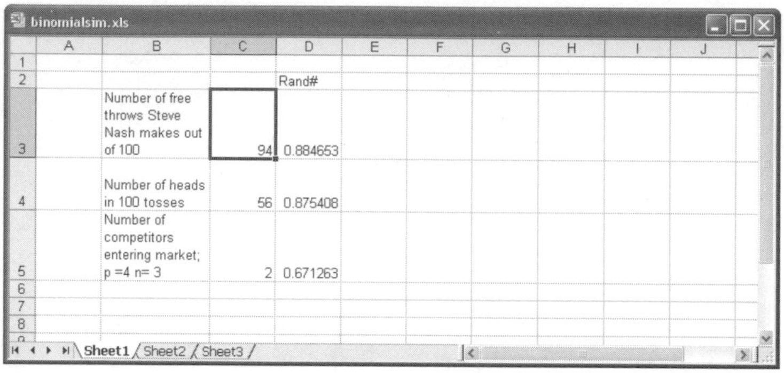

Figure 59-1 Examples of simulating a binomial random variable.

How can I determine whether a continuous random variable should be modeled as a normal random variable?

Suppose we are bidding on a construction project that we estimate will cost $25,000 to complete. If we assume that each competitor could choose any amount as their bid, we should model each competitor's bid as a continuous random variable. If each competitor's bid is limited to a finite number of values, we should model each competitor's bid as a discrete random variable. To determine whether a normal random variable is appropriate, we first determine the mean bid. For a normal random variable, the mean is also the most likely value (remember that the probability density function—PDF—for the normal peaks at the mean).

Let's suppose we feel that the most likely bid by a competitor is $50,000. Recall that the normal PDF is symmetric about its mean. Therefore, to determine whether a normal random variable can be used to model a competitor's bid, we need to test for symmetry about the bid's mean. If the competitor's bid exhibits symmetry about the mean of $50,000, bids of $40,000 and $60,000, $45,000 and $55,000, and so on should be approximately equally likely. If the symmetry assumption seems reasonable, we can then model each competitor's bid as a normal random variable with a mean of $50,000.

How might we estimate the standard deviation of each competitor's bid? Recall from the rule of thumb discussed in Chapter 35 that data sets with symmetric histograms have roughly 95 percent of their data within two standard deviations of the mean. Similarly, a normal random variable has a 95 percent probability of being within two standard deviations of its mean. Suppose that we are 95 percent sure that a competitor's bid will be between $30,000 and $70,000. This implies that *2*(standard deviation of competitor's bid) = $20,000*, or the standard deviation of a competitor's bid equals $10,000.

Assuming the symmetry assumption is reasonable, we could now simulate a competitor's bid with the formula *NORMINV(rand(), 50000, 10000)*. (See

Chapter 58 for details about how to model normal random variables using the NORMINV function.)

How can I use simulation to determine the optimal bid for a construction project?

Let's assume that we're bidding on a construction project that will cost us $25,000 to complete. It costs us $1,000 to prepare our bid. There are six potential competitors, and we estimate that there is a 50 percent chance that each competitor will bid on the project. If a competitor places a bid, their bid is assumed to follow a normal random variable with a mean equal to $50,000 and a standard deviation equal to $10,000. Also suppose we are only considering bids that are exact multiples of $5,000. What should we bid to maximize expected profit? Remember, the low bid wins! Our work is in the file Bidsim.xls, shown in Figures 59-2 and 59-3.

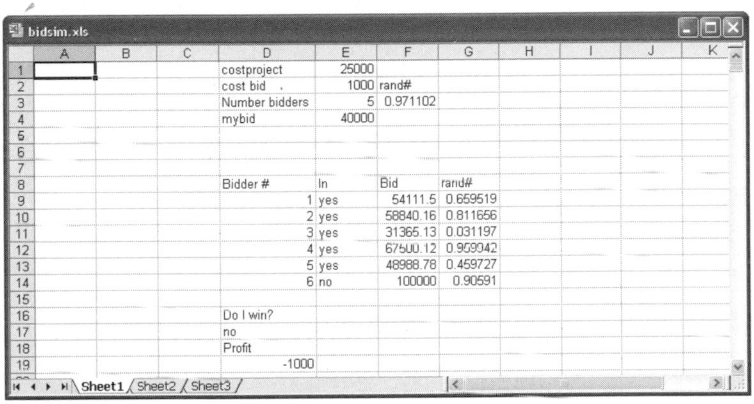

bidsim.xls

	D	E	F	G
1	costproject	25000		
2	cost bid .	1000	rand#	
3	Number bidders	5	0.971102	
4	mybid	40000		
5				
6				
7				
8	Bidder #	In	Bid	rand#
9	1	yes	54111.5	0.659519
10	2	yes	58840.16	0.811656
11	3	yes	31365.13	0.031197
12	4	yes	67500.12	0.959042
13	5	yes	48988.78	0.459727
14	6	no	100000	0.90591
15				
16	Do I win?			
17	no			
18	Profit			
19	-1000			

Sheet1 / Sheet2 / Sheet3

Figure 59-2 Bidding simulation model.

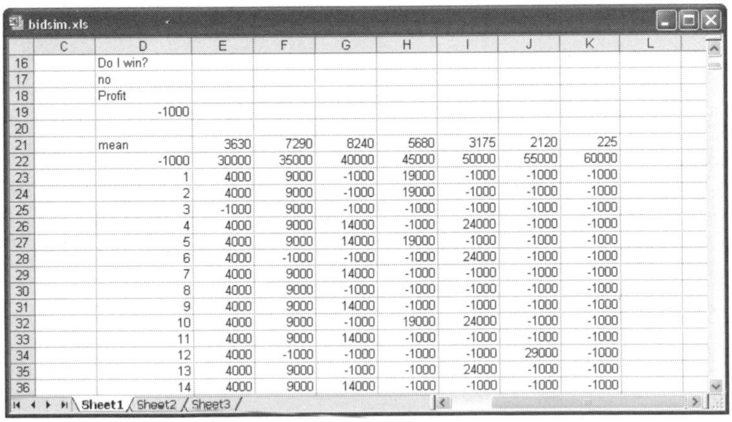

bidsim.xls

	D	E	F	G	H	I	J	K
16	Do I win?							
17	no							
18	Profit							
19	-1000							
20								
21	mean	3630	7290	8240	5680	3175	2120	225
22	-1000	30000	35000	40000	45000	50000	55000	60000
23	1	4000	9000	-1000	19000	-1000	-1000	-1000
24	2	4000	9000	-1000	19000	-1000	-1000	-1000
25	3	-1000	9000	-1000	-1000	-1000	-1000	-1000
26	4	4000	9000	14000	-1000	24000	-1000	-1000
27	5	4000	9000	14000	19000	-1000	-1000	-1000
28	6	4000	-1000	-1000	-1000	24000	-1000	-1000
29	7	4000	9000	14000	-1000	-1000	-1000	-1000
30	8	4000	9000	-1000	-1000	-1000	-1000	-1000
31	9	4000	9000	14000	-1000	-1000	-1000	-1000
32	10	4000	9000	-1000	19000	24000	-1000	-1000
33	11	4000	9000	14000	-1000	-1000	-1000	-1000
34	12	4000	-1000	-1000	-1000	-1000	29000	-1000
35	13	4000	9000	-1000	-1000	24000	-1000	-1000
36	14	4000	9000	14000	-1000	-1000	-1000	-1000

Sheet1 / Sheet2 / Sheet3

Figure 59-3 Bidding simulation data table.

Our strategy is as follows:

- Generate the number of bidders.

- For each potential bidder who actually bids, use the normal random variable to model their bid. If a potential bidder does not bid, we assign them a large bid (say $100,000) to ensure that they do not win the bidding.

- Determine whether we are the low bidder.

- If we are the low bidder, we earn a profit equal to our bid, less project cost, less $1,000 (the cost of making the bid). If we are not the low bidder, we lose the cost of the bid, $1,000.

- Use a two-way data table to simulate each possible bid (say $30,000, $35,000, … $60,000) one thousand times and choose the bid with the largest expected profit.

To begin, I've assigned the names in the cell range D1:D4 to the range E1:E4. We determine in cell E3 the number of bidders with the formula *CRITBI-NOM(6,0.5,F3)*. Cell F3 contains the *=RAND()* formula. Next we determine which of our potential bidders actually bid by copying from E9 to E10:E14 the formula *IF(D9<=Number_bidders,"yes","no")*.

We then generate a bid for each bidder (nonbidders are assigned a bid of $100,000) by copying from cell F9 to F10:F14 the formula *IF(E9="yes",NORM-INV(G9,50000,10000),100000)*. Each cell in the cell range G9:G14 contains the *=RAND()* function. In cell D17, I determine whether I am the low bidder and win the project with the formula *IF(mybid<=MIN(F9:F14),"yes","no")*. In cell D19, I compute my profit with the formula *IF(D17="yes",mybid-costproject-cost_bid,-cost_bid)*, recognizing that I only receive the amount of the bid and pay project costs if I win the bid.

Now we can use a two-way data table (shown in Figure 59-3) to simulate one thousand bids between $30,000 and $60,000. We copy our profit to cell D22 by entering the formula *=D19*. Then we select the table range D22:K1022. We choose Data, Table to specify the input values for the data table. Our column input cell is any blank cell in the spreadsheet, and our row input cell is E4 (the location of our bid). Clicking OK in the Table dialog box simulates the profit from each bid 1000 times.

Copying from E21 to F21:K21 the formula *AVERAGE(E23:E1022)* calculates the mean profit for each bid. Each time we press F9, we see that our mean profit for one thousand trials is maximized by bidding $40,000.

Problems

1. How would our optimal bid change if there were 12 competitors?

2. Suppose we are bidding for an oil well that we believe will yield $40 million (including the cost of developing and mining the oil) in profits. Three competitors are bidding against us, and each competitor's bid is assumed to follow a normal random variable with a mean of $30 million and a standard deviation of $4 million. What should we bid (within $1 million)?

3. A commonly used continuous random variable is the uniform random variable. A uniform random variable—written as $U(a, b)$—is equally likely to assume any value between two given numbers a and b. Explain why the formula $a + (b-a)*RAND()$ can be used to simulate $U(a,b)$.

4. Superior investor Peter Finch is bidding to take over a biotech company. The company is equally likely to be worth any amount between $0 and $200 per share. The company itself knows its true value. Peter is such a good investor that the market will immediately estimate the firm's value to equal 50 percent more than the firm's true value. What should Peter bid per share for this company?

60

Simulating Stock Prices and Asset Allocation Modeling

■ I recently bought 100 shares of GE. What is the probability that during the next year this investment will return more than 10 percent?

■ I'm trying to determine how to allocate my investment portfolio between stocks, Treasury bills, and bonds. What asset allocation over a 5-year planning horizon will yield an expected return of at least 10 percent and minimize risk?

The last few years have shown us that future returns on our investments are highly uncertain. In this chapter, I'll explain a relatively simple approach that can be used to assess uncertainty in future investment returns. This approach is based on the idea of *bootstrapping*. Essentially, bootstrapping simulates future investment returns by assuming that the future will be similar to the past. For example, if we want to simulate the stock price of GE in one year, we can assume that each month's percentage change in price is equally likely to be one of, say, the last 60 months' percentage change in the value of the stock. This method allows us to easily generate thousands of scenarios for the future value of our investments. In addition to scenarios that assume that future variability and average returns will be similar to the recent past, we can easily adjust bootstrapping to reflect a view that future returns on investments will be less or more favorable than the recent past.

After we've generated future scenarios for investment returns, it's a simple matter to use the Excel Solver to work out the asset allocation problem—that is, how should we allocate our investments to attain the level of expected return we want with minimum risk?

The following two examples will demonstrate the simplicity and power of the bootstrapping approach.

I recently bought 100 shares of GE. What is the probability that during the next year this investment will return more than 10 percent?

Let's suppose GE stock is currently selling for $28.50. We have data for the monthly returns on GE (as well as Microsoft and Intel) for the months between August 1997 and July 2002. You can find the data in the file Gesim.xls, shown in Figure 60-1. For example, in the month ending on August 2, 2002 (this is basically July 2002), GE lost 12.1 percent. These returns include dividends (if any) paid by each company.

	A	B	C	D	E	F	G	H
1								
2								
3			mean	0.014746	0.006237	0.008828		
4		Code		MSFT	INTC	GE		
5		1	8/2/2002	-0.08316	-0.15397	-0.12112		
6		2	7/2/2002	-0.12285	0.028493	0.108434		
7		3	6/2/2002	0.074445	-0.33853	-0.06139		
8		4	5/2/2002	-0.02583	-0.03464	-0.01276		
9		5	4/2/2002	-0.13348	-0.05894	-0.15658		
10		6	3/2/2002	0.033768	0.064867	-0.02849		
11		7	2/2/2002	-0.08429	-0.18514	0.041088		
12		8	1/2/2002	-0.03834	0.114295	-0.07314		
13		9	12/1/2002	0.031771	-0.03709	0.045898		
14		10	11/1/2002	0.104213	0.337433	0.057167		
15		11	10/1/2002	0.136408	0.194417	-0.02102		
16		12	9/1/2002	-0.10307	-0.26889	-0.08653		
17		13	8/1/2002	-0.13809	-0.06181	-0.05957		
18		14	7/1/2002	-0.09329	0.019172	-0.10944		
19		15	6/1/2002	0.055218	0.082654	0		
20		16	5/1/2002	0.021107	-0.12601	0.009701		

Figure 60-1   GE, Microsoft, and Intel stock data.

The price that GE stock will have in one year is uncertain, so how can we get an idea about the range of variation in the price GE might have one year from now? The bootstrapping approach simply estimates a return on GE during each of the next 12 months by assuming that the return during each month is equally likely to be any of the returns for the 60 months listed. In other words, the return on GE next month is equally likely to be any of the numbers in the cell range F5:F64. To implement this idea, we use the function RAND-

BETWEEN(1,60) to choose a "scenario" for each of the next 12 months. For example, if this function returns 7 for next month, we use the GE return in cell F11 (4.1 percent), which is the seventh cell in the range, as next month's return. The results are shown in Figure 60-2. (You'll see different values because the RANDBETWEEN function recalculates random values when you open the spreadsheet.)

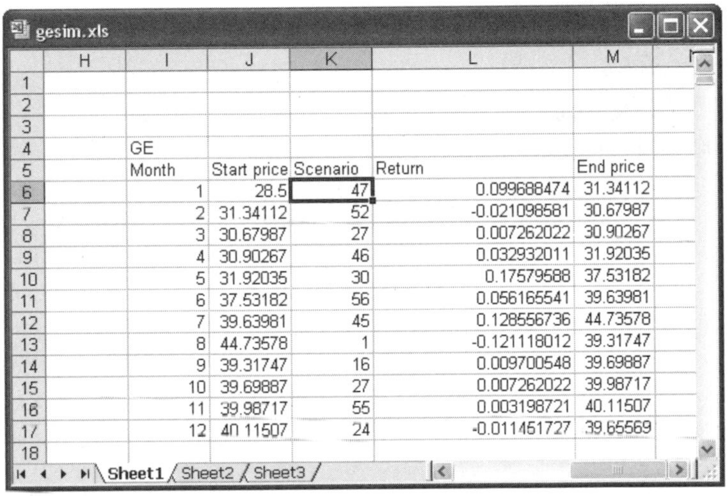
gesim.xls

	H	I	J	K	L	M
1						
2						
3						
4		GE				
5		Month	Start price	Scenario	Return	End price
6		1	28.5	47	0.099688474	31.34112
7		2	31.34112	52	-0.021098581	30.67987
8		3	30.67987	27	0.007262022	30.90267
9		4	30.90267	46	0.032932011	31.92035
10		5	31.92035	30	0.17579588	37.53182
11		6	37.53182	56	0.056165541	39.63981
12		7	39.63981	45	0.128556736	44.73578
13		8	44.73578	1	-0.121118012	39.31747
14		9	39.31747	16	0.009700548	39.69887
15		10	39.69887	27	0.007262022	39.98717
16		11	39.98717	55	0.003198721	40.11507
17		12	40.11507	24	-0.011451727	39.65569
18						

Sheet1 / Sheet2 / Sheet3

Figure 60-2 Simulation of GE price in one year.

To begin, we enter GE's current price ($28.50) in cell J6. Then we generate a scenario for each of the next 12 months by copying from K6 to K7:K17 the formula *RANDBETWEEN(1,60)*. Next we use a lookup table to obtain the GE return based on our scenario. To do this, simply copy from L6 to L7:L17 the formula *VLOOKUP(K6,lookup,5)*. As the formula indicates, the range B5:F64 is named *Lookup*, and the returns for GE are in the fifth column of the lookup range. In the scenarios shown in Figure 60-2, we see, for example, that our return for GE two months into the future is equal to our 5/1/1998 data point (a -2 percent return).

Copying from M6 to M7:M17 the formula *(1+L6)*J6* determines each month's ending GE price. The formula takes the form *(1+ month's return)*(GE's beginning price)*. Finally, copying from J7 to J8:J17 the formula *=M6* computes the beginning price for each month as equal to the previous month's ending price.

We can now use a data table to generate 1000 scenarios for GE's price in one year and the one-year percentage return on our investment. The data table is shown in Figure 60-3. In cell J19, we copy our ending price with the formula *=M17*. In cell K19, we enter the formula *(M17-$J$6)/$J$6* to compute our one-year return as *(Ending GE price – Beginning GE price)/Beginning GE price*.

	H	I	J	K	L	M	N	O
18			End Price	End Return				
19			37.18515	0.304742004				
20		1	28.66472	0.005779684	Prob lose money	0.394		
21		2	27.25956	-0.043524344	Prob make more than 10%	0.457		
22		3	39.39399	0.382245214	Make between 0 and 10%	0.149		
23		4	36.80815	0.291514146	Lose between 0 and 10%	0.151		
24		5	44.50568	0.56160267	Lose More than 10%	0.243		
25		6	31.08327	0.090641093				
26		7	33.31544	0.168962763				
27		8	26.72289	-0.062354563				
28		9	32.34277	0.134834125				
29		10	25.53561	-0.104013783				
30		11	29.03599	0.018806753				
31		12	26.63438	-0.065460361				
32		13	52.66948	0.848052069				
33		14	30.29268	0.062901124				
34		15	22.33703	-0.216244558				

Figure 60-3   Data table for GE simulation.

Next we select our table range (J19:K1019) and select Data, Table. We set up a one-way data table by selecting a blank cell as our column input cell. After we click OK in the Table dialog box, we have generated 1000 scenarios for GE's stock price in one year. (The calculation option for this workbook has been set to Automatic Except For Tables on the Calculation tab in the Options dialog box. You need to press F9 if you want to see the simulated prices change.)

In cells M20:M24, I used the COUNTIF function (see Chapter 19 for details about this function) to summarize the range of returns that can occur in one year. For example, in cell M20, I computed the probability that we will lose money in one year with the formula *COUNTIF(returns,"<0")/1000*. (I named the range containing our 1000 simulated returns as *Returns*.) Our simulation indicates that based on the 1997–2002 data, there is roughly a 39 percent chance that our GE investment will lose money during the next year. Similarly, we find the following results:

- There is a 46 percent probability we will make more than 10 percent.

- There is a 15 percent probability that we will make between 0 and 10 percent.

- There is a 15 percent chance that we will lose between 0 and 10 percent.

- There is a 24 percent chance that we will lose more than 10 percent.

- Average return for the next year will be approximately 11 percent.

Many pundits believe that future stock returns will not be as good as the recent past. Suppose we feel that in the next year, GE will perform 5 percent worse per year on average than it performed during the 1997–2002 period for which we have data. We can easily incorporate this assumption into our

simulation by changing the final price formula for GE in cell M17 to
(1+L17)*J17-0.05*J6. This simply reduces our ending GE price by 5 percent of
its initial price, which will reduce our returns for the next year by 5 percent.
You can see these results in the file GesimLess5.xls, shown in Figure 60-4.

	L	M	N	O	P	Q	R	
19	Mean	0.061264						
20	Prob lose money	0.478						
21	Prob make more than 10%	0.39						
22	Make between 0 and 10%	0.132						
23	Lose between 0 and 10%	0.143						
24	Lose More than 10%	0.335						

Figure 60-4 Pessimistic view of the future.

Note that we now estimate that there is a 48 percent chance that the price
of GE stock will decrease during the next year. Our average is not exactly 5 percent lower than the previous simulation because each time we run 1000 iterations, the simulated values change.

I'm trying to determine how to allocate my investment portfolio between stocks, Treasury bills, and bonds. What asset allocation over a 5-year planning horizon will yield an expected return of at least 10 percent and minimize risk?

A key decision made by individuals, mutual fund managers, and other investors
is how to allocate assets between different asset classes given the future uncertainty about returns for these asset classes. A reasonable approach to asset allocation is to use bootstrapping to generate 1000 simulated values for the future
values of each asset class and then use Excel's Solver to determine an asset allocation that yields an expected return and minimizes risk. As an example, suppose we are given annual returns on stocks, Treasury bills, and bonds during
the period 1972–2001. We are investing for a 5-year planning horizon, and
based on the historical data, we want to know what asset allocation yields a
minimum risk (as measured by standard deviation) of annual returns and yields
an annual expected return of at least 10 percent. You can see this data in the file
Assetallsim.xls, shown in Figure 60-5. (Not all the data is shown.)

assetallsim.xls

	A	B	C	D	E	F
7	Year	Stocks	T.Bills	T.Bonds		
8	1972	18.76%	4.01%	2.82%		
9	1973	-14.31%	5.07%	3.66%		
10	1974	-25.90%	7.45%	1.99%		
11	1975	37.00%	7.15%	3.61%		
12	1976	23.83%	5.44%	15.98%		
13	1977	-6.98%	4.35%	1.29%		
14	1978	6.51%	6.07%	-0.78%		
15	1979	18.52%	9.08%	0.67%		
16	1980	31.74%	12.04%	-2.99%		
17	1981	-4.70%	15.49%	8.20%		
18	1982	20.42%	10.85%	32.81%		
19	1983	22.34%	7.94%	3.20%		
20	1984	6.15%	9.00%	13.73%		
21	1985	31.24%	8.06%	25.71%		
22	1986	18.49%	7.10%	24.28%		
23	1987	5.81%	5.53%	-4.96%		
24	1988	16.54%	5.77%	8.22%		
25	1989	31.48%	8.07%	17.69%		
26	1990	-3.06%	7.63%	6.24%		

Sheet1 / Sheet2 / Sheet3

Figure 60-5 Historical returns on stocks, bonds, and T-bills.

To begin, we use bootstrapping to generate 1000 simulated values for stocks, T-bills, and bonds in five years. We assume that each asset class has a current price of $1. (See Figure 60-6.)

assetallsim.xls

	G	H	I	J	K	L	M	N	O
7									
8						2	3	4	
9	Year	Stock value	Bill value	Bond value	Scenario	End stock	End bill	End bond	
10	1	1	1	1	1976	1.2383	1.0544	1.1598	
11	2	1.2383	1.0544	1.1598	1990	1.200408	1.134851	1.232172	
12	3	1.200408	1.13485072	1.232172	1991	1.563291	1.21134	1.416997	
13	4	1.563291	1.211339659	1.416997	1974	1.158399	1.301584	1.445195	
14	5	1.158399	1.301584463	1.445195	1978	1.233811	1.380591	1.433923	
15			5 yr stock	5 year bill	5 yr bond				
16			1.23381067	1.380591	1.433923				
17		1	1.244557338	1.567836	1.738831				
18		2	1.337944133	1.344457	1.460524				
19		3	1.22054568	1.361073	1.551765				
20		4	0.913847764	1.476809	1.250252				
21		5	2.608751815	1.51106	2.966516				
22		6	2.029491225	1.398894	1.043079				
23		7	3.197047916	1.346503	1.571979				
24		8	2.04480827	1.266579	1.861445				

Sheet1 / Sheet2 / Sheet3

Figure 60-6 Simulated 5-year returns on stocks, T-bills, and bonds.

To begin, we enter an initial unit price for each asset class of $1 in the cell range H10:J10. Next, by copying from K10 to K11:K14 the formula *RANDBETWEEN(1972,2001)*, we generate a "scenario" for each of the next 5 years. For example, for the data shown, next year will be similar to 1976, the year after, similar to 1990, and so on. Copying from L10 to L10:N14 the formula *H10*(1+VLOOKUP($K10,lookup,L$8))* generates each year's ending value for each asset class. For stocks, for example, this formula computes the following:

```
(Ending year t stock value) = (Beginning year t stock value)*(1 + Year t stock
return)
```

Copying the formula *=L10* from H11 to H11:L14 computes the value for each asset class at the beginning of each successive year.

We can now use a one-way data table to generate 1000 scenarios of the value of stocks, T-bills, and bonds in 5 years. Begin by copying the ending year 5 value for each asset class to cells I16:K16. Next, select our table range (H16:K1015), and then click Data, Table. Use any blank cell as the column input cell to set up a one-way data table. After clicking OK in the Table dialog box, we obtain 1000 simulated values for the value of stocks, T-bills, and bonds in 5 years. It is important to note that our approach models the fact that stock, T-bills, and bonds do not move independently. In each of our 5 years, the stock, T-bill, and bond returns are always chosen from the same row of data. This enables the bootstrapping approach to reflect the interdependence of returns on these asset classes that has been exhibited during the recent past. (See Problem 7 at the end of this chapter for concrete evidence that bootstrapping properly models the interdependence between the returns on our three asset classes.)

We are now ready to find the optimal asset allocation, which I've calculated in the file Assetallocationopt.xls, shown in Figure 60-7. To start, I copy the 1000 simulated 5-year asset values to a blank worksheet and paste them into the cell range C4:F1003. In cells C2:E2, I enter trial fractions of our assets allocated to stocks, bonds, and T-bills, respectively. In cell F2, I add these asset allocation fractions with the formula *SUM(C2:E2)*. Later, I'll add the constraint *F2 = 1* to our Solver model, which will ensure that we invest 100 percent of our money in one of the three asset classes.

	A	B	C	D	E	F	G	H	I	J	K
1			stock	bill	bond	total					
2			0.452984	0.362552	0.184464	1					
3		Iteration#	5 yr stock	5 yr bill	5 yr bond	final value	annual return		mean	0.1	
4		1	2.415411	1.35984	1.108607	1.791653	0.12370102		stdev	0.040506	
5		2	1.603314	1.33449	1.702971	1.524234	0.087953549				
6		3	1.03961	1.386724	1.087423	1.174227	0.032652262				
7		4	1.070247	1.442663	1.295489	1.246816	0.045106348				
8		5	1.984675	1.372362	1.504565	1.674116	0.108554718				
9		6	2.590193	1.35308	1.562307	1.952067	0.14313876				
10		7	2.182375	1.490447	1.915396	1.882267	0.134844236				
11		8	2.985769	1.399561	1.107142	2.064147	0.155974163				
12		9	1.461413	1.316099	1.734171	1.459044	0.078483862				
13		10	1.393477	1.524212	1.397079	1.44154	0.075883679				
14		11	1.72976	1.325904	1.344169	1.512213	0.086232064				

Figure 60-7   Optimal asset allocation model.

Next we want to determine our final portfolio value for each scenario. To make this calculation, we can use a formula such as *(Final portfolio value) = (Final value of stocks) + (Final value of T-bills) + (Final value of bonds)*. Copying from cell F4 to F5:F1003 the formula *SUMPRODUCT(C4:E4, $C$2:$E$2)* determines our final asset position for each scenario.

We now want to determine the annual return over the 5-year simulated period for each scenario we generated. Note that $(1+ Annual\ return)^5 = (Final\ portfolio\ value)/(Initial\ portfolio\ value)$. Because the initial portfolio value is just $1, this tells us that $Annual\ return = (Final\ portfolio\ value)^{1/5} - 1$.

Therefore, by copying from cell G4 to G5:G1003 the formula *(F4/1)^(1/5)-1*, we compute the annual return for each scenario during our 5-year simulated period. After naming the range G4:G1003 (which contains the simulated annual returns) as *Returns,* I computed the average annual return in cell J3 with the formula *AVERAGE(returns)* and the standard deviation of our annual returns in cell J4 with the formula *STDEV(returns)*.

Now we're ready to use Solver to determine the set of allocation weights that yields an expected annual return of at least 10 percent and minimizes the standard deviation of our annual returns. The Solver Parameters dialog box set up to perform this calculation is shown in Figure 60-8.

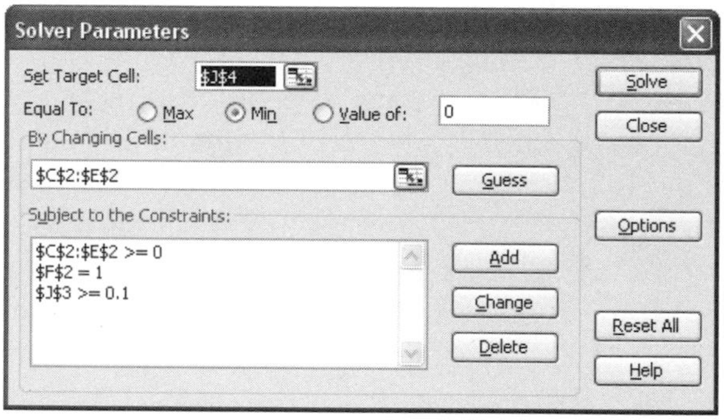

Figure 60-8 The Solver Parameters dialog box set up for our asset allocation model.

- We try to minimize the standard deviation of our annual portfolio return (cell J4).

- Our changing cells are our asset allocation weights (cells C2:E2).

- We must allocate 100 percent of our money to the three asset classes (F2 = 1).

- Our expected annual return must be at least 10 percent (J3>=.1).

■   We assume that no short sales are allowed, which is modeled by forcing the fraction of our money in each asset class to be nonnegative, (C2:E2)>=0.

We find that the minimum risk asset allocation is 45.3 percent stocks, 36.3 percent T-bills, and 18.4 percent bonds. This portfolio yields an expected annual return of 10 percent and an annual standard deviation of 4.1 percent. Deleting the constraint C2:E2>=0 yields the same solution, so it appears there is no benefit to short selling.

Suppose we believe that the next 5 years will, on average, produce returns for stocks that are 5 percent worse than the last 30 years. It is easy (see Problem 4 at the end of the chapter) to incorporate these expectations into our simulation.

Problems

Problems 1–3 utilize the data in file Gesim.xls.

1.   Assume that the current price of Microsoft stock is $28. What is the probability that in 2 years the price of Microsoft will be at least $35?

2.   Redo Problem 1 with the assumption that during the next 2 years, Microsoft will on average perform 6 percent better per year than it performed during the 1997–2002 period for which we have data.

3.   Assume that the current price of Intel is $20. What is the probability that during the next 3 years, we will earn at least a 30 percent return (for the three-year period) on a purchase of Intel stock?

4.   Suppose you believe that over the next 5 years, stocks, on average, will produce returns that are 5 percent worse per year than our 1972–2001 data. Find an asset allocation between stocks, T-bills, and bonds that yields an expected annual return of at least 6 percent and minimizes risk.

5.   Suppose you feel that it is two times more likely that investment returns for each of the next 5 years will be more like the period 1992–2001 than the period 1972–1991. For example, the chance that next year will be like 1993 has twice the probability that next year is like 1980. This sense causes our bootstrapping analysis to give more weight to the recent past. How would you factor these beliefs into our portfolio optimization model?

6. Many mutual funds and investors hedge the risk that stocks will go down by purchasing put options. (See Chapter 63 for more discussion of put options.) How could our asset allocation model be used to determine an optimal hedging strategy using puts?

7. Determine the correlations (based on our 1972–2001 data) between annual returns on stocks, T-bills, and bonds. Then determine the correlation (based on our 1000 scenarios created by bootstrapping) between the final values for stocks, T-bills, and assets. Does it appear that the bootstrapping approach picks up the interdependence between the returns on stocks, T-bills, and bonds?

61

Fun and Games: Simulating Gambling and Sporting Event Probabilities

- What is the probability of winning at craps?

- In five-card draw poker, what is the probability of getting three of a kind?

- Before the 2003 Super Bowl, Oakland was favored by 3 points. What was the probability that Tampa Bay would beat Oakland?

- Going into the 2003 NCAA men's basketball Final Four, what was the probability of each team winning the tournament?

Gambling and following sporting events are popular pastimes. I think gambling and sports are exciting because you never know what's going to happen. Monte Carlo simulation provides a powerful tool that can be used to estimate gambling and sporting event probabilities. Essentially, we estimate probability by playing out our gambling or sporting event situation many times. If, for example, we have Excel play out craps 10,000 times and we win 4900 times, we would estimate the probability of winning at craps to equal 4900/10,000, or 49 percent. If we play out the 2003 NCAA men's Final Four 1000 times and Syracuse wins 300 of our iterations, we would estimate Syracuse's probability of winning the championship as 300/1000, or 30 percent.

What is the probability of winning at craps?

In the game of craps, a player tosses dice. If the player tosses the combination 2, 3, or 12, the player loses. If the player rolls 7 or 11, the player wins. If the dice combine for a different number, the player continues tossing the dice until he or she either matches the number thrown on the first roll (called the *point*) or tosses a 7. If the player rolls the point before rolling a 7, the player wins. If the player rolls a 7 before rolling the point, the player loses. By complex calculations, we can show that the probability that a player wins at craps is .493. We can use Excel to simulate the game of craps many (I chose 2000) times to demonstrate this probability.

In this example, it is crucial to keep in mind that we don't know how many rolls the game will take. We can show that the chance that a game requires more than 50 rolls of the dice is highly unlikely, so we'll play out 50 rolls of the dice. After each roll, we keep track of the game status as follows:

- 0 equals the game is lost

- 1 equals the game is won

- 2 equals the game continues

Our output cell will keep track of the status of the game after the fiftieth toss. A 1 will indicate a win, and a 0 will indicate a loss. You can find the work I did in the file Craps.xls, shown in Figure 61-1.

	A	B	C	D	E	F	G	H	AX	AY
1	TOSS#	1	2	3	4	5	6	7	49	50
2	Die Toss 1	2	6	2	2	2	2	4	5	5
3	Die Toss 2	2	2	2	1	6	6	5	3	6
4	Total	4	8	4	3	8	8	9	8	11
5	GAME STATUS	2	2	1	1	1	1	1	1	1
6		WIN??	1							
7										
8				prob win	0.502					
9					1					
10				1	1					
11				2	1					
12				3	0					
13				4	1					
14				5	1					
15				6	0					
16				7	1					
17				8	1					
18				9	0					
19				10	0					
20				11	1					

Figure 61-1 Craps simulation.

In cell B2, I used the RANDBETWEEN function to generate the number of the first die on the first toss by using the formula *RANDBETWEEN(1,6)*. The RANDBETWEEN function ensures that each of its arguments is equally likely, so each die has an equal (1/6) chance of yielding a 1, 2, 3, 4, 5, or 6. Copying this formula to the range B2:AY3 generates 50 tosses of the dice. (In Figure 61-1, I've hidden tosses 8-48.)

In the cell range B4:AY4, I compute the total dice roll for each of the 50 rolls by copying from B4 to C4:AY4 the formula *Sum(B2:B3)*. In cell B5, I determine the game status after the first roll with the formula *IF(OR(B4=2,B4=3,B4=12),0,IF(OR(B4=7,B4=11),1,2))*. Remember that a roll of 2, 3, or 12 results in a loss (entering a 0 in the cell); a 7 or 11 results in a win (1); and any other roll results in the game continuing (2).

In cell C5 I compute the status of the game after the second roll with the formula *IF(OR(B5=0,B5=1),B5,IF(C4=$B4,1,IF(C4=7,0,2)))*. If the game ended on the first roll, we maintain the status of the game. If we make our point, we record a win with a 1. If we roll a 7, we record a loss. Otherwise, the game continues. Note that I added a dollar sign in the reference to column B ($B4) in this formula to ensure that on each toss, we try to match the point thrown on the first toss. Copying this formula from C5 to D5:AY5 records the game status after rolls 2 through 50.

The game result is in cell AY5, which is copied to C6 so that we can easily see it. I then use a one-way data table to play out the game of craps 2000 times. In cell E8, I enter the formula *=C6*, which tracks the final outcome of the game (0 if a loss or 1 if a win). Next I select the table range (D9:E2009), and then click Data, Table. I choose a one-way table with any blank cell being our column input cell. After pressing F9, I've simulated the game of craps 2000 times.

In cell E8, I can compute the fraction of our simulations that result in wins with the formula *AVERAGE(E10:E2009)*. For our 2000 iterations, we won 50.2 percent of the time. If we had run more trials (say, 10,000 iterations), we would have come much closer to the true probability of winning at craps. For information about using a one-way data table, see Chapter 15.

In five-card draw poker, what is the probability of getting three of a kind?

An ordinary deck of cards contains four cards of each type—four aces, four deuces, and so on up to four kings. To estimate the probability of getting a particular poker hand, we'll assign the value 1 to an ace, 2 to a deuce, and on up the deck so that a jack is assigned the value 11, a queen is assigned 12, and a king is assigned 13.

In five-card draw poker, you are dealt five cards. Many probabilities are of interest, but let's use simulation to estimate the probability of getting three of a kind, which requires that you have three of one type of card and no pairs. (If you have a pair and three of a kind, the hand is a full house.) To simulate the five cards drawn, we proceed as follows. (See the file Poker.xls, shown in Figure 61-2.)

■   Associate a random number with each card in the deck.

■ The five cards chosen will be the five cards associated with the five smallest random numbers, which gives each card an equal chance of being chosen.

■ Count how many of each card (ace through king) are drawn.

	Drawn hand	Rank		Rand#			How many	
1	11	11	1	0.173806			1	0
2	11	9	1	0.166648			2	0
3	7	21	1	0.299832			3	0
4	11	6	1	0.066262			4	0
5	6	30	2	0.519683			5	0
		15	2	0.214663			6	1
		19	2	0.283556			7	1
		45	2	0.798174			8	0
		20	3	0.294141			9	0
		35	3	0.616052			10	0
		51	3	0.971928			11	3
		27	3	0.378423			12	0
		31	4	0.549715			13	0
		36	4	0.616151				
		23	4	0.323426			three of kind?	1
		28	4	0.501769				
		48	5	0.864718				1
		13	5	0.187801	prob 3 of kind		1	0
		25	5	0.341266	0.01925		2	0
		14	5	0.203932			3	0

Figure 61-2 Poker simulation for estimating the probability that we'll draw three of a kind.

To begin, we list in cells D3:D54 all the cards in the deck: four 1s, four 2s, and so on up to four 12s, and four 13s. Then we copy from cell E3 to E4:E54 the RAND() function to associate a random number with each card in the deck. Copying from C3 to C4:C54 the formula *RANK(E3,$E$3:$E$54,1)* gives the rank (ordered from smallest to largest) of each random number. For example, in Figure 61-2, you can see that the first 3 in the deck (row 11) is associated with the 20th smallest random number. (You will see different results in the worksheet because the random numbers are recalculated when you open the worksheet.)

The syntax of the RANK function is *RANK(number, array, 1 or 0)*. If the last argument of the RANK function is 1, the function returns the rank of the number in the array with the smallest number receiving a rank of 1, the second smallest number a rank of 2, and the like. If the last argument to the RANK function is 0, the function returns the rank of the number in the array with the largest number receiving a rank of 1, the second largest number receiving a rank of 2, and so on.

When ranking random numbers, no ties can occur (because the random numbers would have to match to 16 digits).

Suppose, for example, we were ranking the numbers 1, 3, 3, and 4 and that the last argument of the RANK function was 1. Excel would return the following ranks:

Number	Rank (smallest number has rank of 1)
1	1
3	2
3	2
4	4

Because 3 is second smallest number, 3 would be assigned a rank of 2. The other 3 would also be assigned a rank of 2. Because 4 is the fourth smallest number, it will be assigned a rank of 4. Understanding the treatment of ties by the RANK function will help you complete Problem 1 at the end of the chapter.

By copying from cell B3 to B4:B7 the formula *VLOOKUP(A3,lookup,2,FALSE)*, we can draw our five cards from the deck. This formula draws the five cards corresponding to the five smallest random numbers. (The lookup table range C3:D54 has been named *Lookup*.) We use *False* in the VLOOKUP function because the ranks need not be in ascending order.

Having assigned the range name *Drawn* to our drawn cards (the range B3:B7), copying from J3 to J4:J15 the formula *COUNTIF(drawn,I3)* counts how many of each card are in our drawn hand. In cell J17 we determine whether we have three of a kind with the formula *IF(AND(MAX(J3:J15)=3,COUNTIF(J3:J15,2)=0),1,0)*. This formula returns a 1 if and only if our hand has three of one kind and no pairs.

We now use a one-way data table to simulate 4000 poker hands. In cell J19, we recopy the results of cell J17 with the formula *=J17*. Next we select our table range (I19:J4019). After choosing Data, Table, we set up a one-way data table by selecting any blank cell as our column input cell. After clicking OK, we have simulated 4000 poker hands. In cell G21, we record our estimated probability of three of a kind with the formula *AVERAGE(J20:J4019)*. We estimate the chance of three of a kind at 1.9 percent. (Using basic probability theory, we can show that the true probability of drawing three of a kind is 2.1 percent.)

Before the 2003 Super Bowl, Oakland was favored by 3 points. What was the probability that Tampa Bay would beat Oakland?

Extensive study by my friend Jeff Sagarin (check out his sports ratings at *http://www.usatoday.com/sports/sagarin.htm*) has shown that the number of points by which the favorite wins a college or professional football or basketball game follows a normal distribution with the mean equal to the bookies' forecast, with a standard deviation of 16 points for professional football, 14 points for college football, 12 points for professional basketball, and 10 points for college basketball. Therefore, the number of points by which Oakland wins the Super Bowl (Oakland winning by negative points means they lose) is normally distributed with a mean of 3 and a standard deviation of 16 points. Again, for Oakland to lose, they must win by 0 points or less.

This problem can be computed with the function *NORMDIST(0,3,16, True)*. (See Chapter 56 for a discussion of the NORMDIST function.) This function yields a 42.6 percent chance for Oakland to lose. As we know, Tampa Bay won the game, but this was not a totally unexpected outcome.

Going into the 2003 NCAA men's basketball Final Four, what was the probability of each team winning the tournament?

Using a methodology similar to that described in Chapter 30, where we used Excel's Solver to rate sports teams, you can use the scores of previous games to develop ratings for each college basketball team. On the eve of the 2003 men's Final Four, the ratings of the four teams were Syracuse, 91.03; Kansas, 92.76; Marquette, 89.01; and Texas, 90.66. Given this information, we can play out the Final Four several thousand times to estimate the chance that each team will win.

Our mean prediction for the number of points by which the home team wins equals *favorite rating – underdog rating*. In the Final Four, there is no home team, but if there were a home team, we would add 5 points to the home team's rating. (In professional basketball, home edge is 4 points; in college and pro football, the home edge is 3 points.) Then we can use the NORMINV function to simulate the outcome of each game. (See Chapter 58 for a discussion of using the NORMINV function to simulate a normal random variable.)

We've calculated the likely outcome of the 2003 Final Four in the file Final4sim.xls, shown in Figure 61-3. The semifinals pitted Kansas against Marquette and Syracuse against Texas.

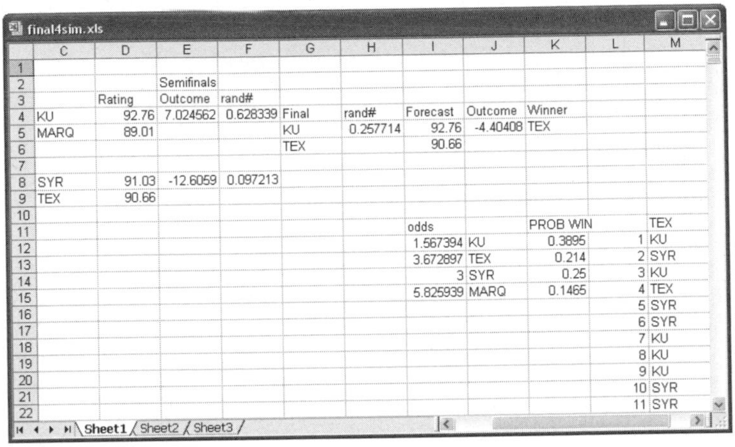

	C	D	E	F	G	H	I	J	K	L	M
1											
2			Semifinals								
3		Rating	Outcome	rand#							
4	KU	92.76	7.024562	0.628339	Final	rand#	Forecast	Outcome	Winner		
5	MARQ	89.01			KU	0.257714	92.76	-4.40408	TEX		
6					TEX		90.66				
7											
8	SYR	91.03	-12.6059	0.097213							
9	TEX	90.66									
10											
11							odds		PROB WIN		TEX
12							1.567394	KU	0.3895	1	KU
13							3.672897	TEX	0.214	2	SYR
14							3	SYR	0.25	3	KU
15							5.825939	MARQ	0.1465	4	TEX
16										5	SYR
17										6	SYR
18										7	KU
19										8	KU
20										9	KU
21										10	SYR
22										11	SYR

Figure 61-3 NCAA 2003 Final Four simulation.

To begin, we enter each team's name and rating in the cell range C4:D9. In cell F4, we use the RAND() function to enter a random number for the Marquette-Kansas game, and in cell F8 we enter a random number for the Syracuse-Texas game. Our simulated outcome is always relative to the top team listed.

In cell E4, we determine the outcome of the Kansas-Marquette game (from the standpoint of Kansas) with the formula *NORMINV(F4,D4-D5,10)*. Note that Kansas is favored by *D4-D5* points. In cell E8, we determine the outcome of the Texas-Syracuse game (from the standpoint of Syracuse) with the formula *NORMINV(F8,D8-D9,10)*. (Remember that the standard deviation for the winning margin of college basketball games is 10 points.)

In cells G5 and G6, we ensure that the winner of each semifinal game moves on to the finals. An outcome of greater than 0 causes the top-listed team to win; otherwise the bottom-listed team wins. Thus in cell G5, we enter the winner of the first game with the formula *IF(E4>0,"KU", vMARQ")*. In cell G6, we enter the winner of the second game by using the formula *IF(E8>0,"SYR","TEX")*.

In cell H5, we enter a random number that will be used to simulate the outcome of the championship game. Copying from I5 to I6 the formula *VLOOKUP(G5,$C$4:$D$9,2,FALSE)* obtains the rating for each team in the championship game. Next, in cell J5, we compute the outcome of the championship game (from the reference point of the top-listed team in cell G5) with the formula *NORMINV(H5,I5-I6,10)*. Finally, in cell K5, we determine the actual champion with the formula *IF(J5>0,G5,G6)*.

Now we can use a one-way data table in the usual fashion to play out the Final Four a couple of thousand times. Our simulated winners are in the cell range M12:M2011. Copying from K12 to K13:K15 the formula *COUNTIF($M$12:$M$2011,J12)/2000* computes the predicted probability for each team winning: 39 percent for Kansas, 25 percent for Syracuse, 21 percent for Texas, and 15 percent for Marquette. These probabilities can be translated to odds using the following formula:

$$odds\,against\,team\,winning = \frac{prob\,team\,loses}{prob\,team\,wins}$$

For example, the odds against Kansas are 1.56 to 1:

$$\left(\frac{1-.39}{.39}\right) = 1.56$$

This means that a bet in which we placed $1 on Kansas to win and a book-maker pay us $1.56 for a Kansas championship is a fair bet. Of course, the bookie will lower these odds slightly to ensure that he makes money. (See Problem 6 at the end of this chapter for a related exercise.)

By the way, our methodology can easily be extended to simulate the entire NCAA tournament. Just use IF statements to ensure that each winner advances and use LOOKUP functions to look up each team's rating. See the file Ncaa2003.xls for a simulation of the 2003 tournament. We gave Syracuse a 4 percent chance to win at the start of tournament.

In this worksheet, I used comments to explain my work, which you can see in Figure 61-4. Here is some background about using comments:

- To insert a comment in a cell, select Insert, Comment. You will see a small red mark in the upper right corner of a cell containing a comment.

- To edit a comment, right-click on the cell containing the comment and select Edit Comment.

- To make a comment always show, right-click the cell and select Show Comment. Selecting Hide Comment causes the comment not to be displayed unless the pointer is in the cell containing the comment.

- If you want to print your comments, click File, Page Setup, and then select the Sheet tab. You can indicate whether you want comments printed on the worksheet or at the end of the worksheet.

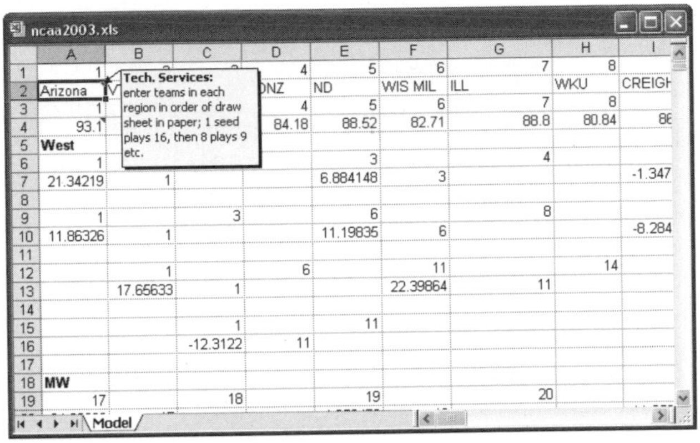

Figure 61-4   Example of comments.

Problems

1. Suppose 30 people are in a room. What is the probability that at least two have the same birthday?

2. What is the probability of getting one pair in five-card poker?

3. What is probability of getting two pair in five-card poker?

4. In the game of keno, 80 balls (numbered 1–80) are mixed up and 20 balls are randomly drawn. Before the 20 balls are drawn, a player chooses 10 different numbers. If at least 5 of the numbers are drawn, the player wins. What is the probability of winning?

5. Going into the 2003 NBA finals, Jeff Sagarin had San Antonio rated 3 points better than New Jersey. The teams play until one team wins 4 games. The first 2 games were at San Antonio, the next three at New Jersey, and the final two games were scheduled for San Antonio. What is the probability that San Antonio will win the series?

6. What odds should the bookmaker give on Kansas winning the Final Four if the bookmaker wants to earn an average of 10 cents per dollar bet?

62

Using Resampling to Analyze Data

- I've produced nine batches of a product using a high temperature and seven batches of a product using a low temperature. What is the probability that the process yield is better at the high temperature?

In our work and personal lives, we often use data to make inferences. In addition to the example described above, we use data to answer questions such as these:

- What is the probability that a new teaching technique improves student learning?

- What is the probability that aspirin reduces the incidence of heart attacks?

- What is the probability that machine 1 is the most productive of our three machines?

You can use a simple yet powerful technique known as *resampling* to make inferences from data. To make statistical inferences by using resampling, you regenerate data many times by sampling with replacement from your data. Sampling from data with replacement means that the same data point can be chosen more than once. Then you make inferences based on the results of this repeated sampling. A key tool in implementing resampling is the RANDBETWEEN function. Entering the function *RANDBETWEEN(a,b)* yields with equal probability any integer between *a* and *b* (inclusive). Thus, for example, *RANDBETWEEN(1,9)* is equally likely to yield one of the numbers 1 through 9, inclusive.

I've produced nine batches of a product using a high temperature and seven batches of a product using a low temperature. What is the probability that the process yield is better at the high temperature?

The file Resampleyield.xls (shown in Figure 62-1) contains the product yield from nine batches of a product manufactured at a high temperature and seven batches produced at a low temperature.

	B	C	D	E	F	G	H	I	J
1									
2									
3		mean	39.74	32.27					
4		Number	High Temp	Low Temp					
5		1	17.55	37.37					
6		2	39.93	43.20					
7		3	48.98	34.85					
8		4	41.40	31.22					
9		5	35.70	26.59					
10		6	42.24	42.67					
11		7	54.75	10.00					
12		8	46.96						
13		9	30.19						

Figure 62-1 Product yields at high and low temperature.

The mean yield at high temperature is 39.74, and the mean yield at low temperature is 32.27. This difference does not prove, however, that mean yield at a high temperature is better than mean yield at low temperature. We want to know, based on our sample data, the probability that yield at a high temperature is better than at low temperature. To answer this question, we can randomly generate nine integers between 1 and 9, which creates a resampling of the high-temperature yields. For example, if we generate the random number 4, the resampled data for high-temperature yields will include a yield of 41.40, and so on. Next we randomly generate seven integers between 1 and 7, which creates our resampling of the low-temperature yields. We can then check the resampled data to see whether the high-temperature mean is larger than the low-temperature mean and use a data table to repeat this process several hundred times. (I repeated the process 400 times in this example.) In the resampled data, the fraction of the time that the high-temperature mean beats the low-temperature mean estimates the probability that the high-temperature process is superior to the low-temperature process.

To begin, we generate a resampling of the high temperature-data by copying from cell C16 to C17:C24 the formula RANDBETWEEN(1,9), as shown in Figure 62-2. A given observation can be chosen more than once or not chosen at all. Copying the formula *VLOOKUP(C16,lookup,2)*—the range C4:E13 has been named *Lookup*—from cell D16 to D17:D24 generates the yields corresponding to our random resampling of the data. Next we generate a resampling from our low-temperature yields. Copying from E16 to E17:E22 the formula *RANDBETWEEN(1,7)* generates a resampling of seven observations from our original low-temperature data. Copying the formula *VLOOKUP(E16,lookup,3)* from F16 to F17:F22 generates the seven actual resampled low-temperature yields.

	B	C	D	E	F	G	H	I	J
15		Resampled	High Temp	Resampled	Low Temp				
16		6	42.24	7	10.00				
17		5	35.70	7	10.00				
18		4	41.40	2	43.20				
19		4	41.40	3	34.85				
20		1	17.55	1	37.37				
21		6	42.24	3	34.85				
22		9	30.19	7	10.00				
23		3	48.98						
24		5	35.70						
25									
26		Average	37.27		25.75				
27									
28									
29		High better	1						
30					Prob high better				
31			1		0.915				
32		1	1						
33		2	1						

Figure 62-2   Implementation of resampling.

In cell D26, I compute the mean of our resampled high-temperature yields with the formula *AVERAGE(D16:D24)*. Similarly, in cell F26, I compute the mean of our resampled low-temperature yields with the formula *AVERAGE(F16:F22)*. In cell D29, I determine whether the resampled mean for high temperature was larger than the resampled mean for low temperature with the formula *IF(D26>F26,1,0)*.

To replay our resampling 400 times, we can use a one-way data table. I copy iteration numbers 1 through 400 to the cell range C32:431. (See Chapter 58 for an explanation of how to use the Edit, Fill Series command to easily create a list of iteration values.) By entering *=D29* in cell D31, I make the formula that records whether high-temperature mean is better than low-temperature mean in the output cell for our data table. After selecting the table range (C31:D431) and then clicking Data, Table, we can choose any blank cell in the spreadsheet as our column input cell. We have now tricked Excel into playing out our resampling 400 times. Each iteration with the value 1 indicates a resampling in which high temperature has the larger mean. Each iteration that evaluates to 0 indicates a resampling for which low temperature has a larger mean. In cell F31, I determine the fraction of time that high-temperature yield has a larger mean by using the formula *AVERAGE(D32:D431)*. In Figure 62-2, our resampling indicates a 92 percent chance that high temperature has a larger mean than low temperature. Of course, pressing F9 will generate a different set of 400 resamplings and will give us a slightly different estimate of the probability that high temperature is superior to low temperature.

Problems

1. We are testing a flu drug. Twenty of twenty-four flu victims who were given the drug felt better, and four felt worse. Nine flu victims were given a placebo. Six felt better, and three felt worse. What is the probability that the drug is more effective than the placebo?

2. Eight workers were given a talk on the dangers of high cholesterol. Each worker's cholesterol before and after the talk is given below. What is the probability that the talk caused the workers to undertake lifestyle changes that reduced their cholesterol?

Cholesterol Before	Cholesterol After
220	210
195	198
250	210
200	199
220	224
260	212
175	179
198	184

3. The *beta* of a stock is simply the slope of the best-fitting line used to predict the monthly return on the stock from the monthly return on the Standard and Poor's (S&P) index. A *beta* that is larger than 1 indicates that a stock is more cyclical than the market, while a *beta* of less than 1 indicates that a stock is less cyclical than the market. The File BetaResampling.xls contains more than 12 years of monthly returns on Microsoft (MSFT), Pfizer (PFE), and the S&P index. Use this data to determine the probability that MSFT has a lower *beta* than Pfizer. You will need to use the Excel SLOPE function to estimate the *beta* for each iteration of resampling.

63

Pricing Stock Options

- What are put and call options?

- What are American and European options?

- As a function of the stock price on the exercise date, what do the payoffs look like for European puts and calls?

- What parameters determine the value of an option?

- How do we estimate the volatility of a stock based on historical data?

- How can I use Excel to implement the Black-Scholes formula?

- How do changes in key parameters change the value of a put or call option?

- How can I use the Black-Scholes formula to estimate a stock's volatility?

- I don't want somebody messing up my neat option-pricing formulas. How can I protect the formulas in my worksheet so that nobody can mess them up?

- How can option pricing be used to help companies make better investment decisions?

During the early 1970s, economists Fischer Black, Myron Scholes, and Robert Merton derived the Black-Scholes option-pricing formula, which enables us to derive a value for a European put or call option. Scholes and Merton were awarded the 1997 Nobel Prize in Economics for their efforts. (Black died prior to 1997, and Nobel prizes are not awarded posthumously.) The work of these economists revolutionized corporate finance. In this chapter, I'll introduce you to their important work.[1]

---

1. For an excellent technical discussion of options, see David G. Luenberger's book *Investment Science* (Oxford University Press, 1997).

What are put and call options?

A *call option* gives the owner of the option the right to buy a share of stock for a price called the *exercise price*. A *put option* gives the owner of the option the right to sell a share of stock for the exercise price.

What are American and European options?

An *American* option can be exercised on or before a date known as the *exercise date*. (The exercise date is often referred to as the *expiration date*.) A *European* option can be exercised only on the exercise date.

As a function of the stock price on the exercise date, what do the payoffs look like for European puts and calls?

Let's look at cash flows from a six-month European call option on shares of Microsoft with an exercise price of $110. Let P equal the price of Microsoft stock in six months. The payoff from a call option on these shares is $0 if $P \leq 110$ and P-110 if $P > 110$. With a value of P below $110, we would not exercise the option. If P is larger than $110, we would exercise the option to buy stock for $110 and immediately sell the stock for P, thereby earning a profit of $P - 110$. Figure 63-1 displays the payoff from this call option. In short, a call option pays $1 for every dollar by which the stock price exceeds the exercise price. The payoff for this call option can be written as *Max(0, P – 110)*. Notice that the call option graph in Figure 63-1 has a slope 0 for P smaller than the exercise price. Its slope is 1 for a value of P greater than the exercise price.

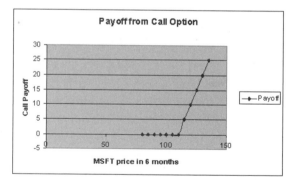

Figure 63-1   Cash flows from a call option.

By the way, we can show that if a stock pays no dividends, it is never optimal to exercise an American call option early. Therefore, for a nondividend-paying stock, an American and European call option have the same value.

Now let's look at cash flows from a six-month European put option on shares of Microsoft with an exercise price of $110. Let P equal the price of Microsoft in six months. The payoff from the put option is $0 if $P \leq 110$ and $P -$ 110 if $P \geq 110$. For a value of P below $110, we would buy a share of stock for P and immediately sell the stock for $110. This yields a profit of $110 - P$. If P is larger than $110, it would not pay to buy the stock for P and sell it for $110, so we would not exercise our option to sell the stock for $110.

Figure 63-2 displays the payoff from this put option. In short, a put option pays us $1 for each dollar by which the stock price is below the exercise price. A put payoff can be written as *Max(0, 110 – P)*. Note that the slope of the put payoff is −1 for P less than the exercise price, and the slope of the put payoff is 0 for a value of P greater than the exercise price.

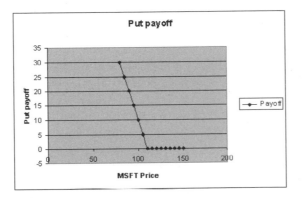

Figure 63-2   Cash flows from a put option.

An American put option can be exercised early, so the cash flows from an American put option cannot be determined without knowledge of the stock price at the times before the expiration date.

What parameters determine the value of an option?

In their derivation of the Black-Scholes option-pricing model, Black, Scholes, and Merton showed that the value of a call or put option depends on the following parameters:

- The current stock price

- The option's exercise price

- The time (in years) until the option expires (referred to as the option's *duration*)

■ The interest rate (per year on a compounded basis) on a risk-free investment (usually Treasury bills) throughout the duration of the investment. This rate is called the *risk-free rate*. For example, if three-month Treasury bills are paying 5 percent, the risk-free rate is computed as *LN(1 + .05)*. (Calculating the logarithm transforms a simple interest rate into a compounded rate.) Compound interest simply means that at every instant, you are earning interest on your interest.

■ The annual rate (as a percentage of the stock price) at which dividends are paid. If a stock pays 2 percent of its value each year in dividends, the dividend rate is .02.

■ The *volatility* of the stock (measured on an annual basis). An annual volatility of, say, 30 percent means that (approximately) the standard deviation of the annual percentage changes in the stock's price is expected to be around 30 percent. During the Internet bubble of the late 1990s, the volatility of many Internet stocks exceeded 100 percent. I'll soon show you two ways to estimate this important parameter.

How do we estimate the volatility of a stock based on historical data?

To estimate the volatility of a stock from data about the stock's monthly returns, we can proceed as follows:

■ Determine the monthly return on the stock for a period of several years.

■ Determine for each month *LN(1 + monthly return)*.

■ Determine the standard deviation of *LN(1 + monthly return)*. This calculation gives us the monthly volatility.

■ Multiply the monthly volatility by

$$\sqrt{12}$$

to convert monthly volatility to an annual volatility.

This procedure is illustrated in the file Dellvol.xls, in which I estimate the annual volatility of Dell stock using monthly prices from the period August 1988 through May 2001. (See Figure 63-3; I've hidden many rows of data.)

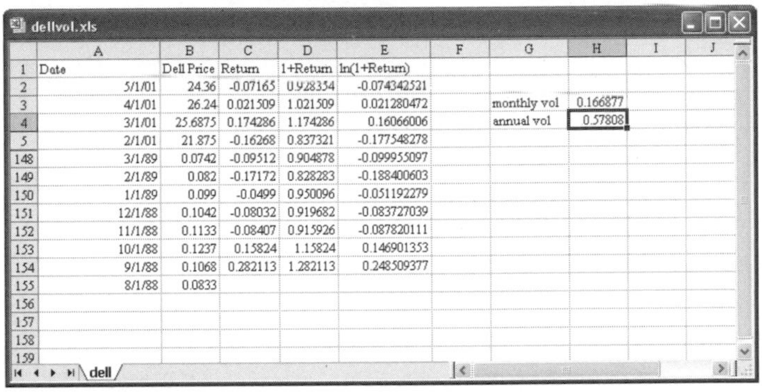

dellvol.xls

	A	B	C	D	E	F	G	H	I	J
1	Date	Dell Price	Return	1+Return	ln(1+Return)					
2	5/1/01	24.36	-0.07165	0.928354	-0.074342521					
3	4/1/01	26.24	0.021509	1.021509	0.021280472		monthly vol	0.166877		
4	3/1/01	25.6875	0.174286	1.174286	0.16066006		annual vol	0.57808		
5	2/1/01	21.875	-0.16268	0.837321	-0.177548278					
148	3/1/89	0.0742	-0.09512	0.904878	-0.099955097					
149	2/1/89	0.082	-0.17172	0.828283	-0.188400603					
150	1/1/89	0.099	-0.0499	0.950096	-0.051192279					
151	12/1/88	0.1042	-0.08032	0.919682	-0.083727039					
152	11/1/88	0.1133	-0.08407	0.915926	-0.087820111					
153	10/1/88	0.1237	0.15824	1.15824	0.146901353					
154	9/1/88	0.1068	0.282113	1.282113	0.248509377					
155	8/1/88	0.0833								
156										
157										
158										
159										

dell

Figure 63-3 Computing the historical volatility for Dell.

Copying from cell C2 to C3:C154 the formula *(B2-B3)/B3* computes each month's return on Dell. Then, copying from D2 to D3:D154 the formula *1+C2* computes for each month *1 + month's return*. Next I compute *LN(1+ month's return)* for each month by copying from E2 to E3:E154 the formula *LN(D2)* and the monthly volatility in cell H3 with the formula *STDEV(E2:E154)*. Finally, I compute an estimate of Dell's annual volatility with the formula *SQRT(12)*H3*. Dell's annual volatility is estimated to be 57.8 percent.

How can I use Excel to implement the Black-Scholes formula?

To apply the Black-Scholes formula in Excel, we need input values for the following parameters:

- *S* = Today's stock price
- *t* = Duration of the option (in years)
- *X* = Exercise price
- *r* = Annual risk-free rate (This rate is assumed to be continuously compounded.)
- σ = Annual volatility of stock
- *y* = Percentage of stock value paid annually in dividends

Given these input values, the Black-Scholes price for a European call option can be computed as follows:

Define

$$d_1 = \frac{LN(\frac{S}{X}) + (r - y + \frac{\sigma^2}{2})t}{\sigma\sqrt{t}}$$

and

$$d_2 = d_1 - \sigma\sqrt{t}$$

The call price C is given by

$$C = Se^{-yt}N(d_1) - Xe^{-rt}N(d_2).$$

Here, N(x) is the probability that a normal random variable with a mean of 0 and a σ equal to 1 is less than or equal to x. For example, N(-1) = .16, N(0) = .5, N(1) = .84, and N(1.96) =.975. A normal random variable with a mean of 0 and a standard deviation of 1 is called a *standard normal.* The cumulative normal probability can be computed in Excel with the NORMDIST function. Entering *NORMDIST(x)* returns the probability that a standard normal random variable is less than or equal to x. For example, entering the formula *NORMDIST(-1)* in a cell will yield .16, which indicates that a normal random variable with a mean of 0 and a standard deviation of 1 has a 16 percent chance of assuming a value less than -1.

The price of a European put P can be written as follows:

$$P = Se^{-yt}(N(d_1) - 1) - Xe^{-rt}(N(d_2) - 1).$$

In the file named Bstemp.xls (see Figure 63-4), I've created a template that computes the value for a European call or put option.[2] Simply enter the parameter values in B5:B10 and read the value of a European call in D13 and a European put in D14.

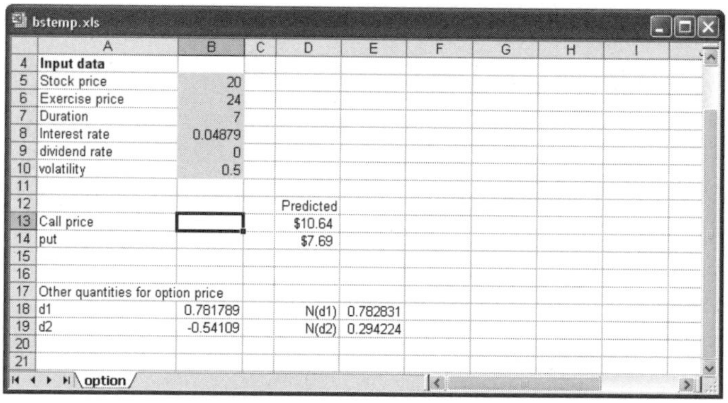

	A	B	C	D	E
4	Input data				
5	Stock price	20			
6	Exercise price	24			
7	Duration	7			
8	Interest rate	0.04879			
9	dividend rate	0			
10	volatility	0.5			
11					
12				Predicted	
13	Call price			$10.64	
14	put			$7.69	
15					
16					
17	Other quantities for option price				
18	d1	0.781789		N(d1)	0.782831
19	d2	-0.54109		N(d2)	0.294224
20					
21					

Figure 63-4 Valuing European puts and calls.

2. Valuing American options is beyond the scope of this book. Interested readers should refer to Luenberger's excellent textbook.

As an example, suppose that Cisco stock sells for $20 today and that we've been issued a seven-year European call option. Assume that the annual volatility of Cisco stock is 50 percent and the risk-free rate during the seven-year period is estimated at 5 percent per year. Compounded, this translates to *LN(1 + .05) = .04879*. Cisco does not pay dividends, so the annual dividend rate is 0. We find the value of the call option to be $10.64. A seven-year put option with an exercise price of $24 would be worth $7.69.

How do changes in key parameters change the value of a put or call option?

In general, the effect of changing an input parameter on the value of a put or call is given in the following table:

Parameter	European Call	European Put	American Call	American Put
Stock price	+	-	+	-
Exercise price	-	+	-	+
Time to expiration	?	?	+	+
Volatility	+	+	+	+
Risk-free rate	+	-	+	-
Dividends	-	+	-	+

- An increase in today's stock price always increases the value of a call and decreases the value of a put.

- An increase in the exercise price always increases the value of a put and decreases the value of a call.

- An increase in the duration of an option always increases the value of an American option. In the presence of dividends, an increase in the duration of an option can either increase or decrease the value of a European option.

- An increase in volatility always increases option value.

- An increase in the risk-free rate increases the value of a call because higher rates tend to increase the growth rate of the stock price (which is good for the call). This situation more than cancels out the fact that option payoff is worth less as a result of the higher interest rate. An increase in the risk-free rate always decreases the value of a put because the higher growth rate of the stock tends to hurt the put, as does the fact that future payoffs from the put are worth less.

Again, this assumes that interest rates do not affect current stock prices, but they do.

■ Dividends tend to reduce growth rate of a stock price, so increased dividends reduce the value of a call and increase the value of a put.

Using one-way and two-way data tables (see Chapter 15 for details about how to work with data tables), we can, if we want, explore the specific effects of parameter changes on the value of puts and calls.

How can I use the Black-Scholes formula to estimate a stock's volatility?

Earlier in this chapter, I showed how to use historical data to estimate a stock's annual volatility. The problem with a historical volatility estimate is that the analysis looks backward. What we really want is an estimate of a stock's volatility looking forward. The *implied volatility* approach simply estimates a stock's volatility as the volatility value that will make the Black-Scholes price match the option's market price. In short, implied volatility extracts the volatility value implied by the option's market price.

We can easily use the Goal Seek command and our input parameters to compute an implied volatility. On July 22, 2003, Cisco was selling for $18.43. An October 2003 call option with a $17.50 exercise price was selling for $1.85. This option expires on October 18 (89 days in the future). Thus, the option has a duration of 89/365 = .2438 years. Cisco does not expect to pay dividends, and we assume a Treasury bill rate of 5 percent and a corresponding risk-free rate of $LN(1 + .05) = .04879$. To determine the volatility for Cisco implied by this option price, we enter the relevant parameters in cells B5:B10 of the file CiscoImpVol.xls, which is shown in Figure 63-5.

	A	B	C	D	E	F	G	H
4	**Input data**							
5	Stock price	18.43						
6	Exercise price	17.5						
7	Duration	0.243836						
8	Interest rate	0.04879						
9	dividend rate	0						
10	volatility	0.340364						
11								
12				Predicted				
13	Call price			$1.85				
14	put			$0.71				
15								
16								
17	Other quantities for option price							
18	d1	0.462898		N(d1)	0.678281			
19	d2	0.294827		N(d2)	0.615937			
20								

Figure 63-5 Using implied volatility to estimate Cisco's volatility.

Next we use the Goal Seek feature (see Figure 63 6) to determine the volatility (the value in cell B10) that makes the call price (the formula in D13) hit a value of $1.85.

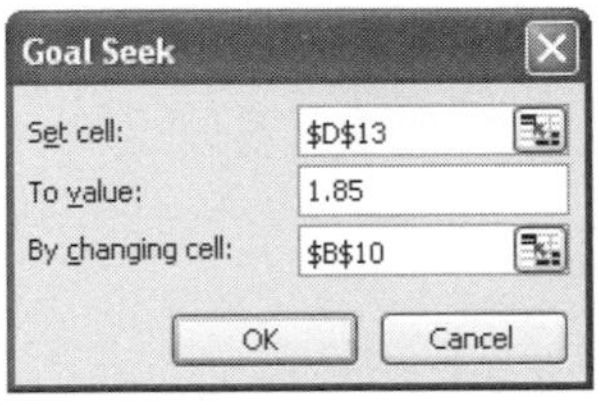

Figure 63-6   Goal Seek settings to find implied volatility.

We find that this option implies an annual volatility for Cisco of 34 percent, as you can see in Figure 63-5.

I don't want somebody messing up my neat option-pricing formulas. How can I protect the formulas in my worksheet so that nobody can mess them up?

I'm sure that you have often sent your spreadsheets to people who then mess up your carefully constructed formulas. Sometimes you want to protect your spreadsheets so that another user can only enter input data but not modify the spreadsheet's formulas. As an example, I'll show you how to protect all the formulas in our Black-Scholes template (see the file Bstemp.xls).

To begin, I "unlock" all the cells in the spreadsheet. First, click the gray box in the upper left corner of the spreadsheet grid (next to the A and the 1). Selecting this box causes any format changes you make to take effect in your entire spreadsheet. For example, if you select a bold format after clicking this box, all the cells in the spreadsheet will use a bold font. Unlock cells by selecting Format, Cells, and then click the Protection tab, shown in Figure 63-7. Clear the Locked option, and then click OK.

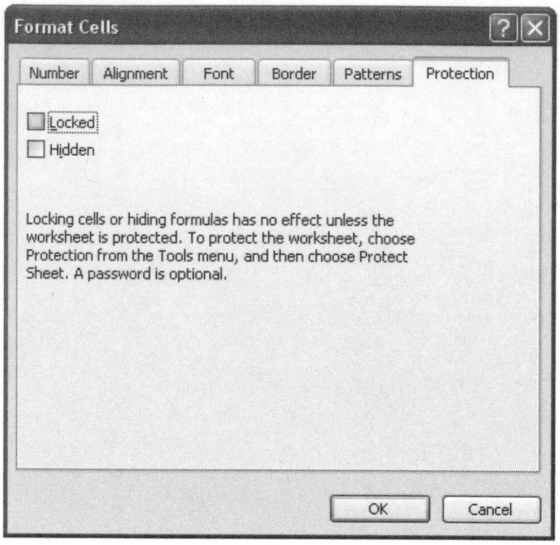

Figure 63-7   Unlocking all cells on the spreadsheet.

Next, I select all the formulas in the spreadsheet. To do this, press F5, which opens the Go To dialog box. Click Special, and then select Formulas. Click OK in the Go To Special dialog box. Click Format, Cells again, and then select the Locked option. Selecting this option "locks" all our formulas.

Now we can protect our worksheet, which will prevent a user from messing up our formulas. Select Tools, Protection, Protect Sheet. In the Protect Sheet dialog box, select the option that will allow all users to select unlocked cells, as shown in Figure 63-8. This option will allow users of our template to select unlocked cells, but our formulas will be off-limits.

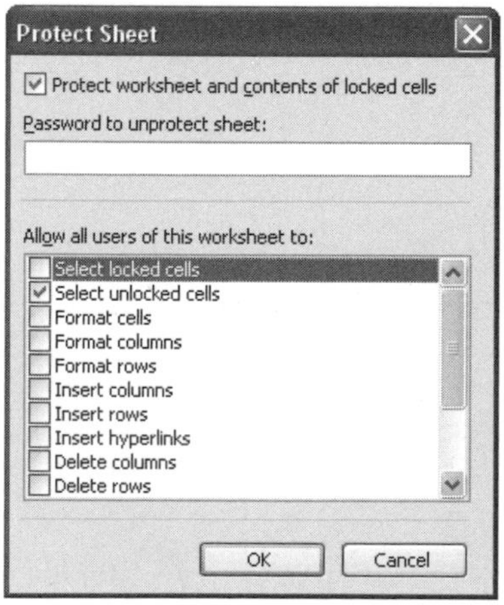

Figure 63-8   Allowing user to access unlocked cells.

Now, when you click on any formulas, you cannot see or change their contents. Go ahead and try to mess up the formulas! The final result of protecting this workbook is saved in the file Bstempprotected.xls.

How can option pricing be used to help companies make better investment decisions?

Option pricing can be used to improve a company's capital budgeting or financial decision-making process. The use of option pricing to evaluate actual investment projects is called *real options*. The idea of real options is credited to Judy Lewent, the chief financial officer of Merck. Essentially, real options let you put an explicit value on managerial flexibility, and the value of managerial flexibility is often missed by traditional capital budgeting.[3] The following two simple examples illustrate the concepts of real options.

Let's say that we own an oil well. Today, our best guess is that the oil in the well is worth $50 million. In five years (if we own the well), we will make a decision to develop the oil well, and it will cost $70 million to develop the well. A wildcatter comes along today and is willing to buy the well for $10 million. Should we sell the well?

Traditional capital budgeting says that the well is worthless because the cost to develop the well is more than the value of the oil in the well. But wait. In five years, the value of the oil in the well will be different because many things (such as the world oil price) might change. Surely there's a chance that the oil will be worth at least $70 million in five years. If the oil is worth $80 million in five years, developing the well in five years would return $10 million.

Essentially, we own a five-year European call option on this well because our payoff from the well in five years is the same as the payoff on a European call option with a stock price of $50 million, an exercise price of $70 million, and a duration of five years. We can assume an annual volatility similar to the volatility of a typical oil company stock (say 30 percent). We will use a Treasury bill rate of 5 percent, corresponding to a risk-free rate of 4.879 percent. In the file Oilwell.xls (see Figure 63-9), we find the value of this call option to be $11.47 million, which means that we should not sell the well for $10 million.

Of course, we do not know the actual volatility for this oil well. Therefore, we can use a one-way data table to determine how the value of the option depends on our volatility estimate. (See Figure 63-9.) From the data table, we find that as long as the oil well's volatility is at least 27 percent, our oil well "option" is worth more than $10 million.

---

3. Again, the reader is referred to Luenberger's book for a more detailed discussion of real options.

oilwell.xls

	A	B	C	D	E	F	G	H	I	J	K
9	dividend rate	0					Volatility	$11.47			
10	volatility	0.3					0.1	2.635248			
11							0.11	3.064456			
12				Predicted			0.12	3.498668			
13	Call price			$11.47			0.13	3.936575			
14	put			$16.32			0.14	4.377212			
15							0.15	4.819845			
16							0.16	5.263906			
17	Other quantities for option price						0.17	5.708942			
18	d1	0.197487		N(d1)	0.578277		0.18	6.15459			
19	d2	-0.47333		N(d2)	0.317988		0.19	6.600548			
20							0.2	7.046562			
21							0.21	7.492419			
22							0.22	7.937931			
23							0.23	8.382936			
24							0.24	8.82729			
25							0.25	9.270862			
26							0.26	9.713537			
27							0.27	10.15521			
28							0.28	10.59577			
29							0.29	11.03514			
30							0.3	11.47322			

buy oil well

Figure 63-9 Oil well real options example.

As a second example, consider a biotech drug company that is developing a drug for a major pharmaceutical firm. The biotech company currently believes the value of the drug is $50 million. Of course, the value of the drug might drop over time. To protect against a price drop, the biotech company wants to receive a guaranteed payment of $40 million in five years. If an insurance company wants to underwrite this liability, what is a fair price to charge?

Essentially, the biotech company is asking for a payment of $1 million in five years for each $1 million by which the value of the drug in five years is below $40 million. This is equivalent to a five-year put option on the value of the drug. Assuming a Treasury bill rate is 5 percent and the annual volatility on comparable drug stocks is 40 percent (see the file Drugabandon.xls, shown in Figure 63-10), the value of this option is $10.51 million. This type of option is often referred to as an *abandonment option*, but it is equivalent to a put option. (We have also included a one-way data table to show how the value of the abandonment option depends on the assumed volatility, ranging from 30 to 45 percent, of the drug's value.)

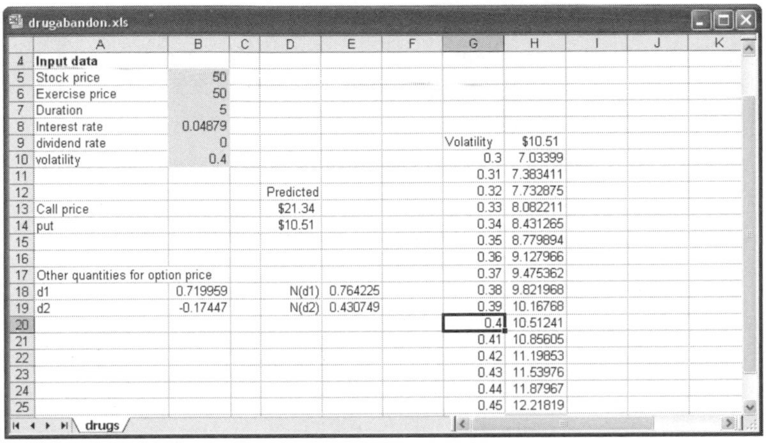

drugabandon.xls

	A	B	C	D	E	F	G	H
4	**Input data**							
5	Stock price	50						
6	Exercise price	50						
7	Duration	5						
8	Interest rate	0.04879						
9	dividend rate	0					Volatility	$10.51
10	volatility	0.4					0.3	7.03399
11							0.31	7.383411
12				Predicted			0.32	7.732875
13	Call price			$21.34			0.33	8.082211
14	put			$10.51			0.34	8.431265
15							0.35	8.779894
16							0.36	9.127966
17	Other quantities for option price						0.37	9.475362
18	d1	0.719959		N(d1)	0.764225		0.38	9.821968
19	d2	-0.17447		N(d2)	0.430749		0.39	10.16768
20							0.4	10.51241
21							0.41	10.85605
22							0.42	11.19853
23							0.43	11.53976
24							0.44	11.87967
25							0.45	12.21819

Figure 63-10 Abandonment option calculations.

Problems

1. Use the monthly stock returns in file Volatility.xls to determine estimates of annual volatility for Intel, Microsoft, and GE.

2. Today a stock is selling for $42. The stock has an annual volatility of 40 percent and the annual risk-free rate is 10 percent.

   - What is a fair price for a six-month European call option with an exercise price of $40?
   - By how much does the current stock price have to increase in order for the purchaser of the call option to break even in six months?
   - What is a fair price for a six-month European put option with an exercise price of $40?
   - How much does the current stock price have to decrease in order for the purchaser of the put option to break even in six months?
   - What level of volatility would make the $40 call option sell for $6? (Hint: Use the Goal Seek command.)

3. On September 25, 2000, JDS Uniphase sold for $106.81. A $100 European put expiring on January 20, 2001, sold on September 25, 2000, for $11.875. Compute an implied volatility for JDS Uniphase based on this information. Use a Treasury bill rate of 5 percent.

4.   On August 9, 2002, Microsoft was selling for $48.58. A $35 European call option expiring on January 17, 2003, was selling for $13.85. Use this information to estimate Microsoft's implied volatility. Use a Treasury bill rate of 4 percent.

5.   You have an option to buy a new plane in three years for $25 million. Your current estimate of the value of the plane is $21 million. The annual volatility for change in the plane's value is 25 percent and the risk-free rate is 5 percent. What is the option to buy the plane worth?

6.   The current price of copper is 95 cents per pound. The annual volatility for copper prices is 20 percent, and the risk-free rate is 5 percent. In one year, we have the option (if we desire) to spend $1.25 million to mine 8 million pounds of copper. The copper can be sold at the copper price in one year. It costs 85 cents to extract a pound of copper from the ground. What is the value of this situation to us?

7.   We own the rights to a biotech drug. Our best estimate is that the current value of these rights is $50 million. Assuming that the annual volatility of biotech companies is 90 percent and the risk-free rate is 5 percent, what is the value of an option to sell the rights to the drug five years from now for $40 million?

8.   Merck is debating whether to invest in a pioneer biotech project. They estimate that the worth of the project is –$56 million. Investing in the pioneer project gives Merck the option to own, if they want, a much bigger technology that will be available in four years. If Merck does not participate in the pioneer project, they cannot own the bigger project. The big project will require $1.5 billion in cash four years from now. Currently, Merck estimates the net present value (NPV) of the cash flows from the bigger project to be $597 million. What should Merck do? Assume a risk-free rate of 10 percent and that the annual volatility of the big project is 35 percent. (This was the example that started the whole field of real options!)

9.   Develop a spreadsheet that uses the following inputs to compute annual profit. Then protect the cells used to compute annual demand and annual profit.

  ❑   Annual fixed cost

  ❑   Unit cost

  ❑   Unit price

Annual demand = 10,000 – 100*(price)

64

Determining Customer Value

- A credit-card company currently has an 80 percent retention rate. How will the company's profitability improve if the retention rate increases to 90 percent or higher?

- A long-distance phone company gives the competition's customers an incentive to switch. How large an incentive should they give?

Many companies undervalue their customers. When valuing a customer, a company should look at the net present value (NPV) of the long-term profits the company earns from the customer. (For detailed information about net present value, see Chapter 8.) Failure to look at the long-term value of a customer often causes a company to make poor decisions. For example, a company might cut its customer service staff by 10 percent to save $1 million, and the resulting decrease in service quality might cause them to lose much more than $1 million in "customer value," which would, of course, result in the company being less profitable. The following two examples show how to compute customer value.

A credit-card company currently has an 80 percent retention rate. How will the company's profitability improve if the retention rate increases to 90 percent or higher?

Our example is based on a discussion in Frederick Reichheld's excellent book *The Loyalty Effect* (Harvard Business School Press, 2001). You can find the sample data we'll use in the file Loyalty.xls, which is shown in Figure 64-1. Reichheld estimates the profitability of a credit-card customer based on the number of years the customer has held a card. For example, during the first year a customer has the credit card, the cardholder generates –$40 profit, which is the result of customer acquisition costs and the cost of setting up the customer's account. During each successive year, the profit generated by the customer increases until a customer who has owned a card for 20 or more years generates $161 per year in profits. (In Figure 64-1, the rows corresponding to years 15-29 are hidden.)

	A	B	C	D	E	F	G	H
2								
3								
4				npv per customer	141.7181			
5								
6		retention rate	0.8					
7		Interest rate	0.15					
8	Year	Mean Profit(if still	Number	Profit		retention rate	141.7181	
9	1	($40.00)	100	($4,000.00)		0.8	141.7181	
10	2	$66.00	80	$5,280.00		0.85	193.1495	
11	3	$72.00	64	$4,608.00		0.9	269.3474	
12	4	$79.00	51.2	$4,044.80		0.95	390.7125	
13	5	$87.00	40.96	$3,563.52		0.99	548.5771	
14	6	$92.00	32.768	$3,014.66				
15	7	$96.00	26.2144	$2,516.58				
16	8	$99.00	20.97152	$2,076.18				
17	9	$103.00	16.77722	$1,728.05				
18	10	$106.00	13.42177	$1,422.71				
19	11	$111.00	10.73742	$1,191.85				
20	12	$116.00	8.589935	$996.43				
21	13	$120.00	6.871948	$824.63				
22	14	$124.00	5.497558	$681.70				
38	30	$161	0.154743	$24.91				
39								

Sheet1 / Sheet2 / Sheet3 /

Figure 64-1   Value of a credit-card customer.

The credit-card company wants to determine how the value of a customer depends on the company's retention rate. Currently, the company has an 80 percent retention rate, which means that at the end of each year, 20 percent (1-.80) of all customers do not renew their card. (We refer to the 20 percent of customers who don't renew as the annual *churn rate.*) The credit-card company wants to determine the long-term value of a customer for retention rates of 80 percent, 85 percent, 90 percent, 95 percent, and 99 percent.

To determine the long-term value of a customer, we start with a cohort of, say, 100 customers. (A cohort is a group of individuals having a statistical factor in common. The size 100 is arbitrary here, but nice round numbers make following the analysis easier.) Then we determine how many of these customers are still around each year with the formula *(Customers around for year t + 1) = (Retention rate)*(Customers around for year t)*. We assume that customers "quit" only at the end of each year. Then we use the NPV function to determine the total NPV (assuming a 15 percent discount rate) generated by our original cohort of 100 customers. The 15 percent discount rate implies that $1 earned one year from now is worth the same as $1.00/$1.15 of profit earned now. Dividing this number by the number of customers in our original cohort (100) gives us the value of an individual customer.

I first assigned the names in the cell range B6:B7 to the cell range C6:C7. Then I entered our number of original customers (100) in cell C9. Copying from cell C10 to the range C11:C38 the formula *retention_rate*C9* generates the number of customers present for each year. For example, we will have 80 customers present in year 2.

I compute the profit earned each year by multiplying the number of remaining customers by each customer's profit. To make this calculation, copy from cell D9 to D10:D38 the formula *C9*B9*. In cell E4, I compute the average NPV generated by an individual customer with the formula *(1+Interest_rate)*NPV(Interest_rate,D9:D38)/100*. We are assuming cash flows at the beginning of the year and a 15 percent annual discount rate. The portion of the formula that reads *NPV(Interest_rate,D9:D38)* computes the average NPV generated by an individual customer assuming end-of-year cash flows. Multiplying by *(1+Interest_rate)* converts the end-of-year cash flow NPV to a beginning-of-year NPV.

With an 80 percent retention rate, we find that the average customer is worth $141.72. To determine how the value of an individual customer varies with a change in annual retention rate, I use a one-way data table. I enter the relevant annual retention rates in the cell range F9:F13. In cell G8, I enter the formula we want the data table to calculate (NPV per customer) with the formula =*E4*. Next, I select the table range (F8:G13) and then choose Data, Table. After entering a column input cell of C6, I obtain the profit calculations shown in Figure 64-1. Notice that increasing our retention rate from 80 percent to 90 percent nearly doubles the value of each customer, which strongly argues for being "nice" to these customers and against pinching pennies on activities related to customer service. Understanding the value of a customer gives most companies a crucial lever that can be used to increase their profitability.

A long-distance phone company gives the competition's customers an incentive to switch. How large an incentive should they give?

Let's say that we work for a phone company in which the average long-distance customer spends $400 per year and the company generates a 10 percent profit margin on each dollar spent. At the end of each year, 50 percent of the company's customers switch to the competition, and without any incentives, 30 percent of the competition's customers switch back to us. We're considering giving the competitors' customers a one-time incentive to switch companies. How large an incentive can we give and still break even?

The key to analyzing this problem (which you can find in the file PhoneLoyalty.xls, shown in Figure 64-2) is to look at the NPV of two situations:

■ Situation 1: 100 customers begin with the competition.

■ Situation 2: We pay the 100 customers with the competition a certain amount to switch to us.

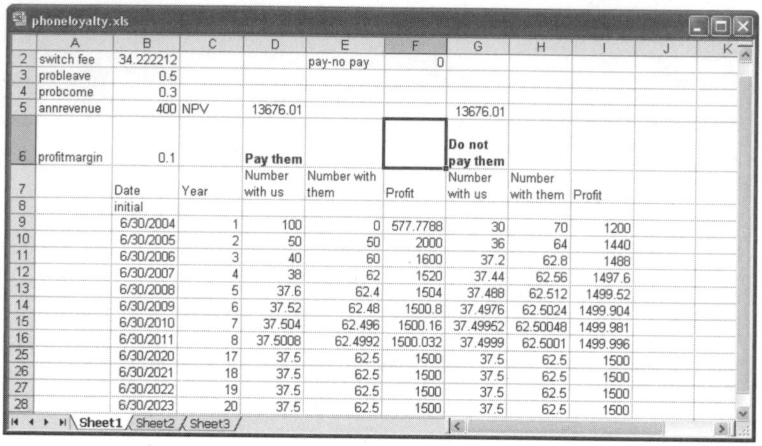
phoneloyalty.xls

	A	B	C	D	E	F	G	H	I
2	switch fee	34.222212			pay-no pay	0			
3	probleave	0.5							
4	probcome	0.3							
5	annrevenue	400	NPV	13676.01			13676.01		
6	profitmargin	0.1		**Pay them**			**Do not pay them**		
7		Date	Year	Number with us	Number with them	Profit	Number with us	Number with them	Profit
8		initial							
9		6/30/2004	1	100	0	577.7788	30	70	1200
10		6/30/2005	2	50	50	2000	36	64	1440
11		6/30/2006	3	40	60	1600	37.2	62.8	1488
12		6/30/2007	4	38	62	1520	37.44	62.56	1497.6
13		6/30/2008	5	37.6	62.4	1504	37.488	62.512	1499.52
14		6/30/2009	6	37.52	62.48	1500.8	37.4976	62.5024	1499.904
15		6/30/2010	7	37.504	62.496	1500.16	37.49952	62.50048	1499.981
16		6/30/2011	8	37.5008	62.4992	1500.032	37.4999	62.5001	1499.996
25		6/30/2020	17	37.5	62.5	1500	37.5	62.5	1500
26		6/30/2021	18	37.5	62.5	1500	37.5	62.5	1500
27		6/30/2022	19	37.5	62.5	1500	37.5	62.5	1500
28		6/30/2023	20	37.5	62.5	1500	37.5	62.5	1500

Sheet1 / Sheet2 / Sheet3

Figure 64-2 Phone incentive analysis.

Following through each situation for a period of time (say 20 years), we can then use Excel's Goal Seek command to determine the dollar amount *x* paid to a person switching back to our company that makes us indifferent between the following two situations:

- Situation 1: We have just paid 100 nonloyal customers $*x* each to switch back to us.
- Situation 2: The market consists of 100 nonloyal customers.

We assume that our analysis begins on June 30, 2004, and that customers switch companies, at most, once per year. I assigned the range names in cells A2:A6 to cells B2:B6. The key step in our analysis is to realize that *(Year t + 1 customers with us) = .3*(Year t competitor customers) + .5*(Year t our customers)*. Similarly *(Year t + 1 customers with competition) = .7*(Year t competition customers) + .5*(Year t our customers)*.

Next, I enter 100 in cell D9 (customers with us) and 0 in cell E9 (customers with the competition). This customer alignment corresponds to the situation right after we give our incentive to 100 customers. We're assuming that customers who receive the incentive must stay with us for at least one year. Copying from D10 to D11:D28 the formula *(1-probleave)*D9+probcome*E9* generates the number of customers we have during each year (years 2012-2019 are hidden in Figure 64-2). Copying the formula *probleave*D9+(1-probcome)*E9* from E10 to E11:E28 gives us the number of customers with the competition during each year.

In cell F9, I generate the profit earned during our first year with the formula *D9*annrevenue*profitmargin – switch_fee*100*. Note that I have subtracted the cost of paying the 100 customers with the competition to switch. Copying from F10 to F11:F28 the formula *D10*annrevenue*profitmargin* generates our profit during later years. In cell D5, I compute the NPV of the profits associated with the incentive by using the formula *XNPV(0.1,F9:F28,B9:B28)*. (See Chapter 8 for a discussion of the XNPV function.)

In a similar fashion, in the cell range G8:I28, I generate the profits earned each year from 100 customers who were originally with the competition. On June 30, 2004, 30 of these 100 customers will have switched to us (even without incentives). In cell F2, I compute the difference between our NPV with the incentive and the NPV without the incentive.

Finally, I use Goal Seek to vary the size of the incentive (cell B2) to set F2 equal to 0. The Goal Seek dialog box is shown in Figure 64-3. We find that an incentive of $34.22 makes the NPV of the two situations identical. Therefore, we could give incentives of up to $34.21 for a customer to switch and still have increased our profitability.

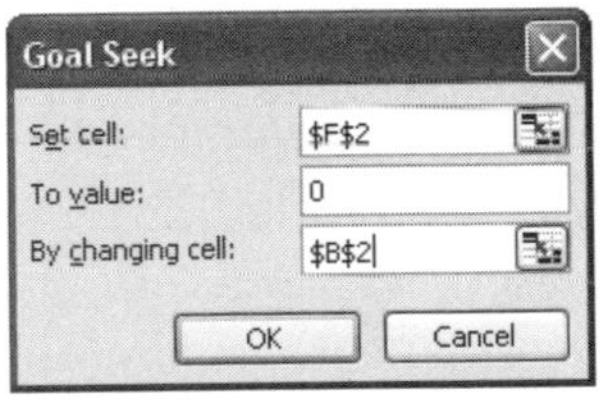

Figure 64-3   Goal Seek settings to determine the maximum incentive that increases profitability.

Problems

1. Whirlswim Appliance is considering giving each of its customers free maintenance on each VCR purchased. They estimate that this proposal will require them to pay an average of $2.50 for each VCR sold today (this cost is in today's dollars). Currently, the market consists of 72,000 consumers whose last purchase was from Whirlswim and 86,000 consumers whose last purchase was from a competitor. In a given year, 40 percent of all consumers purchase a VCR. If their last purchase was a Whirlswim, there is a 60 percent chance that their next purchase will be a Whirlswim. If their last purchase was not a Whirlswim, there is a 30 percent chance that their next purchase will be a Whirlswim. A purchase during the current year will lead to $20

profit. The contribution to profit (and maintenance cost per purchaser) from a purchaser grows at 5 percent per year. Profits (over a 30-year horizon) are discounted at 10 percent per year.

Suppose that we give free maintenance. If the customer's last purchase was a Whirlswim, the probability that their next purchase will be a Whirlswim will increase by an unknown amount between 0 percent and 10 percent. Similarly, if we give free maintenance and the customer's last purchase was not a Whirlswim, the probability that their next purchase is a Whirlswim will increase by an unknown amount between 0 percent and 10 percent. Do you recommend that Whirlswim adopt the free maintenance policy?

2. Mr. D's Supermarket is determined to please their customers with a customer advantage card. Currently, 30 percent of all shoppers are loyal to Mr. D's. A loyal Mr. D's shopper shops at Mr. D's 80 percent of the time. A nonloyal Mr. D's shopper shops at Mr. D's 10 percent of the time. Assume that a typical customer spends $150 per week and that Mr. D's is running on a 4 percent profit margin.

The customer advantage card will cost Mr. D's an average of $.01 per dollar spent. We believe Mr. D's share of loyal customers will increase by an unknown amount between 2 percent and 10 percent. We also believe that the fraction of the time a loyal customer shops at Mr. D's will increase by an unknown amount between 2 percent and 12 percent. Should Mr. D's adopt a customer advantage card? Should they adopt the card if their profit margins are 8 percent?

65

The Economic Order Quantity Inventory Model

- An electronics store sells 10,000 PDAs per year. Each time an order is placed for a supply of PDAs, the store incurs an order cost of $10. The store pays $100 for each PDA, and the cost of holding a PDA in inventory for a year is assumed to be $20. When the store orders PDAs, how large an order should it place?

- A PC manufacturing plant produces 10,000 PCs per year. The cost to produce each PC is $2,000. The cost to set up a production run of PCs is $200, and the cost to hold a PC in inventory for a year is $500. The plant can, if it wants, produce 25,000 PCs per year. When the plant produces PCs, how large a batch should it produce?

Consider a store that orders an item repeatedly. A natural question is what quantity should the store order each time it places an order? If the store orders too many items, it incurs excessive inventory or holding costs. If the store orders too few items, it will place many orders and incur excessive ordering costs. Somewhere, there must be a happy medium that minimizes the sum of annual inventory and order costs.

Similarly, consider a manufacturing plant that produces batches of a product. What batch size minimizes the sum of annual inventory and setup costs? The two examples in this chapter show how to use the Economic Order Quantity formula (developed in 1913 by F. Harris of Westinghouse Corporation) to answer these questions.

An electronics store sells 10,000 PDAs per year. Each time an order is placed for a supply of PDAs, an order cost of $10 is incurred. The store pays $100 for each PDA, and the cost of holding a PDA in inventory for a year is assumed to be $20. When the store orders PDAs, how large an order should be placed?

The size of an order that minimizes the sum of annual inventory and ordering costs can be determined after the following parameters are known.

■ K = Cost per order

■ h = Cost of holding one unit in inventory for a year

■ D = Annual demand for product

You can follow an example of how to work with these parameters using the worksheet EOQ in the file Eoq.xls, which is shown in Figure 65-1.

	A	B	C	D	E	F	G	H
1								
2	cost/order	K	10					
3	annual holding cost per unit	h	20					
4	annual demand	D	10000					
5	order quantity	EOQ	100					
6	holding cost per year	annhc	$1,000.00					
7	order cost per year	annoc	$1,000.00					
8	total annual cost (excluding purchasing)	anncost	$2,000.00					
9	orders per year	annorders	100					
10								
11								
12								
13								

Figure 65-1   EOQ template.

If q equals order size, annual inventory cost equals $.5qh$. (Throughout this example, I'll refer to this equation as equation 1.) We derive equation 1 because our average inventory level ($.5q$) will be half the maximum inventory level. To see why the average inventory level is $.5q$, note that we can compute the average inventory level for a cycle (the time between arrival of orders). At the beginning of a cycle, an order arrives and our inventory level is q. At the end of the cycle, we are out of stock and our inventory level is 0. Because demand occurs at a constant rate, the average inventory level during a cycle is simply the average of 0 and q or $.5q$. Maximum inventory level will equal q because orders are assumed to arrive at the instant that the inventory level is reduced to 0.

Because D/q orders are placed per year, annual ordering cost equals $(D/q)*K$. (I'll refer to this equation as equation 2.) Using calculus or the Excel Solver, we can show that the annual sum of inventory and ordering costs is minimized for a value of q equal to the economic order quantity (EOQ), which is calculated using the following formula (which I'll refer to as equation 3).

$$EOQ = \sqrt{\frac{2KD}{h}}$$

From this formula, we see the following:

- An increase in demand or ordering cost will increase the EOQ.

- An increase in holding cost will decrease the EOQ.

In the file Eoq.xls, I used equation 3 to determine EOQ in cell C5. I determined annual holding cost in cell C6 by using equation 1. I determined annual ordering cost in cell C7 with equation 2. Notice that for EOQ, the annual ordering cost equals the annual holding cost, which will always be the case. In cell C8, I determined the total annual cost (ignoring the purchasing cost, which does not depend on our ordering strategy) with the formula *C6+C7*.

Of course, you can use one-way and two-way data tables to determine the sensitivity of the EOQ and various costs to variations in K, h, and D. For our example, we have $K = \$10$, $D = 10,000$ PDAs per year, and $h = \$20$ per PDA. Inserting these values in cells C2:C4, we find the following:

- Each order should be for 100 PDAs.

- Annual holding and ordering costs each equal $1,000. The EOQ always sets annual holding costs equal to annual ordering costs.

- Total annual costs (exclusive of purchasing costs) equal $2,000.

When you are working with EOQ, keep the following in mind:

- The presence of quantity discounts invalidates the EOQ because the annual purchase cost would now depend on the order size.

- The EOQ assumes that demand occurs at a relatively constant rate throughout the year. The EOQ should not be used for products for which demand is highly seasonal.

- Annual holding cost is usually assumed to be between 10 percent and 40 percent of a product's unit purchasing cost.

- I've included (in the worksheet named Protected in the file Eoq.xls) a version of the EOQ spreadsheet in which all formulas are protected. When the sheet is protected, it ensures that nobody can mess up our formulas. See Chapter 63 for instructions about how to protect a worksheet.

- For further discussion of inventory modeling, interested readers can use my book *Operations Research: Applications and Algorithms* (Duxbury Press, 2003).

A PC manufacturing plant produces 10,000 PCs per year. The cost to produce each PC is $2,000. The cost to set up a production run of PCs is $200, and the cost to hold a PC in inventory for a year is $500. The plant can, if it wants, produce 25,000 PCs per year. When the plant produces PCs, how large a batch should it produce?

With the EOQ model, we assume an order arrives the instant the order is placed. When a company manufactures a product instead of ordering it, an order must be produced and cannot arrive instantaneously. In such situations, instead of computing the cost-minimizing order quantity, we need to determine the cost-minimizing batch size. When a company produces a product internally instead of purchasing the product externally, the batch size that minimizes costs depends on the following parameters:

- K = Cost of setting up a batch for production

- h = Cost of holding one unit in inventory for a year

- D = Annual demand for product

- R = Annual rate at which the product can be produced. For example, IBM might have the capacity to produce 25,000 PCs per year.

If q equals the size of each production batch, the annual holding cost equals $.5*(q/R)*(R-D)*h$. (I'll refer to this equation as equation 4.) Equation 4 follows because each batch takes q/R years to produce and, during a production cycle, inventory increases at a rate of $R-D$. Our maximum inventory level, which occurs at the completion of a batch, can be calculated as $(q/R)*(R-D)$. Our average inventory level will thus equal $.5*(q/R)*(R-D)$.

Because D/q batches are produced per year, annual setup cost equals KD/q (equation 5). Using calculus or the Excel Solver, we can show that the batch size that minimizes the sum of annual setup and production-run costs is given by the following (which I'll refer to as equation 6). We call this model the Economic Order Batch Size (EOB).

$$\text{Economic Order Batch size} = \sqrt{\frac{2KDR}{h(R-D)}}$$

From this formula, we find the following:

- An increase in K or D will increase the economic order batch size.

- An increase in h or R will decrease the EOB.

In the worksheet Cont Rate EOQ in the file Contrateeoq.xls, I've constructed a template to determine the EOB, annual setup, and holding costs. The worksheet is shown in Figure 65-2.

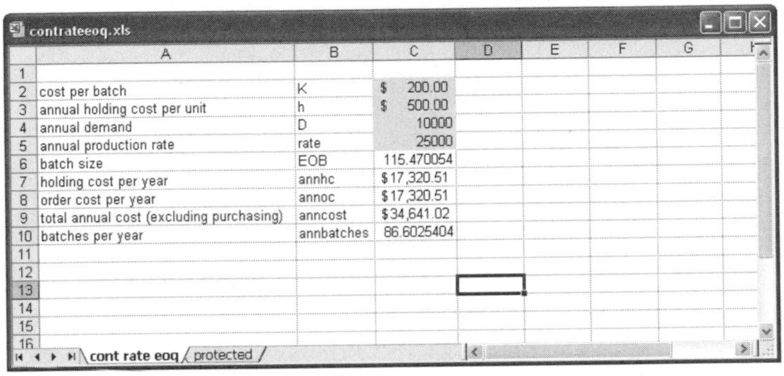

	A	B	C
1			
2	cost per batch	K	$ 200.00
3	annual holding cost per unit	h	$ 500.00
4	annual demand	D	10000
5	annual production rate	rate	25000
6	batch size	EOB	115.470054
7	holding cost per year	annhc	$17,320.51
8	order cost per year	annoc	$17,320.51
9	total annual cost (excluding purchasing)	anncost	$34,641.02
10	batches per year	annbatches	86.6025404

Figure 65-2 Template for computing EOB.

For our example, K = \$200, h = \$500, D = 10,000 units per year, and R = 25,000 units per year. After entering these parameter values in the cell range C2:C5, we find the following:

- The batch size that minimizes costs is 115.47 PCs. Thus, we should produce 115 or 116 PCs in each batch.
- The annual holding cost and setup costs equal $17,320.51. Again, the EOB will always set annual holding cost equal to annual setup cost.
- Total annual cost (exclusive of variable production costs) is $34,641.02.
- 86.6 batches per year will be produced.

When you are working with the EOB model, keep the following in mind:

- If the unit variable cost of producing a product depends on the batch size, the EOB model is invalid.
- The EOB assumes that demand occurs at a relatively constant rate throughout the year. The EOB should not be used for products for which demand is highly seasonal.
- The annual holding cost is usually assumed to be between 10 percent and 40 percent of a product's unit purchasing cost.
- I've included (in the worksheet named Protected in the file Contrateeoq.xls) a version of the EOB spreadsheet in which all formulas are protected. See Chapter 63 for instructions about how to protect a worksheet.

Problems

1. An appliance store sells plasma TVs. Annual demand is estimated at 1000 units. The cost to carry a TV in inventory for one year is $500, and the cost to place an order for plasma TVs is $400.

    ❑ How many TVs should be ordered each time an order is placed?

    ❑ How many orders per year should be placed?

    ❑ What are the annual inventory and ordering costs?

2. Waterford Glass Company can produce up to 100 iced tea pitchers per day. Annual demand (the plant is open 250 days per year) is for 20,000 pitchers. The cost to hold a pitcher in inventory for a year is $10, and the cost to set up the facility to produce iced tea pitchers is $40.

    ❑ What batch size would you recommend for iced tea pitchers?

    ❑ How many batches per year should be produced?

    ❑ What are the annual setup and inventory costs for iced tea pitchers?

66

Determining the Reorder Point: How Low Should I Let My Inventory Level Go Before I Reorder?

- At what inventory level (called the *reorder point*) should I place an order if my goal is to minimize the sum of annual holding, ordering, and shortage costs?

- What does the term *95 percent service level* mean?

In Chapter 65, we used the economic order quantity (EOQ) to determine an optimal order quantity and production batch size. We assumed that demand occurred at a constant rate. Thus, if annual demand occurred at a rate of, say, 1200 units per year, during each month demand would equal 100 units. As long as demand occurs at a relatively constant rate, the EOQ is a good approximation of the cost-minimizing order quantity.

In reality, demand during any time period is uncertain. When demand is uncertain, a natural question is how low I should let my inventory level go before I place an order. We call the inventory level at which an order should be placed the *reorder point*. Clearly, a high reorder point will lower shortage costs and increase holding costs. Similarly, a low reorder point will increase shortage costs and lower holding costs. At some intermediate value for the reorder point, the sum of shortage and holding costs will be minimized. Our first example shows how to determine a reorder point that minimizes the sum of expected ordering, shortage, and holding costs under two assumptions:

- Each unit we are short is back ordered by a customer, and a shortage cost c_B is incurred for each unit we are short.

- Each unit we are short results in a lost sale, and a shortage cost $c_{LS} > c_B$ is incurred for each unit short.

The second example shows how to determine the optimal reorder point based on a *service level* approach. For example, a 95 percent service level means that we set the reorder point at a level ensuring that on average, 95 percent of all demand is met on time. It is usually difficult to determine the cost of a shortage in either the back-ordered or lost sales case. For that reason, most companies set reorder points using the service level approach.

> **Note**   On this book's companion CD, I've included a worksheet in which all formulas are protected for both the back-ordered and lost-sales cases. You can use these worksheets as templates.

At what inventory level (called the *reorder point*) should I place an order if my goal is to minimize the sum of annual holding, ordering, and shortage costs?

As I indicated in Chapter 65, the economic order quantity (EOQ) depends on the following parameters:

- K = Cost per order

- h = Cost of holding one unit in inventory for a year

- D = Annual demand for the product

Because demand is now uncertain, we will let D stand for the expected annual demand for the product.

The back-order case   See the file ReorderPoint_Backorder.xls, shown in Figure 66-1, for the data I'm using in this example. Let's first suppose that each shortage results in the short units being back ordered. In other words, a shortage does not result in any lost demand. We assume that each unit we are short incurs a cost c_B. In this case, the reorder point depends on the following quantities:

- EOQ is the economic order quantity (the quantity ordered each time an order is placed).

- *K* is the cost per order.

- *h* is the annual holding cost per unit.

- *D* is the mean annual demand.

- *SOC* is the cost per unit short.

- *annsig* is the standard deviation of annual demand.

- *meanLT* is the average *lead time*; that is, the average time between placing an order and the time the order is received.

- *sigmaLT* is the standard deviation of lead time.

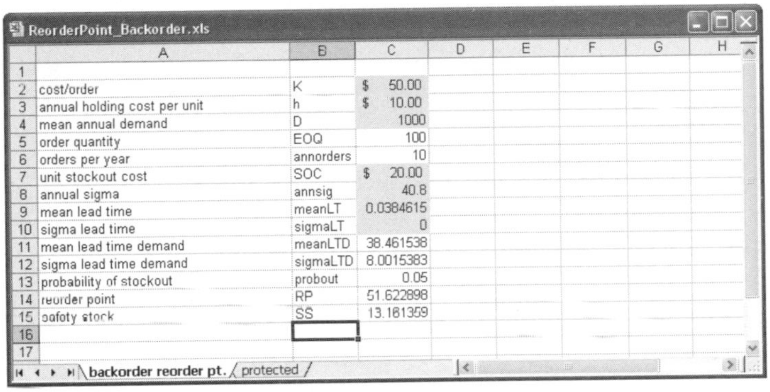

	A	B	C	D	E	F	G	H
1								
2	cost/order	K	$ 50.00					
3	annual holding cost per unit	h	$ 10.00					
4	mean annual demand	D	1000					
5	order quantity	EOQ	100					
6	orders per year	annorders	10					
7	unit stockout cost	SOC	$ 20.00					
8	annual sigma	annsig	40.8					
9	mean lead time	meanLT	0.0384615					
10	sigma lead time	sigmaLT	0					
11	mean lead time demand	meanLTD	38.461538					
12	sigma lead time demand	sigmaLTD	8.0015383					
13	probability of stockout	probout	0.05					
14	reorder point	RP	51.622898					
15	safety stock	SS	13.161359					
16								
17								

backorder reorder pt. / protected /

Figure 66-1   Determination of reorder point when shortages arc back ordered.

Let's suppose that a department store wants to determine an optimal inventory policy for ordering electric mixers. They have the following information:

- It costs $50 to place an order for mixers.

- It costs $10 to hold a mixer in inventory for a year.

- On average, demand during a year is for 1000 mixers.

- All customers who try to purchase a mixer when the store is out of stock return at a later date and buy the mixer when the mixer is in stock. The store incurs a penalty cost of $20 for each unit it is short.

- The annual demand for mixers (based on historical data) has a standard deviation of 40.8.

- Lead time is always two weeks (which equals .038 years), with a standard deviation of 0.

After we input K, h, and D in cells C2:C4, our spreadsheet computes the *EOQ* (100 mixers) in C5. After we enter *SOC, annsig, meanLT*, and *sigmaLT* in cells C7:C10, our spreadsheet computes in cell C14 the reorder point that minimizes the sum of expected annual holding and shortage costs (51.63 mixers). Thus, our department store should order 100 mixers whenever their stock decreases to 51.63 (say 52) mixers.

The *safety stock level* associated with a given reorder point is *reorder point – mean lead time demand*. The department store maintains a safety stock level of 51.62 – 38.46 = 13.16 mixers, computed in cell C15. Essentially, the safety stock is always in inventory, resulting in extra holding costs. A higher level of safety stock will, of course, reduce shortages.

Finally, in cell C13, our spreadsheet reports the probability of a stock outage associated with our cost-minimizing reorder point. The sum of expected shortages and holding costs is minimized by failing to meet 5 percent of our demand on time.

The lost-sales case   Now suppose that each shortage results in a lost sale. The cost associated with a lost sale is usually estimated as the back-order penalty plus the profit associated with a unit sold. Suppose that the department store earns a $20 profit on each mixer it sells. The unit shortage cost for the lost-sales case is then $40 (*$20 lost profit + $20 back-order penalty*).

In the file ReorderPoint_LostSales.xls, shown in Figure 66-2, you can see the work I did to estimate the reorder point for the lost-sales case. After inputting in cell C7 of the spreadsheet the lost-sales cost of $40, we find the optimal inventory policy is to order 100 mixers and place an order when inventory is down to 54.23 mixers. Our safety stock level is 15.77 mixers, and 2.4 percent of our demand for mixers will be unmet. Notice that the assumption of a lost sale has increased our reorder point and reduced the probability of a shortage. This happens because the increased cost of a shortage (from $20 to $40) makes us more eager to avoid shortages.

	A	B	C	D	E	F	G	H
1								
2	cost/order	K	$ 50.00					
3	annual holding cost per unit	h	$ 10.00					
4	mean annual demand	D	1000					
5	order quantity	EOQ	100					
6	orders per year	annorders	10					
7	lost sales cost	LSC	$ 40.00					
8	annual sigma	annsig	40.8					
9	mean lead time	meanLT	0.0384615					
10	sigma lead time	sigmaLT	0					
11	mean lead time demand	meanLTD	38.461538					
12	sigma lead time demand	sigmaLTD	8.0015383					
13	probability of stockout	probout	0.0243902					
14	reorder point	RP	54.228612					
15	safety stock	SS	15.767074					
16								

Figure 66-2   Reorder point determination when a sale is lost.

Increased uncertainty greatly increases the reorder point. For example, in the lost-sales case, if the standard deviation for lead time is one week (0.019 years) rather than 0, the reorder point increases to 79.50 mixers and the safety stock more than doubles from the case in which our lead time was known with certainty.

What does the term *95 percent service level* mean?

A 95 percent service level simply means that we want 95 percent of our demand to be met on time. Because estimating the back-order penalty and/or the penalty that results from a lost sale is often difficult, many companies set safety stock levels for products by setting a service level. The file ServiceLevelReorder.xls (shown in Figure 66-3) enables us to determine the reorder point corresponding to any service level we want.

	A	B	C	D	E	F	G
1	Service level	SL	0.95				
2	cost/order	K	$ 50.00				
3	annual holding cost per unit	h	$ 10.00				
4	mean annual demand	D	1000				
5	order quantity	EOQ	100				
6	orders per year	annorders	10				
7	annual sigma	annsig	69.28				
8	mean lead time	meanLT	0.0833333				
9	sigma lead time	sigmaLT	0				
10	mean lead time demand	meanLTD	83.333333				
11	sigma lead time demand	sigmaLTD	19.999413				
12	reorder point	ROP	**90.230075**				
13	standardized reorder point	SROP	0.3448472				DIFF
14	normal loss for stand. ROP	NLSTANDROP	0.2500074 =		0.250007		6.43673E-08
15	safety stock	SS	6.8967417				
16							
17							
18							

Figure 66-3 Determination of reorder point using the service level approach.

As an example, consider a pharmacy that is trying to determine an optimal inventory policy for a drug they stock. They would like to meet 95 percent of their demand on time. The following parameters are relevant.

■ Each order for the drug costs $50.

■ The cost to hold a unit of the drug in inventory for a year is $10.

■ Average demand per year for the drug is 1000 units.

■ The standard deviation of annual demand is 69.28 units.

■ The time required to receive a shipment of the drug always takes exactly1 month (0.083 years).

We enter the service level (0.95) we want in cell C1 and all other parameters in cells C2:C4 and C7:C9. To determine the reorder point yielding the desired service level, select Tools, Solver and click the Solve button. Our solver model adjusts the reorder point until the percentage of demand met on time matches the service level we want. We find that we should order 100 units of the drug whenever our inventory level drops to 90.23 units. This reorder point corresponds to a safety stock level of 6.90 units.

In the following table, I've listed the reorder point and safety stock levels corresponding to service levels between 80 percent and 99 percent.

Service Level Percentage	Reorder Point	Safety Stock
80	65.34	-17.99
85	71.85	-11.48
90	79.57	-3.76
95	90.23	6.90
99	108.44	25.11

Notice that moving from an 80 percent to a 99 percent service level increases the reorder point by almost 67 percent! Also note that we can attain a 90 percent service level with a reorder point less than our mean lead time demand (refer back to cell C10 in Figure 66-3). This service level results in a negative safety stock level, which is possible because shortages only occur during the lead time and our lead times usually cover a small portion of a year.

Problems

In working with Problems 1 and 2, assume that a restaurant uses an average of 5000 bottles of wine per year. The standard deviation of the annual demand for wine is 1000 bottles. The holding cost for a year for a bottle of wine is $1. It costs $10 to place an order for the wine, and it takes an average of 3 weeks (with a standard deviation of 1 week) for the wine to arrive.

1. Assume that the restaurant incurs a penalty of $5 as the result of lost goodwill when it is out of wine. Also, the restaurant earns $2 profit per bottle of wine. Determine an optimal ordering policy for the wine.

2. Determine an inventory policy for wine that yields a 99 percent service level.

3. A reorder point policy is often referred to as a *two-bin policy*. How can a reorder point policy be implemented in a situation in which two bins are used to store inventory?

67

Queuing Theory: The Mathematics of Waiting in Line

■ What factors affect the time we spend waiting in line and the number of people waiting in line?

■ Under what conditions can we talk about the average time spent in a queuing system or the average number of people present in a queuing system?

■ Why does variability degrade the performance of a queuing system?

■ Can I easily determine the average time a person spends at airport security or waiting in line at a bank?

We have all spent a lot of time waiting in lines, and you'll soon see that a slight increase in service capacity can often greatly reduce the size of the lines we encounter. If you run a business, ensuring that your customers do not spend too much time in line is important. Therefore, businesspeople need to understand the mathematics of waiting in line, which is usually referred to as *queuing theory*. In this chapter, I'll show you how to determine the amount of service capacity needed to provide adequate service.

What factors affect the time we spend waiting in line and the number of people waiting in line?

In this chapter, we will consider queuing problems in which all arriving customers wait in a single line for the first available server. This model is a fairly accurate representation of the situations we face when we wait at a bank, at an airline ticket counter, or at the post office. By the way, the idea of having customers wait in a single line started around 1970. Although waiting in a single line does not reduce the average time spent waiting, it does reduce the variability of our time in line, thereby creating a "fairer" system.

Three main factors influence the time we spend in a queuing system:

- The number of servers. Clearly, the more servers, the less time on average we spend in line, and fewer people on average will be present in the line.

- The mean and the standard deviation of the time between arrivals. (We call the time between arrivals *interarrival time*.) If the average time between arrivals increases, the number of arrivals decreases, which results in shorter lines and less time spent in a queuing system. As you'll soon see, an increase in standard deviation of interarrival times increases the average time a customer spends in a queuing system and the average number of customers present.

- The mean and standard deviation of the time needed to complete service. If the average service time increases, we will see an increase in the average time a customer spends in the system and the number of customers present. As you'll see, an increase in the standard deviation of service times increases the average time a customer spends in a queuing system and the average number of customers present.

Under what conditions can we talk about the average time spent in a queuing system or the average number of people present in a queuing system?

When analyzing the time spent waiting in lines, mathematicians talk about *steady state* characteristics of a system. Essentially, steady state means that a system has operated for a long time. More specifically, we would like to know the value of the following quantities in the steady state:

- W = Average time a customer spends in the system.

- W_q = Average time a customer spends waiting in line before the customer starts to be served.

- L = Average number of customers present in the system.

- L_q = Average number of customers waiting in line.

By the way, it is always true that L equals *(1/mean interarrival time)*W* and L_q equals *(1/mean interarrival time)*W_q*.

To discuss the steady state of a queuing system meaningfully, the following must be the case:

- The mean and standard deviation of both the interarrival times and the service times changes little over time. The technical phrase is that the distribution of interarrival and service times is *stationary* over time.

- *(1/mean service time)*(number of servers) > (1/(mean interarrival time))*. I'll refer to this equation as equation 1.

Essentially, if equation 1 is true, we can serve more people per hour than are arriving. For example, if *mean service time* equals *2* minutes (or 1/30 of an hour), and *mean interarrival time* equals 1 minute (or 1/60 of an hour), equation 1 tells us that *30*(number of servers) > 60,* or that the number of servers must be greater than or equal to 3 for a steady state to exist. If you cannot serve customers faster than customers arrive, eventually you fall behind and never catch up, resulting in an infinite line.

Why does variability degrade the performance of a queuing system?

To see why variability degrades the performance of a queuing system, consider a single server system in which customers arrive every 2 minutes and service times always equal 2 minutes. There will never be more than one customer in the system. Now suppose that customers arrive every 2 minutes, but half of all service times are .5 minutes and half are 3.5 minutes. Even though arrivals are totally predictable, the uncertainty in service times means that eventually we will fall behind and a line will form. For example, if the first four customers have 3.5 minute service times, after 12 minutes, we will have four customers waiting, which is illustrated in the following table.

Time	Event	Number Present after event
0	Arrival	1
2	Arrival	2
3.5	Service completed	1
4	Arrival	2
6	Arrival	3
7	Service completed	2
8	Arrival	3
10	Arrival	4
10.5	Service completed	3
12	Arrival	4

Can I easily determine the average time a person spends at airport security or waiting in line at a bank?

The file QueuingTemplate.xls (in the worksheet named Model) contains a template that you can use to determine approximate values for L, W, L_q, and W_q (usually within 10 percent of their true value). The worksheet is shown in Figure 67-1.

	A	B	C	D
1				
2				
3	Arrival rate	0.077736		
4	Service rate	0.01297		
5	s	6		
6	Mean interarrival time	12.864		
7	Mean service time	77.102		
8	Standard deviation of interarrival times	4.439		
9	Standard deviation of service times	48.051		
10	CV arrive	0.119074		
11	CV service	0.388395		
12	u	5.993626		
13	ro	0.998938		
14	R(s,mu)	0.735525		
15	E$_C$(s,mu)	0.997054		
16	W$_q$	3060.035		
17	L$_q$	237.8758		
18	W	3137.137		
19	L	243.8694		
20				

Figure 67-1   Queuing template.

After entering the following inputs, the template computes W_q, L_q, W, and L. The parameters in cells B6:B9 can easily be estimated by using past data:

- Number of servers (cell B5)

- Mean interarrival time (cell B6)

- Mean service time (cell B7)

- Standard deviation of interarrival times (cell B8)

- Standard deviation of service times (cell B9)

Here's an example of the template in action. We want to determine how the operating characteristics of an airline ticket counter during the 9 A.M. to 5 P.M. shift depend on the number of agents working. In the worksheet Queuing Data in the file QueuingTemplate.xls, shown in Figure 67-2, I've tabulated interarrival times and service times. (Some rows have been hidden.)

	A	B	C	D	E	F	G	H	I
1	mean	12.86440678	77.10169492	seconds!					
2	sigma	4.43908047	48.05051039						
3		Interarrival times	Service time						
4		5	95						
5		17	240						
6		12	71						
7		18	68						
8		9	90						
9		16	117						
10		15	291						
11		15	116						
12		10	107						
13		11	100						
14		9	28						
15		15	119						
16		19	98						
17		9	72						
18		16	127						
57		13	74						
58		11	27						
59		13	84						
60		19	90						

Figure 67-2   Airline interarrival and service times.

By copying from cell B1 to C1 the formula *AVERAGE(B4:B62)*, we find the mean interarrival time to be 12.864 seconds and the mean service time to be 77.102 seconds. Because mean service time is almost six times as large as mean interarrival time, we will need at least six agents to guarantee a steady state. Copying from cell B2 to C2 the formula *STDEV(B4:B62)* tells us that the standard deviation of the interarrival times is 4.439 seconds, and the standard deviation of the service times is 48.051 seconds.

Returning to the queuing template in the worksheet named Model, if we enter these values in cells B6:B9 and enter six servers in cell B5, we find that disaster ensues. In the steady state, nearly 244 people will be in line (cell B19). You've probably been at the airport in this situation.

I used a one-way data table (shown in Figure 67-3) to determine how changing the number of agents affects the system's performance. In cells F10:F14, I entered the number of agents we want to consider (6 through 10). In cell G9, I enter the formula to compute *L* (*=B19*) and in H9, I enter the formula to compute *W* (*=B18*). Next, I select the table range (F8:H14) and then choose Data, Table. After choosing cell B5 (the number of servers) as the row input cell, we obtain the data table shown in Figure 67-3. Notice that adding just one ticket agent to our original six agents reduces the expected number of customers present in line from 244 to fewer than 7. Adding the seventh agent reduces a customer's average time in the system from 3137 seconds (53 minutes) to 90 seconds (1.5 minutes). This example shows that a small increase in service capacity can greatly improve the performance of a queuing system.

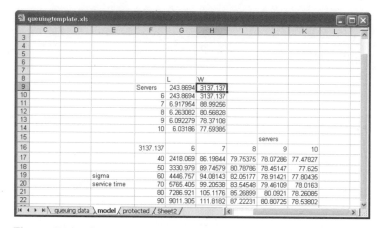

Figure 67-3 Sensitivity analysis for an airline ticket counter.

In cells F16:K22, I used a two-way data table to examine the sensitivity of the average time in the system (*W*) to changes in the number of servers and standard deviation of service times. The row input cell is B5, and the column input cell is B9. When seven agents are working, an increase in the standard deviation of service times from 40 to 90 seconds results in a 29 percent increase in the mean time in the system (from 86.2 seconds to 111.8 seconds).

Note   Readers who are interested in a more extensive discussion of queuing theory should refer to my book *Operations Research: Applications and Algorithms* (Duxbury Press, 2003).

Problems

A bank has six tellers. Use the following information to answer problems 1-5:

■   Mean service time equals 1 minute.

■   Mean interarrival time equals 25 seconds.

■   Standard deviation of service times equals 1 minute.

■   Standard deviation of interarrival times equals 10 seconds.

1.   Determine the average time a customer waits in line.

2.   On average, how many customers are present in the bank?

3.   Would you recommend adding more tellers?

4.   If the bank could decrease the standard deviation of service times by 50 percent, by how much would average time in the bank be reduced?

5.   Suppose it costs $20 per hour to have a teller working and we value a customer's time at $15 per hour. How many tellers should we have working?

68

Estimating a Demand Curve

- What do I need to know to price a product?

- What is the meaning of elasticity of demand?

- Is there any easy way to estimate a demand curve?

- What does a demand curve tell us about a customer's willingness to pay for our product?

Every business must determine a price for each of its products. Pricing a product properly is difficult. In Chapters 68-71, I'll describe some simple models that might aid you in pricing a product to maximize profitability. For further insights into pricing, refer to the excellent book *Power Pricing*, by Robert J. Dolan and Hermann Simon (Free Press, 1996).

What do I need to know to price a product?
Let's consider a product such as a candy bar. In order to determine a profit-maximizing price, we need to know two things:

- The variable cost of producing each unit of the product (call this *UC*).

- The product's demand curve. Simply put, a demand curve tells us the number of units of our product a customer will demand at each price. In short, if we charge a price of p per unit, the demand curve gives us a number $D(p)$, which equals the number of units of our product that will be demanded at price p. Of course, a firm's demand curve is constantly changing and often depends on factors beyond the firm's control (such as the state of the economy and a competitor's price).

Once we know *UC* and the demand curve, the profit corresponding to a price of $p is simply *(p – UC)*D(p)*. After we have an equation for *D(p)*, which gives the quantity of the product demanded for each price, we can use the Excel Solver to find the profit-maximizing price, which we'll do in Chapter 69 and Chapter 70.

What is the meaning of elasticity of demand?

Given a demand curve, the *price elasticity* for demand is the percentage decrease in demand resulting from a 1 percent increase in price. When elasticity is larger than 1, demand is price elastic. When demand is price elastic, a price cut will increase revenue. When elasticity is less than 1, demand is price inelastic. When demand is price inelastic, a price cut will decrease revenue. Here are some observed estimates of elasticities:

- Salt, 0.1 (very inelastic)

- Coffee, 0.25 (inelastic)

- Legal fees, 0.4 (inelastic)

- TV sets, 1.2 (slightly elastic)

- Restaurant meals, 2.3 (elastic)

- Foreign travel, 4.0 (very elastic)

A 1 percent decrease in cost of foreign travel, for example, will result in a 4 percent increase in demand for foreign travel.

Is there any easy way to estimate a demand curve?

Using *q* to represent the quantity demanded of a product, the two most commonly used forms for estimating demand curves are as follows:

- **Linear demand curve**   In this case, demand follows a straight line relationship of the form $q = a - bp$. For example, $q = 10 - p$ is a linear demand curve. (Here *a* and *b* can be determined using a method that I'll describe later in the chapter.) When the demand curve is linear, the elasticity is constantly changing.

- **Power Demand Curve**   In this situation, the demand curve is described by a power curve of the form $q = ap^b$, $b < 0$. (See Chapter 43 for a discussion of the power curve.) Again, a and b can be determined by the method I'll describe later in the chapter. The equation $q = 100p^{-2}$ is an example of a power demand curve. If demand follows a power curve, for any price, the elasticity equals –b. Thus, for the demand curve $q = 100p^{-2}$, the price elasticity of demand always equals 2.

Suppose that a product's demand curve follows a linear or power demand curve. Given the current price and demand for a product and the product's price elasticity of demand, determining the product's demand curve is a simple matter. Here are two examples.

A product is currently selling for $100 and demand equals 500 units. The product's price elasticity for demand is 2. Assuming the demand curve is linear, we want to determine the equation of the demand curve. Our solution is in the file Linearfit.xls, which is shown in Figure 68-1.

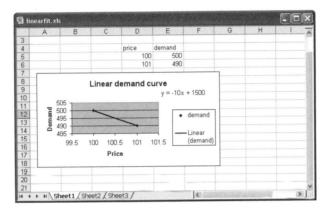

Figure 68-1   Fitting a linear demand curve.

Given two points, we know that there is a unique straight line that passes through those two points. We actually know two points on our demand curve. One point is $p = 100$ and $q = 500$. Because elasticity of demand equals 2, a 1 percent increase in price will result in a 2 percent decrease in demand. Thus, if $p = 101$ (a 1 percent increase), demand will drop by 2 percent of 500 (10 units), or 490. Thus $p = 101$ and $q = 490$ is a second point on our demand curve. We can now use the Excel trend line to find the straight line that passes through the points (100, 500) and (101, 490).

We begin by entering these points in our worksheet in the cell range D5:E6, as shown in Figure 68-1. Then we select the range D4:E6 and choose Insert, Chart. After selecting the first option for an XY (Scatter) chart and clicking Next in the Chart Wizard, we indicate to Excel that data is in columns (otherwise, because there are only two data points, Excel will not understand that each row is a separate data point). After completing the wizard to create the graph of our two points, we right-click on one of the points, choose Add Trendline, and then choose the Linear option. On the Options tab of the Add Trendline dialog box, select the option Display Equation On Chart. After clicking OK in the Add Trendline dialog box, you will see the straight line plot, complete with the equation shown in Figure 68-1. Because x is price and y is demand, the equation for our demand curve is $q = 1500 - 10p$. This equation means that each increase in price of $1 costs us 10 units of demand. Of course, demand cannot be linear for all values of p because for large values of p, a linear demand curve will yield negative demand. For prices near the current price, however, the linear demand curve is usually a good approximation to the product's true demand curve.

As a second example, let's again assume that a product is currently selling for $100 and demand equals 500 units. The product's price elasticity for demand is 2. Now let's fit a power demand curve to this information. See the file Powerfit.xls, shown in Figure 68-2.

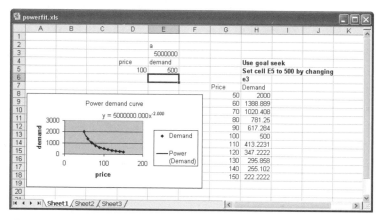

Figure 68-2   Power demand curve.

In cell E3, we enter a trial value for a. Then, in cell D5, we enter the current price of $100. Because elasticity of demand equals 2, we know that the demand curve has the form $q = ap^{-2}$, where a is unknown. In cell E5, we enter the demand for a price of $100 corresponding to the value of a in cell E3 with the formula $a*D5\text{^}-2$. Now we use the Goal Seek command (for details, see Chapter 16) to determine the value of a that makes our demand for price $100 equal to 500 units. I simply set cell E5 to the value of 500 by changing cell E3. I find that a value for a of 5,000,000 yields a demand of 500 at a price of $100. Thus, our demand curve (graphed in Figure 68-2) is given by $q = 5,000,000p^{-2}$. For any price, the price elasticity of demand on this demand curve equals 2.

What does a demand curve tell us about a customer's willingness to pay for our product?

Let's suppose we are trying to sell a software program to a Fortune 500 company. Let q equal the number of copies of the program the company demands, and let p equal the price charged for the software. Suppose we have estimated that the demand curve for software is given by $q = 400 - p$. Clearly, our customer is willing to pay less for each additional unit of our software program. Locked inside this demand curve is information about how much the company is willing to pay for each unit of our program. This information is crucial for maximizing profitability of sales.

Let's rewrite our demand curve as $p = 400 - q$. Thus, when $q = 1, p = \$399$, and so on. Now let's try and figure out the value our customer attaches to each of the first two units of our program. Assuming that our customer is rational, the customer will buy a unit if and only if the value of the unit exceeds our price. At a price of $400, demand equals 0, so the first unit cannot be worth $400. At a price of $399, however, demand equals 1 unit. Therefore, the first unit must be worth somewhere between $399 and $400. Similarly, at a price of $399, the customer does not purchase the second unit. At a price of $398, however, the customer is purchasing two units, so the customer does purchase the second unit. Therefore, the customer values the second unit somewhere between $399 and $398.

It can be shown that the best approximation to the value of the ith unit purchased by the customer is the price that makes demand equal to $i - .5$. For example, by setting q equal to 0.5, we find that the value of the first unit is $400 - 0.5 = \$399.50$. Similarly, by setting $q = 1.5$, we find that the value of the second unit is $400 - 1.5 = \$398.50$.

Problems

1.   Suppose we are charging $60 for a board game we invented and have sold 3000 copies during the last year. Elasticity for board games is known to equal 3. Use this information to determine a linear and power demand curve.

2.   For each of your answers in problem 1, determine the value consumers place on the 2000th unit purchased of your game.

69

Pricing Products with Tie-Ins

- How does the fact that customers buy razor blades as well as razors affect the profit-maximizing price of razors?

Many products that are purchased by a customer result in the customer purchasing related products, or tie-ins. Here are some examples:

Original Purchase	Tie-In Product
Razor	Razor blades
Men's suit	Shirt and/or tie
Personal computer	Consulting services to set up a network
Video game console	Video game

Using the techniques I described in Chapter 68, it's easy to determine a demand curve for the product that's originally purchased. We can then use Excel's Solver to determine the price for the original product that maximizes the sum of the profit earned from the original and the tie-in products. The following example shows how this analysis is done.

How does the fact that customers buy razor blades as well as razors affect the profit-maximizing price of razors?

Suppose that we're currently charging $5.00 for a razor and we're selling 6 million razors. Assume that the variable cost of producing a razor is $2.00. Finally, suppose that the price elasticity of demand for razors is 2. What price should we charge for razors?

Let's assume (incorrectly) that no purchasers of razors buy blades. We determine our demand curve (assuming a linear demand curve) as shown in Figure 69-1. (You can find this data and the chart on the worksheet named No Blades in the file RazorsAndBlades.xls.) Two points on the demand curve are price = $5.00, demand = 6 million razors and price = $5.05 (an increase of 1 percent), demand = 5.88 million (2 percent less than 6 million). Using the Chart Wizard, we find the demand curve equation is $y = 18 - 2.4x$. Since x equals price and y equals demand, we can write the demand curve for razors as follows: *demand (in millions) = 18 − 2.4(price)*.

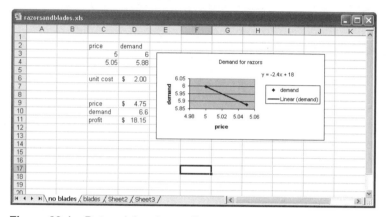

Figure 69-1   Determining the profit-maximizing price for razors.

I've associated the names in cell C6 and the range C9:C11 with cells D6 and D9:D11. Next I enter a trial price in D9 and determine demand for that price in cell D10 with the formula *18-2.4*price*. Then I determine in cell D11 the profit for razors with the formula *demand*(price-unit_cost)*.

Next I use Solver to determine the profit-maximizing price. The Solver Parameters dialog box is shown in Figure 69-2.

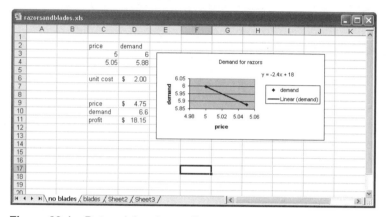

Figure 69-2   Solver Parameters dialog box set up for maximizing razor profit.

We choose to maximize our profit cell (cell D11) by changing our price (cell D9). The model is not linear because our target cell multiplies together two quantities—*demand* and *(price – cost)*—that each depend on our changing cell. Solver finds that by charging $4.75 for a razor, we can maximize our profit. (Maximum profit is $18.15 million.)

Now let's suppose that the average purchaser of a razor buys 50 blades and that we earn $0.15 of profit per blade purchased. How does this change the price we should charge for a razor? We assume that the price of a blade is fixed. (In Problem 3 at the end of the chapter, we will allow the blade price to change.) Our analysis is in the worksheet named Blades, which is shown in Figure 69-3.

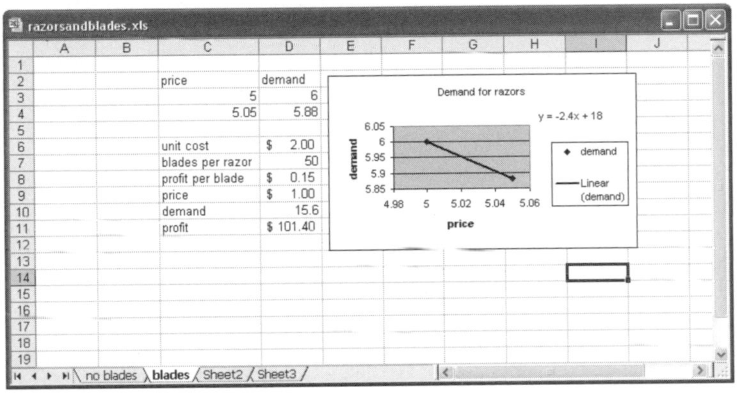

Figure 69-3   Price for razors with blade profit included.

I used the Insert, Name Create command to associate the names in cells C6:C11 with cells D6:D11. (For example, cell D10 is named *Demand*.)

> **Note**   The astute reader will recall that I also named cell D10 of the worksheet named No Blades as *Demand*. What does Excel do when you use the range name *Demand* in a formula? Excel simply refers to the cell named *Demand* in the current worksheet. In other words, when we use the range name *Demand* in the worksheet Blades, Excel refers to cell D11 of that worksheet, and not to cell D10 in the worksheet No Blades.

In cells D7 and D8, I've entered the relevant information about blades. In D9, I enter a trial price for razors, and in D10, I compute our demand with the formula *18-2.4*price*. Next, in cell D11, I compute total profit from razors and blades with the formula *demand*(price-unit_cost)+ demand*blades_per_razor*profit_per_blade*. Notice that *demand*blades_ per_razor*profit_per_blade* is our profit from blades.

Our Solver set up is exactly as was shown earlier in Figure 69-2: change price to maximize profit. Of course, now our profit formula includes the profit earned from blades. We find that profit is maximized by charging only $1.00 (half the variable cost!) for a razor. This price results from making so much money from the blades. We are much better off ensuring that many people have razors even though we lose $1.00 on each razor sold. Many companies do not understand the importance of the profit from tie-in products. This leads them to overprice their primary product and not maximize their total profit.

Problems

1. We are trying to determine the profit-maximizing price for a video game console. Currently we are charging $180 and selling 2 million consoles per year. It costs $150 to produce a console, and price elasticity of demand for consoles is 3. What price should we charge for a console?

2. Now assume that on average, a purchaser of our video game console buys 10 video games and we earn $10 profit on each video game. What is the correct price for consoles?

3. In our razor and blade example, suppose the cost to produce a blade is $0.20. If we charge $0.35 for a blade, a customer buys an average of 50 blades from us. Assume the price elasticity of demand for blades is 3. What price should we charge for a razor and for a blade?

70

Pricing Products Using Subjectively Determined Demand

- Sometimes I don't know the price elasticity for a product. In other situations, I don't believe a linear or power demand curve is relevant. Can I still estimate a demand curve and use Solver to determine a profit-maximizing price?

- How can a small drugstore determine the profit-maximizing price for lipstick?

Sometimes I don't know the price elasticity for a product. In other situations, I don't believe a linear or power demand curve is relevant. Can I still estimate a demand curve and use Solver to determine a profit-maximizing price?

In situations when you don't know the price elasticity for a product or don't think you can rely on a linear or power demand curve, a good way to determine a product's demand curve is to identify the lowest price and highest price that seem reasonable. You can then try to estimate the product's demand with the high price, the low price, and a price midway between the high and low prices. Given these three points on the product's demand curve, you can use the Excel trendline feature to fit a quadratic demand curve with the following form (which I'll call equation 1):

$$\text{Demand} = a(\text{price})^2 + b(\text{price}) + c$$

For any three specified points on the demand curve, values of *a*, *b*, and *c* exist that will make equation 1 *exactly* fit the three specified points. Since equation 1 fits three points on the demand curve, it seems reasonable to believe that the equation will give an accurate representation of demand for other prices. We can then use equation 1 and Solver to maximize profit, which is given by the formula *(price – unit cost)*demand*. The following example shows how this process works.

How can a small drugstore determine the profit-maximizing price for lipstick?

Let's suppose that a drugstore pays $0.90 for each unit of lipstick it orders. The store is considering charging between $1.50 and $2.50 for a unit of lipstick. They believe (see Figure 70-1 and the file LipstickPrice.xls) that at a price of $1.50, they will sell 60 pieces per week. At a price of $2.00, they think they will sell 51 pieces per week, and at a price of $2.50, they will sell 20 pieces per week. What price should they charge for lipstick?

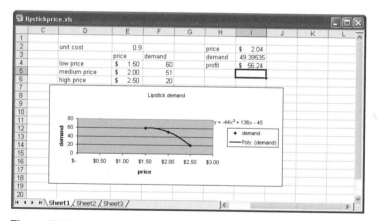

Figure 70-1   Lipstick pricing model.

We begin by entering the three points with which we'll chart our demand curve in the cell range E3:F6. After selecting E3:F6, we click the Chart Wizard button and then select the first option for an XY (Scatter) chart. We can then right-click on a data point and select Add Trendline. In the Add Trendline dialog box, we choose Polynomial and select 2 in the Order box (to obtain a quadratic curve of the form of equation 1). Finally, we click the Options tab and select the option Display Equation On Chart. You will see the chart shown in Figure 70-1. Our estimated demand curve (equation 2) is *Demand = -44*Price² + 136*Price – 45*.

Next we insert a trial price in cell I2. We compute our product demand using equation 2 in cell I3 with the formula *-44*price^2+136*price-45*. (I've named cell I2 *Price*.) Then we compute our weekly profit from lipstick in cell I4 with the formula *demand*(price-unit_cost)*. (Cell E2 is named *Unit_Cost* and cell I3 is named *Demand*.) Then we use Solver to determine the price that maximizes profit. The Solver Parameters dialog box is shown in Figure 70-2. Note that we constrain our price to be between the lowest and highest specified prices ($1.50 to $2.50). If we allow Solver to consider prices outside this range, the quadratic demand curve might slope upward, which implies that a higher price would result in larger demand. This result is unreasonable, so we constrain our price to be between $1.50 and $2.50.

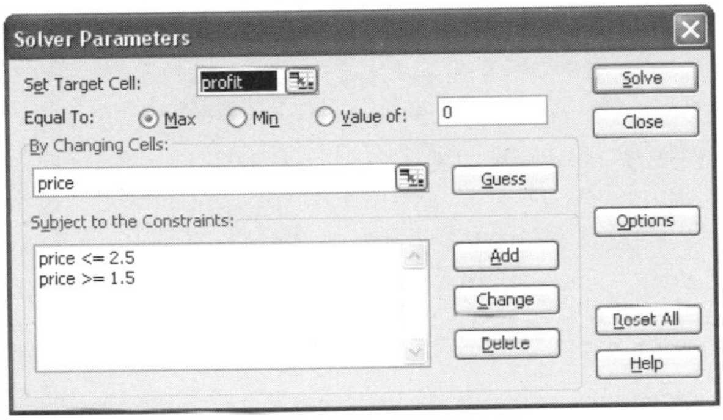

Figure 70-2   Solver Parameters dialog box set up to calculate lipstick pricing.

We find that our drugstore should charge $2.04 for a piece of lipstick. This yields sales of 49.4 units per week and a weekly profit of $56.24.

The approach to pricing outlined in this chapter requires no knowledge of the concept of price elasticity. Inherently, the Solver considers the elasticity for each price when it determines the profit-maximizing price. This approach can easily be applied by organizations that sell even thousands of different products. The only data that needs to be specified for each product is its variable cost and the three given points on the demand curve.

Problems

1. Suppose it costs $250 to produce a video game console. A price of between $200 and $400 is under consideration. Estimated demand for the game console is as follows.

    Each game owner buys an average of 10 video games. We earn $10 profit per video game. What price should we charge for the game console?

Price	Demand (in millions)
$200	2
$300	.9
$400	.2

2. We are trying to determine the correct price for a new weekly magazine. The variable cost of printing and distributing a copy of the magazine is $0.50. We are thinking of charging between $0.50 and $1.30 per copy. The estimated weekly sales of the magazine are as follows:

Price	Demand (in millions)
$0.50	2
$0.90	1.2
$1.30	.3

    In addition to sales revenue from the magazine, we can charge $30 per thousand copies sold for each of the 20 pages of advertising in each week's magazine. What price should we charge for the magazine?

71

Nonlinear Pricing

- What is linear pricing?

- What is nonlinear pricing?

- What is bundling, and how can it increase profitability?

- How can I find a profit-maximizing nonlinear pricing plan?

What is linear pricing?

In Chapters 69 and 70, I showed how to determine a profit-maximizing price for a product. We made the implicit assumption, however, that no matter how many units a customer purchases, the customer is charged the same amount per unit. This model is known as *linear pricing* because the cost of buying x units is a straight line function of x (cost of x units = *(unit price)*x*). We will see in this chapter that *nonlinear pricing* can often greatly increase a company's profit.

What is nonlinear pricing?

A nonlinear pricing scheme simply means that the cost of buying x units is not a straight line function of x. We have all encountered nonlinear pricing strategies. Here are some examples:

- **Quantity discounts**   For example, the first five units might cost $20 each and the remaining units $12 each. Quantity discounts are commonly used by companies selling software and computers. An example of the cost of purchasing x units is shown in the worksheet Nonlinear Pricing Examples in the file Nlp.xls, which is shown in Figure 71-1. Notice that the graph has a slope of 20 for units purchased less than or equal to 5 and a slope of 12 for units purchased more than 5.

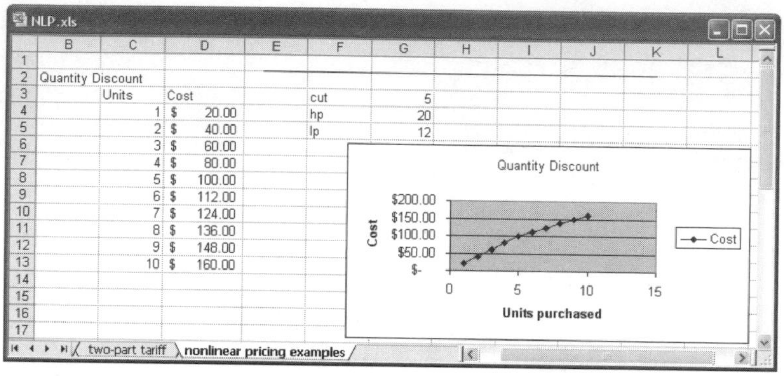

Figure 71-1   Cost of quantity discount plan.

■   **Two-part tariff**   When you join a golf or country club, you usually
     pay a fixed fee for joining the club and then a fee for each round of
     golf you play. Suppose that your country club charges a membership
     fee of $500 per year and charges $20 per round of golf. This type of
     pricing strategy is called a *two-part tariff*. For this pricing policy, the
     cost of purchasing a given number of rounds of golf is shown in Fig-
     ure 71-2. Again, look at the worksheet Nonlinear Pricing Examples
     in Nlp.xls. Note that the graph has a slope of 520 between 0 and 1
     units purchased and a slope of 20 for more than 1 unit purchased.
     Because a straight line must always have the same slope, we can see
     that a two-part tariff is highly nonlinear.

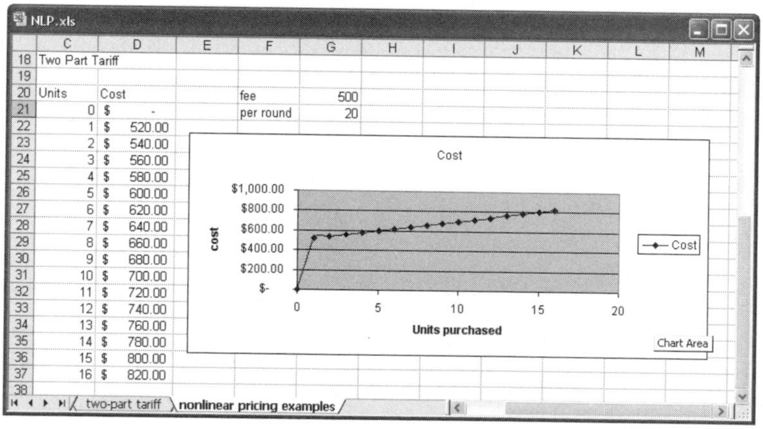

Figure 71-2   Cost of two-part tariff.

What is bundling, and how can it increase profitability?

Price bundling involves offering a customer a set of products for a price less than the sum of the products' individual prices. To analyze why bundling works, we need to understand how a rational consumer makes decisions. For each product combination available, a rational consumer looks at the value of what we are selling and subtracts the cost to purchase it. This yields the *consumer surplus* of the purchase. A rational consumer buys nothing if the consumer surplus of each available option is negative. Otherwise, the consumer purchases the product combination having the largest consumer surplus.

So how can bundling increase our profitability? Suppose that we sell computers and printers and have two customers. The values each customer attaches to a computer and a printer are shown here:

Customer	Computer value	Printer value
1	$1000	$500
2	$500	$1000

We only offer the computer and printer for sale separately. By charging $1000 for a printer and for a computer, we will sell one printer and one computer and receive $2,000 in revenue. Now suppose we offer the printer and computer in combination for $1,500. Each customer buys both the computer and the printer, and we receive $3,000 in revenue. The act of bundling enables us to extract more of the consumer's total valuation. Bundling works best if customer valuations for the bundled products are negatively correlated. In our example, the negative correlation between the values for the bundled products is a consequence of the fact that the customer who places a high value on a printer places a low value on a computer, and the customer who places a low value on a printer places a high value on a computer.

We know that when you go to a theme park such as Disneyland, you don't buy a ticket for each ride. You either buy a ticket to enter the theme park or you don't go. This is an example of *pure bundling* because the consumer does not have the option of paying for a subset of the offered products. This approach reduces lines (imagine a line at *every* ride) and also results in more profit.

To see why this bundling approach increases profitability, suppose there is only a single customer and that the number of rides the customer wants to go on is governed by a demand curve that is calculated as *(Number of rides) = 20 − 2*(Price of ride)*. From the discussion of demand curves in Chapter 68, we know that the value the consumer gives to the ith ride is the price that makes demand equal to $i - .5$. Thus, we know that $i - .5 = 20 - 2*(value of ride i)$ or, solving for the value of ride i, we find *(value of ride i) = 10.25 − (i/2)*. The first ride is worth $9.75, the second ride is worth $9.25 … the twentieth ride is worth $0.25.

Assume we charge a constant price per ride and that it costs us $2 in variable costs per ride. We seek the profit-maximizing linear pricing scheme. In the worksheet named OnePrice in the file Nlp.xls, shown in Figure 71-3, I show how to determine the profit-maximizing price per ride.

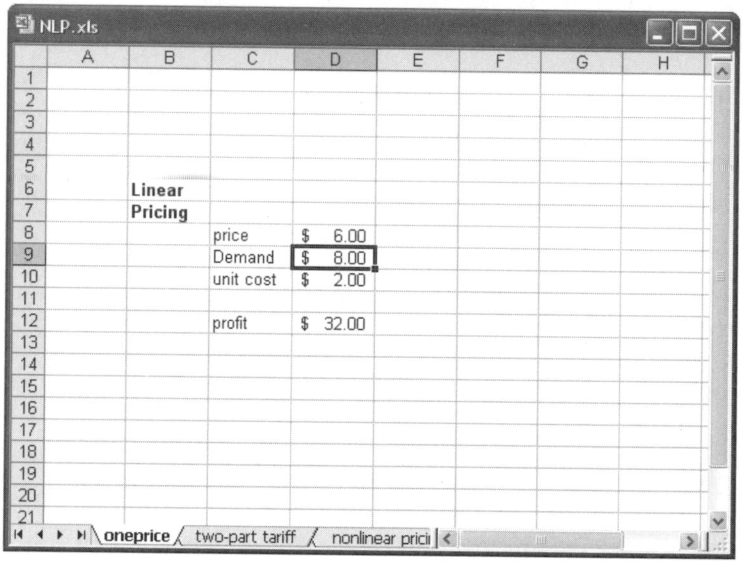

Figure 71-3   Profit-maximizing linear pricing scheme.

I've associated the range names in C8:C12 with cells D8:D12. I enter a trial price in cell D8 and compute the number of ride tickets purchased in cell D9 with the formula *20-(2*D8)*. Then I compute our profit in cell D12 with the formula *Demand*(price-unit_cost)*. I can now use Excel's Solver to maximize the value in D12 (profit) by changing cell D8 (price). We find that a price of $6 results in 8 ride tickets being purchased. We earn a maximum profit of $32.

Now let's pretend we're like Disneyland and offer just a bundle of 20 rides to the customer. We set a price equal to the sum of the customer's valuations for each ride ($9.75 + $9.25 + …. $0.75 + $0.25 = $100). The customer values all 20 rides at $100, so the customer will buy a park entry ticket for $100. We earn a profit of $100 – $2(20) = $60, which almost doubles our profit from linear pricing.

How can I find a profit-maximizing nonlinear pricing plan?

In this section, I'll show how you can determine a profit-maximizing, two-part-tariff pricing plan for our amusement park example. We'll proceed as follows:

■   Hypothesize trial values for the fixed fee and the price per ride.

■   Determine the value the customer associates with each ride (*Value of ride i = 10.5 − .5i*).

- Determine the cumulative value associated with buying *i* rides.

- Determine the price charged for *i* rides, *Fixed fee + i*(price per ride)*.

- Determine the consumer surplus for buying *i* rides, *Value of i rides – price of i rides*.

- Determine the maximum consumer surplus.

- Determine the number of units purchased. If the maximum consumer surplus is negative, no units are purchased. Otherwise, we'll use the MATCH function to find the number of units yielding the maximum surplus.

- Use a VLOOKUP function to look up our revenue corresponding to the number of units purchased.

- Compute our profit as *revenue – costs*.

- Use a two-way data table to determine a profit-maximizing fixed fee and price per ride.

Our work is in the worksheet Two-Part Tariff in the file Nlp.xls, which is shown is Figure 71-4.

	B	C	D	E	F	G	H	I	J
1						0	Units bought	15	
2		cost		fixed fee	$ 56.00		Revenue	$ 93.50	
3		$ 2.00		price per ride	$ 2.50		Prod Cost	$ 30.00	
4						Max surplus	0.25	
5				Unit	Value	Cum Value	Price paid	Surplus	Profit
6				1	9.75	9.75	58.5	-48.75	$ 63.50
7				2	9.25	19	61	-42	
8				3	8.75	27.75	63.5	-35.75	
9				4	8.25	36	66	-30	
10				5	7.76	43.75	68.5	-24.75	
11				6	7.25	51	71	-20	Fixed
12				7	6.75	57.75	73.5	-15.75	
13				8	6.25	64	76	-12	
14				9	5.75	69.75	78.5	-8.75	
15				10	5.25	75	81	-6	
16				11	4.75	79.75	83.5	-3.75	
17				12	4.25	84	86	-2	
18				13	3.75	87.75	88.5	-0.75	
19				14	3.25	91	91	0	
20				15	2.75	93.75	93.5	0.25	
21				16	2.25	96	96	0	
22				17	1.75	97.75	98.5	-0.75	

Figure 71-4 Determination of optimal two-part tariff.

To begin, I associate the range names in E2:E3 with cells F2:F3. I enter trial values for the fixed fee and the price per ride in cells F2 and F3. Next, I determine the value the consumer places on each ride by copying from cell E6 to E7:E25 the formula *10.25-(D6/2)*. We find that the customer places a value of $9.75 on the first ride, $9.25 on the second ride, and so on.

To compute the cumulative value of the first i rides, I copy from F6 to F7:F25 the formula *SUM($E$6:E6)*. This formula adds up all values in column E that are in or above the current row. By copying from G6 to G7:G25 the formula *fixed_fee+price_per_ride*D6*, I compute the cost of i rides. For example, five rides cost $68.50.

Recall that the consumer surplus for i rides equals *(Value of i rides) – (Cost of i rides)*. By copying from cell H6 to the range H7:H25 the formula *F6-G6*, I compute the consumer's surplus for purchasing any number of rides. For example, the consumer surplus for purchasing five rides is $-24.75, which is the result of the large fixed fee.

In cell H4, I compute the maximum consumer surplus with the formula *MAX(H6:H25)*. Remember that if the maximum consumer surplus is negative, no units are purchased. Otherwise, the consumer will purchase the number of units yielding the maximum consumer surplus. Therefore, entering in cell I1 the formula *IF(H4>=0,MATCH(H4,H6:H24,0),0)* determines the number of units purchased (in our case 15). Notice that the MATCH function finds the number of rows we need to move down in the range H6:H24 to find the first match to the maximum surplus.

We now name the range D5:G25 as *Lookup*. We can then look up our total revenue in the fourth column of this range based on the number of units purchased (which is already computed in cell I1). Our total revenue is computed in cell I2 with the formula *IF(I1=0,0,VLOOKUP(I1,lookup,4))*. Notice that if no rides are purchased, we earn no revenue. We compute our total production cost for rides purchased in cell I3 with the formula *I1*C3*. In cell J6, I compute our profit as revenues less costs with the formula *I2-I3*.

Now we can use a two-way data table to determine the profit-maximizing combination of fixed fee and price per ride. The data table is shown in Figure 71-5. (Many rows and columns are hidden.) In setting up the data table, we will vary the fixed fee between $10 and $60 (the values in the range K10:K60) and vary the price per ride between $.50 and $5.00 (the values in L9:BE9). We recomputed profit in cell K9 with the formula *=J6*.

We now select the table range (cells K9:BE60), and then choose Data, Table. Our column input cell is F2 (the fixed fee) and row input cell is F3 (the price per ride). After clicking OK in the Table dialog box, we've computed our profit for each fixed fee and price per ride combination represented in the data table.

J	K	L	M	N	AE	AF	BB	BC	BD	BE
$ 63.50				$ 63.50						
		Var								
	$ 63.50	0.5	0.6	0.7	2.4	2.5	4.7	4.8	4.9	5
	10	$ (18.50)	$ (16.60)	$ (14.70)	$ 16.00	$ 17.50	$ 39.70	$ 38.00	$ 39.00	$ 40.00
Fixed	11	$ (17.50)	$ (15.60)	$ (13.70)	$ 17.00	$ 18.50	$ 40.70	$ 39.00	$ 40.00	$ 41.00
	12	$ (16.50)	$ (14.60)	$ (12.70)	$ 18.00	$ 19.50	$ 41.70	$ 40.00	$ 41.00	$ 42.00
	13	$ (15.50)	$ (13.60)	$ (11.70)	$ 19.00	$ 20.50	$ 42.70	$ 41.00	$ 42.00	$ 43.00
	14	$ (14.50)	$ (12.60)	$ (10.70)	$ 20.00	$ 21.50	$ 43.70	$ 42.00	$ 43.00	$ 44.00
	15	$ (13.50)	$ (11.60)	$ (9.70)	$ 21.00	$ 22.50	$ 44.70	$ 43.00	$ 44.00	$ 45.00
	16	$ (12.50)	$ (10.60)	$ (8.70)	$ 22.00	$ 23.50	$ 45.70	$ 44.00	$ 45.00	$ 46.00
	17	$ (11.50)	$ (9.60)	$ (7.70)	$ 23.00	$ 24.50	$ 46.70	$ 45.00	$ 46.00	$ 47.00
	18	$ (10.50)	$ (8.60)	$ (6.70)	$ 24.00	$ 25.50	$ 47.70	$ 46.00	$ 47.00	$ 48.00
	19	$ (9.50)	$ (7.60)	$ (5.70)	$ 25.00	$ 26.50	$ 48.70	$ 47.00	$ 48.00	$ 49.00
	20	$ (8.50)	$ (6.60)	$ (4.70)	$ 26.00	$ 27.50	$ 49.70	$ 48.00	$ 49.00	$ 50.00
	21	$ (7.50)	$ (5.60)	$ (3.70)	$ 27.00	$ 28.50	$ 50.70	$ 49.00	$ 50.00	$ 51.00
	22	$ (6.50)	$ (4.60)	$ (2.70)	$ 28.00	$ 29.50	$ 51.70	$ 50.00	$ 51.00	$ 52.00
	23	$ (5.50)	$ (3.60)	$ (1.70)	$ 29.00	$ 30.50	$ 52.70	$ 51.00	$ 52.00	$ 53.00
	24	$ (4.50)	$ (2.60)	$ (0.70)	$ 30.00	$ 31.50	$ 53.70	$ 52.00	$ 53.00	$ 54.00
	54	$ 25.50	$ 27.40	29.30	$ 60.00	$ 61.50	$ -	$ -	$ -	$ -
	55	$ 26.50	$ 28.40	30.30	$ 61.00	$ 62.50	$ -	$ -	$ -	$ -
	56	$ 27.50	$ 29.40	31.30	$ 62.00	$ 63.50	$ -	$ -	$ -	$ -
	57	$ 28.50	$ 30.40	32.30	$ 63.00	$ -	$ -	$ -	$ -	$ -

oneprice \ **two-part tariff** / nonlinear pricing examples

Figure 71-5   Two-way data table computes optimal two-part tariff.

To highlight the profit-maximizing two-part tariff, I used conditional formatting. First, I computed our maximum profit in cell N6 with the formula *MAX(L10:BE60)*. Then I selected the range L10:BE60 and used conditional formatting to highlight the cell yielding the maximum profit. The Conditional Formatting dialog box set up to find the maximum profit is shown in Figure 71-6. Entering *=L10=$N$6* while the cursor is in cell L10 ensures that any fixed fee and price per ride yielding the maximum profit will be highlighted in red. We find that a fixed fee of $56 and a price per ride of $2.50 earns us a profit of $63.50, which almost doubles the profit from linear pricing. A fixed fee of $59.00 and a price per ride of $2.30 also yields a profit of $63.50.

Figure 71-6   Conditional formatting highlights the profit maximizing pricing strategy.

Because a quantity discount plan involves selecting three variables (cutoff, high price, and low price), we cannot use a data table to determine a profit-maximizing quantity-discount plan. You might think we could use a Solver model (with changing cells set to cutoff, high price, and low price) to determine a profit-maximizing quantity-discount strategy. Unfortunately, the Excel Solver often has difficulty determining optimal solutions when the target cell is computed using formulas containing IF statements. Therefore, the Solver might fail to find a profit-maximizing quantity-discount plan. For details about how to set up Solver models involving IF statements, look at Chapter 15 of my book *Introduction to Mathematical Programming* (Duxbury Press, 2003).

Problems

Both problems refer to the following situation. You own a small country club and have three types of customers who value each round of golf they play during a month as shown below:

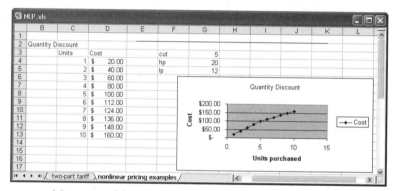

It costs you $5 in variable costs to provide a customer with a round of golf.

1. Find a profit-maximizing two-part tariff.

2. Suppose you are going to offer a pure bundle. For example, a member can play up to five rounds of golf for $60 per month. The member has no other option to choose from other than the pure bundle. What pure bundle maximizes your profit?

72

Array Formulas and Functions

- What is an array formula?

- How do we interpret formulas such as *(D2:D7)*(E2:E7)* and *SUM(D2:D7*E2:E7)*?

- I have a list of names in a single column. These names change often. Is there any easy way to transpose the listed names to a single row so that changes in the original column of names are reflected in the new row of names?

- I have a list of monthly stock returns. Is there a way to determine the number of returns between -30 percent and -20 percent, -10 percent and 0 percent, and so on that will automatically update if I change the original data?

- Can I write a single formula that will sum up the second digit of a list of integers?

- Is there a way to look at two lists of names and determine which names occur on both lists?

- Can I write a formula that averages all numbers in a list that exceed the list's median value?

- I have a sales database for a small makeup company that lists the salesperson, product, units sold, and dollar amount for every transaction. I know I can use database statistical functions to summarize this data, but can I also use array functions to summarize the data and answer questions such as how many units of makeup did Jen sell, how many units of lipstick did Jen sell, and how many units were sold by Jen or were lipstick?

■   What are array constants and how can I use them?

■   How do I edit array formulas?

■   Given quarterly revenues for a toy store, can I estimate the trend and seasonality of the store's revenues?

What is an array formula?

Array formulas often provide a shortcut or more efficient approach to performing complex calculations with Excel. An array formula can return a result in either a single cell or in a range of cells. Array formulas perform operations on two or more sets of values, called *array arguments*. Each array argument used in an array formula must contain exactly the same number of rows and columns.

When entering an array formula, you must first select the range in which you want Excel to place the array formula's results. Then, after entering the formula in the first cell of the selected range, *you must press Ctrl+Shift+Enter.* If you fail to press Ctrl+Shift+Enter, you'll obtain incorrect or nonsensical results. I'll refer to the process of entering an array formula and then pressing Ctrl+Shift+Enter as *array-entering* a formula.

Excel also contains a variety of *array functions.* You met two array functions (LINEST and TREND) in Chapters 45 and 46. As with an array formula, to use an array function you must first select the range in which you want the function's results placed. Then, after entering the function in the first cell of the selected range, you must press Ctrl+Shift+Enter. In this chapter, I'll introduce you to three other useful array functions: TRANSPOSE, FREQUENCY, and LOGEST.

As you'll see, you cannot delete any part of a cell range that contains results computed with an array formula. Also, you cannot paste an array formula into a range that contains both blank cells and array formulas. For example, if you have an array formula in cell C10 and you want to copy it to the cell range C10:J15, you cannot simply copy the formula to this range because the range contains both blank cells and the array formula in cell C10. To work around this difficulty, copy the formula from C10 to D10:J10 and then copy the contents of C10:J10 to C11:J15.

The best way to learn how array formulas and functions work is by looking at some examples, so let's get started.

How do we interpret formulas such as *(D2:D7)*(E2:E7)* and *SUM(D2:D7*E2:E7)*?

In the worksheet Total Wages in the file Array.xls, I've listed the number of hours worked and the hourly wage rates for six employees, as you can see in Figure 72-1.

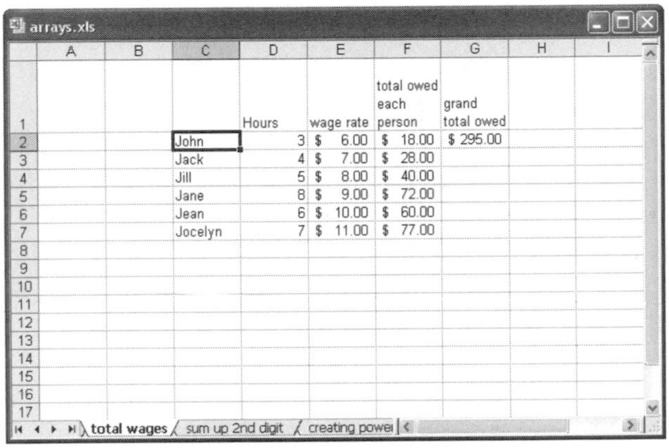

Figure 72-1   Using array formulas to compute hourly wages.

If we wanted to compute each person's total wages, we could simply copy from F2 to F3:F7 the formula *D3*E3*. There is certainly nothing wrong with that approach, but using an array formula provides a more elegant solution. Begin by selecting the range F2:F7, where you want each person's total earnings to be computed. Then enter in cell F2 the formula *(D2:D7*E2:E7)* and press Ctrl+Shift+Enter. You will see that each person's total wages has been correctly computed. Also, if you look at the formula bar, you'll see that the formula appears as *{(D2:D7*E2:E7)}*. The curly brackets are Excel's way of telling us that we've created an array formula. (You don't enter the curly brackets that show up at the beginning and end of an array formula, but to indicate that a formula is an array formula in this chapter, we'll show the curly brackets.)

To see how this formula works, click in the formula bar, highlight *D2:D7* in the formula, and then press F9. You will see *{3;4;5;8;6;7}*, which is Excel's creation of the cell range D2:D7 as an array. Now select E2:E7 in the formula bar, and then press F9 again. You will see *{6;7;8;9;10;11}*, which is Excel's creation of an array corresponding to the range E2:E7. The inclusion of the asterisk (*) tells Excel to multiply the corresponding elements in each array. Because the cells' ranges we are multiplying include six cells each, Excel creates arrays with six items, and because we selected a cell range of six cells, each person's total wages is displayed in its own cell. Had we selected a range of only five cells, the sixth item in the array would not be displayed.

Suppose we want to compute the total wages earned by all employees. One approach would be to use the formula *SUMPRODUCT(D2:D7,E2:E7)*. Again, however, let's try to create an array formula to compute total wages. We begin by selecting a single cell (I chose cell G2) in which to place our result. Then we enter in cell G2 the formula *SUM(D2:D7*E2:E7)*. After pressing Ctrl+Shift+Enter, we obtain (3)(6) + (4)(7) + (5)(8) + (8)(9) + (6)(10) + (7)(11) = 295. To see how this formula works, select the *D2:D7*E2:E7* portion in the formula bar and then press F9. You will see SUM({18;28;40;72;60;77}), which shows that Excel created a six-element array whose first element is 3*6 (18), whose second element is 4*7 (28), and so on, until the last element, which is 7*11 (77). Excel then adds up the values in the array to obtain the total of $295.

I have a list of names in a single column. These names change often. Is there any easy way to transpose the listed names to a single row so that changes in the original column of names are reflected in the new row of names?

In the worksheet named Transpose in the file Array.xls, shown in Figure 72-2, I've listed a set of names in cells A4:A8. We want to list these names in a single row (the cell range C3:G3). If we knew that the original list of names would never change, we could accomplish this goal by copying the cell range and then using the Transpose option in the Paste Special dialog box. (See Chapter 13 for details.) Unfortunately, if the names in column A change, the names in the row 3 would not reflect those changes if we use Paste Special, Transpose. What we need in this situation is Excel's TRANSPOSE function.

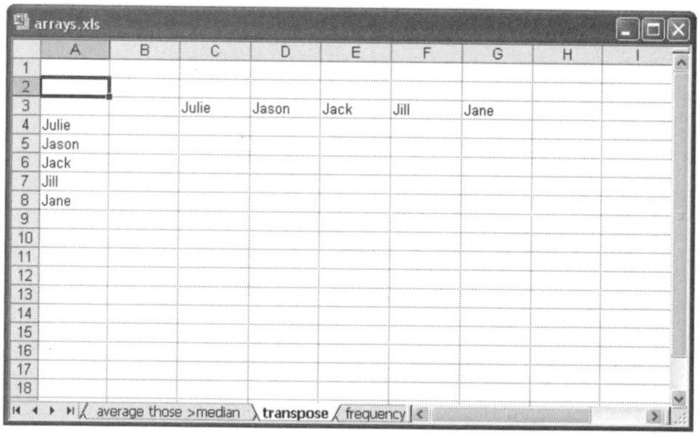

Figure 72-2   Example of using the TRANSPOSE function.

The TRANSPOSE function is an array function that changes rows of a selected range into columns and vice versa. To begin using TRANSPOSE, we select the range C3:G3, where we want our transposed list of names to be placed. Then, in cell C3, we array-enter the formula *{TRANSPOSE(A4:A8)}*. The list of names is now displayed in a single row. More importantly, if we change any of the names in A4:A8, the corresponding name will change in the transposed range.

I have a list of monthly stock returns. Is there a way to determine the number of returns between -30 percent and -20 percent, -10 percent and 0 percent, and so on that will automatically update if I change the original data?

This problem is a job for the FREQUENCY array function. The FREQUENCY function counts how many values in an array (called the *data array*) occur within given value ranges (specified by a bin array). The syntax of the FREQUENCY function is *FREQUENCY(data array, bin array).*

To illustrate the use of the FREQUENCY function, look at the worksheet named Frequency in the file Array.xls, shown in Figure 72-3. I've listed monthly stock returns for a fictitious stock in the cell range A4:A77.

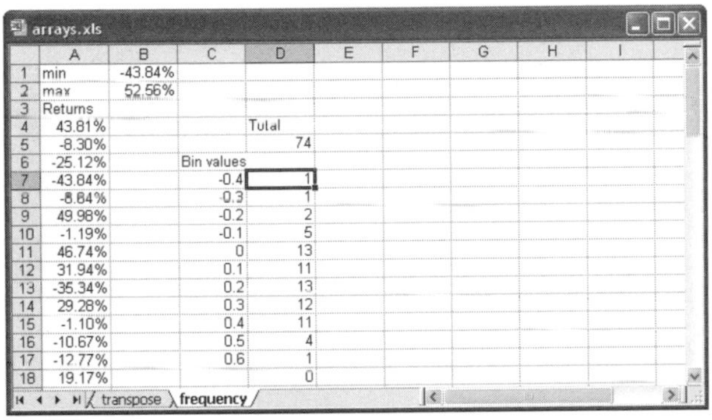

	A	B	C	D
1	min	-43.84%		
2	max	52.56%		
3	Returns			
4	43.81%			Total
5	-8.30%			74
6	-25.12%		Bin values	
7	-43.84%		-0.4	1
8	-8.64%		-0.3	1
9	49.98%		-0.2	2
10	-1.19%		-0.1	5
11	46.74%		0	13
12	31.94%		0.1	11
13	-35.34%		0.2	13
14	29.28%		0.3	12
15	-1.10%		0.4	11
16	-10.67%		0.5	4
17	-12.77%		0.6	1
18	19.17%			0

Figure 72-3 Use of the FREQUENCY function.

We found in cells A1 and A2 (using the MIN and MAX functions) that all returns are between -44 percent and 53 percent. Based on this information, I set up our bin value boundaries in cells C7:C17, starting at -0.4 and ending at 0.6. Now I select the range D7:D18, where I want the results of the FREQUENCY function to be placed. In this range, cell D7 will count the number of data points less than or equal to -0.4, D8 will count the number of data points greater than -0.4 and less than or equal to –0.3, and so on. Cell D17 will count all data points greater than 0.5 and less than or equal to 0.6, and cell D18 will count all the data points that are greater than 0.6.

I enter in D7 the formula *FREQUENCY(A4:A77,C7:C17)*, and then press Ctrl+Shift+Enter. This formula tells Excel to count the number of data points from A4:A77 (the data array) that lie in each of the bin ranges defined in C7:C17. We find, for example, that 1 return is greater than -0.4 and less than or equal to -0.3. Thirteen returns are greater than 0.1 and less than or equal to .2. If you change any of the data points in the data array, the results generated by the FREQUENCY function in cells D7:D17 will reflect the changes in your data.

Can I write a single formula that will sum up the second digit of a list of integers?

In the cell range A4:A10 in the worksheet Sum Up 2nd Digit in the file Array.xls, I've listed seven integers. (See Figure 72-4.) We would like to write a single formula that will sum up the second digit of each number. Of course, we could obtain this sum by copying from B4 to B5:B10 the formula *VALUE(MID(A4,2,1))*. This formula returns (as a numerical value) the second character in cell A4. Then we could add up the range B4:B10 and obtain the total of 27.

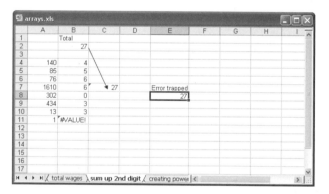

Figure 72-4   Summing second digits in a set of integers.

An array function makes this process much easier. Simply select cell C7 and array-enter the formula *{SUM(VALUE(MID(A4:A10,2,1)))}*. Your array formula will return the correct answer, 27.

To see what this formula does, highlight *MID(A4:A10,2,1)* in the formula bar and then press F9. You will see {"4";"5";"6";"6";"0";"3";"3"}. This string of values shows that Excel has created an array consisting of the second digit (viewed as text) in the cell range A4:A10. The VALUE portion of the formula changes these text strings into numerical values, which are added up by the SUM portion of the formula.

Notice that in cell A11, I entered a number with 1 digit. Because this number has no second digit, the MID portion of our formula returns #VALUE. How can we modify our array formula to account for the possible inclusion of one digit integers? Simply array-enter in cell E8 the formula *{SUM(IF(LEN(A4:A11)>=2,VALUE(MID(A4:A11,2,1)),0))}*. This formula replaces any one-digit integer by a 0, so we still obtain the correct sum.

Is there a way to look at two lists of names and determine which names occur on both lists?

In the worksheet Matching Names in the file Array.xls, I've included two lists of names (in columns D and E), as you can see in Figure 72-5. We want to determine which names on List 1 also appear on List 2. To accomplish this, we select the range C5:28 and array-enter in cell C5 the formula *{MATCH(D5:D28,E5:E28,0)}*. This formula loops through the cells C5:C28. In cell C5, the formula checks whether the name in D5 has a match in column E. If a match exists, the formula returns the position of the first match in E5:E28. If no match exists, the formula returns #NA (for not available). Similarly in C6, the formula checks to see whether the second name on List 1 has a match. We see, for example, that Artest does not appear on the second list but Harrington does (first matched in the second cell in the range E5:E28).

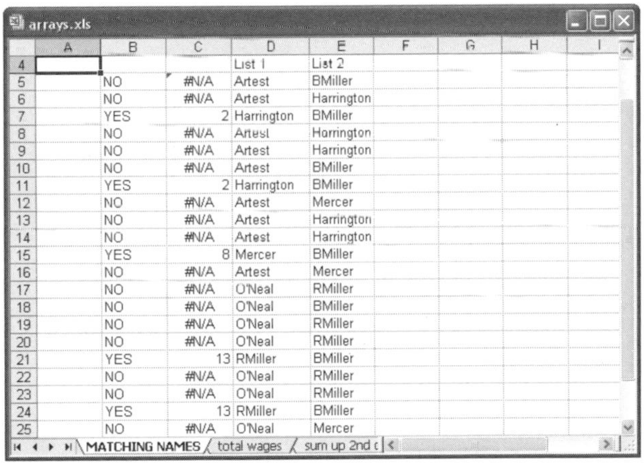

	A	B	C	D	E
4				List 1	List 2
5		NO	#N/A	Artest	BMiller
6		NO	#N/A	Artest	Harrington
7		YES	2	Harrington	BMiller
8		NO	#N/A	Artest	Harrington
9		NO	#N/A	Artest	Harrington
10		NO	#N/A	Artest	BMiller
11		YES	2	Harrington	BMiller
12		NO	#N/A	Artest	Mercer
13		NO	#N/A	Artest	Harrington
14		NO	#N/A	Artest	Harrington
15		YES	8	Mercer	BMiller
16		NO	#N/A	Artest	Mercer
17		NO	#N/A	O'Neal	RMiller
18		NO	#N/A	O'Neal	BMiller
19		NO	#N/A	O'Neal	RMiller
20		NO	#N/A	O'Neal	RMiller
21		YES	13	RMiller	BMiller
22		NO	#N/A	O'Neal	RMiller
23		NO	#N/A	O'Neal	RMiller
24		YES	13	RMiller	BMiller
25		NO	#N/A	O'Neal	Mercer

Figure 72-5 Finding duplicates in two lists.

To enter Yes for each name in List 1 with a match in a List 2, and No for each List 1 name without a match, select the cell range B5:B28 and array-enter the formula *{IF(ISERROR(C5:C28),"NO","YES")}* in cell B5. This formula displays No for each cell in C5:C28 containing the #NA message and Yes for all cells returning a numerical value.

Can I write a formula that averages all numbers in a list that are greater than or equal to the list's median value?

In the worksheet Average Those > Median in the file Array.xls, shown in Figure 72-6, the range D5:D785 (named *Prices*) contains a list of prices. We'd like to average all prices that are at least as large as the median price. In cell F2, I've computed the median with the formula *Median(prices)*. In cell F3, I compute the average of numbers greater than or equal to the median by entering the formula *SUMIF(prices,">="&F2,prices)/COUNTIF(prices, ">="&F2)*. This formula adds up all prices that are at least as large as the median value (243) and then divides by the number of prices that are at least as large as the median. We find that the average of all prices at least as large as the median price is $324.2977.

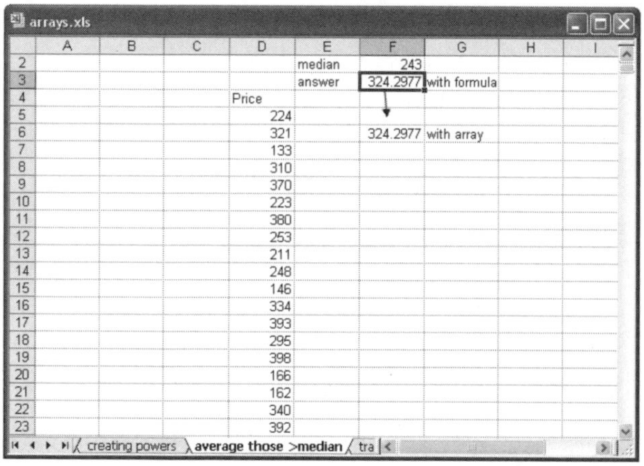

Figure 72-6   Averaging prices at least as large as median price.

An easier approach is to select cell F6 and array-enter the formula *{AVERAGE(IF(prices>=MEDIAN(prices),prices," "))}*. This formula creates an array that contains the row's price if the row's price is greater than or equal to the median price or a space otherwise. Averaging this array gives us the results we want.

I have a sales database for a small makeup company that lists the salesperson, product, units sold, and dollar amount for every transaction. I know I can use database statistical functions to summarize this data, but can I also use array functions to summarize the data and answer questions such as how many units of makeup did Jen sell, how many units of lipstick did Jen sell, and how many units were sold by Jen or were lipstick?

The file MakeupArray.xls contains a list of 1900 sales transactions made by a makeup company. For each transaction, the transaction number, salesperson, transaction date, product sold, units sold, and dollar volume are listed. You can see some of the data in Figure 72-7.

	H	Trans Number	Name	Date	Product	Units	Dollars	O	P
4		Trans Number	Name	Date	Product	Units	Dollars		
5		1	Betsy	4/1/2004	lip gloss	45	$ 137.20		
6		2	Hallagan	3/10/2004	foundation	50	$ 152.01		
7		3	Ashley	2/25/2005	lipstick	9	$ 28.72		
8		4	Hallagan	5/22/2006	lip gloss	55	$ 167.08		
9		5	Zaret	6/17/2004	lip gloss	43	$ 130.60		
10		6	Colleen	11/27/2005	eye liner	58	$ 175.99		
11		7	Cristina	3/21/2004	eye liner	8	$ 25.80		
12		8	Colleen	12/17/2006	lip gloss	72	$ 217.84		
13		9	Ashley	7/5/2006	eye liner	75	$ 226.64		
14		10	Betsy	8/7/2006	lip gloss	24	$ 73.50		
15		11	Ashley	11/29/2004	mascara	43	$ 130.84		
16		12	Ashley	11/18/2004	lip gloss	23	$ 71.03		
17		13	Emilee	8/31/2005	lip gloss	49	$ 149.59		
18		14	Hallagan	1/1/2005	eye liner	18	$ 56.47		
19		15	Zaret	9/20/2006	foundation	-8	$ (21.99)		
20		16	Emilee	4/12/2004	mascara	45	$ 137.39		
21		17	Colleen	4/30/2006	mascara	66	$ 199.65		
22		18	Jen	8/31/2005	lip gloss	88	$ 265.19		

Figure 72-7   Makeup database.

This data can easily be summarized using database statistical functions, as I described in Chapter 37. As you'll see in this section, array functions provide an easy, powerful alternative to database statistical functions.

How many units of makeup did Jen sell?   We can easily answer this question by using the SUMIF function. In this worksheet, I named the cell range J5:J1904 *Name* and the cell range M5:M1904 *Units*. I entered in cell E7 the formula *SUMIF(Name,"Jen",Units)* to sum up all the units sold by Jen. We found that Jen sold 9537 units. We can also answer this question by array-entering in cell E6 the formula *{=SUM(IF(J5:J1904="Jen",M5:M1904,0))}*. This formula creates an array that contains the units sold for a transaction made by Jen and a 0 for all other transactions. Therefore, summing this array also yields the number of units sold by Jen, 9,537, as you can see in Figure 72-8.

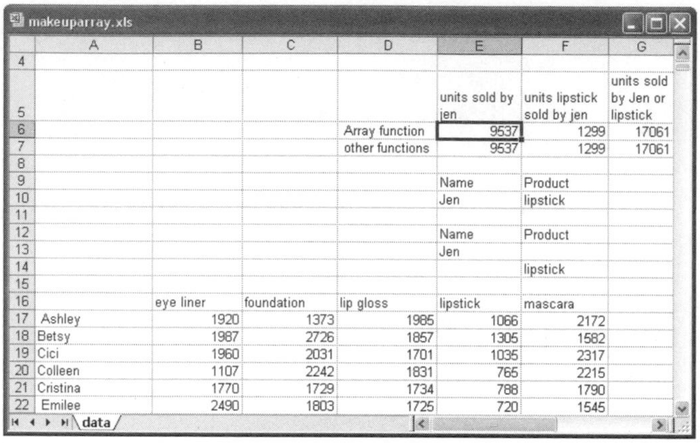

makeuparray.xls

	A	B	C	D	E	F	G
4							
5					units sold by jen	units lipstick sold by jen	units sold by Jen or lipstick
6				Array function	9537	1299	17061
7				other functions	9537	1299	17061
8							
9					Name	Product	
10					Jen	lipstick	
11							
12					Name	Product	
13					Jen		
14						lipstick	
15							
16		eye liner	foundation	lip gloss	lipstick	mascara	
17	Ashley	1920	1373	1985	1066	2172	
18	Betsy	1987	2726	1857	1305	1582	
19	Cici	1960	2031	1701	1035	2317	
20	Colleen	1107	2242	1831	765	2215	
21	Cristina	1770	1729	1734	788	1790	
22	Emilee	2490	1803	1725	720	1545	

data

Figure 72-8 Summarizing data with array formulas.

How many units of lipstick did Jen sell? This question requires a criterion that uses two columns (Name and Product). We could answer the question using the database statistical function formula *DSUM(J4:N1904,4,E9:F10)*, which is entered in cell F7. This formula shows that Jen sold 1299 units of lipstick. We can also obtain this answer by using the array formula entered in cell F6, *{=SUM((J5:J1904="jen")*(L5:L1904="lipstick")*M5:M1904)}*.

To understand this formula, you need to know a bit about Boolean arrays. The portion of this formula that reads *(J5:J1904="jen")* creates a Boolean array. For each entry in J5:J1904 that equals *Jen,* the array includes the value True, and for each entry in J5:J1904 that does not equal *Jen,* the array contains False. Similarly, the *(L5:L1904="lipstick")* portion of our formula creates a Boolean array with a True corresponding to each cell in the range that contains the word *lipstick* and a False corresponding to each cell in the range that does not. When Boolean arrays are multiplied, another array is created using the following rules:

- True*True = 1
- True*False = 0
- False*True= 0
- False*False = 0

In short, multiplying Boolean arrays mimics the AND operator. Multiplying the product of our Boolean arrays by the values in the range M5:M1904 creates a new array. In any row in which Jen sold lipstick, this array contains the units sold. In all other rows, this array contains a 0. Summing this array yields Jen's total lipstick sales (1,299).

How many units were sold by Jen or were lipstick?   In cell G7, I used the database statistical function *DSUM(J4:N1904,4,E12:F14)* to find that all units that were sold by Jen or that were lipstick total 17,061. In cell G6, I computed the number of units that were sold by Jen or that were lipstick by array-entering the formula *{SUM(IF((J5:J1904="jen")+(L5:L1904="lipstick"),1,0)*M5:M1904)}*.

Again, the portion of our formula that reads *(J5:J1904="jen")+(L5:L1904="lipstick")* creates two Boolean arrays. The first array contains True if and only if Jen (the formula is not case sensitive) is the salesperson. The second array contains True if and only if the product sold is lipstick. When Boolean arrays are added, the following rules are used:

- False + True = 1

- True + True = 1

- True + False = 1

- False + False = 0

In short, adding Boolean arrays mimics the OR operator. Therefore, our formula will create an array in which each row where Jen is the salesperson or lipstick is the product sold has the number of units sold multiplied by 1. In any other row, the number of units sold is multiplied by 0. We obtain the same result as the database statistical formula (17,061).

Can I summarize the number of units of each product sold by each salesperson?
Array formulas make answering a question such as this a snap. We begin by listing each salesperson's name in the cell range A17:A25 and each product name in the cell range B16:F16. Now we array-enter in cell B17 the formula: *{SUM(($J$5:$J$1904=$A17)*($L$5:$L$1904=B$16)*$M$5:$M$1904)}*.

This formula counts only units of eye liner sold by Ashley (1920 units). By copying this formula to C17:F17, I compute the units of each product sold by Ashley. Next, I copy the formulas in C17:F17 to C18:C25 and compute the number of units of each product sold by each salesperson. Notice that I add a dollar sign to A in the reference to cell A17 so that I always pull the person's name, and I add a dollar sign to the 16 in the reference to cell B16 so that I always pull the product.

> **Note**   The astute reader might ask why I simply didn't select the formula in B17 and try to copy it in one step to fill in the table. Remember that you cannot paste an array formula into a range that contains both blank cells and array formulas, which is why I first copied the formula in B17 to C17:F17 and then dragged it down to complete the table.

What are array constants and how can I use them?

You can create your own arrays and use them in array formulas. Simply enclose the array values in curly brackets, { }. You need to enclose text in double quotation marks as well. You can also include the logical values True and False as entries in the array. Formulas or symbols such as dollar signs or commas are not allowed in array constants.

As an example of how an array constant might be used, look at the worksheet named Creating Powers in the file Array.xls, shown in Figure 72-9.

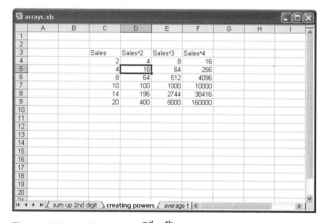

Figure 72-9   Creating 2nd–4th power of sales.

In this worksheet, we're given sales during six months, and we want to create for each month the 2nd, 3rd, and 4th power of sales. Simply select the range D4:F9, which is where we want the resulting computation to be placed. Array-enter in cell D4 the formula {C4:C9^{2,3,4}}. In the cell range D4:D9, this formula loops through and squares each number in C4:C9. In the cell range E4:E9, the formula loops through and cubes each number in C4:C9. Finally, in the cell range F4:F9, the formula loops through and raises each number in C4:C9 to the 4th power. The array constant {2,3,4} is required to let us loop through different power values.

How do I edit array formulas?

Suppose we have an array formula that creates results in multiple cells and we want to edit, move, or delete the results. For example, consider our last example, which placed results in the cell range D4:F9. If we select a cell in this range (say E6) and try and delete the cell, we receive the message *You cannot change part of an array.* You also receive this message if you try and edit any cell in the range D4:F9 and then press Enter. If you want to edit a single cell in an array range (say, cell D4, which is where we entered our array formula), select the cell, edit it, and then press Ctrl+Shift+Enter.

Given quarterly revenues for a toy store, can I estimate the trend and seasonality of the store's revenues?

The file Toysrustrend.xls, shown in Figure 72-10, contains quarterly revenues (in millions of dollars) for a toy store during the years 1997–2002. We would like to estimate the quarterly trend in revenues as well as the seasonality associated with each quarter (First quarter = January–March; second quarter = April–June; third Quarter = July–September; fourth Quarter = October–December). A trend of, say, 1 percent per quarter, means that sales are increasing at 1 percent per quarter. A seasonal index for the first quarter of, say, .80, means that sales during quarter 1 are around 80 percent of an average quarter.

	C	D	E	F	G	H	I	J
2								mean quarter
3								
4					1	2	3	index
5	Year	Quarter	Sales	Quarter#	Q1 dummy	Q2 dummy	Q3 dummy	Forecast
6	1997	1	1646	1	1	0	0	1853.104665
7	1997	2	1738	2	0	1	0	1826.702203
8	1997	3	1883	3	0	0	1	2025.018084
9	1997	4	4868	4	0	0	0	4366.196216
10	1998	1	1924	5	1	0	0	1917.500329
11	1998	2	1989	6	0	1	0	1890.180377
12	1998	3	2142	7	0	0	1	2095.387765
13	1998	4	4383	8	0	0	0	4517.922188
14	1999	1	2043	9	1	0	0	1984.133752
15	1999	2	2020	10	0	1	0	1955.864428
16	1999	3	2171	11	0	0	1	2168.202803
17	1999	4	4338	12	0	0	0	4674.920659
18	2000	1	2186	13	1	0	0	2053.082697
19	2000	2	2204	14	0	1	0	2023.83101
20	2000	3	2465	15	0	0	1	2243.548175
21	2000	4	5027	16	0	0	0	4837.374851
22	2001	1	2319	17	1	0	0	2124.427627
23	2001	2	1994	18	0	1	0	2094.15944
24	2001	3	2220	19	0	0	1	2321.51181
25	2001	4	4799	20	0	0	0	5005.474351
26	2002	1	2061	21	1	0	0	2198.251805

Figure 72-10   Toy revenue trend and seasonality estimation.

The trick to solving this problem is to use Excel's LOGEST function. Suppose that we are trying to predict a variable y from independent variables $x1$, $x2$, ... xn, and we believe that for some values of a, $b1$, $b2$, ... bn, the relationship between y and $x1$, $x2$, ... xn is given by $y = a(b1)^{x1}(b2)^{x2}(bn)^{xn}$. (I'll call this equation 1.)

The LOGEST function is used to determine values of *a*, *b*1, *b*2, ... *b*n that best fit this equation to the observed data. To use the LOGEST function to estimate trend and seasonality, note the following:

- *y* equals quarterly revenues.

- *x*1 equals quarter number (listed in chronological order, the current quarter is quarter 1, the next quarter is quarter 2, and so on).

- *x*2 equals 1 if the quarter is the first quarter of the year, and 0 otherwise.

- *x*3 equals 1 if the quarter is the second quarter of the year, and 0 otherwise.

- *x*4 equals 1 if the quarter is the third quarter of the year, and 0 otherwise.

We need to choose one quarter to leave out of the model, and I've arbitrarily chosen the fourth quarter. This approach is similar to the one we used with dummy variables in Chapter 46. The model we choose to estimate is then $y = a(b1)^{x1}(b2)^{x2}(b3)^{x3}(b4)^{x4}$. When the LOGEST function determines values of *a*, *b*1, *b*2, *b*3, and *b*4 that best fit the data, the values are interpreted as follows:

- *a* is a constant used to scale the forecasts.

- *b*1 is a constant that represents the average per quarter percentage increase in toy store sales.

- *b*2 is a constant that measures the ratio of first quarter sales to the omitted quarter's (fourth quarter) sales.

- *b*3 is a constant that measures the ratio of second quarter sales to the omitted quarter's sales.

- *b*4 is a constant that measures the ratio of third quarter sales to the omitted quarter's sales.

To begin, I created the dummy variables for quarters 1-3 in the cell range G6:I27 by copying from G6 to G6:I27 the formula *IF($D6=G$4,1,0)*. Remember that a fourth quarter is known to Excel because all three dummy variables equal 0 during the fourth quarter, which is why we can leave out the dummy variable for this quarter.

We now select the cell range K6:O6, where we want LOGEST to place the estimated coefficients. The constant *a* will be placed in the right-most cell, followed by the coefficients corresponding to the ordering of the independent variables. Thus, the trend coefficient will be next to the constant, then the quarter 1 coefficient, and so on.

The syntax for the LOGEST function is *LOGEST(y range, x range, TRUE, TRUE)*. After array-entering in cell K6 the formula *{LOGEST(E6:E27, F6:I27, TRUE, TRUE)}*, we obtain the coefficient estimates shown in Figure 72-11. Our equation to predict quarterly revenues (in millions) is as follows:

$$4219.57*(1.0086)^{\text{quarter number}}*(.435)^{\text{Q1dummy}}*(.426)^{\text{Q2dummy}}*(.468)^{\text{Q3dummy}}$$

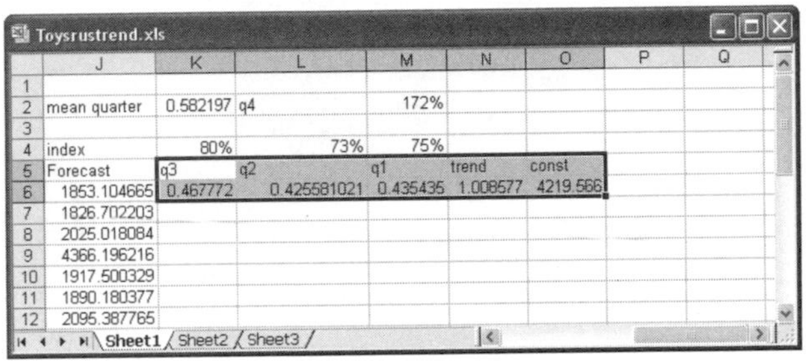

Figure 72-11   LOGEST estimates trend and seasonality.

During the first quarter, the Q1 dummy equals 1 and the Q2 and Q3 dummies equal 0. (Recall that any number raised to the power 0 equals 1.) Thus, during a first quarter, we predict quarterly revenues to equal $4219.57*(1.0086)^{\text{quarter number}}*(.435)$.

During a second quarter, the Q1 dummy and the Q3 dummy equal 0 and the Q2 dummy equals 1. During a second quarter, we predict quarterly revenues to equal $4219.57*(1.0086)^{\text{quarter number}}*(.426)$. During a third quarter, the Q1 dummy and the Q2 dummy equal 0 and the Q3 dummy equals 1. We predict quarterly revenues during a third quarter to equal $4219.57*(1.0086)^{\text{quarter number}}*(.468)$. Finally during a fourth quarter, the Q1, Q2, and Q3 dummies equal 0. During a 4th quarter, we predict quarterly revenues to equal $4219.57*(1.0086)^{\text{quarter number}}$.

In summary, we have estimated a quarterly upward trend in revenues of 0.9 percent (around 3.6 percent annually). After adjusting for trend, we find the following:

■   Quarter 1 revenues average 43.5 percent of quarter 4 revenues.

■   Quarter 2 revenues average 42.6 percent of quarter 4 revenues.

■   Quarter 3 revenues average 46.8 percent of quarter 4 revenues.

To create a seasonal index for each quarter, we give the omitted quarter (quarter 4) a value of 1, and we find an average quarter has a weight equal to

$$\frac{.435 + .426 + .468 + 1}{4} = .582$$

(See cell K2 in Figure 72-11.)

Then we can compute the relative seasonal index for quarters 1–3 by copying from K4 to L4:M4 the formula *K6/$K$2*. The quarter 4 seasonality is computed in cell M2 with the formula *1/K2*. After adjusting for trend, we conclude that:

- Quarter 3 sales are 75 percent of a typical quarter.

- Quarter 2 sales are 73 percent of a typical quarter.

- Quarter 1 sales are 80 percent of a typical quarter.

- Quarter 4 sales are 172 percent of a typical quarter.

Suppose we want to generate the forecast for each quarter corresponding to our fitted equation (equation 1). We can use the Excel GROWTH function to make this forecast. The GROWTH function is an array function with the syntax *GROWTH(known ys, known xs, new xs, True)*. This formula will give the predictions for the new *x*s when equation 1 is fitted to the data contained in the ranges specified by *known ys* and *known xs*. Thus, selecting the range J6:J27 and array-entering in cell J6 the formula *{GROWTH(E6:E27,F6:I27,F6:I27, TRUE)}* generates forecasts from equation 1 for each quarter's revenue. For example, our forecast for quarter 4 of 1997 using equation 1 is $4.366 billion.

Problems

All data for Problems 1-5 is in the file Chapter72data.xls.

1. The worksheet named Duplicate contains two lists of names. Use an array formula to count the number of names appearing on both lists.

2. The worksheet named Find Errors contains some calculations. Use an array function to count the number of cells containing errors. (Hint: Use the ISERROR function in your array formula.)

3. The worksheet named Sales contains 48 months of sales at a toy store. Create an array formula to add (beginning with month 3) every fifth month of sales. (Hint: You might want to use the Excel MOD function. *MOD(number, divisor)* yields the remainder after the number is divided by the divisor. For example, *MOD(7,5)* yields 2.)

4. Use an array function to compute the 3rd, 5th, and 7th power of each month's sales.

5. The worksheet Product contains sales during April through August of products 1–7. Sales for each month are listed in the same column. Rearrange the data so that sales for each month are listed in the same row and changes to the original data will be reflected in the new arrangement you have created.

6. Use the data in file HistoricalInvest.xls to create a count of the number of years in which stock, bond, and T-bill returns are between -20 percent to -15 percent, -15 percent to -10 percent, and so on.

7. An m by n matrix is a rectangular array of numbers containing m rows and n columns. For example,

$$\begin{bmatrix} 1 & 2 & 3 \\ 3 & 4 & 5 \\ 1 & 3 & 1 \end{bmatrix}$$

is a 3-by-3 matrix. Consider two matrices, A and B. Suppose that the number of columns in matrix A equals the number of rows in matrix B. Then you can multiply matrix A times matrix B. (The product is written as AB.) The entry in row I and column J of AB is computed by applying the SUMPRODUCT function to row I of A and column J of B. AB will have as many rows as A and columns as B. The Excel MMULT function is an array function that allows you to multiply matrices. Use the MMULT function to multiply the following matrices:

$$A = \begin{bmatrix} 1 & 2 & 3 \\ 4 & 5 & 6 \\ 7 & 7 & 0 \end{bmatrix}$$

and

$$B = \begin{bmatrix} 1 & 2 & 3 \\ 1 & 2 & 0 \\ 3 & 3 & 0 \end{bmatrix}$$

8. A square matrix has the same number of rows and columns. Given a square matrix A, suppose there exists a matrix B having AB equal a matrix in which each diagonal entry equals 1 and all other entries equal 0. We the say that B is the inverse of A. The Excel array function MINVERSE finds the inverse of a square matrix. Use the MINVERSE function to find the inverse for matrices A and B in problem 7.

9. Suppose we have invested a fraction f_i of our money in investment i (i = 1, 2, ... n). Also, suppose the standard deviation of the annual percentage return on investment i is s_i and the correlation between the annual percentage return on investment i and investment j is $ñ_{ij}$. We would like to know the variance and standard deviation of the annual percentage return on our portfolio. This may easily be computed using matrix multiplication. Create the following three matrices:

❑ Matrix 1 equals a 1 by n matrix whose ith entry is s_if_i.

❑ Matrix 2 equals an n by n matrix whose entry in row i and column j is $ñ_{ij}$.

❑ Matrix 3 is a n by 1 matrix whose ith entry is s_if_i.

The variance of the annual percentage return on our portfolio is simply (Matrix 1)*(Matrix 2)*(Matrix 3). The data in HistoricalInvest.xls gives annual returns on stocks, bonds, and T-bills. Use the MMULT and TRANSPOSE functions to estimate (based on the given historical data) the variance and standard deviation of a portfolio that invests 50 percent in stocks, 25 percent in bonds, and 25 percent in T-Bills.

Problems 10–13 use the data in file MakeupDb.xls.

10. How many dollars' worth of lip gloss did Jen sell?

11. What was the average number of units of lipstick sold when Jen made a sale in the East region?

12. How many dollars of sales were made by Emilee or in the East region?

13. How many dollars' worth of lipstick were sold by Colleen or Zaret in the East region?

14. Use the data in file Chapter50data.xls to estimate the trend and seasonal components of the quarterly revenues of Ford and GM.

15. In the toy store example, use the data for 1999–2001 to forecast quarterly revenues for 2002.

73

Picking Your Fantasy Football Team

- What is fantasy football?

- What information do I need to pick a good team?

- How can I use the Excel Solver to pick my team?

What is fantasy football?

To play fantasy football, you choose a team (usually 10 players) and receive rewards based on player performances during the current season. In the league I entered, each player chooses the following positions:

- One quarterback (QB)

- One place kicker (K)

- Three running backs (RB)

- Three wide receivers (WR)

- One tight end (TE)

- One team's defense (Team)

Each choice of player or team is assigned a price based on the player's or team's ability. For example, the great quarterback Michael Vick is assigned a price of $19 million. You have a total of $100 million to spend on your team. During a game, you earn points on the basis of the following rules:

- A QB earns one point for each 25 yards passing, six points for each TD pass or TD run, and one point for every 10 yards rushing. A QB loses two points for each interception thrown.

- A RB earns one point for every 10 rushing or receiving yards and six points for each TD rushing or receiving.

- A kicker earns one point for each 1-point conversion, three points for each field goal, and three points extra for each field goal that is 50 yards or longer.

- A WR or TE earns one point for every 10 receiving or rushing yards and six points for each TD receiving or rushing.

- A team receives six points for each defensive or special team touchdown, six points for each safety, four points for each fumble recovery or interception, two points for each sack, and ten points for each defensive shutout. In addition, the team is awarded points on the basis of the game's score. You get six points for each game in which the team defense allows 1–6 points, four points for each game in which the defense allows 7–13 points, two points for each game in which the defense allows 14–20 points, and 0 points for each game in which the defense allows 21–27 points. You get –2 points for each game in which 28–34 points are allowed, –4 points in games in which 35–41 points are allowed, and –6 points for each game in which at least 42 points are allowed.

What information do I need to pick a good team?

Essentially, you need to predict the performance of each player or team for the upcoming season. These predictions can be made using past performances from recent seasons or human judgment. In the file Fantasy2.xls, shown in figure 73-1, I've entered predictions for 167 players or teams during the 2003 season.

For example, we predicted that Priest Holmes (who costs $16.5 million) would gain 1,450 yards rushing and 550 yards passing and score 14 rushing and 2 receiving TDs. For each team, I've computed—based on points per game yielded last season—the probability of each range of points given up (0, 1–6, and so on) in a game. I assumed that the number of points given up during a game follows a Poisson random variable (see Chapter 55 for details about working with Poisson random variables) with a mean equal to the number of points given up last season. For example, in cell K110, I computed the probability that Tampa Bay gives up 0 points in a game with the formula *POISSON(0,F110,FALSE)*. In cell L110, I computed the probability that Tampa Bay gives up between 1 and 6 points in a game with the formula *POIS-SON(6,F110,TRUE)-POISSON(0,F110,TRUE)*. This formula computes the probability of giving up 6 or less points and subtracts the probability of yielding 0 points to derive the probability of giving up 1–6 points during a game.

	C	D	E	F	G	H	I	J	K	L
1										
2	POS	Player	Cost	EP		FG	FG>50			
3	K	M. GRAMETICA	8	40	30	5				
30				YDS PASS	TD PASS	INT	YDSRUN	TDS RUN		
31	QB	D. Mcnabb	20	3550	26	11	600	6		
54				YDS RUSH	TD RUSH	YDS PASS	TD PASS			
55	RB	P. HOLMES	16.5	1450	14	550	2			
90				YDS	TDS					
91	TE	T. GONZALES	7	800	7					
109				PPG	TD	Safety	Fumble+Int	Sack		0 1-6
110	TEAM	TAMPA BAY	14.5	12.3	6	0	38	43	4.55174E-06	0.038723294
111	TEAM	PHILLY	14.3	15.1	4	0	38	56	2.76792E-07	0.007161929
112	TEAM	GB	14	20.5	4	0	45	43	1.25015E-09	0.000177872
113	TEAM	PITT	13.6	21.6	2	0	36	50	4.1614E-10	7.95834E-05
114	TEAM	NO	13.3	24.3	6	1	38	39	2.79669E-11	1.04542E-05
115	TEAM	MIAMI	13.1	18.8	2	0	30	47	6.84327E-09	0.000598105
116	TEAM	BALT	13	22.1	6	0	31	33	2.52402E-10	5.4961E-05
117	TEAM	OAK	12.8	19	7	0	31	43	5.6028E-09	0.00051965
118	TEAM	NE	12.7	21.6	6	0	29	34	4.1614E-10	7.95834E-05
119	TEAM	ATL	12.6	19.6	3	0	39	47	3.07488E-09	0.000339657
120	TEAM	SF	12.6	21.9	2	0	27	32	3.08284E-10	6.37538E-05
121	TEAM	STL	12.5	23.1	3	0	26	38	9.28533E-11	2.60034E-05
137				YDS	TD	YDSR	TDR			
138	WR	T. OWENS	13.5	1400	14	40				
175										
176										
177										

Figure 73-1   Fantasy football inputs.

How can I use the Excel Solver to pick my team?

Our model is very similar to the capital budgeting project-selection model described in Chapter 28. Our changing cells are 0 or 1 binary variables for each player or team. A value of 1 indicates that a player or team is selected, and a value of 0 indicates that the player or team is not selected. Our target cell is to maximize the predicted total points scored by our selections. Our constraints are as follows:

- Spend at most $100 million.

- Choose exactly 1 K, 1 TE, 1 QB, 3 WR, 3 RB, and one Team.

   This model is linear for the following reasons:

- Our target cell is computed by adding together terms of the form *(0 or 1 changing cell for player or team)*(predicted points for player or team)*.

- The budget constraint is constructed by adding up terms such as *(0 or 1 changing cell for player or team)*(price of player)*.

- Our constraints on the number of each type of player simply add up changing cells, so they are linear as well.

To proceed, enter trial values of 0 or 1 for each player or team in column A, as shown in Figure 73-2. I created the following range names to help keep track of formulas.

- KICK for binary changing cells for kickers (A3:A29).

- QB for binary changing cells for quarterbacks (A33:A53).

- RUN for binary changing cells for running backs (A55:A89).

- TE for binary changing cells for tight ends (A91:A108).

- TEAM for binary changing cells for teams (A110:A136).

- WR for binary changing cells for wide receivers (A138:A174).

	A	B	C	D	E
2	Pick?	Pts	POS	Player	Cost
3	0	145	K	M. GRAMETICA	8
30					
31	0	372	QB	D. Mcnabb	20
54					
55	0	296	RB	P. HOLMES	16.5
90					
91	0	122	TE	T. GONZALES	7
109					
110	0	327.5474	TEAM	TAMPA BAY	14.5
111	1	328.6967	TEAM	PHILLY	14.3
112	0	306.0033	TEAM	GB	14
113	0	266.9745	TEAM	PITT	13.6
114	0	270.6282	TEAM	NO	13.3
115	0	249.7667	TEAM	MIAMI	13.1
116	0	234.688	TEAM	BALT	13
117	0	274.8539	TEAM	OAK	12.8
118	0	230.9745	TEAM	NE	12.7
119	0	288.1147	TEAM	ATL	12.6
120	0	193.6027	TEAM	SF	12.6
121	0	202.1149	TEAM	STL	12.5
137					
138	0	228	WR	T. OWENS	13.5
139	0	227	WR	M. HARRISON	13

Figure 73-2 Changing cells for player and team selection and estimated points.

To compute the target cell value (expected points earned by our selected players), we need to enter a formula that computes for each type of player or team the number of points that will be earned if our forecasted performance becomes reality. For place kickers, we compute the number of points earned by copying the formula *3*G3+3*H3+F3* from cell B3 to B4:B29. For quarterbacks, we compute the number of points earned by copying from B31 to B32:B53 the formula *6*G31-2*H31+(F31/25)+6*J31+(I31/10)*. For running backs, we compute the number of points earned by copying from B55 to B56:B89 the formula *(F55/10)+6*(G55+I55)+(H55/10)*. For tight ends, we compute the number of points earned by copying from B91 to B92:B108 the formula *(F91/10)+6*G91*. For each team, we compute the number of points earned by copying from B110 to B111:B136 the formula *6*G110+6*H110+4*I110+2*J110+16*(10*K110+6* L110+4*M110+2*N110+0*O110-2*P110-4*Q110-6*R110)*.   Note that we multiply the probability of each range of points given up by 16 because each team plays 16 games.

We now compute our target cell in cell L12 as the sum of the points earned by each type of player or team. For example, in cell L9, we compute the total points earned by wide receivers with the formula *SUMPRODUCT(WR,B138:B174)*, as shown in Figure 73-3.

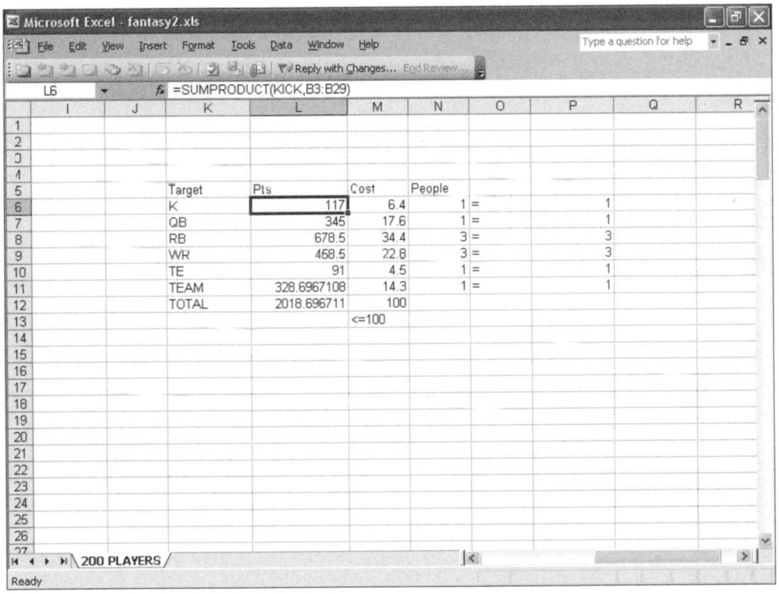

Figure 73-3   Calculations for constraints and target cell of Solver model.

Similarly, in cells M6:M11, we compute the total cost for each type of player or team, and in cell L12, we add up the total cost of all types of players or teams. For example, in cell M9, we compute total cost of wide receivers with the formula *SUMPRODUCT(WR,E138:E174)*.

Next, we compute the number of players of each type (or number of teams) selected in cells N6:N11. For example, we compute the number of teams selected in cell N11 with the formula *SUM(TEAM)*. In cells P6:P11, we enter the number of players (or teams) of each type needed.

Now we're ready to enter our model into Solver. Our Solver dialog box is shown in Figure 73-4. Our target cell is to maximize total points earned by our team (cell L12). Our changing cells are the ranges KICK, QB, RUN, TE, TEAM, and WR. To enter multiple ranges of changing cells, you can separate them by commas or hold down the Ctrl key while you enter the ranges. The constraint $M$12<=100 ensures that we spend at most $100 million. The constraint $N$6:$N$11= $P$6:$P$11 ensures that we choose the right number of players or team of each type. Finally, we add that each range of changing cells is binary. Open the Solver Options dialog box, and select the Assume Linear Models option.

Figure 73-4   Solver window for fantasy football team selection.

After pressing solve, the Solver selects the following team and players:

■   Kicker: Paul Edinger

■   QB: Jeff Garcia

■   RBs: Clinton Portis, Edgerin James, and Stacey Mack

■   TE: Alge Crumpier

■   Team: Philadelphia Eagles

■   WRs: Torry Holt, Keeshawn Johnson, and Bill Schroeder

We used conditional formatting to highlight our selected players in red. We selected the cell range D3:D174 (which contains the player and team names) and filled in (after selecting cell D3) the Conditional Formatting dialog box as shown in Figure 73-5.

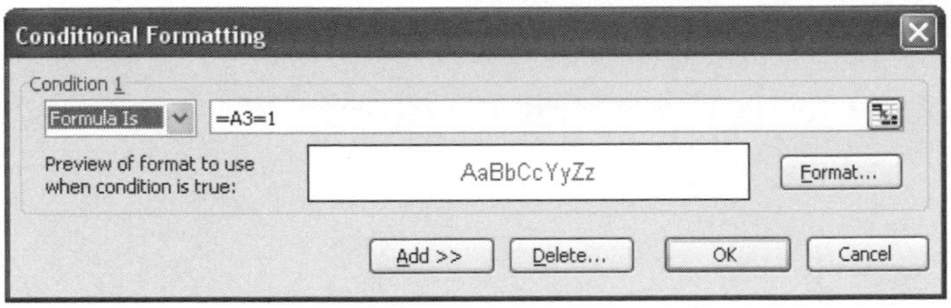

Figure 73-5   Formatting selected players in red.

Whenever column A has a 1 (indicating a selected player or team), conditional formatting will display column D (player or team name) in red, as we've specified.

Of course, the same methodology I've described in this chapter for selecting a fantasy football team can be applied to baseball or basketball fantasy leagues. Enjoy!

Note   By the way, the Excel Solver can handle only up to 200 changing cells and 200 constraints in linear models. Therefore, I prescreened the players and teams in order to reduce the number of available players and teams below 200.

Index

Symbols

A

About the Author

Wayne L. Winston is a professor of decision sciences at the Indiana University Kelley School of Business. He has earned MBA teaching awards for 18 consecutive years and regularly teaches business analysts how to use Microsoft Excel to make better decisions. Wayne also consults for several Fortune 500 clients, including Bristol-Myers Squibb Company; Cisco Systems, Inc.; Eli Lilly and Company; Ford Motor Company; General Motors Corporation; Intel Corporation; Microsoft Corporation; NCR Corporation; Owens Corning; Pfizer, Inc.; Proctor & Gamble; the U.S. Army; and the U.S. Department of Defense. He and business partner Jeff Sagarin developed the statistics tracking and rating system used by the Dallas Mavericks professional basketball team. Wayne is also a two-time Jeopardy! Champion.

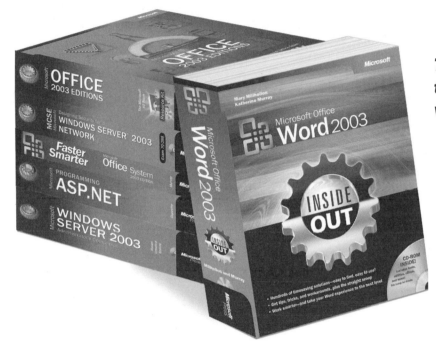

Self-paced

training that works
as hard as you do!

Information-packed STEP BY STEP courses are the most effective way to teach yourself how to complete tasks with the Microsoft Windows operating system and Microsoft Office applications. Numbered steps and scenario-based lessons with practice files on CD-ROM make it easy to find your way while learning tasks and procedures. Work through every lesson or choose your own starting point—with STEP BY STEP'S modular design and straightforward writing style, *you* drive the instruction. And the books are constructed with lay-flat binding so you can follow the text with both hands at the keyboard. Select STEP BY STEP titles also prepare you for the Microsoft Office User Specialist (MOUS) credential. It's an excellent way for you or your organization to take a giant step toward workplace productivity.

Microsoft Press also has STEP BY STEP titles to help you use earlier versions of Microsoft software.

- **Home Networking with Microsoft® Windows® XP Step by Step**
  ISBN 0-7356-1435-0

- **Microsoft Windows XP Step by Step**
  ISBN 0-7356-1383-4

- **Microsoft Office XP Step by Step**
  ISBN 0-7356-1294-3

- **Microsoft Word Version 2002 Step by Step**
  ISBN 0-7356-1295-1

- **Microsoft Project Version 2002 Step by Step**
  ISBN 0-7356-1301-X

- **Microsoft Excel Version 2002 Step by Step**
  ISBN 0-7356-1296-X

- **Microsoft PowerPoint® Version 2002 Step by Step**
  ISBN 0-7356-1297-8

- **Microsoft Outlook® Version 2002 Step by Step**
  ISBN 0-7356-1298-6

- **Microsoft FrontPage® Version 2002 Step by Step**
  ISBN 0-7356-1300-1

- **Microsoft Access Version 2002 Step by Step**
  ISBN 0-7356-1299-4

- **Microsoft Visio® Version 2002 Step by Step**
  ISBN 0-7356-1302-8

Microsoft Press® products are available worldwide wherever quality computer books are sold. For more information, contact your book or computer retailer, software reseller, or local Microsoft Sales Office, or visit our Web site at microsoft.com/mspress. To locate your nearest source for Microsoft Press products, or to order directly, call 1-800-MSPRESS in the United States. (in Canada, call 1-800-268-2222).

Prices and availability dates are subject to change.

microsoft.com/mspress

Get a **Free**
e-mail newsletter, updates,
special offers, links to related books,
and more when you

register online!

Register your Microsoft Press® title on our Web site and you'll get a FREE subscription to our e-mail newsletter, *Microsoft Press Book Connections.* You'll find out about newly released and upcoming books and learning tools, online events, software downloads, special offers and coupons for Microsoft Press customers, and information about major Microsoft® product releases. You can also read useful additional information about all the titles we publish, such as detailed book descriptions, tables of contents and indexes, sample chapters, links to related books and book series, author biographies, and reviews by other customers.

Registration is easy. Just visit this Web page and fill in your information:
http://www.microsoft.com/mspress/register

Microsoft®

Proof of Purchase

Microsoft® Excel Data Analysis and Business Modeling
0-7356-1901-8

CUSTOMER NAME

Microsoft Press, PO Box 97017, Redmond, WA 98073-9830